Cherokee National Forest Hiking Guide

Cherokee National Forest Hiking Guide

Second Edition

Edited by William H. Skelton

Written by the Harvey Broome Group of the Tennessee Chapter of the Sierra Club

Foreword by Lamar Alexander

Outdoor Tennessee Series

Jim Casada, Series Editor

THE UNIVERSITY OF TENNESSEE PRESS / KNOXVILLE

The Outdoor Tennessee Series covers a wide range of topics of interest to the general reader, including titles on the flora and fauna, the varied recreational activities, and the rich history of outdoor Tennessee. With a keen appreciation of the importance of protecting our state's natural resources and beauty, the University of Tennessee Press intends the series to emphasize environmental awareness and conservation.

The first edition of this work appeared under the title *Wilderness Trails of Tennessee's Cherokee National Forest.*

This book is printed on acid-free paper.

Library of Congress Cataloging-in-Publication Data

Cherokee National Forest hiking guide / edited by William H. Skelton; written by the Harvey Broome Group of the Tennessee Chapter of the Sierra Club; foreword by Lamar Alexander.— 2nd ed.
    p. cm. — (Outdoor Tennessee series)
Rev. ed. of: Wilderness trails of Tennessee's Cherokee National Forest. 1992.
Includes bibliographical references and index.
ISBN 1-57233-374-X (pbk.)
    1. Hiking—Tennessee—Cherokee National Forest—Guidebooks.
2. Cherokee National Forest (Tenn.)—Guidebooks. I. Skelton, William H., 1942– II. Sierra Club. Tennessee Chapter. Harvey Broome Group.
III. Wilderness trails of Tennessee's Cherokee National Forest. IV. Series.
GV199.42.T22C447 2005
917.68'8—dc22

2004018769

Dedicated to the thousands of people who worked for passage of the two Cherokee National Forest Wilderness Acts and who continue to work for protection of the Cherokee's special natural areas. This book is also dedicated to two individuals who were involved in those efforts and who helped with the preparation of the first edition of this book, and who will be long remembered as strong advocates for wilderness preservation: Arthur Smith, of Kingsport (1921–1999), and Dan Dillon, of Church Hill (1950–2003).

This book is intended only as a general guide to the Cherokee National Forest's natural areas and trails and is not a substitute for individual outdoor skills, including survival and route finding. Each user of the Cherokee National Forest should possess those outdoor skills, or be accompanied by an individual who does, since the specific information provided herein has been compiled from a variety of sources and is subject to the ever-changing natural and human-made environment.

Contents

SECTION C Northern Cherokee National Forest: French Broad and Nolichucky Rivers 189

SECTION D Southern Cherokee National Forest:
Tellico and Ocoee Rivers   281

Illustrations

Figures

Maps

Foreword to
the Second Edition

Near our cabin in West Miller's Cove outside Maryville, Tennessee, there are three trails. Walk in back of the cabin and you will find a hunter's trail. It leads up the ridge to some coonhunter's shack. There are plenty of places to lie down and watch leaves float and see clouds through branches and listen to the wind making trees creak, so you know for sure you are a long way away.

To the north of our cabin, another trail runs along Trunk Branch through two miles of land that the National Park Service wanted in the 1930s but couldn't afford even at ten dollars per acre. Walk those two miles—including the steep horse-slide at the end (so named because horses slide when they try to walk down it)—and you come to the Boundary Trail along the edge of the Great Smoky Mountains National Park. This Boundary Trail was once so overgrown that it was too rough to travel; today it is so well used that not many sprouts in the trail survive.

Go south from our cabin and you can find a network of old trails that will take you back through early history in East Tennessee—trails that run across the mountain to Maryville, or to the mouth of Abrams Creek or over to Cades Cove. A century ago mountaineers ran these ridges to the city to swap honey for salt and pepper; now the trails are busy again with refugees from the city looking for quiet.

The problem is, the quiet is getting hard to find. Too many people know these trails in and around the Great Smoky Mountains. When I was a boy it was different. We could walk the Appalachian Trail from Davenport Gap to Newfound Gap and rarely see a soul, never giving a thought to the possibility that there might not be a vacancy at the trail shelters. Now hikers must have permits to use the shelters, and once you are there the surrounding area can be as busy as an RV campground. Some trails are so worn that they might as well be paved. Some trails are paved.

Congestion in the Smokies is one reason why this guidebook about trails in the Cherokee National Forest is so welcome. Think of the Cherokee National Forest this way: the border of Tennessee and North Carolina meanders along the crest of the highest and most magnificent mountains in the eastern United States. The Great Smoky Mountains are a slice from the middle of this border. The Cherokee National Forest is everything else—larger than the Smokies, not nearly as well known, and, as a result, as untrampled as the Smokies were when I was a boy.

They are part of God's same quilt, but there are parts of the Cherokee National Forest that even the Smokies cannot match. Have you ever walked the Highlands of Roan Mountain in June, at 6,000 feet, the wind blowing so that wearing a poncho invites flying, the grasses bent to the ground, old yellow birches bending, the rhododendron in display? These are the most beautiful views along the entire Appalachian Trail. They are a part of the Cherokee National Forest. So is the John Muir National Recreation Trail along the Hiwassee, of which Muir in 1814 wrote: ". . . a most impressive mountain river . . . with its surface broken to a thousand sparkling gems, and its forest walls vinedraped and flowery as Eden."

This guidebook's dedication to the "thousands of people who worked for passage of Tennessee's Cherokee National Forest Wilderness Acts" should alert you: this is more than a guidebook. It is a political statement—and why should it not be? It is hard to discover the backcountry of these mountains without wanting to save them. In a nation this diverse it is important for those who know these mountains best to make their case.

I recall how in 1984 I thought the United States Congress would unanimously want to make most of the Great Smoky Mountains National Park a wilderness as a part of the park's fiftieth birthday celebration. The Smokies already were being managed like a wilderness in order to absorb the visits from nine million people each year. A permanent wilderness designation made sense.

Western U.S. senators had a different perspective. The federal government owns most of the West, and many westerners see more wilderness as a threat, the government owning too much more. But the government owns very little land in the East. Protecting the mountains along the border of North Carolina and Tennessee is a case that must be made.

Through this guidebook runs the enthusiasm of thousands of hikers who have discovered the Cherokee National Forest and who have worked to protect it. These friends of the Cherokee National Forest give us plenty of advice. About what to wear and how to camp. About rock formations. About what trees and flowers and plants grow in the Cherokee National Forest and what flies or moves at daybreak and at dusk. About speckled trout and where the rainbows hide. About the recent arrival of humans. And, of course, about how you can join their efforts to make certain that some of this wilderness remains as civilization encroaches.

One hundred years from now when my great-great-grandchildren will be as old as I am today, the main trails of Cherokee National Forest will be at least as populated as are today's trails through the Smoky Mountains. Campsites in the Cherokee National Forest will be crowded. There may even be, perish the thought, paved trails.

What there will not be, one hundred years from now, is still another Cherokee National Forest to explore and save. In Tennessee there are no more high mountains, grassy balds, rushing creeks. All there will be more of one hundred years from now are people and the residue of people.

This guidebook is welcome, first, because it is a road map to enjoyment, up Rattlesnake Ridge, down Stony Creek, over Pond Mountain, through the Doe River Gorge. (Let us not become so preoccupied with saving the forest that we forget to enjoy it!) And, second, it is welcome because it will multiply the thousands who have worked to protect the Cherokee National Forest into the larger army of tens of thousands who love walking a trail to some resting place where the noises are trees creaking, the smells of wet moss and leaves, the colors pure, and the world at peace.

A couple of salutes are in order. First, to Will Skelton and the members of the Harvey Broome Group of the Tennessee Chapter of the Sierra Club, not only for their work on this guidebook but because no Tennesseans have been more consistent and effective in reminding us that the outdoors surrounding us are worth saving.

A second salute goes to the University of Tennessee. The *Cherokee National Forest Hiking Guide* is another one of those UT Press guidebooks that everyone who cares about our mountains will want two of—one for the bookshelf, one for the backpack.

Lamar Alexander
West Miller's Cove
August 1, 2003

Preface to the Second Edition

When I read the original manuscript for the first edition of this book, I knew that it would enjoy a warm reception from a wide and varied audience. Despite having some of the problems inherent in any group literary effort, certain salient features made the book most attractive. Foremost among these was the fact that every contributor, no matter their literary ability or lack thereof, wrote with passion and with a sense of intimate familiarity with their subject. It was clear that the Harvey Broome Group of the Tennessee Chapter of the Sierra Club had a dedicated membership that cherished the good earth and cared deeply about protecting the natural world as well as sharing its wonder with others.

More than a decade has passed since the original publication of this book (under the title *Wilderness Trails of Tennessee's Cherokee National Forest*). Thanks to dramatic changes over that period, ranging from new trails to troubling developments on the environmental front, the work cried out for updating. Furthermore, the fact that the original work covered only those trails that penetrated protected areas, as opposed to comprehensive coverage of all maintained trails in the Cherokee National Forest (CNF), it cried out for expanded coverage. The result is the current book. Its new title provides an accurate reflection of precisely what the work embodies, and as the first comprehensive guide to the trails of this Tennessee wonderland, the work seems certain to become an essential companion for those who cherish the CNF.

Once again Will Skelton brings solid editing (and, one suspects, leadership) skills to the fore in marshalling an impressive array of contributors along with putting their contributions together in a tidy fashion. The product of his labors, along with those of fellow hikers and Sierra Club members, is a thoroughly updated, revised, and expanded coverage of trail hiking in the CNF. Would that every Sierra Club chapter was as farsighted, active, and committed.

This is a trail guide, with no attempt to cover off-trail activities. That is right and sensible, since such ventures should be undertaken only by those with a high level of woodsman's skills. That being said, there are real joys to be garnered from adventures that truly place one back of beyond, as the more intrepid of the hunters, fishermen, hikers, and campers who venture into the CNF know. Perhaps coverage of the skills, training, and knowledge required to go off trail could be the subject of another book by the Harvey Broome Chapter, for the information found in these pages makes it abundantly clear that the group includes plenty of members who know their backwoods stuff.

For now, though, suffice it to say that this little addendum to my original preface (which stands in its own right) comes with a real sense of pride in being connected, albeit remotely and only as series editor, with the fine folks who have done yeoman duty in making this book a reality. Over the years I have been privileged to speak to Sierra Club chapters along with a lot of other conservation organizations. Many of them are composed of dedicated members who do a great deal of good when it comes to protecting our precious natural heritage. Yet I can honestly say, even though I view matters from afar and have never addressed the Harvey Broome Chapter or even knowingly met any of its members, that this is the most impressive effort associated with a conservation organization that I have ever encountered.

For the average user of this work, that may not matter a great deal, but it is something I felt needed to be said. With that out of the way, settle into a model trail guide. It is one that deserves to become dog-eared with use, for any time you trek into the fascinating fastnesses of the CNF it should be a handy companion in your daypack or backpack.

Jim Casada
Series Editor

Preface to the First Edition

Today we typically find material sustenance in the cities, but it is the high, remote hills that offer food for the soul. The Cherokee National Forest (CNF) is such a place—one where solitude beckons those who find solace amidst nature's splendor. This is not primeval wilderness, for earlier generations cut the region's virgin hardwood forests and eked out a precarious existence in its secluded coves and hollows. The healing hand of time has worked wonders, though, and today extensive portions of the CNF appear much as they did before pioneering settlers first began to fell trees and till soil along the west-facing spine of the Appalachians. Only the knowing, discerning eye detects the vestiges of human presence, even though, just a few generations back, surprising numbers of hardy mountain folk wrested a hardscrabble existence over much of the CNF.

Here a pair of boxwoods, bright green where the gray of midwinter dominates, mark the path leading to an old home place. Piles of stones, the occasional rock wall, and house foundations recall backbreaking labor of proud, self-sufficient men and women who lived close to the earth. The springtime pilgrim in the high country may find rambling roses, tiger lilies, or ancient fruit trees abloom. In isolated spots, usually atop a hill with a breathtaking view, one sometimes encounters slabs of stone marking long-forgotten grave sites. As a rule these crude stones are mute, for rarely could the hill folk afford the luxury of an engraved marker. Still, for those of a reflective nature, they bear poignant, powerful testament to a world we have lost. For the most part, though, the scars left by man are well hidden, with only isolated pockets of recent timber cutting striking a discordant note in this world of visual harmony.

Those who lived here in yesteryear saw it as a land full of hope and promise, and today we can look on the CNF in similar fashion. Those who once lived here sought fulfillment of basic physical needs; as visitors we look for mental peace and escape from the madding crowd. There are other differences as well. The regal monarch that once dominated Appalachian hardwood forests, the American chestnut, is gone, the victim of a virulent imported blight. With its passage we lost much, for the tree and its myriad benefits—rich nuts to feed man and beast, tannic acid unexcelled for leatherworking, virtually rot-proof fence posts, shingles sure to stand the test of the most adverse weather conditions, and the wood to make beautiful furniture—loomed large in the lifestyles of southern highlanders. Today the American chestnut is almost gone from living memory. Sadly, the inhabitant of cold, pristine streams, the brook trout, may be traveling the same road, albeit at a slower pace. Siltation, acid rain, competition from rainbow and brown trout, and a host of other factors threaten this sprightly, strikingly beautiful fish. For now, though, "speckled trout," as they are known throughout the mountains, still survive in the laurel-shaded headwaters of the CNF, a lovely linchpin joining us to bygone days. For every species lost or threatened, however, there are dozens of survivors. Pink lady slippers blooming on a dry pinewoods ridge; a dozen different species of trilliums thriving in the moist, acid-rich soil; showy orchis catching the springtime wayfarer's eye; or a regiment of mayapples in their lime-green uniforms, standing shoulder-to-shoulder as they savor the warmth of earth's annual rebirth. These and countless other sights offer a visual feast no matter what the season, and the other senses of those who traverse the CNF encounter similar delights. Keen ears detect the raucous cry of the raven about the high ridges; the startling sound of a pileated woodpecker readily explains why it is known as the "Lord God bird" in some regions of the South; and always there are gray squirrels chirring and chipmunks squealing. Along with sound and sight, smell is accorded its due. Spring means the alluring fragrance of azaleas and the heady aroma of sweetshrub; summer brings the rank odor of rotting fungi blended with the tempting smell of ripening blackberries; autumn is characterized by the tangy essence of ripening persimmons and the pungency of pawpaws; and even in the dead of winter one can savor the sweetness of honey locust pods or the pleasingly acrid odor of spruce.

These sensations are all a part of the CNF's complex character, and the only real way to know this world of wonder is to walk through it. Roads do not reach its more remote fastnesses, and even if they did the automobile is ill suited to knowing the forest in intimate fashion. The CNF demands ample quantities of that priceless quality, time, but those who do tread its hidden footpaths and beckoning byways are richly rewarded. This is something the members of the Harvey Broome Group of the Tennessee Chapter of the Sierra Club have long recognized, and now, in a collective labor of love, they have seen fit to share their treasured experiences with others.

The result, *Wilderness Trails of Tennessee's Cherokee National Forest*, is a work eminently suited to the Outdoor Tennessee Series.

From the outset, one intent of this series has been to make Tennesseans, as well as others, more fully aware of the variegated offerings the Volunteer State presents to those who cherish the outdoor experience. Until now, there has been no truly suitable guide to the CNF, although the nearby Great Smoky mountains National Park, along with that portion of the Appalachian Trail that traces its way along the North Carolina–Tennessee border, has attracted considerable attention. Works such as Carson Brewer's *Hiking in the Great Smokies* (1962), Dick Murlless and Constance Stallings's *Hiker's Guide to the Smokies* (1973), Rodney and Priscilla Albright's *Walks in the Great Smokies* (1979, 1990), and the Appalachian Trail Conference's *Appalachian Trail Guide to Tennessee–North Carolina* (9th ed., 1989), among others, come to mind. Yet we have had no work focusing solely on the CNF's trails, and only a handful of books, such as Evan Means's *Tennessee Trails* (3rd ed., 1989) and Robert Brandt's *Tennessee Hiking Guide* (1982), have touched on the region at all.

With the appearance of *Wilderness Trails,* we have a work that fills a gap in the literature of hiking and constitutes a model for this genre. Featuring well over a score of contributors, the volume draws on literally hundreds of years and untold thousands of miles of hiking experience. Often efforts of this type are disjointed or of uneven quality, but thanks to Will Skelton's solid grip on the editorial tiller, the present work steers well clears of such shoals.

Instead, what we have is a guide that bids fair to serve hikers in the CNF, and serve them exceptionally well, for many years to come. That being said, let me hasten to add that the book is much more than just another handy reference tool to be stowed away in one's backpack for occasional consultation. *Wilderness Trails* is a truly comprehensive work. It not only gives the reader details on intended routes but also provides a solid overview of the CNF's natural and human history. A number of appendixes add to the book's usefulness; novices will find a helpful chapter on the "dos and don'ts" of safe hiking; detailed maps, which are essential to a guide of this sort, are present. In sum, this easily understood work is reader friendly.

Wilderness Trails will appeal to a wide audience. Hikers will find it indispensable, as will bird watchers, wildlife photographers, and those who find joy in the simple act of communing closely with nature. Sportsmen, too, especially those of a more adventurous nature, will discover grist for their mills here. For example, any angler worth his salt is always looking for forgotten creeks, for trout-filled waters that are, as that consummate outdoorsman Horace Kephart put it, "back of beyond." These pages suggest avenues to such treasure troves for fisherman (and hunters), as indeed they open up enticing vistas for all who appreciate what oneness with the natural world can mean.

Finally, and perhaps most important, devotion to keeping the CNF forever wild runs as a bright ribbon of hope throughout the work. As a volume forming part of a series devoted to environmental awareness and conservation, that is only as it should be. With that in mind, as you use this book remember that the good earth, properly treated, will never, ever, let mankind down.

Jim Casada
Series Editor

Acknowledgments

We would like to acknowledge the efforts of all the people who worked on this book, many of whose names are indicated as contributors in a separate section. George Ritter, Steve McGaffin, Hiram Rogers, and T. J. Tolnas deserve special thanks for their hiking and writing about an extraordinary number of trails, many of them new to this book. Will Fontanez, of the University of Tennessee Cartography Laboratory, and his staff member, Will Albaugh, prepared the excellent maps. Roger Jenkins coordinated and provided many of the photographs, contributed substantial sections of the book, and was more generally involved in the book's preparation than anyone other than the editor. Others also helped in both large and small ways, and many are recognized in the Contributors section.

We would like to thank the public officials and elected representatives who made possible the protection of the wilderness areas described in this book, many of whom are listed in the "Political History" section. Former senators James Sasser and Al Gore consistently supported the protection of wilderness in the Cherokee National Forest and deserve special thanks. Former governor, and now senator, Lamar Alexander, former senator Howard Baker, former congressman James Quillen, and the late congressman John J. Duncan Sr. also deserve special thanks for introducing and/or supporting the acts that designated the Cherokee National Forest's existing wilderness areas.

We thank the University of Tennessee Press and its staff, whose contributions resulted in many improvements in this book. We thank the Cherokee National Forest and several of its employees for their help with trail and forest information, especially Doug Byerly, recreation program manager, and Delce Dyer, recreation planner.

Finally, we would like to acknowledge a gift that helped make both the initial edition and the second edition of this book possible. The Lana S. Lombardo Wilderness Trust Fund was established by Mrs. Lombardo's husband, Thomas G. Lombardo, family, and friends in her memory after her death in an automobile accident in 1985 at the age of forty-one. The trust was established to help maintain, expand, and preserve wilderness and hiking areas in East and Middle Tennessee and western North Carolina. Lana Lombardo was an avid hiker and a lover of wilderness trails. Her legacy has helped to provide funding both to support the passage of the 1986 Tennessee Wilderness Act and the publication of this book. We are thankful, as will be many future generations of Cherokee National Forest hikers.

Statement of Purpose

Members of the Harvey Broome Group of the Sierra Club's Tennessee Chapter have roamed the world in search of wilderness places and experiences, to the world's highest mountains in Nepal, the canyons of Utah, the summit of Mount Kilimanjaro, and Alaska's Brooks Range. But they always come home to the southern Appalachians and especially the mountains, ridges, and valleys in Tennessee's Cherokee National Forest along the eastern Tennessee–western North Carolina state line. Here are spectacular vistas, looking west over the broad, gentle, and green Tennessee Valley or east to a succession of misty, high, blue mountaintops. You also see crystal-clear mountain streams cascading over mountain rocks and waterfalls and a veritable cornucopia of wildflowers that match any artist's palette. There are historical echoes of long-gone Cherokee Indians and pioneer settlers, as well as extinct species like the cougar, bison, elk, and gray wolf. These southern Appalachian forests also provide one of the few remaining refuges of the black bear and other species that have suffered from encroachments of our modern society.

The CNF is an asset to present and future generations because a portion has been protected, we hope for all time, in a variety of land-use categories that generally prohibit clear-cutting, road building, motor vehicles, and development. Hiking and backpacking in these natural areas are truly experiences to be treasured, experiences that will not be marred by society's seemingly endless need to destroy natural areas.

This edition is the first comprehensive guidebook to all of the trails of the CNF. The first edition covered only the trails in protected areas, whereas this edition describes every official trail and some unofficial trails in the forest. This book was prepared for two interrelated reasons. The first is to encourage and help people visit, hike, backpack, hunt, fish, bird-watch, and otherwise enjoy these natural areas. The second, and most important, is to encourage the public to demand that our elected United States representatives and senators and the US Forest Service keep the trails and natural areas described in this book forever wild and natural. The CNF's protected areas are protected only by statutes or administrative decision, both of which can be changed or modified by the US Congress and the US Forest Service. The US Forest Service reviews its administrative protection of natural areas approximately every ten years, and as this book goes to press in 2004, the CNF has just adopted a revised management plan (see "Political History"). It is now up to the public to see that the natural areas included in this book continue to be protected from timber harvesting, road building, and development that would destroy the very attributes that resulted in their protection. That is our goal, and we seek your help in ensuring that it is realized.

The benefits of protecting the natural areas of the CNF are numerous and include the following:

1. Watershed protection. Stable soil found in natural areas protects streams from erosion resulting in clean water for streams and rivers.

2. Baseline information. Natural areas provide places where human influences have not drastically modified natural processes, thus allowing comparison from time to time to see how human-impacted areas are faring.

3. Education and research. Natural areas provide educational opportunities for both individuals and numerous Tennessee and southeastern United States educational institutions, ranging from elementary school field trips to university researchers.

4. Diversity of forest trees. The US Forest Service proposes substantial clear-cutting of much of the CNF within the next fifty years. Natural areas will ensure that a significant portion of the CNF continues to be covered with large trees—"late successional species" in the US Forest Service's terminology—which many people want to see when they visit a national forest.

5. Diversity of wildlife habitat. Different animal species have different habitat requirements. Some species, especially the black bear, bobcat, and cougar, require large roadless tracts, which natural areas provide. Other species, such as brook trout, squirrel, raccoon, and ruffed grouse, will also do well in natural areas.

6. Diversity of plant species. Different species of plants also require different habitats and some plant species survive better in natural habitats.

7. Recreation. Purely and simply, hiking in a natural area is a pleasure for many people for many reasons—adventure, exploration, exercise, and solitude. The assurance that there will be no off-road vehicle traffic and noise, no clear-cuts,

and no roads makes for a special experience. These attributes also improve the recreational aspects of many other uses of natural areas, including horseback riding, hunting, fishing, bird watching, and backpacking.

8. Living museum. An almost endless forest once covered most of the southern Appalachian Mountains and, indeed, most of the eastern United States. We have been steadily reducing that forest, year by year, to a bare remnant of what once existed. Although the natural areas in this book contain only traces of that virgin forest, they are primarily covered with older trees. Protecting those areas will provide a living museum of what once existed for our study and enjoyment.

How to Use This Guidebook

This book is both a resource for general information on the CNF and a source of detailed descriptions of areas and trails and their access. General information on the CNF is presented in section A, including the natural, human, and political environments that have made the forest what it is today. Sections B, C, and D provide detailed trail descriptions for the CNF (presented in geographical order from north to south). The appendixes provide various lists of helpful information about the forest. The trails themselves are generally arranged by geographic area, often using the principal protected area in which the trails are located (for example, a designated wilderness or scenic area). The list of trails is intended to be comprehensive and to include all official CNF trails and, in some cases, other unofficial trails and/or USFS roads that are used by hikers. Our list of 195 trails is based on the set of three National Geographic Society/Trails Illustrated maps for the Cherokee National Forest (http://maps.nationalgeographic.com/trails). We were advised by the CNF that those maps contain the "official" CNF trail list as of 2003. Those maps are described in detail in appendix 1.

This book is not intended to be a how-to-hike or backpack book and does not provide the information and skills necessary for those activities. If you lack the necessary skills, you should, before striking out on your own, obtain such skills through a variety of sources. Several excellent how-to books are listed in the bibliography. Many colleges and universities, including the University of Tennessee, offer noncredit courses in hiking and backpacking. Numerous environmental and hiking groups have an active outings program, often featuring one or more beginner backpacks. Several backpacking and outfitter shops located near the CNF are listed in appendix 4 and are a good source of practical information and, in some cases, backpacking courses. Friends and acquaintances who know something about backpacking and hiking are also invaluable. The Tennessee Chapter of the Sierra Club and, particularly, its East Tennessee groups in Knoxville, Chattanooga, and the Bristol–Kingsport–Johnson City area probably have the greatest concentration of outings to the CNF. These groups and other environmental and outing clubs in the area are listed in appendix 3.

Once you have the necessary skills, your principal problem will be which trails to choose. This book will help in that respect by giving you a general idea of the attributes of the various areas and trails. You may want to scan the descriptions to determine whether a particular area or trail appeals to you (note that alternate trail names are sometimes shown in parentheses). Or you may choose an area based on proximity to your residence (see the CNF General Maps) or a friend's recommendation. Once you have focused on a particular area—because of location, attributes, or a recommendation—you may want to buy a Trails Illustrated map and/or US Geological Survey topographic map of the area. You can also buy CD-ROMs that show the area, or you can download a map from an Internet site (see appendix 1 for information on where to obtain these maps). The maps in this book were prepared from topographic maps but do not show all topographic features, such as elevation contours. Before getting started, many people choose to make photocopies of the relevant pages from guidebooks (and perhaps even the topographic maps) rather than lugging along the book itself, since most of the book will usually relate to trails you are not hiking on a specific day. You may also want to note various GPS readings (appendix 1) for the area you plan to hike. Such information can be obtained from either print copies or Internet versions of US Geological Survey topographical maps. We have given some GPS readings in this book, especially for difficult-to-find areas and junctions; however, such listings are not comprehensive.

In describing the trails in this book, reference is sometimes made to old logging grades and roads (which are not current USFS roads but which often are used for trails). These are old routes that were used to remove timber from the area both prior to it becoming an NF and since then. The timber was removed by various means, including logging trains, steam powered skidders, rubber tired skidders, tractors, trucks, mules, horses, and oxen. The grades and roads vary in width from that of a logging train or truck to a very narrow track used by working animals. Some are quite obvious but others are very obscure and even unnoticeable to many hikers.

This book also contains a wealth of information, other than trails, on aspects of the CNF that many people will want to read before or after visiting an area. For example, if you saw a rock outcrop and wondered what it meant geologically, there is a section on geology. Other sections cover history, both political and human, and the wildlife and vegetation of the CNF. With a topographical map and this book, you can get to the trailhead and have a pretty good idea of where to go and what to expect.

At this point we want to say a word about the difficulty of trails. In the first edition of this book we chose not to assign a difficulty rating to each trail, based on the authors' years of experience with other guidebooks whose difficulty ratings were often inconsistent. One person's easy trail is often another person's hard trail. However, because most guidebooks contain such ratings, as do the Trails Illustrated maps, we elected to use the simple Trails Illustrated and CNF difficulty ratings: Easy, Moderate, and Difficult. However, we did not necessarily assign the trails the same rating as the Trails Illustrated maps. We assigned our own rating based on our hiking of the trails. We have also mentioned particularly steep and difficult trail sections, and we have provided low- and high-point elevations. The information in this book, along with topographical maps, will give you a general idea about the difficulty of a trail. However, always know your limitations. If a trail seems too difficult, turn back.

Each of the trails in this book was hiked and wheel-measured and then described by members of the Harvey Broome Group whose names appear in the contributors section at the end of this book. Some attempt has been made to make the descriptions consistent; however, there will necessarily be some variance, depending on each hiker's style of writing and the degree of detail they provide.

It is particularly important to remember when using this book and topographical maps that the CNF trail system is a "living system" that is constantly being changed by both human and environmental impacts. Most of the trails included herein were hiked during 2002. It is possible that some of the trails will have changed by this book's publication date. Human changes can include official relocation of trails in order to correct trail erosion, changes in permitted uses (such as from hiker use only to horse and hiker use), and changes in trail blazes, names, and numbers. Trails are also changed by hikers who sometimes find what they think is a better route and move the trail location by use. Environmental changes may include bridges that are washed out, trees that are blown down over the trail, and trails that are overgrown due to lack of maintenance. In addition to dating the information in this book, such changes can be even more pronounced with regard to roads, trails, and developments shown on the topographical maps. Most of the topographical maps you will use are not really current and some date back to the 1950s.

We must also advise the potential user of the trails that, unlike many National Park and State Park trails, including especially the GSMNP, the CNF's trails run the gamut from clearly visible and well maintained to unmaintained. A surprising number of the CNF's trails are poorly maintained. Some have never seen any maintenance and are only open, to the extent they are passable, as the result of use by hikers or maintenance by users. Often the trail descriptions will mention trails that are difficult to follow because of this lack of maintenance. In the past, trail maintenance and new trail construction have not been a high priority of the CNF, and the lack of attention shows on many of the trails. We hope that more maintenance will become the norm in the future.

Hikers and backpackers will find this book of invaluable benefit. However, we want to make it clear that numerous other users of the CNF will also find valuable information in this book. Anglers looking for trail access to a trout stream, hunters looking for a backcountry campsite near a favorite hunting area, horseback riders looking for a good trail ride, birdwatchers looking for a particular species, and botanists looking for a particularly beautiful flower will all benefit from this book. Hunting and fishing are legitimate uses of our national forests, provided there is compliance with applicable state game and fish laws and seasons. Horseback riding is also a legitimate use on designated horse trails, which are identified in this book. All users can enjoy and benefit from the CNF's trails, and all we ask is that you respect the natural beauty of the forest and leave it just as natural and beautiful when you leave.

We would appreciate your letting us know of any significant changes in the trails and areas included herein, any errors you feel may have slipped through our editing process, and any other comments to help us in connection with future editions of this book. Send your comments to William H. Skelton, editor, *Hiking Guide to the Cherokee National Forest,* c/o The University of Tennessee Press, Suite 110, Conference Center, Knoxville, TN 37996-4108.

We hope to see you on one of the many CNF trails.

Abbreviations

We will use the following abbreviations throughout this book:

2 WD	Two-Wheel-Drive Vehicles
4 WD	Four-Wheel-Drive Vehicles
AT	Appalachian Trail
CNF	Cherokee National Forest
CCC	Civilian Conservation Corps
FS ____	US Forest Service Road Number
FS Trail ____	US Forest Service Trail Number
GA	Georgia
GSMNP	Great Smoky Mountains National Park
GPS	Global Positioning System
I-____	Interstate Highway Number
NC	North Carolina
NC ____	North Carolina Highway Number
NF	National Forest
NPS	National Park Service
ORV	Off-Road Vehicle
TN	Tennessee
TN ____	Tennessee Highway Number
TI ____	National Geographic/Trails Illustrated Map Number
TVA	Tennessee Valley Authority
TWRA	Tennessee Wildlife Resources Agency
US ____	United States Highway Number
USFS	United States Forest Service
USGS	United States Geological Survey
VA	Virginia
WMA	Wildlife Management Area

Semiprimitive Nonmotorized Recreation Opportunity Areas (both Motorized and Nonmotorized), as designated under the 1988 CNF Management Plan, will be referred to as "Primitive Areas," while those areas designated Remote Backcountry Recreation Areas (both Few Open Roads and Nonmotorized) under the CNF's 2004 management plan will be referred to as "Backcountry Areas."

SYMBOL GUIDE TO TRAIL MAPS

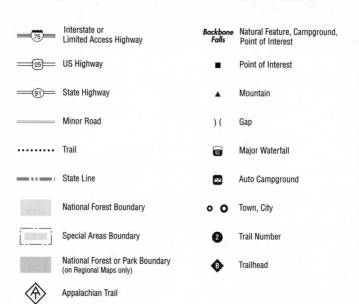

Interstate or Limited Access Highway	Natural Feature, Campground, Point of Interest (*Backbone Falls*)
US Highway	Point of Interest
State Highway	Mountain
Minor Road	Gap
Trail	Major Waterfall
State Line	Auto Campground
National Forest Boundary	Town, City
Special Areas Boundary	Trail Number
National Forest or Park Boundary (on Regional Maps only)	Trailhead
Appalachian Trail	

General Information

1. The Cherokee National Forest

The CNF consists of approximately 640,000 acres of forested federal lands generally located along the TN-NC state line, extending from GA to VA. The GSMNP also lies on the TN-NC state line and divides the CNF into two portions. The northern CNF (see map, p. 55) extends north from the GSMNP to the VA-TN state line and includes 340,969 acres. There are two ranger districts on the northern CNF: the Watauga District on the north and the Unaka/Nolichucky District on the south (the Unaka and Nolichucky were formerly separate but were merged in the late 1900s). The southern CNF (see map, p. 280) includes 298,998 acres and extends south from the GSMNP and the Little Tennessee River to the GA-TN state line. Two ranger districts are also located on the southern CNF: the Tellico District on the north and the Ocoee/Hiwassee District on the south (the Hiwassee and Ocoee were again formerly separate districts but were merged in the late 1900s) (see appendix 2 for ranger district addresses).

The CNF is part of the national forest system managed by the USFS. As a national forest, the CNF is managed according to different statutory guidelines from national parks. National parks, pursuant to the National Park Service Organic Act of 1916, are managed so as to "conserve the scenery and the natural and historic objects and the wildlife therein," but, at the same time, the management must "provide for the enjoyment of the same in such a manner and by such means as will leave them unimpaired for the enjoyment of future generations." Preservation is therefore the principal requirement of national park management. On the other hand, national forests are managed for a variety of multiple uses pursuant to the National Forest Management

Act of 1976 and related statutes. Such uses include a variety of bene-fits including water, forage, wildlife, wood, minerals, and recreation. Timber production, often by the use of clear-cutting, is an important part of the USFS's legislative mission.

Although much of the CNF is not managed as a park, significant portions have, under the multiple-use concept, been recognized by the USFS as having outstanding scenic, wildlife, and recreation qualities. Such acres are protected in a variety of management categories by the USFS, including wilderness areas, scenic areas, and backcountry areas. Many, but not all, of the trails in this book are located in those areas. We also will refer in this book to roadless areas. These are areas iden-tified by the USFS for their roadless character. However, the protection provided by that identification is uncertain as of 2004 (see the com-ments below). The following are short descriptions of the management categories used by the CNF that protect the forest from timber har-vesting and road building.

WILDERNESS AREAS

Wilderness designation of federal lands by Congress under the 1964 Wilderness Act is the best protection and most secure in that only Congress can change it. The 1964 Wilderness Act defines *wilderness* as a natural environment where "the earth and its community of life are untrammeled by man, where man himself is a visitor who does not remain." Further, it should be "an area of undeveloped Federal land retaining its primeval character and influence, without permanent improvements or human habitation." Commercial and other timber harvesting, motorized vehicles (including ORVs), development, and construction (other than trails) are prohibited, leaving these areas as natural as possible. Hiking, backpacking, hunting (in national forests but not national parks), fishing, horseback riding (but only on trails designated for horse use), and nature study are all allowed in wilder-ness areas. The use of vehicles and timber cutting are allowed, with proper approval, for fighting forest fires, search and rescue, and treat-ing insect infestation. The USFS's wilderness management guidelines are as follows: "The physical and biological components are managed so that natural processes, excluding naturally occurring wildfire, pro-ceed unrestricted by human activities. . . . Visitor use will be managed to a level compatible with the wilderness resource to prevent loss of soli-tude or unacceptable depreciation of wilderness qualities."

ROADLESS AREAS

Roadless areas are national forestlands evaluated for potential wilderness that meet preliminary criteria for wilderness evaluation. Roadless areas were identified on the CNF by the Roadless Area Review Evaluation (RARE) II process that was completed in 1979 as required by the Wilderness Act. An updated roadless inventory was performed as a part of the 1996 Southern Appalachian Assessment. The CNF roadless inventory was finalized in 1998 as part of the management plan revision process. Regulations that implement the National Forest Management Act require that roadless areas be evaluated for possible recommendation as wilderness study areas as a part of the planning process. In addition, the Clinton administration issued the Final Rule for Roadless Area Conservation on January 12, 2001. This rule recognized that roadless areas should be protected for the long term even if they are not recommended for wilderness areas in a forest plan. It offers a layer of protection to roadless areas beyond the prescriptions assigned in a forest plan and should guide these prescription designations in the plans. The rule received more comments than any other environmental rulemaking in history, and the vast majority of these comments were in favor of the rule. However, the status of this rule is uncertain. Although it has been challenged by several lawsuits by western states and the timber industry, it emerged triumphant from the first injunction that delayed its initial implementation. The rule can, however, be replaced by additional administrative rulemaking. The Bush administration has indicated its intention to amend the rule.

SCENIC AREAS

The USFS designates as scenic areas those blocks of land that feature outstanding scenic characteristics. These areas are only administratively protected, and such designation may be changed by the USFS pursuant to Forest Management Plans, which are revised every ten to fifteen years. The initial plan for the CNF was adopted on August 4, 1988, and a revised plan was released on January 30, 2004. The protection is of a lesser degree than for wilderness, although it is significant since logging is generally prohibited. The guidelines state simply that "timber will not be managed," although limited cutting is allowed for hazard prevention, vista enhancement, and pest-infested tree removal. Roads and vehicles are allowed under strict guidelines, which means that vehicle use should be limited to a very few existing roads.

The overall management criteria are to "provide an environment for a high quality dispersed recreation opportunity and . . . maintain and protect the ecological, scenic, and botanical attributes of the areas."

BACKCOUNTRY AREAS

In the CNF's 1988 management plan, backcountry areas were designated by the USFS as primitive areas to maintain the resources and attributes most desirable for those types of outdoor recreation practiced in a semiprimitive environment. Although they were officially called semiprimitive, nonmotorized (or motorized) recreation areas by the USFS, we referred to these areas in the first edition of this book as primitive areas for brevity's sake. Primitive areas, as designated in the 1988 plan, were protected in the CNF management plan; they generally do not allow timber harvesting, road construction/reconstruction, or ORV use. Within this category are several subcategories. Most did not have any timber harvesting or motor vehicle use. However, a few primitive areas allowed limited timber harvesting, but with less than twenty-acre clear-cuts and with road access being closed after any timber operation. Two areas also allowed motor vehicles, but only on specific roads. The areas that allowed some timber and road management were called primitive areas (managed) in the first edition of this book.

The new management plan for the CNF , released on January 30, 2004, provides a new framework. Under this plan, remote backcountry recreation—nonmotorized (or motorized) areas, or simply backcountry areas, take the place of primitive areas. In this book we have used the designations in the new management plan. The backcountry designation in the new plan closely parallels the old primitive designation. As with the old primitive area designation, the backcountry area designation has subcategories. The more restrictive subcategories prohibit salvage, road construction/reconstruction, and ORV use (Prescription 12A), while the less restrictive subcategories allow existing ORV use to continue and allow temporary road construction, existing road reconstruction, and salvage timber operations (Prescription 12B). Unless otherwise specified, backcountry areas will be in the roadless, nonmotorized category. These management designations are revised when the plan is revised, every ten to fifteen years. Because these designations are not permanent, all of these backcountry areas are at risk, and continued efforts by conservationists will be necessary to protect them through the USFS's current and future forest plans.

As to the trails themselves, hiking is a legal use of all the routes covered by this book. In many cases trails are designated by the USFS for a variety of other additional uses, including equestrian (horse), mountain bike, motorcycle, ORV, and 4 WD. Hikers may use all of these trails. Under CNF rules, if uses other than hiking are not specifically authorized, such use is prohibited. Most of the trails covered in this book will therefore be specified as hiking (meaning foot travel only), equestrian (meaning horse or foot travel), and/or mountain bike (meaning nonmotorized mountain or other bikes). In a few cases, motorcycle, ORV, and/or 4 WD trails and/or primitive roads will be listed and described if they provide access to or are located within a protected area. However, motor vehicles are prohibited on most of the trails described in this book.

2. Some Warnings and Advice

Hiking in the southern Appalachians brings one into intimate contact with nature. These encounters should be a delight to the senses and should not be threatening. It is important to act as responsible hikers. If you are just getting started in hiking, there are a number of fine books to help you on your way, some of which are listed in the bibliography. John Hart's *Walk Softly in the Wilderness*, Colin Fletcher and Chip Rawlins's *The Complete Walker IV*, and Ray Jardine's *Beyond Backpacking: Ray Jardine's Guide to Lightweight Hiking* are three of the best, with much more detail than would be appropriate for this book. Nevertheless, we will provide some specific advice for the CNF.

Because of hunting pressure, CNF black bears tend to be more wary and less of a problem than their counterparts in the GSMNP. So consider yourself fortunate if you see a bear, but be careful. Small cubs are usually within earshot of their mothers, and mama bears often act unpredictably if they sense that their cubs are threatened. Give bears, wild boars, and any other wild animals plenty of distance. Relax, enjoy your experience, but remember: it is *their* home; *you* are just a visitor.

As much as you may enjoy wild animals, do not ever feed them, intentionally or otherwise. The "otherwise" is usually the major problem. Protect your food and never underestimate the cleverness or resourcefulness of a panhandling bear. Remember that if a bear is of the panhandling type, it sees that brightly colored stuff sack hanging in the tree much as a human might see the Golden Arches, an announcement of food availability. Hang your food well off the ground, at least six feet from any trunk or branch big enough to support a small bear, and several feet below the branch on which it is hanging. Little animals, such as mice and squirrels, also get hungry and cold, and they can ruin a pack or stuff sack if they try to get to food or a nesting place. So here is a tip. If you leave your pack out overnight, do not leave any food in it, and open up all the pockets before you put your rain cover over it. It is better to have a mouse actually make a nest out of your wool hat than to have it first chew through your pack to get to the wool hat.

Copperheads and timber rattlesnakes are present in the CNF, although rarely seen. If you do see one, enjoy its beauty and remember that snakes are important to nature's balance. Do not even think of doing them harm. Show them the same respect that you would want. After all, would you like to be stepped on? Also, be careful where you put your hands and feet. Always look on the other side of a log before you step over it. The chance of a careful hiker being bitten is extremely small, but you should be prepared with first-aid knowledge and equipment. Indeed, a rudimentary knowledge of first aid should be a prerequisite for wilderness travel. *Medicine for Mountaineering*, published by the Mountaineers, is excellent (see the bibliography). More likely than snake bites are stinging insects. The biggest problem seems to be in early September and the fall, when yellow jackets become particularly ornery. Know before you start hiking whether you might be susceptible to allergic reactions. It is usually a long way to medical help. And with the growing spread of Lyme disease, it is always a good idea to inspect for ticks at least twice a day.

The perception of weather in the southern Appalachians can be deceiving. It can be eighty-eight degrees and sweltering in the TN Valley while a thunderstorm rages on the high peaks with the thermometer reading forty-five degrees. Or it can be raining in Knoxville and partly cloudy on top of Fodderstack. The point is that the mountains can often create their own weather, and it is best to be prepared for anything nature might throw at you. A good rule of thumb is that, for every one thousand feet of elevation increase, the temperature will drop about three degrees Fahrenheit. It can often be windier in the mountains. And wind, combined with rain, can really accelerate the loss of body heat. That's why smart hikers in the CNF never leave home without rain gear (see "Ten Essentials," below). The tops of the mountains in TN are within a couple of inches of rainfall from being officially classified as a rain forest. Keep that in mind.

Lightning is something with which all sensible hikers concern themselves. Many people advise not waiting out a thunderstorm in a metal-roofed or gated trail shelter. People have perished in the GSMNP in such structures. Instead, get off the high ground. If you are hiking on a long ridgecrest, drop down in the woods a hundred yards or so, the lower the better. If you are caught out in the open and cannot get to lower ground, many advise to keep moving; do not stand still. If you do, you run the risk of allowing static charges to accumulate on your body, acting as your own lightning rod.

The streams of the Cherokee can be delightful, especially in the summertime. But after a good rain, the water levels can rise very quickly and turn a babbling brook into a treacherous or impassable torrent. If you have any doubt about your ability to negotiate a stream safely, have one of the more sure-footed members of your party test the waters—without a pack. Stay away from large rocks in the stream, as currents near them can be especially hazardous. A rope tied across the stream can restore the confidence of the more timid party members and can be helpful in an emergency. If anyone ends up taking an unscheduled swim, watch out for the early signs of hypothermia (shivering, slow speech, loss of coordination). Many streams can feel like an ice bath in any season. If you decide you cannot ford a stream safely, do not panic. Stop and review your maps. You might find that some creative route alteration (or a bit of thrashing through the bushes) can obviate the need to ford the creek. The CNF is also blessed with a number of lovely waterfalls. Do not be tempted to climb on them. Moss or algae-covered rocks can be unbelievably slippery and can be very unforgiving if your head or knee hits them at the right angle.

In most cases, the direction from which the trail is described in this book is from the trailhead that provides the easiest access. However, it should be obvious, though it deserves stating explicitly, that all of the trails can be hiked in either direction, often giving quite different views, experiences, and impressions. When necessary, one should be able (we hope) to decipher the directions in reverse. An additional point regarding trails: trail mileage measurement is something of an art, and you may find the mileage in this book sometimes differing from other sources, including posted mileage. Although each trail was walked with a measuring wheel, you should not rely absolutely on specific distances. Besides, hiking a poorly maintained trail for five miles can wear you out much more than walking a well maintained tread for ten miles. Be wary when you start thinking, "Boy, it seems like we should have come farther than that." Many of the trails in this book are rugged and entail a bit of route finding, which can slow your pace substantially.

TEN ESSENTIALS

With all the excitement that the wilderness can throw at you, it seems to be only common sense that the hiker should be ready to meet it with at least the bare minimum of equipment. This minimum is usually referred to in hiking guides as the Ten Essentials (the exact number and composition of such a list can often consume hours of debate around the campfire, or anyplace else where hikers congregate). Briefly, the Ten Essentials are those items that you should never leave the trailhead without. And that means NEVER! EVER! It is absolutely amazing how many hikers have heard this and yet fail to heed the advice. Why not? Laziness. Stupidity. The old "It can't happen to me" syndrome. Well, maybe not. But are you willing to bet your life on it? Some folks have and have either lost or come dangerously close to losing. The couple of pounds that the essentials represent are not "extra." They are absolutely critical. There is no way to emphasize this point too much. "OK, OK," you say. "I'll carry them—but what are they?" Again, the list will vary depending on whom you talk to, but the following are some that almost everyone can agree on.

First Aid Kit. As a casual hiker, you can purchase ready-made kits or fabricate your own. You don't have to be prepared for cardiac bypass surgery on the trail. Keep it simple: a few Band-Aids, some gauze and adhesive tape, an elastic bandage for twisted knees or ankles, butterfly bandages for deep cuts, a few antihistamines for bee stings, and some painkillers are most of what is needed for day hiking. For extended backpacking trips, you might want to add a few more things. A lightweight (few ounces) flexible splint can be a welcome addition in case of an unfortunate accident. Talk to your family doctor about which prescription medications you might want to have.

Maps. At least carry copies of the relevant pages of this book with you. Better yet, also carry topographic maps. You say you don't know how to read the maps? Learn. It is easy, and anyone intelligent enough to read a highway map and get to the trailhead is intelligent enough to read a topographic map. The complexity of the terrain in the CNF is almost unbelievable. Unless you are on a very well maintained trail, it is easy to get onto a less well maintained spur, and before you know it, you are in the next valley. You can purchase topographic maps from a number of sources (see appendix 1).

Compass. Do not assume you can find north on a cloudy day without instrument assistance. Yes, moss does grow on the north side of a tree. But in the near rain forests of the CNF, it also grows on the south side, on the east side, etc. You probably spent five or ten bucks worth of gas getting to your hike; you do not have to spend much more on a good compass. And invest ten minutes worth of your valuable time reading the material that came with it. It can be really amazing to learn how many people carry compasses and do not know how to use them.

Rain Gear. The comments above should have convinced you to take rain gear, even on a bright, sunny day. But do not feel that you cannot leave the trailhead without a $250 Gore-Tex rain suit. Sure, they are great, but so is anything that will keep you dry: garbage sacks, ponchos, coated nylon rain suits. Some hikers even carry umbrellas. And, you backpackers, don't forget a cover for your pack. Even the coated nylon pack bags will let water seep in and dampen your sleeping bag or extra clothes.

Extra Clothes, Including a Wool or Fleece Hat. You lose 35 to 40 percent of your total body heat through your head. That loss can make a tremendous difference in cool weather. It may be the thing that keeps you alive through an unscheduled night out. But most of all, it keeps the brain warm so that you can think your way out of any predicament in which you find yourself.

Matches. Get the waterproof variety, or put the regular ones in a waterproof container. Cigarette lighters are very convenient, especially for starting backpacking stoves. But try to use them after the flint has gotten wet, and you will see why people who carry them also carry matches. And remember that starting a fire in the CNF can sometimes be a nontrivial matter, especially when it has been raining for a few days—or even a few hours. Do not be afraid to assist the start-up with a little toilet paper or a few pinecones.

Knife. We are not talking here about the forty-tool, everything-including-the-kitchen-sink Swiss Army variety. Just a simple, one or two-bladed type will do, to cut fabric, shave kindling, cut cord, etc.

Flashlight. This one seems to raise the most eyebrows among novice hikers. "Why do I have to take a flashlight for a day hike?" Of course, the answer is because it is only light about half of the time. Sometimes it is difficult to judge the amount of time it will take to complete a hike. Or maybe you just want to watch the sunset from an overlook four miles up the trail. There are any number of reasons why you might be out after dark. But walking in the dark on a trail, without a light, can be a terrifying experience, especially after the fourth fall. Just make sure that the batteries are reasonably fresh or that you are carrying spares. For extended trips, always carry a spare bulb or two.

Extra Food. "Extra" implies that you have some food with you to begin with. We know that no one is likely to starve to death even going without food for a week or two. But that extra snack bar will give your body a little charge to help keep warm on a cold day and may help you think straight. And relax. Don't worry about nutrition. Anything that is high in carbohydrates will be fine. This is your one chance to justify all of those things that you don't eat the rest of the time because you want to stay healthy. So go ahead, pour in the Twinkies and the M&Ms. This is not the time to be dieting.

The Tenth Essential. This is your call. *Think* about what might be important to you. For some it might be a handheld GPS or strong insect repellent or water purification tablets; for others, toilet paper, a hairbrush, make-up, or the latest Tom Clancy novel. Everyone should try to take along a good load of common sense.

In addition to these essentials, it is advisable to leave your trip itinerary with family, friends, and/or the USFS. Sometimes problems do arise, and even experienced backpackers can be unavoidably delayed. If the USFS is contacted to look for someone, it is a big help to know the lost party's location rather than simply "somewhere in the CNF." And with regard to getting lost, remember the common advice for the southern Appalachian Mountains: you can usually follow any creek downstream and along a succession of larger streams to a road or other source of help. This advice does not necessarily apply in other parts of the United States or the world, but the relatively small size of most natural areas and population density make it appropriate for the southern Appalachians.

A lot of people seem to shy away from hiking during hunting season. That is too bad, because that is often when the mountains are in their finest colors. Incidents of hikers being shot by accident are very rare in TN. Nevertheless, it is probably a good idea to wear bright colors (preferably hunter or international orange) during that time of year. Remember that probably the most dangerous thing you will do on your entire journey is to *drive* to the trailhead. Wear your seat belt when you do.

One final note of caution: The maintenance level of the trails in this book varies greatly, from well-marked, cleared, and graded trails to those receiving very little or no maintenance at all. The CNF's record in such matters is spotty at best, and the USFS should be encouraged to maintain all of the designated trails. Many trails are also not marked with signs. Pending better maintenance and signage, hikers should watch their maps and the trails carefully. Of course, there are always those who prefer the more adventurous course: off-trail. This can be an exciting experience, but it is not for beginners. Hiking off-trail in this part of the country can require anywhere from two to ten times the energy expenditure per mile as on-trail hiking. Good compass and map skills are absolutely critical to a successful off-trail trip, and an altimeter and/or GPS—and the knowledge to use it properly—can really help. If you are hiking off-trail in the foothills, there is always the risk that you will stumble onto a still or a marijuana patch. If you do, and it is during growing season, beat a hasty and quiet retreat.

3. Geology

The CNF is positioned along the western edge of the Blue Ridge Mountains that form the boundary between TN and NC. Although the mountains appear as a nearly continuous chain, they are divided into three separate ranges aligned north to south as the Unaka, Great Smoky, and Unicoi Mountains. The Unaka and Unicoi ranges got their name from the Cherokee word *unega,* meaning white. This is evidently a reference to the white race that populated lands east of the mountain range. Some other early sources refer to this range as the Great Iron or Iron Mountains in reference to the many forges that operated in the hills in the early days of colonization. Geologist James Safford named the Great Smoky Mountains in the 1860s.

In addition to the main ranges, there are several other named portions of the main range, such as Stone Mountain in northeast TN and the Bald Mountains near Greeneville. There also are subsidiary ranges and foothills just west of the main ranges, such as Holston Mountain, Iron Mountain, and Buffalo Mountain in the northeast, then a broken line of outlying ridges farther southwest called Meadow Creek, English, Chilhowee, and Starr Mountains. These front ranges may technically not even be part of the Blue Ridge Mountains at all, but rather have more in common with the neighboring Valley and Ridge that separates the Unakas from the Cumberland Mountains on the western edge of the Appalachians. It turns out that the geology of the CNF provides an explanation of why these mountains are where they are, and why they are different from the broader ranges to the east. They also have provided nearly two centuries of geologists a unique picture of what the underside of a mountain range looks like, allowing them a glimpse into to the forces that build mountains.

Despite the differences in their names, these mountains share a common ancestry. The history of the TN mountains began about 760 million years ago, during the Late Proterozoic era. An early continent (known as Laurentia) began to split apart through a process called rifting. Volcanic activity accompanied the rifting, and a new ocean (called Iapetus after one of the Titans of Greek mythology) filled the basin left by the spreading crust. Great volumes of gravel, sand, silt, and mud were shed off Laurentia and the chain of volcanoes. Deposition of these sediments into Iapetus continued for more than 200 million years.

The break up of Laurentia was followed by the three successive mountain-building events (orogenies). The Taconic Orogeny was the first and began during Ordovician time. The early rift was squeezed shut during the orogeny, plastering the volcanic islands and their associated sediments onto the continent. The region soon (give or take 50 million years) experienced a second mountain-building event, the Acadian Orogeny, beginning in Devonian time. This episode saw a microcontinent named Avalonia (after a peninsula in Newfoundland where its rocks are well exposed, or after the mythic island where King Arthur healed his wounds after the battle of Camlan, depending on your bent) smashed onto Laurentia. This was accompanied by 150 to 200 million years of deposition as thousands of feet of sediment were eroded off the early mountains. Then the final and most impressive mountain-building event, the Appalachian (or Alleghanian) Orogeny began about 250 to 300 million years ago during the Late Paleozoic era, and continued for almost 100 million years. This episode saw the closing of Iapetus and the inclusion of Laurentia into the supercontinent Pangaea.

The Appalachian Orogeny corresponds to emergence of the dinosaurs, which witnessed a lofty mountain range stretched from the present-day Alabama to Newfoundland and beyond. While the dinosaurs flourished, the pervasive forces of climate and gravity were eroding the young Appalachians. The catastrophic splitting of the range with the breakup of Pangaea followed this, when half of the range moved eastward on the African continent as the Atlas Mountains and the present-day Atlantic Ocean began to form. The entire Appalachian range may have been reduced to a high, sloping plain by the time the dinosaurs disappeared, about 65 million years ago. However, increased erosion during the Pleistocene glacial episodes wore down the less resistant rocks, but the harder, older rocks in the center of the range remained. The result was complete removal of the highlands that are now the TN Valley and the Carolina Piedmont, leaving only the thin ranges of metamorphic and igneous rocks we see today.

Anyone who has hiked both ranges will notice that the rock structure of the TN Unakas is very different from that found in the eastern Blue Ridge. The Unakas are composed mostly of folded and faulted sedimentary strata, while the rocks of the eastern Blue Ridge are metamorphic and igneous in origin. This is apparent in the character of the mountains themselves. The Blue Ridge Mountains are arched and rounded, with expansive smooth granite faces reminiscent of Yosemite. The Unaka peaks are sharper and sometimes craggy. These characteristics are derived from the way the rocks weather, and in turn the weathering process is dependent on the internal makeup of the rocks. Rocks in the CNF are composed of hard, brittle metamorphic sandstone and are full of cracks of all sizes (called fractures). These fractures are left over from when they were pushed up and over each other during the Appalachian Orogeny. The rocks tend to separate along the sharp intersections of fractures as they weather, and the blocky nature of the resulting rock mass is reflected in the general shape of the mountains. As you would expect, the rocks of Blue Ridge, on the other hand, were deformed while they were still hot and more plastic and therefore contain fewer cracks. These rocks tend to weather along broad curving surfaces like a peeled onion. Hikers may notice that the trails in the CNF are steep and rocky, so blame the Appalachian Orogeny, and not the trail builders, next time you slog up a slope of loose, sharp-edged rock.

The rocks in the CNF also differ somewhat from north to south in age and composition. The Unakas north of the French Broad River are composed primarily of Cambrian-period sandstone, conglomerate, dolostone, and shale deposited after the Acadian Orogeny, along with Precambrian-era granite and gneiss. The Cambrian rock forms the impressive cliffs seen on Bald Mountain Ridge, Holston Mountain, and Iron Mountain at the western rim of the Unakas. The Precambrian igneous and metamorphic rock found primarily in the vicinity of the Roan Highlands and Flag Pond, TN, forms the core of the range.

South of the French Broad River, the mountains are primarily made up of massive units of Precambrian sandstone, slate, and conglomerate formed during the initial breakup of Laurentia. Unlike the younger Cambrian rocks composed of similar material, these rocks have been more intensely deformed by heat and pressure and are very hard and brittle. The Cambrian rocks that compose much of the northern Unakas are found only in the long ridges that form the foothills in the southern part. Chilhowee Mountain, Starr Mountain (part of which is in the Gee Creek Wilderness), and much of English Mountain all comprise rocks similar to those found throughout the northern section of the CNF.

The oldest rocks of the CNF are found in the northeastern part of the state, in easternmost Johnson, Unicoi, and Carter counties. These rocks include the remains of the continent of Laurentia and are referred to as the basement complex because they comprise the "cellar" of the continent upon which all later sediments were deposited. These metamorphic rocks are composed of schist and gneiss and include some igneous rocks such as granite and gabbro. Much of the schist and gneiss originated as sandstone and shale deposited nearly one billion years ago. These rocks were deformed and intruded by molten rock (magma), which cooled to form granite (a pink, white, or light gray rock, rich in silica) and gabbro (a darker, iron-rich type). The rocks were then further altered by heat and pressure, destroying much of their original character. The basement complex is not very common in the CNF, although it makes up most of the eastern Blue Ridge in NC and GA. The best place to observe the ancient basement rocks in the CNF are in road cuts along US 19E near the town of Roan Mountain, where the pink and white granite is very common. On the bald summits around Roan Mountain itself, look for the dark green or black gabbro and banded gneiss and schist.

Sand and gravel shed of the ancestral mountains in the Precambrian collected in a thick sequence of sandstone, conglomerate, and slate called the Ocoee Supergroup. This great mass of rock is subdivided into three large rock units: the Snowbird Group (named for rock exposures on Snowbird Mountain in the CNF), the Great Smoky Group, and the Walden Creek Group. The Snowbird Group is well exposed along I-40 near the TN-NC border and the Devil's Backbone Primitive Area. These rocks exhibit strong cleavage that forms through the realignment of mineral orientation in response to the stress produced during mountain building. Construction of the highway undercut the smooth cleavage planes, causing massive rockslides. Repairs to the interstate from rockslides are very costly and are nearly an annual occurrence. The slides have caused at least one death and permanently scarred a beautiful gorge. This enormous cost could have been avoided by routing the road through a less sensitive area.

The Great Smoky Group and Walden Creek Group form the backbone of the mountains of the southern CNF. The Great Smoky Group is composed mainly of massive, coarse-grained sandstone, with thin units of shale. The Great Smoky Group forms the high summits along the state line from Mount Cammerer in the GSMNP, south to Copperhill, TN, and into GA. The Walden Creek Group is characteristically composed of thick beds of conglomerate sandwiched between contorted shale and siltstone. The Walden Creek Group is believed to have been deposited at the edge of the continental shelf, where ancient submarine canyons avalanched great masses of sediment deep onto the ocean floor.

The Great Smoky and Walden Creek groups are well exposed along road cuts throughout the transmountain highways in the CNF. The massive sandstone of the Great Smoky Group can be seen on the Cherohala Skyway located on the spine of Sassafras Ridge above the Jeffery Hell portion of the Citico Creek Wilderness. Farther along the road, near the state line, a conspicuous road cut exposes reddish brown and black slate on both sides of the road. This is the Anakeesta Formation, noted for its tendency to leach acids into surface runoff. Disturbance of this rock type has been blamed for fish kills in creeks below the construction of the Cherohala Skyway, the rerouting of the NC portion of US 441 through the GSMNP, and the infamous Northshore Road or "Road to Nowhere" in the GSMNP. Close examination of this rock reveals small cubes of an iron sulfide mineral, the brassy-colored pyrite (fool's gold). When rainwater reacts with these sulfides, it creates sulfuric acid that drains into streams. Another place to view the Walden Creek and Great Smoky groups is along US 64 above Parksville Dam on the Ocoee River, through the gorge, and into Ducktown.

The Great Smoky Group in the Copper Basin is well exposed, affording excellent observation of the highly deformed metamorphosed greywacke and arkose. This rock was also enriched with sulfide minerals, most notably copper. Copper was collected here by the Cherokee and discovered by European settlers in 1843. Copper, sulfur, and even TNT were produced from these acidic ores until 1987. The environmental impact of copper production in the Copper Basin is legendary. Acid fumes from copper smelting operations denuded 32,000 acres, prompting some of the original environmental lawsuits in the United States. The area has recovered slowly, thanks to more than 14 million tree plantings, several exotic species of plants, and copious use of fertilizer. The area has recently received Superfund cleanup monies in the latest phase of a 150-year ecologic calamity. Much of the damage was confined to Copper Basin; the Little Frog Wilderness lies just to the west.

The Walden Creek Group is clearly exposed in road cuts at two locations in the CNF and vicinity. One is just outside the CNF boundary along US 129 as it runs beside Chilhowee Lake and the GSMNP. Just past Chilhowee Dam are coarse-grained sandstone and conglomerate with conspicuous pebbles of bright white quartz, with some Feldspur and other minerals. Farther up the road, past the Foothills Parkway, a road cut on the left reveals numerous tight folds in the shale and siltstone, testament to the forces required to transport these massive deposits of rock from deep beneath the earth to the high mountains that once stood there. Impressive folding in the Walden Creek Group is also seen along the lower section of the Cherohala Skyway (TN 165) paralleling the Tellico River. To the right of the road before the first newer bridge, thick sandstone units are bent into several large folds with smaller folds within the larger ones. A mile or so farther, where a vertical face was blasted into the rock, are hundreds of small folds of pink quartzite between thin layers of shiny, black and blue-green rock called phyllite.

Much as the rock of the Precambrian Ocoee Supergroup forms the peaks of the Great Smokies and southern Unakas, Cambrian strata make up the rugged ridgetops of the northern Unaka range. The Cambrian rocks in the CNF are, for the most part, members of the Chilhowee Group. The Chilhowee Group comprises about 3,000 to 6,000 feet of brown, white, and gray sandstone and shale. The Chilhowee can be further subdivided into several smaller units, with names that indicate places where they are found. The Erwin Formation, Hesse Sandstone, Hampton Formation, and Unicoi Formation are all named for various East TN towns, creeks, and counties where these rocks were first described. A striking difference between the sandstone of the Chilhowee and the Ocoee Supergroup is the presence of fossils and animal burrows in the former.

The Chilhowee, being Cambrian in age, was deposited about 550 million years ago as a diverse fauna of marine creatures such as sponges, brachiopods, trilobites, and jellyfish proliferated on the shallow sea floor. Some small, bizarre sea creatures did exist during "Ocoee time," but no definitive fossils have been found in these rocks. Another distinguishing feature of the Chilhowee sandstones is their tendency to display impressive cliffs visible from the TN Valley, with gentler slopes inclined toward the east. These features reflect the tilted strata that moved up to seventy miles along thrust faults during the collision of North America and Africa some 250 to 300 million years ago in the Appalachian Orogeny. The oldest Chilhowee rocks (Unicoi Formation) are found directly on top of the Precambrian Ocoee rocks and on the basement rocks as well. The sediments that were to become the Chilhowee Group were deposited in shallow seas that accumulated lime mud produced by the early life forms. The lime mud became carbonate rock that is now exposed in many of the valleys in the northeastern CNF, such as a dolomite named for Shady Valley. Deposition of lime by marine organisms generally continued for nearly 200 million years thereafter, resulting in the extensive limestone deposits found throughout the TN Valley and outwards through middle TN and Kentucky to as far away as Minnesota.

The Chilhowee Group can be viewed in numerous locations throughout the CNF, especially in the northeastern Unakas along US 19E, 19W, and 321. Holston and Iron Mountains, incidentally, are composed of the same units as the Chilhowee, bent into a broad U or syncline. The excavation for Watauga Dam, near the Big Laurel Branch

Wilderness, affords spectacular exposure of the Chilhowee and the associated Iron Mountain Fault. A particularly scenic exposure of the Chilhowee Group occurs in the southern Unicois where the Hiwassee River gorge has cut through a ridge of Chilhowee and into the Ocoee Supergroup below. Paddlers on the Hiwassee, and hikers on the John Muir Trail, enjoy expansive views of the cliffs on Chestnut Mountain (to the northeast) and Bean Mountain (on the opposite bank) that contain an almost complete geologic section of the Chilhowee.

There are few rocks in the CNF that are younger than the Cambrian sandstone. This is because the younger rocks have been eroded from the mountaintops over the past 20 million years. Much of the erosion that left the mountains as we see them today occurred during glacial episodes in response to widespread global cooling. Although snowfields may have existed year-round during these times, no true glaciers existed in the southern Appalachians. Much of the southern Appalachians during the Pleistocene show geologic evidence of being periglacial, or near glacial. The Unakas were sparsely vegetated in tundra and taiga reminiscent of the northern portions of modern-day Alaska and Canada. The various microclimates of the southern Appalachians acted as a refuge for northern and temperate plant species during this time of climatic change. As the climate warmed and the continental glaciers receded, the mountains were covered by a diverse forest that retained much of its northern character. The boulder fields and talus created by freezing and thawing of rocks in the extreme climate were later stabilized by one of the richest forests on Earth, which remained relatively unchanged until the Europeans arrived about 250 years ago.

The rocks of the Unakas are the result of a complex history of past mountain ranges, coastlines, dawning organisms, and long-term erosion. However, the visitor will be most impressed by the present beauty of these mountains and can only reflect on their past. Perhaps the geologist James Safford, describing the geology of the Unakas in the 1860s, summarized these feelings best when he wrote the following: "when the great and magnificent views of the world below and around them are associated, they become in truth, sublime. They must be visited to be appreciated. There is a fascination about them which cannot be told."

4. Vegetation

The CNF supports a great diversity of plant species. Although there have been no botanical surveys of the forest as a whole, a measure of its diversity can be gleaned from surveys of portions of the forest and adjacent areas. The vascular plants, which include flowering plants, conifers, ferns, fern allies, and club mosses, have been most extensively studied. A total of 536 species and varieties of vascular plants are found in the Citico Creek Wilderness; 70 species of these are trees. A total of 476 species and varieties of vascular plants are found in the Big Frog Mountain Area, consisting of Big Frog Mountain Wilderness and a small section of Cohutta Wilderness.

The most thoroughly studied area of the region in terms of its biological richness is the GSMNP, where approximately 1,500 species of vascular plants have been found, including 100 species of native trees, the highest number for any of the national parks. No absolute conclusions about the species diversity of the CNF can be drawn from what is known about GSMNP because the park contains the highest portion of the Unaka Mountains and was left with more old-growth forest than the CNF. However, most or all of the habitat types found in the GSMNP can be found in the CNF. In addition, the CNF extends both farther north and south than the GSMNP. Perhaps the most significant indicator of plant species diversity in the CNF is that there are 2,391 species and varieties of plants known to inhabit the Blue Ridge Province, of which the CNF is a part.

The nonvascular plants of the CNF have been studied even less than the vascular plants. More than 1,400 nonvascular plants have been identified in GSMNP and literally thousands more are expected to be discovered in an all-taxa-biodiversity inventory currently being conducted in the park. Approximately 2,250 species of fungi (not technically a plant) have been identified in GSMNP, and this total is expected to eventually reach 20,000 after the park is thoroughly surveyed. Species of fungi, algae, lichens, liverworts, and mosses are very diverse in the CNF and make notable contributions to the forest environment.

VEGETATION HISTORY OF THE BLUE RIDGE PROVINCE

The CNF lies in the Unaka Mountains of the Blue Ridge Province, a physiographic province in eastern North America, consisting of mountains of great antiquity (see "Geology"). Mountains have been present in what is now eastern North America since at least the end of the Paleozoic era (230 million years ago), and they have gone through several cycles of uplift and erosion. The southern portion of the Blue Ridge has been continuously vegetated since the Cretaceous extinction

65 million years ago, and some elements of plant life probably survived even through this massive worldwide die-off. The Blue Ridge has thus played a crucial role in the vegetational history of North America and the world. While other areas have been submerged under seas, covered by glaciers, or subjected to great climatic change, the southern Blue Ridge has remained as a refuge for plants.

The ancestral forests of the Blue Ridge Province actually developed during the Tertiary period, which began 65 million years ago. These forests consisted of a broad-leaved forest with a diverse herbaceous layer known as the Arcto-Tertiary forest. It extended over much of the northern portion of present-day North America and Eurasia and is thought to have extended south along high-elevation chains such as the Blue Ridge while subtropical flora dominated nearer sea level in the south. This ancient forest is thought to closely resemble in structure and types of species the present-day mixed mesophytic or cove hardwood forests of the Blue Ridge and Cumberland mountains.

Climatic changes in the later Tertiary period led to more temperate conditions and an expansion of the Arcto-Tertiary forest at the expense of more tropical species. Essentially, all the elements of the modern forest were present by 34 million years ago in the Arcto-Tertiary forest, the dominant forest in eastern North America. The gradual rise of mountains in western North America resulted in increasing dryness in the western interior. The Arcto-Tertiary forest retreated eastward, to be replaced with grassland. The oak-hickory forest also developed during this period, in response to dry conditions. The mixed mesophytic forest was retained in the cove and uplands of the Blue Ridge. An oak-chestnut forest began to dominate the Ridge and Valley Province around the Blue Ridge and the drier ridges of the mountains, and an oak-pine forest began to develop in the Piedmont Region.

The Pleistocene epoch of the Quaternary period that began about two million years ago was characterized by periods of cold lasting about 100,000 years, during which glaciers moved south. These periods were interrupted by periods of relative warmth, lasting 10,000 to 30,000 years, during which the glaciers receded. Four to ten such periods occurred. The southern Blue Ridge was south of the ice sheets but was nevertheless greatly affected by them. Periods of cooling were associated with southward migrations of plant species; interglacial warming was associated with northward migrations as the ice sheet receded. The migration to the south as the climate cooled is thought to have occurred much more slowly than the northward migration following warming of the climate. The northward migration would have been into bare or sparsely occupied land; southern plant migrants would have had to compete with plants in relatively closed communities. The faster northward migration has been estimated at forty-eight miles per century.

There is evidence that climatic cooling produced a timberline on the higher mountains of GSMNP and displaced vegetation to lower elevations and to the south. During interglacial periods vegetation would have been displaced upward and to the north again. Vegetation may have been displaced upward 1,000 to 1,300 feet above present levels during the dry warm period following glaciation.

The importance of the Blue Ridge in preserving species during this period cannot be overemphasized. The mountain ranges in the Blue Ridge run generally south to north, allowing plants to migrate up or down the chain. In contrast, the mountains of Europe run east to west and formed a barrier to plant migration, resulting in the elimination of most species of plants north of the mountains. In addition, the mountains of the Blue Ridge are deeply cut by stream valleys and side ridges, creating a diversity of local climates varying in elevation (temperature), moisture, and aspect. These local climates provided a continuum of conditions that allowed plants to migrate, not only north and south along the mountain chains but up and down and around the mountains to find suitable habitat.

Another important marker of the major climatic changes and plant migrations in the Blue Ridge Province is disjunct populations of plants. As plants migrated in response to climatic change, some populations were able to adapt to conditions in particular areas, such as mountaintops, but were not able to survive in the surrounding areas. When the main population of the species reached an equilibrium in faraway places, the disjunct population was left isolated from the main population. Such isolated species of plants occur frequently in the Blue Ridge.

DYNAMICS IN THE OLD-GROWTH FOREST

Characteristic of all life, individual trees and plants in an old-growth forest become established, mature, reproduce, age, die, and decay. In general, these milestones will be different for each species of plant. The trees, being the largest living structures, will tend to dominate the forest. Each species of tree has different requirements for light, moisture, soil, temperature, and other conditions. Some species of trees will tend to be more "dominant" than others, and a number of tree species will tend to share dominance.

Gaps in the canopy of the forest, which allow light to penetrate to the forest floor, occur for many reasons. Old age may cause the death of a giant old tree; lightning may strike a tree standing higher than its neighbors; fire may burn an area; ice may strip the limbs from one or more trees; wind may blow over one weakened tree or a group of trees. All of these disturbances open up gaps that allow light to penetrate to the floor of the forest. Saplings in the understory of the forest take advantage of the light and compete to fill the gap. Some of the saplings will win the struggle and become larger; others will die or grow very little. Another tree that falls may give some of the trees a spurt of growth. Through the creation of a series of adjacent gaps over the years, some of the trees will eventually become dominant or subdominant in the forest, while most will die. The tree species that thrive and grow in this cycle will depend on the amount of light created in these gaps, the moisture in the area, the trees producing seeds in the area, and the seed and seedling characteristics. Through this process, a characteristic canopy of dominant and subdominant tree species will form. Distinctive layers of vines, shrubs, and herbaceous plants will form under the canopy.

FOREST VEGETATION TYPES

Forest vegetation types have been classified in various ways. In 1956 the ecologist R. H. Whittaker studied species distribution with variations in elevation and moisture. Although this study was for the GSMNP, the vegetation types would seem to have a broader application and will be used to describe the natural vegetation of the CNF.

Cove Hardwood Forest. These beautiful and very diverse forests occupy the valleys (coves) below 4,500 feet. In old-growth cove hardwood forests the canopy trees are three to four feet in diameter, with occasional tulip trees reaching six to seven feet in diameter. The crowns of the trees are 75 to 100 feet above the forest floor, with the tops of the trees reaching 100 to 150 feet and occasionally 200 feet. Below the canopy, smaller trees form a broad foliage layer. Ferns and herbs cover the floor of the forest. The forest has an open, parklike appearance. Eastern hemlock, silverbell, buckeye, basswood, sugar maple, and yellow birch are usually the dominant trees. Often tulip tree and American beech share dominance of the canopy. A number of other trees share dominance with these eight trees in dispersed quantities. These species, which are widespread but never numerous, include white ash, green ash, northern red oak, cucumber tree, bitternut hickory, red maple, and wild black cherry.

Trees of small and medium stature that form another layer below the canopy trees include umbrella magnolia, blue beech, Fraser magnolia, yellowwood, holly, and hop hornbeam. Mountain maple and serviceberry occur at high elevations.

A shrub layer, although frequently absent or poorly developed, may include strawberry bush and spicebush at low elevations. Alternate leaf dogwood, hobblebush, and dogberry occur at higher elevations. Wild hydrangea occurs at all elevations. Rhododendron occurs along streams and, with doghobble, under hemlock and in other sites.

The herbaceous species development is the richest in the mountains, with more than a hundred different species represented in this vegetation type. The herbaceous layer itself is stratified with canopy herbs and an undergrowth of prostrate herbs. A large variety of spring wildflowers is very well represented in the cove hardwood forests, including blue cohosh, squirrelcorn, dutchman's breeches, bleeding heart, umbrella-leaf, trout lily, wild geranium, sharp-lobed hepatica, dwarf crested iris, bishop's cap, showy orchis, mayapple, Solomon's seal, bloodroot, black snakeroot, false Solomon's seal, giant chickweed, foamflower, several species of trillium, and numerous species of violets.

The foliage of some of the spring wildflowers persists through the summer. Others die back, and herbs characteristic of the summer come to dominate. Herbaceous cover during the summer is as high as 80 percent. The most abundant herbs during the summer are white snakeroot, black cohosh, blue cohosh, jewel weed, wood-nettle, heart-leaved aster, wood fern, and silvery glade fern. Underneath these herbs are smaller species, such as giant chickweed, foamflower, bedstraw, and strawberry bush.

Eastern Hemlock Forest. Hemlock forests commonly form dense, shaded stands along streams, on north-facing slopes, and on ridgetops. Tree stems of three and four feet diameter are common in the hemlock forest, and the canopy crowns reach over 100 feet. At higher elevations these stands may be almost entirely hemlock; at lower elevations, mesic tree species characteristic of the cove forest are increasingly represented. Below 2,500 feet the hemlock forest gradually blends into the cove forests. Hemlock is a large tree and grows very densely. It can therefore dominate a forest that contains a number of other species.

Hemlock forests tend to have a dense, dark appearance. This impression is often heightened by a dense shrub layer of rhododendron that, at high elevations, may cover 60 to 80 percent of the ground. The understory and shrub layer species include rosebay rhododendron, mountain rosebay, dog hobble, wild hydrangea, and mountain laurel.

The herbaceous layer is usually nonexistent or sparse in a well-developed hemlock forest. The already dark conditions are exacerbated by a thick heath shrub layer. The superficial root systems of the heaths result in drying of the soil. In addition, the bed of hemlock needles and heath leaves on the floor of the forest tends to promote very acidic conditions unfavorable to herbaceous plants. Where heath coverage is low, an herbaceous coverage may occur, with wood fern, partridge berry, rattlesnake plantain, and foamflower being the most represented. Rock cap fern can be found on many exposed rocks and roots.

Gray Beech Forest. High-elevation beech forests occur above 4,500 feet. The American beech trees are gray from lichens and appear stunted with rounded crowns. These forests on north-facing slopes could be considered a continuation of the upper cove hardwoods and may contain yellow birch, buckeye, and a low tree layer of mountain maple, striped maple, and serviceberry. Witch hobble, alternate-leaf dogwood, and wild hydrangea occur in the shrub layer. The herb layer is similar to that of higher elevation cove forests, with the addition of sedges, coneflower, and twisted stalk.

The south-facing beech forests are characterized by a preponderance of beech, with silverbell as a second species. The small tree and shrub layer is largely absent, and wild hydrangea appears only sporadically. The south-facing beech forests are distinctive in their herb layer of sedges that cover up to 80 to 90 percent of the forest floor. Scattered plants of most of the herb species of the upper coves and north slopes occur with the sedges.

Oak-Hickory Forest. At elevations of 2,500 to 3,000 feet, oak-hickory forests occupy areas slightly more dry than the cove hardwoods. These forests are dominated by northern red oak, pignut hickory, white oak, and mockernut hickory. Stands usually include black oak, sweet pignut hickory, chestnut oak, American chestnut, black gum, and tulip tree. Red maple, flowering dogwood, and sourwood are important understory trees. Huckleberry and mountain laurel are most prevalent in the shrub layer, with rosebay rhododendron, flame azalea, buffalo nut, and other shrubs also present.

Herb coverage in these forests is generally only 1 to 10 percent. Christmas fern, goldenrod, false foxglove, and galax are the most frequent herbs. Spear-leaved violet, pipsissewa, beggar lice, downy rattlesnake plantain, gall-of-the-earth, false Soloman's seal, and bellwort also occur.

Chestnut Oak–Chestnut Forest. This forest, which has drastically changed since the chestnut blight, is the most extensive of the lower and middle elevations. It is now dominated by chestnut oak, formerly by American chestnut. Chestnut made up probably 30 to 70 percent of this forest type, with chestnut oak making up much of the rest. Components of northern red oak, white oak, black oak, black gum, red maple, tulip tree, and small percentages of hickories and cove species also occur. Oak-chestnut forests and oak-chestnut heaths (described below) occur on almost all slopes except those facing south and southwest. It is believed that before settlement and the blight, forests of large chestnut trees grew in lower coves and in broad open valleys away from streams. Chestnut trees on the slopes probably reached four to five feet in diameter. Chestnut oak, northern red oak, and red maple have replaced nearly half the dead chestnut. Other replacement trees are hemlock, silverbell, sourwood, black locust, scarlet oak, tulip tree, sweet birch, white oak, beech, and flowering dogwood.

Shrub coverage is high, especially above 2,500 feet. Mountain laurel, flame azalea, rosebay, and huckleberry are the most important shrubs. Buffalo nut, sweet pepperbush, sweet-shrub, and highbush blueberry are also usually present.

The herb layer is similar to that of the oak-hickory forest. The dominant species are false foxglove, gall-of-the-earth, wood betony, beggar lice, downy rattlesnake plantain, hellebore, and galax. Herb coverage ranges from a low of about 1 percent up to about 30 percent in higher elevations and moister sites.

Chestnut Oak–Chestnut Heath. The oak-chestnut heath occurs on the drier slopes. Tree canopy coverage can fall below 40 to 50 percent. Large chestnut oak and chestnut were widely scattered. Under the open forest, the shrub layer is closed, being covered by continuous evergreen heath made up of mountain laurel, with sweet pepperbush, male-blueberry, rosebay, buffalo nut, and highbush blueberry. A low shrub layer of huckleberry is usually below the higher shrub layer. Galax is the dominant herbaceous plant, with other minor components. Herbaceous cover is only about 1 to 5 percent.

Red Oak-Chestnut Forest. This vegetation is somewhat moist in species composition and is the high-altitude equivalent of the chestnut oak–chestnut forest. Northern red oak and chestnut formed 70 to 80 percent of the canopy. Red maple, basswood, black cherry, yellow birch, buckeye, and white ash are important associates below 4,500 feet. Red maple and American beech are important associates above 4,500, feet and silverbell has come in thickly since the chestnut blight above 4,500 feet.

Shrub coverage above 4,500 feet is sparse, with flame azalea and highbush blueberry being the major species. The herbaceous layer above 4,500 feet resembles that of the south-slope beech stands, but with less coverage. Sedges and ferns predominate. Below 4,500 feet the herb layer is essentially the same as in the chestnut oak–chestnut forests; only the subalpine species painted trillium, goldenrod, and umbrella leaf distinguish it from the chestnut oak–chestnut forest. Herb coverage is from 10 to 40 percent at lower elevations and 20 to 60 percent above 4,500 feet.

White Oak–Chestnut Forest. Below 4,500 feet, the white oak–chestnut forests are not distinguishable from the red oak–chestnut. Above 4,500 feet, white oak becomes strongly dominant on some exposed southwest ridges, with an open growth of rather small trees and a diverse herbaceous layer of grasses, ferns, and herbs. American chestnut formerly shared dominance with white oak. Northern red oak is almost always present. Pignut hickory and chestnut oak occupy the canopy at lower elevations. Subdominant trees of red maple, sourwood, and black locust also occur.

Shrubs are predominantly flame azalea, highbush blueberry, and mountain laurel, with coverage from 20 to 60 percent. Herb coverage is 10 to 50 percent. New York fern, southern lady fern, bracken fern, and a variety of other herbs and grasses are represented.

Virginia Pine Forest. In low elevations Virginia pine is dominant in stands on south-facing slopes and in old fields. Shrub coverage is 10 to 40 percent with mountain laurel and lowbush blueberry usually dominant. Herb coverage is from 2 to 10 percent and includes such species as little bluestem, broomstraw, panic grass, bracken fern, goat's rue, wild indigo, tickseed sunflower, asters, and goldenrod.

Pitch Pine Forest. Pitch pine dominates pine stands in the elevation range of 2,200 feet to 3,200 feet. Scarlet oak sometimes shares dominance. Also present are chestnut oak and American chestnut. Shrub coverage is 40 to 50 percent and consists of mountain laurel, lowbush blueberry, and blueberry. Herb coverage is 5 to 20 percent and consists of little bluestem, bracken fern, trailing arbutus, and wintergreen.

Table Mountain Pine Heath. At higher elevations table mountain pine becomes more and more dominant. At the upper end of the pine heaths it is strongly dominant. The stands are usually small, low, and open. The shrub layer is usually dominated by blueberry or huckleberry, with 60 to 90 percent coverage. Herb coverage is 5 to 20 percent, with little bluestem, galax, trailing arbutus, and wintergreen.

Spruce-Fir Forest. The spruce-fir forests are generally above 5,000 feet in elevation. These dense, moist forests of red spruce and Fraser fir are characteristic of much more northerly forests. Associated species include yellow birch, mountain maple, striped maple, serviceberry, and mountain ash. The canopy is dominated by spruce and, to a lesser extent, yellow birch. The shrub and herbal layers are highly variable. In their most developed form, they show a characteristic five-tier layering. Mosses and herbs form the lowest layer. A low herb layer of wood sorrel is overtopped by a high herb layer of woodfern, bluebead-lily, aster, Rugel's ragwort, wake robin, and twisted stalk. A low shrub layer of bearberry is followed by a high shrub layer of hobblebush. Mountain maple and the other small trees form a low tree layer.

Grassy Balds. Grassy balds are distinctive meadows covered with grass and herbs. The transition from forest to bald is quite abrupt, except for a gradual decrease in tree stature. However, the trees end in a distinct tree line of dwarfed trees of the surrounding forest. Usually these forests are beech and oak-chestnut. Shrubs in this tree line include highbush blueberry, flame azalea, and male-blueberry. Mountain oak grass is strongly dominant on the balds. Some introduced grasses are also prevalent. Sedges occur and various herbs are scattered throughout the grass. Five fingers is the most abundant herb, with hedge nettle, goldenrod, rattlesnake root, catbriar, bluets, coneflower, gentian, and giant chickweed also present, as well as a number of introduced weeds. Scattered shrubs of flame azalea, highbush blueberry, and blackberry may occur over the balds.

The origin of the balds and the means of their prehistoric maintenance are subject to much controversy. Everything from Indian fires to parasitic insects and large grazing animals has been used to explain the balds. Many of the bald areas were grazed by early settlers. Other areas were cleared by settlers for grazing purposes and are not true balds. Reinvasion by trees on both natural balds and human-made balds is a current management issue.

Heath Balds. The heath balds occur throughout the elevations of the subalpine forest down to 4,000 feet. These balds are composed of blueberry and other heath shrubs, the particular species depending on the elevation. The shrubs approach full coverage and are often impenetrable, forming dense thickets three to ten feet high that are sometimes known as "hells." Herbal coverage is well below 5 percent. Wintergreen, galax, cow wheat, Indian cucumber root, and painted trillium are the main herbal species. Tree seedlings that may be present at high altitudes are Fraser's fir, red spruce, mountain ash, and fire cherry. At lower elevations, seedlings of cherry birch, red maple, American chestnut, sourwood, sassafras, table mountain pine, black locust, and witch-hazel can be found.

HUMAN IMPACT ON VEGETATION

There is a long history of human use of the southern Appalachian forests, including the CNF. It is probable that prehistoric native Americans used the mountains for hunting. There is also some evidence that they used fire as a tool to shape the forest. American Indians used the forested mountains for hunting, fishing, and other purposes. With the coming of European settlers the clearing of the more accessible portions of the CNF occurred, slowly at first and then at an accelerated rate. Settlers also intensified the use of fire to create better livestock browse and to clear the forest. Later, in the early twentieth century, large timber companies moved in with massive logging operations. The end result of settlement and timber operations was a forest left ravaged by huge timber cuts, wildfires, and erosion. The land was to some extent rendered undesirable, and much of the land was bought by the US government for incorporation into the new national forest system.

Little logging took place under early USFS management. The forests were protected from fires and were allowed to recover. This stewardship, coupled with the remarkable recuperative power of southern Appalachian forests, resulted in recovery of much of the botanical diversity in the CNF. Such diversity continues to recover and will improve as sections of the forest approach old-growth conditions. However, biological diversity is not synonymous with timber productivity. As the forest has aged, the USFS has increased timbering activities. Conservation organizations have pressed for greater emphasis on other uses of the national forests, including recreation, wildlife habitat, watershed and wilderness preservation, and nature study. In addition, they have supported the continued biological recovery of the national forests through wilderness and other special-area designations, longer rotation ages, and alternative methods of harvesting timber.

One of the greatest impacts on the vegetation of the CNF and on the forests of eastern North America in general has been the introduction of exotic organisms. Examples are legion, but none has had the impact or so changed the character of the forests as the inadvertent introduction of the chestnut blight. The blight, which is caused by the fungus *Endothia parasitica,* is fatal to American chestnut trees. The fungus was brought to America from Asia on Asiatic chestnut trees, which are resistant to the fungus. The blight was discovered in New York City in 1904. Over the next few decades it slowly spread throughout the natural range of the American chestnut, frustrating efforts to eradicate it.

The American chestnut was one of the largest and most important trees of the southern Appalachian forests. Heights of 120 feet and stem diameters of eight feet were reached. The nut of the chestnut was a very important wildlife food; it was much more reliable than that of the oak, which is subject to major fluctuations in production from year to year. The American chestnut was a shade-tolerant tree and could regenerate well in mature forest. It was thus a dominant species of the old-growth forest and helped determine the environment of the forest. It was also a major component of many of the forest types. Its demise affected the whole forest ecosystem. Other trees have replaced it in the forest, but they fall short of filling its place in the ecosystem. Stump sprouts from the trees' root systems, which are not affected by the fungus, can still be seen in the CNF. There is ongoing research attempting to genetically breed the fungal resistance of the Asiatic species into the American chestnut. Other research indicates that forms of the fungus that are harmless may protect against the virulent forms. The American Chestnut Foundation (http://www.acf.org) has taken the lead in attempting to bring back the chestnut, and we can only hope that this great tree will someday grow once again throughout our forests.

EDIBLE AND MEDICINAL PLANTS

A large number of the plants found in CNF have been used for food and medicine. Native Americans were dependent on many of the berries, nuts, fruits, and roots of the forest for food and used many herbs for medical treatments and as tonics. The pioneers helped preserve much of this knowledge. Science has shown the value of many of these remedies, and some of the herbs are used as the basis for modern medicines. Others have not been fully investigated.

You should definitely know what you are doing before ingesting anything found in the wild. The possibility of poisoning is very real. There are many poisonous plants, and many of the plants used as herbs or medicines have the potential for poisoning if the wrong plant part or the wrong dose is taken. This book does not cover the identification and preparation of the edible plants, but there are many other knowledgeable people and excellent guides to edible and medicinal plants.

A few of the more tasty treats to be found in the CNF are blueberries, huckleberries, blackberries, pawpaw (the pioneer's banana), persimmon, common greenbriar, wild grapes, hickory nuts, common elderberry, wood sorrel, violets, ramps, and wild strawberries. Native

Americans used acorns (especially from the white oak) for flour, but this required special preparation to remove the tannins. Before being eliminated by blight, the American chestnut was one of the most important sources of food found in the CNF.

RARE, ENDANGERED, AND THREATENED PLANTS

You will need a sharp eye to see these plants—there are very few of them, and for obvious reasons their exact locations are not publicized. They have persisted through centuries of change in the CNF and we hope that favorable management practices will allow them to continue. An endangered species is in danger of extinction, while a threatened species is likely to become endangered in the future. Four plant species listed as endangered and three listed as threatened by the US Fish and Wildlife Service are found in the CNF. Sensitive species are plant and animal species identified by the regional forester for which global population viability is a concern. There are 101 sensitive species that have been identified in the CNF. Many additional "locally rare species" that have forestwide, state, or regional viability concerns are located in the CNF. A complete catalog of the threatened, endangered, and sensitive species of plants and animals is included in appendix 6.

The hiker of the CNF's trails will leave with many impressions. One of the strongest and most memorable and pleasant will be of diverse and beautiful vegetation, ranging from vistas of soft green-blanketed ridges and valleys, to giant oak trees, to the smallest of bluet flowers. The land, the wildlife, but also the vegetation, make these areas special and worthy of efforts to preserve and protect them.

5. Wildlife

The typical CNF hiker will see little wildlife, a few birds, a snake or lizard in the summer, or occasionally a deer. However, a little patience and knowledge will reveal a variety of wildlife in the diverse habitats provided by the CNF. Since the CNF is managed for multiple uses, including timber harvesting, its wildlife habitats range from protected wilderness to clear-cuts. Each habitat is important to different species of wildlife. The areas described in this book will often feature what are called "late successional" habitats by foresters, or "big, old trees," to laymen. This section will emphasize wildlife species dependent on such late successional habitats that are rare in TN. It should be noted that the all-taxa-biodiversity inventory currently being conducted in the GSMNP will reveal many species of both flora and fauna that could also be found in the adjacent CNF.

BIRDS

More than 120 bird species may be found in the CNF, including wild turkey, seven species of woodpeckers, ruffed grouse, five kinds of owls, hawks, vultures, ravens, warblers, and much more. Birds are often difficult to see, so to see more than an occasional few you will need to learn where and when to look. A good bird guidebook, knowledge of the songs of birds, and a pair of binoculars are essential. Those who make the effort may be rewarded by the sight of some rare and interesting birds, possibly a red-cockaded woodpecker, a hooded warbler, a wild turkey, a golden eagle, or a peregrine falcon.

The red-cockaded woodpecker is the size of a cardinal, about 8.5 inches long. The cockade, for which it is named, is a small red patch behind the male's eye that is very difficult to see in the field. The best field mark is the bird's white cheek, which no other North American woodpecker has. The red-cockaded woodpecker is in trouble all over the southeastern United States. There are only a few areas where the population is stable; everywhere else they are declining. The red-cockaded was once a common bird in the Southeast, including TN, extending as far north as NJ and PA. However, habitat changes have caused it to decline in numbers.

The red-cockaded requires both large, live pine trees, usually 70 to over 100 years old, in which to build their nest cavities, and sparse understory. Red-cockadeds build their cavities below the lowest branches on a tree, usually about fifteen feet above the ground. When nearby vegetation gets as high as the cavity, they abandon it. Originally, the sparse understory required by the red-cockaded was naturally maintained by wildfire. Fire suppression has generally eliminated this aspect of their habitat even where old-growth pine forests persist.

Red-cockaded woodpeckers were not known to exist in the CNF until a single colony was found in 1987. With help and encouragement from conservationists, the USFS has been searching for other colonies. The USFS has also modified its timber-harvesting practices to avoid adverse impacts, but it remains to be seen whether the red-cockaded will survive in the CNF.

The hooded warbler is another of the fascinating birds that may be found in the CNF's special areas. It is named for the male's black hood that covers the top of the head, the throat, and chin. The underparts and face are bright yellow, and the wings, back, and tail are olive green. The female looks like a faded version of the male without the hood. The hooded warbler breeds in the mature deciduous forests with well-developed understories. They glean insects from trees and understory vegetation and seldom forage more than fifteen feet above the ground.

Hooded warblers are characterized as forest-interior species because they avoid edge habitats and need relatively large uninterrupted tracts of forest for successful breeding. Hooded warblers have disappeared from forest fragments as large as 1,200 acres. Why they need such large forest tracts is not completely clear, but it appears to be related to their susceptibility to nest predators (e.g., blue jays) and nest parasites (brown-hooded cowbirds) that frequent forest edges.

Because of the decline and fragmentation of mature deciduous forests in eastern North America, large expanses of forest like the CNF are important for survival of the hooded warbler and other birds that are dependent on the interior of a forest. The CNF's protected areas that are the subject of this book, especially the larger ones, are important refuges for the hooded warbler and may be crucial to its long-term survival. Listen for its song as you hike and enjoy the wilderness even more by knowing wilderness helps to preserve this and other parts of our natural heritage.

The wild turkey is a wildlife success story. The turkey was eliminated from East TN by overhunting and habitat loss as the virgin forests were removed. However, they are now plentiful due to their reintroduction and management by the TWRA and the regrowth of the forests under supervision of the USFS. Wild turkeys are much more intelligent than their barnyard cousins, and only the lucky or persistent hiker is likely to see them. Those who do will have no trouble identifying them. Except for eagles and condors, no North American bird approaches their size.

In recent years, the USFS and the TWRA have been reintroducing bald eagles and peregrine falcons in the CNF and adjacent areas. The initial results of these efforts are positive and if these birds return to live and breed again in the CNF, they will be an invaluable addition to TN's natural heritage.

MAMMALS

The USFS lists forty-seven species of mammals that may be found in the CNF. Among the most interesting are black bears, flying squirrels, red and gray fox, and bobcats. Red and gray fox are particularly elusive, while flying squirrels and bobcats are nocturnal. Of these mammals, you are therefore most likely to see bears. However, because they are hunted in some areas of the CNF during season and often poached at other times, you are less likely to see them than in the nearby GSMNP. Other mammals you may see include raccoons, opossums, cottontail rabbits, and river otters. And, of course, there are the mice, shrews, voles, moles, bats, and many other important small-animal citizens of the CNF. Small and large, there are many fascinating mammals to observe and enjoy.

The larger protected areas of the CNF discussed in this book constitute, with the GSMNP, the principal habitats of the black bear in TN. The historic range of the eastern black bear has declined significantly in the wake of deforestation and heavy exploitation, and the species now exists on less than 10 percent of its former range in the Southeast. Increasing human populations and developments continue to fragment the black bear population. As a result the bear now exists primarily on federal lands containing designated or de facto wilderness.

The survival of the black bear in the Southeast depends on the abundance of a diversity of late-successional trees (especially oaks over 100 years old), availability of seed and berry plant species, an adequate supply of old-growth forest distributed throughout its range, limitations on future road developments, greatly increased educational and enforcement activities by responsible resource agencies, and regular and systematic population monitoring. Of these requirements, food is obviously very important. Although black bears are omnivores, they primarily eat berries and nuts. Berries are the predominant food in the summer. In the fall, bears begin to make physiological and behavioral changes that allow them to accumulate body fat. They must accumulate enough body fat to carry them through three to four months of winter denning (during which they eat nothing) and another month of scarce early spring foods. For bears to accumulate body fat, they often abandon their typical summer range and feed almost continuously over extensive areas. It is not uncommon for bears to gain one or two pounds per day during the peak of this "feeding frenzy" period. In the Southeast, nuts are their predominant fall food. In the CNF, acorns provide almost all of their fall and winter energy needs.

Black bears also require high-quality denning sites. Bears are adaptable enough to den in a number of different kinds of sites. However, adult females need highly protected sites for their newborn cubs. The best sites occur in old-growth forests under the root mass or in cavities in large trees. Males are less demanding and can often take advantage of thickets created by fallen trees or timber-cutting activities.

As more and more of the private lands near the CNF come under intensive management, the bear becomes more dependent on the national forest. The protected areas described in this book are therefore essential to the black bear's future.

Bobcats are nocturnal and hunt by stealth. Alert hikers may find evidence of the bobcat's presence in scats or their scrapes, piles of dirt, or duff that they sometimes use to mark their territories. Large rodents and rabbits are bobcats' dominant foods, but they also eat birds, mice, eggs, reptiles, and squirrels. Bobcats are capable of killing deer but seldom do so.

The white-tail deer is another of TN's wildlife success stories. After being hunted nearly out of existence, regulated hunts and reintroductions have made the deer one of the most plentiful animals in the state. The deer's high fecundity and preference for edge habitat created by clear-cuts have allowed them to support remarkably high hunting pressures. Hikers may see them, especially at dawn and dusk, and especially in the northern CNF. They are less numerous in the southern CNF.

Coyotes are moving into the CNF from the west, including western TN, where their numbers are higher. Coyotes are highly omnivorous with principal items in the diet being rodents (mice, rats, and rabbits), squirrels, insects, berries, fruit, birds, and carrion. Rabbits are the largest part of the diet overall, but carrion may be largest in the winter. Berries and fruits are important in the fall, whereas insects are consumed chiefly in the spring and early summer. Occasionally a group of coyotes will gang up on a larger animal, usually the young of deer, sheep, or cows. However, these larger animals make up a small portion of the coyote's diet. Coyotes breed rapidly and at a young age, are extremely adaptable, and will den almost anywhere. Although the coyote's original habitat is the dry and open intermountain basin areas in the American West, it has successfully colonized nearly every habitat on the continent, including urban areas. Its numbers are expected to grow in the entire Southeast, including in the CNF.

A discussion of CNF mammals would not be complete without mention of the European wild boar. This exotic game animal causes serious damage to plants of the forest by rooting for tubers. It also competes with native wildlife for food. A typical adult boar can consume 1,300 pounds per year of acorns, the most important wildlife food in the southern Appalachians. Many conservationists support elimination of this nonnative animal from the forests of the state, while some hunters value it as a game animal in spite of its adverse impact on native species.

The wild boar was introduced to the mountains of NC in 1912 by an entrepreneur named George Moore. Moore's intention was to build a hunting preserve for wealthy businessmen on approximately 1,500 acres of fenced Hooper Bald land. By 1920, when financial difficulties caused him to abandon his venture and release the boars, his original population of 14 boars had increased to over 100. Those few boars have prospered, multiplied, and caused unending damage in the mountains of East TN and western NC.

The NPS spends substantial sums each year for trapping and hunting to keep the population of wild boar in the GSMNP at acceptable levels. Many of the boars trapped in the GSMNP are released in TN and NC national forests, where the principal controls on boar numbers are hunters and starvation in years with mast crop failures. They are managed as a game species in the national forests. The boar has therefore grown in numbers and remains a problem today.

REPTILES, AMPHIBIANS, AND FISH

The USFS recognizes thirty reptiles as residents of the CNF, including eastern and three-toed box turtles, nine lizard species, and nineteen snake species. The snake species include northern copperheads and timber rattlesnakes that were once common in the region but now are more likely to be found in remote areas like the CNF. They are not especially common in the CNF, but care should be taken to avoid them. Snakes are a part of the mountains. Admire them but do not harm them.

The USFS recognizes forty-six amphibians as residents of the CNF. Thirty-two of these are salamanders, many of which are found only in the southern Appalachians. Salamanders are most commonly found in moist areas near streams. In such places, lifting large stones and fallen logs may give you the pleasure of finding one of these interesting amphibians. Salamanders eat insects and worms, making them the top predators of the leaf litter on the forest floor.

The habitat needs of many of these reptiles and amphibians are not well known. There is a considerable amount of uncertainty about the effects of clear-cuts on the amphibians, particularly salamanders. Most salamanders live near streams, which receive protection from clear-cuts; however, some species live a considerable distance from streams and may not survive in clear-cut areas. Further, because they move slowly and do not migrate, it is uncertain whether they will recolonize cutover areas before they are clear-cut again.

As trout fishermen know, the CNF contains the most important cold-water fishing in TN, especially in places like the Citico Creek Wilderness. Good rainbow trout fishing in the mountains is a tribute to the cold, clean water that comes off the forested mountains.

Unfortunately, much of the rainbow fishing exists at the expense of the native brook trout. Competition from rainbow trout, a native of the Pacific Northwest that was introduced to the southern Appalachians, has driven the brook trout to the brink of extinction on many streams. Trout Unlimited and the USFS are restoring brook trout to some of the streams in the CNF. Conservationists support these efforts and look forward to restoration of the brook trout throughout the CNF, especially in wilderness areas.

THREATENED AND ENDANGERED SPECIES

A remote and relatively undisturbed area, the CNF is the last refuge of many animal species that were once common in TN. The US Fish and Wildlife Service has identified a number of species that are listed or proposed for listing as threatened or endangered and either live in the CNF or have habitat in it. The federal list of the CNF's endangered and threatened wildlife species is included in appendix 6. Endangered species are defined as species in danger of becoming extinct, while threatened species are likely to become endangered. As you look this list over, realize that these species, without careful management or, in most cases, lack of human interference with their habitat, can soon be lost forever. There are probably many other species in the CNF that either have not yet been found or are in much worse condition than is presently known. The protected areas described in this book are therefore important refuges for much of the wildlife discussed in this chapter.

While walking the trails of the CNF, take some time to search for the wildlife that is there but not easy to see. Remember that hiking is not only a means of transportation but also a pilgrimage to our roots. When the hour gets late or you get tired of walking, let your mind wander to an earlier time when the cougar, the wolf, and the elk walked the forest. Ask yourself if it is not time to begin to put the pieces back into the wilderness. Think how thrilling it would be to hear the wolf's song, to glimpse a cougar on a rock outcrop, or to hear the clashing antlers of bull elk in rut. These visions and sounds could be within our grasp if we work to put the wild back in the wilderness. The future of the CNF is in our hands.

6. Human History

The trails of the CNF often provide solitude, a momentary respite from the cares of the world. And yet even on the most remote forest trail one cannot escape the human imprint, for the history of the area is long and filled with many different peoples.

No one knows when the first Indians hunted in these forested mountains and valleys, but archaeological evidence suggests it was perhaps 12,000 years ago. Hundreds of generations later, local Indians adopted a diversified economy featuring a corn-based agriculture, settled in semipermanent communities, and developed complex cultural patterns. When the Spanish conquistador Hernando de Soto arrived in 1540, he encountered well-established tribal groups, although it is not clear to what extent these correspond to later tribes. For more than 100 years after de Soto, this area remained a mystery to white settlers. Not until the late 1600s did English traders operating out of VA and SC establish contact with the Cherokees, who occupied a number of scattered villages in the southern Appalachians. Maps of the 1720s and 1730s show Cherokee towns along the Little Tennessee, Hiwassee, and Tellico rivers in the southern part of today's CNF. For a time, Chota, on the Little Tennessee River, was the "principal town" of the Cherokees and the center of tribal diplomacy and ceremonies.

Because of their strategic location, the Cherokees assumed great importance in the colonial wars between Britain and France. Near Chota, in 1756–57, the British built Fort Loudon, their first major fortification west of the Appalachians. Fort Loudon was the scene of a memorable siege and massacre in 1760 when the long-suffering Cherokees vented their frustration on the garrison. British troops retaliated by destroying many Cherokee towns. A restored version of the fort, near Vonore, TN, makes a nice side trip for a visitor to the CNF. Sequoyah, the famous inventor of the Cherokee alphabet, was born in the area and is honored by a modern museum near the restored fort.

Despite the absence of permanent Cherokee habitations in the northern part of the CNF, the tribe still claimed the area and hunted there frequently. A few white adventurers also visited periodically, including famous "long hunters" like Daniel Boone. The first white residents settled along the Watauga, Holston, and Nolichucky rivers in the early 1770s (in defiance of British law) and quickly aroused resentment among the Cherokees, resulting in widespread Indian raids during the American Revolution. The frontiersmen responded with brutal efficiency, laying waste to Cherokee villages. In 1780 these same backwoodsmen, the so-called Over-the-Mountain Boys, marched eastward across the mountains and helped defeat British troops at the battle of King's Mountain. The Overmountain Victory National Historic Trail (FS Trail 193) through the Highlands of Roan Scenic Area commemorates the Overmountain trek. The frontier soldiers began their march at Sycamore Shoals, a famous gathering place on the Watauga and today the site of the Sycamore Shoals State Historic Park in Elizabethton. Visitors may also want to see nearby Jonesborough, the state's oldest white settlement.

Following the Revolutionary War, American settlers quickly spread across the Appalachians into the Ohio, Mississippi, and Tennessee River valleys. During the 1830s most of the indigenous tribes were forced to leave their homelands and migrate westward to present-day Oklahoma. For the Cherokees it literally became a Trail of Tears, with thousands perishing during the ordeal. Red Clay State Historic Park, near the CNF headquarters in Cleveland, is the site of the last tribal council held before removal. A few Indians in the more isolated mountain areas were able to avoid eviction and became the ancestors of today's Eastern Band of Cherokees, a federally recognized tribe occupying a reservation on the NC side of the GSMNP.

With the vast interior of the continent offering readily accessible fertile lands, most whites chose to bypass the valleys, coves, and highlands of today's CNF. It became predominantly an isolated region of subsistence farming, although a few areas—such as Cades Cove in the GSMNP—remained surprisingly dynamic and cosmopolitan. The people of these mountains were a mixture of Scotch-Irish, German, English, and other ethnic stock, all melding together into a fiercely independent yet pious people. Francis Asbury, America's first Methodist bishop and circuit rider, regularly crossed the mountains in the northern part of what is now the CNF as he conducted his ministerial duties in a growing America.

Because the mountainous part of East TN was a region of small farms, few whites owned any slaves and, indeed, some resented the social and economic influence of slaveholders. Among many there was also a deep attachment to the Union, explaining why Confederate leaders viewed the area as a nest of subversion during the Civil War. Escaped Union prisoners of war often found safety there, amid a society of divided loyalties. Bushwhacking and other forms of violence were common as old scores were settled and animosities lingered for years afterward.

Not until the late nineteenth and early twentieth centuries did the area begin to develop economically, as northern mining and lumber interests moved in. Once geographically isolated, the region opened up as railroads spanned the mountains and reached into remote valleys to make exploitation easier. These ranged from temporary narrow-gauge lines to standard-gauge track still in use. The virgin forests were especially attractive to entrepreneurs, and before long, large corporations were logging hundreds of thousand of acres. In the extreme southern part of the CNF, at Copperhill and Ducktown, the railroads opened mining operations that proved ecologically disastrous, creating an eerie, barren landscape that astronauts have seen from space. Such considerations were secondary, however, as times were good and jobs plentiful in a region that had been economically depressed. The Ducktown Basin Museum has displays telling this story well. Even though the heyday of mining, milling, and railroading is long past, locomotives are occasionally dusted off and polished for excursions of sightseers who wish to enjoy a few hours amid the forest's autumn colors.

Even in the boom days, some people had a grander vision for the forest. They were interested in protecting watersheds, managing forests for sustained yields, and preserving a portion of these mountains through the creation of a new national park. The allure of money was also a part of this new concern. Prominent citizens of East TN and western NC, envisioning a possible tourist bonanza, organized a campaign during the 1920s that finally led to creation of the GSMNP, which was formally dedicated in 1934.

The genesis of the CNF was different. In 1911 Congress authorized the federal government to acquire lands for protecting the headwaters of navigable streams, and the following year the United States began purchasing units in the extreme southeastern part of TN as well as in GA. In 1920 President Woodrow Wilson officially proclaimed these combined lands to be Cherokee National Forest. On July 8, 1936, President Franklin D. Roosevelt issued another proclamation, enlarging the CNF and redrawing its boundaries so that it was exclusively within TN. The southern part, the Cherokee Division, consisted mostly of earlier-acquired forestlands, while the portion north of the national park, the Unaka Division, consisted of new acquisitions and cessions from the Unaka and Pisgah NFs.

Roosevelt's New Deal had other important consequences for the CNF. The TVA, established in 1933, built a series of dams throughout the region, impounding reservoirs like Watauga and South Holston Lakes in the north. In the south, reservoirs earlier impounded by ALCOA, a private corporation, were joined by TVA projects like Ocoee and, most recently, Tellico Lake. TVA brought jobs, flood control, and electric power to a desperately needy region—and it brought controversy over environmental issues. Whatever its merits, TVA has provided a different kind of recreation for visitors, from boating on reservoirs to whitewater rafting, canoeing, and kayaking on dam-controlled streams.

Today the visitor taking any major highway in the CNF will inevitably confront the powerful presence of the federal government.

Paradoxically, this same presence has created avenues of escape. The CNF is latticed by a network of paved and gravel roads offering access to remote trailheads where it is possible to escape for a time most of life's pressures and to find solace amid the trees and rushing streams. In a few areas one can even find small stands of virgin timber. But even along the most isolated pathway one is still brought back to the forest's human history by encountering the unexpected: some crumbling foundations, perhaps, or a meandering stone wall—mute, lichen-covered mementos linking past with present.

7. Political History

The CNF's protected natural areas are outstanding botanical, wildlife, and recreation preserves. They are and will remain wild only because, quite simply, of politics. The most permanent protection is, of course, wilderness areas designated by the US Congress under the 1964 Wilderness Act. USFS administrative designation of special management areas in forest plans provide an additional layer of protection, albeit subject to change in revised management plans. In the CNF only a very small number of acres were part of the national Wilderness Preservation System until the 1980s. This shortcoming was somewhat corrected in 1984 and 1986 when literally thousands of hours of lobbying by individuals and groups dissatisfied with the lack of CNF wilderness led to the passage of wilderness bills by Congress. The resolution of an appeal of the Forest Management Plan in August of 1988 further contributed to the administrative protection of additional areas, and the 2004 plan revision added additional areas.

The history of protection of wilderness and special areas in the CNF is a long one. The earliest mention of formal protection for a portion of the CNF occurred in 1935 when the USFS proposed designating a primitive area in the Citico Creek watershed to be called "Citico-Cheoah Primitive Area." No action, however, was taken on the proposal.

The road to wilderness in the CNF must therefore begin with the passage of the Wilderness Act, which authorized wilderness protection for federal lands. It was enacted by Congress in 1964 and provided for protection of only three small wilderness areas in the eastern United States while a substantial amount of wilderness was designated in the western United States. No areas were designated in TN's CNF. In subsequent years, the correction of this imbalance was a priority of national environmental groups, particularly the Sierra Club and the Wilderness Society.

The first formal recognition of wilderness for the CNF was the Eastern Wilderness Areas Act that was passed by Congress and signed by President Gerald Ford on January 3, 1975. This act designated three small wilderness areas (only 1.3 percent of the total CNF acreage) and two large wilderness study areas in the CNF. The Wilderness areas were an extension of the Cohutta Wilderness from GA into TN, an extension of the Joyce Kilmer-Slickrock Wilderness from NC into TN, and the small Gee Creek Wilderness located wholly within TN. The wilderness study areas were Big Frog Mountain and Citico Creek. The 1974 effort was led by Citizens for Eastern Wilderness; Dave Saylor (Washington, DC) was the overall coordinator, Felix Montgomery (Chattanooga) was the southeastern-US coordinator, and Ray Payne (Knoxville) was the TN coordinator. TN's Third District congressman, LaMar Baker, cosponsored the Eastern Wilderness Areas Act in the House of Representatives and deserves much of the credit for the act, as does Ernie Dickerman of the Wilderness Society. Ernie spent untold hours and lobbied for enactment of the bill during the waning hours of the 93rd Congress.

The principal obstacle to the TN-NC portions of the Eastern Wilderness Areas Act was a proposed road between Tellico Plains, TN, and Robbinsville, NC. The route for the road ran directly through the most scenic portion of the proposed Joyce Kilmer–Slickrock Wilderness (along the Hangover, Naked Ground, and Bob's Bald mountain crest). Accordingly, the proroad forces, headed by Mayor Charles Hall of Tellico Plains, were squarely faced off against Ted Snyder and the Joyce Kilmer Wilderness Advocates. A compromise was thus in order, and the parties were brought together by the efforts of Dr. Houston Lowry of Madisonville. Advocates for the road agreed to reroute it across the less scenic Beech Gap while the Wilderness Advocates agreed not to oppose the road along its new route.

After passage of the 1974 act, TN conservationists began looking toward additional TN areas to be protected as wilderness. A principal candidate was the Bald River watershed. Ray Payne and Will Skelton met with CNF Supervisor Bob Lusk and various interested parties to discuss its protection but were essentially stonewalled. Supervisor Lusk maintained, as did official USFS policy at that time, that there were no lands that qualified for wilderness in the East. So there was much work to be done.

Conservationists throughout the nation worked on an unprecedented scale for the election of Jimmy Carter as president in 1976. President Carter ran as a candidate sympathetic to the idea of wilderness and, once elected, implemented a formal procedure for correcting the eastern-western wilderness designation imbalance. The procedure was called RARE II (Roadless Areas Review and Evaluation; the "II" reflects that a previous review had been conducted only in the western United States). The first RARE II function in TN was a meeting conducted by the USFS in Knoxville on July 29, 1977. Areas possessing some potential for wilderness designation were to be identified by participants. The meeting seemed to go very well, as conservationists took maps of the CNF and generally were able to agree with the other interest groups on areas that "might" possess some potential for wilderness. However, much later, environmentalists were told that this innocuous meeting was at least part of the beginning of vehement wilderness opposition in eastern TN. The meeting was conducted in small subgroups, and apparently a wilderness proponent in one of the subgroups was overly eager and came across as somewhat of a fanatic, urging that the entire CNF be designated wilderness. This scared other members of that subgroup, and they promptly went home and began organizing against wilderness, particularly in the Elizabethton and Tellico Plains areas. The opposition in Elizabethton was led by the Carter County Sportsmen's Club, a hunting and fishing group, while the opposition in Tellico Plains was led by Save Our Recreational Environment ("SORE") organized by Mayor Hall of Tellico Plains. SORE subsequently produced the most active opposition.

A variety of reasons were given by opponents of wilderness for their position. Deer are a principal large-game species in East TN, and hunters were concerned with loss of deer habitat. Many hunters feel that deer thrive in a forest that is managed for timber harvesting, which wilderness designation would not allow. Wilderness proponents responded that, aside from disagreement by other hunters about the need for managed habitat, other important species such as black bear clearly need the nonmanaged habitat provided by wilderness. Individuals involved with the timber industry were concerned that wilderness acres would be taken out of the CNF timber base. Wilderness proponents responded that the amount of commercial timber in the proposed areas was small, especially in view of the rugged topography that made it difficult to harvest large amounts of timber. Motor vehicle interests were concerned that wilderness areas would be closed to ORVs. Wilderness proponents responded with lists of the negligible mileage involved in road closures and the need to have a few areas off-limits to ORVs. The USFS was a reluctant wilderness supporter in the beginning, largely because many USFS employees felt timber harvesting was a necessary part of good forest management. However, they gradually came to accept wilderness as a legitimate use of the national forests within a multiple-use context. Other reasons given for opposition to wilderness often resulted from misunderstandings of the Wilderness Act. The most common was the false belief that hunting would be banned in wilderness areas. Some wilderness opposition was also based on deliberate misinformation, as discussed below.

The RARE II process continued with the USFS identifying twenty-one possible wilderness designations in a draft Environmental Impact Statement released on June 15, 1978. Written comments were then solicited on those areas during the summer of 1978, but no hearings were scheduled. The USFS advised conservationists, both orally and in writing, that their comments should be site-specific and substantive to help the USFS make a professional decision. They further advised that form letters and petitions would not be considered. The CNF Wilderness Coalition was formed to coordinate the preparation of these comments by conservationists. Will Skelton served as coordinator of the coalition, which was initially composed of the TN Chapter of the Sierra Club, Great Smoky Mountains Hiking Club, TN Citizens for Wilderness Planning, Trout Unlimited, and TN Council of the Audubon Society. Other groups were subsequently added. John Thomas of Knoxville served for some time as assistant coordinator.

Meanwhile, on the other side of the issue, SORE was producing input in a totally different way. SORE essentially collected petitions and form letters, contrary to the USFS's request. There were also reports of false information being disseminated by unknown parties with regard to wilderness. For example, "They are going to close all of the roads in the National Forest"; "They are closing the campgrounds"; "If you own land outside the National Forest, it will also be managed as Wilderness"; and "You will not be able to hunt in the National Forest anymore." When the coalition learned what was happening, it was too late. The antiwilderness people submitted 12,586 petitions and form letters opposing wilderness (and 7,492 supporting multiple use) but almost no substantive, site-specific letters opposing wilderness. The coalition submitted, in addition to detailed reports on each area, 724 site-specific substantive letters supporting wilderness, but submitted few form letters. The coalition's comments to the USFS were, without question, the most detailed and substantive public comments on wilderness ever received by the CNF. The coalition won the site-specific battle 87.6 to 12.4 percent but lost the petition and form letter battle. Who was to win the war itself was still unclear.

With this input, CNF Supervisor Marvin Laurisen obviously had a problem. He elected to change horses in the middle of the stream, accepted the antiwilderness petitions and form letters, and made his decision based on them. The result was a devastating defeat in terms of numbers for wilderness designation. The USFS announced their final RARE II recommendations at a press conference held in the Howard Johnson's West in Knoxville on January 4, 1979. The wilderness recommendations were few. Only Bald River Gorge was recommended for wilderness designation, while Little Frog Mountain, Citico Creek, Big Frog Mountain, Flint Mill, and Pond Mountain were recommended for further planning. Pond Mountain Addition and Unaka Mountain were later added as further planning areas, after numerous protests by environmentalists.

The Wilderness Coalition vowed not to be a victim of the USFS's misrepresentation again. Accordingly, shortly after the RARE II process was over, it began collecting petition signatures with the aim of fighting fire with fire in the event other hearings were held. Since the process is essentially political, the coalition also began obtaining letters to East TN Congressmen John Duncan and James Quillen and TN senators Howard Baker and James Sasser. Finally, in an effort to combat the misinformation about wilderness during RARE II, Ken and Susie McDonald, with the help of other members of the Harvey Broome Group of the Sierra Club's TN Chapter, produced and subsequently began presenting a multimedia slide show entitled "Wilderness for Tomorrow," which contained beautiful pictures of the CNF, together with answers to the most frequently asked questions about wilderness.

Various efforts at compromise over the years helped to humanize the people on both sides of the issue. Ray Payne, Will Skelton, and Sandy Hodge met with SORE's president, Mayor Charles Hall of Tellico Plains, on several occasions, all friendly and helpful, but inconclusive. In northeast TN the Carter County Club and the Greene County Hunting and Fishing Club in Greeneville were the principal sources of opposition to wilderness. The Greene County Club refused to meet with the coalition. The coalition did meet with the Carter County Club on two occasions in the late 1970s, but without success. The initial meeting was in Elizabethton on June 6, 1978, and, in spite of being fairly friendly, resulted in a letter that stated, after a vote by their club, "It is now a matter of record that our Club will oppose your Coalition in every way we can." However, after some passage of time, the coalition tried again in October of 1979 and, although another vote of the Carter County Club was close, it was again antiwilderness. These failed compromise efforts made it clear that, if the coalition wanted wilderness, an easy compromise was not possible.

The first opportunity to test whether the coalition's activities after RARE II were having any effect was the USFS's hearings on Citico Creek and Big Frog Mountain. The USFS was required by the 1974

Eastern Wilderness Areas Act to study these two areas for wilderness by December 31, 1979. They did not make that deadline, but on June 10, 1982, the USFS distributed its draft Environmental Impact Statement on the areas and conducted public hearings. From the substantive, site-specific standpoint, Lance McCold, of Knoxville, organized a committee to critique the draft statement in detail and produce a written analysis. A massive petition effort coordinated by Will Skelton resulted in 20,642 petition signatures versus only 10,313 anti-wilderness signatures. A change in public opinion was also reflected at the public hearings in Chatsworth, GA, and Athens, TN, with sixty-seven witnesses for wilderness and only sixteen against.

After the Citico Creek and Big Frog hearings, the next logical step was to convince Congressman John Duncan, in whose district all of the areas in the southern CNF were located, that he should introduce a wilderness bill. Such effort included forwarding Congressman Duncan copies of the 20,642 petition signatures (plus additional signatures obtained after 1982), meeting with him in Sweetwater and showing him the slide show, and soliciting additional letters supporting wilderness from a wide variety of people. On November 1, 1983, Congressman Duncan introduced HR 4263, the southern CNF Wilderness Act. The bill provided for the designation of Citico Creek, Bald River Gorge, and Big Frog Mountain as wilderness, while Little Frog Mountain would be a wilderness study area. The real suspense with regard to HR 4263 was the USFS's attitude, since they had not released the final Environmental Impact Statement on Citico Creek and Big Frog Mountain. However, about this time the wilderness cause was fortunate to gain a new supervisor of the CNF, Don Rollens. His experience with western USFS wilderness resulted in a greater willingness to view wilderness as a legitimate use of the CNF.

The US House of Representatives moved quickly on the bill as public hearings were held by the Public Lands Subcommittee of the Interior Committee on March 29, 1984, by Congressman John Seiberling. Max Petterson, the chief of the USFS, testified and supported the bill, as did Charles Howell, the commissioner of the TN Department of Conservation. Congressman Duncan also testified in favor of the bill. Their testimony was followed by Will Skelton on behalf of the coalition and Dr. Houston Lowry of Madisonville, who testified as a local resident for wilderness. S 590, the Senate version of HR 4263, was introduced on April 25, 1984, by both TN senators, Howard Baker and James Sasser. Hearings were held before the Forestry Subcommittee of the Senate's Agriculture Committee on May 24, 1984, and were chaired by Iowa senator Roger Jepsen. The USFS representative, Lamar Beasley, again supported the bill. Walter Criley, director of planning of the TN

Department of Conservation, likewise supported the bill. Will Skelton also testified on behalf of the coalition, and Ralston Bailey, a Benton resident and the president of the Cherokee Sportsmen's Association, testified in favor of the bill.

The Senate passed the bill on October 2, 1984, just before adjournment. The House thereafter acted promptly and repassed the Senate version of the bill. President Ronald Reagan then signed the act into law on October 30, 1984.

After the passage of the southern CNF Wilderness Act, the coalition's efforts were directed toward the northern CNF and Congressman James Quillen, who was not willing to introduce a bill in 1984. The first real opportunity to influence the USFS toward a wilderness recommendation for the northern CNF was the legal requirement of the National Forest Management Practices Act that the USFS prepare a management plan for the CNF. The draft Forest Management Plan was released in mid-January of 1985, with wilderness recommendations that were an improvement over RARE II but still considered inadequate by the coalition. The coalition prepared comments on wilderness while the TN Chapter of the Sierra Club, TN Citizens for Wilderness Planning, and Smoky Mountains Hiking Club prepared comments on the management aspects of the forest plan. Both sets of comments were thorough and comprehensive and presented factual arguments. The coalition, remembering past lessons, also ensured that they had the "numbers," and 4,387 petition signatures were delivered to the USFS; 1,384 of those were from Congressman Quillen's First Congressional District.

One of the problems facing the legislation was the largest RARE II area in the northern CNF, the Jennings Creek area located near Greeneville. Jennings Creek is a large, unique, and beautiful area located on the western slopes of the Bald Mountain Ridge. The area contains everything from large waterfalls to grassy balds and the AT. It was also the source of perhaps the toughest site-specific controversy in the northern CNF. District Ranger Bill Sweet encouraged the various parties to work out a compromise. Efforts in that regard were subsequently led by Tony Campbell and the TN Conservation League. A public meeting on January 25, 1985, was followed by a more productive meeting and hike among the leaders. The final compromise had something for everyone: a new Bald Mountain Ridge Scenic Area that encompassed most of the old Jennings Creek area, two dead-end roads left open, and an adjacent Sampson Mountain Wilderness.

The final management plan was released on April 1, 1986, and contained a much improved wilderness recommendation for additional CNF wilderness: four wilderness areas in upper East TN (Pond Mountain,

Unaka Mountain, Sampson Mountain, and Big Laurel Branch) and the Little Frog and Big Frog Mountain Addition in southeast TN. These recommendations created the hope that Congressman Quillen would go along with the wilderness designation. Ed Williams and Will Skelton met with Congressman Quillen on June 27, 1986, and asked him to introduce a bill. The State of Franklin Sierra Club Group and the Watauga Audubon Society also met with Congressman Quillen shortly afterward and presented him with additional petitions and showed him the wilderness slide show. Congressman Quillen then gave his aides the go-ahead on the bill, leaving primarily a problem of logistics in completing passage during the remainder of the legislative year.

The bill was introduced as HR 5166 in the House of Representatives by Congressmen Duncan and Quillen on July 15, 1986, and in the US Senate as S 2685 by Senators James Sasser and Al Gore on July 24, 1986.

Hearings were promptly held in the House of Representatives on July 31, 1986. Dan Lady and Will Skelton testified from TN and worked, with the USFS, on resolving several problems that had arisen. These included the discovery of a rare mineral, niobium, in the proposed Big Laurel Branch Wilderness (the USFS overcame this one by continuing to recommend wilderness designation because of plentiful existing supplies in Canada and Brazil); the concern over whether boaters could continue to dock their boats on the Big Laurel Branch/ Watauga Lake shoreline (resolved by the conclusion that such was allowed under the Wilderness Act); the desire by some residents for a road from Butler to Blue Springs across the proposed Big Laurel Branch Wilderness; and the demand of Unicoi County that approximately 100 acres of USFS land be given to the county. The last two were bigger problems and required some negotiations and work. The road issue was settled by a USFS report reflecting that, if the road were built, the most practical location would be outside the wilderness (and even then very expensive and environmentally questionable). The Unicoi issue was resolved by a committee report encouraging the parties to settle the land transfer issue.

With those issues out of the way, Senate hearings were held on September 25, 1986. Only Senators Gore and Sasser presented "live" testimony in view of the noncontroversial nature of the bill and the lack of time due to the pending end of the session. Thereafter, with the support of Senators Sasser and Gore as well as Congressmen Quillen and Duncan, the TN Wilderness Act of 1986 was passed by the US House of Representatives on September 22, 1986, and by the Senate on October 3, 1986, with President Ronald Reagan signing it on October 16, 1986.

With wilderness designation being settled by the 1984 and 1986 acts, environmentalists turned to an appeal of the CNF management plan to obtain administrative protection for areas left out of the Wilderness Acts. A formal appeal of the management plan was filed by the Sierra Club, Wilderness Society, Smoky Mountain Hiking Club, TN Citizens for Wilderness Planning, and TN Audubon Council soon after the plan was released in 1986. The initial phase of the appeal was to the USFS Regional Forester in Atlanta under USFS rules. Shortly thereafter, settlement negotiations commenced and were consummated in July of 1988. Those who filed the appeal were represented in the negotiations by Bill Bumpers, a Washington, DC, attorney. The Wilderness Society's Ron Tipton and Peter Kirby coordinated the appeal from a national standpoint while Ray Payne coordinated the TN efforts. Other individuals participating in the appeal negotiations for TN conservation groups were Hugh Irwin, Lance McCold, Roger Jenkins, Will Skelton, Dana Eglinton, Arthur Smith, John Doyal, and Kirk Johnson. Both timber harvesting practices and special area protection were considered and were the subject of many negotiating sessions. The last roadblock to a settlement was the Upper Bald River area, which had persistently defied final agreement. Finally, in July of 1988 discussions between Mike Murphy of the USFS, Ken Arney of TWRA, and Will Skelton of the Sierra Club forged a resolution that allowed an overall settlement. The agreement protected a significant number of additional scenic and primitive areas, reduced the amount of future clear-cutting, and contained provisions designed to help the CNF's black bear population.

The settlement was announced in Knoxville on August 4, 1988, at a joint press conference by the USFS, the appellants, and the interveners (TN Conservation League, TWRA, TN Valley Sportsmen's Club, Appalachian Chapter of Trout Unlimited, TN Forestry Association, TN Forestry Commission, Kentucky-TN Society of American Foresters, and Multi-Use Council of the Southeast). At the time the settlement was signed, the USFS issued an amendment to the CNF management plan that incorporated the settlement items (except for changes in timber harvest methods and volumes that required a supplemental Environmental Impact Statement and certain issues of national scope that were forwarded to the chief of the USFS for decision). Finally resolved for the duration of the management plan was the fate of numerous wild areas protected under various management categories.

A new coalition, Cherokee Forest Voices, was subsequently organized by the appellants, with Hugh Irwin as coordinator. Hugh served as coordinator until 1996, when Arthur Smith assumed this role. Catherine Murray became coordinator after Arthur's death in 1999. The organization's principal purpose has been to monitor the CNF's compliance with the management plan and obtain improved conservation management of the forest. Cherokee Forest Voices has actively reviewed, critiqued, and challenged activities in the forest to safeguard the remaining unprotected areas of the CNF. The wildland character of many of the areas in this book have been protected through these efforts.

Changes in USFS philosophy and direction during the 1990s promised a focus on wildland protection. This culminated in 2000 with a new USFS national policy that placed roadless areas off-limits for logging and road building. This policy has been challenged by timber interests and western states, and its future is uncertain. The Bush administration is attempting, as this book goes to press in 2004, to open up many of the inventoried roadless areas to timber harvesting. In addition, a series of USFS policy changes in 2002 and 2003 threaten many of the environmental safeguards that have guided national forest management for decades.

One of the main concerns conservationists had with the 1980s management plans for national forests in the region was that they were based on political boundaries rather than ecological or landscape concerns. This concern was addressed by federal agencies prior to the start of revisions of management plans in the southern Appalachians. The USFS, NPS, Fish and Wildlife Service, and TVA, as well as other federal and state agencies, cooperated on the most comprehensive environmental assessment ever performed for the southern Appalachians. The southern Appalachian Assessment, which was coordinated by the Southern Appalachian Man and the Biosphere Program, was released in 1996. One of its purposes was to serve as the basis for national forest plan revisions in the region.

The CNF began its plan revision in 1996 in coordination with most of the other forests in the region. The planning process has continued under two administrations and with funding that has at times disappeared. However, a draft plan was officially released on March 21, 2003, and the final management plan was released on January 30, 2004. Few changes occurred between the draft and the final plan. The final plan recommends several wilderness additions to existing wilderness areas. The largest of these additions include a 4,930-acre addition to Big Laurel Branch Wilderness, a 3,069-acre addition to Sampson Mountain Wilderness, and a 1,964-acre addition to Joyce Kilmer–Slickrock Wilderness (also adjacent to Citico Wilderness). There are also small additions to Big Frog Wilderness and Little Frog Wilderness. Only one stand-alone area is recommended for wilderness designation: 9,112 acres of the Upper Bald River area. In all, the recommended wilderness additions total 20,417 acres. Of course it would take passage of wilderness legislation to actually designate the areas as wilderness.

Many of the areas that were managed as primitive areas in the 1986 plan are now in backcountry prescriptions under the 2004 recommended plan revision, which offer a similar degree of protection. Further, the 2004 plan provides for the protection of several significant additional backcountry areas, and other designations within the plan provide a degree of protection as well. Areas inventoried as roadless have also generally been placed in protective prescriptions, although portions of some areas do not appear to be in prescriptions that would protect their roadless values. Several significant areas long supported by conservationists for protection, but which were not inventoried as roadless, will be subject to timber management if the plan is implemented.

This status of the management plan revision highlights the ongoing need for protection efforts to keep many of the areas in this book wild. Wilderness is the most permanent and lasting protection, but even this cannot be taken for granted. Proposals over the years have sometimes threatened their integrity. The areas prescribed as scenic and backcountry areas in the 2004 plan revision are not permanently protected. This protection will only last for the life of the plan, which is intended to be about ten to fifteen years. Future national forest policy changes could jeopardize most areas, except designated wilderness areas. Politics is if anything a changeable process, and continued vigilance will be necessary to keep these areas wild.

8. Maintaining and Protecting the Trails

As you visit the natural areas included in this book, remember that all of these areas have been lived on, logged, or otherwise used within the past hundred years. They have recovered immensely from those times and will continue to recover if we allow them to do so.

Such recovery will be ensured if everyone practices no-trace camping, meaning leave no significant evidence of having hiked or camped in an area. This can be a challenge, but every effort to maintain natural conditions will reward you and others on future hikes. A littered campsite and trail versus a campsite and trail that appear to be part of the natural environment will make a difference in your wilderness experience. John Hart's *Walk Softly in the Wilderness* (see bibliography) is one of the best guidebooks on no-trace camping. The key phrase is "pack it in, pack it out." Some other specific suggestions include the following.

Campfires. If you can avoid a campfire by using a backpacking stove, you've made a huge contribution to your campsite's environment. Campfires, together with litter, create the most adverse visual and ecological impacts of backcountry camping. The fire ring detracts from the naturalness of the area by introducing blackened rocks and piles of ash, charcoal, and unburned wood. The wood for the fire also removes dead wood critical to a healthy forest's ecosystem. If you do choose to build a campfire, remember several guidelines. Use an existing fire ring, or, if none exists, choose a site with little or no vegetation and do not build an unnecessary fire ring. Keep the fire small and burn only dead and down wood that can be broken by hand; leave saws and axes at home. Never leave the fire unattended. Afterward, completely erase the campfire. Make sure it is dead out; remove unburned foil, plastic, or other foreign materials; scatter the ashes; and camouflage the burned area with organic matter. If there was an existing fire ring, you may want to scatter the rocks and erase the fire ring unless it is in a popular area where it is likely to be rebuilt. Scatter any unused firewood in the forest.

Campsites. Many people hope for a "virgin" campsite and avoid the "used" campsite. Actually, it is preferable to use existing campsites that are in acceptable condition (where understory vegetation is worn away on some or most of the site but humus, litter, leaves, or needles cover most of the ground). If everyone develops a "new" campsite, the area will soon be littered with campsites. However, you should avoid overused sites that need to rest (where the entire area is bare ground with eroding soil, damaged trees, tree stumps, and exposed roots). Also avoid lightly used campsites that are near an established site. When in camp, minimize your impact. Avoid "site engineering" by digging, cutting, and moving the natural environment. Also avoid spreading out and expanding the area. Prepare and eat meals in one location.

When leaving camp, pack out *all* trash and garbage and make a conscious effort to leave the site in as good, if not better, condition than when you arrived. The littered and overused sites will not improve by themselves; give nature a helping hand.

Sanitation. Proper disposal of human waste is a critical part of no-trace camping (everything else should be burned or carried out). A cathole should *always* be used for human excrement; no exceptions. It should be located at least 100 feet from water sources and campsites.

Dig the hole at least six to eight inches deep. After using it, burn your toilet paper (carry a matchbook with your toilet paper) and then refill the hole with soil. Scatter organic matter on top to camouflage the site. A group cat-hole can be used, in which case it should be larger and deeper, with only a light layer of soil placed in the hole after each use.

Horse Use. If you are riding horses, make a particular effort to see that horse manure does not foul campsites, streams, and trails. Keep the horses well away from campsites and trails during stops and at night. Remember that horses can do a tremendous amount of damage to dirt trails. Stay on trails that have been constructed to withstand the high "pounds per square inch" levels of horses and their riders and gear.

As you visit these areas, remember that their protection as wilderness, scenic, and backcountry areas did not come easily; many people worked many hours for their protection. You can thank those people by taking care of our natural areas and reporting to the CNF any abuse you observe (the most likely abuse will be ORVs; they are absolutely prohibited in wilderness areas and should not be present; they are allowed in scenic and primitive areas only on existing roads where specifically authorized). Call or write the CNF district ranger or supervisor (see appendix 2 for addresses and telephone numbers).

You can also help these areas and trails by volunteering to maintain trails or work for the future protection of the natural areas in this book; in either case, contact the Sierra Club Group nearest you or the CNF (see appendix 2 for addresses). Finally, you can help by simply writing your congressperson (US House of Representatives, Washington, DC 20515) or senator (US Senate, Washington, DC 20510) and the CNF supervisor (see appendix 2 for address) and telling them that areas you have hiked should continue to be protected from timber harvesting, road building, vehicle use, and development. (Note that since the anthrax attacks on members of Congress in 2001, using traditional mail to contact your congressperson is likely to result in a multiweek delay in their hearing from you. It is typically more effective to send a fax or e-mail. You can get contact information for your representatives or senators at http://www.house.gov or http://www.senate.gov.)

9. Global Positioning Systems (GPS) and Digital Maps

Perhaps two of the most important aids to the hiker that have been developed since the first edition of this book are inexpensive handheld global positioning receivers and digital mapping software. The purpose of this section is to acquaint those hikers and mountain bikers that still may be unfamiliar with such. It is hard to imagine where the technology will be in another decade, so we will not even speculate. This section is not meant to be a tutorial, as the reader can find much more extensive treatises on the Internet, which also was not in common use twelve years ago.

Handheld GPS units are essentially very sensitive radio receivers and timing devices. They take advantage of a constellation of twenty-four satellites that over the past couple of decades have been lofted by the US military into earth orbits about 12,000 miles high. Without going into much detail, a small unit can take the signals from a minimum of four satellites and compute its position on the surface of the planet. (The units can make an estimate of position with only three satellite signals, but the quality of the estimate is vastly improved with the addition of one more signal.) The sensitivity of the units has improved dramatically over the past few years, to the point where a view to the sky unobstructed by vegetation is no longer required for a position fix. Theoretically, anyone with a detailed topographical map and a functioning GPS should be able to pinpoint his or her position on the planet to within a few meters. Never ever getting lost can be a powerful incentive for owning one of these units.

Owning a GPS and a topo map will not do you a whole lot of good, however, unless you know how to use them. Like most things in life, a few skills are needed. A GPS can tell you where you are, but you have to be able to translate that information to a topo map. That means you have to have some rudimentary knowledge of coordinate systems. Most hikers rely on Universal Transverse Mercator coordinates, and all the coordinates given in this book are in UTM format (NAD 27, or North American Datum 1927 grid). UTM coordinates tend to be easier to understand than latitude and longitude, because the coordinates are in distances (easier for most of us to digest) rather than degrees, minutes, and seconds. UTM coordinates give a position in terms of the distance north of the equator and east of the western boundary of the zone in which an individual is hiking. Once you get the hang of it, you will never want to go back to latitude and longitude. Almost all of the topo maps covering the forest have UTM coordinates on them. You just need to learn how to find and read them.

Some of the higher-end handheld GPS units have the capability to display electronic versions of simple topo maps on their screens along with the unit's position. This may be a handy feature and something with which to impress your friends, but somehow relying on a map, of which you can only see a few square inches at a time and has little detail, seems unsatisfying. The point of having a map is not only to provide a position, but also to provide context for that position. Four of five square inches of view just does not provide a lot of context.

Clearly, with the availability of powerful, low cost personal computers and color printers, digital mapping products are becoming increasingly competitive with that hiker's staple, the 7.5-minute quad topo. One reason is simple economics. As of this writing, the cost of the standard USGS topographical map is $6–$8. To cover just the southern part of the CNF, it takes something like twenty-seven topo maps. However, you can currently purchase software with the same quality of maps for the entire state of Tennessee for $100. You do the math. Sure it costs some paper and ink to print the maps, but the economics still support digital maps. Another important feature is convenience. Have you ever planned to head for the mountains on a Saturday morning, only to remember, after digging through the pile of fifty or sixty quads you have stored so conveniently under your bed, because there is nowhere else in the house to put those huge sheets of paper, that the last time you hiked in the Citico Creek area your Whiteoak Flats topo got so soggy from the rain that you tossed it? With digital maps, the solution is simple: just print yourself a new one. Beats having to wait for the local backpacking shop to open up, with you hoping that they have not sold out of the map you need.

Another convenience of electronic/digital maps is the ability to customize, both the region of coverage and what features the map depicts. A running joke among hikers is that inevitably a particular area of interest will always fall right at the junction of four topo maps. Since virtually all digital maps these days offer seamless viewing and printing, you just have to highlight the area you want to print, even if it is at the intersection of four maps, and print away.

Most digital maps provide features that are simply not possible with paper maps. For example, you can trace the route you want to hike on the map and immediately generate an elevation profile of your route. That way, there are no surprises when you get to that steep stretch of trail that gains 1,100 feet in less than a mile. Even better, most modern software permits the integration of your handheld GPS unit through a serial cable connected to your computer. This will permit you to identify and name key waypoints on your digital map and upload them to your GPS unit, vastly easier than entering them by hand directly on your GPS unit. Alternatively, you can turn on the tracking feature of your GPS, throw it in the very top of your pack, and it will keep an exact record of where you hiked. This feature is particularly useful for trail mapping (we used such for some of the trails in this book and found that some existing maps had significant mistakes as to trail locations) and for figuring out where you actually went on your off-trail hike.

Like all technological approaches to solving problems, there are limitations. For example, using digital maps requires spending a few minutes understanding the differences among coordinate grids. And, as of this writing, most handheld GPS units do not come bundled with interface cables for personal computers. You have to purchase them separately, and that requires a basic knowledge of how to connect the two. Currently, virtually all handheld units connect to a PC through the old-fashioned—and slow—serial port, which is likely to go the way of the 3.5-inch floppy disk. It will be interesting to see what manufacturers dream up to interface the high speed computers of tomorrow with the relatively low data throughput of the GPS units.

Probably the most significant limitation with handheld GPS units is potential positional error. Despite vast improvements in sensitivity and the shift to simultaneous multisatellite reception in the past few years, even the best units will occasionally place you in the middle of that lake over there, 400 meters to the west. Two of the biggest problems are signal scatter and signal bounce. The former is pretty easy to discern. In the rain, under a significant leaf canopy, your chances of getting an accurate fix are extremely limited. Your chances of getting any kind of a position fix are only slightly better. The wet leaves act as signal reflectors and it will appear as though the GPS simply cannot make up its mind as to where it is. Perhaps more insidious is the problem of signal bounce. That is, the signal from a particular satellite will bounce off a cliff face or rock wall before it reaches the GPS. This problem is usually minimized if you can pick up signals from six or eight satellites at one time. But often in the mountains, the terrain limits the view to the horizon and you may be stuck with only four signals. You take a reading, more or less to confirm where you think you are, and the GPS places you several hundred meters away in a spot that simply does not make sense, based on what you can see around you. If this happens, or if the reading you get is a bit suspicious, walk 30 to 50 meters away from your original spot, and take another reading. I was once near the confluence of two major creeks in the GSMNP. I knew exactly where I was, but I pulled out my GPS anyway. I got a reading that did not make any sense. I looked around me, and there was a big rock face up on the hill behind me. I moved about 20 meters, and watched as the GPS corrected its position. This does not happen frequently, but it does happen, so pay attention to the surrounding landscape while you are getting your position fix.

The latter phenomenon is a good reminder. All the fancy hardware is not a substitute for good map reading skills when you go into the wilderness. It is sometimes too easy to rely on technology, only to learn too late that you did not really know how to use it or that the batteries were about to run down. Enjoy the technological advances, but do not forget or ignore the basics. And carry spare batteries.

Note: See the area and trail descriptions and the appendixes for what is available in topographical maps and where to get them.

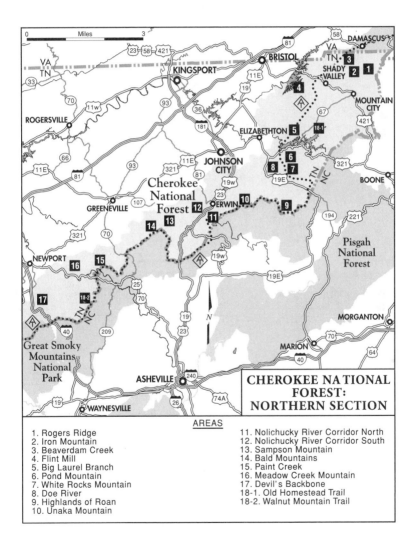

CHEROKEE NATIONAL
FOREST:
NORTHERN SECTION

AREAS

1. Rogers Ridge
2. Iron Mountain
3. Beaverdam Creek
4. Flint Mill
5. Big Laurel Branch
6. Pond Mountain
7. White Rocks Mountain
8. Doe River
9. Highlands of Roan
10. Unaka Mountain
11. Nolichucky River Corridor North
12. Nolichucky River Corridor South
13. Sampson Mountain
14. Bald Mountains
15. Paint Creek
16. Meadow Creek Mountain
17. Devil's Backbone
18-1. Old Homestead Trail
18-2. Walnut Mountain Trail

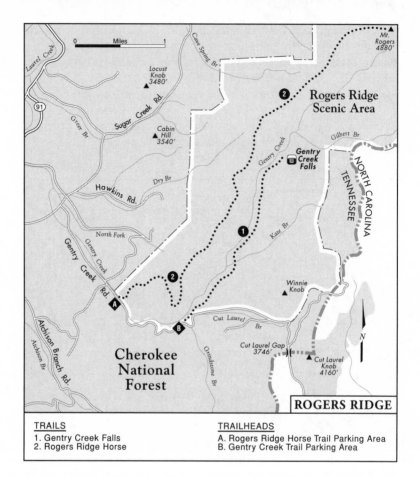

0 Miles 1

Laurel Creek

Cave Spring Br

Mt. Rogers 4880'

Locust Knob 3480'

91

Gryer Br

Sugar Creek Rd.

❷ Rogers Ridge Scenic Area

Cabin Hill 3540'

Gilbert Br

Gentry Creek

Gentry Creek Falls

Dry Br

Hawkins Rd.

NORTH CAROLINA

TENNESSEE

North Fork

Gentry Creek

❶

Kate Br

Gentry Creek Rd.

❷

Winnie Knob

A

N

B

Cut Laurel Br

Cut Laurel Gap 3746'

Atchison Branch Rd.

Atchison Br.

Cherokee National Forest

Grindstone Br

Cut Laurel Knob 4160'

ROGERS RIDGE

TRAILS
1. Gentry Creek Falls
2. Rogers Ridge Horse

TRAILHEADS
A. Rogers Ridge Horse Trail Parking Area
B. Gentry Creek Trail Parking Area

Northern Cherokee National Forest

South Holston and Watauga Lakes
(TI Map 783)

▌ Rogers Ridge

(Includes Rogers Ridge Scenic Area, Rogers Ridge Backcountry Area, and Rogers Ridge Roadless Area)

The Rogers Ridge area is located in the extreme northeastern corner of TN in Johnson County and the Watauga Ranger District. The significant natural qualities of the area were recognized by the USFS in its Southern Appalachian Assessment when it identified the 4,753-acre Rogers Ridge Roadless Area (plus another 180 acres in the Jefferson NF). An area greater than the roadless area is protected in the CNF's 2004 plan revision, including the 5,530-acre Rogers Ridge scenic area and the 2,548-acre Rogers Ridge backcountry area. The outstanding feature of the area is the high grassy ridges that provide truly spectacular vistas to range after range of mountain highlands, including Mount Rogers and Whitetop to the north and Roan Mountain and Grandfather Mountain to the south. The balds on Rogers Ridge are among the most beautiful and extensive in the southern Appalachians. They were severely damaged by ORV traffic prior to designation of the Rogers Ridge scenic area in 1988. The scenic area classification prohibited ORV access and there has been some recovery. However, illegal ORV use continues to be a management problem. Perhaps the finest "up-close" scenery is on Gentry Creek where two beautiful 30-foot waterfalls tumble over high rock walls into clear pools.

In addition to the marvelous views, the area contains a variety of wildflowers, including the rare silverling, Robbins ragwort, Rock skullcap, Roan rattlesnake root, Fraser's sedge, mountain bitter cress, Appalachian twayblade, rosy twisted-stalk, and Minnie bush. Some of the gaps contain high mountain bogs, which are important biological ecosystems. Wildlife in the area includes abundant deer and turkey populations. Of special note is that one of the last authenticated sightings of the eastern panther in TN was in the Rogers Ridge area.

HISTORY

Most of the area was logged within the past century, but only traces of this activity can still be found. Logging and fires may be partially responsible for the extensive grassy balds in the area. However, the exact origin of the balds is still a mystery, with fires set by Indians and pioneers being a frequently mentioned possibility. ORV use, particularly in areas accessed from private land in NC east of the area, has traditionally been a management problem. Backcountry and scenic area designations have brought some improvement. The CNF's 1988 management plan protected a 3,865-acre scenic area (which incorporated the even earlier 1,297-acre Gentry Creek scenic area) and a 1,390-acre primitive area. The CNF's 2004 plan revision continues the protection of those areas in enlarged scenic area and backcountry area designations.

TRAILHEADS AND MAPS

The trailheads for the area are located just east of Laurel Bloomery, TN. Laurel Bloomery is reached by taking TN 91 7.6 miles north from the US 421, TN 91, and TN 67 intersection in Mountain City, TN. Directions from Laurel Bloomery to nearby trailheads are described below. Gentry Creek Road (FS 123) turns east off TN 91 in Laurel Bloomery but is not marked. When approaching from Mountain City, Gentry Creek Road turns right at 7.6 miles just before crossing the bridge over Gentry Creek. Note the flag and volunteer fire department on the other side of the bridge. There is a very small sign on the right at this point stating "Gentry Creek 3 Miles." Although the scenic area is in TN, it is also very accessible from VA. From I-81 at Abingdon, VA, take US 58 12 miles to Damascus, VA. Proceed past the "Red Caboose" visitor's center through downtown on US 58 for about 1.5

miles to the US 58/VA 91 junction. Turn right on VA 91 and follow it south for 5.7 miles from the US 58/VA 91 junction. Note that VA 91 becomes TN 91 at the state line. At 5.7 miles note a volunteer fire department building on the left, usually with a flag out front. Immediately cross a bridge (over Gentry Creek) and turn left on FS 123.

Rogers Ridge Horse Trail Parking Area and Gentry Creek Trail Parking Area Trailheads

Whether approaching from north or south, drive up the paved Gentry Creek Road 0.7 mile, past two churches, to an intersection where there is a street sign for "Gentry Creek Road" to the right. Two trailheads are reached from this intersection ("Gentry Creek Intersection"), both after turning right at the Gentry Creek Intersection. The road continues to be a paved road and you will pass two ponds on the left. At 1.8 miles from TN 91, the pavement turns to rough gravel that is usually passable by 2 WD vehicles. At 2.0 miles a spur road turns left into the gravel Rogers Ridge Horse Trail Parking Area (UTM 17S 0433890E/4044434N). The Rogers Ridge Horse Trail starts at the back left side of the parking lot, which is often littered and sometimes used by locals for parties. For the Gentry Creek Trailhead, continue on up the Gentry Creek Road to the right, past the parking area. The road becomes difficult but not usually impassable for high clearance 2 WD automobiles. At 3.2 miles the road ends in the oval and gravel Gentry Creek Trail Parking Area. The Gentry Creek Trail goes off into the woods at the backside of the parking area. Note a rough road angling up to the right at the back-right side of the parking area. This is the Gentry Creek ORV road (FS 123), which climbs up to Cut Laurel Gap and then north to Winnie Knob and Haw Gap. It is badly washed out and is used only by ORVs.

TOPOGRAPHIC MAPS: USGS Grayson, TN-NC-VA; Laurel Bloomery, TN-VA. TI Map 783, South Holston and Watauga Lakes, CNF.

TRAIL DESCRIPTIONS

I. GENTRY CREEK TRAIL (GENTRY CREEK FALLS) (FS TRAIL 51, TI TRAIL 12)

LENGTH: 2.3 miles

ELEVATION CHANGE: Low point, 2,840 feet; high point, 3,600 feet

DIFFICULTY: Easy (difficult near Gentry Creek Falls)

TRAILHEADS: Gentry Creek Trail Parking Area

TRAIL CONNECTIONS: Kate Branch off-trail route

USE: Hiking

TOPOGRAPHIC MAPS: USGS Grayson, TN-NC-VA; Laurel Bloomery, TN-VA

COMMENTS: The good-quality and maintained Gentry Creek Falls Trail leads to Gentry Creek Falls, one of the scenic area's most outstanding sights. Above the falls the trail is not maintained but provides an off-trail connection to the Kate Branch off-trail route and opportunities for loop trips. The trail generally follows Gentry Creek and is periodically marked with dark green plastic signs, posted by the Gentry Falls Trail Club, a local hiking group. They have substantially improved both the signage and maintenance of the trail in the early 2000s, including the construction of several bridges, placement of rocks for crossing the creek, and a "cut-off" to avoid creek crossings. Gentry Creek is usually easily fordable except in heavy rains. This trail is also known as Gentry Creek Falls Trail. Depending on your vehicle, you may want to park in the Rogers Ridge Trail Parking Area and walk up to the Gentry Creek Trailhead since the road connecting the two is rather primitive in places, especially after rains. The road portion is about 1.2 miles. The parking area for the trail (UTM 17S 435165E/4044347N) is sometimes used by people for camping and is rather primitive.

DETAILS: The trail begins at the backside of the parking area in a shady grove of white pine and rhododendron. Note that between the trailhead and Kate Branch, the trail is not the trail shown on USGS topographical maps. The Gentry Creek Trail stays near the creek, while the trail shown on the maps is an old railroad grade.

At 0.1 mile from the trailhead the Kate Branch off-trail route veers off to the right while the Gentry Creek Trail goes straight ahead. The Gentry Creek Trail is marked at this point with dark green plastic signs and the sign "Gentry Creek Falls 2⅓ Miles." Gentry Creek Trail continues along Gentry Creek, through a carpet of wildflowers in the early spring. The trail is generally dirt but quite rocky in some places. The predominant tree along the creek is the yellow birch, with its characteristic peeling bark. A high canopy of second-growth hardwoods, poplar and maple, provides dense shade and leaves the forest floor remarkably open except for the mounds of rhododendrons. In early morning, shafts of sunlight pierce the canopy and create an inspiring pattern of light in the morning mist.

After passing through a relatively level area and crossing several side streams, at 0.56 mile the trail crosses to the west side of the creek. This is the first of numerous crossings, most of which require rock-hopping or fording. At 0.8 mile note a USFS property sign and yellow "bearing tree" sign on the left. At 0.85 mile there is an interesting low rock cliff on the left displaying cubic fractures. Even in the thick growth of summer, the character of the gorge is influenced by the rock faces that outcrop, revealing thick and thin bands of sediment laid down in basins that preceded today's mountain ridges. Piles of talus from the gorge walls accumulate on the otherwise broad, flat valley bottom. At 1.0 mile an old logging railroad grade on the left side of the creek goes back and up to the left of the trail.

The trail ascends very gradually through the steep-sided gorge, crossing and recrossing the creek numerous times before reaching Gentry Falls. At 1.36 miles go straight up a usually dry rocky stream-bed instead of taking an obvious trail across the streambed to an island area. At 1.4 miles the rock changes to quartzite, which in places

Hiker and dog cross Gentry Creek on log. Photograph by Will Skelton.

forms the stream bottom, channeling the water into slides and small cascades. The gorge in this area features prolific ferns and nettles. In midsummer, mountain hydrangea and crimson bee balm (oswego tea) bloom along the creek.

At 1.55 miles there is an old FS bridge. On at 1.83 miles the trail crosses the creek on a well-constructed split-log bridge with rock support structures on each end. Just beyond the bridge is a huge fire ring in the middle of the trail. At 1.86 miles an old railroad grade goes off and up to the left and is followed by another creek crossing. Just above the creek crossing is a sign for the "Gentry Creek Cut-Off Trail," which was constructed by the Gentry Creek Trail Club to avoid two creek crossings. The new trail goes to the right above the east bank of Gentry Creek, while the old trail goes left.

The trail gradually becomes more and more rocky as you approach Gentry Falls, and the walking is accordingly more difficult. Finally at 2.3 miles, the approach to Gentry Falls is heralded as the trail goes around the left side of a huge, high boulder covered with leathery lichen. Once around the boulder, go down to the creek. From this beautiful vantage point below the falls, both an upper and lower cascade are visible, each 30 feet high, and tucked into a limestone gorge. The water spills over two broad rock ledges that span the width of the gorge. To the right a fern-covered slope ascends from the pool beneath the falls.

Beyond the lower falls the ascent steepens and becomes more challenging. The official trail and the trail as shown on the TI map end at this point. If you proceed, be extremely careful and do not continue unless you have off-trail hiking experience. As of 2002, located below a tree between the two falls, cards and mementos were left in memory of a hiker who died falling off the cliffs. To continue the hike to the upper falls, climb the steep talus pile beside the left wall of the lower falls and scramble up a stack of rocks. Then traverse over to the right; the trail crosses the stream between the upper and lower falls. The pool between the two is more delightful than the one below, with deep water under a jutting rock face sprouting rhododendrons. The falls are a logical destination for a day hike, including a swim in the heat of summer.

The ascent continues up the right side of the upper falls; there is no trail at this point, and extreme caution is advised. Once on top of the cliff above the falls, descend to the left down to the creek and trail above the falls. From the top of the falls at 2.4 miles the trail levels out and the character of the woods changes. The stream is quieter and the understory increasingly dense.

The trail is fairly well defined above the falls and is occasionally marked with yellow ribbons. At 2.66 miles you will pass two pieces of metal from the railroad logging days. One has printed on it "Built By Meadow Mill Co., N. Wilkesboro, N.C." A short distance on, you will see the remnants of an old stove and an obvious fork in the trail. This is the Gilbert Branch and the end of the Gentry Creek Trail as we describe it. However, the Kate Branch off-trail route continues both up Gentry Creek straight ahead and up Gilbert Branch to the right. Just up the railroad grade to the right are the remains of an old cabin, including bedsprings.

In case you are making a loop hike, we will briefly describe the route up Gentry Creek (see also the Kate Branch off-trail route below). To follow the Kate Branch off-trail route, continue by crossing the creek and proceeding upstream. At 2.9 miles a railroad grade descends from the right (this is where the Kate Branch off-trail route comes down to Gentry Creek). The trail will continue up the valley to about 3.6 miles. At that point the route will climb steeply for 0.1 mile out of the gorge to an old road. The old road then leads 0.5 mile to join the Rogers Ridge Trail in a clearing at 4.16 miles. It will switchback to the right just before reaching the clearing. At the clearing the Rogers Ridge Horse Trail leads along Rogers Ridge left to the Gentry Creek watershed. To the right it goes up to the Rogers Ridge summit and acres of grassy balds. Straight across the clearing an ORV road leads down into Seng Cove.

2. ROGERS RIDGE TRAIL (ROGERS RIDGE HORSE TRAIL) (FS TRAIL 192, TI TRAIL 35)

LENGTH: 6.23 miles

ELEVATION CHANGE: Low point, 2,680 feet; high point, 4,880 feet

DIFFICULTY: Moderate

TRAILHEADS: Rogers Ridge Trail Parking Area

TRAIL CONNECTIONS: Kate Branch off-trail route

USE: Equestrian, hiking

TOPOGRAPHIC MAPS: USGS Grayson, TN-NC-VA; Laurel Bloomery, TN-VA

COMMENTS: The Rogers Ridge Trail is the major trail in the Rogers Ridge Scenic Area. Much of the trail runs along bald ridgetops, offering beautiful views all year long. There is a good campsite at the highest spot along the trail, complete with a freshwater spring that runs most of the year. However, the spring may be dry during very dry seasons or periods of drought. The trail is sometimes well blazed, sometimes not. The blazes vary but are usually a vertical yellow slash and/or a metal horse-and-rider logo. The first 4.0 miles of the trail up Rogers Ridge from the Rogers Ridge Trail Trailhead to the first of three grassy gaps is the official USFS trail as shown on the TI map. However, there is a trail/road that extends on to the high grassy balds. From those balds, in the prior edition of this book, we described an extension that allowed a large loop trip, southward from Tri-State Corner along the TN-NC state line to Haw Gap and then FS 123 to get back to the starting trailhead. However, private land in the middle of this route has been gated off and the route is no longer feasible.

DETAILS: The Rogers Ridge Trail starts at the left side of the parking area (do not follow the trail at the far end of the parking area, which is a fisherman's trail that follows the creek). The Rogers Ridge Trail immediately crosses Gentry Creek, which is usually easily fordable. A steep climb follows on the other side of the creek, and then the trail alternates between steep areas and more level areas as it traverses around the right side of a ridge. At 0.2 mile there is a small clearing on the left. At 0.6 mile the top of a low ridge is reached, overlooking Negro Shanty Hollow. The much higher Rogers Ridge is visible to the east. At 0.86 mile the remnant of an old road turns left and continues straight up Negro Hollow Shanty, while the trail continues at an easy grade to the right.

At 1.36 miles the trail finally reaches Rogers Ridge, turns northeast, and subsequently traverses along Rogers Ridge and involves hiking up and over numerous high points along the ridge, although progress is gradually upward toward the summit of Rogers Ridge. The trail continues to be in a forested area for some distance, although there are good views when the leaves are down in the winter. You are hiking above Gentry Creek and its trail to the right, which are no more than 0.5 mile away. Much of the trail is relatively level.

At 2.7 miles an old dirt road angles off to the left, with the trail continuing straight along with the ridge. Sometimes the trail will be on one side or the other of the ridge, but it never varies far from the ridgetop. At 3.5 miles there is a junction where the trail appears to go straight ahead at the side of the ridge; instead, take a hard turn back to the right and climb steeply toward the top of the ridge. The trail straight ahead ends up at the same place but passes through private property and should be avoided. In another 0.1 mile, after reaching the top of the ridge, there is a yellow USFS boundary marker and an elevation marker. The former trail goes straight ahead along the ridge on private property, while the official trail slants down onto the right side of the ridge. This portion of the trail was built in the late 1990s by the USFS with the use of a small bulldozer. As a result, it is quite wide in many places. The trail looked terrible during construction, but it is slowly beginning to look more like a trail than a road.

After descending and then climbing again, the newly constructed trail intersects a roadbed running left and right at 4.0 miles. The roadbed comes up from private property and is not maintained. Turn right on the roadbed and follow it over a low rise to a gap that has some grassy areas. This is the first of three grassy gaps. In the gap there is an intersection of a more obvious dirt road on the left at 4.06 miles. The road comes up from private property along Piney Knob Ridge and permits ORV abuse of the trail. The trail as shown on the TI map ends at this grassy gap; however, continuing on is both easy and rewarding. Turn right on the dirt road and continue walking on the dirt road to the northeast.

After some fairly easy walking, a big grassy gap is reached at 5.0 miles. In this gap there is also a dirt road coming up from private property that angles down to the left and also permits ORV access. The road you are walking on angles to the right side of the ridge, while the trail continues straight ahead along the ridgetop and appears to be a trail instead of a road. This gap at 5.0 miles provides access to the Kate Branch off-trail route. To go down the Kate Branch Trail (and to make a loop hike using the Gentry Creek Trail), look to the right (south) and you will see an obvious old road that traverses back to the south side of the ridge (UTM 17S 437115E/4047891N). Follow it about 0.6 mile down to Gentry Creek.

At 4.66 miles you will enter another large grassy area and notice an old upside-down school bus off to the left at the northeast corner. At the east end of the clearing an old road turns to the left and heads straight up the side of the ridge, while the trail you are on continues straight ahead out the side of the ridge. At this point, when the leaves are off the trees, you can begin to see the Tri-Corner Knob where NC, TN, and VA come together and the grassy balds of Rogers Ridge.

At 5.27 miles, after a long and fairly continuous climb, the trail emerges into the beginning of a grassy bald that is pretty much continuous to the summit of Rogers Ridge, with lots of blackberry bushes, a few blueberries, and grass everywhere. A few hundred feet on, the trail reaches a junction, with the more used road portion turning left to a couple of cabins located on the side of the ridge. The trail, however, turns right and continues to ascend along the ridge. At this point the views really begin to get spectacular. On a clear day you can see the TN Valley and a series of smaller valleys lying to the west and a succession of southern Appalachian peaks to the east in the NC.

The remainder of the hike is probably the best part of the hike, with many grassy balds and scenic vistas. At 5.2 miles, just below the ridgetop, there is "V" junction and you should take the right one to the top of the ridge. The left one goes out to an overlook. At 5.8 miles you are at the ridge on which the Rogers Ridge Summit is located. You can walk to the left out to a 4,760-foot knoll for a look on the TN side of the mountain. A wonderful campsite is located straight ahead in the forested saddle where Catface Ridge joins Rogers Ridge. Water can be found below Rogers Ridge summit (see below). However, to follow the trail turn right (south), toward a wooden gate/fence that serves no purpose, as it is not gated or continuous enough to prevent access. After going through the gate, you will enter an evergreen forest area, and the trail follows a circuitous route toward the summit.

At 6.0 miles you will emerge from the woods onto a beautiful grassy bald. You will reach the summit of Rogers Ridge at 4,880 feet in another 0.23 mile along the grassy ridgetop. Plan to stop somewhere in that 0.23 mile and simply enjoy the panoramic vistas. The summit is generally grassy but with lots of blackberry bushes and some trees. The Gentry Creek Valley is below to the south and pro-

Winter backpackers near summit of Rogers Ridge. Photograph by Will Skelton.

vides opportunities for off-trail hiking. To the south you can also see Sugar Mountain Ski Resort and the ugly condominium project built on a ridge nearby that resulted in NC banning high elevation ridgetop developments like that one. You will also see, directly to the east, the Tri-Corner Knob and, just south of there, a road leading up to a large house constructed on private property at substantial expense by a man from Charlotte, NC. The house and the Sugar Mountain Condominiums both reflect how our high elevation mountains can be abused. If you want to camp, there are lots of available areas. However, water is the only problem and is located in the bowl almost due south of the ridgetop (UTM 17S 438705E/4048831N).

OFF-TRAIL HIKING OPPORTUNITIES

Kate Branch and Gilbert Branch

This route is an unauthorized trail that has been constructed by horse riders mainly by use rather than real trail construction, and it is extremely poorly routed in places. Sometimes it follows creek beds, sometimes it goes straight up the sides of hills. The route's length is about 5.5 miles from the Gentry Creek Trailhead to the Rogers Ridge Trail, and it is sometimes marked with yellow ribbons and yellow blazes with a horse on top of the blaze. The trailhead is the same as for the Gentry Creek Trail. The route begins at the backside of the parking area in a shady grove of white pine and rhododendron. Note that between the trailhead and Kate Branch, the route is the trail shown on USGS topographical maps on the side of the ridge, while the Gentry Creek Trail stays near the creek and is not shown on the maps. At 0.1 mile from the trailhead the Kate Branch off-trail route veers off to the right, while the Gentry Creek Trail goes straight ahead. The Gentry Creek Trail is marked at this point with dark green plastic signs and the sign "Gentry Creek Falls 2⅓ Miles." Instead, follow the old road up to the right and over an earthen ORV barrier. For nearly a mile to Kate Branch the route follows an old railroad grade and is very easy walking.

At 0.96 mile the route reaches its namesake, Kate Branch. After crossing Kate Branch, the route continues up the left side of the Kate Branch valley. The route is often frustrating for the next mile, as it generally follows Kate Branch, sometimes in the creek, sometimes along the creek, and sometimes following old roadbeds above the creek. The route is generally obvious but sometimes difficult. At 1.73 miles the route climbs out of the creek gorge to the right and ascends into a once open area. A nice beech tree sits in the middle of the area. Most of the valley is covered with a mixture of deciduous and evergreen trees, with lots of rhododendrons in the understory. At this point there is good walking for a way on an old road grade. A large metal can sits at 1.9 miles.

At 1.95 miles, after another creek crossing, the route veers sharply to the left, up and away from the creek valley and straight up a rocky drainage. Although it appears the route is going to go on up the drainage, it then quickly veers to the left, on what is probably an old road, away from the drainage. The ascent up and over a high ridge to Gilbert Branch begins at this point. The climb is often very steep, usually when the route connects old roads together. There is no apparent trail construction, simply use by horses. The top of the ridge is reached at 2.47 miles where there are often cool breezes in the summer (UTM 17S 437147E/4046741N). The route turns slightly to the left and proceeds down the other side to the left (northwest). However, after only 50 feet, the route again takes a hard right down an old roadbed; another old roadbed continues straight ahead, but you should avoid it. A clump of metal lies at the intersection where you turn right. At 2.7 miles the old road you are on continues straight down the side of the mountain, whereas the Kate Branch route takes another old road but ascends to the right. Evidence of old road construction is apparent in many places, including not only cuts into the side of the ridges but also built-up piles of rock to support the roads. Most of these were logging roads. Cross over a ridge at 2.8 miles and at 3.0 miles and ascend to a gap. The route reaches a junction (UTM 17S 437861E/4047034N) with a good trail that heads both left and right. Do not take the trail to the right, which leads to private property where you may see a yellow "Posted Private Property" sign prohibiting access to Cherokee Hunt Club Lands. Instead, turn left and follow the clear trail over a low ridge.

On the other side of the ridge the route descends toward Gilbert Branch and is wide and clear following an old roadbed. The creek is crossed at 3.4 miles, after which the route climbs over a small ridge to a wet weather drainage. At the wet weather drainage the route makes a hard left turn. It is important to avoid going straight at that point. Instead, turn left and proceed down the valley. The route will cross a creek and at 3.63 miles will cross an area of large bare rocks. After this point the walk gradually becomes much easier as an old roadbed traverses above the creek down toward Gentry Creek.

At 4.1 miles, the route reaches Gentry Creek. To the left there is a rough off-trail route down to Gentry Falls and the Gentry Creek Trail.

Remnants of an old stove are located at the junction. To follow the Kate Branch off-trail route, turn right and continue up Gentry Creek for almost 0.7 mile, where the route will leave the creek to the left and follow an old logging road 0.6 mile to the Rogers Ridge Horse Trail.

McQueen Gap and Whetstone Branch

This route is entirely in the scenic area, mostly just south of the TN-VA state line. It is shown on the Grayson TN-VA USGS topographic map as a trail, but it is not an official trail and is not maintained. The trail as shown on the map starts at the upper end of Dry Branch and then traverses across to McQueen Gap. Although it is possible to begin or end the trail at Dry Branch, permission of the owners of the private property at that trailhead must be obtained and may not be given; ordinarily it is preferable to hike in and out from McQueen Gap. The route starts on the south side of McQueen Gap and follows an old jeep road surrounded by rhododendron blooming in the early summer months. At about 0.3 mile, the trail crosses Richardson Branch at its confluence with Valley Creek. The USGS map shows a side trail heading up Richardson Branch to Flat Springs Ridge, which affords excellent views. The trailhead to this side trail is barricaded with a small earthen mound, and the trail quickly disappears along the creek. Proceeding up Richardson Branch is possible but moderately difficult and should only be attempted with the aid of a topographic map. Continue up Whetstone Branch, a small but beautiful area. At 1.0 mile the trail crosses Whetstone Branch. Immediately after the crossing, tempting blueberries are within reach in season. The USFS boundary is posted at about 2.2 miles. Just on the other side of the boundary, the trail climbs moderately to its highest elevation at about 3,920 feet and begins to narrow as it descends along Dry Branch to the Dry Branch road, about 1.0 mile further.

Tri-State Corner

This route provides the shortest access to Tri-State Corner and the grassy balds just beyond. It can be beautiful in winter when snow often keeps ORVs out, but at other times ORVs will intrude. The route begins at the end of a road just west of Bearpen Ridge on the USGS Grayson TN-VA map. Proceed straight up the narrow valley on an ORV road. At the head of the valley, the trail will circle around an old logging operation as it gradually gains elevation. Some views are outstanding, and portions of the route are not used by ORVs. After ascending to Flat Spring Ridge at about 1.2 miles, the trail makes a very sharp turn to the left; other trails go right toward a grassy bald. Proceed southeast and at around 1.6 miles you will come to the ridge-crest, where a picturesque cabin is located. Roads lead up to that and other houses from the valley below and to the northeast. Vehicle use is frequent in this area. At the cabin you can turn right and follow the road up the ridge to the Tri-State Corner at 2.3 miles. TN, VA, and NC meet here. You can then continue about 0.5 mile up the ridge to USFS property and the summit balds of Rogers Ridge. The summit is the official end of the Rogers Ridge Trail, which comes from the south.

2 Iron Mountain

(Includes London Bridge Backcountry Area, Iron Mountain Back-country Area, and Iron Mountain Roadless Area)

Iron Mountain is a long mountain ridge that stretches more than 34 miles from Damascus and the TN-VA state line south to US 19E near Hampton, TN. Another 30 plus miles of the mountain also extends into VA. The TN portion of the ridge is continuous and unbroken except for the Watauga River gorge near its southern terminus. The Iron Mountain Trail, at slightly more than 18.0 miles, provides one of the best long-distance hiking opportunities, other than the AT, in the CNF. This trail follows the ridgetop and features wildflowers, large high-elevation hemlock trees, and outstanding views of the valleys on both sides of the ridge. The northern half of TN's Iron Mountain, from TN 91 to the TN-VA state line, is included in this section of this guide. The southern half is included in the Big Laurel Branch section. The outstanding roadless qualities of the area were recognized by the USFS's Southern Appalachian Assessment identification of the 3,431-acre (plus 853 acres on the Jefferson NF) Iron Mountain Roadless Area. The roadless area is located on the steep, forested slopes on the northernmost portion of Iron Mountain. An area greater than the roadless area is protected in the CNF's 2004 plan revision, including the 3,416-acre London Bridge Backcountry Area (no roads), a 1,239-acre London Bridge Backcountry Area (few open roads), and a 544-acre Iron Mountain Backcountry Area (no roads). The area is generally located in Johnson County, TN, and is in the Watauga Ranger District.

HISTORY

This corner of northeast TN was originally a part of NC although it was supposed to be in VA. In 1749 when the land was surveyed, the surveyor made a mistake in the rough mountain topography, designating the land as part of NC instead of VA. When the mistake was

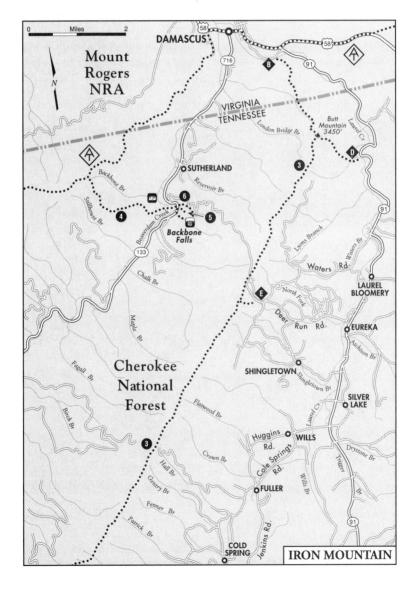

discovered, an aide was sent back to correct the error, but he left the lines as originally drawn (probably wanting to avoid walking the difficult terrain again). NC ceded the land to TN when TN became a state. The CNF's 1988 management plan protected a 2,550-acre primitive area. The CNF's 2004 plan revision provides for the protection of a larger area in backcountry area designations. There are several old clear-cuts in the area that have almost completely regrown. Outside of the backcountry areas, a 200-foot corridor protects the Iron Mountain Trail.

The Iron Mountain Trail description below only includes the 18.0-mile hiking trail running south from Damascus, VA, to Cross Mountain

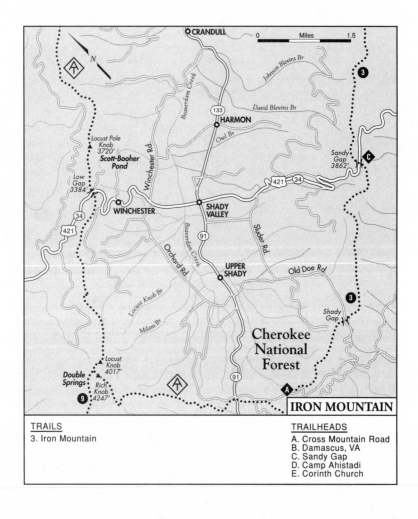

TRAILS
3. Iron Mountain

TRAILHEADS
A. Cross Mountain Road
B. Damascus, VA
C. Sandy Gap
D. Camp Ahistadi
E. Corinth Church

Road (near TN 91). Another multiuse bike, hike, and equestrian trail follows the Iron Mountain Ridge as it extends into VA and the Jefferson NF.

TRAILHEADS AND MAPS

Trailheads for Hiking the Entire Southern Length of the Iron Mountain Trail

CROSS MOUNTAIN ROAD TRAILHEAD

From Elizabethton, TN, drive north on TN 91 for 19.0 miles (the AT crosses TN 91 at 18.9 miles and Cross Mountain Road is on the right, 0.1 mile past the AT crossing). Turn right on Cross Mountain Road (no road sign) and drive approximately 1.2 miles to the trailhead, which is located on the left side of the road (radio towers on the right). The trailhead is an old, rutted USFS road marked only by a blue blaze on a pine tree on the left side of the trail. There are neither trail signs nor parking at the trailhead, so a shuttle is advisable. An alternate approach from the north is from Damascus, VA, and the intersection of VA 58 and VA 133, Drive south on VA 133 for 17.1 miles to Cross Mountain Road, which will be on the left. Turn left on Cross Mountain Road and drive 1.2 miles to the trailhead on the left. The trailhead is not signed, but there is a blue blaze on a large pine tree on the left-hand side of the trail. Again there are no trail signs or parking at the trailhead.

DAMASCUS, VA, TRAILHEAD

From Mount Rogers Outfitters in the middle of downtown Damascus, drive east to the intersection of VA 58 and VA 91 (0.3 mile). Turn right and drive south on VA 91 for 0.2 mile (past Cowboy's Food Market on the right). At the point where the road curves sharply to the left, go straight onto Orchard Hill Road and cross the narrow one-lane bridge. The trailhead is located 1.0 mile from the turnoff to Orchard Hill Road. The trailhead is marked by an iron gate across the trail, a trail sign on the left side behind the iron gate, and mile marker 15 in front of the gate. No parking is available at the trailhead, so it is advisable to park in Damascus and walk to the trailhead or arrange a shuttle.

*Trailheads for Hiking Shorter Sections of the
Iron Mountain Trail*

SANDY GAP TRAILHEAD

From Shady Valley, TN, and the junction of US 421, TN 91, and TN 133, drive southeast on US 421 for 4.2 miles to Sandy Gap. From Mountain City, TN, and the junction of US 421, TN 67, and TN 91, drive northwest on US 421 6.8 miles to Sandy Gap. The Iron Mountain Trailhead is on the north side of the road in the gap. Stone steps lead up the side of the bank. A small parking area is on the south side of the road.

CAMP AHISTADI AND CORINTH CHURCH TRAILHEADS

From Damascus, VA, take VA 91 south to the intersection with US 58 (1.0 mile outside of Damascus). From the intersection, drive 3.1 miles to Camp Ahistadi, a Methodist church camp. Parking is available outside the metal gate. Go through the gate or fence, cross a bridge, and turn right to reach the trailhead. To find the Corinth Church Trailhead, drive 10.2 miles past Camp Ahistadi and look for the sign for Corinth Church. Turn right at the sign and drive 1.7 miles to the church.

From Mountain City, TN, and the junction of US 421 and TN 91, drive 9.4 miles north on TN 91 to the sign for the Corinth Church. Turn left at the sign and drive 1.7 miles to the church. To reach the Camp Ahistadi Trailhead from Mountain City, drive 19.6 miles north on TN 91 from the junction of TN 91 and US 421. Parking and the entrance to Camp Ahistadi are on the left.

TOPOGRAPHIC MAPS: USGS Laurel Bloomery, TN-VA; Shady Valley, TN-VA; Doe, TN. TI Map 783, South Holston and Watauga Lakes, CNF.

TRAIL DESCRIPTIONS

3. IRON MOUNTAIN TRAIL (FS TRAIL 54, TI TRAIL 16)

LENGTH: 18.0 miles

ELEVATION CHANGE: Low point, 1,930 feet; high point, 4,200 feet

DIFFICULTY: Moderate

TRAILHEADS: Damascus, VA (start), and Cross Mountain Road (end)

USE: Hiking

TOPOGRAPHIC MAPS: USGS Laurel Bloomery, TN-VA; Shady Valley, TN-VA, and Doe, TN

COMMENTS: The Iron Mountain Trail is maintained by the Mid-Appalachian Highlands Club, located in Elizabethton, TN (http://jat.esmartweb.com/hikers/mid-app-hiland-club.htm). The club has positioned yellow triangular mileage markers at one-mile intervals along the trail for the purpose of sectioning the trail for maintenance. Although the trail is generally well maintained during the summer months, stinging nettle can be a problem. This is a "no-nonsense" trail following the spine of Iron Mountain with few switchbacks.

This trail offers one of the best long-distance hiking opportunities in the CNF. The Iron Mountain Trail terminates a mile or so (walking distance) from the Mount Rogers Outfitters parking lot in downtown Damascus. If you are hiking the trail end to end, it is advisable to park your car there and hire a shuttle to the Cross Mountain Road Trailhead. No parking is available at either trailhead.

When coupled with the AT, the Iron Mountain Trail can be hiked as a 45-mile loop. To do the loop hike, start at the Iron Mountain Trailhead in Damascus, VA, hike that trail to Cross Mountain Road, then take a right on Cross Mountain Road and follow the road for 1.2 miles to TN 91. Pick up the AT just west and across the two-lane highway and hike back to Damascus.

Since most of the Iron Mountain Trail follows the ridgeline, the availability of water is of particular concern, especially during the summer months and/or if rainfall has been scarce. Use caution if hiking during hunting season. Information (free), maps, parking, and shuttle service (charge) are available at Mount Rogers Outfitters (on the AT), 110 Laurel Avenue, Damascus, VA, 276/475-5416.

DETAILS: The Iron Mountain Trail begins with a steady climb. At the 0.5 mile mark, several downed trees have been notched out to make way for the trail. Ferns and hardwood trees are abundant on this section. The trail levels off briefly but becomes an uphill climb again at the double blue blaze located at the 0.7 mile point. A sign noting that you are leaving VA's Mount Rogers National Recreation Area and going into the CNF in TN is located at the 1.3 mile mark.

This section of the trail is well groomed and easy, following just below the mountain's rocky ridgetop. The trail reaches the ridgetop at 2.5 miles and thereafter follows the spine of the mountain for much of the hike. The 3,450-foot Butt Mountain is located at this north end of the ridgetop. Shortly thereafter you will see a trail junction and a side trail on the left that descends 1.9 miles to the Camp Ahistadi Trailhead.

The following is a brief description of that side trail, with the mileage starting at the junction. The side trail descends from Iron Mountain and passes rock outcroppings and rock slides at 0.2 mile, with good views of the valley and mountains. Flame azaleas bloom here in late spring. At 0.4 mile the trail descends sharply for approximately 0.5 mile. Yellow star grass blooms here in late spring. At 0.7 mile the trail levels off among Fraser magnolias and striped maples and turns east. At 0.9 mile the trail begins a very sharp descent of Butt Mountain as it leaves Iron Mountain, and the first of several switchbacks appears. At 1.0 mile the trail reaches a small stream and then follows it down the valley. Crested dwarf iris and fire pink grow here as the trail leaves the pine-oak forest and enters the cove hardwoods. At 1.2 miles the trail levels out and abandons the small stream, which continues into Laurel Creek. At 1.5 miles a side road, used by the Methodist Church's Camp Ahistadi, enters from the right. Continue straight for 200 feet and come to a gravel road and turn left. Cross the bridge and 100 yards ahead is the gate to Camp Ahistadi and the parking area by TN 91.

The Iron Mountain Trail continues along the ridgetop. A good campsite is located at 4.3 miles in a flat, wooded area, although a water source is not visible in the immediate vicinity.

At 4.8 miles an open grassy area is located on the right side of the trail. The grassy area is large enough for several tents. To find water, walk toward the growth of trees at the west-end of the campsite and look for a creek bed. If water is not flowing out of the white pipe, keep walking along the creek bed and water should eventually appear. A spring is also located on the left side of the trail a few hundred feet beyond the campsite. It is bigger and easier to access than the creek bed.

Just beyond the stream, the trail ascends steeply to the ridgetop and levels out at 5.1 miles. The first vista can be enjoyed at this point from the left side of the trail. Mount Rogers, White Top, and Doe Valley are visible. The terrain becomes rougher and rockier here, although it is still fairly easy to walk on.

At 5.2 miles, a jeep road, FS 322, crosses the trail. A small "home-made" trail sign covered in plastic is located on a large three-trunk Tulip Poplar, which is growing on the right side of the trail. The sign indicates mileage to a number of sites as well as 13 miles to the end of the Iron Mountain Trail. Left on the jeep road (south) 0.7 mile is the Corinth Church Trailhead. To the right on the jeep road, approximately 3.0 miles, is TN 133, near Backbone Rock Recreational Area.

Utility poles and a series of cables are visible about 0.2 mile ahead. Several small antennas are also erected here. Nice views can be seen from both sides of the trail, and although the vista on the left side is almost overgrown, you can see Doe Valley and Doe Mountain. At 5.6 miles, evidence of a fire is visible on the right side of the trail. The bottom of the trees and the downed wood is scorched, but otherwise little damage is visible. The effects of the fire are seen for several miles.

At 6.4 miles, the trail weaves through several large rock outcrops and leaves the ridgetop. At 7.0 miles, the trail skirts the right side of the ridge among rue anemone and makes a steep ascent back to the ridgetop, arriving at a small clearing at 7.4 miles.

For the next 0.6 mile, the trail alternately climbs and descends gradually. At 8.0 miles the trail once again ascends through large rocks, and at 9.4 and 9.9 miles large rock outcrops are located on the left side of the trail. As the trail continues to ascend and descend, summer-blooming flowers including bladderwort, Oswego tea, and Carolina lilies are scattered along the trail view shed.

At mile marker 11.1 and 11.5 miles, streams cross the trail in a valley surrounded by a hardwood forest. At 12.7 miles is an open grassy area on the right, which can serve as an unprotected campsite. The trail skirts the south side of Grindstone Knob, which is the high

Iron Mountain Trail near Sandy Gap. Photograph by Will Skelton.

point of the trail at 4,200 feet. (A large black bear was observed on the trail below the Knob while hiking the trail for this book.) The trail then descends toward Sandy Gap. At 13.4 miles the trail crosses US 421 (see Sandy Gap Trailhead information for early-out option).

Another small campsite with fire ring is available at 13.9 miles with no visible source of water in the area. The trail descends steeply into Shady Gap, crosses the gravel Old Doe Road (FS 6054), and ascends steeply up the other side. The trail then follows the ridgetop for about a mile before a gradual descent to Cross Mountain Road at 18.0 miles.

3 Beaverdam Creek

(Includes Beaverdam Creek Roadless Area and Beaverdam Creek Backcountry Area)

The Beaverdam Creek area includes the forested eastern slopes of northern Holston Mountain, from which the scenic Beaver Creek and several of its tributaries flow. Beaverdam Creek was named for the large population of beavers that once inhabited the area and built dams along the creek, creating marshes and ponds. However, beavers were hunted out of existence in this area in the 1700s. The area is located in northern Johnson County, TN, just southeast of Damascus, VA, and is in the Watauga Ranger District. The significant natural qualities of the area were recognized by the USFS's Southern Appalachian Assessment identification of the 5,130-acre (plus 1,133 acres on the Jefferson NF) Beaverdam Creek Roadless Area. Portions of that roadless area are protected in the CNF's 2004 plan revision, including the 2,792-acre Beaverdam Creek Backcountry Area.

The Backbone Rock Recreational Area lies within the area approximately 5.0 miles south of Damascus, VA, and 10.0 miles north of Shady Valley, TN, on TN 133. Backbone Rock is a unique sandstone rock formation located in a spur ridge of the Holston Mountain that ends sharply at a large bend in Beaverdam Creek. The Backbone Rock Recreational Area has several picnic areas with large shelters and bathroom facilities, an 11-site creek-side campground with on-site host, and several areas for parking. All facilities, including parking, are fee-paid. Beaverdam Creek offers swimming opportunities (at your own risk) and is considered an excellent trout stream.

In the bottomlands of the area, and especially along the creeks, there are a variety of wildflowers, including some rare species. The rare Carolina saxifrage grows near Backbone Rock, as does the beautiful grass-of-parnassus. The upper portions of the area contain scattered specimens of Carolina hemlock, a fuller, richer tree than the more common eastern hemlock.

The longest trail in the area is the 2.2-mile Backbone Rock Trail (TI Trail 53), which dead-ends at the AT on Holston Mountain. The highlights of the area are the 0.25-mile spur trail over the Backbone Rock formation (no trail number) and the Backbone Falls Trail (TI Trail 198), which is a 0.5 mile loop showcasing a waterfall, a rock gorge, and some very nice CCC stonework.

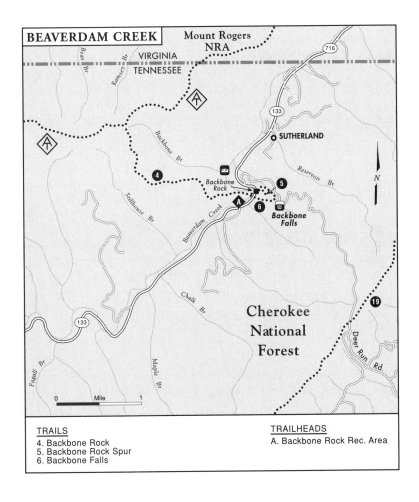

TRAILS
4. Backbone Rock
5. Backbone Rock Spur
6. Backbone Falls

TRAILHEADS
A. Backbone Rock Rec. Area

HISTORY

In the early 1900s, private rail companies operated a rail system that extended from the main line in Abington, VA, to Damascus, over Whitetop Mountain, and down into NC. A narrow gauge extension into TN along Beaverdam Creek was called the Beaverdam Creek Railroad. For many years, the trains provided a source of transportation carrying mail, passengers, and virgin timber harvested from the area, but ultimately all were closed. The rail bed between Abingdon and Whitetop is now the hiking/biking trail known as the Virginia Creeper Trail. A road replaced another part of the rail bed, which became TN 133.

The Backbone Rock tunnel is locally known as the "shortest tunnel in the world." The tunnel was drilled through the Backbone Rock in 1901 to allow passage of the railroad. The total height of Backbone Rock is 76 feet at the tunnel, and it is 22 feet wide through its narrowest point. In 1913, the USFS purchased 22,000 acres of land, including Backbone Rock, to become a part of the emerging eastern United States national forest system. In the 1930s, during the era of President Franklin D. Roosevelt's New Deal, the picnic and camping areas were constructed by the CCC. These recreational facilities were extensively reworked in the 1960s and again during 1994–95.

The CNF's 1988 management plan protected a 1,145-acre Beaverdam Creek Primitive Area. The CNF's 2004 plan revision provides for the protection of a larger area in the backcountry area designation.

TRAILHEADS AND MAPS

Backbone Rock Recreation Area Trailhead

The approach can be made from US 421 (TN side) or US 58 (VA side). From the US 421–TN 133 intersection in Shady Valley, TN, head north on TN 133, 9.5 miles to the Backbone Rock parking area (on the left before the tunnel entrance). From the US 58–VA 716 intersection located in downtown Damascus, VA, head south on VA 716 for approximately 5.0 miles to the Backbone Rock parking area (on the right just past the tunnel). The highway turns into TN 133 south of the tunnel.

TOPOGRAPHIC MAPS: USGS Laurel Bloomery, TN-VA. TI Map 783, South Holston and Watauga Lakes, CNF.

TRAIL DESCRIPTIONS

4. BACKBONE ROCK TRAIL (FS TRAIL 53, TI TRAIL 3)

LENGTH: 2.2 miles

ELEVATION CHANGE: Low point, 2,100 feet; high point, 3,250 feet

DIFFICULTY: Moderate

TRAILHEADS: Backbone Rock Recreation Area (start); AT (end)

USE: Hiking

TOPOGRAPHIC MAP: Laurel Bloomery, TN-VA

COMMENTS: The trail begins in the parking area for the Backbone Rock Recreation Area and ends at a junction with the AT on the crest of Holston Mountain. The trail is blue-blazed and well maintained by the TN Eastman Hiking and Canoe Club, which uses the Backbone Rock Trail to access a portion of the 127 miles of AT they are responsible for maintaining. The trail is enclosed by forest and offers an opportunity for solitude rather than scenic vistas. Although the hiking surface is relatively easy, the trail has a moderate rating due to several steep climbs.

Old Railroad Tunnel (now TN 133) through Backbone Rock. Photograph by Will Skelton.

DETAILS: Ascend the stone steps from the parking area. At the top of the steps, follow the blue blazes to the left fork to hike the Backbone Rock Trail. The fork to the right leads to a spur trail across the Backbone rock formation. Although the early part of the hike is through a grove of rhododendron, most of the hiking is in a second-growth hardwood forest.

The 0.5 mile point is marked by a large blowdown covering the trail. A secondary trail has been developed to the right. At 1.1 miles the trail narrows, although it is clear, well blazed, and easy to follow. The steepest section of the trail begins at about 1.5 miles and continues to 1.7 miles. There are no switchbacks in this area and the climb is straight up (tighten your bootlaces on the way down to keep your toes from jamming into the ends of your boots).

The trail dead-ends at the AT. A right on the AT will lead you north to the town of Damascus, VA (4.2 miles). A left will take you south to US 421 (10.4 miles). Consult the "AT Guidebook to TN-NC" for a specific description of the AT. The AT white blazes are clearly visible in both directions. Several large logs make this spot a nice area to sit and rest before the return hike back to Backbone Rock parking area.

5. BACKBONE ROCK SPUR TRAIL (NO FS OR TI TRAIL NUMBERS)

LENGTH: 0.25 miles

ELEVATION CHANGE: Insignificant

DIFFICULTY: Easy

TRAILHEADS: Backbone Rock Recreation Area

USE: Hiking

TOPOGRAPHIC MAP: Laurel Bloomery, TN-VA

COMMENTS: The spur trail goes across the top of the Backbone Rock Tunnel and winds down the side of the formation via a stone staircase. The trail ends in a picnic area on the north side of the rock formation. Exercise caution, especially in damp conditions; the trail footing across the top of the tunnel is smooth, flat rock. A fence has been constructed to the left of the trail but there is no protection on the right side.

DETAILS: The hike across Backbone Rock Tunnel begins at the steps in the Backbone Rock Recreation Area parking area. Ascend the steps and go right at the trail fork (the left fork is the Backbone Rock Trail and is blue-blazed). After the trail has crossed over the tunnel it forks again. The trail to the left (look for the banister) is the best route back to the road. Go down the rock steps to the picnic area. From the picnic area, the Backbone Rock Recreation Area parking area is across the street and through the tunnel.

There is an assortment of very short dead-end trails to explore on top of Backbone Rock. Most lead to a rock ledge and views of Beaverdam Creek.

6. BACKBONE FALLS TRAIL (FS TRAIL 198, TI TRAIL 2)

LENGTH: 0.5 mile

ELEVATION CHANGE: Insignificant

DIFFICULTY: Easy

TRAILHEADS: Backbone Rock Recreation Area

USE: Hiking

TOPOGRAPHIC MAP: Laurel Bloomery, TN-VA

DETAILS: This loop trail is located across the street from the Backbone Rock Parking Area. The trailhead is located on the right side of the stone wall. The trail to the left of the stone wall eventually leads back to Beaverdam Creek. Take the right trail up several steps, where the trail opens into a lookout area over a creek. The trail turns left and is surrounded by a dense thicket of rhododendron. Follow the trail along the creek to where it twists to the right at the top of the waterfall. The waterfall is long and narrow, falling into a beautiful rock gorge below. A series of 100 stone steps follow the gorge down to creek level. Stone benches are built into the rock gorge, offering an opportunity to stop and enjoy the area. The trail ends at TN 133, and a short walk to the right along the highway leads back to the Backbone Rock Recreation Area Trailhead.

4 Flint Mill

(Includes Stoney Creek Scenic Area, Flint Mill Backcountry Area, and Flint Mill Gap Roadless Area)

The Flint Mill area is located near the center of the 30-mile-long ridge of Holston Mountain that stretches from the town of Damascus, VA, to Elizabethton, TN, and forms the southeastern backdrop to upper East TN's pastoral Holston Valley. Elevations in the areas range from 2,600 feet at the base of the mountain to over 4,200 feet at Rich Knob. The northwest slopes of the mountain are very steep and dominated by short spur ridges clothed in table mountain pine and other

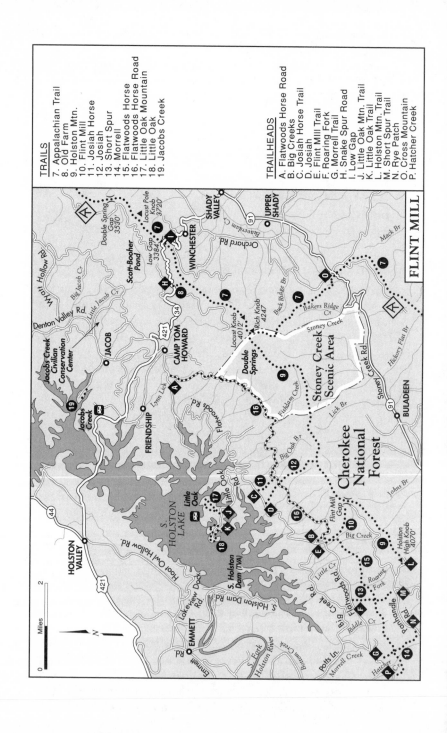

FLINT MILL

TRAILS
7. Appalachian Trail
8. Old Farm
9. Holston Mtn.
10. Flint Mill
11. Josiah Horse
12. Josiah
13. Short Spur
14. Morrell
15. Flatwoods Horse
16. Flatwoods Horse Road
17. Little Oak Mountain
18. Little Oak
19. Jacobs Creek

TRAILHEADS
A. Flatwoods Horse Road
B. Big Creeks
C. Josiah Horse Trail
D. Josiah
E. Flint Mill Trail
F. Roaring Fork
G. Morrell Trail
H. Snake Spur Road
I. Low Gap
J. Little Oak Mtn. Trail
K. Little Oak Trail
L. Holston Mtn. Trail
M. Short Spur Trail
N. Rye Patch
O. Cross Mountain
P. Hatcher Creek

fire-dependent pine species. There are numerous rock outcroppings on these ridges that offer outstanding views of the Holston Valley, the best-known being Flint Rock. The main ridge and southeastern slopes of the mountain are more gradual and covered with cove and upland hardwoods. The area is located in Carter, Sullivan, and Johnson counties, TN, and is in the Watauga Ranger District. The outstanding wilderness qualities of the area were recognized by the USFS's Southern Appalachian Assessment identification of the 9,629-acre roadless area. That roadless area and additional acres are protected in the CNF's 2004 plan revision, including the 2,606-acre Stoney Creek Scenic Area and the 7,981-acre Flint Mill Backcountry Area. The scenic area is located along the AT Corridor, while the backcountry area is located to the south of the scenic area.

Many small streams drain the Flint Mill area, creating scenic waterfalls and providing habitat for brook trout and many species of wildflowers. The two most scenic of these are Fishdam Creek and North Fork Stony Creek. Large mammals inhabiting the area include deer, bear, and bobcat. Turkeys are common, as are many other woodland bird species. Four rare plants are found in the area: round-leaved orchis, kidney-leaved twayblade, large purple-fringed orchid, and Frazier's sedge. A hiker following the trails gets a good taste of the area, but many outstanding scenic features, including waterfalls, overlooks, rare plants, and old-growth timber, reveal themselves only to those willing to hike off-trail.

HISTORY

The value of Holston Mountain was first recognized in the USFS's RARE II process in the late 1970s. The CNF's 1988 management plan protected a 3,920-acre Stoney Creek Scenic Area, and a 2,620-acre Flint Mill Primitive Area. The CNF's 2004 plan revision continues the protection of a significantly larger area in scenic area and backcountry area designations. The current protected areas have given up land from both ends of the previous RARE II tract but have added the northwest slopes of the mountain. Most important is the protection given to the scenic Fishdam Creek Gorge.

Most of the protected areas were destructively logged by private timber companies after the turn of the twentieth century, and old logging grades are abundant. The top of Rich Knob was a bald used for pasture and still shows signs of old field conditions, with blackberries and locusts. There are also prehistoric sites in the area.

TRAILHEADS AND MAPS

FS 87 Trailheads: Flatwoods Horse Road, Josiah Horse Trail, Josiah, Big Creek, Flint Mill, Roaring Fork, Morrell, and Hatcher Creek Trailheads

From the US 421 bridge over South Holston Lake east of Bristol continue southeast on 421 for 3.8 miles and turn right on Camp Tom Howard Road at a USFS sign to Little Oak Campground. Camp Tom Howard Road begins as a paved road but becomes the gravel road FS 87, which follows Flatwoods and Old Flatwoods Roads to the southwest. All the following trailhead mileages start from the turnoff from US 421 to Camp Tom Howard Road.

At 0.4 mile the paved road turns to gravel at an intersection with Sharps Creek Road. At 1.0 mile there is a gated USFS gravel road on the left that is the Flatwoods Horse Road Trailhead, the northeast trailhead for the 9.7-mile-long Flatwoods Horse Road. At 6.5 miles is an intersection at Three Rocks where FS 87G heads right for 1.5 miles to the Little Oak and Little Oak Mountain Trailheads (for FS Trails 52 and 601). Continuing southwest on Flatwoods Road, at mile 7.5 is the Josiah Horse Trail Trailhead (FS Trail 45) and at mile 7.9 the Josiah Trailhead (FS Trail 50). At 9.8 miles on the left is the Big Creek Trailhead at a gated USFS road that is normally open. This is the southwest trailhead for the Flatwoods Horse Road and the northeast trailhead for the Flatwoods Horse Trail (FS 46). At 10.0 miles along the Flatwoods Road is the Flint Mill Trailhead (FS Trail 49), and at 11.5 miles, immediately after a power line crossing, is the Roaring Fork Trailhead for the Short Spur Trail (FS 48).

At mile 12.9 you will reach Hickory Tree Crossroads, the junction of Big Creek Road and Flatwoods Road. Here FS 87 turns left onto Big Creek Road but continues as FS 87. Heading down Big Creek Road, at mile 13.3 (from US 421), just past a smaller power line, is the Morrell Trailhead (FS Trail 47) and at mile 13.7 is the Hatcher Creek Trailhead, the southwest trailhead for the Flatwoods Horse Trail (FS Trail 46). All of the trailheads along FS 87 are on the left as you travel southwest.

Snake Spur Road and Low Gap Trailheads

These trailheads are reached from the southeast end of the bridge over South Holston Lake (as above). At mile 6.4, Snake Spur Road, a gated, gravel USFS road is on your right. The Old Farm Trail (not maintained as a USFS trail) begins on the uphill side of Snake Spur Road. Park without blocking the gate. For the AT Low Gap Trailhead proceed on up US 421 to mile 7.8, where the trailhead and parking are on the right just before you reach Low Gap at the top of the mountain. A larger parking area is on the left at the gap. These trailheads also can be reached by driving 2.8 miles west of Shady Valley, TN, to Low Gap and 1.4 miles farther to Snake Spur Road.

Little Oak Road (FS 87G) Trailheads: Little Oak Mountain Trail Trailhead and Little Oak Trail Trailhead

This road turns off the Flatwoods Road (FS 87) described above and proceeds northward toward South Holston Lake. The trailhead for the Little Oak Mountain Trail will be reached first at 1.5 miles, on the right, and a short distance on will be the trailhead for the Little Oak Trail.

FS 202 Trailheads: Holston Mountain Trail, Short Spur and Rye Patch Trailheads

Take Panhandle Road (FS 56) north from TN 91 starting at a junction that is 9.9 miles northeast of US 19E in Elizabethton, TN, and 11.8 miles southwest of US 421 in Shady Valley, TN. The first 0.8 mile of Panhandle Road is paved, and then it becomes a gravel road. At mile 4.3 you will reach the crest of Holston Mountain at a backcountry parking area beside the closed gate to the Holston High Knob Fire Tower access road (FS 56A). This is the trailhead for the Holston Mountain Trail (FS Trail 44) and the beginning of FS 202. Just a few yards to the southwest, on the right side of FS 202 and just before a power line crossing, is the Short Spur Trailhead (FS Trail 48), and 1.2 miles farther southwest on FS 202 is the Rye Patch Trailhead for the Morrell Trail (FS Trail 47). The Morrell Trail begins 25 yards in, and on the left side of, a short turn-off on the right of FS 202. There is another, smaller power line crossing FS 202 about 150 yards beyond the turn-off for the Rye Patch Trailhead. The USFS closes Panhandle Road during periods of freezing weather, so check with the Watauga Ranger Station in Unicoi (423/735-1500) if you plan to use this road between December and April.

Cross Mountain Trailhead

Beginning at the new intersection US 19E, TN 37, and TN 91 (this is 0.4 mile north of the US 321, US 19E, and TN 91 intersection) in

Elizabethton, TN, go north on paved TN 91. At 18.7 miles the AT crosses the road just below the top of Cross Mountain. However, continue to the gap at mile 18.8 and a gravel parking lot for the AT on the right. This trailhead can also be approached from the north. From the US 421, TN 91, and TN 133 junction in Shady Valley, follow TN 91 for 3.6 miles south to the gap just above where the AT crosses TN 91.

TOPOGRAPHIC MAPS: USGS Shady Valley, TN-VA; Carter, TN; Doe, TN; Holston Valley, TN. TI Map 783, South Holston and Watauga Lakes, CNF.

TRAIL DESCRIPTIONS

7A. APPALACHIAN TRAIL (FROM US 421 TO DOUBLE SPRINGS SHELTER) (FS TRAIL 1, TI TRAIL 1)

LENGTH: 3.5 miles

ELEVATION CHANGE: Low point, 3,380 feet; high point, 4,100 feet

DIFFICULTY: Moderate

TRAILHEADS: Low Gap (start), Double Springs Shelter (end)

USE: Hiking

TOPOGRAPHIC MAP: USGS Shady Valley, TN-VA

COMMENTS: This section of the AT is protected by an AT Corridor designation and provides access to the northeast end of Holston Mountain Trail. It is a very pleasant hike in any season. The trail has vertical white blazes.

DETAILS: From the parking area on US 421 below Low Gap (UTM 17S 0415070E/4043914N), head southwest on the AT, which follows the crest of Holston Mountain. At 1.3 miles the trail comes to the edge of an old farm and at 1.4 miles (UTM 17S 0413470E/4042881N) is joined by an old road known as the Old Farm Trail, which comes up from Snake Spur Road Trailhead and US 421. At 1.9 miles the trail turns left out into an old field. There are excellent views of Shady Valley and Iron Mountain, with Whitetop and Rogers Ridge in the background. The trail reenters the woods at 2.0 miles and goes over a knoll. After descending, the trail climbs and passes over Locust Knob at 3.0 miles. It then curves to the right around Rich Knob and at 3.4 miles, in a small opening (UTM 17S 0411736E/4040714N), the AT turns left, with Holston Mountain Trail going straight ahead. On the AT just 0.1 mile past that clearing is the Double Springs Shelter, with a spring several hundred feet behind it. The shelter is constructed of concrete blocks and accommodates six. See description below of the AT from TN 91 for the details on the rest of the AT within the area.

7B. APPALACHIAN TRAIL (TN 91 TO DOUBLE SPRINGS SHELTER) (FS TRAIL 1, TI TRAIL 1)

LENGTH: 3.5 miles

ELEVATION CHANGE: Low point, 3,500 feet; high point, 4,200 feet

DIFFICULTY: Moderate

TRAILHEAD: Cross Mountain (start); Double Springs AT Shelter (end)

TRAIL CONNECTIONS: Holston Mountain Trail

USE: Hiking

TOPOGRAPHIC MAPS: USGS Doe, TN; Shady Valley, TN-VA

COMMENTS: This section of the AT follows the northeast boundary of the Flint Mill Area and provides access to the northeast end of Holston Mountain Trail. It generally follows the crest of Cross Mountain, constantly gaining in elevation to Rich Knob and the junction with Holston Mountain Trail. Cross Mountain is the connector in the "H" created by Holston Mountain to the west and Iron Mountain to the east. The trail is entirely within a deciduous forest.

DETAILS: The trail begins (UTM 17S 0413923E/4037559N) at the Johnson/Carter County line where the AT crosses TN 91, 0.1 mile south of the crest of Cross Mountain. There is limited parking at the gap and absolutely no parking at the trailhead. In the first 0.25 mile the trail crosses three small creeks, the last one on a wooden bridge. It then generally ascends until just before it reaches Double Springs Shelter. At 2.5 miles it passes a good campsite with water. The springs here are the headwaters of Stony Creek. At 2.6 miles the trail turns sharply right (to the left is Old Road Ridge). At 3.5 miles are the Double Springs Shelter and spring on the left. The junction with the Holston Mountain Trail (UTM 17S 0411736E/4040714N) is also on the left several hundred feet beyond the shelter. To the right at this junction the AT continues northeast 3.5 miles to the trailhead on US 421 at Low Gap (see trail description for "AT from US 421 to Double Springs Shelter" above).

8. OLD FARM TRAIL (NO FS OR TI TRAIL NUMBERS; NOT MAINTAINED AS USFS TRAIL)

LENGTH: 0.7 mile

ELEVATION CHANGE: Low point, 3,150 feet; high point, 3,450 feet

DIFFICULTY: Easy

TRAILHEADS: Snake Spur Road (start), AT (end)

TRAIL CONNECTIONS: AT

TOPOGRAPHIC MAP: USGS Shady Valley, TN-VA

COMMENTS: This trail is not maintained but is a very pleasant and open trail for hiking. It is a constant, but not extreme, uphill grade on an old logging road.

DETAILS: The route begins at the junction of US 421 and the Snake Spur logging road (FS 6098) (UTM 17S 0413334E/4043542N). The trail begins at the top of the bank on the uphill side of the road junction. For the first 0.2 mile the trail parallels US 421 heading east; then it curves around to the south and continues up the mountain. At 0.7 mile the trail joins the AT at 1.4 miles from US 421 and Low Gap (UTM 17S 0413470E/4042881N).

9. HOLSTON MOUNTAIN TRAIL (FS TRAIL 44, TI TRAIL 15)

LENGTH: 8.8 miles

ELEVATION CHANGE: Low point, 3,380 feet; high point, 4,200 feet

DIFFICULTY: Moderate

TRAILHEADS: FS 202 (Holston Mountain Trail) (start), Double Springs AT Shelter (end)

USE: Hiking

TOPOGRAPHIC MAPS: USGS Carter, TN; Doe, TN; Holston Valley; TN; Shady Valley, TN-VA

COMMENTS: The Holston Mountain Trail follows the crest of Holston Mountain for most of the distance between its two trailheads. It passes through hardwood forests with occasional views of Iron Mountain to the southeast and Holston Valley to the northwest. The view from the former Holston High Knob fire tower is excellent. Holston Mountain Trail connects several other trails in the area and provides a jumping-off point for off-trail exploration. The trail has blue blazes. This is also known as the Holston Trail.

DETAILS: The trail begins on FS 202 (UTM 17S 0402419E/ 4035334N) at the closed gate blocking access to the Holston High Knob fire tower. The first mile is on the gravel road to the former fire tower. At 0.2 mile there is a fork in the fire tower road. Take the right fork, the one that follows the power line toward the tower. At 1.0 mile the road takes a sharp hairpin turn to the left and the base of the tower is visible at the end of the road. Here the trail leaves the road to the right (northeast) and becomes a hiking trail only. The trail descends through hardwoods to Flint Mill Gap and a junction at 3.1 miles (UTM 17S 0405584E/4037071N). An old jeep road enters this junction from the northwest and exits to the northeast. The Flint Mill Trail enters from the north, and an old, unmaintained section of the Flint Mill Trail exits to the southeast. Take the old jeep road to the northeast (right). In about 80 yards the jeep road turns left into an FS wildlife field and the trail continues straight ahead. Within that 80 yards, avoid an old logging road that bears off to the right.

The next section of the trail occasionally follows an old logging road for short distances but often leaves the road to follow the ridgecrest, where some good views of the Holston Valley exist. At 4.4 miles the Josiah Trail angles in from the left rear (UTM 17S 0407129E/ 4038252N). At 4.6 miles there is an intersection (UTM 17S 0407452E/ 4038147N) with another old logging road that comes in from the right rear. There is a spring in the cove to the left. The Holston Mountain Trail follows this old road for about 30 yards and then veers to the right up the ridge. Be alert here to avoid heading off (straight ahead) on the old road (unless you are heading for the grove of old-growth trees described at the end of this section). From here the trail climbs steeply to the top of a small knob at 4.8 miles. From this point Red Eye Ridge extends off-trail to the southeast (right); 0.25 miles off-trail to the north (left) is that grove of large old-growth poplars and oaks that apparently escaped the logger's ax. In a dip at 5.4 miles is a campsite and spring to the left of the trail in a small cove. At 5.8 miles avoid an ORV trail heading off to the right on a ridge just west of Upper Hinkle Branch. The trail begins a large curve to the left at 7.1 miles and descends to a saddle at 7.4 miles (UTM 17S 0410500E/ 4039329N). This is a good jumping-off point for off-trail hiking to Fishdam Creek on the left and North Fork Stony Creek on the right. (See the discussion below on off-trail hiking.)

The trail climbs from the saddle to the ridgetop, reaching it at 7.7 miles. This is the ridge leading northeast to Rich Knob, and the trail follows it for the remaining distance. At 7.9 miles the trail passes to the left of a knob. After that, where the ridgecrest is narrow, the trail is easily followed; but where the crest is broad, the trail often becomes indistinct. At such times, stay more to the southeast (right) side of the crest until the trail again becomes visible. At 8.7 miles, just short of the highest crest, the trail bears slightly to the right of the crest and at 8.8 miles comes into the clearing where it intersects the AT (UTM 17S 0411736E/4040714N).

10. FLINT MILL TRAIL (FS TRAIL 49, TI TRAIL 11)

LENGTH: 1.4 miles

ELEVATION CHANGE: Low point, 2,000 feet; high point, 3,380 feet

DIFFICULTY: Difficult

TRAILHEAD: FS 87 (Flint Mill) (start); Holston Mountain Trail (end)

TRAIL CONNECTIONS: Holston Mountain Trail

USE: Hiking

TOPOGRAPHIC MAP: USGS Carter, TN

COMMENTS: Flint Mill Trail is a short, very steep trail beginning on Flatwoods Road, climbing the northwest slope of the mountain and

View from Flint Rock of Holston Lake. Flint Mill Primitive Area. Photograph by Roger Jenkins.

ending at Flint Mill Gap on the main ridge. The Flint Mill Gap area is a special area, with outstanding views from Flint Rock, rare flowers at a small bog, a large wildlife field, and an excellent but small campsite. The trail has blue blazes and the upper section will be mucky and slippery in wet weather. A good round-trip hike utilizing this trail is described under the Josiah Trail below. Flint Rock provides outstanding views of the Holston Valley, and a small bog near the top of the mountain offers some unusual vegetation.

DETAILS: The trail begins as an old logging road. At 0.1 mile a horse trail goes to the left at a wildlife food plot. The horse trail leaves the Flint Mill Trail to the right at 0.15 mile. The trail climbs steeply upward and leaves behind evidence of prior logging at 0.5 mile. For the next 0.5 mile the trail is very steep and eroded. At 0.6 mile the trail passes out of the upland hardwood forest and into dry ridge vegetation dominated by Table Mountain and other pines, with an understory of laurel. This section of the trail is beautiful when the laurel is in bloom in June. The trail is extremely steep in places and will probably require the use of your hands to ascend.

At 1.0 mile the trail climbs up and around Flint Rock. In clear weather the rock provides an exceptional view of South Holston Lake and the Holston Valley, with VA's Clinch Mountain as a backdrop. At this point the trail levels out through pine woods until it crosses a small stream and bog at 1.3 miles. A little exploration will turn up quite a list of orchids blooming at various times during the spring and summer. The bog and surrounding area provide habitat for pink and yellow lady's slippers, whorled pogonia, Adder's mouth, yellow fringed orchis, pale green orchis, dwarf rattlesnake plantain, and the rare kidneyleaf twayblade. The bog is also a good place to catch a glimpse of a hooded warbler. There is a good campsite beside the stream.

The trail continues on through hardwoods to its junction with the Holston Mountain Trail at 1.4 miles (UTM 17S 0405584E/4037071N), near a large wildlife management field. The topographic map shows the trail continuing down the other side of the mountain, which it does as an overgrown logging road. It disappears into a maze of old roads from a long-abandoned mine on the edge of FS property.

11. JOSIAH HORSE TRAIL (FS TRAIL 45, TI TRAIL 19)

LENGTH: 0.7 mile

ELEVATION CHANGE: Low point, 1,730 feet; high point, 2,080 feet

DIFFICULTY: Easy

TRAILHEADS: FS 87 (Josiah Horse Trail) (start); Flatwoods Horse Road (end)

TRAIL CONNECTIONS: Flatwoods Horse Trail

USE: Hiking, equestrian, mountain bike

TOPOGRAPHIC MAP: USGS Holston Valley, TN

COMMENTS: A pleasant and well-defined hiking trail, although it is heavily used by horses and could be muddy in wet weather. The nearby Josiah Hiking Trail is a better choice for hiking, but this trail could be used in conjunction with it for a short round-trip. The trail is marked with yellow blazes.

DETAILS: The trailhead is not marked (UTM 17S 0405977E/ 4040470N). The trail ends on Flatwoods Horse Road (FS 87A), which is a very good hiking trail behind locked gates. The Flatwoods Horse Road is covered elsewhere in this section.

12. JOSIAH TRAIL (FS TRAIL 50, TI TRAIL 18)

LENGTH: 2.2 miles

ELEVATION CHANGE: Low point, 1,800 feet; high point, 3,530 feet

DIFFICULTY: Difficult

TRAILHEAD: FS 87 (Josiah) (Start); Holston Mountain Trail (End)

TRAIL CONNECTIONS: Holston Mountain

USE: Hiking

TOPOGRAPHIC MAPS: USGS Holston Valley, TN; Carter, TN

COMMENTS: This trail provides access to the top of Holston Mountain and the Holston Mountain Trail. The last 0.5 mile of the trail, as it nears the top of Holston Mountain, is very difficult and would be extremely difficult in wet weather. This trail, together with the Holston Mountain Trail, Flint Mill Trail, and FS 87B, makes a good round-trip hike of about 8.0 miles to the top of Holston Mountain. The trail is marked with blue blazes.

DETAILS: The first section of the trail is through open deciduous forest with only a moderate upgrade following old logging roads. At 0.6 mile the trail crosses FS 87B (UTS 17S406236/4039712). This is also part of the Flatwoods Horse Trail and makes a very pleasant hiking trail. At about 0.1 mile past FS 87B the trail bears left off an old logging road. Be careful not to follow the old logging road.

The trail gradually becomes steeper, and it is very steep near the crest of Holston Mountain, where it intersects with the Holston

Mountain Trail (UTM 17S 0407129E/4038252N). There is a small spring 0.2 mile to the left down Holston Mountain Trail. The spring is in the cove to the left of the trail. At the end of May the vicinity of the trail junction has quite a variety of azaleas.

13. SHORT SPUR TRAIL (FS TRAIL 48, TI TRAIL 36)

LENGTH: 1.7 miles

ELEVATION CHANGE: Low point, 2,150 feet; high point, 3,780 feet

DIFFICULTY: Difficult

TRAILHEADS: FS 202 (Short Spur) (start); FS 87 (Roaring Fork) (end)

USE: Hiking

TOPOGRAPHIC MAP: USGS Carter, TN

COMMENTS: Because of its extreme steepness, it may be preferable to hike this trail as the descending return leg of a loop hike that goes up one of the other trails on Holston Mountain. This description starts at the top. One short section of Short Spur is so nearly vertical that hiking it is essentially an off-trail scramble. The trail is marked with blue blazes.

DETAILS: The Roaring Fork Trailhead (UTM 17S 0402403E/4035308N) is immediately west of the FS 202 junction with FS 56, Panhandle Road. Parking at that junction can be used for both the Short Spur Trail and the Holston Mountain Trail, which heads northeast along the mountain crest from here. The Short Spur Trail begins at a Trail 48 sign just northeast of the power line crossing FS 202. The trail angles left and enters the power line clearing just a few yards from the road. There is a terrific view of the Holston Valley to the north here. In the clearing, descend about 20 yards and turn left to enter the woods. This left turn is about 20 yards above the next set of power line poles down the hill. Enter the woods at a hiker sign and bear slightly left. At 0.1 mile you will reach a good spring (UTM 17S 0402273E/4035374N) with sufficient flow in dry weather to provide a drink.

After the spring, the trail descends gradually on the crest of the ridge until, at 0.2 mile, it turns right and begins a series of extremely steep, short switchbacks in a brushy drainage parallel to the power line. This is the nearly vertical section referred to above. Each switchback leg is only about five yards long. After about a 200-foot descent, the trail climbs slightly to the left and slabs around the nose of the ridge. At 0.4 mile it begins descending switchbacks through rhododendron and laurel on the nose of the ridge. These switchbacks are less steep and are longer than those encountered above, but they are very steep by any measure. Watch for signs of black bear in this area. At 0.9 mile the trail turns right and descends less steeply straight down a rocky drainage and then down the nose of the ridge through open woods.

At 1.0 mile it intersects the Flatwoods Horse Trail (UTM 17S 0402022E/4036051N) and then descends more gradually following an old road on the crest of a broad ridge. At 1.6 miles you will reach a steep bank above Flatwoods Road. Turn right and proceed 40 yards parallel to Flatwoods Road to a point where the bank is less steep and the Short Spur Trail sign appears at the trailhead (UTM 17S 0402072E/ 4037005N).

14. MORRELL TRAIL (FS TRAIL 47, TI TRAIL 28)

LENGTH: 2.2 miles

ELEVATION CHANGE: Low point, 2,320 feet; high point, 4,050 feet

DIFFICULTY: Difficult

TRAILHEADS: FS 87 (Morrell) (start), FS 202 (Rye Patch) (end)

USE: Hiking, equestrian

TOPOGRAPHIC MAP: USGS Carter, TN

COMMENTS: This trail is a steep but very scenic path to the top of Holston Mountain. A series of long switchbacks carry it back and forth across a small power line clearing, and the views of South Holston Lake and Holston Valley to the north are magnificent. On a clear day one can see the city of Bristol and even Clinch Mountain some 23 miles to the NW. Yellow blazes mark the trail.

DETAILS: The Morrell Trailhead on Old Flatwoods Road (UTM 17S 0399779E/4035912N) is 30 yards west of a small phone and power line that crosses Flatwoods Road. The trail starts on an old road, but at a point 0.1 mile up the trail, turn right off the old road on a footpath. In 15 or 20 yards turn left again, avoiding the mistake of continuing east on this little jog in the trail. At a point 0.4 mile up the trail there is an intersection with the Flatwoods Horse Trail (UTM 17S 0400144E/4035446N). To the left, the Flatwoods Horse Trail goes a few yards and turns south, following the power line up the slope until it turns east into the woods. To the right, the Flatwoods Horse Trail goes east and north 0.8 mile to Old Flatwoods Road. The Morrell Trail continues more steeply uphill parallel to the power line. Soon it bears left to cross the power line clearing for the first of 11 times as the trail switches back and forth to gain elevation at a steep but reasonable rate. Each crossing brings successively broader panoramic views to the north. At 2.0 miles, just before the last power line crossing, the trail turns back to the left and becomes less steep. After the last crossing the trail passes a flat, brushy area and reaches the trailhead (UTM 17S 0400804E/4034463N) on a short turnoff from FS 202. To the left, it is 1.2 miles on FS 202 to the trailheads for the Short Spur and Holston Mountain Trails.

15. FLATWOODS HORSE TRAIL (FS TRAIL 46, TI TRAIL 10)

LENGTH: 5.1 miles

ELEVATION CHANGE: Low point, 2,100 feet; high point, 2,600 feet

DIFFICULTY: Moderate

TRAILHEADS: FS 87A (Big Creek) (start), FS 87 (Hatcher Creek) (end)

USE: Horse, hiking, mountain bike

TOPOGRAPHIC MAP: USGS Carter, TN

COMMENTS: This trail can be combined with gated gravel roads (FS 87A and 87B) for a total length of 14.8 miles. The USFS refers to that entire length as the Flatwoods Horse Trail. While mountain bikes are permitted on this trail, the frequent rocky stretches make it a tough bike trip. The gravel road sections of the Flatwoods Horse Road to the northeast are better suited to mountain bikes. The trail described here intersects four other trails that climb from Flatwoods Road to the crest of Holston Mountain. It offers a convenient route for foot travel loop hikes on those trails. The trail is marked with yellow blazes.

DETAILS: The beginning trailhead for the Flatwoods Horse Trail is the Big Creek Trailhead, at the intersection of FS 87 with gated FS 87A. This is also the ending trailhead for the Flatwoods Horse Road. The Flatwoods Horse Trail begins 0.3 mile up FS 87A (UTM 17S 0404280E/4037961N) at an easy-to-find intersection marked with the standard fiberglass stakes with the number 6. At 0.2 mile the trail reaches the Flint Mill Trail, where it jogs left about 50 yards, then turns right, descends, and crosses a small branch of Big Creek. Yellow blazes mark most of the route as the trail alternately climbs and descends, working its way southwest along the base of Holston Mountain. At 1.8 miles the trail makes a right turn and descends steeply along a weak (or dry) branch. A seep makes the trail quite muddy for several yards. At 1.9

miles the trail crosses a strong branch and turns left, ascending through a boulder field. In about 100 yards the route bears around to the right on the boulders and heads downhill for a short distance before turning left and heading uphill again on an old road. At 2.4 miles you will reach a power line and a terrific view to the north. In the power line clearing, turn left uphill, go about 10 yards, and turn right, into woods.

At 2.6 miles there is a junction (UTM 17S 0402022E/4036051N) with Short Spur Trail (foot traffic only). To the right, this trail descends 0.7 mile to Flatwoods Road. To the left, it reaches FS 202 on the crest of Holston Mountain after an extremely steep climb of 1.0 mile. Flatwoods Horse Trail goes straight ahead here, well defined and blazed yellow. At 3.6 miles, after descending northwest across a broad ridge, the trail intersects an old trail that also has yellow blazes. Keep straight ahead here rather than taking the trail to the right.

At 4.1 miles there is a clearing (for a smaller power line) with a nice view to the north. Turn right, descend 0.1 mile along the power line, and then turn left. About 20 yards into the woods on the other side is the junction with the Morrell Trail (UTM 17S 0400144E/4035446N). The Morrell Trail goes left 1.8 miles to FS 202 on the crest of Holston Mountain, and to the right it reaches Big Creek Road in 0.4 mile. The Flatwoods Horse Trail crosses the Morrell Trail, heading generally west. At 4.3 miles avoid a side trail that comes up from the right. After crossing three small branches the trail turns right and at 5.0 miles reaches its western trailhead, Hatcher Creek, on Big Creek Road (UTM 17S 0399383E/4035494N).

16. FLATWOODS HORSE ROAD (FS 87A AND 87B)

LENGTH: 9.7 miles

ELEVATION CHANGE: Low point, 2,020 feet; high point, 2,600 feet

DIFFICULTY: Moderate

TRAILHEADS: Flatwoods Horse Road (start); Big Creek (end)

USE: Horse, hiking, mountain bike

TOPOGRAPHIC MAPS: USGS Shady Valley, TN-VA; Holston Valley, TN; Carter, TN

COMMENTS: This trail can be combined with the Flatwoods Horse Trail (FS Trail 46) for a total one-way length of 14.8 miles. The USFS refers to that entire length as the Flatwoods Horse Trail, and Trail 46 signs appear throughout. The Flatwoods Horse Road described here is almost entirely on gravel USFS roads and is well suited for hikers, equestrians, or mountain bikers. It follows a graded route along the northwest flank of Holston Mountain and has several junctions with other trails.

DETAILS: The trail starts at Flatwoods Road (FS 87) at a point (UTM 17S 0410210E/4043800N) 1.0 mile southwest of US 421. The trail climbs gradually for about the first 2.0 miles. At 3.2 miles pass an unmarked trail to the right (UTM 17S 0409534E/4040709N). At 5.2 miles the graveled road ends (UTM 17S 0407562E/4040170N) and the route turns sharply left on a bulldozed trail marked with yellow blazes. In a few hundred yards the yellow blazes lead off to the right on an unmarked and narrow trail. This trail soon leads to another bulldozed trail, still marked with yellow blazes, that leads straight downhill to the previously followed road at 5.8 miles (UTM 17S 0407311E/4039675N). The TI map does not clearly show such discontinuation of the gravel road. At 6.5 miles the Flatwoods Horse Road heads to the southwest at a point where the Josiah Horse Trail (FS 45) intersects from the northwest, having come up 0.7 mile from its trailhead on Flatwoods Road. At 6.8 miles pass a good trail with no markings. This is the old Josiah Trail shown on the 1969 USGS topographic map (Carter, TN). At 7.0 miles (UTM 17S 0406225E/4039653N) cross the intersection with the Josiah Foot Trail (FS Trail 50). To the right, the Josiah Foot Trail descends 0.6 mile to its trailhead on Flatwoods Road, and to the left it ascends 1.6 miles to the crest of Holston Mountain. At 7.8 miles pass a closed gate, where the road improves substantially. At mile 9.4 pass an intersection that is the start of the Flatwoods Horse Trail (UTM 17S 0404280E/4037961N), and at mile 9.7 reach the southwest end of the Flatwoods Horse Road (FS 87A) and the Big Creek Trailhead at an intersection with Flatwoods Road (FS 87) (UTM 17S 0404066E/4038283N).

17. LITTLE OAK MOUNTAIN TRAIL (FS TRAIL 601, TI TRAIL 26)

LENGTH: 1.2 miles

ELEVATION CHANGE: Low point, 1,760; high point, 2,020 feet

DIFFICULTY: Easy

TRAILHEADS: Little Oak Mountain

USE: Hiking

TOPOGRAPHIC MAP: USGS Holston Valley, TN

COMMENTS: This trail, along with Little Oak Trail, provides pleasant day-hiking for campers at Little Oak Campground. This blue-blazed trail consists of a loop of 0.8 mile with two access connectors and one spur at the eastern end. Both connectors and the spur are 0.2 mile. The mileage given above includes one access connector hiked both ways. If the spur is included, add another 0.4 mile to go out and back that spur. Numerous benches and interpretive signs make this a pleasant and educational walk. The bench at the end of the spur provides a lovely view of Holston Lake.

DETAILS: One access connector starts inside the campground a few yards south of the campground entrance pay station. It climbs around the western end of Little Oak Mountain and joins the loop trail at a point where it follows an old service road. To traverse the loop counterclockwise, turn right on the road, go 0.1 mile, and reach an intersection where the trail leaves the road to the left. Follow the arrow indicating that this is the way "To Road." In another 100 yards, you will come to the intersection where the loop continues slightly left and the access connector with the road turns back to the right. Continue left on the loop another 0.3 mile, where the trail splits. The spur trail goes down to the right and the loop continues up to the left. The hike out the spur is well worth the time and effort. In another 0.4 mile after the spur trail, the loop trail reaches that old service road near a concrete water vault and turns left. Follow the old road about 20 yards down to where the access connector to the camp turns back to the right. A sign here says "To Camp."

The other access connector starts from Little Oak Road (FS 87G) at a point 150 yards outside the gated campground entrance. It is just to the right of a gated service road. If you start here, you will reach the loop trail after a 0.2 mile climb along the side of Little Oak Mountain. At 0.5 mile reach the spur trail and continue as in the above description.

18. LITTLE OAK TRAIL (FS TRAIL 52, TI TRAIL 25)

LENGTH: 1.9 miles

ELEVATION CHANGE: Low point, 1,750 feet; high point, 1,760 feet

DIFFICULTY: Easy

TRAILHEADS: Little Oak

USE: Hiking

TOPOGRAPHIC MAP: USGS Holston Valley, TN

COMMENTS: This trail, along with Little Oak Mountain Trail, provides pleasant day-hiking for campers at Little Oak Campground.

The trail consists of a loop of 1.9 miles, but the first 0.4 mile and last 0.1 mile simply follow on or near campground roads and are not really a trail. They are included to provide a complete loop. Numerous benches, interpretive signs, and views of Holston Lake make this a pleasant and educational walk. One viewpoint is of South Holston Dam and another provides a great view of Holston Mountain including the fire tower on Holston High Top.

DETAILS: A loop hike on this trail could start and end at almost any point along the shoreline of the campground. The counter clockwise loop described here starts at a "Trail 52" sign a few yards to the northeast of the campground entrance pay station. Follow along the edge of the woods and then the campground road. In 0.2 mile, 20 yards after passing campsite 27, an old road drops off to the right providing a shortcut to the end of this northeast arm of Little Oak Campground. Emerging from the old road at campsite 41, continue around the circle to campsite 48, where there is a vehicle gate. Proceed through or around the gate and out to the grassy open space toward a lake inlet. At 0.4 mile from the original start, reach a point near the water and turn left where there is a trail sign. The trail now becomes discernable and follows the shoreline around three small peninsulas that make up the eastern end of the campground. There are occasional blue blazes. At 1.7 miles the trail passes beside a small amphitheater, and at 1.8 miles it reaches the head of a lake inlet. Here turn away from the lake and proceed up the road to the pay station to complete the loop.

19. JACOBS CREEK TRAIL (FS TRAIL 604, TI TRAIL 17)

LENGTH: 0.3 mile

ELEVATION CHANGE: Insignificant

DIFFICULTY: Easy

TRAILHEADS: FS 604C (Jacobs Creek Road) (start and finish)

USE: Hiking

TOPOGRAPHIC MAP: USGS Holston Mountain, TN

COMMENTS: A well-used trail along one side of Jacobs Creek Campground and beside a narrow inlet of South Holston Lake. There should be good leaf color in the fall along this trail. The Jacobs Creek Road turns off Denton Valley Road, which in turn turns north off US 421 southeast of South Holston Lake; because of the campground and other facilities the Jacobs Creek area is well signed.

DETAILS: The trail begins on the left side of the Jacobs Campground Road 900 feet before the campground fee collection station. The trail ends at the turnaround at the far end of the campground.

OFF-TRAIL HIKING OPPORTUNITIES

Of the top scenic attractions in the area, only the Flint Mill Trail, with its overlook and bog, is directly accessible by the trail system. The others require off-trail exploration and are the North Fork Stony Creek drainage, with its wildflowers and outstanding waterfall; Fishdam Creek Gorge, with its many small waterfalls and interesting rock outcroppings; the north fork of Sulphur Spring Branch, with its waterfall and outstanding view; and the grove of old-growth poplars and oaks on the main ridge of the mountain opposite Red Eye Ridge. Another interesting exploration is provided by hiking Upper Stony Creek.

Direction finding is generally not too difficult in the area, as there is only one main ridge with small drainages dropping off to either side. If you get oriented to the proper drainage with a topographical map, you can experience these other areas. The terrain, however, can be challenging. Slopes are often steep and there are plenty of rhododendron thickets. Patience and a pace suited to the terrain are the key; the rewards in wildlife, solitude, and scenery are well worth the effort. Brief descriptions of the off-trail routes are provided below.

The North Fork of Stony Creek has its beginnings in the springs next to the Double Creek AT Shelter. If you are very fond of rhododendron thickets, start here and head downstream about 1.6 miles to the falls. An easier way to reach the most scenic part of the watershed is to begin at the junction of the AT and Holston Mountain Trail and head southwest on Holston Mountain Trail. At 1.4 miles out you will be at the low point in the saddle between North Fork Stony and Fishdam Creeks (this is the same place used as a jump-off for Fishdam Creek and is described coming from the other direction in the Fishdam Creek Gorge section below). Turn left (east) off the trail and follow the drainage 0.4 mile down to the creek. Head downstream and in another 0.4 mile you will come to the falls of North Fork Stony, the premier falls in this area. The stream drops 30 feet over a semicircular cliff into a beautiful rock amphitheater. Scramble down on the right side. If you continue down the stream there are nice wildflowers in the spring, but after about 1.6 miles from the falls you will eventually come out *on private property that you need permission to cross.*

The Upper Stony Creek Trail is not maintained and should also be considered an off-trail hike. The lower portion from the TN 91 trailhead off TN 91 is used by fishermen and can easily be followed. However, after a mile the trail disappears. Essentially the route is directly up Stony Creek. Take the left fork at 0.7 mile when Water Hollow comes in from the right. Otherwise, follow the creek to a junction with the AT at about 2.2 miles. The trail generally follows old logging grades.

The southeastern trailheads for the above North Fork Stony Creek and Upper Stony Creek routes can be reached by road as follows: Beginning at the new intersection US 19E, TN 37, and TN 91 (this is 0.4 mile north of the US 321, US 19E, and TN 91 intersection) in Elizabethton, TN, go north on paved TN 91. At 14.6 miles from the intersection a dirt road turns left (west); there is a "Keep Out" sign on a tree on the left as you turn onto this road. Drive 0.2 mile to a fork, take the right fork, and go 0.1 mile to where it dead-ends at the unmarked trailhead for the North Fork of Stony Creek Trail. *This is private property; permission must be secured from an adjacent landowner to park at the trailhead.* If you continue on TN 91 to 16.2 miles from the TN 19E and TN 91 junction in Elizabethton, you will reach a small unmarked parking area on the right (east) side of the road. The Upper Stony Creek Trailhead is on the opposite (west) side of the road. These trails can also be approached from the north and the US 421, TN 91, and TN 133 junction in Shady Valley. Follow TN 91 3.6 miles south to the gap just above where the AT crosses TN 91; the Upper Stony Creek Trailhead is 2.5 miles from the gap, and the North Fork of Stony Creek Trailhead is 4.1 miles from the gap.

Fishdam Creek Gorge is accessed via Holston Mountain Trail or Flatwoods Road (FS 87). Traveling northeast on the Holston Mountain Trail from Holston High Knob Trailhead, look for the saddle at 7.4 miles where the main ridge is offset and, at the low point of the saddle, turn left (west) and follow the drainage down the mountain. It is approximately 2.0 miles to the horse trail at the base of the mountain. As you descend, gradually at first, keep alert for three rare plants: Frazier's sedge, round leaf orchid, and large purple fringed orchid. At the point where the gorge begins to drop steeply, Vulture Rock rises above the creek on the left. It is a bit of a scramble, but the view is excellent. The purple rhododendron, mountain laurel, and white rhododendron are beautiful from the end of May to the beginning of July. Also at this point there is an old logging grade to the right (described below) that offers a short hike out to another overlook and an alternative exit from the gorge. Below this point the stream is very steep and rocky, with many small waterfalls and pools.

To approach the gorge from Flatwoods Road, park at Fishdam Creek (4.8 miles southwest on FS 87 from US 421) and head up the creek. It is approximately 1.0 mile to the horse trail and the mouth of the gorge. A longer but easier entrance to the gorge from Flatwoods Road involves parking your car at Sulphur Spring Branch (3.8 miles southwest on FS 87 from US 421). Follow the modern logging roads up the mountain for 1.25 miles until you cross the horse trail. At this point continue up the mountain into the woods. After several hundred yards you will hit an old logging grade. Turn right and follow it southwest up and across the face of the mountain. It is about 1.0 mile to the gorge. There are several places where the grade has been washed out, and one where it makes a double switchback. As the grade wraps around into the gorge it passes a large rock offering an outstanding view of the mountain, the gorge, and the Holston Valley. Another 0.25 mile and the grade reaches the creek just above the steepest part of the gorge.

Sulphur Spring Branch (North Fork) features a nice waterfall. To reach the falls and overlook on Sulphur Spring Branch, begin where the Sulphur Spring Branch crosses Flatwoods Road (3.8 miles southwest on FS 87 from US 421). Head southeast toward Holston Mountain on the logging road to the right of the creek. The upper part of this area has been recently logged, and there are several road choices, but keep heading toward the mountain and remember that all logging roads lead to bigger roads. You will soon arrive on the Flatwoods Horse Trail. It is approximately 1.25 miles from Flatwoods Road to the horse trail, and you should emerge on it between the two forks of Sulphur Spring Branch. Turn left (northeast), and the first stream you cross will be the north fork. The best tactic here is to head right up the streambed. In several hundred yards you will enter the Scenic Area, and in 0.25 mile you will reach the falls. Follow the cliff line that creates the falls up through the woods to the left (north). Climb up to the ridgeline through one of the breaks in the cliff and come down the nose of the ridge to the best vantage point on Holston Mountain. The view down the mountain over the Flatwoods is great; you can also see back up the watershed and out over the Holston Valley. Unfortunately, this is also rattlesnake heaven, and the best ledge to sit on is one of their favorite sunning spots. Remember this if you visit the area in the warm months.

There are several coves near the main ridgeline on the northwest slope of the Holston Mountain that contain some very large trees. The largest are poplars, but there are also oak and ash. Many have fallen in recent years, but some are still standing. The trees are along a shoulder of the mountain below the main ridgeline but before the steep drop-off. On the USGS topographical map this area is across the main ridgeline from Red Eye Ridge. To reach the area, hike northeast on Holston Mountain Trail from the Holston High Knob Trailhead. At 4.6 miles (UTM 17S 0407452E/4038147N) the trail crosses a logging road. Instead of bearing right on the trail, continue straight ahead following the logging road several hundred yards till it dead-ends. At this point continue out onto the shoulder of the mountain, and within 0.5 mile you should find the trees. Backtrack or head up the slope to the trail.

5 Big Laurel Branch

(Includes Big Laurel Branch Wilderness, Big Laurel Branch Wilderness Study Area, Big Laurel Branch Roadless Area, and Hickory Flat Branch Backcountry Area)

The principal feature of the area is the 6,360-acre Big Laurel Branch Wilderness, which includes the completely forested southern end of Iron Mountain. At this lower end, Iron Mountain consists of double parallel crests that enclose the secluded Big Laurel Branch and Little Laurel Branch valleys. A unique sense of isolation and solitude is thus provided to those willing to travel cross-country (no maintained trails lead into the Big Laurel Valley). The southeast side of the wilderness rises steeply—1,100 to 1,400 feet from Watauga Lake to the crest of the mountain. The AT follows the crest of Iron Mountain, sometimes

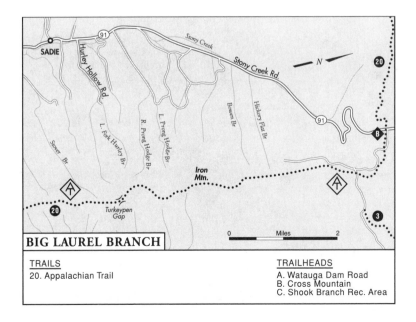

TRAILS	TRAILHEADS
20. Appalachian Trail	A. Watauga Dam Road
	B. Cross Mountain
	C. Shook Branch Rec. Area

at the base of high and lengthy outcroppings of rock, with several spectacular views from the tops of cliffs up to 40 feet high. Numerous creeks cut deep, steep-sided ravines in the beautiful northwest side of the mountain, including Big Laurel Branch itself. Wilbur Lake resembles a fjord because of the mountain wall, which rises precipitously over 600

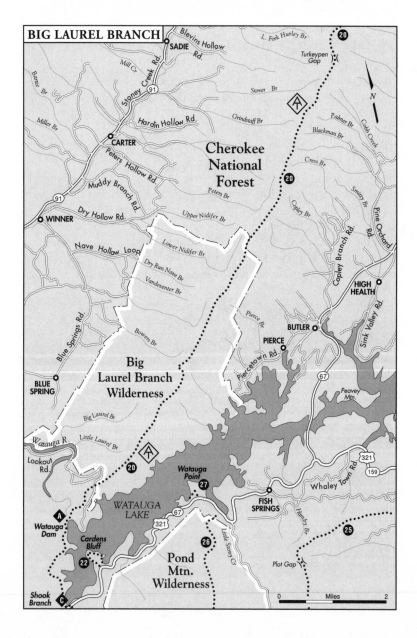

feet from the water's edge at the southwest end of the wilderness; a graceful 50-foot waterfall tumbles over the cliffs. The area includes thriving stands of the Carolina hemlock and specimens of the rare Fraser's sedge.

In addition to the Big Laurel Branch Wilderness, the USFS in its Southern Appalachian Assessment identified a 5,589-acre Roadless Area north of the wilderness, along Iron Mountain toward Cross Mountain Road. An area greater than the roadless area is protected in the CNF's 2004 plan revision, including the 4,930-acre Big Laurel Branch Wilderness Study Area, the 1,297-acre Big Laurel Branch Backcountry Area, and the 4,220-acre Hickory Flat Branch Backcountry Area. The area is located approximately 10 miles east of Elizabethton, TN, at the southern end of Iron Mountain, between TN 91 and the Watauga River (impounded as Wilbur Lake), and is in Carter and Johnson counties, TN, and the Watauga Ranger District.

HISTORY

In 1963 the area was the site of the severe and extensive Blue Springs Fire, which burned approximately 2,800 acres along the mountain crest. Both the north and south slopes were burned in places, and bulldozers were used to create firebreaks. The forest has regenerated itself

Blooming rhododendrons in Big Laurel Branch Wilderness. Photograph by Suzanne McDonald.

very well. Old logging and wagon roads penetrated the area but have become overgrown. The Bowers Branch and Vandeventer Branch jeep roads were closed more recently. These old roads provide the opportunity for some off-trail hiking in the area. The US Congress designated the Big Laurel Branch as wilderness in 1986. The CNF's 1988 management plan did not protect the balance of Iron Mountain northward to Cross Mountain Road; however, most of Iron Mountain north of the wilderness is to be protected in wilderness study area and backcountry area designations.

TRAILHEADS AND MAPS

Watauga Dam Road Trailhead

The principal trail in the area is the AT, and the principal access to its trailhead is near Watauga Dam. From Elizabethton, TN, and the east end of Broad Street (junction of TN 91, US 19E, US 321, and TN 67), go south on US 321 for 0.5 mile. Turn left (east) on Siam Road and follow it to the Watauga River. At the river turn right (no signs) on Watauga Dam Road without crossing the river, and follow the Watauga Dam signs up the river and past Wilbur Dam and Wilbur Lake (the wilderness is on the other side of the lake) and across Wilbur Lake. After crossing the lake, Watauga Dam Road goes up to the crest of the ridge, where the AT crosses. From the Elizabethton junction, it is 8.6 miles to this crossing. AT signs are clearly visible, and parking areas are provided nearby, with the largest parking area being 0.7 mile down the road on Watauga Lake.

Cross Mountain Trailhead

The area can also be reached by hiking 9.8 miles down the AT from the north, starting at TN 91 on Cross Mountain. From the east end of Broad Street (junction of TN 91 with US 19E, US 321, and TN 67) in Elizabethton, TN, follow TN 91 north 18.7 miles. The AT crosses TN 91 about 100 feet south of the Carter County–Johnson County line. A parking area is 0.1 mile farther on the right. From the AT crossing it is 6.8 miles north on TN 91 to the junction with US 421 in Shady Valley, TN. The AT crossing of the road is well signed. Proceed south on the AT.

Most of the northwest side of the wilderness can be reached from farther south on TN 91, particularly along the former jeep roads that proceed up Bowers Branch, Vandeventer Branch, and Lower Nidifer

Branch, from the Blue Spring Community. To reach the Blue Spring Community take the Blue Spring Road south from milepost 9 on TN 91. However, topographical maps are necessary to locate these old roads.

Shook Branch Recreation Area Trailhead

The Big Laurel Branch Wilderness can be reached by hiking 4.0 miles north on the AT from the Shook Branch Recreation Area. From Elizabethton, TN, take US 19E south for about 5.0 miles and turn left onto US 321/TN 67 at Hampton, TN. There is a convenience market at this road junction. Drive 3.2 miles east on US 321, the Shook Branch Recreation Area will be on the left. Overnight parking is not allowed in the recreation area, so you will need to park in the small gravel pull-off at the sign to the Shook Branch Recreation Area on US 321. The trailhead is at the west end of the recreation area and may be reached from the parking area by walking through the woods to the recreation area.

TOPOGRAPHIC MAPS: USGS Watauga Dam, TN; Carter, TN; Doe, TN. TI Map 783, South Holston and Watauga Lakes, CNF.

TRAIL DESCRIPTIONS

20. APPALACHIAN TRAIL (TN 91 TO WATAUGA DAM ROAD SECTION) (FS TRAIL 1, TI TRAIL 1)

LENGTH: 15.9 miles

ELEVATION CHANGE: Low point, 2,240 feet; high point, 4,190 feet

DIFFICULTY: Moderate

TRAILHEADS: Cross Mountain Road, Watauga Dam Road, and Shook Branch Recreation Area

USE: Hiking

TOPOGRAPHIC MAPS: Watauga Dam, Carter, and Doe, TN

COMMENTS: The AT is the only trail in Big Laurel Branch Wilderness. The trail is described from north to south, the preferred hiking direction so one descends from the ridgetop to Watauga Lake. Hiking north to south involves a modest climb of 2,600 feet, but hiking south to north requires a difficult 3,900 feet climb. This trail provides several wonderful views of the Watauga Lake and the surrounding area as you descend to the lake. An alternate ending (or beginning) point, Shook Branch Recreation Area, is also given for those wanting to complete the short section of the AT that lies between the Big Laurel Branch Wilderness and the Pond Mountain Wilderness. Only a brief description of that section is included here.

DETAILS: From the parking area on TN 91 at Cross Mountain Road, the trail begins a 2.0 mile ascent to the ridgetop. Being a part of the AT, the entire length of the trail is well maintained and easy to follow. At 2.7 miles there is a side trail to a water source, marked with a small silver trail sign. This is reported to be the most dependable water source for the Iron Mountain Shelter during the dryer months. The shelter is an additional 1.8 miles south along the AT. At 3.2 miles you reach a monument built in honor of Nick Grindstaff. He was an orphan who, at the age of 26, moved up on Iron Mountain, where he lived for 46 years. The inscription on the monument reads, "Uncle Nick Grindstaff / Born Dec. 26, 1851 / died July 22, 1923 / Lived alone, suffered alone, and died alone."

At 4.5 miles you reach the Iron Mountain Shelter. This shelter is a single rack for six to eight hikers. It is constructed of cinder block, as are all of the shelters in this area. Several tent sites are available at the shelter. Just 0.2 mile beyond the shelter a small stream crosses the trail. In July, when we hiked the trail for this book, there was water flowing; however, during long dry spells this stream might be dry. The trail con-

Grandfather and grandson rest from hiking AT. Photograph by Will Skelton.

tinues on or just off the ridge reaching Turkeypen Gap at 6.5 miles. At this point the trail opens into a small grassy area with blackberry brambles, providing a great seasonal treat. Although not obvious, an unmaintained side trail leads from this point down to TN 91. At 7.4 miles there is a large campsite, and at 7.5 miles a smaller campsite. Water for both campsites can be found on a clearly marked side trail.

At 10 miles the trail drops off the ridge at the division between Lower Nidifer Branch and Peters Branch. At this point there is a sign marking the entrance to the Big Laurel Branch Wilderness. After entering the wilderness the trail climbs back to the ridgecrest, and at 11.5 miles you reach the Vandeventer Shelter. This shelter is another open-front block shelter with a single rack for six to eight hikers. Tent sites are very limited here. Water can be found down a side trail just beyond the shelter. The blue-blazed trail drops quickly off the ridge. Be mindful of the stinging nettles covering the lower part of this trail, they can be painful on uncovered legs. Behind the shelter a large rock outcrop provides a place to sit and enjoy excellent views of Watauga Lake and the surrounding area. This is the first good view of the lake. Just less than one mile farther south is another large rock outcrop, again providing excellent views of the lake.

The trail continues on and off the ridge for the next 2.0 miles. There are a couple of established tent sites along this stretch. At 12 miles there is a small water source, but it may not be reliable during dry periods. At 13.5 miles the trail begins a steep descent toward Watauga Lake, reaching the Watauga Dam Road at 15.9 miles. This marks the end of the AT in the Big Laurel Branch Wilderness.

For those wishing to complete this section of the AT to the Shook Branch Recreation Area, cross the Watauga Dam Road and continue. The trail circles the ridge before dropping again and crossing the road. At this point, walk along the road and across the dam where the trail reenters the woods. The trail then follows the edge of the lake. Several campsites along this portion of the trail provide easy access to the lake, a great place for summer camping. At 2.2 miles from the Watauga Dam Road you reach the Watauga Lake Shelter. Although not on the lake, it is only a short distance from the lake. Water is available at the shelter.

At 19.8 miles (from TN 91) the trail ends at the west end of Watauga Lake at the Shook Branch Recreation Area. The AT crosses US 321 at this point and continues into the Pond Mountain Wilderness.

6 Pond Mountain

(Includes Pond Mountain Wilderness)

Just east of Hampton, TN, is a prominent and beautiful mountain, much of which is protected by the 6,929-acre Pond Mountain Wilderness. The wilderness is in Carter County, TN, and lies within both the Unaka and Watauga ranger districts. The area is characterized by rugged terrain with elevations ranging from about 1,900 feet along Laurel Fork Creek to 4,329 feet at the summit of Pond Mountain. The majority of Pond Mountain is in stands of upland hardwoods, with some small stands of cove hardwoods. The area also contains some stands of virgin timber that were inaccessible to loggers. Perhaps the major attraction of the wilderness is the spectacular Laurel Fork Gorge. Sheer rock cliffs rise 100 to 200 feet from the banks of the stream, and wooded slopes rise over 1,000 feet from the streambed to the top of Black Mountain, at 3,231 feet. Laurel Falls is big, 40 feet high and 50 feet wide, and is quite picturesque, with a deep, wide pool at its base. Above the falls are rock promontories crowned with evergreens. The nearby slopes of Black Mountain contain some virgin timber. The gorge also features Potato Top and Buckled Rock. Potato Top is a large rocky promontory shaped much like a potato hill with a forest cover. Laurel Fork makes a loop around Potato Top. Buckled Rock is a vertical cliff rising from the creek. About 150 feet high, it derives its name from the pattern of bends in the strata.

Vegetation found in the area includes flame azalea, mountain laurel, rhododendron, Carolina hemlock, Fraser's sedge, mountain mint, and Allegheny cliff fern. There are several trails in the area, with the AT being the best maintained. There is an AT shelter along the AT as well as good campsites on Pond Mountain and in the gorge. Laurel Fork Creek is a popular trout-fishing stream, and deer and grouse hunters also use the area.

HISTORY

The Laurel Fork Valley was timbered from 1911 to 1925, with a railroad being constructed from Braemar (adjacent to Hampton), up the gorge, and into the Dennis Cove Valley above. This railroad bed now provides the location for the AT through much of the gorge. The US Congress designated the area as wilderness in 1986.

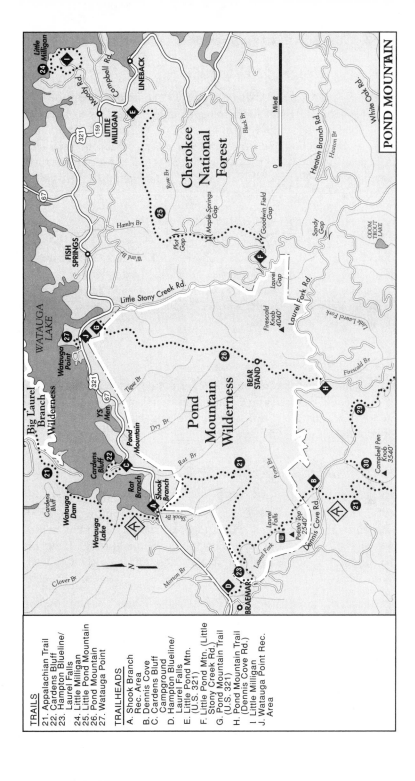

POND MOUNTAIN

TRAILS
21. Appalachian Trail
22. Cardens Bluff
23. Hampton Blueline/
    Laurel Falls
24. Little Milligan
25. Little Pond Mountain
26. Pond Mountain
27. Watauga Point

TRAILHEADS
A. Shook Branch
   Rec. Area
B. Dennis Cove
C. Cardens Bluff
D. Hampton Blueline/
   Laurel Falls
   Campground
E. Little Pond Mtn.
F. Little Pond Mtn. (Little
   Stony Creek Rd.)
G. Pond Mountain Trail
   (U.S. 321)
H. Pond Mountain Trail
   (Dennis Cove Rd.)
I. Little Milligan
J. Watauga Point Rec.
   Area

TRAILHEADS AND MAPS

All trailheads are reached by taking US 19E south out of Elizabethton, TN, for about 5.0 miles and turning left onto US 321/TN 67 at Hampton, TN. Or you can drive north on 19E from NC and Roan Mountain, TN, to the junction and turn right. There is a convenience market at this road junction. All directions and distances are given from this intersection of US 19E, US 321, and TN 67 in Hampton. Turn east on US 321/TN 67.

Shook Branch Recreation Area Trailhead

Drive 3.2 miles east on US 321 from the US 19E junction in Hampton, TN. There is a gravel parking area on US 321 at the sign for the CNF. Park here and walk across US 321 and up the road across from the parking area for 0.1 mile. The AT begins at the point where a side road comes in from the left.

Dennis Cove Trailhead

Drive through Hampton on US 321 0.8 mile to Dennis Cove Road (County 50). Turn right on County 50, which is not marked. Continue for 3.9 miles on a narrow, steep, winding paved road to the FS parking lot for the AT on the left.

Cardens Bluff Campground Trailhead

Drive 4.1 miles east on US 321 from the US 19E junction in Hampton, TN. The entrance to the Cardens Bluff Campground will be on the left. Enter the campground, go past the pay station, turn right after the first bathhouse (a three-way split), and continue through the campground until you reach the trailhead. The trail is on the left across from campsite 12.

Hampton Blueline/Laurel Falls Trailhead

Drive 1.3 miles east on US 321 from the junction in Hampton, TN. The parking area is on the right immediately after you cross the second of two bridges (the first is over Laurel Creek and the second is over a tributary). The trail goes up the creek at the back of the parking area. Vandalism of cars left overnight has been a problem at this trailhead.

Little Pond Mountain (US 321) Trailhead

Drive 9.3 miles east on US 321 to the junction with TN 67; US 321 turns right at the junction. Continue on US 321 another 2.3 miles, then turn right onto FS 6031. This road is unmarked. Continue on FS 6031 about 0.25 miles where the power lines cross the road. There is a small off-road parking area on the left under the power lines. The trailhead is 0.5 mile farther up the road and on the right. If you are in a 4 WD vehicle, you can continue farther up the road to other parking areas closer to the trailhead. Parking is not available at the trailhead.

Little Pond Mountain (Little Stony Creek Road) Trailhead

Drive 7.2 miles east on US 321 from the US 19E junction in Hampton. Turn right on Little Stony Creek road (unmarked) and go 3.3 miles to FS 6034. This is a gated road entering from the left. Off-road parking for two cars is available across Little Stony Creek Road from the FS road. The trailhead is about 50 yards down the FS road, on the right. At the time of this writing the trail sign is missing.

Pond Mountain Trail (US 321) Trailhead

Drive 6.9 miles east on US 321 from the US 19E junction in Hampton, TN. Just past the Watauga Point Recreation Area is a gravel pull-off on the left with a picnic table down by the lake. Cross the highway and look for the post marking the trail. Yellow blazes mark the Pond Mountain Trail.

Pond Mountain Trail (Dennis Cove Road) Trailhead

Drive 0.8 mile east on US 321 from the US 19E junction in Hampton, TN. Turn right onto the Dennis Cove Road (County 50). Follow County 50 past the parking lot for the AT (at 3.9 miles) described above, past the CNF Dennis Cove Campground (5.3 miles), past some private homes, and onto FS 50, which is gravel. Continue up the mountain to the Pond Mountain Trail Trailhead on the left at 7.3 miles. There is limited parking at this trailhead. This trailhead can also be reached by continuing on US 321 past the Watauga Point Recreation Area Trailhead and turning right onto Little Stony Creek Road (FS 39). Follow it until it forms a "T" with FS 50, turn right (west), and go another 2.5 miles to the trailhead on the right (north).

Little Milligan Trailhead

Drive 9.3 miles east on US 321 to the junction with TN 67; US 321 turns right at the junction. Continue on US 321 for 1.5 miles and look for Little Milligan Church on the left and Little Milligan School on the right. At 0.1 mile beyond the church, turn left on Moody Road and continue on Moody to the Little Milligan boat launch. The trailhead is in the parking area for the boat launch.

Watauga Point Recreation Area Trailhead

Drive 6.5 miles east on US 321 from the US 19E junction in Hampton, TN. Turn left into the entrance of the Watauga Point Recreation Area and then immediately right into a small parking lot. The trail begins and ends at the parking lot.

TOPOGRAPHIC MAPS: USGS Elizabethton, TN; Watauga Dam, TN. TI Map 783, South Holston and Watauga Lakes, CNF.

TRAIL DESCRIPTIONS

21. APPALACHIAN TRAIL (SHOOK BRANCH RECREATION AREA TO DENNIS COVE SECTION) (FS TRAIL 1, TI TRAIL 1)

LENGTH: 8.5 miles

ELEVATION CHANGE: Low point, 1,900 feet; high point, 3,760 feet

DIFFICULTY: Moderate/difficult

TRAILHEADS: Shook Branch Recreation Area and Dennis Cove

USE: Hiking

TOPOGRAPHIC MAPS: Elizabethton and Watauga Dam, TN

COMMENTS: This section of the AT is maintained by the TN Eastman Hiking Club and includes a trail shelter in Laurel Fork Gorge. There is no preferred direction to hike this trail; steep ascents are required either way (north to south, 3,200 feet; south to north, 2,900 feet). Hiking north to south, the way we describe it here, the ascent is gradual and the descent is steep. In the other direction, there is a steep ascent with a gradual descent. This is a very good hike either way. For a shorter and easier day hike to see Laurel Falls and the lower portions of this trail, begin the hike at the Dennis Cove Trailhead. Take the AT to Laurel Falls and beyond to the intersection with the blue-blazed

Laurel Falls Access Trail, which will take you back to US 321 at the Laurel Creek Trailhead. This route is generally downhill the entire way, but a car shuttle is necessary.

DETAILS: This description is written as a hike starting at the Shook Branch Recreation Area and ending at the Dennis Cove Trailhead. Hiking in this direction provides good views of the Watauga Lake, the southern end of the Iron Mountain range, and the Big Laurel Branch Wilderness. One good view in particular is located just one mile up the trail off a blue-blazed side trail. The trail continues to climb through a series of switchbacks over 3.5 miles to Pond Mountain Flats. This area is a frequent camping spot and a spring crosses the trail less than 100 yards up the trail from the campsite. The site is large enough for several tents.

Beyond the Pond Mountain Flats the trail continues on a gentle grade for 1.0 mile before descending into the Laurel Fork gorge. The descent is quite steep, dropping almost 2,000 feet in just over 1.0 mile. After the steep descent, the trail widens and follows an old railroad grade until reaching the intersection with the Hampton Blueline/Laurel Falls Trail, which enters from the right at 5.8 miles. Following the Blueline trail, 1.7 miles takes you to US 321 and the Laurel Creek Trailhead. Staying on the AT (going left) the trail continues along an essentially flat, wide trail following Laurel Creek. At two places you

Day hikers playing in water at foot of Laurel Falls. Photograph by Will Skelton.

cross footbridges that were replaced in the late 1900s after being washed out. Several campsites are located along this section of the trail. At 6.5 miles the trail narrows and begins a short ascent to a ridgeline.

At 6.7 miles a blue-blazed side trail enters from the left. This trail leads up to the Laurel Fork Shelter and is an AT bypass trail during times when Laurel Creek is swollen from rain. At 7.2 miles the AT descends to Laurel Creek. At this point the trail appears to descend into a large rock outcrop on a worn path. The AT, however, circles the rock to the right, almost entering the creek bed, then continues along the creek and reaches Laurel Falls at 7.4 miles. Swimming in the pool below the falls is prohibited due to a strong undertow created by the water coming over the falls. From this point the trail turns away from the creek and begins its ascent out of the gorge.

At 7.4 miles a blue-blazed trail enters from the left. This is the AT high-water bypass and Laurel Fork shelter trail. At 7.6 miles a side trail (0.2 mile) takes you out to Potato Top, where the hiker is rewarded with views of the Laurel Fork gorge. Continuing along the AT, the trail widens and again picks up the railroad grade for the balance of the trail and at times passes beside Laurel Creek. Along this section of the trail you pass through several rock cutouts made for train passage into the gorge. At 8.0 miles there is a large campsite by the creek in a hemlock stand. The Dennis Cove trailhead is reached at 8.5 miles.

22. CARDENS BLUFF TRAIL (FS TRAIL 55, TI TRAIL 5)

LENGTH: 0.7 miles

ELEVATION CHANGE: Insignificant

DIFFICULTY: Easy

TRAILHEAD: Cardens Bluff Campground

USE: Hiking

TOPOGRAPHIC MAPS: Watauga Dam, TN

COMMENTS: This is mainly a campground trail and there is no parking at the trailhead itself.

DETAILS: The trail is a nice and easy walk while staying in the Cardens Bluff Campground. It follows along the shoreline and passes through areas of the campground that are undeveloped. At many points the trail has easy access to water for fishing and swimming. About half of the trail circles the developed campground area and as a result you pass between many campsites and the lake. The trail is not a full loop and ends at a bathhouse a short distance from the entrance to the campground off TN US 321.

23. HAMPTON BLUELINE/LAUREL FALLS TRAIL (FS TRAIL 501, TI TRAIL 13)

LENGTH: 1.7 miles

ELEVATION CHANGE: Insignificant

DIFFICULTY: Easy

TRAILHEADS: Hampton Blueline/Laurel Falls

USE: Hiking

TOPOGRAPHIC MAPS: Elizabethton, TN

DETAILS: This trail follows Laurel Creek for the majority of its length. With the exception of a small uphill section about 0.1 mile from the trailhead the trail is flat and easy to traverse. At 0.25 mile the trail splits; stay left to continue on the Blueline trail. At 0.4 mile from US 321 there is a sign stating that you are entering the Pond Mountain Wilderness. Just beyond this point the trail splits again; stay right following Laurel Creek. At 1.0 mile the trail intersects the AT. To the left (north) the AT traverses over Pond Mountain; to the right (south) it travels on to Laurel Falls. As you look down the trail, notice that the blazes change from blue to white, showing that it becomes the AT.

24. LITTLE MILLIGAN TRAIL (FS TRAIL 602, TI TRAIL 24)

LENGTH: 1.7 miles

DIFFICULTY: Easy

ELEVATION CHANGE: Insignificant

TRAILHEADS: Little Milligan

USE: Hiking

TOPOGRAPHIC MAPS: Watauga Dam, TN

COMMENTS: The trail is an easy loop trail through the woods around the Little Milligan boat launch.

DETAILS: The trail begins in the far corner of the parking area. Depending on the season, you could find yourself in a lot of poison ivy near the beginning of the trail. The trail opens with a walk through an area of pine trees and starts along the lake. At 0.2 mile it turns west, heading away from the lake and into the woods. At 0.3 mile the trail turns left across a shallow ravine and continues. This ravine might contain water during heavy rains. The trail continues its northwest direction. At 0.4 mile the trail goes left at a trail junction and at 0.5 mile crosses Moody Road after a roundabout through the woods. After crossing the road, the trail drops into the woods again. Watch for holly bushes around a trail split at 0.6 mile. The trail meanders through the woods as it makes its way toward the lake. At 1.3 miles it passes an old cemetery on the left. The cemetery only has two markers, both for children. The trail eventually returns to Moody road. Turn left and it is a short walk down the road to the boat launch area.

25. LITTLE POND MOUNTAIN TRAIL (FS TRAIL 41, TI TRAIL 27)

LENGTH: 5.3 miles

ELEVATION CHANGE: Low point, 2,520 feet; high point, 3,400 feet

DIFFICULTY: Moderate/Difficult

TRAILHEADS: US 321 and Little Stony Creek Road

USE: Hiking

TOPOGRAPHIC MAPS: Watauga Dam, TN

COMMENTS: Although an official CNF trail, the Little Pond Mountain Trail has not been maintained. It should be considered, as of the early 2000s, an off-trail hike.

DETAILS: Beginning at the trailhead off FS 60301, the trail heads south and ascends straight up the mountain 0.2 mile before reaching a series of switchbacks that lead to the ridgecrest. At 0.5 mile the trail turns northwest and continues to climb along the ridge toward the crest that is reached at 0.7 mile. This area of the CNF was burned in a 1991 forest fire. As a result, most of the old growth was lost and the area is being reforested, primarily by pine that line the trail as you ascend to the ridgecrest. The fire also opened the area up for understory growth of plants such as mountain laurel, which are growing in and off the trail. First- and second-year hardwoods are also making their appearance in the trail. With continued lack of trail maintenance, these plants and trees will eventually claim the trail and completely obscure it. Trail blazes are virtually nonexistent, probably due to the fire claiming most of the mature trees in the area. The lack of blazes and the plant growth in the trail make it more difficult to follow in places.

The fire also opened up several vistas. As you climb the ridge, there are wonderful views of Watauga Lake to the north and Sheffield Ridge to the south. Once reaching the ridge, the trail follows it in a

generally west/southwest direction for another 2.0 miles before turning south and dropping off the ridge into Plot Gap. The trail then
ascends a smaller ridge and follows it for 1.0 mile and descends into
Maple Spring Gap. At Maple Spring Gap the trail crosses FS 6034.
This road will take you to Little Stony Creek Road and the trailhead.
Maple Spring Gap is currently a recommended termination (or beginning) point for the trail due to lack of trail maintenance and the lack
of a trail marker at the beginning of the trail. For those wanting to
continue on-trail from Maple Spring Gap, the trail turns southeast
from the road and ascends a small ridge. It then follows the ridge for
about 1.0 mile before descending through a rhododendron thicket to
FS 6034.

26. POND MOUNTAIN TRAIL (FS TRAIL 31, TI TRAIL 40)

LENGTH: 4.5 miles

ELEVATION CHANGE: Low point, 1,968 feet; high point,
4,040 feet

DIFFICULTY: Difficult

TRAILHEADS: US 321 (Pond Mountain) and Dennis Cove Road
(Pond Mountain)

TRAIL CONNECTIONS: Bear Stand off-trail route

USE: Hiking

TOPOGRAPHIC MAPS: Watauga Dam, TN

COMMENTS: This trail is a rugged 4.5-mile hike. The trail is not
well maintained and in many places goes straight up the fall line. With
much use, severe erosion will take place. There is no reliable water on
the trail. The yellow blazes that mark the trail are often obscure and
the trail itself is often obscure, making this trail more challenging for
the experienced hiker. The lack of switchbacks on the steep ascents
adds to the trail's difficulty. The trail is described north to south.

DETAILS: Cross US 321 from the trailhead parking area and you
will see a treated post on your left marked "Pond Mountain Trail."
The trail proceeds to the left. Just beyond the post is a covered kiosk
where a map and general description of the area may be found. The
trail begins beyond the kiosk, turning right and heading up the mountain. Within 100 feet of the kiosk the trail disappears; however, if you
follow the ridgeline straight up the mountain you will reconnect with
a more obvious trail in a couple hundred yards. The trail ascends very
steeply, very quickly. You will pass under power lines and through a

rhododendron thicket before regaining the trail. The wilderness begins just beyond the power lines. At 0.2 mile an old road intersects with the trail. Go left on the road for 30 feet and then turn right onto the trail. Look for yellow blazes, which are faint in many places. At 0.3 mile the trail bends to the right and continues a steep ascent through hardwood forest and rhododendrons. During the winter months look back for views of Watauga Lake as you ascend the mountain.

The ridgecrest is at 0.4 mile. Descend from the ridge into a small gap and then back up another ridge. At 0.5 mile the trail turns right and begins another steep ascent. At 0.7 mile you reach the ridgeline and continue along the ridge. As you scramble to the next high point along the ridge, there are nice views of the lake and surrounding valleys. At l.0 mile the trail turns left and descends into another small gap. For the next 0.5 mile, walk along the ridge, climbing gently. At 1.5 miles climb steeply again and reach the top of the ridge at 2.0 miles.

The next 0.4 mile is gentle ridge walking. At 2.4 miles you enter a broad open wooded area with a number of large oak trees. Continue straight ahead and ascend, with the trail turning left up the ridge for

Backpacker cooks dinner at campsite atop Pond Mountain. Photograph by Will Skelton

0.2 mile to the ridgetop. Continue along the ridge. At 2.8 miles a junction is reached; the trail turns left and leaves the ridge with a steep descent, while the former Bear Stand Trail proceeds straight ahead to the AT. However, the Bear Stand Trail is not maintained and should be considered off-trail. It essentially follows the crest of Pond Mountain along a fairly easy grade (see off-trail hiking opportunities below). At 2.9 miles the trail enters a small grassy gap where it intersects with an old skid road. There are three other trails, presumably used by hunters, which leave from this area. Turn left on the old logging road and follow it for 1.6 miles to the Dennis Cove trailhead.

27. WATAUGA POINT TRAIL (FS TRAIL 59, TI TRAIL 39)

LENGTH: 0.4 mile

ELEVATION CHANGE: Insignificant

DIFFICULTY: Easy

TRAILHEADS: Watauga Point Recreation Area

USE: Hiking

TOPOGRAPHIC MAPS: Watauga Dam, TN

DETAILS: This is a short, easy loop trail suited for the whole family. The trail is mostly level and parts have been covered with crushed gravel for easier travel. The trail crosses a few small streams, but there are bridges at each one. At 0.3 mile the trail comes to a junction. The trail goes left, but there is a path to the right that goes to Watauga Lake. From this junction the trail follows the lake around for a short distance before turning away from the lake and heading up to the trailhead. The trail comes out in the same parking lot where you began.

OFF-TRAIL HIKING OPPORTUNITIES

The Pond Mountain Wilderness is also a good area for off-trail hiking on now-abandoned trails. A few of the options are listed here for those wishing that type of adventure.

Dry Branch

Formerly FS Trail 134, this route leads you into the heart of the former Watauga Scenic Area, which formed the core of the subsequently designated Pond Mountain Wilderness. This is also known as Watauga

Scenic Area Trail. The trailhead is at the Watauga Shooting Range on US 321, and the end is at about 2.2 miles on a 3,280-foot knoll overlooking much of the wilderness. However, as of the early 1990s, this is more of an off-trail route than a trail; it has not been maintained and is very difficult to follow. Accordingly, it cannot be described in detail. With a topographical map and the map in this book, however, you can follow the route up Dry Branch, proceeding generally southeast. At about the 3,000-foot contour, the route turns sharply to the left and to the northeast; you will almost be heading back toward the direction you came from earlier. The knoll is less than 0.5 mile ahead on the horizon. The trailhead is the Watauga Shooting Range. Drive 4.8 miles east on US 321 from the US 19E junction in Hampton, TN. A short gravel road, FS 344, is on the right and is signed "Rifle Range-Pond Mountain." Follow the gravel road 0.1 mile into the woods. At its end the shooting range is on the right, and the trailhead is straight ahead at several earth mounds that block ORVs. Be careful because of shooting activities in the area.

Bear Stand

Formerly FS Trail 166, this route connects the AT to the Pond Mountain Trail. The first 1.0 mile was formerly the AT and is in good shape, but the last 0.8 mile has not been maintained for years and is very obscure and difficult to follow. Occasionally, you will see old faded yellow blazes on trees. It may be cleared and maintained in the future. The trailhead from the Pond Mountain Trail is difficult to find. At 2.8 miles on the Pond Mountain Trail (from US 321), that trail turns left and leaves the ridge, while the Bear Stand Trail continues straight ahead. There is neither sign nor clear evidence of a trailhead; you must simply follow the ridge.

The Bear Stand route leaves Pond Flats and heads southeast, to the left of the knoll, with a quite level trail. At 0.3 mile the route ascends along a narrow crest. At 0.9 mile, veer left off the crest and skirt left, descending gently. At 1.0 mile the trail ascends to the right and proceeds along the ridge, while the former AT goes straight and begins descending steeply. This junction can be a problem, so be careful. From this point the Bear Stand route is difficult to follow, as it leads 0.8 mile on to the Pond Mountain Trail. In places it is obvious; in others it is very obscure. Perhaps the best advice for hiking this route is to attempt to stay on the ridgecrest for the entire length of the route and use a topographical map. Although forested, the trail features occasional outstanding views of the surrounding mountains. The route ends at 1.8 miles at the Pond Mountain Trail.

7 White Rocks Mountain

(Includes Slide Hollow Backcountry Area and Slide Hollow Roadless Area)

The White Rocks Mountain area is an often ignored hiking area located between the more visited Pond Mountain Wilderness and the Highlands of Roan. It is perhaps ignored because, except for the AT Corridor and the nearby Slide Hollow Backcountry Area, it does not contain any protected areas. However, it has several good hiking opportunities. The White Rocks Mountain to the south and Walnut Mountain to the north form the valley through which the Laurel Fork flows. These rough borders encompass an estimated 20 square miles of excellent wild lands. The Laurel Fork, which actually begins well east of and beyond the area, is fed by no less than sixteen named streams and branches, as well as many unnamed springs and seasonal water sources. The sheer volume of water received by the surrounding hillsides and the valley below has resulted in a destination of great charm and beauty. Many excellent, secluded campsites may be found throughout the management area, and, as one might expect, water is generally nearby. Elevation ranges between a high of 4,200 feet along the AT to a low of 2,850 feet at Frog Level in the valley. The Frog Level area is more or less centrally positioned within the management area and intersects the Laurel Fork Trail near the Lacy Trap Trailhead. This makes it an excellent destination from which one may combine all or portions of several trails into a variety of outings ranging from as little as 4.0 miles to over 15.0 miles, with overnight stays possible in a multitude of outstanding campsites. The USFS's Southern Appalachian Assessment identified the substantial 4,195-acre Slide Hollow Roadless Area nearby; it is separated by a mountain ridge from the White Rocks Mountain area. Portions of that roadless area are protected in the CNF's 2004 plan revision, including the 2,464-acre Slide Hollow Backcountry Area (few open roads). The roadless area presents opportunities for off-trail exploration, although, except for the AT at the edge of the area, there are no official trails. The area is generally located southeast of Hampton, TN, in Johnson County and the Watauga Ranger District.

HISTORY

The AT runs along the crest of White Rocks Mountain, and its corridor has been protected from logging. However, other portions of the

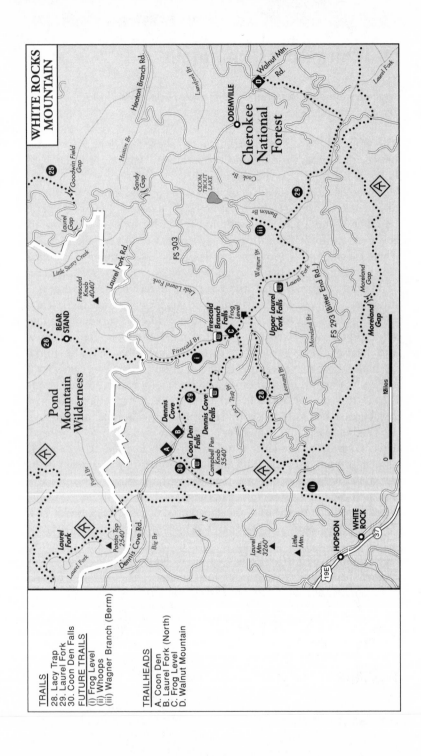

Cherokee National Forest

Pond Mountain Wilderness

ODOM TROUT LAKE

Legend labels on map:

Walnut Mtn. Rd.
Laurel Fork
Lunsford Br
Heaton Branch Rd.
ODEMVILLE
Heaton Br
Goodwin Field Gap
Laurel Gap
Sandy Gap
Cook Br
Burton Br
Little Stony Creek
Laurel Fork Rd
FS 303
Firescald Knob 4040'
BEAR STAND
Little Laurel Fork
Firescald Br
Wagner Br
Laurel Fork
Firescald Branch Falls
Frog Level
Upper Laurel Fork Falls
Moreland Br
Moreland Gap
FS 293 (Bitter End Rd.)
Leonard Br
Moreland Gap
Dennis Cove
Coon Den Falls
Dennis Cove Falls
Campbell Pen Knob 3540'
Lacy Trap Br
Pond Br
Potato Top 2540'
Dennis Cove Rd.
Big Br
Laurel Fork
Laurel Fork
Laurel Mtn. 3260'
Little Mtn.
HOPSON
WHITE ROCK
19E
37

Miles

0

N

25
26
29
28
29
30

A
B

Trailhead/trail markers: i, ii, iii

TRAILS
28. Lacy Trap
29. Laurel Fork
30. Coon Den Falls
FUTURE TRAILS
(i) Frog Level
(ii) Whoops
(iii) Wagner Branch (Berm)

TRAILHEADS
A. Coon Den
B. Laurel Fork (North)
C. Frog Level
D. Walnut Mountain

area have been logged, and a fair number of open logging roads remain. Much of the area is included in the Laurel Fork WMA, although this designation does not prevent logging and road building. Portions of undisturbed forest remain, however, especially along the Laurel Fork. The designation of the Slide Hollow Backcountry Area, on the south side of the Elk River, in the CNF's 2004 plan revision provides the first protection for the area, other than the AT Corridor.

TRAILHEADS AND MAPS

Coon Den, Laurel Fork (North), and Frog Level Trailheads

These trailheads are reached by taking US 19E south out of Elizabethton, TN, for 5.1 miles and turning left onto US 321/TN 67 at Hampton, TN. Or you can drive north on 19E from NC and Roan Mountain, TN, to the junction and turn right. There is a convenience market at this road junction. From this point, all directions and distances are from this intersection of US 19E, US 321, and TN 67 in Hampton. Drive 0.6 mile east through Hampton on US 321 to Dennis Cove Road (County 50). Turn right on County 50, which becomes FS 50 and is not marked. Continue on a narrow, steep, winding paved road. You will ascend the southwest side of Black Mountain, go over Cedar Gap, and begin the descent into the Laurel Fork valley. At 4.0 miles the AT crossing is passed, with a parking area at the northern (left) side. Laurel Fork now appears to your left and is alongside the roadway until just before reaching Dennis Cove Campground. Continue past the Laurel Creek Lodge, a hostel used by many AT hikers. At 4.7 miles the Coon Den Trailhead is passed on the right; there is no parking immediately at the trailhead.

Continue on FS 50 to the Laurel Fork (North) Trailhead at 5.6 miles; the trailhead parking area is on the left just before crossing a one-vehicle bridge. Just 0.1 mile farther is the Dennis Cove Campground. A fee is required for this pleasant, rather small, car camping area offering water, toilets, no bathing facilities, and a limited number of campsites, a few of which are alongside the Laurel Fork. The road becomes gravel at 6.4 miles but is more than adequate for most 2 WD vehicles throughout the portion relevant to this area. Proceed to an intersection with FS 50F at 7.6 miles and take the extreme right fork on FS 50F to begin a fairly constant descent into the Laurel Fork valley. The road dead-ends in the parking area at 9.8 miles above the area known as Frog Level, where one will find the Laurel Fork (south) and Lacy Trap trailheads. A rough ORV road continues at this point.

Walnut Mountain Trailhead

The trailheads for the Slide Hollow off-trail hiking area and Laurel Fork Trail are located on the Walnut Mountain Road (FS50). Beginning in the city of Elizabethton at the intersection of US 321/TN 37/US 19E, proceed 17.4 miles south on US 19E/TN 37 to the city of Roan Mountain and the TN 143 intersection. Restart your mileage at that intersection and continue 1.4 miles on US 19E/TN 37 to Buck Mountain Road on the left; there is a sign (note the TI map wrongly identifies the road as Dolan Hollow Road). Follow Buck Hollow Road up the mountain. At 3.0 miles continue right as the Old Buck Mountain Road turns left and makes a loop back to join the Buck Mountain Road at 3.3 miles. At 4.0 miles Bluegrass Road (which is an alternate route to the trailhead from US 19W) joins the Buck Mountain Road from the right. Continue on the Buck Mountain Road to 4.85 miles, where you turn left on Walnut Mountain Road. Look carefully, as Walnut Mountain Road angles left to the east, rather than turns off, at this point and may be missed! Mountain View Lane also angles off on the left to the west at that three-way intersection. In a long gap at 5.8 miles, just past a Christmas tree farm, the pavement ends and a gravel road begins. As the road starts up the ridge past the gap, at 6.1 miles, you will see an old gated road on the right with parking spaces for several vehicles. This is the trailhead (UTM 17S 409761E/4008556N) for the Slide Hollow Valley off-trail hiking described below. Continuing on the gravel Walnut Mountain Road to 8.4 miles will bring you to the Walnut Mountain Trailhead for the Laurel Fork Trail; the trail ascends to enter Walnut Mountain Road on the left, just as the road curves right. The trail is poorly marked, with little blaze visible, but it is an obvious trail.

TOPOGRAPHIC MAPS: USGS White Rocks Mountain, TN; Watauga Dam, TN. TI Map 783, South Holston and Watauga Lakes, CNF.

TRAIL DESCRIPTIONS

28. LACY TRAP TRAIL (FS TRAIL 36, TI TRAIL 20)

LENGTH: 3.6 miles

ELEVATION: High point, 3,937 feet; low point, 2,857 feet

DIFFICULTY: Moderate

TRAILHEAD: Frog Level, or 2.5 miles along the AT, starting at Dennis Cove Road

USE: Hiking, equestrian, mountain bike

TOPOGRAPHIC MAPS: White Rocks Mountain, TN-NC

COMMENTS: This trail begins at Frog Level and ascends the northeastern side of White Rocks Mountain, where it connects with the AT. It is a less than spectacular trail in that it shares use of an old, seldom-used roadway for much of the hike. It is marked with yellow blazes. The trail ascends fairly consistently until about the three mile point, at which it gradually drops 130 feet from the trail's high elevation of 3,937 feet to 3,807 feet at the AT junction during the last 0.6 mile. The central location of the Lacy Trap Trail makes up for any lack of appeal by providing flexibility in planning, permitting a connection between the Laurel Fork Trail and the AT, then to the Coon Den Falls Trail, for an outing of under 7.0 miles when begun at Dennis Cove Road/Laurel Fork crossing. There are also possibilities for longer circuitous hikes of varying portions and lengths combining the AT, Laurel Fork Trail, Coon Den Falls Trail, and the Lacy Trap Trail

DETAILS: From Frog Level, begin by crossing the branch at the southeast corner and following the old roadbed, which will cross two more streams at 0.1 mile and 0.15 miles. With the Laurel Fork to your right, proceed to a "Trail 36/39" junction marker at 0.24 miles, bear left following the vehicle path to a final stream crossing at 0.3 mile, and enter a large field of perhaps six acres in size. You may follow either side around the field to encounter FS Trail 36/20, either choice taking you eventually to the small, (50 feet +/-) pond at the southeasternmost end of the field. At this point the trail begins an ascent behind the south side of the pond at 0.45 miles, reentering the forest with the trail bounded by dense rhododendron.

The trail continues through perhaps the longest section of rather steep trail of this hike until 0.75 miles, where the forest opens up to larger trees and much less dense low growth. Just beyond, at 0.8 mile, a first "plateau" is reached and the trail will be found less strenuous and generally not as steep from this point on. The last 1.2 miles is a pleasant stroll on trail leading through the hardwood and hemlock forest common to the area, ending at the AT. Continuing to 1.0 mile the trail intersects the old roadway onto which you will turn left and begin to follow it to 2.1 miles. At this point you will note a large, open field, probably a combination of horse camp/wildlife management clearing. The roadway passes through the clearing and turns sharply right as you exit the area at 2.3 miles. Just past the intersection to the right of a shorter, dead-end section of roadway, the trail crosses the road and, diverging to the right, once again ascends, leading away from the roadway for a short distance, intersecting and crossing the road again at 2.4 miles, where it ascends into the woodland. At 2.5 miles, a short descent will place the roadway curving in toward the trail from the left, eventually to be within approximately 25 feet. The trail begins an ascent to the maximum elevation point of this hike at 2.95 miles and 3,937 feet and turns to a southwesterly heading to begin a descent where the old roadway is rejoined at 3.2 miles. A small brook will be crossed at 3.4 miles, and the vehicular barrier at the AT is reached at 3.6 miles.

29. LAUREL FORK TRAIL (FS TRAIL 39, TI TRAIL 21)

LENGTH: 7.9 miles

ELEVATION: High point, 3,515 feet; low point, 2,822 feet

DIFFICULTY: Dennis Cove to Frog Level, difficult (due to stream crossings); Walnut Mountain to Frog Level, moderate

TRAILHEADS: Laurel Fork (north), Frog Level, and Walnut Mountain

USE: Dennis Cove to Frog Level, hiking; Walnut Mountain to Frog Level, hiking and mountain bike

TOPOGRAPHIC MAP: White Rocks Mountain, TN-NC

GENERAL COMMENTS: Although this is one continuous trail, it is being described in two sections due to their distinct differences, thus permitting better planning. The northern section is Dennis Cove to Frog Level. The southern section is Walnut Mountain to Frog Level. Access to Frog Level by a good gravel road, suitable to standard 2 WD vehicles, permits beginning or ending of either section at Frog Level.

NORTHERN SECTION

COMMENTS (DENNIS COVE TO FROG LEVEL): This is the most challenging section. It begins at the one-lane bridge 0.1 mile from Dennis Cove Campground and continues to Frog Level. Beyond the first stream crossing at the trailhead, this trail is very poorly marked and maintained, sometimes making it difficult to locate. *Many stream crossings are required, several of which are rather deep, and at least two crossings require "rock-hopping" technical skills.* Having a change of footwear and perhaps convertible type pants is highly recommended, as is a staff or hiking pole. Caution is strongly recommended in attempting to hike this section during any time of significant rainfall or snowmelt, as the Laurel Fork is the recipient of all run-off in the Laurel Fork Wildlife Management Area and is fed by no less than sixteen named streams and branches, as well as a profusion of unnamed springs and seasonal runoff areas not shown on the map. On the positive side, this seldom-used trail offers the opportunity to access an area in which one will find a representation of the best stream valley flora and perhaps a better chance to view wildlife—all in a relatively level, if somewhat wet, hike of about 2.0 (plus) miles.

DETAILS (DENNIS COVE TO FROG LEVEL): Beginning at the Dennis Cove Road trailhead, the trail ascends to the first crossing of Laurel Fork at 0.5 mile, one requiring a combination of rock-hopping and wading. Following the trail through a rough, rock-strewn escarpment will place you at the next crossing, at 0.6 mile. Approaching a short drop in the trail at 1.1 miles, follow the left trail, as you will find a right turn leads to a dead-end at a campsite that overlooks a small waterfall in the stream, which is several feet below the camp. Two crossings await at 1.4 and 1.7 miles, respectively, with the latter being a broader, shallower crossing where the trail leads diagonally upstream. At 1.9 miles the deepest crossing point may be difficult to see, but the exit point is diagonally upstream of, and marked by the presence of, a cable. The final crossing, at 2.15 miles, is at an area adjacent to the westernmost field of the Frog Level area. It is actually two crossings, under normal conditions, as the trail crosses at the point where an island exists. This may be the least difficult, shallow, but widest crossing. Following the Laurel Fork eastward thru the fields at Frog Level will bring you to the Lacy Trap Trailhead at approximately 2.75 miles and the southern section of the Laurel Fork Trail.

SOUTHERN SECTION

COMMENTS (WALNUT MOUNTAIN TO FROG LEVEL): While a large number of stream crossings make applicable the warning used in the northern section, the crossings tend to be through shallower areas of streams accessed by well-defined trail. Most stream crossings would be defined as "wading," requiring (in drier weather) only perhaps a change of shoes, although this writer remained dry when wearing leather hiking boots. The moderately steep descent from Walnut Mountain Road/FS 50 into Laurel Fork Valley is along a good trail through pleasant stands of mature hardwoods, hemlocks, and rhododendron. The valley floor tends to be fairly broad and surprisingly consistent in descent, having only slight undulations, resulting in a trail that is very good to hike and one that experienced hikers will find to be effortless to trek. There is little difficulty in identifying the trail en route. Many streamside areas would make excellent campsites. One minor point to consider is that while progress along the trail may be monitored using major or named brooks and streams, the sheer number of unnamed sources emptying into Laurel Fork can be rather confusing and make the precise tracking of one's position a bit tedious if these are used as references.

DETAILS (WALNUT MOUNTAIN TO FROG LEVEL): Arriving at the Walnut Mountain Trailhead on Walnut Mountain Road/FS 50, close attention must be given to the odometer, as no marker for the trail is evident. One will, however, note blue blazes indicating the trailhead, which begins at left of the roadway in a westbound descent toward the valley floor. At this point, the trail leads through heavy stands of large rhododendron along a good trail; however, many fallen trees lay across and throughout this hillside portion of the trail. Within the first 0.25 mile, the beginning of Hays Branch will be noted and crossed, but it is so small it may not be evident in the dry season. Hays Branch will be crossed again within 300 feet, and the trail makes a short but sharp ascent to the right, placing Hays Branch to the left at 0.4 mile. The stream will be crossed just before arriving at a small waterfall.

A gravel roadway intersects the trail at 0.7 mile and the trail resumes across this road and then to the right on a second, gated, unimproved road with a trail marker bearing "Laurel Fork Trail." Grassland gives way to bogs in the depressed areas of the road/trail, and a number of wetlands will be visible, as is a pond of 30 foot diameter at the right side of the trail at just under 1.0 mile. The trail widens

Hiker enjoys rest stop at a bridge over Laurel Fork. Photograph by Steve Dyer.

at approximately 1.1 miles, and entry into a field of several acres in size occurs. Following either the right-hand side of this field or heading toward the southwest corner will lead to the exit from this area at 1.2 miles, where multiple blazes will be found marking what has once again become a hiking trail of good condition and leading to a first crossing of Laurel fork at 1.35 miles. The trail continues alongside Laurel Fork to the right for 180 feet and leads through a narrow but somewhat open area sheltered by hardwoods, where one might expect to recross Laurel Fork. Looking instead to the left, a short but somewhat steep ascent (15 feet vertically) over tree roots will be taken to a visibly more open area, where a right turn at the top will resume a rough parallel to Laurel Fork.

The trail continues on a west-northwest path through bushy, low growth overhanging the trail that is bounded by Laurel Fork to the right. At 1.6 miles a fairly large outcropping of rock will be found. The trail drops to the right toward Laurel Fork in approximately 210 feet farther on, where a trail marker will be found to the left indicating an old roadway. A connection to the Bitter End Road, which leads south and out of the valley, is found to the left at 1.7 miles. Two crossings of Laurel Fork, at 1.75 miles and 1.95 miles, precede a crossing of an unnamed small stream that descends to the trail from the left at just over 2.0 miles. Arrival at Cook Branch is at 2.35 miles, with Cook Branch emerging from the right to join Laurel fork, which you cross once again.

At 2.5 miles, entry into a valley floor field occurs, one surrounded by rhododendron at the edges and bisected by Laurel Fork and further subdivided by vegetative lines of growth into three areas of diminishing size for a total length of approximately 600–800 feet. This is an outstanding area that receives adequate sun to support grasses and reed-type growth in the flat, open floor and invites camping within earshot of Laurel Fork. Stream access is easy, and, where permissible, this would be an excellent camp destination for those wanting only a short backpack, as well as a perfect day-trip stopover.

Upon exiting the field, expect two more stream crossings, one at 2.6 miles and another at Bunton Branch, which ascends from the right and intersects Laurel Fork to your immediate left as you cross at 2.9 miles. At 3.2 miles, a more obvious but still very gradual descent is now apparent, and Laurel Fork flows below and to the left of the trail over a series of rapids stretching approximately 150–200 feet. Moreland Branch intersects Laurel Fork unseen and above Upper Laurel Fork Falls (there is no *Lower* Laurel Fork Falls unless Laurel Falls in the Pond Mountain Wilderness is such) at 3.6 miles. Upper Laurel

Falls is a small waterfall dropping through a series of "pockets" worn into the boulders that constrict the stream rather than allowing water to cascade over a precipice in a long, steady fall. Viewing is possible from vantage points that require some rock-hopping onto fairly slick areas overlooking the falls. There are also views from the trail and slightly downstream.

At 4.5 miles, note an overhead cable on your left and the diagonal stream crossing that will lead to where the trail emerges at a short but steep embankment and becomes an old roadbed in appearance. Your final crossing, of Leonard Branch occurs within 200 feet of Frog Level and signals your arrival there at 5.0 miles. Continuing through Frog Level will place the trailhead for Lacy Trap Trail to the left when very near Leonard Branch and, in an additional 0.7 miles, the northern section of the Laurel Fork Trail.

30. COON DEN FALLS TRAIL (FS TRAIL 37, TI TRAIL 6)

LENGTH: 1.25 miles

ELEVATION: High point, 3,433 feet; low point, 2,568 feet

DIFFICULTY: Moderate

TRAILHEADS: Coon Den and AT (1.25 miles south of Dennis Cove Road, FS 50)

USE: Hiking

TOPOGRAPHIC MAPS: White Rocks Mountain, TN-NC

COMMENTS: The trailhead marker is placed away from the roadway on Dennis Cove Road and is approximately 0.7 miles east of the AT crossing, but slightly west of Coon Den Branch. The trail ascends toward the southwest from the valley through which Laurel Fork flows; then it connects with the AT at the crest of the White Rocks Mountain. It is a short but picturesque hike and is somewhat steep in some sections. Two waterfalls will be encountered on the left of the trail. The first is a slender, unnamed ribbon that is perhaps 20 feet high; the other is farther up the trail and is the larger Coon Den Falls. Above the falls and toward the AT there is an abundance of rhododendron. The trail follows Coon Den Branch until the last few hundred feet before reaching the saddle and an intersection with the AT. An excellent outing would be to combine the Coon Den Falls Trail with the AT. Go left/south on the AT and turn left at about 1.25 miles. Follow the Lacy Trap Trail to Frog Level, then go west onto the northern section of the Laurel Fork Trail, which ends at Dennis Cove Road near the campground. The trail is often used as an exit point for the Laurel Creek AT hostel. The trail is blue blazed.

DETAILS: Beginning as a moderate ascent, the trail soon merges with Coon Den Branch; the creek is on the left thereafter. At 0.36 miles, a small, unnamed waterfall is encountered, and the trail begins a more strenuous ascent toward Coon Den Falls. Nearing Coon Den Falls, at 0.46 miles, the main trail turns sharply to the right (west), away from the creek. A short 150-foot access trail turns left and slightly uphill as it leads to the bottom of Coon Den Falls. This waterfall, while not of great width, is of impressive height, the top obscured by the rhododendron and laurel, whose growth intertwines at the narrow source to make any "eyeball" estimate of the height questionable. That having been said, Coon Den Falls appears to drop, nearly vertically, for about 60 feet, forming a mostly unbroken ribbon until near the bottom, where several small steps break and divide the falling water. As with many waterfalls, it will be more impressive after a rainstorm.

Continuing to the right on the main trail beyond the falls (do not try to climb beside the falls), the trail is quite steep as it ascends in a loop away from and then back toward and above the creek. Large rocks in the trail make travel more difficult, especially if coming off the AT heading toward Dennis Cove Road. The trail will rejoin the branch at very nearly 1.0 mile and then generally follow the branch for a short distance before intersecting the AT at 1.24 miles. Following the AT to the right will begin a descent to the Dennis Cove Road at 1.10 miles and 0.9 mile west of the entry point. Turning left will begin an ascent that will lead to the Lacy Trap Trail junction, on the left at 1.25 miles. You may descend to Frog Level from here.

Off-Trail Hiking Opportunities

The 4,395-acre Slide Hollow Roadless Area is located just east of the Laurel Fork valley area, outside the Laurel Fork watershed but nearby in the Elk River watershed. The access roads are the same as the directions for reaching the Walnut Mountain Trailhead described above, except that you stop short of the Laurel Fork Trail. The main access to the valley is at 6.1 miles on the Walnut Mountain Road, as described in the trailhead section above; there will be an old gated road on your right. After the gate and several earth ORV barriers, the old road provides access into Slide Hollow on a short 0.1-mile descent to the AT. The AT goes left and right at this point, and Slide Hollow is just on the other side of the AT. You can follow the old road along Flint Ridge or, better, turn right on the AT (east) and follow it down the valley. The AT was relocated in the area in the early 2000s. The AT descends to cross Slide Hollow Creek on a footbridge, then continues above the creek for a short distance down the valley to a camping area signed "Tent Site." The AT then leaves the valley and heads up to the ridge. At this point (UTM 17S 410802E/4009015N) an old logging road, blocked by several trees that have been cut across the trail, angles left, while the AT traverses out the side of the mountain. The USGS topographical map (USGS Elk Park, TN-NC) shows this old road making a large loop down toward the Elk River and then back up Slide Hollow. However, true off-trail experience is required to follow the old road, as it is very much overgrown, especially with rhododendron. The ultimate goal of reaching the beautiful Twisting Falls on the Elk River (shown on the USGS map) is difficult to achieve; two groups exploring for this book turned back before reaching it. Slide Hollow was a favorite area of Arthur Smith (1921–99), one of East TN's most effective environmentalists and one of the people most responsible for the protection of many CNF areas as wilderness and other protected land-use categories.

FUTURE TRAILS

Several new trails are planned in the White Rocks area, with construction to be accomplished sometime after 2003. These trails include the following:

Whoops Trail (FS Trail 36A)

This new trail will generally follow the old White Rocks Road grade. It will be approximately 1.75 miles in length and will connect to the White Rocks Road on both ends, with trail access junctions with the AT, Lacy Trap Trail, and Bitter End Road. Parking will be available at White Rocks Road Gate No. 1. The western access will be just off US 19E. The trail will be for mountain biking and hiking.

Wagner Branch Trail (Berm Trail) (FS Trail 392)

Another new mountain biking and hiking trail is to be built as a spur off FS 303. It will be about 1.0 mile in length and will connect Wagner Branch Road to Laurel Fork Trail. It is sometimes referred to as the Berm Trail. Parking will be provided at Wagner Branch Road gate.

Frog Level Trail (FS Trail 391)

A final trail to be constructed in the White Rocks area will be an approximately 1.5-mile mountain biking and hiking trail that will follow the old Frog Level Road grade and parallel FS 50F. It will connect the Laurel Fork Road (FS 50) with the Laurel Fork Trail. Parking will be available at Walnut Mountain Road or Frog Level Parking Area.

Bitter End Road (FS 303)

This is a gravel road that is often referred to as a "trail," especially for mountain biking. However, it has not been reclassified as a trail by the CNF. It roughly parallels the AT to the north (and below the AT) and provides a good connection for traversing the Laurel Fork valley.

8 Doe River Gorge

(Includes Doe River Gorge Scenic Area)

The Doe River Gorge Scenic Area is a hidden treasure of the CNF. It is located in a valley of the Doe River in Carter County just southeast of Elizabethton, in the Nolichucky/Unaka Ranger District. The scenic area contains 2,652 acres and is to be protected as such by the CNF's 2004 plan revision. Two hikes can be taken into the area. One is on USFS land and follows an old FS road to the top of Fork Mountain. The other, entirely on private land, starts at the Christian Camp and Conference Center, proceeds through an abandoned hand-dug railroad tunnel, a unique keyhole entry into the gorge, and follows the old railroad grade above the Doe River. The tunnel entrance is the most spectacular access to the area and follows a section of abandoned railroad right-of-way passing through three tunnels as it leads you into this secluded pocket of pristine beauty.

The Doe River is a steeply dropping mountain stream with numerous swimming holes between boulder-strewn rapids. The Doe River Trail, which follows the abandoned railroad right-of-way, is very gradual and easy walking. Spectacular views down to the river and up to the exposed rock cliffs and ridges make the hike interesting. The rocks exposed by the river's downcutting are early Cambrian quartzite that has been metamorphosed, leaving the original bedding lines folded in interesting configurations. The vegetation is mixed hardwoods with abundant common wildflowers and a number of rare plant species.

HISTORY

The principal cultural feature of the gorge is the East TN and Western NC (ETWNC) Railroad, on which construction began in 1868. From its rather early history, the line has been referred to as the Tweetsie Railroad. This affectionate name is thought to have been given to the line by young girls riding as passengers on their way to the exclusive camps of western NC; they referred to the train as "the tweetsie" because of the sound of its whistle. Unlike most of the rail lines in the CNF, which were built for lumber hauling, the ETWNC served the iron industry first, connecting the Cranberry Iron Works near Elk Park, NC, with blast furnaces in Johnson City.

After a false start in 1868, construction of the narrow-gauge rail line was begun in 1880 and finished in 1882, from Johnson City to Cranberry, a distance of 34 miles. The five tunnels on the line were manually dug and pass through the rocky spurs that extend from the high ridges to the valley bottom. To speed construction on the line, the tunnels were dug from both ends, with the assistance of many small mules. The animals were lifted over the ridges with block and

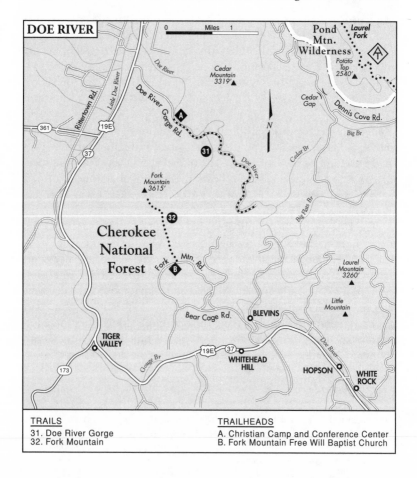

TRAILS	TRAILHEADS
31. Doe River Gorge	A. Christian Camp and Conference Center
32. Fork Mountain	B. Fork Mountain Free Will Baptist Church

tackle, the cliffs on the side of the gorge being too sheer to risk the loss of the mules.

In addition to hauling iron ore, the line also offered passenger service and general freight, including timber, supplied by the numerous small branch lines in the area. The railroad opened a very remote area isolated from the developing communities in the valley, delivering social liberation to its inhabitants through numerous personal services offered by the train crew. From the early years, the line ran excursion trains to picnics, church socials, reunions, baptisms, and other events of importance to the local people.

Operation of the Tweetsie line was extremely informal; there was always time for the train to stop for a visit with the crew. For many years the crew consisted of the same four men, serving as engineer, brakeman, fireman, and conductor, who knew every family along the line and were known to occasionally provide such service as accompanying children to their door while the train waited. Conductor Cy Crumley reminisced, "I guess I've carried everything from a spool of thread to a kitchen range, and stopped at the house to take them in. I liked doing it. The biggest trouble was buying something that didn't suit, then having to take it back and exchange it!"

Heavy rains and flooding were a periodic menace to the lines. In 1901 a cloudburst washed the line out in 39 locations. In August 1904 sections of the track in NC were lost. Maintenance costs and declining use resulted in the closure of many mountain railroads in the first half of the twentieth century. Service on the line through the gorge declined in the early 1940s, down to three round-trips a week from the heyday when trains ran daily, including Sunday. By 1950 a request to abandon the gorge section was filed and granted. Subsequently, the lower part of the line through the gorge was rebuilt and operated by the Doe River Railroad Company as a tourist attraction. However, use was discontinued in 1975. The tracks remain in place, but the old bridge trestles have largely been destroyed or barricaded because of their hazardous conditions.

The CNF's 1988 management plan protected a 1,783-acre Doe River Gorge Scenic Area. The CNF's 2004 plan revision continues the protection of a larger 2,652-acre scenic area.

TRAILHEADS AND MAPS

Christian Camp and Conference Center Trailhead

This trailhead is reached by driving southeast from Elizabethton, TN, on US 19E toward Roan Mountain. At the junction of US 19E and US

321 with TN 67 and TN 91, check the mileage and drive 5.0 miles to the split of US 19E and US 321 in Hampton, TN. Continue on US 19E another 1.1 miles to Doe River Road. The road is marked with a street sign and the Christian Camp's train mailbox, which is labeled "Doe River Gorge." Turn left onto Doe River Road and drive about 0.5 mile. The road dead-ends at the Doe River Christian Camp and Conference Center office and caboose gift shop. The Christian Camp and Conference Center ministry owns the Doe River Gorge trail property. Access procedures may change from time to time, but as of the early 2000s it is necessary to sign a registration and release form before entering the gorge via this trail. The form can be found on a clipboard that hangs at the door of the camp's office. The gorge is surrounded by CNF land that starts at approximately the 2,000-foot contour in the lower gorge.

Fork Mountain Free Will Baptist Church Trailhead

This trailhead is reached by driving southeast of Elizabethton, TN, on US 19E toward Roan Mountain. From the intersection of US 19E with TN 91N (eastside of Elizabethton), drive 10.9 miles to Bear Cage Road (County 5307). Turn left and follow signs to the Fork Mountain Free Will Baptist Church. The road forks at 0.6 mile (marked with a Free Will Baptist Church sign). Take the left fork onto Fork Mountain Road. Another 0.8 mile brings you to the church parking lot. The trailhead is directly across the road from the church. The trailhead is an unmarked old FS road. There are several dirt and gravel driveways in the area, so look for the overgrown metal gate/fence. The trailhead is just to the left of the gate. This rural area is developing with a number of homes and trailers. You are likely to be greeted by dogs barking and residents watching.

TOPOGRAPHIC MAPS: USGS Elizabethton, TN; Iron Mountain Gap, TN. TI Map 783, South Holston and Watauga Lakes, CNF.

TRAIL DESCRIPTIONS

31. DOE RIVER GORGE TRAIL (NO FS OR TI NUMBERS)

LENGTH: 2.4 miles

ELEVATION CHANGE: Low point, 1,960 feet; high point, 2,200 feet

DIFFICULTY: Easy

TRAILHEAD: Christian Camp and Conference Center (start and dead-end)

USE: Hiking

TOPOGRAPHIC MAPS: USGS Elizabethton, TN; Iron Mountain Gap, TN

COMMENTS: This trail is not on USFS land and is not included in the CNF trail system. It follows the abandoned tracks and gravel rail bed of the Tweetsie Railroad. In the late spring (mid-May) the gorge is abloom with dogwood, Carolina rhododendron, purple phacelia, fire pink, Solomon's seal, wild iris, jack-in-the-pulpit, and bleeding heart. The blooming season is considerably delayed due to the lack of sunshine in the steep-sided gorge. In the summer, the stream offers numerous trout-filled fishing and swimming holes. Turtle head, wild grapes, and wild raspberries persist into the fall, with a display of colors offered by the mixed hardwoods. In the winter, icicles hang in abundance from the rocks in the gorge.

DETAILS: The trail begins behind the camp's swimming pool and an abandoned water tower (follow the railroad tracks from the camp office). It immediately enters a rock tunnel, emerging 200 feet later above the Doe River Gorge. At 0.3 mile a side trail on the left leads to a "ropes" challenge course used by the camp. This trail is marked with a "do not enter" sign. Another side trail goes to the left just before the entrance to the second rock tunnel. The side trail is a gentle 0.2-mile hike through a rhododendron thicket to the sandy shores of the Doe River. The views of the gorge walls are spectacular from this vantage point.

The main trail proceeds through the rock tunnel, emerging at 0.9 mile to another excellent viewpoint. A scramble over the rocks at the left puts you atop a cliff overlooking the Doe River, with a view up several hundred feet to the ridgeline atop an impressive exposure of folded rock strata. It is in this area that some of the more unusual plant species in the gorge occur on the cliff base to the right of the tracks.

A rockslide marks the 1.5-mile point. At 2.3 miles the river diverges from the track at a broad open clearing. The trail continues through a narrow cut another 0.1 mile, ending at 2.4 miles at a bridge trestle crossing of the Doe River. The bridge, high above the river, is rotting and dangerous. Barely visible on the other side of the trestle is a third rock tunnel, which is followed immediately by a second and less sound bridge crossing of the river. Crossing of either bridge is prohibited by posted signs and is inadvisable due to the hazardous condition of both the structures and the track bed.

Hikers in old railroad tunnel along Doe River Trail. Photograph by Will Skelton.

32. FORK MOUNTAIN TRAIL (NO FS OR TI TRAIL NUMBERS)

LENGTH: 1.5 miles

ELEVATION CHANGE: Low point, 2,600 feet; high point, 3,615 feet

DIFFICULTY: Moderate

TRAILHEAD: Fork Mountain Free Will Baptist Church (start and dead-end)

USE: Hiking

TOPOGRAPHIC MAPS: USGS Elizabethton, TN; Iron Mountain Gap, TN

COMMENTS: This trail is unmarked and is not included in the CNF trail system. The views are good only in late fall, winter, and early spring, when leaves are off the trees. Hiking during the summer in this area is a muggy, "snaky" experience. Locals ride ORV's through the area and there are a number of trails that lead nowhere at the base of the mountain.

DETAILS: The road (trail) heads north and passes behind a small house on the right as it enters FS land. At a little less than 0.1 mile the trail forks, bear to the right. At 0.3 mile the road forks in several directions. Take the middle fork, which follows alongside an area that was clear-cut in the late 1970s and is now regenerating in maple and sourwood. The road winds upward for almost a mile through an older forested area that was likely last harvested in the 1930s. The top of the first peak is reached at 1.2 miles with a vehicle turnaround on the left. The elevation at this point is 3,560 feet. The road turns into a trail and gradually descends. The trail reaches 1.3 miles at a point directly below the saddle between the two peaks of Fork Mountain (on the left). Hike up the side of the mountain (0.1 mile) to the ridgetop using the saddle as a guide. There is no visible trail and the climb is steep but not difficult.

Turn right at the ridgetop onto a faint path. The path ascends steeply through mountain laurel and rock outcrops to the top of Fork Mountain at 1.5 miles. The elevation is 3,615 feet. In the winter when the leaves are down there are decent views in all directions. To the north, the lip of the Doe River Gorge is seen, and to the south Strawberry Mountain dominates.

9 Highlands of Roan

(Includes Highlands of Roan Scenic Area)

The Highlands of Roan is the spectacular range of mountains along the TN-NC state line from US 19E on the east to near NC 226/TN 107 on the west. Most of the area is above 4,000 feet in elevation, and many of the mountaintops and ridges between 5,400 feet and 6,100 feet are grassy balds. For over 17 of its 2,100 miles, the AT traverses the Highlands of Roan, which many consider to be one of the most

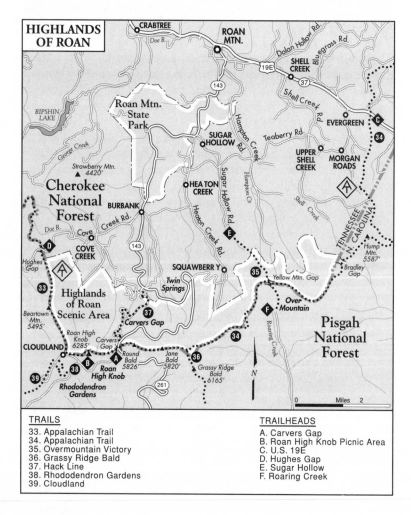

HIGHLANDS OF ROAN

TRAILS
33. Appalachian Trail
34. Appalachian Trail
35. Overmountain Victory
36. Grassy Ridge Bald
37. Hack Line
38. Rhododendron Gardens
39. Cloudland

TRAILHEADS
A. Carvers Gap
B. Roan High Knob Picnic Area
C. U.S. 19E
D. Hughes Gap
E. Sugar Hollow
F. Roaring Creek

rewarding portions of the entire AT. The USFS in its 1974 Composite Plan for the Highlands of Roan stated: "The Highlands of Roan present an exceptional recreational opportunity for the Appalachian Trail hiker to experience the most extensive area of mountain balds on the entire 2,000 miles of the Trail. . . . There is no other area . . . that offers such extensive panoramic views of the high mountain country of the southern Appalachians. Unique is not, at least in this sense, misleading."

The Highlands of Roan is a vast high country with great balds that undulate in every direction and are the most extensive in the southern Appalachians. The balds are treeless areas of sedges, grasses, and wildflowers covering several hundred acres along rounded ridges and peaks. Wild yet tranquil, rugged yet fragile, this place is unlike any other. Winds, averaging 25 miles per hour year-round, ripple the sedges and hair grass like seaweed in a great tide. Great rocks, weathered and timeworn into strange and fascinating shapes, jut from the knee-deep grasses. Wind-wracked, rocky crags edge the balds. Ancient many-colored lichens, centuries old, creep across the rocks at the rate of only a quarter of an inch every century.

In season, wildflowers carpet the trails. Acres of white-fringed phacelia cover the ground in May, accented with splotches of may apples, white and purple violets, trout lilies, and many other early spring flowers.

Gnarled tree on the open balds of the Highlands of Roan. Photograph by Roger Jenkins.

A month later the balds streak yellow and red with hawkweed, rag-wort, and other sun-loving flowers.

Scattered along the edges of the meadows, the heath shrubs produce great bursts of color. The flame azaleas range from pale lemon yellow to deep, brilliant, sunburst orange, and the Catawba rhododendron, purplish-pink in color, light up 600 acres along the mountain each June. These natural but gardenlike displays occur throughout the area, especially at the western end, where you can find the best displays of Catawba rhododendron in the world.

The Highlands of Roan are notable for such biotic diversity. More than 300 species of plants are found there, including the rare Gray's lily. From a botanist's perspective, the Roan Mountain massif is superlative because of the outstanding diversity of plant species and the exceptional quality and variety of plant communities found there. In an ecological evaluation of the area for the NPS in 1981, L. L. Gaddy, consulting biologist, wrote, "The Roan Mountain massif is, without doubt, nationally significant."

Gaddy reported that there are more nationally or regionally ranked rare species on the Roan massif than at any other site in the high mountains of the southern Appalachians, which would include the GSMNP, an area noted for its ecological diversity. An updated version of Gaddy's listing of the rare plants of Roan shows that there are 54 currently recognized rare plant species on the massif, including the Blue Ridge goldenrod, Roan Mountain bluet, and spreading avens.

The northern hardwood forests surrounding the balds are among the best examples of this community type anywhere in the Blue Ridge. One yellow birch tree in this forest is over 385 years old. At the edge of the balds, dwarf beeches, only 12 inches in diameter, are as old as 250 years. A mature stand of table-mountain pine, a southern Appalachian endemic, and the dwarfed yellow buckeye, an "orchard" of which is in one of the gaps, are other unique forest species there.

The Highlands also has varied and abundant wildlife, which can be attributed to its exceptional habitat diversity, a product of latitude, altitude, physiography, vegetation, and even history. The Roan massif is a vast, high-altitude island surrounded and isolated by low and narrow valleys and rolling hills. Because its slopes vary in steepness, soils, orientation, and drainage, it supports a mosaic of vegetation types and microhabitats, and these are of sufficient total area to sustain substantial animal populations. The area's ice-age history transformed the 18-mile ridge into a faunal melting pot of northern, southern, and local animals. These factors, helped by the low level of human activities, have created living space for a wide array of animal species.

A few species, such as the New England cottontail and bog lemming, are at or near their southern limits and may be relics of a past ice age. Others, like the opossum and southern flying squirrel, are warm-climate species that periodically invade the upper slopes. Some species are confined to one type of habitat on a permanent or seasonal basis. For example, meadow mice inhabit the grass balds, a habitat used by the rare snow bunting only in winter. Other species occupy the adjacent parts of two vegetation zones; the threatened northern flying squirrel frequents the lower spruce-fir and upper northern hardwood forests. Still other animals (shrews, jumping mice, salamanders, and many invertebrates) require certain microhabitats within a zone to provide special foods or refuges. Finally, active carnivores (least weasels, spotted skunks), large species (bear, bobcats, and foxes), and fliers with special needs (owls, bats, hummingbirds) must range widely over the mountain and, in fact, would probably not survive if confined to a single area.

The area is located in Carter County, TN, and Avery and Mitchell counties, NC, southeast of the town of Roan Mountain, TN. The CNF's 2004 plan revision places 4,601 acres of the area in a special management category for bald management (herein called a "scenic area"). Those management guidelines provide for maintaining the grassy balds but otherwise do not permit timber harvesting and road building. The NC side of the Highlands of Roan, located in the Pisgah NF, has similar management plan protections. Substantial additional private lands in the area are at risk of development. The Southern Appalachian Highlands Conservancy (http://www.appalachian.org), based in Asheville, NC, was formed to help protect the Highlands of Roan from development. Although the Highlands of Roan remain its "flagship project," the conservancy later expanded its efforts to include other southern Appalachian mountains. The Conservancy and other land trusts have acquired in excess of 15,000 acres in the Highlands of Roan area, on which they hold conservation easements.

HISTORY

Recorded history of the area goes back to at least the 1770s, when the Overmountain Men mustered at Sycamore Shoals (now Elizabethton, TN) and marched across the Highlands through Yellow Mountain Gap to help the North Carolinians defeat the British at King's Mountain, a turning point of the Revolutionary War. The Overmountain Victory National Historic Trail has been designated along this route, crossing the Highlands of Roan near its center.

Throughout the nineteenth century, botanists from around the world visited the Highlands in their studies of Appalachian flora. Elisha Mitchell, for whom the East's highest mountain is named, worked in the area. Sierra Club founder John Muir visited the area and wrote of his 1898 trip to the Cloudland Hotel on Roan High Knob: "We drove through the most beautiful deciduous forest I ever saw. All the landscapes in every direction are made up of mountains, a billowing sea of them without bounds as far as one can look."

Gen. John T. Wilder, an industrialist and Civil War hero, organized the Roan Iron Company in the area in 1867. A decade later, in 1877, he built a 20-room spruce log structure on the top of Roan High Knob. Almost another decade later, in 1885, he built the three-story Cloudland Hotel nearby. It was located at an elevation of over 6,200 feet and was probably the highest human residence east of the Rockies. The advertisements for the hotel exclaimed: "Come up out of the sultry plains to the Land of the Sky—magnificent views above the clouds where the rivers are born—a most extended prospect of 50,000 square miles in seven different states—one hundred mountain tops over 4,000 feet high, in sight." Room and board were $2 per day or $10 per week. Access to the hotel was by horse-drawn carriages up the extremely narrow and steep "Hack Line Road" from the valley below; the current Hack Line Trail generally follows the route of the road (see below). An interesting method was used to get materials to this high mountain site. Railroad tracks were laid from the valleys in NC and TN up to the hotel site; railroad cars were then connected by cable and one car was filled to act as a counterbalance to pull the other car up to the site; the process was then reversed. The hotel initially enjoyed success, but by the turn of the century it was declining and was abandoned by 1910. The hotel was thereafter dismembered by looters and weather, and only the stone foundations remain. Some timber harvesting followed. With USFS acquisition of much of the mountain, in recent decades the area has been increasingly patronized by day visitors who enjoy the rhododendron and views.

In the mid-1960s, the USFS, cooperating with the Appalachian Trail Conference, initiated an acquisition program in the area. A central core has to date been protected as public lands, especially along the AT Corridor, but significant acres remain unprotected. The Southern Appalachian Highlands Conservancy, a regional private land trust, is leading current efforts to complete the mountain's protection and to assure management excellence. The USFS has created special management categories for the Highlands in both TN and NC, essentially creating a scenic/scientific area that will be free from timber harvesting.

The CNF stated in its 1988 management plan for the area: "This management area on Roan Mountain contains some of the most unique flora and fauna in the Eastern United States. Much national attention has been directed to identifying and classifying these unique features as well as being recognized for its outstanding scenic qualities of high mountain balds, rhododendron gardens, and spruce-fir timber types. This area is unsuitable for timber production."

The CNF's 1988 management plan protected a 2,867-acre Highlands of Roan Scenic Area. The CNF's 2004 plan revision continues the protection of a larger 4,601-acre scenic area.

TRAILHEADS AND MAPS

Carvers Gap and Roan High Knob Picnic Area Trailheads

Follow TN 143 south from the intersection of US 19E and TN 143 in Roan Mountain, TN, for 12.7 miles to an obvious gap (UTM 17S 400024E/3996117N). At that point there will be "NC State Line" and "Mitchell County" signs on TN 143 and a USFS sign pointing to the right for the Roan Mountain Gardens. There is a small parking lot, picnic area, and primitive restrooms. The paved road to the right leads to the natural concentrations of Catawba rhododendron on the mountains to the west and Roan High Knob Picnic Area, another trailhead for this section of the AT. The road to Roan High Knob and the Gardens and Cloudland Trail is open from April to November, and a fee station is located about 1.7 miles up this road, near the site of the former Cloudland Hotel.

The AT crosses TN 143 in the gap. To the west the trail to Hughes Gap enters the forest while to the east the AT begins an ascent of the huge grassy Round Bald. Carvers Gap may also be approached from the NC side by following NC 261 14.0 miles north of Bakersville, NC.

US 19E Trailhead

Follow US 19E 3.85 miles east from the junction of US 19E and TN 143 in Roan Mountain, TN. The trailhead (UTM 17S 409056E/4003862N), which is easily missed, is located shortly after a highway passing lane begins, on the right in a break in the metal guardrail. Several white blazes mark the small parking area. Recurring vandalism of vehicles continues to be a problem at this trailhead and has only gotten worse in the last decade. WE DO NOT RECOMMEND THAT YOU LEAVE A CAR OVERNIGHT ANYWHERE NEAR THIS TRAILHEAD. Any recommendation for a particular shuttle service may be out of date by the time you read this. Instead, contact the Appalachian Trail Conference (http://www. appalchiantrail.org) or call and ask local businesses or the Roan Mountain State Park Headquarters as to suggestions for current shuttle services. From NC the trailhead is on the left 3.0 miles west from the junction of US 19E and NC 194 north in Elk Park, NC; it is also 0.9 mile west of the TN-NC state line.

Hughes Gap Trailhead

From Roan Mountain, TN, follow TN 143 south from the junction of TN 143 and US 19E for 5.3 miles. Turn right (west) on County 2680, Cove Creek Road (no sign), at the signs for Calvary Baptist and Cove Creek Presbyterian churches. Immediately cross a bridge and follow a paved road upward for 3.1 miles to an obvious gap marked by "NC State Line" and "Mitchell County" signs. The AT trailhead is on the left. Parking is limited, and overnight parking is not recommended. Hughes Gap may also be approached from Bakersville, NC. Drive north from Bakersville on NC 226 for 12.1 miles to Buladean, NC. Turn right on paved NC 1330 (Hughes Gap Road) and drive 4.4 miles to Hughes Gap (the uppermost 1.1 miles is gravel but in good shape).

Sugar Hollow Trailhead

From the junction of US 19E and TN 143 in Roan Mountain, TN, follow TN 143 south for 2.3 miles. Turn left on paved and narrow Sugar Hollow Road; this road is not signed, but there is a sign for Sugar Hollow F. W. B. Church. Caution: a second road turns left off TN 143 just 0.1 mile farther and is Heaton Creek Road. Proceed 2.3 miles on Sugar Hollow Road to the trailhead at its upper end, opposite the Shell residence. If possible, check at the house for parking suggestions, as space is limited. Avoid taking up all of the turning space to the right of the pavement and below a garage; a school bus needs this space for turning. Also do not block the gravel private road extending beyond the pavement; other residences use this road for access. The route proceeds up this gravel road, but you will not feel like you are on an actual trail until after the way passes a small pond and goes through a fence line.

Roaring Creek Trailhead

Find the junction of paved NC 1132 (Roaring Creek Road) and US 19E 3.0 miles north of Plumtree, NC, and 4.5 miles south of Minneapolis,

NC, on US 19E. At the intersection are McCoury's Rock F. W. Baptist Church and a historical marker commemorating the Overmountain Men's march. Follow narrow and winding NC 1132 for 2.2 miles to its end at a Y intersection where NC 1200 (Old Roaring Creek Road) turns right and NC 1133 (Jerry's Creek Road) turns left. Turn right and follow NC 1200 up the valley. At 3.5 miles NC 1200 ends and the gravel, unsigned FS 5545 continues. Both NC 1200 and FS 5545 are narrow. Notice at 3.95 miles, on the left, a vandalized metal plaque on a boulder commemorating the Overmountain Men. The trailhead is reached at 4.6 miles at a USFS gate on FS 5545. There is parking for several vehicles, and the trail proceeds up the road behind the gate.

TOPOGRAPHIC MAPS: USGS White Rocks Mountain, TN-NC; Carvers Gap, NC-TN; Bakersville, NC; Iron Mountain Gap, TN-NC. TI Map 783, South Holston and Watauga Lakes, CNF.

Trail Descriptions

33. APPALACHIAN TRAIL (CARVERS GAP TO HUGHES GAP) (FS TRAIL 1, TI TRAIL 1)

LENGTH: 4.9 miles

ELEVATION CHANGE: Low point, 4,040 feet; high point, 6,150 feet

DIFFICULTY: Moderate

TRAILHEADS: Carvers Gap (start), Hughes Gap (end), and Roan High Knob Picnic Area

TRAIL CONNECTIONS: AT north of Carvers Gap

USE: Hiking

COMMENTS: The AT is well marked with white blazes and offers some fine opportunities to hike through real spruce-fir forest. In addition to the beginning and ending trailheads, this section of the AT is also accessible from two parking lots near the Cloudland Hotel site on the Roan Mountain Gardens Road. Avoid leaving your car near Hughes Gap overnight. Vandalism continues to be a problem.

DETAILS: The trail begins at the southeast corner of the Carvers Gap parking lot, beside an information shelter. It proceeds inside a log fence, with the Roan Mountain Gardens Road on the other side. After a short distance the trail passes an AT mileage sign. The trail then enters a dense fir and spruce forest and climbs steeply on an eroded trail. At 0.15 mile the trail turns right on an old road, now grassy, that comes up from the left. The trail proceeds up an easy incline on a trail that is wide and clear and has a good surface. At 0.25 mile the first of several wet-weather streams is crossed. Such streams sometimes run in the trail. At 0.3 mile is the first of six switchbacks, which provide the easy grade up the mountain. Ferns are frequent beside the trail. The trees are mainly evergreens, predominantly Fraser or balsam fir and some red spruce (the last spruce and fir between this area and New England except for Mount Rogers National Recreation Area and Shenandoah National Park). A fair number of dead trees reflect possible acid rain and insect problems.

At 1.1 miles the trail reaches the top of a ridge and then proceeds along the southeast and then northeast sides of the ridge. A partially clear opening to the right at 1.17 miles allows views out over the valley below. The side-trail to the Roan High Knob AT Shelter, reflected by a wooden sign, is reached at 1.3 miles; the shelter is 0.1 mile to the left. The shelter is an old fire warden's cabin with a large downstairs room and upstairs sleeping loft. Water from a pipe can be found 50 feet below the shelter on a blue-blazed trail. The shelter is the highest on the entire AT, at 6,285 feet.

Past the shelter the trail inclines down the north side of the ridge, heading toward Tool House Gap. A series of rock outcrops is passed at 1.55 miles, and the trail goes through a small open grassy area at 1.6 miles. At this point the Roan Mountain Gardens Road is just below the trail and cars can be heard. The trail passes to the right of a small gravel parking lot at 1.7 miles; simply go by the lot and reenter the forest. Just behind the lot at 1.8 miles the trail goes around a sturdy 14-foot chimney that remains from an old cabin. The trail then proceeds up a ridge and is quite open.

At 1.9 miles the trail reaches a large, open grassy area and turns sharply to the right. A short walk to the left across the grassy area leads to the Roan High Knob Picnic Area, an alternate trailhead. At the edge of the grassy area is a historical marker for the site of the former Cloudland Hotel at 6,150 feet. The hotel is described in more detail in the history section above. The trail proceeds to the north of the hotel site, past a series of campfire rings, and at 1.93 miles climbs steeply up to the hotel site and then to the right across its back side. At 1.96 miles the trail begins a long descent toward Hughes Gap. This less used section of the trail is more narrow and closed-in by vegetation. It passes through a principally deciduous, rather than evergreen, forest. The route is often steep and is generally down a ridge where lush grass appears, possibly indicating the location of a former bald.

At 2.1 miles the trail passes around several rugged outcrops and continues the descent. Several slick rocks are crossed at 2.28 miles. A one-tent campsite, no water, is at 2.6 miles. Many ferns and blackberries are located in this section. The trail levels off in Ash Gap at 2.8 miles, providing a good large campsite, with open grassy forest. Water is located a short distance to the left. The trail continues along the ridgetop, inclining slightly upward at first and then becoming more level. After passing around a large rounded rock at 3.2 miles, the trail reaches the top of a knoll known as Beartown Mountain, which offers good views when the leaves are off the trees. The trail then continues to descend along a narrow ridge to a possible small campsite in a grassy area at 3.27 miles. A steep descent follows, at a rate of about 1,000 feet per mile.

Several large rocks are passed at 3.3 miles, and at 3.5 miles a short trail to the left leads to a large, picturesque beech tree and views of the valley below. The trail then continues steeply down through second-growth beech forest with a few level areas and several large beech trees. At 4.0 miles the trail turns left to the side of the ridge and begins a series of switchbacks. The forest changes to predominant oak at around 4.1 miles and levels off several times. At 4.4 miles the trail returns to the ridge and cuts to the right side through an open oak forest. Several switchbacks follow; at 4.7 miles the trail continues the switchbacks on an old road. At 4.9 miles the trail ends at a paved road at Hughes Gap. Note that if reversing the route described, an ORV track goes straight up the mountainside at Hughes Gap, while the AT angles off to the left and upward.

34. APPALACHIAN TRAIL (CARVERS GAP TO US 19E SECTION) (FS TRAIL 1, TI TRAIL 1)

LENGTH: 13.54 miles

ELEVATION CHANGE: Low point, 2,900 feet; high point, 5,900 feet

DIFFICULTY: Moderate

TRAILHEADS: Carvers Gap (start) and US 19E (end)

TRAIL CONNECTIONS: Grassy Ridge Bald Trail and Overmountain Victory National Historic Trail

USE: Hiking

TOPOGRAPHIC MAPS: USGS Carvers Gap, TN-NC; White Rocks Mountain, TN-NC

COMMENTS: This trail is one of the most spectacular hikes described in this book. The combination of magnificent vistas, open grassy balds, unusual vegetation, and marvelous campsites makes this traverse of the spine of the Appalachians from Carvers Gap to US 19E a classic. However, the steep ascents and descents, combined with sometimes difficult footing, make this not a trip for the novice backpacker. The route is described from south to north, the easier direction, and is often hiked as a two-day backpack. The one-way trip requires a shuttle; check with local businesses to see who might provide such a service, but *do not leave your car parked overnight at the US 19E terminus of this hike.*

DETAILS: The trail starts by going through a wooden fence at the western base of Round Bald. The trail switchbacks a bit and at 0.16 miles enters a wonderful patch of high elevation evergreen forest. Pause a bit and drink in the smells and delicate images all around. This may be the most intimate part of this stretch of trail. After a couple more switchbacks, you will break out into the open and reach the summit of Round Bald (5,826 feet) at 0.63 miles. Another 0.1 mile of level walking provides superb views of Grassy Ridge Bald and Big Hump Mountain, the latter being a day's walk away. For the next 1.3 miles, the vistas are nearly overwhelming. At 0.8 mile, begin a moderate descent and notice the interesting moss and lichen growing in patches, with pink rounded tops. Huckleberry bushes can be seen nearby. At 1.0 mile, end the descent at Engine Gap, amidst carpets of wildflowers. At 1.16 miles, begin the ascent of Jane Bald, topping out at 1.27 miles at a large rock formation. The trail starts another descent at 1.32 miles, arriving at a low saddle at 1.46 miles. A moderate ascent starts at 1.6 miles, and the junction with the Grassy Ridge Bald Trail is reached at 1.81 miles (UTM 17S 402292E/3995977N). This side trip is separately described and is well worth the short climb.

At its junction with the Grassy Ridge Bald Trail, the AT forks left and traverses around the north side of Grassy Ridge Bald, encountering the first of many springs at 1.9 miles. At 2.0 miles, the trail passes through a tunnel of rhododendrons, ferns, and beech trees. Following a very slight uphill stretch, the trail begins a steep descent of the northeast spur of Grassy Ridge Bald through deep woods. Watch your footing. There is a small sheltered campsite at 2.38 miles, but you would have to carry water from the springs previously described. The descent moderates somewhat at 2.86 miles, arriving at the Roan Highlands AT Trail Shelter (5,050 feet) at 3.24 miles. This wooden shelter accommodates six. There is water about 250 yards down a small side trail to the south. At 3.34 miles, following a moderate ascent through somewhat open terrain, there is a classic view of the east face of Grassy Ridge. Around mid-June this is seen as being pink from the blooming rhododendron. But do not miss the wild strawberries growing at your feet. And keep an eye out for the rare Gray's lily. As this area has become more protected, this 30-inch-high, deep orange flower is making a strong comeback. The trail tops out at 3.45 miles, then enters woods and begins a moderate descent. At 4.06 miles, the trail flattens out. Over the next 0.8 mile, the trail undulates. At 4.9 miles, it reaches

Lone backpacker makes her way through head-high Cow Parsnips along the Appalachian Trail in the Highlands of Roan. Photograph by Roger Jenkins.

a small knoll with space for three tents. At times, the cow parsnip can be well over the tallest hiker's head. After a short descent, Yellow Mountain Gap is reached at 5.14 miles. The Overmountain Victory National Historical Trail crosses the AT in this gap and is separately described. There is a small campsite with potential, but not certain, water about 300 yards down a side trail to the left (north). There is also usually water at 0.1 mile on a side trail to the right (south). To the immediate south and west is a barnlike structure used as a trail shelter. Known as the Overmountain Shelter or Yellow Mountain Barn, it accommodates 20 or more. It is not visible from the trail unless you get out into the field to the south.

At 5.2 miles, the trail leaves the woods, enters an open meadow, and begins a steep ascent. At 6.17 miles, an old fence stile is reached. Note that the trail turns left, crosses the fence line, and leaves the old roadbed. After passing by some woods on the left, the trail breaks out into the open. There are only 150 feet of climbing left to the summit of Little Hump Mountain. At 6.74 miles the summit, one of the most spectacular campsites on the TN-NC state line, is reached. There is room for numerous tents, the sunsets are magnificent, and the views in every direction make you feel like you are flying. But be mindful of the exposure. With wind-driven rain and fog, it can be an intimidating place. There are some more sheltered spots on the south side of the bald near some small beech trees. The easiest route to water is to follow the path that parallels the tree line on the south side of the bald. It descends about 130 feet, curls around to the north, enters the woods, and follows an old road grade as it further descends before crossing a nice spring. The total distance amounts to a 15-minute stroll. Water can also be found near the AT, farther along the trail.

At 6.8 miles, the trail begins a very steep and somewhat difficult descent in woods, passing a small clearing at 6.92 miles. Descending more moderately, the trail enters woods at 7.0 miles. Here is a small campsite, and water can be found on the old road grade to the south about 200 yards. At 7.15 miles, there is a small side trail to some water (sign on the tree) to the right. At 7.2 miles, the trail enters open meadows with trees, and Bradley Gap is reached at 7.53 miles. For the next 1.75 miles, the views are even more outstanding. Take a deep breath and begin the steep, 600 foot climb of Big Hump Mountain. Frequent rest stops can be easily justified on the basis of the increasingly grander views. Note, however, that dense fog is frequently encountered on this stretch, and very close attention to the white blazes marking the AT is critical. It is easy to lose your way. Near the summit of Big Hump Mountain (8.38 miles), the trail takes a very sharp right-hand turn, reaching the summit at 8.42 miles (5,587 feet). Relax and pretend you are Julie Andrews in *The Sound of Music*. The settlements nestled in the valleys have a postcard quality.

As the trail begins a moderate descent of the southeast spine of Big Hump Mountain, carpets of yellow wildflowers in June make this an unforgettable experience. Pay attention in fog at 9.18 miles, as the trail leaves the main ridge, turns left, and crosses open fields before entering woods at 9.3 miles. Here the trail begins a shallow traversing descent of the northeast face of Big Hump Mountain on a frustratingly rocky section of trail. At 10.2 miles, the trail crosses a spring, the first high-quality water actually crossing the trail for the last 8.0 miles. At 10.67 miles, the edge of a steep meadow is reached, and the trail arrives at Doll Flats at 10.83 miles. Here is good camping among shade trees and large rocks, with a spring nearby. At 10.86 miles, the AT crosses an old fence line. The aforementioned spring can be found by turning left, going about 50 yards, turning right, and following the old roadbed about 200 yards. A small side trail leaves the roadbed to the right, and a spring can be heard gurgling in the woods. The AT bears slightly right at the fence line and begins a descent that at times can be very steep and slippery. At 11.21 miles, there is a side trail leading 75 feet to the left to a fine, unobstructed view of the valley. At 11.33 miles, the first of many switchbacks is reached as the trail zigzags down to lose elevation as fast as possible. At 11.83 miles, cross a fence line. At 12.02 miles, cross a small field. At 12.32 miles, the trail merges with an old roadbed and turns very sharply left. After a sharp turn to the right, the roadbed narrows to the width of a path (12.42 miles). At 12.64 miles, the trail takes a sharp left near a small streambed, passes a side trail on the right to the site of an old mine, and reaches the Apple House AT Trail Shelter at 12.98 miles. This shelter was originally used to store explosives for a quarry in the hollow below as well as tools for nearby orchards. At 13.37 miles, the trail enters a small field, crosses a small bridge at 13.41 miles, and reaches the US 19E Trailhead at 13.54 miles.

35. OVERMOUNTAIN VICTORY NATIONAL HISTORIC TRAIL (FS TRAIL 193/308, TI TRAIL 30)

LENGTH: 2.6 miles

ELEVATION CHANGE: Low point, 3,250 feet; high point, 4,617 feet

DIFFICULTY: Moderate

TRAILHEADS: Sugar Hollow Creek (start) and Roaring Creek (end)

TRAIL CONNECTIONS: AT

USE: Equestrian, hiking

TOPOGRAPHIC MAPS: USGS Carvers Gap, TN-NC; White Rocks Mountain, TN-NC

COMMENTS: Only the portion of this trail that passes through the area is described. It is described from the north (TN) to the south (NC). The entire trail extends for approximately 315 miles from Craig's Meadow in Abingdon, VA, to the King's Mountain National Battlefield in SC and is, for most of its distance, a motor vehicle route. About 12 miles are hiking trail, including the portion through the Highlands. The frontiersmen who answered the call to battle camped in the Highlands on the way to King's Mountain. The battle of King's Mountain resulted in the death of British Maj. Patrick Ferguson on October 7, 1780, and the defeat of his army, a turning point in the Revolutionary War. The trail offers an exit to/entry from civilization, but only history buffs are likely to "really" enjoy the steep grade through ordinary woods. Also, note that blazes are very spotty on the northern half of the trail, and the TI map *incorrectly* shows the trail's northern terminus on the east side of Hampton Creek Ridge. Actually, the trail starts on the western side of the ridge in the upper drainage of Sugar Hollow Creek.

DETAILS: Proceed up the private gravel road from the trailhead. At 0.12 mile there is water at a spring box overflow on the left and a picnic table/shelter that the Shells welcome hikers to use, although permission should be requested. Proceed through a road-width gate in a white board fence and pass a small pond on the right. At 0.19 mile, go through another trail-width gate in a woven wire fence. At this point (UTM 17S 403968E/4000000N) the trail leaves private land and enters protected lands, first owned by the Southern Appalachian Highlands Conservancy and then the USFS. The trail continues up an old farm road in rapidly growing young trees. A stream is soon crossed. At 0.39 mile another stream is crossed at a large boulder on the left. Pay close attention, as there are numerous old roads leading off in other directions. The topographical map shows the trail going through open country, but in fact the trail is in the woods from the start. At about 0.75 miles, the trail leaves the immediate vicinity of the headwaters of Sugar Hollow Creek and, climbing at the same 700-plus feet per mile grade, heads for the crest of Hampton Creek Ridge.

At 0.88 mile the trail crosses to the left through a break in an old fence line. A faint unmarked side trail continues straight up the ridgeline; care should be taken not to follow it. The trail continues along the left (east) side of the ridge and is fairly level. The trail is now in the watershed of the westernmost fork of Hampton Creek. There are traces of an old road or trail a short way down the ridge, roughly paralleling the trail. At 1.23 miles the trail enters an interesting "rock garden" and seepage area as it curves left across a cove drainage system. There is poor footing at this point, and the rocks can be slippery. A local resident believes that the jumble of rocks at this point was caused by the tremendous flood of May 20–23, 1901. At 1.34 miles, leave the rock garden and seepage area and continue steeply uphill.

At 1.4 miles, on the ridgeline, the trail joins the old cross-mountain Yellow Mountain Road at its uppermost switchback and makes a sharp turn to the right (UTM 17S 405210E/3998780N). The trail continues up the old road, with the road section not being blazed. At 1.62 miles, there is often—but not always—water on the left at the lower end of a steel culvert pipe under the road. Farther up, an earth mound across the road was constructed by the USFS to discourage motorized vehicles. Almost immediately thereafter, at 1.74 miles, the trail leaves the road, bearing slightly left into the woods. Again the trail becomes blazed, with the trail being relocated through the woods to avoid a series of trees felled across the road to block motorized vehicles. At 1.8 miles leave the woods and reenter the road, continuing upward.

At 1.82 miles, the trail reaches historic Yellow Mountain Gap and intersects with the AT. This is the high point of the trail, and there is a small campsite just to the left on the AT. Water may usually be found 0.1 mile south on the trail. The Overmountain Men on their march to King's Mountain are said to have camped around this gap on September 27, 1780. That night was cold, and the ground was covered with snow that was "shoemouth deep." One militiaman is said to have frozen to death; his grave may be nearby. The Yellow Mountain Road originally crossed the mountain at this point but is no longer maintained as a road. This was also the location of an early migration route from western NC to eastern TN known as "Bright's Trace."

Beyond the AT the trail passes into North Carolina and becomes Trail 308. It goes through an old fencerow and enters a field where there is a sign and a trail junction. To the right is a blue-blazed trail leading to the Overmountain Shelter (Yellow Mountain Barn), a converted barn with a loft for sleeping and cooking on the ground floor. A short distance down this side trail, there is water on the left from a small pipe; however, this source can fail in droughts.

The Overmountain Victory Trail heads across the field following yellow blazes. It soon starts downhill on an overgrown wagon track with woods on the right and a bank on the left. As the trail begins to descend more steeply, the path becomes more of a rocky road. A water source is passed on the right, although a large downed tree hampers access. The trail breaks out of the woods into a field (2.4 miles) where there is a double-blazed turn to the left. The trail crosses between a lower and an upper field for a short distance before turning sharply right back onto a distinct road. At this point a creek comes in from the left. The trail follows the stream closely as it drops rather steeply to its terminus at a gate. (Note: the TI map incorrectly shows the trail being away from the creek.) At 2.6 miles, FS 5545 is beyond the gate and there is parking for a few vehicles.

36. GRASSY RIDGE BALD (NO FS OR TI TRAIL NUMBERS)

LENGTH: 0.8 mile

ELEVATION CHANGE: Low point, 5,900 feet; high point, 6,200 feet

DIFFICULTY: Easy

TRAILHEAD: AT (1.81 miles east of Carvers Gap) (start and dead-end)

USE: Hiking

TOPOGRAPHIC MAPS: Carvers Gap, TN-NC

COMMENTS: This spectacular spur trail is a great way to extend a day hike across the high balds of the Roan Highlands. Note that it is dead-end trail, ending in a saddle on the ridge. Experienced cross-country hikers may want to explore further but should note that much of Grassy Ridge is privately owned.

DETAILS: The beginning of the trail is reached by hiking east (northbound) on the AT, 1.81 miles from the Carvers Gap Trailhead. The trail begins in a nice, grassy area but quickly becomes narrow and rutted, with many rocks underfoot. The views are so distracting that it is hard to pay attention to the placement of your feet. At 0.21 mile, there are dense rhododendron on both sides of the trail. At 0.3 mile, the trail reaches a false summit in open, nearly tundralike surroundings at about 6,100 feet. The true summit (6,200 feet) of Grassy Ridge is reached at 0.53 mile. Stop for a moment, look around, and savor the 360-degree views. You will truly feel like you are on top of the world. Nearby is a plaque in memory of Cornelius Peake, who used to own most of this ridge. At 0.61 mile, the trail begins an easy descent to a saddle at 0.79 mile (6,070 feet), where the trail ends for purposes of this book. Here is a very good, albeit exposed and sometimes windy, campsite. Water can be found about 100 yards down a path on the east side of the saddle. Consider this a stoves-only camp, as dead vegetation is quite sparse. Beyond the saddle to the south, a path leads out the right (west) side of the ridge through rhododendron bushes and along a series of rocky outcrops to a wonderful overlook at the end of the ridge. A few secluded campsites are located along the path.

37. HACK LINE ROAD TRAIL (FS 53281; NO TI NUMBER)

LENGTH: 3.6 miles

ELEVATION CHANGE: Low point, 3,830 feet; high point, 5,430 feet

DIFFICULTY: Easy (downhill)

TRAILHEADS: Carvers Gap (start) and TN 143 (end)

USE: Hiking, equestrian, mountain bike

TOPOGRAPHIC MAP: USGS Carvers Gap, TN-NC

COMMENTS: The Hack Line Road Trail follows the former road that leads to the former Cloudland Hotel located near Roan High Knob. Built in the 1870s, it was the route followed by buggies (hacks) hauling guests to the rustic but elegant hotel. Even John Muir rode to the top of Roan High Knob this way. With the demise of the hotel in 1910, the road was converted into a toll road in 1931 and was used by cars. You can tell this route did not start out as a hiking trail: when looking at an elevation profile of the route, the grade is an amazingly constant 444 feet per mile. While the trail is on USFS land, the route is maintained sporadically by the State of Franklin Group of the Sierra Club and/or the CNF. Since there is currently virtually no parking at the trail's lower terminus (about 370 feet up a side road off TN 143 that leaves TN 143 at UTM 17S 400942E/3998143N), it is recommended that you hike in the downhill direction and have friends pick you up at the bottom. This spot is 2.2 miles south of the intersection of TN 143 and CO 2680. Because of the unclear terminus, it is recommended that you pay very close attention to the trail description (and UTM waypoints) in the lower section. There are a large number of side roads that take off from the main trail, and it can be very difficult to stay on track in some places. The CNF has plans to construct a parking lot for the trail, but as of mid-2004 it has not been constructed.

DETAILS: The trail starts at a break in the guardrail on the west side of TN 143 around 600 feet north of Carvers Gap proper (UTM

17S 400019E/3996341N), at a sign announcing to southbound travelers the directions to Roan Mountain. There is no trail sign, and as you start down into the woods, you might feel like, "Hey, this is going to be adventuresome." Within around 330 feet or so, you will encounter a roadbed coming in from the left. If you follow this back into the woods a ways, you will come to an unofficial picnic area. Our trail heads straight ahead and curves to the northeast as it parallels TN 143. At 0.17 miles, the trail makes its first switchback to the left. Around 650 feet past the first switchback, the woods are particularly lovely, with lots of grass and beech trees. At 0.45 miles, the trail comes alongside a small creek and makes a switchback to the right. Be careful about drinking this water untreated, as the creek has its headwaters close to the bathrooms near Carvers Gap.

The trail continues to descend on switchbacks through the woods. At some places, the foot bed is grassy; at others it is heavily eroded. A note to mountain bikers: while hiking the trail for this book, we found two damaged and abandoned mountain bikes. Such suggests that this is not a trail for mountain bike novices. After another switchback, at about 0.85 miles (UTM 17S 400053E/3996683N), the trail crosses a small stream. This is probably the first good water source on the trail. At 1.15 miles, the trail crosses a creek on a very rickety wooden bridge. In damp conditions, this can be extremely slippery, so be careful. The trail makes its first stream crossing since the rickety bridge at 1.96 miles, and there are nice pools to cool your feet on a warm summer day. At 2.7 miles (UTM 17S 401110E/3997544N), the trail comes to an apparent fork. While both forks rejoin soon, take the left fork. A few hundred feet farther, the trail comes to another fork (UTM 17S 401121E/3997626N). Stay left and do not descend toward the clearing. At 2.92 miles, the trail feels a lot more like an old road and passes a small anthropogenic pond on the right. At 3.23 miles, there is a hairpin turn to the right. If you are traveling uphill, make sure that you do not follow the steep uphill route that would be straight ahead. At 3.3 miles (UTM 17S 400853E/3997881N), there is an old road leading off to the right. Stay left.

At 3.45 miles (UTM 17S 401043E/3997959N), the trail arrives at a very confusing intersection. Bear left at the switchback. There are red blazes on some of the trees, but they quickly peter out. About 400 feet past the switchback, there is an old road grade heading off to TN 143. Stay straight. The trail finally intersects a paved road, about 370 feet west of the road's intersection with TN 143. There is no sign, and not really any parking at the terminus. Because the "trailhead" is so brushy and difficult to find, we suggest that you navigate to it by using coordinates (UTM 17S 400879E/3998072N).

38. RHODODENDRON GARDENS TRAIL (FS TRAIL 290; NO TI NUMBER BUT SHOWN ON TI MAP)

LENGTH: 0.75 miles

ELEVATION CHANGE: Low point, 6,050; high point, 6,150 feet (negligible loss/gain)

DIFFICULTY: Easy

TRAILHEADS: 1.7 miles from Carvers Gap

USE: Hiking

TOPOGRAPHIC MAPS: Bakersville, TN-NC

COMMENTS: This is an easy, partially paved trail that winds through the beautiful rhododendron gardens and spruce-fir forest atop the high ridge that is Roan Mountain. The entire trail forms a figure-eight loop; the starting loop is paved and thus handicap accessible. There are restrooms and a seasonal information center located at the start of the trail. Ample parking is available.

DETAILS: The trail begins just past the information center. At this point there are restrooms located to the left and picnic tables to the right. At .02 mile there is a junction that starts the first loop of the figure eight. Turning right, the trail winds among large Catawba rhododendrons. There are picnic tables off to the right at .09 miles. At 0.23 miles, there is a wooden ramp on the right that leads to a nice overlook. Continuing on, an intersection with the second loop is reached at 0.26 miles.

The second loop is unpaved and a bit rocky in places. Shortly after leaving the paved trail, there is a four-way junction. Turning left, the trail passes through stands of spruce-fir interspersed with rhododendrons for about a quarter of a mile before returning to the four-way junction. Turning left at the junction, the trail meets the paved trail again just west of the wooden ramp. Turn right to complete the loop and return to the parking area.

39. CLOUDLAND TRAIL (ROAN HIGH BLUFF TRAIL) (NO FS OR TI NUMBERS BUT SHOWN ON TI MAP)

LENGTH: 1.2 miles

ELEVATION CHANGE: Low point, 6,100 feet; high point, 6,267 feet

DIFFICULTY: Easy

TRAILHEADS: Parking area 1.7 miles west of Carvers Gap

USE: Hiking

TOPOGRAPHIC MAP: USGS Bakersville, TN-NC

COMMENTS: This is a moderate hike through spruce-fir forest to a constructed overlook at Roan High Bluff. For part of its length, it parallels the road and parking areas atop Roan Mountain. There is ample parking available at the Cloudland parking area.

DETAILS: The trail begins at the west end of the Cloudland parking area. It passes through spruce-fir forest and crosses the gravel road in about a half a mile just southwest of the end of the bus parking area. It enters another stretch of spruce-fir before crossing the road again at about 0.68 miles. On the other side of the road the trail becomes paved and crosses an open area with picnic tables before climbing gradually through classic spruce-fir forest. At 0.93 miles, the pavement ends and the trail becomes a bit rougher. It continues to climb slightly and ends at 1.2 miles at Roan High Bluff, where a wooden platform has been constructed, affording breathtaking, 180-degree views.

10 Unaka Mountain

(Includes Unaka Mountain Wilderness, Unaka Mountain Scenic Area, Stone Mountain Roadless Area, and Stone Mountain Backcountry Area)

Much of this area is contained in the 4,496-acre Unaka Mountain Wilderness on the north slope of lofty Unaka Mountain (5,180 feet), with steep slopes and numerous waterfalls. Two of the most outstanding falls are Red Fork Falls (about 80 feet high at the top of a series of five falls beside a steep, rhododendron-covered cliff) and Rock Creek Falls (about 50 feet high in a shady glen framed by overhanging cliffs). Complementing the waterfalls are virgin timber stands—including huge eastern hemlocks, heath balds, cliffs, and ridges that provide panoramas of the TN Valley—and a dense forest cover, consisting of about 60 percent upland hardwoods. Along the higher elevations red spruce are found.

Flora of both the eastern US and Canadian life zones are present in the area. Several rare plants have been found, including Fraser's sedge, rattlesnake root, gentian, mountain mint, and Mitchell's St. John's wort. Unaka Mountain provides good black bear habitat, although whitetail deer and ruffed grouse are the primary game species. Many other mammals and birds inhabit the area as well. An 11.4-mile section of the AT and its protected corridor border the area on the south,

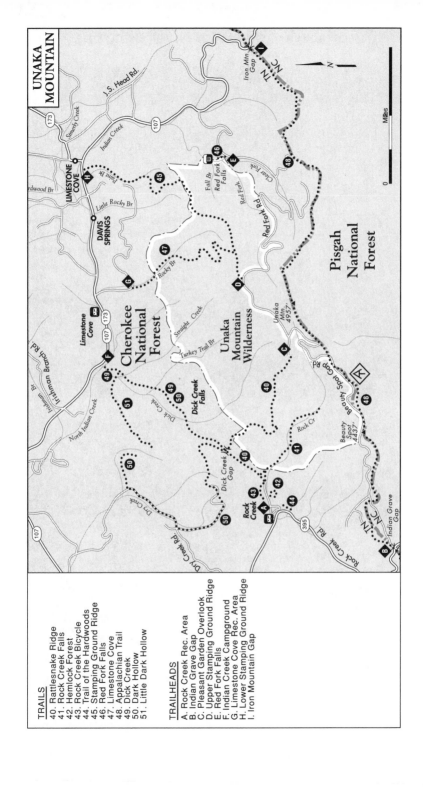

UNAKA MOUNTAIN

Pisgah National Forest

Cherokee National Forest

Unaka Mountain Wilderness

TRAILS
40. Rattlesnake Ridge
41. Rock Creek Falls
42. Hemlock Forest
43. Rock Creek Bicycle
44. Trail of the Hardwoods
45. Stamping Ground Ridge
46. Red Fork Falls
47. Limestone Cove
48. Appalachian Trail
49. Dick Creek
50. Dark Hollow
51. Little Dark Hollow

TRAILHEADS
A. Rock Creek Rec. Area
B. Indian Grave Gap
C. Pleasant Garden Overlook
D. Upper Stamping Ground Ridge
E. Red Fork Falls
F. Indian Creek Campground
G. Limestone Cove Rec. Area
H. Lower Stamping Ground Ridge
I. Iron Mountain Gap

traversing the crest of Unaka Mountain. A gravel road, FS 230, runs roughly parallel to the AT between it and the wilderness. The area is in Unicoi County, southeast of Erwin, TN, in the Nolichucky/Unaka Ranger District.

In addition to the wilderness, the CNF's 2004 plan revision provides for the protection of a 708-acre Unaka Mountain Scenic Area.

Day hiker looks over Unaka Mountain Wilderness. Photograph by Will Skelton.

Across the valley to the west is another significant area that was recognized by the USFS's Southern Appalachian Assessment, the 5,373-acre Stone Mountain Roadless Area. An area slightly larger than the roadless area is protected in the CNF's 2004 plan revision as the 5,457-acre Stone Mountain Backcountry Area. Although it has no official trails, the backcountry area provides excellent off-trail hiking opportunities.

HISTORY

Unaka Mountain is part of the Appalachian Mountain chain, and its geology is similar to the rest of the area, reflecting a history of mountain building, including uplifting, folding, and faulting of the strata. The Unaka Mountain Quartzite takes its name from this prominent peak in the northern CNF. Much of the area was logged prior to acquisition by the USFS. Those logging activities during extremely dry weather resulted in a major fire on the mountain in 1925. Hiking in the area provides a good opportunity to see how nature has healed the land after some 60 years and allows for comparison with areas not touched by the fire. A fire in 1978 also burned 180 acres, which are now recovering. Silver and copper exploration is reported to have occurred in the area years ago, but no silver was found and the copper proved too expensive to mine. Because of the steepness of the slopes, little logging was carried out by the USFS except for a large clear-cut on Stamping Ground Ridge over 20 years ago and two very small clear-cuts in the 1970s.

The wilderness was designated by the US Congress in 1986 and incorporated a previously designated Unaka Mountain Scenic Area. The CNF's 1988 management plan protected a 910-acre Scenic Area and a 1,248-acre primitive area. The CNF's 2004 plan revision continues the protection of a slightly smaller scenic area but not the primitive area. Such revision also designates the Stone Mountain Backcountry Area across the valley on Stone Mountain.

TRAILHEADS AND MAPS

Rock Creek Recreation Area Trailheads

From Erwin, TN, take TN 395 (Tenth Street, Rock Creek Road) east toward NC. At 3.1 miles from the traffic light in Erwin (UTM 17S 378171E/3999791N), turn left into the Rock Creek Recreation Area. Pay $2 day-use fee at entrance ($1 for Golden Age Passport holders).

Go straight ahead 0.3 mile to the swimming pool parking area to park for hiking on Rattlesnake Ridge, Rock Creek Falls, Hemlock Forest Trails, or for the Rock Creek Bicycle Trail. For the Trail of the Hardwoods, take the first right inside the recreation area entrance and follow the narrow road 0.5 mile to park at that trailhead.

Unaka Mountain Road: Indian Grave Gap, Pleasant Garden Overlook, Upper Stamping Ground Ridge, and Red Fork Falls Trailheads

From Erwin, TN, take TN 395 (Tenth Street, Rock Creek Road) east toward NC for 6.1 miles to a gap known as Indian Grave Gap. At that point (UTM 17S 377482E/3996883N) the AT crosses TN 395 and a gravel road turns left (TN 395 continues 4.0 miles to Poplar, NC, and is known as NC 230). The road to the left is Unaka Mountain Road (aka Beauty Spot Gap Road) FS 230 (no signs identify this road). Turn left on FS 230. This road is rocky and rutted and should only be driven in a high road-clearance vehicle with good tires. However, the route provides several terrific views of the mountains to the north and south. Proceed on FS 230 for 2.1 miles from Indian Grave Gap to a fork in the road. To the left, FS 230 continues east. To the right, it is 0.1 mile up to the dead-end turnaround at Beauty Spot. The open bald at Beauty Spot provides one of the premier views on the AT and is a favorite stop for AT through-hikers. There is no shelter, but there is a water source less than a half-mile to the northeast on the trail. Back on FS 230 continue east another 3.1 miles to a second fork (UTM 17S 382399E/3999386N). To the left it is 0.2 mile to the Pleasant Garden Overlook Trailhead for the Rattlesnake Ridge Trail. To the right FS 230 continues northeast another 1.2 miles to the Upper Stamping Ground Ridge Trailhead (UTM 17S 383698E/4000537N). Continue another 4.6 miles past the upper trailhead for the Stamping Ground Ridge Trail to reach the Red Fork Falls Trailhead (UTM 17S 386702E/4001026N).

TN 107: Indian Creek Campground, Limestone Cove Recreation Area, Lower Stamping Ground Ridge, Red Fork Falls, Upper Stamping Ground Ridge, and Iron Mountain Gap Trailheads

From Unicoi, TN, take paved TN 107 east toward Buladean, NC. To reach Unicoi, exit the interstate from Johnson City (I-181 and US 19 and US 23) at Exit 23. Go 0.3 mile southeast to a stop sign and turn right. Go 0.8 mile south to the intersection where TN 107 and TN 173 turn east. Measure mileage on TN 107 from the turn in Unicoi. At 2.5 miles from Unicoi (UTM 17S 381850E/4003912N) reach Indian Creek Campground and trailhead for FS Trails 27, 28, and 280, Dick Creek, Little Dark Hollow and Dark Hollow. Indian Creek is a private campground with an entrance about 30 yards off the highway. Just before and to the right of that entrance there is some trailhead parking space.

At 3.6 miles from Unicoi, just after the Limestone Cove Recreation Area entrance on the left, reach a camping area turn-off on the right (UTM 17S 383468E/4004062N) leading to the trailhead for the Limestone Cove Trail (FS Trail 30). To reach that trail turn right here, and in about 0.1 mile, where the paved road to the campsites bears right, keep left on a gravel road that is FS 4343. Soon bear right at a fork and, at 0.3 mile from Rte TN 107, reach a closed gate that is the start of FS Trail 30 (UTM 17S 383523E/4003687N).

At 5.1 miles from Unicoi pass Walter Garland Road, and at 5.4 miles reach Limestone Cove Church on the left and Shell Lane on the right. The wooded area on the right between Walter Garland Road and Shell Lane is an allowable access to the lower end of Stamping Ground Ridge Trail; see the trail description for details. Jada Blevins, at the Grand View Ranch and RV Park, just 0.2 mile farther up TN 107, has obtained the rights to travel through those privately owned woods and is graciously willing to share them with hikers. She also provides overnight accommodations for folks wanting to hike in the area (423/743-3382). See the trail description for directions on finding the trail in those woods.

At 7.6 miles from Unicoi, Red Fork Road, FS 230, intersects TN 107 on the right just after a CNF sign. Turn right on FS 230, which is paved for the first 2.1 miles. The Red Fork Falls Trailhead is reached after traveling 1.2 miles up this road. At that point (UTM 17S 386702E/4001026N), the paved road passes through a gap where there is a wide place on the right, and the trail (following an ORV route) heads down to the west. Continue another 4.6 miles on FS 230 past the Red Fork Falls Trailhead to reach the upper trailhead for the Stamping Ground Ridge Trail.

At 10.1 miles from Unicoi on TN 107, reach Iron Mountain Gap (UTM 17S 389029E/4000289N). The AT enters from the left rear and exits at the far right along the left side of the ridge.

TOPOGRAPHIC MAPS: USGS Unicoi, TN; Iron Mountain Gap, TN. TI Map 783, South Holston and Watauga Lakes, CNF.

TRAIL DESCRIPTIONS

40. RATTLESNAKE RIDGE TRAIL (FS TRAIL 26, TI TRAIL 32)

LENGTH: 4.0 miles

ELEVATION CHANGE: Low point, 2,400 feet; high point, 4,850 feet

DIFFICULTY: Moderate

TRAILHEADS: Rock Creek Recreation Area (start) and Pleasant Garden Overlook (end)

USE: Hiking

TOPOGRAPHIC MAP: USGS Unicoi, TN-NC

COMMENTS: This is a well-defined trail that is somewhat overgrown by laurel at the upper elevations. Terrific winter views are obscured by vegetation in summer. There is an excellent display of laurel blooms in season.

DETAILS: The trail starts at the bulletin board at the top of the Rock Creek Campground. To reach it, walk from the swimming pool parking area up the paved road past the camping areas. The paved road passes through a very pleasant grove of sweet gum, hemlock, tulip poplar, rhododendron, and other vegetation. In 0.3 mile, where the paved road ends, there is a sign pointing straight ahead to "Trailheads." Continue another 0.1 mile to the bulletin board. The Rattlesnake Ridge Trail starts on the left, crossing a bridge. At 0.4 mile there is a split and the Rattlesnake Ridge Trail heads left. The trail then runs in a northerly direction through laurel slicks and will cross over a small, nearly dry stream several times. Continue on the trail as it climbs around the side of a wooded hill. You will note pines overhead, along with trailing arbutus, galax, and other species found in warm dry exposures.

At 0.8 mile reach Dick Creek Gap (UTM 17S 379806E/4000950N). Here the Dick Creek and Dark Hollow Trails enter from the northeast and the Dark Hollow Trail continues by turning and climbing along the ridge to the north. Turn sharply right (southeast) and begin a steep ascent up Rattlesnake Ridge. At 1.3 miles, pass a wilderness boundary sign. The Rattlesnake Ridge Trail climbs a dry exposed ridge covered with table mountain pines, along with bracken, clubmosses, teaberry, lichen, and reindeer moss. Bear sign can often be spotted. In winter, the view from the trail reveals the ridge to be climbed ahead and more distant ridges to the west. Near the top of the ridge the trail passes through open woods with grassy areas. Eastern hemlock, Fraser magnolia, and red spruce are predominant species at this elevation. Black-berries and blueberries will reward the climber in season, as will good views of Unaka and other mountains in the area. At 3.7 miles the trail enters a laurel thicket and then comes out of the thicket at the Pleasant Garden Overlook after 4.0 miles. The view from Pleasant Garden is terrific—mountain after mountain as far as the eye can see.

41. ROCK CREEK FALLS TRAIL (FS TRAIL 148, TI TRAIL 34)

LENGTH: 1.7 miles

ELEVATION CHANGE: Low point, 2,400 feet; high point, 3,400 feet

DIFFICULTY: Moderate

TRAILHEAD: Rock Creek Recreation Area

USE: Hiking

TOPOGRAPHIC MAP: Unicoi, TN-NC

COMMENTS: The trail begins as a USFS road but converts to a trail. Rock Creek Falls is a small but beautiful series of cascades at the base of Unaka Mountain.

DETAILS: The trail starts at the bulletin board at the top of the Rock Creek Campground. To reach it, walk from the swimming pool parking area up the paved road past the camping areas. In 0.3 mile, where the paved road ends, there is a sign pointing straight ahead to "Trailheads." Continue another 0.1 mile to the bulletin board. The Rock Creek Falls Trail goes right from this point. At 0.2 mile from the bulletin board, pass a bridge on the left where the bicycle trail comes in from the left rear. There are four crossings of the creek as the trail ascends: to the left side at 0.4 mile, to the right at 0.7 mile, left at 1.0 mile, and finally to the right side at 1.3 miles. The trail climbs moderately, passing several smaller falls and laurel-covered rock outcroppings. Rock Creek Falls is reached at 1.7 miles. Rock Creek Falls is a two-step falls set at the end of a rock grotto with vertical rock walls. The water cascades over sculptured rocks in a dark, shaded area of the forest. It is very beautiful setting, but the rocks are quite slippery; be careful.

42. HEMLOCK FOREST TRAIL (FS TRAIL 179, TI TRAIL 14)

LENGTH: 0.3 mile

ELEVATION CHANGE: Low point, 2,280 feet; high point, 2,360 feet

DIFFICULTY: Easy

TRAILHEAD: Rock Creek Recreation Area

USE: Hiking

TOPOGRAPHIC MAP: USGS Unicoi, TN-NC

COMMENTS: This short trail provides a very easy hike for campers at the Rock Creek Recreation Area. It is reached by walking from the swimming pool parking area, around the swimming pool, to the entrance to the small amphitheater. Just inside the entrance, the trail begins on the left where a USFS trail sign is posted. There are blue blazes.

DETAILS: Just 65 yards from the start, the trail splits where a large rock in the middle has a blue arrow pointing up to the right. To hike the loop counterclockwise, follow the arrow. At 0.2 mile the trail reaches its highest elevation and curves around to the left. Another footpath enters from the right as the path passes near the camping area. Back at the split, turn right to return to the starting point.

43. ROCK CREEK BICYCLE TRAIL (FS TRAIL 178, TI TRAIL 33)

LENGTH: 0.9 mile

ELEVATION CHANGE: Low point, 2,280 feet; high point, 2,450 feet

DIFFICULTY: Easy

TRAILHEAD: Rock Creek Recreation Area

USE: Hiking, mountain bike

TOPOGRAPHIC MAP: USGS Unicoi, TN-NC

COMMENTS: This short trail in the Rock Creek Recreation Area provides an easy walk or bike ride that includes some of the lower portions of the Rock Creek Falls and Rattlesnake Ridge trails. The trail passes through a very pleasant grove of sweet gum, hemlock, tulip poplar, rhododendron, and other vegetation, and travels alongside Rock Creek. To reach the bicycle trailhead, go up the road from the swimming area parking lot 0.1 mile to a spot just 20 yards above and across from the entrance to Camping Loop B. There is a trail sign here on the left. The trail is blue-blazed.

DETAILS: At 0.3 mile reach an intersection with a foot trail at a bridge over Rock Creek. To the right there is a bulletin board at the start of the Rock Creek Falls and Rattlesnake Ridge trails. The bicycle trail (and the start of the Rattlesnake Ridge Trail) goes across the bridge to the left. At 0.4 mile there is a split; Rattlesnake Ridge Trail heads left and the bicycle trail goes right. Turn right and at 0.6 mile reach a second bridge over Rock Creek. Across the bridge, the bicycle trail turns right and the Rock Creek Falls trail goes left 1.5 miles to the falls. At 0.8 mile the trail is back at the bulletin board that is the start of the Rock Creek Falls and Rattlesnake Ridge trails. Turn left toward the campground. At 0.9 mile reach a gate at the paved road at the end of Campground Loop C. Coming from the other direction, a sign points back in the opposite direction, with an arrow to "Trailheads." This is the end of the bicycle trail.

44. TRAIL OF THE HARDWOODS (FS TRAIL 525, TI TRAIL 38)

LENGTH: 0.2 mile

ELEVATION CHANGE: Low point, 2,280 feet; high point, 2,360 feet

DIFFICULTY: Easy

TRAILHEAD: Rock Creek Recreation Area

USE: Hiking

TOPOGRAPHIC MAP: USGS Unicoi, TN-NC

COMMENTS: The trail leaves the right end of the parking area where a sign provides the trail name and number. This is an interpretive trail with some 15 numbered positions. The descriptions for the numbered positions are available from the USFS or from the campground host, who is located at Campsite 1, Loop A.

DETAILS: The trail climbs gently around the ridge and soon enters a rhododendron tunnel. A USFS sign marks the trail's end at 0.2 mile.

45. STAMPING GROUND RIDGE TRAIL (STAMPING GROUND) (FS TRAIL 110, TI TRAIL 37)

LENGTH: 4.2 miles

ELEVATION CHANGE: Low point, 2,360 feet; high point, 4,700 feet

DIFFICULTY: Moderate

TRAILHEADS: Upper Stamping Ground Ridge (start) and Lower Stamping Ground Ridge (end)

USE: Hiking, equestrian

TOPOGRAPHIC MAP: USGS Unicoi, TN-NC

COMMENTS: The upper end of this trail begins at a parking lot on FS 230 near the top of Unaka Mountain. The trail is overgrown with laurel in some areas and the blossoms are beautiful in June. The trail ends in a mass of rhododendron and blowdowns on private land 0.4 mile from TN 107. To find the lower trailhead from TN 107, enter the woods across from the Limestone Cove Church and hike (bushwack) parallel and close to Shell Lane until you are past the private property on the left. Here a drainage comes down from the left front (from the south-southeast) and the trail starts in that drainage. At one time a narrow trail entered the woods from Shell Lane just above a small shed, but that route entails crossing posted private property and permission should be obtained. By late 2003 Grand View Ranch (where Jada Blevins has obtained the rights to pass through the unposted woods) may have developed a better access to this trail, and it will probably start closer to Walter Garland Road.

DETAILS: Starting from the parking area at the upper end (UTM 17S 383698E/4000537N), the first 0.3 mile crosses a grassy heath bald with beautiful views of the mountains and valleys to the north and of Unaka Mountain back to the south. Tread carefully, timber rattlers have been spotted here. The vegetation includes red spruce, and club moss carpets the ground. At 0.4 mile pass the junction where the Limestone Cove Trail comes up from Rocky Branch (UTM 17S 384343E/4000711N). Begin traveling through a rhododendron thicket. However, there is no brush on the trail, and in some areas the trail forms a very pleasant tunnel through the rhododendron. At 0.9 mile begin a steep descent, and at 1.0 mile pass a small spring. Stone Mountain is visible straight ahead across Limestone Cove. Vegetation in the area includes galax, trailing arbutus, pipsissewa, and scrubby trees. At 2.1 miles the trail leaves a heavily overgrown area near a wilderness boundary sign. At 3.8 miles there is a USFS end-of-trail sign. The balance of the hike will be on private land in the woods between Shell Lane and Walter Garland Road. At 4.0 miles buildings are visible and the trail essentially disappears in rhododendron and blowdowns. Several "No Trespassing" signs warn against crossing onto the private property on the right. At 4.2 miles emerge from the woods onto TN 107 near Limestone Cove Church (UTM 17S 386285E/4004349N).

46. RED FORK FALLS TRAIL (NO FS OR TI NUMBERS)

LENGTH: 0.25 mile

ELEVATION CHANGE: Low point, 3,000 feet; high point, 3,160 feet

DIFFICULTY: Difficult

TRAILHEAD: Red Fork Falls

USE: Hiking

TOPOGRAPHIC MAP: USGS Unicoi, TN-NC

COMMENTS: Red Fork Falls is a major falls of about 80 feet, including a picturesque series of cascades above and below. The falls gets its name from the rainbow of colors present when the setting sun hits the water. This is no longer an official trail.

DETAILS: Start down the old road heading west from the trailhead (UTM 17S 386702E/4001026N). There are no trail signs or blazes. At 0.1 mile reach a fire ring next to a stream crossing and turn right across the stream, which is Clear Fork. On the other side, continue straight ahead toward another stream beyond some rhododendron. Avoid a strong ORV trail that heads up to the left to a number of campsites. Also avoid a faint trail to the right. In another 50 yards, reach the second stream (Red Fork) and head straight across it. On the far side, a fairly well-defined trail heads up through the rhododendron and then to the right, downstream. Just inside the rhododendron there is a USNF sign indicating the start of the Unaka Mountain Wilderness. At 0.2 mile the trail begins a very steep descent beside Red Fork Falls. *Be very careful here,* and do not venture out on the falls or cascades. Numerous fatal falls have occurred to hikers here. The climb down beside the falls should only be undertaken by strong, active hikers or climbers. While there are numerous steps in the rocks and handholds on roots or small trees, the descent is nearly vertical. At 50 or 60 feet below the last crest there is a vantage point for viewing the upper falls. Further descent is possible but even more dangerous.

47. LIMESTONE COVE TRAIL (FS TRAIL 30, TI TRAIL 22)

LENGTH: 3.5 miles

ELEVATION CHANGE: Low point, 2,320 feet; high point, 4,520 feet

DIFFICULTY: Moderate

TRAILHEADS: Limestone Cove Recreation Area (start) and Upper Stamping Ground Ridge (end)

USE: Hiking, equestrian

TOPOGRAPHIC MAP: USGS Unicoi, TN-NC

COMMENTS: This is a good, easy-to-follow, graded trail. It gains 2,200 feet in 3.5 miles through forest thick with rhododendron and laurel. It is now marked with blue blazes and was previously marked with yellow blazes. At some locations the blue paint has flaked off, revealing the yellow paint underneath. The trail description begins at the lower end of the trail.

DETAILS: Begin hiking at the locked gate on FS 4343 (UTM 17S 383523E/4003687N). Mileages are measured from that gate, although the actual trail does not start for another 0.4 mile. The trail begins as a gentle climb on a wide grassy trail. Old roads crossing or connecting can cause confusion in spots, and one should look for the blue blazes. At 0.4 mile the trail leaves the road to the right at a 90-degree angle (UTM 17S 383634E/4003162N). There is a USFS sign here, but it is set back about 30 feet from the road and could be missed. After the USFS sign is passed, there follows a gentle climb to Rocky Branch. Then, at 0.9 mile the trail crosses the branch and begins a steady, moderate, and sometimes steep winding climb up to Stamping Ground Ridge. The trail is shaded for much of the route up the mountain. Water can be found at several locations. The trail uses the remains of old logging roads and is in good shape and easy to follow. At 3.5 miles the trail joins the Stamping Ground Ridge Trail (UTM 17S 384343E/4000711N) 0.4 mile from the Upper Stamping Ground Ridge Trailhead. The junction is well marked.

48. APPALACHIAN TRAIL (IRON MOUNTAIN GAP TO INDIAN GRAVE GAP) (FS TRAIL 1; TI 1)

LENGTH: 11.4 miles

ELEVATION CHANGE: Low point, 3,360 feet; high point, 4,957 feet

DIFFICULTY: Difficult

TRAILHEADS: Iron Mountain Gap (start) and Indian Grave Gap (end)

USE: Hiking

TOPOGRAPHIC MAPS: USGS Unicoi, TN-NC; Iron Mountain Gap, TN-NC

COMMENTS: While the net elevation change for this hike is 356 feet, it includes 3,056 feet of climb and 3,412 feet of descent over its 11.4 miles. That, combined with a frequently steep and rocky path, constitutes a good test of lungs (going up) and knees (going down). There are numerous camping sites along this stretch, including a shelter at Cherry Gap. Water sources are available at various locations down from the trail. The view from Beauty Spot is one of the premier views on the entire AT. When hiking the AT in the late winter and spring, one often encounters through-hikers, those starting in Georgia and going to Maine. Take some extra apples or oranges for them; they will appreciate it.

DETAILS: The trail enters the woods at the southwest side of Iron Mountain Gap (UTM 17S 389029E/4000289N) heading southwest along the left side of the ridge, left of a USFS road. There is an AT trail sign inside the entrance, and the trail is marked with the familiar white AT blazes, two inches wide and six inches high. The trail is well traveled and well blazed in most areas, and staying on the trail is relatively easy. The first 1.4 miles are a fairly steady climb to the top of Little Bald Knob. Then, at 2.3 miles from TN 107, the trail passes near the summit of Piney Ball (as opposed to "bald"). A side trail leads up to, and some good views exist at, the top. At 2.5 miles pass through Cherry Gap, and at 2.9 miles reach Cherry Gap Shelter. There is a spring 250 feet southwest on a blue-blazed trail.

At 3.9 miles come into Low Gap and start the long climb up Unaka Mountain. In the next 1.9 miles the trail gains 1,260 feet of elevation. At 5.0 miles there is a piped spring just below trail in a rhododendron slick. The trail now becomes very steep, with steps in many places. At 5.3 miles reach a broad shoulder of the mountaintop and bear left. The remaining climb is very gentle. At 5.8 miles reach the survey marker at the crest and bear left, starting down. At 6.9 miles the trail approaches within 50 yards of FS 230 and then switches back sharply to the left and descends through a series of short switchbacks. It now passes through rocky terrain in deciduous woods, with the USFS road often visible below and to the right.

At 7.4 miles reach Beauty Spot Gap at a point where the trail is about 10 yards from the road. A sign points across the road to a water source. The trail continues roughly parallel to the road as both climb southwest out of Beauty Spot Gap. At 7.9 miles reach an open field and begin a long climb up through the field. Many flowers bloom here in season, and terrific views exist to the southeast in NC, as well as back to Unaka Mountain and Pleasant Garden. Reenter the woods at 8.1 miles, and reach a seasonal spring at 8.3 miles. In this area there are abundant mountain laurel and flame azalea in June, and one can often hear the flutelike song of the veery, an American thrush.

At 8.7 miles reach FS 230 at a rail fence. The trail turns left and parallels the road across the fence. A sign points across the road to a blue-blazed trail to a water source. The trail now climbs toward Beauty Spot. At 8.9 miles enter an open field and turn left. At 9.0 miles reach crest of Beauty Spot. From this pleasant bald, Unaka Mountain and

Pleasant Garden are visible to the east; the mountains of NC, to the southeast; and the area around Erwin and the Nolichucky River, to the northwest. A fire ring exists at the summit, and the road access can be seen immediately to the north. The AT continues southwest through a slight gap and then across another, lower bald, where it begins the descent to Indian Grave Gap.

At 9.3 miles turn left and enter the woods. At 10.2 miles cross FS 230 and continue to descend on an old logging road. At 10.7 miles cross a power line with a nice view to the north. The trail now enters an area burned in a fire circa 1997. The understory is recovering with laurel and rhododendron growth. Many taller trees were not burned. At 11.4 miles come into Indian Grave Gap and the end of this section of the AT (UTM 17S 377482E/3996883N).

49. DICK CREEK TRAIL (FS TRAIL 27, TI TRAIL 8)

LENGTH: 2.6 miles

ELEVATION CHANGE: Low point, 2,100 feet; high point, 2,850 feet

DIFFICULTY: Easy

TRAILHEADS: Indian Creek Campground (start) and Dick Creek Gap (end)

USE: Hiking, mountain bike, equestrian

TOPOGRAPHIC MAP: USGS Unicoi, TN-NC

COMMENTS: This trail is entirely on an old road that is still used by 4 WD vehicles, and it has many intersections with other, often-used roadways. One must pay particular attention to staying on the right track. The following details cover each intersection, but the abundance of them can create confusion. The details for the Dick Creek Trail also apply to the initial segment of the Dark Hollow Trail (FS Trail 280), since the two trails are the same to Dick Creek Gap. In addition, the beginning of the Little Dark Hollow Trail follows the first 0.6 mile of the Dick Creek Trail.

DETAILS: The trail starts on a rocky road just off TN 107 at the entrance to Indian Creek Campground (UTM 17S 381850E/ 4003912N). The trail (old road) descends about 50 yards and fords Indian Creek. At low water periods the ford may be crossed on rocks, but usually requires a wade. Hikers may prefer to carry their boots from the trailhead and put them on once across the ford. At 0.1 mile the road forks. Take the left fork and pass through a pair of USFS gateposts. At 0.2 mile there is another fork; go right following the rocky road. At 0.5 mile reach an intersection and proceed straight ahead on the rocky road. Avoid the truck road heading left at a 45-degree angle and the ORV trail to the right. At 0.6 mile another ORV trail enters from the right (UTM 17S 381408E/4003193N). This right turn is the continuation of FS Trail 28, Little Dark Hollow. See the description for that trail elsewhere in this section.

At 1.5 miles reach a major fork in the road that may still be marked with blue flags (UTM 17S 380838E/4002069N). Take the right fork, descend slightly, and proceed to a crossing over Dick Creek. The trail then turns left and ascends on the right side of a branch of Dick Creek. (Just before crossing the creek there is a trail to the left that climbs a short distance to Dick Creek Falls.) At 2.5 miles reach a trail split. The trail to the left goes down and dead-ends shortly. The trail to the right is the trail to Dick Creek Gap. At 2.6 miles reach Dick Creek Gap and the end of Dick Creek Trail. Straight ahead the Rattlesnake Ridge Trail descends 0.8 mile to Rock Creek Campground. To the left, that same trail climbs 3.2 miles to Pleasant Garden. To the right, an old road that climbs up gradually to the northeast is the continuation of FS Trail 280, Dark Hollow Trail. See the description for that trail elsewhere in this section.

50. DARK HOLLOW TRAIL (FS TRAIL 280, TI TRAIL 7)

LENGTH: 7.5 miles

ELEVATION CHANGE: Low point, 2,100 feet; high point, 3,000 feet

DIFFICULTY: Moderate

TRAILHEAD: Indian Creek Campground

USE: Hiking, mountain bike, equestrian

TOPOGRAPHIC MAP: USGS Unicoi, TN-NC

COMMENTS: This trail and the Little Dark Hollow Trail are being built by the Northeast TN Mountain Biking Association (http://www.ntmba.org) in cooperation with the USFS. This trail combines several old roads and former trails with some new trails to make a loop that will eventually be about 9.5 miles long. In 2002 the trail dead-ends in an area of dense rhododendron and one should backtrack to return. An alternate, exit trailhead exists at the south end of Dry Creek Road but entails crossing private property. The owner's permission should be obtained before using this exit. A second alternate exit is available over FS 4365 from Nelson Gap to Rock Creek Road in Erwin. The initial segment of this trail follows the Dick Creek Trail. Refer to that trail description elsewhere in this section. The details commence at the end of the Dick Creek Trail in Dick Creek Gap.

DETAILS: Leave Dick Creek Gap to the northeast (a sharp right turn) on an old, grassy road. At 3.0 miles from the trailhead at Indian Creek Campground there is an opening on the right with good views up Rattlesnake Ridge and Horseback Ridge to the southeast. At 3.1 miles the trail turns left and climbs more steeply. In a few yards it jogs right and left to continue climbing on a newer section of trail. At 3.3 miles, after crossing a saddle, the newer trail ends and now follows an old roadbed, sometimes overgrown. At 3.6 miles cross a drainage and descend due north along drainage. At 3.8 miles the trail swings northwest and climbs to an open field. Turn left in the field and step into an intersection of old roads at 3.9 miles. Take the road down to the right on a heading of 186 degrees, avoiding another road straight ahead across the ridge and an ORV track that goes steeply up the crest to the right.

At 4.0 miles there are some nice views to the north toward Nelson Gap and Nelson High Point. At 4.2 miles reach a junction. Proceed straight ahead, descending and avoiding the left and right intersecting roads. At 5.4 miles, after passing two intersecting roads on the left, enter Nelson Gap. Take a sharp right and descend on a heading of 170 degrees on the road that is the Dark Hollow Trail, avoiding three other intersecting roads. The one going left is FS 4365 leading down 1.5 miles to Rock Creek Road in Erwin. The other two are an ORV track up the ridge and a gated logging road out the right side of the ridge. At 5.7 miles the road switches back sharply to the left at a trashed-up turnaround with a fire ring. The trail now descends along the creek in Dark Hollow. The Hollow is aptly named, as it is in a dense pine forest with a heavy rhododendron understory. At 6.8 miles reach a split where Dry Fork Road goes left and FS Trail 28 goes right, climbing on old roadbed (UTM 17S 378894E/4003429N). The trail now climbs gently around the end of the ridge between Dark Hollow and Little Dark Hollow.

At 7.5 miles reach the bottom of Little Dark Hollow. As of 2002 the route ends here near the dry creek bed. An old roadbed exists here and will probably be used for the continuation of Dark Hollow Trail up Little Dark Hollow to join the Little Dark Hollow Trail, FS Trail 28. To exit the CNF from this point it is 7.5 miles back to the starting trailhead at Indian Creek Campground. An alternate exit down Dry Creek is 0.7 mile back to Dry Creek Road and 0.6 mile out that road to the paved road. The last 0.1 mile of this route is across privately owned land. The other alternate is back 2.1 miles to Nelson Gap and then 1.5 miles down FS 4365 to Rock Creek Road. Both these alternates are many road miles from the starting trailhead and would require a second vehicle.

51. LITTLE DARK HOLLOW TRAIL (FS TRAIL 28, TI TRAIL 23)

LENGTH: 2.2 miles

ELEVATION CHANGE: Low point, 2,100 feet; high point, 2,800 feet

DIFFICULTY: Moderate

TRAILHEAD: Indian Creek Campground

USE: Hiking, mountain bike, equestrian

TOPOGRAPHIC MAP: USGS Unicoi, TN-NC

COMMENTS: This trail and the Dark Hollow Trail are being built by the Northeast TN Mountain Biking Association (http://www.ntmba .org) in cooperation with the USFS. This trail starts out on the Dick Creek Trail and dead-ends near the bottom of Little Dark Hollow. Future plans are to extend it to a point farther up Little Dark Hollow, where it will connect with the Dark Hollow Trail. The TI map shows extensions of this trail to Nelson Gap at the southwest end and to Stanley Road near TN 107 at the northeast end, but these two extensions are not part of the present plans.

DETAILS: The trail starts, along with Dick Creek Trail, on a rocky road just off TN 107 at the entrance to Indian Creek Campground (UTM 17S 381850E/4003912N). The trail (old road) descends about 50 yards and fords Indian Creek. At low water periods the ford may be crossed on rocks, but usually requires a wade. Hikers may prefer to carry their boots from the trailhead and put them on once across the ford. At 0.1 mile the road forks. Take the left fork and pass through a pair of USFS gateposts. At 0.2 mile there is another fork; go right following the rocky road. At 0.5 mile reach an intersection and proceed straight ahead on the rocky road. Avoid the truck road heading left at a 45-degree angle and the ORV trail to right. At 0.6 mile another ORV trail enters from the right (UTM 17S 381408E/4003193N). This right turn is the beginning of Trail 28, Little Dark Hollow.

Turn to right on well-traveled jeep road, leaving the Dick Creek Trail. Soon cross Dick Creek. After the creek crossing, the evidence of vehicular travel disappears, but evidence of much foot travel continues. At 0.9 mile intersect old trail and turn right (north). Soon pick up new trail construction that bears left and continues at a constant elevation.

Much work has been done digging the trail into the side of the mountain. At 1.4 miles the dug-out trail work ends, but the trail right-of-way has been cleared of brush. At 1.9 miles reach a flat area and begin following an old trail that has been cleared of brush. This portion is a very fine trail. At 2.2 miles the old trail continues but has not been cleared of brush and the rhododendron is very thick. In 2002 the route ends here. Plans are to extend it farther up Little Dark Hollow to a point where it will join FS Trail 280.

FUTURE TRAILS

The CNF and Northeast TN Mountain Biking Association are planning other trails in the area to the southwest of Limestone Cove. Information on these new trails may be obtained from either organization as the trails are completed and put into use.

OFF-TRAIL HIKING OPPORTUNITIES (STONE MOUNTAIN ROADLESS AREA)

The USFS in its Southern Appalachian Assessment identified a large, 5,373-acre, roadless area along the crest of Stone Mountain north of the Unaka Wilderness. The CNF's 2004 plan revision also designated 5,457 acres as a backcountry area. Interestingly, there are at least three Stone Mountains in the northern CNF: one is located just north of Hartford and I-40; another is located north of US 321 and southeast of Watauga Lake; and the Stone Mountain identified as a roadless area is located in between. Specifically, the southwestern boundary of the backcountry area is Brummett Creek, the northwestern boundary is the USFS property line just south of Scotio Road, the northeastern boundary is TN 361, and the boundary on the southeastern side is the USFS boundary. The area is only 8.5 miles from Johnson City. Equally interesting, especially considering the size of the area, is the fact that there are no designated trails within either the roadless area or the backcountry area, so exploration is limited to off-trail hiking.

The crest of Stone Mountain is relatively level, and the northwestern slopes gradually descend toward the valley, with numerous streams and valleys. However, the southeastern slopes are very steep. Accordingly, off-trail hiking is probably best accomplished along the ridgetop. The ridgetop rises to just over 3,600 feet and, for over 3.0 miles, the elevation varies only between 3,000 and 3,650 feet. The mountain itself is about 8.0 miles long. There are outstanding views from the top of Johnson City and the developed TN Valley to the north, as well as the vast expanse of the Unaka Mountains to the south. No roads or trails lead to the long summit, although numerous old logging roads, and the resultant evidence of clear-cuts, surround the lower elevations of the mountain.

Access to the area is limited on the long northwest and southeast sides of the mountain by private land and expanding subdivisions. The best access to the area and the ridgetop is probably from the southeast by gated FS 53351 and FS 53352, both reached by a paved county road known as Piney Grove Road. The county road makes a loop off TN 173 and is shown on the TI map; however, care must be taken, as the FS roads are not signed. There is also a gated access road from the southwest known as FS 313, the Irishman Branch Road. It turns northeast off TN 173 and TN 107 and is likewise shown on the TI map.

11 Nolichucky River Corridor North

The Nolichucky River is in one of several major river valleys that cut through the Appalachian Mountains from east to west. The areas on both the north and south sides of the river have wonderful recreational opportunities. On the north side, a substantial amount of acreage is protected as the 2,189-acre AT Corridor in the CNF's 2004 plan revision. The area is a forested triangle formed by the TN-NC state line, the Nolichucky River corridor, and the AT Corridor. It is located in Unicoi County and is under the jurisdiction of the Nolichucky/Unaka Ranger District. The only trail in the area is the AT; however, off-trail hiking provides the opportunity for one to enjoy an isolated and otherwise inaccessible portion of the Unaka Mountains. Open forests of large hemlocks and protected watersheds of numerous clear streams that flow into the Nolichucky River and Jones Branch are among the area attractions. Five species of rare fauna have their habitat in the Nolichucky River just outside the area: three species of river snail and two species of pearly mussel.

HISTORY

Much of the area was logged 40 years or so ago but has since recovered almost completely. The geographical isolation provided by the TN-NC state line, the Nolichucky River, and Johnson Rock Ridge has protected much of the area, although some ORV use is present. The current and past management plan designations have eliminated most ORV abuse in the area. The CNF's 1988 management plan protected a 1,970-acre Nolichucky Primitive Area. The CNF's 2004 plan revision continues the protection of that area as part of the AT Corridor.

TRAILHEADS AND MAPS

Nolichucky Gorge Campground Trailhead

Approach via either TN 107 or US 19. From the intersection of TN 107/81 and US 23/19 (just outside Erwin, TN), drive south on the four-lane US 23/19 for 2.8 miles, at which point the four lanes are reduced to two. Six-tenths of a mile beyond this point, turn left off the highway onto a side road marked with a small brown sign (also on the

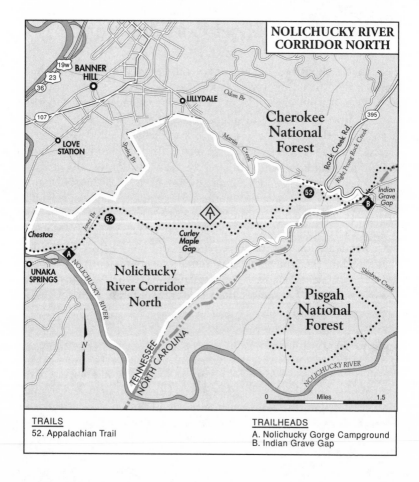

NOLICHUCKY RIVER CORRIDOR NORTH

TRAILS
52. Appalachian Trail

TRAILHEADS
A. Nolichucky Gorge Campground
B. Indian Grave Gap

left side of the highway): "Cherokee N.F.—Chestoa .75 Mile." After 0.4 mile, cross a two-lane bridge (with a protected walkway for AT hikers) over the Nolichucky River and immediately turn right onto a paved road. The Jones Branch section of the AT terminates at this Nolichucky River Bridge. Chestoa Recreation Area, 0.25 mile ahead on the right, has parking for several cars. Continue on to the end of the paved road, 1.4 miles from the bridge, at Nolichucky Expeditions Base Camp, a commercial whitewater rafting operation. The AT passes by here, and the Nolichucky River off-trail route begins here. For help in arranging a car shuttle, three facilities are available: (1) USA Raft (a whitewater rafting company; http://www.usaraft.com; 423/743-7111 or 800-USA-RAFT); (2) Nolichucky Gorge Campground and Resort (a campground with tent and cabin facilities; http://www.angelfire.com/tn/nolichucky; 423/743-8876); and (3) Nolichucky Hostel (an AT hostel located at the Nolichucky River Bridge mentioned above, 151 River Road, Erwin, TN 37650; 423/735-0548; http://www.unclejohnnys.net).

Indian Grave Gap Trailhead

Indian Grave Gap Trailhead is located where TN 395 (paved) intersects with the AT. A paved pull-off will hold several parked cars. A gravel road runs steeply northeast from Indian Grave Gap about 3.0 miles to Beauty Spot on the AT. To reach Indian Grave Gap, drive northeast through Erwin, TN, on Mohawk Drive, then turn right onto Tenth Street, which soon becomes Rock Creek Road and TN 395. A highway sign for Mitchell County marks the end of TN 395, the TN-NC state line, and Indian Grave Gap. Driving distance to the gap is 12.0 miles from Erwin. The road continues into NC as NC 1323 for 4.0 miles to Poplar. To find the AT, walk directly across the highway from the paved parking strip at the end of TN 395 and look for a white AT blaze on a series of stone steps leading up the bank.

TOPOGRAPHIC MAPS: USGS Huntdale, TN-NC; Chestoa, TN-NC. TI Map 783, South Holston and Watauga Lakes, CNF.

TRAIL DESCRIPTIONS

52. APPALACHIAN TRAIL (JONES BRANCH SECTION) (FS TRAIL 1, TI TRAIL 1)

LENGTH: 8.4 Miles

DIFFICULTY: Moderate

ELEVATION CHANGE: Low point, 1,720 feet; high point, 3,480 feet

TRAILHEADS: Indian Grave Gap (start) and Nolichucky Gorge Campground (end)

USE: Hiking

TOPOGRAPHIC MAPS: USGS Huntdale, NC-TN; Chestoa, TN-NC

COMMENTS: This section of the AT is maintained by the Tennessee Eastman Hiking Club (http://www.tehcc.org) and includes a shelter at Curley Maple Gap. AT through-hikers will usually travel this section from south to north; however, day hikers may prefer to hike it from north to south since a car shuttle can be arranged to permit a downhill trip. The description below is from Indian Grave Gap to the Nolichucky Gorge Campground, the downhill route.

DETAILS: Climb the stone steps up the steep bank at Indian Grave Gap and note the small metal sign reading "Appalachian Trail: Curley Maple Gap Shelter 4.1 Mi.; Nolichucky River 8.4 Mi." After an initial steep climb, the trail climbs gently for nearly a mile before leveling off. At 0.4 mile a side trail on the left runs uphill 100 yards to a grassy meadow with a few trees. It has been used as a campsite but has no water. The trail passes over a rounded crest at 1.0 mile to begin a steady descent all the way to the Nolichucky River. Mixed hardwoods and patches of rhododendron characterize this portion of Jones Branch. In season there is an abundance of diverse wildflowers— tradescantia, coreopsis, whorled loosestrife, and blue-bead lily, to name a few. Farther on, where the trail is drier, the heath family is abundantly represented, with arbutus, laurel, wintergreen, and azalea.

At 1.5 miles, the trail crosses the ridge and continues to descend, but with the valley on the left instead of the right. A switchback is encountered at 1.6 miles. The trail passes beneath frequent long rhododendron tunnels; the abundance of vegetation precludes good views from this altitude, but at about 2.0 miles the hiker is offered one of the few glimpses into the valley below. The trail crosses small streams at 2.8, 3.0, and 3.6 miles.

The trail crosses an abandoned dirt road at 4.0 miles, with the foundation of an old CCC shelter nearby. A bit farther, the concrete-block Curley Maple Gap AT shelter with a corrugated metal roof is nestled beside the trail. It accommodates six people, and tent sites are nearby. A spring is 100 feet south on the AT. The spring may be disappointingly stagnant at first, but you will find running water by following the stream downhill where it becomes Jones Branch after several confluences. The stream falls rapidly away from the trail, and soon it becomes audible only in the distance. The trail then descends and plays catch-up to the creek by means of switchbacks at 5.0 and 5.3 miles, enabling the hiker to rock-hop across Jones Branch at mile 5.5. Leucothoe, nettles, and sedges become plentiful in this narrow, flat valley. The narrow nature of this floodplain is responsible for occasional trail destruction by heavy rains. Five additional stream crossings are encountered at miles 5.7, 6.3, 6.6, 6.7, and 7.0—most of them aided by means of improved log bridges.

At 7.1 miles, the AT emerges from a rhododendron and hemlock forest onto a gravel road bordering the Nolichucky Gorge Campground. At 7.2 miles the AT abruptly turns right to cross a gully with the aid of a well-constructed footbridge, although there is no water in dry weather. The Nolichucky Gorge Campground Trailhead and the USA Raft facilities are on the left. However, the AT can be continued from this trailhead area to the bridge downstream across the Nolichucky River.

From the gully bridge the AT gradually climbs a steep ridge while running parallel to Nolichucky River and to the paved road leading to Nolichucky Expeditions Base Camp. The river is continuously visible due to the steep terrain. The AT eventually levels out and traverses a couple of small swampy areas where old railroad ties provide stepping

Nolichucky River canoeist in the Nolichucky River Gorge. Photograph by Will Skelton.

stones. After crossing the Clinchfield Railroad tracks at 8.3 miles, the AT descends easily to the paved road and Nolichucky River at 8.4 miles. Here a two-lane bridge with protected walkway facilitates the AT crossing of Nolichucky River. Although the Jones Branch section of the AT terminates here, the AT continues toward No Business Knob and an AT shelter.

OFF-TRAIL HIKING OPPORTUNITIES

The former Nolichucky River Trail (FS Trail 157) is no longer maintained and is washed out in places. However, the route provides a great opportunity to see the beautiful Nolichucky River close up. The route starts at the back and riverside area of the Nolichucky Gorge Campground Trailhead. Simply follow the riverbank upstream. The old trail extended for about 2.0 miles to the TN-NC state line. It often crosses sand bars, which are subject to flood washouts. In view of the river, any exploration of this route should only be by experienced hikers and at their own risk.

Northern Cherokee National Forest

French Broad and Nolichucky Rivers
(TI Map 782)

12 Nolichucky River Corridor South

As with the northern side of the Nolichucky River, there are also excellent hiking opportunities on the south. The AT of course continues its southward march toward GA, and there are several hiking trails both south and north of Erwin, TN, and I-26 (formerly US 19W) that extend from TN into NC. The trails closer to the Nolichucky River are located north of I-26. Two "official" CNF trails start near the river; however, they are very poorly maintained by the CNF. Other than the AT Corridor and small Scenic River and Rare Communities acreage, there are no designated protected areas within this area.

TRAILHEADS AND MAPS

Mine Flats Trailhead (Temple Hill Trail, North End)

At the intersection of North Main Street and Route 107 in Erwin, head west several blocks on Main Street following old Route 23. Turn left onto Love Street, following the "To Asheville" signs. After several blocks, turn right onto Ohio Avenue, again following the "To Asheville" signs. When the road forks, bear left onto Chestoa Pike, leaving old Route 23. Continue on Chestoa Pike across the bridge over the

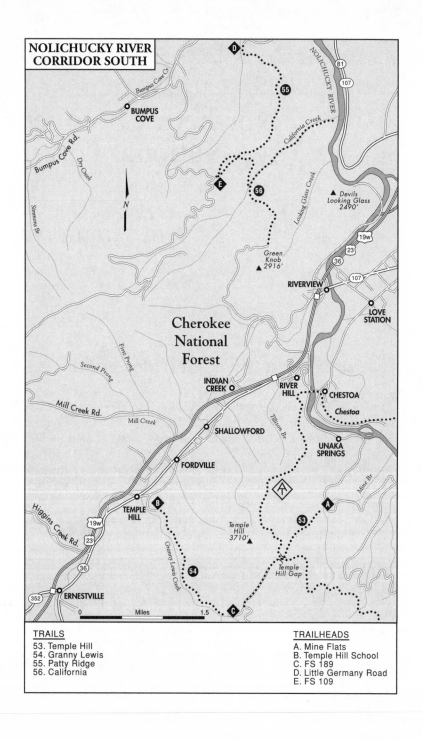

NOLICHUCKY RIVER CORRIDOR SOUTH

TRAILS
53. Temple Hill
54. Granny Lewis
55. Patty Ridge
56. California

TRAILHEADS
A. Mine Flats
B. Temple Hill School
C. FS 189
D. Little Germany Road
E. FS 109

Nolichucky River. Immediately after crossing the bridge, turn left onto Unaka Springs Road. The Nolichucky Hostel sits at the far right corner of the intersection. Continue past the CNF sign found at 1.2 miles from the bridge. At 1.3 miles turn left off the paved road to head up a rocky gravel road. A high road-clearance vehicle with sturdy tires is recommended for this road. Reach Mine Flats at 2.2 miles to find a turnaround just short of an FS gate and a stream (UTM 17S 369899E/ 3994359N). The Temple Hill Trail can be found to the right, up a steep bank.

Temple Hill School Trailhead (Granny Lewis Creek Trail, West End)

Take Exit 12 off the new limited-access I-26 that brings routes former US 23, US 19W, and TN 36 south from Erwin. Route US 19W exits here to head southwest on a two-lane blacktop road. At the stop sign where US 19W turns to the right, turn left onto old Route 23. Proceed northeast 0.2 mile to turn right onto Old Highway Road. Continue

Nolichucky River rafters on Nolichucky River. Photograph by Will Skelton.

0.1 mile on Old Highway Road. Immediately past Temple Hill School, turn right onto a private drive. At 0.1 mile along this driveway, find the Granny Lewis Creek Trailhead on the left (UTM 17S 366385E/ 3994536N). There is no trail sign until the FS boundary, 0.2 mile farther along. Note: This is private property. Obtain permission from the adjacent landowner to park at the trailhead.

FS 189 Trailheads: Temple Hill Trail, South End, and Granny Lewis Creek Trail, East End

Follow the new limited-access highway that brings former US 23, US 19W, and TN 36 south from Erwin. Take Exit 12 to follow Route US 19W as it leaves to head southwest. Turn right at the stop sign. At 1.1 miles from Exit 12 turn left just before a bridge, following US 19W toward Spivey Gap. At 7.4 miles, turn left onto a gravel road, FS 189. A sign identifies this area as a Cherokee Wildlife Management Area. A high road-clearance vehicle with good tires will do best on this rocky, rutted road. Bear to the right, staying on FS 189, when FS 189A splits off to the left. Allow about 30 minutes to travel the next three and one-half miles. The southern trailhead for the Granny Lewis Creek Trail appears on the right at 10.9 miles (UTM 17S 368319E/3992636N). At 11.1 miles, FS 189 dead-ends at the eastern trailhead for the Temple Hill Trail (UTM 17S 368172E/3992323N).

Little Germany Road Trailhead (Patty Ridge Trail, North End)

From Erwin take TN 81 toward Jonesborough. At 6.3 miles turn left onto Bumpass Cove Road. Follow Bumpass Cove Road for 1.0 mile, turning left onto Little Germany Road for 0.5 mile to the bridge over Patty Creek. Turn right onto a gravel road just on the other side of the creek. Follow the public gravel road 0.1 mile to a small parking area with a USFS co-op sign. Please respect the private property adjacent to the gravel road.

FS 109 Trailhead (Patty Ridge Trail, South End)

Follow TN 81 from Erwin 6.3 miles and turn left onto Bumpass Cove Road. Proceed 1.0 to the junction with Little Germany Road and continue on Bumpass Cove for 0.9 mile to FS 190. Turn left on FS 90 and drive roughly 3.0 miles to the small sign on the left marking the start of the upper Patty Ridge Trail (UTM 17S 367786E/4000692N).

FS 109 is a rough, rocky road. A high road-clearance vehicle with sturdy tires is recommended.

TOPOGRAPHIC MAPS: USGS Chestoa, TN. TI 782, French Broad and Nolichucky Rivers, CNF.

TRAIL DESCRIPTIONS

53. TEMPLE HILL TRAIL (FS TRAIL 524, TI TRAIL 35)

LENGTH: 1.7 miles

ELEVATION CHANGE: Low point, 2,120 feet; high point, 2,850 feet

DIFFICULTY: Moderate

TRAILHEADS: Mine Flats (start) and FS 189 (end)

USE: Hiking

TOPOGRAPHIC MAP: USGS Chestoa, TN

COMMENTS: The Temple Hill trail offers an enjoyable hike through the forest. The trail follows a streambed up to Temple Hill Gap between No Business and Temple Hill Ridges. At the gap, the trail intersects the AT then descends to end not far from Granny Lewis Creek.

DETAILS: Scramble up the steep bank to find the trail sign several yards in from the trailhead. The trail sign states, incorrectly, that this is the Granny Lewis Creek Trail. The USFS may subsequently correct this discrepancy. Blue blazes mark the trail. The Temple Hill Trail, an old roadbed, climbs beside a tributary stream of Mine Branch. The trail itself serves as an intermittent streambed. Some stretches of the trail are quite rocky. At 0.4 mile the trail divides. Stay to the left. The trail begins to climb steeply, crossing a small stream at 0.5 mile. The trail forks again at 0.8 mile. Again, stay to the left. After crossing another small stream, the trail levels out. The AT angles in from the left rear at 0.9 mile. Proceed with the AT to the right another 50 yards to reach Temple Hill Gap (UTM 17S 368974E/3993448N).

The AT continues to the right (3.3 miles to the Nolichucky River Bridge), while the Temple Hill Trail heads left, down a small draw. The trail, a well-defined roadbed, forks at 1.3 miles. Take either side. At 1.4 miles the forks rejoin near a small cabin to the left (east) in the woods. The trail reaches FS 189 at 1.7 miles. Two signs name this as the Temple Hill Trail. The old sign identifies the trail as FS Trail 24 (an old designation) and lists mileages of 1.0 mile to the AT and 2.0 miles to Mine Flats. The actual distances measure 0.8 and 1.7 miles respectively. The newer sign shows the trail as FS Trail 524. Note: the TI map incorrectly shows the end of the Temple Hill Trail farther up the mountain, near the AT. Turn right on FS 189 for 0.2 mile to reach the Granny Lewis Creek Trailhead.

54. GRANNY LEWIS CREEK TRAIL (FS TRAIL 108, TI TRAIL 11)

LENGTH: 2.2 miles

ELEVATION CHANGE: Low point, 1,800 feet; high point, 2,320 feet

DIFFICULTY: Moderate

TRAILHEADS: FS 189 (start); Temple Hill School (end)

USE: Hiking

TOPOGRAPHIC MAP: USGS Chestoa, TN

COMMENTS: This trail follows the course of Granny Lewis Creek, crossing it several times, from the dead-end of FS 189 to Temple Hill School. The final 0.2 mile of the trail lies on private land. No right-of-way has been acquired.

DESCRIPTION: Turn to the right at the end of FS 189 to find the Granny Lewis Creek Trail. The sign found here incorrectly states this is the Temple Hill Trail. The FS may have corrected this inconsistency. Blue blazes mark the trail. The first yards of the trail pass through a large messy campsite. At 0.1 mile, rock-hop across to the left side of Granny Lewis Creek. Then rock-hop back to the right side at 0.2 mile. When hiking upstream at this crossing, take care to bear to the left after crossing the creek, following the blue blazes. Avoid the branch to the right. Rock walls, remnants of an old home site, parallel the trail at 0.3 mile. More rock-hops follow, first to the left and then to the right of Granny Lewis Creek at 0.4 and 0.5 mile.

A short distance beyond, a significant blowdown marks the point at which the trail begins a gradual climb along the hill beside the creek. At 1.0 mile, the trail descends steeply over a rock face to circumvent a large, uprooted stump. The trail crosses a side stream at 1.3 miles as it slabs around at constant elevation. The trail begins to descend at 1.5 miles, steeply at first, then gradually. At 1.8 miles, the trail enters a beautiful pine forest with a dense canopy overhead and ground carpeted with pine needles. A trail sign at 2.0 miles indicates the official end of the Granny Lewis Creek Trail, FS 108. Barbed wire posted with "no trespassing" signs parallels the right side of the trail from this point on. The trail continues past a private home on the left at 2.1 miles. The trail ends at 2.2 miles, just above a private road directly behind the Temple Hill School.

55. PATTY RIDGE TRAIL (FS TRAIL 113, TI TRAIL 25)

LENGTH: 2.7 miles

ELEVATION CHANGE: Low point, 1,650 feet; high point, 2,500 feet

DIFFICULTY: Difficult (Lower Patty Ridge Trail), moderate (Upper Patty Ridge Trail to Broad Shoal Creek)

TRAILHEADS: Little Germany Road (start); FS 190 (end)

USE: Hiking

TOPOGRAPHIC MAP: USGS Chestoa, TN

COMMENTS: The lower (north) end of Patty Ridge has not been maintained for many years and is an excellent example of the fairly frequent lack of maintenance of trails by the CNF. Although many trails are shown on their maps, they often do not exist on the ground because they are not maintained. Hiking this trail, therefore, constitutes a difficult off-trail exploration. No blazes are visible. What graded trail can be found is blocked due to numerous blowdowns. From the FS 190 (south) trailhead, the Patty Ridge Trail initially follows an old roadbed marked with blue blazes. The Patty Ridge Trail soon bears off to the left of the blazed roadbed at an unmarked junction. The blazed roadbed continues onward for about a mile to Broad Shoal Creek, where it offers access to a wildlife field. The USFS plans to clean up and blaze the Patty Ridge Trail, although when this will come about remains uncertain. The presently blazed south end of the trail actually connects with the (indistinct) California Trail at that wildlife field.

DETAILS (PATTY RIDGE FROM THE BOTTOM, NORTH END): This description is of the initial stretch of the lower Patty Ridge Trail. At the Little Germany Road trailhead, start hiking west on an old roadbed, immediately crossing Patty Creek. A gate across the road is posted with a "No Trespassing" sign. The road runs parallel to the creek. The streambed itself offers the only nontrespassing route. At 0.1 mile, the road crosses to follow the left side of Patty Creek. A small branch enters the creek at 0.2 mile (UTM 17S 368343E/4000286N). Turn left here to ascend along the branch. There is no visible trail; the route follows the branch up to the back of the hollow, gaining about 120 feet. At 0.3 mile (UTM 17S 368576E/4000301N), take a sharp left turn at the branch. The old graded trail becomes visible for the first time. The trail makes a second switchback, this time turning sharply to the right at 0.4 mile. A succession of blowdowns block the trail as it works its way toward Patty Ridge. With the promise of countless more to come, after about 0.5 mile any further progress is an extremely difficult off-trail hike.

DETAILS (PATTY RIDGE TO BROAD SHOAL CREEK FROM THE UPPER, SOUTH END): Begin hiking at the gated roadbed that heads northeast along the left side of the ridgecrest. The blue-blazed trail initially follows the mapped route of the Patty Ridge trail. At 0.4 mile, the road passes through a gap, passing to the right of the ridge. The old, faint Patty Ridge Trail heads up the ridgecrest to the left. Following the old route along the ridge to connect with the lower end of Patty Ridge should be considered difficult, off-trail hiking. Continuing along the blazed roadbed, a parallel road becomes visible above and to the left at 0.6 mile. The roadbeds meet at 0.7 mile. The blue-blazed trail turns right and descends from the ridge. At 1.2 miles, the trail passes through a swampy area. A short detour to the left will keep your feet dry. Just beyond, the trail fords a creel to end in a wildlife field on the other side. A man-made pond supports a healthy frog population on the far side of the grassy field. To the right, about 100 yards upstream, a small stone dam makes a pretty waterfall. To the left, vestiges of the California Trail head downstream to the northeast. Above the pond, evidence of the California Trail can be seen heading to the southeast.

56. CALIFORNIA TRAIL (FS TRAIL 114, TI TRAIL 6)

LENGTH: 4.5 miles

ELEVATION CHANGE: Low point, 1,600 feet; high point, 2,600 feet

DIFFICULTY: Difficult

TRAILHEADS: West bank of Nolichucky River across from Stony Point (start); FS 53987 (end)

USE: Hiking

TOPOGRAPHIC MAP: USGS Chestoa, TN

COMMENTS: This is an excellent example of no trail maintenance and confusion on the part of the CNF in written reports about the nature of its trails. It is an "official" trail in name only. The CNF reports that fishermen use the lower, northern portion of the California Trail along the Nolichucky River. However, there is no road access to that north end of the trail, though both the USGS and TI maps show a bridge leading from TN 81 across the Nolichucky River at Stony Point. The remaining trailhead is accessible only by traveling along a private drive and across private property to reach FS 53987. The USFS has no plans to develop alternate access to this trailhead. Note that there are several discrepancies between the USGS and TI maps for the California Creek Trail area. The USGS map shows California Creek to the southeast of and roughly parallel to Broad Shoal Creek. The TI map shows Broad Shoal Creek, but names it California Creek. The TI map also shows California Creek, but names it Looking Glass Creek. The USGS map does not name Looking Glass Creek, although it does show a short, unnamed creek to the south of California Creek, draining to the northeast of Looking Glass Mountain.

13 Sampson Mountain

(Includes Sampson Mountain Wilderness, Sampson Mountain Wilderness Study Area, and Sampson Mountain Roadless Area)

The 7,992-acre Sampson Mountain Wilderness and the adjacent 3,069-acre roadless area are rugged and beautiful but often inaccessible, both because of terrain and access problems. They are dominated by very steep slopes and drained by swift-flowing, rock-bottomed streams. A number of impressive, precipitous, and very high falls and cascades occur in the area. The most outstanding of these are the 475-foot-high Buckeye Falls and the 200-foot-high Painter Creek Falls. Although a portion of these falls would probably more accurately be classified as cascades, they are nonetheless very impressive, especially when water flow is plentiful. Some accounts claim Buckeye Falls to be the highest waterfall in the eastern United States. The outstanding wilderness qualities of the area were recognized by the designation of the wilderness and the USFS's Southern Appalachian Assessment identification of the Sampson Mountain Roadless Area. The roadless area is protected in the CNF's 2004 plan revision as the 3,069-acre Sampson Mountain Wilderness Study Area. The area is located in Washington, Unicoi, and Greene counties and the Nolichucky/Unaka Ranger District.

The Sampson Mountain Wilderness is a portion of an outstanding outdoor recreation area, adjacent to the 8,696-acre Bald Mountain Ridge Scenic Area and 3,833-acre Bald Mountain Backcountry Area to the south. A 10,977-acre roadless area also lies across the AT in the Pisgah NF. Balds, high cliffs, and rock outcrops afford magnificent views of the TN Valley to the west and the mountains of NC to the east. Wildlife is varied and abundant in the area. The Sampson Mountain Wilderness, along with the other protected areas to the south, is probably the best bear habitat north of the GSMNP in TN. Black bear or their sign is frequently seen, despite heavy hunting pressure. Trout fishing is excellent in several of the swift-flowing, rock-bottomed streams.

The area is covered in second-growth forest, having been logged in the early part of the century and extensively burned. However, a number of large trees can be found in the area. A wide diversity of shrubs is also found, including laurel, rhododendron, flame azalea, and blue-

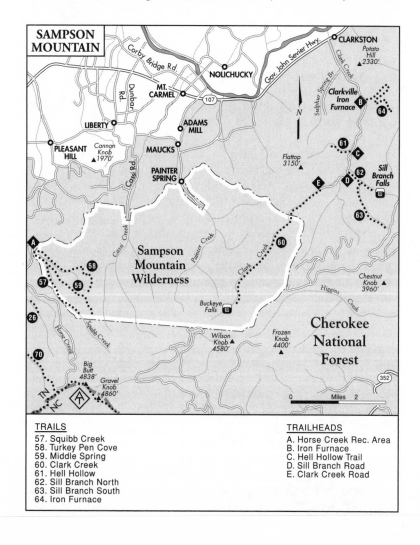

TRAILS
57. Squibb Creek
58. Turkey Pen Cove
59. Middle Spring
60. Clark Creek
61. Hell Hollow
62. Sill Branch North
63. Sill Branch South
64. Iron Furnace

TRAILHEADS
A. Horse Creek Rec. Area
B. Iron Furnace
C. Hell Hollow Trail
D. Sill Branch Road
E. Clark Creek Road

berry. There is also an excellent variety of wildflowers, such as violets, bloodroot, anemone, trillium, lady's slipper, showy orchis, and foam- flowers. There have been few botanical surveys in the protected areas, but rare species found outside the protected areas probably also occur in the area. These species include turkeybeard, long-flowered alum- root, and Buckleya.

The trail system in the area is in great need of maintenance and expansion. Many of the trails lead up creek valleys and gradually fade out, going nowhere. Confusing old roadbeds that go nowhere lead off the main trails. Few circuit hikes are possible at this time because of the lack of trail connections. Despite these limitations, the area has high potential for future trail development and improvement. There are several opportunities to connect trails that would take relatively little construction. If these connecting trails were built, some present trails extended and maintained, and the confusing maze of old road- beds allowed to fade under the vegetation, the area could have an excellent trail system tying into the AT and the adjoining Bald Moun- tain Ridge Scenic Area.

HISTORY

Much of the area was logged in the 1930s. Signs of logging roads can still be seen, especially on the lower slopes of the Clark Creek water- shed. In 1952 a large section was burned to the mineral soil. Some timber-salvage operations took place after the fire. Another fire in 1981, the Painter Creek fire, burned 1,600 acres. These past abuses are still somewhat in evidence, but the area has greatly recovered and the streams run clear and sparkling. Substantial flooding in 2001 washed out many bridges in the general area, including access bridges on the Clark Creek Road.

The Sampson Mountain Wilderness was designated by the US Con- gress in 1986. The CNF's 1988 management plan protected a 6,308-acre primitive area (motorized), a 380-acre Coldspring Mountain Primitive Area, and a 480-acre Flint Mountain Primitive Area. The CNF's 2004 plan revision roughly cuts in half the protected area and recommends a wilderness study area for the protected portion located west of Clark Creek.

TRAILHEADS AND MAPS

Access to the trails in Sampson Mountain Wilderness is from TN 107. Take it east from the junction with the US 11E bypass in Greeneville.

Go through Tusculum and cross the Elbert Kinser Bridge at 4.0 miles. All of the distances below are from the TN 107/US 11E junction.

Horse Creek Recreation Area Trailhead

At 6.7 miles along TN 107, turn right onto FS 94, Horse Creek Road, at a NF Recreation Site sign immediately before several dumpsters. A sign for Horse Creek Recreation Area appears 0.3 mile along the road. There is another Horse Creek Recreation sign at 0.8 mile, when the road takes a sharp right. At 2.8 miles enter USFS land and pass the turnoff to Old Forge Campground at 2.9 miles. Horse Creek Campground is on the left. After you pass the campground, the pavement ends in a parking and picnic area that provides access to Squibb Creek Trail, Turkey Pen Cove Trail, and Middle Spring Ridge Trail, as well as much of Bald Mountain Ridge Scenic Area.

Iron Furnace, Hell Hollow Trail, Sill Branch Road, and Clark Creek Road Trailheads

At mile 15.4 on TN 107, turn right on Clark Creek Road just before TN 107 crosses Clark Creek. The pavement ends at the boundary to CNF, but continue along the gravel road (FS 25). Near the boundary, about 1.6 miles from TN 107, the road crosses Clark Creek on a bridge. The bridge was washed out in a flash flood in 2001 but is being reconstructed in 2004. Until the bridge is completed, these trailheads are accessible only by crossing the creek and hiking FS 25 to the trailheads. The Iron Furnace Trailhead to the Sally Hole Trail (FS Trail 109) is just across the creek to the left of the road; look for a trail marker. At 2.8 miles, the Hell Hollow Trail (FS Trail 24) begins on the right side of the road just after a side stream comes in from the right. It begins as a dirt road that angles up to the right. After approximately 3.4 miles an old dirt road leads off to the left, but access is blocked by large rocks. This road was formerly the Sill Branch Road, FS 25A. It follows Sill Branch for approximately 0.5 mile to the confluence of the North Fork and the South Fork of Sill Branch. The Sill Branch North and Sill Branch South trails begin at the confluence.

Continuing up Clark Creek Road, at 4.2 miles the road ends at rock barricades just before a crossing of Clark Creek. This is the Clark Creek Road Trailhead. An ORV road formerly continued up Clark Creek but is now blocked by rock barriers and is the initial portion of Clark Creek Trail.

TOPOGRAPHIC MAPS: USGS Greystone, TN; Flag Pond, TN-NC. TI Map 782, French Broad and Nolichucky Rivers, CNF.

TRAIL DESCRIPTIONS

57. SQUIBB CREEK TRAIL (FS TRAIL 23, TI TRAIL 33)

LENGTH: 2.2 miles

ELEVATION CHANGE: Low point, 1,920 feet; high point, 2,800 feet

DIFFICULTY: Moderate

TRAILHEAD: Horse Creek Recreation Area (start and dead-end)

TRAIL CONNECTIONS: Turkey Pen Cove Trail and Middle Spring Ridge Trail

USE: Hiking

TOPOGRAPHIC MAPS: USGS Greystone, TN-NC; Flag Pond, TN-NC

COMMENTS: The Squibb Creek Trail follows Squibb Creek to a lovely waterfall. The trail dead-ends at this point, but Turkey Pen Cove Trail and Middle Spring Ridge Trail lead off of Squibb Creek Trail. In fact, USGS topographic maps label Middle Spring Ridge Trail as part of Squibb Creek Trail. However, these topographic maps do not show a trail extending up Squibb Creek, nor do they show Turkey Pen Cove Trail. The trail is rated moderate due to the creek crossings.

DETAILS: Take the Horse Creek Road that begins at the parking area near Horse Creek Campground and follows Horse Creek upstream. After 0.12 mile, look for the remains of a washed-out wooden bridge across Horse Creek and the Squibb Creek Trail. The Squibb Creek Trail begins at the washed out bridge; the bridge may be replaced in the future.

Cross Horse Creek by fording and parallel Squibb Creek along the left bank. At 0.2 mile on the Squibb Creek Trail another wooden bridge takes the trail to the right bank of the creek. At 0.3 mile the trail crosses another wooden bridge to the left side of the creek. At 0.4 mile the trail emerges into a clearing that contains an A-frame cabin. The cabin is on a parcel of private land within the NF. Note the red blaze on the tree to the left of the cabin. Cross in front of the cabin and note another set of double blazes. Angle to the right down to the creek, cross the creek, and continue upstream on the right side of the creek. At 0.49 mile cross back to the left side of the creek. At 0.54 mile cross a side stream that comes in from the left. At 0.56 mile cross another stream that comes in from the left. The Turkey Pen Cove Trail is on the left immediately past a concrete structure that sits low to the ground. Squibb Creek Trail climbs out of the streambed and cuts back toward Squibb Creek. At 0.6 mile look closely for the Middle Spring Ridge Trail as it turns left up over a mound.

To continue on Squibb Creek Trail follow the yellow blazes up Squibb Creek. At 0.9 mile the trail crosses Squibb Creek to the right bank, and at 1.2 miles the trail crosses back to the left side. Look for double blazes at 1.3 miles; the trail turns sharply left up the bank. After this point the trail may be difficult to follow. Continue following the creek as the trail crosses it several times. Watch for yellow blazes. At 2.2 miles the trail ends at a small waterfall.

58. TURKEY PEN COVE TRAIL (FS TRAIL 15, TI TRAIL 36)

LENGTH: 1.8 miles

ELEVATION CHANGE: Low point, 2,000 feet; high point, 3,440 feet

DIFFICULTY: Difficult

TRAILHEADS: Horse Creek Recreation Area (Squibb Creek Trail) (start) and Middle Spring Ridge Trail (end)

USE: Hiking

TOPOGRAPHIC MAPS: USGS Greystone, TN-NC; Flag Pond, TN-NC

COMMENTS: The Turkey Pen Cove Trail leaves the Squibb Creek Trail and travels up Turkey Pen Cove Branch. It then ascends a side ridge of Middle Spring Ridge and intersects the Middle Spring Ridge Trail 0.57 mile from the wilderness boundary. It appears to follow an old road for part of its length. You will need to watch the ground carefully, as the trail is difficult to follow in places. It is rated difficult due to elevation gain and difficulty of following the trail in places at its lower elevations.

DETAILS: Take the Squibb Creek Trail for 0.56 miles. Cross a tributary coming in from the left. Watch for the second tributary and a low concrete structure on the left. At this point turn left onto the Turkey Pen Cove Trail. There is a slight green blaze on the right of Turkey Pen Cove Trail shortly after turning onto the trail. The trail starts on the left bank of the stream and passes through rhododendron, hemlock, and hardwoods. At 0.2 mile cross to the right side of the stream. In places the trail is overgrown with rhododendron. After 0.34 mile, the trail heads uphill into a narrow cove on an old roadbed. At 0.42 mile the trail leaves the roadbed, angles to the right across the slope above the stream, and crosses a small side stream at 0.48 mile. The trail then descends to cross the main stream at 0.51 mile. At 0.56 mile cross the stream back to the right side and continue upstream on an old roadbed. In this section blazes are few and the trail confusing, so follow directions carefully and watch closely for blazes.

At 0.6 mile the trail appears to fork. Take the right-hand fork; the left fork fades out and disappears quickly. The trail crosses a side branch that comes in from the right at 0.63 mile. Bear right along the left bank of this tributary. The other tributary is off to the left through thick rhododendron, running roughly parallel to the one you are following. At 0.75 mile the trail crosses the stream to the right side and heads up the slope away from the stream into more open forest. Cross back to the left of the small stream near its source at 1.05 miles and traverse the slope. Between 1.13 and 1.33 miles the trail goes through a series of switchbacks as it goes up the side of the ridge through pines. At 1.39 miles the trail passes over the point of the ridge and heads up the left side of the ridge and then along the ridgeline. There are spectacular views along this section. At 1.57 miles the trail goes up steeply over rock outcrops with great views to the northeast. The trail continues to travel along the ridgecrest as it levels out. The trail intersects the Middle Spring Ridge Trail at 1.8 miles. To the right, at 1.45 miles, is the intersection with the Squibb Creek Trail; to the left, at about 2.2 miles, is Big Butt.

59. MIDDLE SPRING TRAIL (FS TRAIL 4, TI TRAIL 22)

LENGTH: 3.6 miles

ELEVATION CHANGE: Low point, 2,000 feet; high point, 4,838 feet

DIFFICULTY: Moderate

TRAILHEADS: Horse Creek Recreation Area (Squibb Creek Trail) (start) and AT (end)

USE: Hiking

TOPOGRAPHIC MAPS: USGS Greystone, TN-NC; Flag Pond, TN-NC

COMMENTS: This trail ascends Middle Spring Ridge between Squibb Creek and Turkey Pen Cove. The trail quickly ascends to the ridgecrest, which it follows as it climbs to Rich Mountain. The trail exits Sampson Mountain Wilderness at 2.0 miles, but the trail itself can be followed to Big Butt. Much of the land outside the wilderness is presently in private ownership, but the USFS hopes someday to purchase it. The trail is not blazed. It is not difficult to follow in the wilderness, but the privately owned land is laced with old roads and trails that make finding the way difficult. Actually getting to Big Butt and connecting to the AT requires cutting through a blueberry heath that separates the end of the trail from the AT.

DETAILS: Take the Squibb Creek Trail for 0.6 mile. After crossing a tributary that comes in from the left, skirt through the edge of the stream and notice a green blaze that marks the Turkey Pen Ridge Trail. Continue on Squibb Creek to the Middle Spring Ridge Trail that goes over a small mound to the left. The trail ascends steeply through rhododendron. Turkey Pen Cove Branch can be heard to the left. The trail continues to climb through tulip trees, maples, and hemlock. A group of particularly large hemlocks can be found at 0.3 mile. The trail levels off somewhat through pine forest. Views into the Squibb Creek Gorge can be seen at 0.8 mile. The trail goes through a series of switchbacks from 1.0 mile to 1.2 miles and then steeply ascends the ridgecrest. The grade gradually lessens, and the Turkey Pen Cove Trail intersects as a side ridge joins the main ridge at 1.45 miles, elevation 3,540 feet. The trail continues to follow the ridge as it gradually climbs. At 2.34 miles the trail comes out of thick mountain laurel into a small clearing. A roadbed leads to the left and the right. To the left, the old roadbed leads down into the Cassi Creek drainage before fading out.

Continue to the right along the roadbed, which intersects another road at 2.37 miles. To the left the road dead-ends after 0.3 mile. Turn right on the road and continue uphill. The road reaches a large clearing of exposed ground on the rounded point of the ridge. At the beginning of the clearing, to the right, is a trail that leads 1.1 miles across the headwaters of Squibb Creek before ending on a knob near the boundary between Sampson Mountain Wilderness and Bald Mountain Ridge Scenic Area. Water is available 0.2 mile down this trail. To reach Big Butt, continue through the bare area and pick up the jeep trail on the far side. The trail goes through switchbacks at 2.6 and 2.7 miles. At the second switchback stay right on the jeep trail. The other jeep trail leads toward Wilson Knob. Switchbacks at 3.0 miles and 3.1 miles bring the trail to the ridgeline. Continue along the ridgeline to a clear area at 3.3 miles. Pass through a rock pile at 3.5 miles. At this point there are many blackberry briars that obscure the trail. Reached at 3.6 miles is an area, formerly a blueberry-covered bald, that is covered with mountain laurel and rhododendron. There are numerous stumps and branches where the trail has been cut through the laurel. To reach Big Butt, a 4,838 foot knoll, and the AT, make your way to the southwest. A few hundred yards of this will bring you to the clearings of Big Butt, which connect to the AT. To the right (southwest) along the AT are the Coldspring Mountain Parking Area, Horse Creek Road (FS 94), and Sarvis Cove Trail, all within the Bald Ridge Mountain Scenic Area.

60. CLARK CREEK TRAIL (NO FS OR TI TRAIL NUMBERS)

LENGTH: 3.6 miles

ELEVATION CHANGE: Low point, 1,840 feet; high point, 3,000 feet

DIFFICULTY: Moderate

TRAILHEAD: Clark Creek Road (start and dead-end)

USE: Hiking

TOPOGRAPHIC MAPS: USGS Greystone, TN-NC; Flag Pond, TN-NC; Telford, TN

COMMENTS: The Clark Creek Trail leads up Clark Creek, which is a swift-flowing, rock-bottomed stream with numerous cascades and clear pools. Numerous creek crossings are required, but the stream's low volume often allows rock-hopping. The trail is a good one for seeing wildflowers, especially large-flowered trillium. On the headwaters of one of the branches of Clark Creek lies Buckeye Falls. Buckeye Falls is at least 475 feet high and by some accounts is the highest falls in the eastern United States. Strictly speaking, much of this height is a cascade and not a true waterfall. Water volume is never great, and it is difficult to see the whole falls at one time because of the great height involved. Nevertheless, Buckeye Falls is spectacular, especially when the stream is running full. Great caution should be taken around this falls, as is true with all waterfalls. This trail is unfortunately not currently a part of the CNF trail system.

DETAILS: As the Clark Creek Road bridge is currently washed out, walk the 4.2-mile road to some rock barriers at the very end of the road. Pass the rock barriers and immediately cross the first stream ford. Continue up the old road as it parallels Clark Creek and crosses the creek four more times. At 0.8 mile a side trail comes in from the right. Continue left, as the right-hand road is a dead-end. Continue along the creek, which is crossed two more times. After the first crossing, enter the wilderness. After the second crossing, you will encounter an old trail register. At 1.3 miles the trail climbs steeply above the creek to the right. At 1.5 miles the jeep trail ends and a foot trail continues above the creek.

Descend steeply to the creek and cross to the left side at 2.0 miles. An alternate is to continue 100 feet on the right and then cross. Continue up the creek, which at this point forms numerous clear pools with a solid rock bottom. The trail becomes rough and rocky. Cross the creek numerous times as the trail continues up the creek. Look for a small and deep triangular pool that is perfect for a summer swim. An old engine block is located at 3.0 miles but may be hard to spot. Shortly afterward, the trail follows a ridge in the middle of the creek before crossing a few more times and then going up the middle of the creek. Look for a branch coming in from the left at about 3.2 miles. At 3.4 miles another branch comes in from the left. A faint trail continues up Clark Creek. Turn left and hike up the branch. You will begin to see a cascade ahead after about 0.1 mile, and then Buckeye Falls. The trail becomes indistinct as it follows the creek and is very steep. At 3.6 miles you will reach the base of the falls. Although the water volume is not great, Buckeye Falls is quite impressive. A huge exposed amphitheater-like rock wall spreads across the mountain. On the right side the cascades tumble down from far above. The view of the upper

The lower portion of 475-foot Buckeye Falls. Photograph by Will Skelton.

portion of the falls is blocked by vegetation. A view of the upper reaches of the falls can be had from the ridge to the right of the falls. However, this is not recommended. The slope leading up to the ridge is very steep and unstable. At least one person has been injured coming down this slope. Wilson Knob lies at the top of this ridge above Buckeye Falls.

61. HELL HOLLOW TRAIL (FS TRAIL 124, TI TRAIL 14)

LENGTH: 0.9 mile

ELEVATION CHANGE: Low point, 1,720 feet; high point, 2,400 feet)

DIFFICULTY: Easy

TRAILHEAD: Hell Hollow (start and dead-end)

USE: Hiking

TOPOGRAPHIC MAPS: USGS Flag Pond, TN-NC; Telford, TN

COMMENTS: The Hell Hollow Trail follows the stream of Hell Hollow up the east flank of Sampson Mountain. As one would expect from the name, the trail travels through dense rhododendron and laurel stands. There is potential for extending this trail to Flattop (elevation 3,150) on Sampson Mountain and for connecting it to trails in the Sampson Mountain Wilderness.

DETAILS: Since the Clark Creek bridge is washed out, park at the bridge and hike the 2.8 miles on FS 25 to the trailhead. If the bridge is replaced, you may be able to drive such distance. Head due west on the left side of the creek up a dirt road. At 0.2 mile cross the creek to the right and head rather steeply uphill through laurel thickets. At 0.7 mile head downhill through pines. Cross the creek to the left side at 0.8 mile and turn to the right up the creek. The trail continues up the creek through hemlock and laurel but fades out at about 0.9 mile.

62. SILL BRANCH NORTH TRAIL (FS TRAIL 115, TI TRAIL 31)

LENGTH: 0.6 mile

ELEVATION CHANGE: Low point, 1,960 feet; high point, 2,400 feet

DIFFICULTY: Easy

TRAILHEAD: Sill Branch North Fork Road (start and dead-end)

USE: Hiking

TOPOGRAPHIC MAPS: USGS Flag Pond, TN-NC; Telford, TN

COMMENTS: Since the Clark Creek bridge is washed out, park at the bridge and hike the 3.4 miles on FS 25 to the Sill Branch Road trailhead. If the bridge is replaced, you may be able to drive such distance. Follow the former Sill Branch Road to a trail junction. Continue on the left-hand fork (north fork) of Sill Branch about 0.6 mile to Sill Branch Falls. Some old maps show a road leading farther up Rich Mountain, and it may be possible to follow the old roadbed.

63. SILL BRANCH SOUTH TRAIL (FS TRAIL 116, TI TRAIL 32)

LENGTH: 0.8 mile

ELEVATION CHANGE: Low point, 1,960 feet; high point, 2,400 feet

DIFFICULTY: Easy

TRAILHEAD: Sill Branch Road (start and dead-end)

USE: Hiking

TOPOGRAPHIC MAPS: USGS Flag Pond, TN-NC; Telford, TN

COMMENTS: Hike up the Sill Branch North Fork trail about 0.5 mile on a former road to a trail junction with Sill Branch South Fork. Follow the trail leading up the right-hand fork (South Fork) of Sill Branch. The trail follows the South Fork of Sill Branch uphill for about 0.8 mile.

64. IRON FURNACE TRAIL (ALSO FURNACE STACK HOLLOW AND FORMERLY SALLY'S HOLE) (FS TRAIL 109, TI TRAIL 16)

LENGTH: 2.0 miles

ELEVATION CHANGE: Low point, 1,580 feet; high point, 2,400 feet

DIFFICULTY: Moderate

TRAILHEAD: Iron Furnace (start and dead-end)

USE: Hiking

TOPOGRAPHIC MAPS: USGS Flag Pond, TN-NC; Telford, TN

COMMENTS: The Iron Furnace Trail climbs up Furnace Stack Hollow to a gap in Embreeville Mountain. It then descends into Bumpus Cove, which is a closed toxic-waste landfill on the Superfund list. It is recommended that you hike only as far as the gap on

Embreeville Mountain. The trail is rated moderate due to steepness at higher elevations.

DETAILS: Park at the washed out bridge near the USFS boundary; cross the creek, and look for the trail marker on the left. The trail goes up the creek bed to the left of the road. The creek is crossed many times as the trail continues up the stream. After 0.5 mile the trail turns sharply to the right. The trail leaves the creek and goes uphill past several large hemlocks and pines. At 0.8 mile the trail reaches the crest of a pine-covered ridge. There are nice views back into the Clark Creek Valley. At 1.2 miles continue straight past an old logging road. A few yards past this road is an intersection. Two logging roads turn off to the right; one logging road turns off to the left. The trail to Bumpus Cove continues straight ahead. The trail reaches the back of Bumpus Cove at 2.0 miles, but this route is not recommended because of aesthetic and health concerns.

OFF-TRAIL HIKING OPPORTUNITIES

Because of the size of this area and especially the protected areas, and the lack of trail construction and maintenance by the USFS, this area presents many opportunities for exploring off-trail, often using old logging roads. In the early spring and late fall it is especially easy to traverse the numerous portions of the area that lack trails.

Cassi Creek

This route was formerly a signed CNF trail but was abandoned by the USFS since it is accessible only by crossing private property. If you decide to hike this area, permission to cross the private property must be obtained from the owner of the property at the end of the road. The easy part of the route is about 2.5 miles long. To reach the trailhead, at mile 11.4 on TN 107, turn right on Maple Swamp Road. Go 1.1 miles until Maple Swamp Road intersects Cassi Creek Road (County 5404) and Liberty Creek Drive. Go straight through the intersection onto Cassi Creek Road. Stay on Cassi Creek Road until the pavement ends at 3.2 miles. A wide place in the road provides limited parking on the right before the dirt road crosses a small creek.

To hike the Cassi Creek route continue up the road, which passes through private property and gradually narrows into a trail. Cross a small tributary stream. Follow yellow blazes past dirt barriers. At 0.3 mile the trail goes up a streambed. At 0.35 mile cross Cassi Creek to a gravel bar, go upstream on the gravel bar a few yards, and then cross back to the right side of Cassi Creek. At 0.43 mile cross West Fork Cassi Creek. The East Fork Cassi Creek Trail bears left and follows the East Fork Cassi Creek. The Cassi Creek Trail turns right along the West Fork. A hiker's sign can be seen a few feet down the trail. Follow yellow blazes up the creek and cross the creek at 0.5 mile. At 1.0 mile the trail crosses the creek to the left side. Shortly afterward a hiker's sign is seen where the trail branches.

One of the trail sections turns right across the creek and follows the West Fork Cassi Creek, with yellow blazes, for about 0.25 mile before fading out. Another 0.5 mile in the direction the trail is heading would connect it with the Turkey Pen Cove Trail. The other section of the trail continues up the Middle Fork of Cassi Creek for another 1.4 miles. Continuing on this section of the trail, which is also marked with yellow blazes, the creek is crossed several times. At 1.5 miles an old roadbed comes in from the right. Continue to follow the yellow blazes as the trail crosses the creek several times, heading upstream. The trail passes through a lovely valley, which then narrows. The last blaze is seen at 2.45 miles, and the trail soon ends at 2.5 miles. Old roadbeds can be seen, but these quickly fade out. There is potential to link this trail with the Middle Spring Ridge Trail.

East Fork Cassi Creek

This route makes possible a trip to the spectacular Painter Creek Falls, but it must be considered an off-trail route because of lack of public access. There is a fairly good old roadbed that the route follows. The route begins the same way as the Cassi Creek route above but leaves the Cassi Creek route at the confluence of the West and East Forks of Cassi Creek. After crossing West Fork Cassi Creek on the Cassi Creek route, bear left up the right bank of East Cassi Creek on an old road-bed. After about 150 feet, cross the creek to the left side. The route crosses the creek again at 300 feet and thereafter five times between 0.1 and 0.7 mile as it gradually gains elevation. The route is on the left of the creek at 0.8 mile when it turns sharply to the left (north) away from the creek and begins to climb the slope. The old roadbed that the route follows parallels a branch of East Cassi Creek that is below to the left. At 1.0 mile an old roadbed comes in from the left; it goes down toward the branch before fading out. The route itself bears to the east. At 1.14 miles the route turns to the southeast and begins to circle the point of a ridge. By 1.5 miles the route has come back around to the east and is going downhill, with the branch getting closer on the left. At 1.7 miles the route crosses the branch and turns to the northeast going uphill. The route climbs the slope through pine, laurel, and rhododendron.

At 1.9 miles the route, which had been heading north and northwest, switches back to the east and parallels the section of the route below. The route turns southeast and then south before switching back to the northeast through young pines at 2.3 miles. The route enters a gap at 2.4 miles. Two other routes leave the gap. One leads uphill to the north and goes 0.38 mile to the top of a knob. The other route goes downhill to the south toward Painter Creek. The route to the south descends quickly and reaches Painter Creek at 2.8 miles. Cross Painter Creek and follow it downstream. A side stream comes in from the right at 2.9 miles. Cross the creek to the left bank just before they join. Cross the creek to the right side at 3.05 miles and back to the left side at 3.2 miles. The route, which has been following an old roadbed, narrows and by 3.4 miles has faded out completely. To reach Painter Creek Falls, continue downstream along the creek for 0.25 mile. Approach cautiously, as the terrain falls off precipitously. The safest descent past the falls appears to be off to the left of the falls. Painter Creek route can be picked up 1.25 miles downstream from the falls (or 1.5 miles downstream from the end of East Cassi Creek route). There are stretches along the creek that appear to be trail; other sections require struggling through rhododendron. Painter Creek Falls is a lovely falls of about 200 feet. As with Buckeye Falls, some of this distance might be classified a cascade. Water flow is considerably greater than Buckeye Falls. The falls itself should be approached with extreme caution. According to a local resident, at least two people have lost their lives in accidents on Painter Creek Falls.

Painter Creek

This route provides an easier access to Painter Creek Falls than the East Fork Cassi Creek route described above. However, again there is a public access problem in that the property at the trailhead is privately owned and permission must be obtained. To reach the trailhead, at mile 12.2 on TN 107, turn right on Painter Creek Road. Continue on it for 2.0 miles. At 2.0 miles a parking area on the right can accommodate several cars. The pavement ends, and a gate blocks the road at 2.1 miles. Parking for several cars can be found to the right of Painter Creek Road shortly before it ends at a gate. To take the route, continue past a house on the right and through the gate. The pavement ends at the gate. Continue up the road. At 0.2 mile turn left off the main road and skirt the left side of a large meadow. The road leads to a house on the other side of the meadow. At 0.3 mile you pass a barn as you enter the forest. At 0.34 miles cross Painter Creek to the right side. Cross the creek four times between 0.41 and 0.54 mile. Continue up the right side of the creek. At 0.9 mile cross the creek to the left side and then cross a side stream that comes in from the left and continue up the creek. At 1.06 miles the roadbed narrows and the route gradually fades out. To continue, cross another tributary stream that comes in from the left at 1.2 miles. Continue up the creek, crossing when necessary to find better terrain. Sections of the creek are easy to negotiate, with the route being worn by hikers coming up the creek; other sections are choked with rhododendron and are difficult. At 2.25 miles the foot of Painter Creek Falls is reached. East Cassi Creek Route can be found 0.25 mile up the creek. The safest route seems to be to skirt the falls far to the right. Extreme caution should be exercised, as the terrain slopes steeply in this area.

14 Bald Mountains

(Includes Bald Mountain Ridge Scenic Area, Bald Mountain Backcountry Area, and Bald Mountain Roadless Area)

The Bald Mountains are the wonderfully scenic mountains on the far skyline as you drive I-81 north of Greeneville, or even more scenic if you are on TN 107 just northeast of Tusculum. Much of what you see is protected, and the AT runs along the top. The scenic area is provided for in the CNF's 2004 plan revision and covers 8,696 acres of the CNF (Nolichucky/Unaka Ranger District) in Greene County, TN, including the steep western side of the Bald Mountains as they rise some 3,000 feet above the valley floor. The plan also includes a 3,833-acre Bald Mountain Backcountry Area. Both areas are included in a larger 11,744-acre roadless area identified by the USFS in its Southern Appalachian Assessment; another 10,971-acre roadless area is located in the Pisgah NF in NC. Together with the Sampson Mountain Wilderness to the north, this is by far the largest combined wild area in the northern CNF. Substantial amounts of forest and wildlife are protected and are comparable to the Citico Creek/Joyce Kilmer–Slickrock and Big Frog/Cohutta areas in the southern CNF. The area is rather rugged for the most part, with many rocky exposures and cliffs fringing the upper slopes of the Bald Mountains. Some of these cliffs offer outstanding views of the TN Valley, such as those

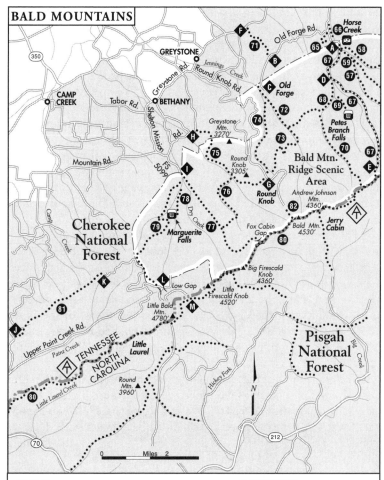

BALD MOUNTAINS

TRAILS

65. Scarlett Oak
66. Horse Creek Recreation
67. Horse Creek Road
68. Poplar Cove
69. Pete' s Branch
70. Sarvis Cove
71. Doctor's Ridge
72. Jennings Creek
73. Cowbell Hollow
74. Little Jennings Creek
75. Davis Creek
76. Artie Hollow
77. Phillips Hollow
78. Marguerite Falls
79. Bullen Hollow
80. Appalachian Trail
81. Greene Mountain
82. Round Knob Connector

TRAILHEADS

A. Horse Creek Rec. Area
B. Doctor' s Ridge (South)
C. Old Forge Campground
D. Horse Creek Road
E. Coldspring Mtn. Parking Area
F. Doctor' s Ridge (North)
G. Round Knob Picnic Area
H. Davis Creek Trail
I. Shelton Mission Road
J. FS 98
K. Kennedy Cabin
L. Low Gap
M. Jones Meadow

near the end of the Horse Creek Road, and the magnificent Blackstack Cliffs on the AT.

Most of the trails into the area follow one of the four major drainages that dissect the main ridge. The streams are not very large, but the trails cross them repeatedly (without the benefit of footbridges) because the steepness of the narrow valley walls leaves little space for both stream and trail. As the streams near the main ridge, they rapidly steepen, and numerous small waterfalls and cascades are found along most of the trails. Care must be followed when hiking several of these trails up to the AT, for although they are marked with yellow or blue blazes, they are rarely used, very steep, and have not received maintenance in several years. In summertime the upper reaches of the Sarvis Cove, Artie Hollow, and Phillips Hollow trails should not be attempted without a topographical map and compass.

The area is covered with a young to middle-aged, second-growth forest, with some large cove hardwoods found in the sheltered hollows. The area has many fine examples of open oak forests on the high ridges, especially above Round Knob and along the AT. Closed oak forests, rich in mountain laurel, rhododendron, blueberry, and flame azalea are especially common on the dry, rocky, south-facing slopes of the lower foothills of Greene Ridge, Greystone Mountain, and Reynolds Ridge. Some of this dry forest was ravaged by fires in the drought years of the late 1980s.

The ruggedness of the terrain in the area makes it prime habitat for reclusive animals, such as wild turkey, ruffed grouse, fox, and black bear. The region around Sarvis Cove and Horse Creek is designated by the TWRA as a bear preserve. Scheduled bear hunts with dogs are conducted in early winter. Check with the CNF before attempting a hike in November and December to avoid these hunts.

HISTORY

The area was extensively clear-cut until it was acquired by the USFS about 1930. Evidence of logging remains on some trails, in the form of old rails, rotted rail ties, and various metal debris. The ruggedness of the terrain generally spared the area from further harvesting until the present time. The area has served as a favorite recreational area for local residents through the years, especially the swimming holes at the campgrounds at Horse Creek and Old Forge, and the grassy balds on Coldspring Mountain. The backcountry trails, however, receive little use, affording a true wilderness experience. The Viking Mountain Resort, a failed resort venture at the southwestern corner of the area between Jones Meadow and Blackstack Cliffs, was auctioned in 1989 and purchased by the USFS; several homes and cottages there have been dismantled. The area is in the center of the former Jennings Creek RARE II area and the subsequently identified roadless area. The CNF Wilderness Coalition supported wilderness designation for this area during the late 1970s and the RARE II process. However, in the early 1980s the USFS issued plans for major road construction and clear-cutting in the area. This action was appealed by the Sierra Club, leading to amendments to the USFS's ambitious plan in 1983. The Sierra Club, in conjunction with the USFS, the TN Conservation League, hunters' groups, and ORV organizations subsequently negotiated a settlement as to the fate of the area. This led to designation of the Sampson Mountain Wilderness in 1986 and the subsequent creation of the 8,653-acre Bald Mountain Ridge Scenic Area from most of the old RARE II area's acreage. The compromise allowed some of the existing roads to remain open but stopped any future road construction and clear-cutting. The scenic area was designated in the CNF's 1988 management plan. The CNF's 2004 plan revision continues the protection of a larger area in scenic and backcountry area designations.

In July and August of 2001, two strong storms hit the area, causing severe flash floods and extensive damage to streambeds, trails, and roads, as well as triggering several landslides. Many of the trails became much more difficult to negotiate due to the flood damage, and some roads were closed. As of 2004, Horse Creek Road (FS 94) is closed to motorized vehicles above the Horse Creek Campground. Greene Mountain Road (FS 98) is also closed between the trailhead for Greene Mountain Trail (FS Trail 13) and Horsehitch Gap. Currently there are no plans to reopen these roads unless government funding is found. Check with the CNF for the current status of these roads.

TRAILHEADS AND MAPS

Horse Creek Recreation Area, Doctor's Ridge Trail (South), and Old Forge Campground Trailheads

Take TN 107 east out of Greeneville off US 11E. Follow TN 107 through Tusculum and across the Nolichucky River about 4.0 miles from Greeneville. Continue on TN 107 about 3.0 miles from the river and turn right onto County 94 (Horse Creek Road) at a USFS sign for the Horse Creek Recreation Area on the right, about 0.3 mile past the second intersection with TN 351. After about 0.8 mile the road takes a sharp right at an intersection. Look for the USFS sign. Just past the intersection Greystone Road enters from the right (west), leading to the trailheads at Round Knob and Shelton Mission Road (see below). The road bears right again at a rocky knoll and travels about 0.3 mile farther to the Horse Creek Recreation Area at 2.7 miles from TN 107. The gravel road (FS 331) to Old Forge Campground enters from the right about 100 yards ahead. To the left is a parking lot for the swimming area. Straight ahead it is about 0.2 mile to the Horse Creek Campground and 0.5 mile to the trailhead for the Horse Creek and Squibb Mountain trails (see the Sampson Mountain section). The lower portion of Horse Creek Road (FS 94) is an ORV trail. However, due to severe flood damage, FS 94 is closed to motorized vehicles beyond the Horse Creek Campground. To reach Old Forge Campground turn right (west) on FS 331. Doctor's Ridge Trail (South) Trailhead is 2.0 miles west on FS 331 and the Old Forge Campground and the Little Jennings Creek and Jennings Creek trails are 2.7 miles at the end of FS 331.

Horse Creek Road (Poplar Cove Trail) and Coldspring Mountain Parking Area Trailheads

The Coldspring Mountain Parking Area can be reached only by four-wheel-drive vehicle and is at the south end of FS 94, the Horse Creek Road, on Coldspring Mountain; FS 94 is often used as a trail and is described in the trail descriptions. The road begins at the Horse Creek Recreation Area Trailhead described above and climbs up toward Coldspring Mountain along Horse Creek. At 0.8 mile the Poplar Cove Trail (FS Trail 22) begins on the right. The road ends at the Coldspring Mountain Parking Area at 4.7 miles. As noted, FS 94 beyond Horse Creek Campground and leading up to Coldspring Mountain Parking Area may be closed to motorized vehicles due to severe flood damage. There are no plans to repair this road unless government funding is found. Check with the CNF for the current status.

Doctor's Ridge Trail (North), Round Knob Picnic Area, Davis Creek Trail, and Shelton Mission Road Trailheads

To get to both Round Knob Picnic Area and Shelton Mission Road trailheads, turn right (west) on Greystone Road, as mentioned above (Greystone Road is on the Horse Creek Road, County 94, about 1.0 mile from the County 94/TN 107 junction). Bear left at the first intersection, passing a church on the right. Doctor's Ridge Trail is on the left at about 2.0 miles as the road passes over a small gap, just after the junction with Middle Creek Road and just before Walters Road. The road curves around a knoll and passes Greystone FWB Church about 3.3 miles from the road to Horse Creek. Follow the road over Jennings Creek at 3.4 miles (you are now on County 2580), then look for the unmarked and paved Round Knob Road on the left at 3.7 miles, just before crossing another creek (Water Fork). Turn left onto Round Knob Road (FS 88). At the fork, stay to the right. The road turns to gravel at 1.0 mile and then climbs another 3.5 miles to the Round Knob Picnic Area and several trailheads. FS 88 continues as a rough and steep 4 WD road from the southern end of the parking lot to climb another 1.5 miles to a dead-end. There are no maintained trails on this section of road.

To reach Shelton Mission Road access, continue past the road to Round Knob, passing a large piped spring on the left. Take the first paved road to the left, 0.25 mile from the road to Round Knob. This is Shelton Mission Road. Follow the road 1.25 miles to a stone foundation on the right. Directly across the road is the Davis Creek Trailhead. There is a trail sign but very little room for parking. Continue along Shelton Mission Road, past Shelton Mission Church. Look for

Grassy Bald and AT on Coldspring Mountain. Photograph by Will Skelton.

Peavine Way on the right. The unmarked and gravel FS 5099 is on the left 0.1 mile past Peavine Way, 1.0 mile from the Davis Creek Trailhead, or 2.3 miles from Greystone Road. Turn left onto FS 5099 to reach the Shelton Mission Road Trailhead; there is a parking area on the left at 0.2 mile, big enough for four cars. Another small pull-off is on the left at 0.3 mile for one car. The road dead-ends at the Phillips Hollow Trailhead at 0.4 mile, where there is parking for several cars.

Shelton Mission Road continues past FS 5099 to another intersection with Greystone Road, 2.3 miles away. Turning left onto Greystone Road from this intersection will take you 4.8 miles to the junction of TN 350 and TN 351. At the four-way stop, turn left to go 7.2 miles to the junction with TN 70. Turn right to cross the Nolichucky River at 1.7 miles and reach Greeneville at about 7.0 miles.

An alternate route to the Round Knob area is on TN 351. When proceeding east on TN 107, take the first right (south) onto TN 351 after crossing the Nolichucky River (Elbert Kinser Bridge). Take TN 351 for about 4.5 miles, taking the fourth left turn in the Bird Island Community. Follow the road 2.0 miles until it descends into another road and turn left. Follow this road about 3.2 miles to Shelton Mission Road or 3.5 miles to the gravel road to Round Knob. To the right, it is about 6.0 miles back to Greeneville along TN 350. After turning left, follow the road past a sand and gravel quarry at 2.0 miles from TN 351. Turn right at the next intersection, following signs to Greystone FWB Church. At 3.2 miles from TN 351 you will pass the Greystone School. At 4.7 miles the Shelton Mission Road turns right. At 5.0 miles FS 88 turns right and proceeds up to the Round Knob Picnic Area.

FS 98 Trailhead

Take TN 70 east from Greeneville about 15 miles to Viking Mountain Road (marked on the Trails Illustrated map as Upper Paint Creek Road), which enters on the left just before crossing Paint Creek and before the state line. There is a sign at the road for a summer camp. If approaching from NC, take NC 208 to the TN-NC state line and look for Viking Mountain Road about 0.5 mile from the state line on the right and immediately after crossing Paint Creek. Follow the paved Viking Mountain Road 1.6 miles; then turn left onto the gravel Greene Mountain Road (FS 98). Follow the gravel road 1.0 mile and look for a horse-trail on the right immediately before a hairpin turn to the right. As of the early 2000s, FS 98 is closed beyond this point and barricaded by downed trees. There is ample parking, but if the road is reopened there is parking space for a couple of cars along the roadside on the left shoulder of the road. There are no plans to repair FS 98 unless government funding is found.

Kennedy Cabin, Low Gap, and Jones Meadow Trailheads

Three trailheads are located off the Viking Mountain Road (Upper Paint Creek Road), a fairly well-maintained road, because of the cellular towers located at the top of the mountain. This road used to provide access to the now defunct Viking Mountain development at Jones Meadow. Use the directions for the FS 98 Trailhead above to locate Viking Mountain Road. Continue on Viking Mountain Road for 3.0 miles past the FS 98 turnoff, at which point the road changes to gravel. Follow the gravel road 1.4 miles. To reach the Kennedy Cabin Trailhead turn left at this point on a gated USFS road (FS 358). Check with the USFS to see if the road will be open. It is a rough road and is only passable by high clearance vehicles. If the road is closed, there is parking near the gate for a few cars. Follow the rough dirt road 0.8 mile to an intersection and bear left. The right fork leads approximately 50 yards to the Bullen Hollow Trail at a small gap. The trail leaves the gap to the right, leading approximately 0.5 mile to Low Gap, and to the left of the gap it goes downhill 2.6 miles to the Shelton Mission Road Trailhead. To reach the Kennedy Cabin Trailhead, proceed on the left fork 0.7 mile, reaching a turnaround in a grassy clearing. The trailhead is to the left, marked by trail signs. There is ample space for parking.

To reach the other two trailheads, continue on the Viking Mountain Road for approximately 0.6 mile from FS 358 to an obvious gap. This is the Low Gap Trailhead, and the Bullen Hollow Trail begins on the left (west) side of the gap. The Jones Meadow Trailhead is reached by continuing on the Viking Mountain Road 1.7 miles until it ends at Jones Meadow at a T intersection with a road that follows the ridgeline. Turn right at the T intersection and go approximately 100 yards to park just before the southwestern edge of the bald and a sign for "Camp Creek Trail/The Oaks." To reach the AT, go directly across the road from the Camp Creek Trail sign and follow what may start as a faint trail in the summer but quickly becomes a very clear trail that leads downhill about 100 yards to the AT. Most of the failed development's land at Jones Meadow has been acquired by the USFS. The gravel road that goes past the ruins of the chalets now leads to communications towers. The Camp Creek Trail is not a USFS trail, but is maintained by The Oaks, a private camp in the Camp Creek Valley. It leads down to the Low Gap Trailhead, follows the Bullen Hollow Trail for 0.5 mile before turning off to go past the Kennedy Cabin Trailhead and then down to The Oaks.

TOPOGRAPHIC MAPS: USGS Greystone, TN-NC; Davy Crockett Lake, TN-NC. TI Map 782, French Broad and Nolichucky Rivers, CNF.

TRAIL DESCRIPTIONS

65. SCARLET OAK TRAIL (FS TRAIL 181, TI TRAIL 30)

LENGTH: 0.5 mile

ELEVATION CHANGE: Low point, 1,750 feet; high point, 2,000 feet

DIFFICULTY: Easy

TRAILHEADS: Horse Creek Campground (loop)

USE: Hiking

TOPOGRAPHIC MAP: USGS Greystone, TN-NC

DETAILS: This is a short loop trail that passes through a pine-oak forest with a thick undergrowth of rhododendron. The trail begins opposite from the entrance for Horse Creek Campground on Horse Creek Road (FS 94) and just past the junction with Old Forge Road (FS 331). After about 50 feet, the trail splits at the beginning of the loop. In either direction the trail climbs gradually up through the rhododendron to the midway point at a small bench next to a stream. Mosses and ferns line the trail in both directions as it curves back down to the beginning of the loop.

66. HORSE CREEK RECREATION TRAIL (FS TRAIL 200, TI TRAIL 15)

LENGTH: 0.4 mile

ELEVATION CHANGE: Low point, 1,750 feet; high point, 1,850 feet

DIFFICULTY: Easy

TRAILHEADS: Horse Creek Recreation Area—Swimming Area Parking (start) and Horse Creek Picnic Area (end)

USE: Hiking, mountain bike

TOPOGRAPHIC MAP: USGS Greystone, TN-NC

DETAILS: This is a short, paved trail that winds its way from the swimming area, through the Horse Creek Campground alongside Horse Creek, and ends at the picnic area. It crosses Horse Creek twice, but the bridges were washed away during the 2001 floods, so it is necessary to rock-hop to get across the fairly wide stream. The trail begins at the Horse Creek Swimming Area across the parking lot from the bathrooms. It crosses a small creek on a covered wooden bridge and continues upstream, working its way through a forest of mature hemlocks and very sparse undergrowth. At 0.1 mile there is a footing for a bridge that used to cross Horse Creek to a trail that paralleled the stream on the other side. Soon after, the pavement is broken and missing due to flood damage and is a minor testament to the power of fast-moving water. After crossing the campground road, the trail winds through the campground and comes to the first crossing of Horse Creek and a missing bridge at 0.3 mile. The trail soon reaches the next crossing and washed-out bridge. Shortly after, the trail ends at the pavilion at the Horse Creek Picnic Area.

67. HORSE CREEK ROAD (COLDSPRING MOUNTAIN ROAD) (FS ROAD 94)

LENGTH: 4.7 miles

ELEVATION CHANGE: Low point, 1,800 feet; high point, 4,550 feet

DIFFICULTY: Moderate

TRAILHEADS: Horse Creek Recreation Area (start) and Coldspring Mountain Parking Area (end)

TRAIL CONNECTIONS: Squibb Creek and Poplar Cove Trails

USE: Hiking, equestrian, mountain bike, motorcycle, ATV, 4 WD. Note: As of the early 2000s, the road is closed to all motorized vehicles due to severe flood damage. Check with the CNF for the current status. All users should use caution. Some sections of the trail have been undercut by the stream and are narrow, rocky, and may be unstable.

TOPOGRAPHIC MAP: USGS Greystone, TN-NC

COMMENTS: The Horse Creek Road (also known as Coldspring Mountain Road) is, for the most part, an ORV road that provides access to the Horse Creek watershed, the AT near Big Butt, and fine views near its terminus on Coldspring Mountain. The road is wide, graded, and receives regular use by ORVs, especially during the summer, and you may want to avoid it during that period. It is otherwise a pleasant walk and may be used to create loop hikes. The road is gated near the AT, where there is a small parking area. No vehicles are allowed on the AT or within an adjacent corridor. The road is not suitable for 2 WD vehicles.

DETAILS: The road begins near the entrance of the Horse Creek Campground, where there are ample parking, toilets, and drinking water. There are no road or trail signs, but the gravel jeep road is quite evident as it follows Horse Creek south away from the campground.

The road passes the concrete footings of what used to be a footbridge leading to the Squibb Creek Trail before crossing Horse Creek at 0.1 mile. The bridge was washed away during the 2001 floods. The Squibb Creek Trail and Middle Spring Ridge Trail can be used to reach the AT (see Sampson Mountain Wilderness, above). The road then follows Horse Creek through mature second-growth forest and among occasional sandstone outcrops. At 0.5 mile the road forks in a grove of white pine and hemlock. Take the left fork, which crosses the creek, then recrosses. At 0.8 mile the road forks again. Here the right fork is the Poplar Cove Trail, which leads to Jennings Creek and to the AT via the Sarvis Cove Trail. The Horse Creek Road veers left along a rutted jeep road, climbing gently. At 1.6 miles the road enters a clearing among the sycamore, pine, and rhododendron. Note the large boulders of white quartzite. At 1.7 miles the road again crosses Horse Creek and continues climbing, leaving the stream. At 2.3 miles the road begins its ascent out of the valley at a wide switchback. The road climbs through a young forest of pine, mountain laurel, and galax.

At about 3.0 miles an abandoned road enters from the right. The Horse Creek Road continues climbing, passing several small branches. The road skirts a boulder field at a switchback at 3.5 miles as the forest becomes rich in beech, birch, and hickory. The road climbs steadily through several switchbacks, passing boulders and outcrops of white quartzite. To the north, there are heath balds near the ridgecrest and fine views of cliffs. The road flattens at 4.4 miles and arrives at a turnaround, where a side trail to the right leads to a clifftop affording excellent views of the valley and ridge in the vicinity of Greeneville, as well as the entire Bald Mountain Ridge Scenic Area. The road continues past the turnaround, reaching a gate at 4.6 miles, where the road goes right to the Coldspring Mountain Parking Area. A trail continues uphill, reaching the junction with the AT at 4.7 miles. To the right (southwest) it is about 0.2 mile to the Sarvis Cove Trail and the grassy bald summit of Coldspring Mountain. To the left (northeast) it is 0.4 mile to the Middle Spring Ridge Trail near Big Butt (4,838 feet).

68. POPLAR COVE TRAIL (FS TRAIL 22, TI TRAIL 28)

LENGTH: 1.6 miles

ELEVATION CHANGE: Low point, 2,030 feet; high point, 2,750 feet

DIFFICULTY: Moderate

TRAILHEADS: Horse Creek Road (start) and Jennings Creek Trail (end)

TRAIL CONNECTIONS: Pete's Branch and Sarvis Cove Trails

USE: Hiking, equestrian, mountain bike

TOPOGRAPHIC MAP: USGS Greystone, TN-NC

COMMENTS: This trail begins in a clearing at 0.8 mile on the Horse Creek Road (FS 94) and provides access from the Horse Creek watershed to Sarvis Cove and Jennings Creek. The trail follows a jeep road to a camping area on Sarvis Creek; afterward, it becomes a well-graded trail leading through an unnamed gap and descending to Jennings Creek. The trail passes mostly through an oak, pine, and laurel forest, typical of south-facing slopes of the southern Appalachians. There is a large campsite at 0.2 mile. Water is accessible for the first 0.7 mile and again at the junction with Jennings Creek Trail at 1.6 miles.

DETAILS: The trail follows the jeep road through the clearing, passing a camping area on the right at 0.2 mile. The trail continues past the boulders placed to prohibit ORV use beyond this point. The trail crosses Sarvis Creek and reaches the trailhead for the Pete's Branch Trail about 75 feet after crossing the creek, where there is a signpost but no trail sign. That trail leads 0.5 mile to a small cascade (Pete's Branch or Sierra Falls). The Poplar Cove Trail ascends above the creek, which is surrounded by pine, rhododendron, and mountain laurel. At 0.7 mile the Sarvis Cove Trail begins on the left, following the creek. The Poplar Cove Trail turns right, ascending beside a dry ravine. The trail climbs steadily along a rocky trail and enters an oak forest. At 1.1 miles the trail reaches a dry gap on Middle Ridge.

A manway leads to the right, following the ridgetop toward Green Ridge. The Poplar Cove Trail descends steeply from the gap, passing through a pine forest that has been heavily damaged by the pine bark beetle, along with oaks, huckleberry, and laurel. The trail tunnels through dense rhododendron and descends into a ravine (Poplar Cove) via a couple of steep switchbacks. The Poplar Cove Trail terminates at 1.6 miles at the Jennings Creek Trail. To the left it is 0.25 mile to the Cowbell Hollow Trail and 1.8 miles to Round Knob Picnic Area. To the right it is 1.0 mile to Old Forge Campground.

69. PETE'S BRANCH TRAIL (FS TRAIL 12, TI TRAIL 26)

LENGTH: 0.5 mile

ELEVATION CHANGE: Low point, 2,160 feet; high point, 2,600 feet

DIFFICULTY: Moderate (flood damage requires scrambling over rocks)

TRAILHEAD: Poplar Cove Trail (start and dead-end)

USE: Hiking

TOPOGRAPHIC MAP: USGS Greystone, TN-NC

DETAILS: This trail leaves the intersection with the Poplar Cove Trail as an overgrown road, tunneling through a rhododendron thicket. It crosses the creek about 100 feet from the trailhead and climbs past a small wooden sign for "Pete's Branch" at 200 feet. The trail enters a flood-damaged area at 0.1 mile that lasts for about 200 feet, crossing and recrossing the stream. At 0.2 mile it crosses the creek to the right side before it climbs to a clearing, where the road fades away. The trail, now a footpath, continues uphill, climbing gently through second-growth timber. It crosses the stream again at 0.4 mile. Passing alongside the eroded streambed the trail climbs gently along Pete's Branch, which stair steps through angular blocks of quartzite. The trail becomes rather rough as it approaches a steep ravine. At 0.5 mile the Pete's Branch Trail reaches Pete's Branch Falls (Sierra Falls) at an impressive rocky bluff. The small waterfall splashes through a cleft in the quartzite face. The large fold on the left wall and the numerous fractures in the bedrock attest to the powerful mountain-building stresses that accompanied the original uplift of this region some 250 million years ago. A rich grove of yellow poplar, buckeye, and hemlock has matured in this steep-sided valley, forming an amphitheater-like setting.

---

70. SARVIS COVE TRAIL (FS TRAIL 14, TI TRAIL 29)

LENGTH: 2.6 miles

ELEVATION CHANGE: Low point, 2,320 feet; high point, 4,560 feet

DIFFICULTY: Moderate

TRAILHEADS: Poplar Cove Trail (start) and AT (end)

USE: Hiking

TOPOGRAPHIC MAP: USGS Greystone, TN-NC

COMMENTS: This trail provides a nice alternate route to the Horse Creek Road, which will be heavily used by ORVs if the Horse

Creek Road is repaired. The trail begins as a wide trail but is steep and may be overgrown in the summer in its last mile. The trail generally follows an old logging road along Sarvis Creek, in a mature second-growth forest through Sarvis Cove. The upper reaches of the cove house a mature grove of fairly large oaks and hemlocks. Water can be found during the first 1.7 miles.

DETAILS: The trail leaves the Poplar Cove Trail at 0.7 mile from the Horse Creek Road. There is a trail sign about 50 feet up the trail. The Sarvis Cove Trail heads left (south) along the creek while the Poplar Cove Trail goes right (west), uphill.

Past the trail intersection, the trail ascends gently along the creek, tunneling through rhododendron in a young forest. Here the trail is wide and walking is pleasant. The trail begins to climb more steeply and crosses Sarvis Creek at 0.4 mile. The forest is largely mature hardwoods, rhododendron, and hemlock. Spring wildflowers grow in profusion in this rich wood. At 1.3 miles the trail crosses the stream again at the confluence of two branches. Flooding has damaged the trail between here and the next stream crossing, about 200 feet away. The trail passes a small waterfall and several smaller rapids and cascades shortly after the last crossing. At about 1.0 mile you will reach another beautiful cascade down a moss-strewn cleft in the bedrock. At 1.7 miles the trail narrows and leaves the creek, turning sharply left at a confluence of two streams, beginning a steep ascent through a hemlock-dominated forest. The trail climbs through switchbacks and is poorly graded until 2.5 miles. The trail may be difficult to follow in summer, so look carefully for yellow blazes. The trail reaches the ridgecrest at 2.5 miles at a rocky crag of white quartzite on the left of the trail. Just past the rocks, a side trail leads to the parking lot at the end of the Horse Creek Road. The Sarvis Cove Trail continues 0.1 mile to meet the old AT at 2.6 miles. To the left the Horse Creek Road is about 0.2 mile. To the right is a nice bald area, across which runs the relocated AT, marked by white blazes. The Sarvis Cove Trail continues another 75 feet straight ahead from the junction with the old AT on a faint footpath to reach the relocated AT.

71. DOCTOR'S RIDGE TRAIL (FS TRAIL 194, TI TRAIL 10)

LENGTH: 1.0 mile

ELEVATION CHANGE: Low point, 1,700 feet; high point, 1,950 feet

DIFFICULTY: Moderate (short steep grades)

TRAILHEADS: Doctor's Ridge North (start) and Doctor's Ridge South (end)

USE: Hiking, equestrian, mountain bike

TOPOGRAPHIC MAP: USGS Greystone, TN-NC

COMMENTS: This short, wide trail follows an old logging road as it winds up and down through forests of pine, oak, and rhododendron. There is a campsite at 0.5 mile in a small valley, next to a creek.

DETAILS: The trail begins on the south side of the gap a short distance above the junction of Greystone Road and Walter's Road. It is marked with an FS trail post. There is parking for a couple of cars on the south side of the road. The Doctor's Ridge Trail immediately begins to climb up through rhododendrons and pine. At 0.1 mile a clear trail enters from the right and joins the Doctor's Ridge Trail as it turns left and continues uphill. The trail climbs nearly to the ridgeline before descending into a small valley and crossing a creek at 0.5 mile. It curves right and climbs the side of the mountain, gradually curving back around to the left to regain the ridgeline at the end of the trail on Old Forge Road. A side trail turns off to the left and leads 100 feet to an overgrown clearing with limited views to the east. The trailhead is marked with an FS trail post and there is parking for a few cars on the side of the road. The Old Forge Campground is 0.7 mile to the right on Old Forge Road and Horse Creek Campground is 2.0 miles to the left.

72. JENNINGS CREEK TRAIL (FS TRAIL 21, TI TRAIL 17)

LENGTH: 1.2 miles

ELEVATION CHANGE: Low point, 1,920 feet; high point, 2,280 feet

DIFFICULTY: Moderate

TRAILHEADS: Old Forge Campground (start) and Cowbell Hollow Trail (end)

Type: Hiking, equestrian, and mountain bike

TRAIL CONNECTIONS: Poplar Cove and Little Jennings Creek Trails

TOPOGRAPHIC MAP: USGS Greystone, TN-NC

COMMENTS: The Jennings Creek Trail follows beautiful Jennings Creek, crossing it repeatedly. The trail is wide and easy to follow to the intersection with the Cowbell Hollow Trail. Old maps show the trail extending up to Chestnutlog Gap on the AT, but this trail is no longer evident and must be considered off-trail hiking. This trail can be used to make a 4.8-mile loop day hike from Old Forge via the Cowbell Hollow and Little Jennings Creek trails with a stop at Round Knob for lunch. This trail has a marvelous show of spring wildflowers, notably wild iris, trillium, trailing arbutus, and several varieties of violets. A small campsite is located at 0.6 mile.

DETAILS: The trail begins at the trail sign and archway at the entrance to the Old Forge Campground. Here, in addition to campsites, there is ample parking, toilets, drinking water, and a swimming hole. The road to Old Forge is closed after the first snow and/or bad weather in winter. The toilets and water are also turned off in winter. If you choose to walk the road to the trailhead, add an additional 2.7 miles from the gate.

The trail leaves the south end of the campground and immediately crosses Jennings Creek. Before the crossing, a side trail heads to the right and through the archway, 50 feet to a swimming hole at a small

Waterfall near Old Forge Campground, just below the Jennings Creek Trail. Photograph by Steve McGaffin.

waterfall. At 0.1 mile the trail crosses a large branch and reaches the Little Jennings Creek Trail (FS Trail 95), which comes down from the right. There is no sign marking this intersection. The topographic map calls this stream "Round Knob Branch." The Jennings Creek Trail continues along Jennings Creek and crosses it at 0.2 mile. At 0.6 mile, after several stream crossings, the trail passes the remnants of an old chimney on the left and enters an area of open forest where wildflowers grow in profusion in late April and early May. Note particularly the large white trillium, foam flower, and abundant wild iris. A small campsite can be found a short distance later. At 1.0 mile the Poplar Cove Trail terminates on the left, having come 0.9 mile from the beginning of the Sarvis Cove Trail and 1.6 miles from the Horse Creek Road. The Jennings Creek Trail continues along the creek through cove hardwoods (buckeye, poplar, hemlock, oak, hickory) and rhododendron. The trail reaches the trailhead of the Cowbell Hollow Trail on the right at 1.2 miles. It leads 1.6 miles to the Round Knob Picnic Area. There is no distinguishable end of Jennings Creek Trail or beginning of Cowbell Hollow Trail and there are no signs. Jennings Creek Trail ends as the trail curves right across a dry, rocky gully and begins to climb away from the creek. This is the beginning of Cowbell Hollow Trail.

73. COWBELL HOLLOW TRAIL (FS TRAIL 24, TI TRAIL 8)

LENGTH: 1.6 miles

ELEVATION CHANGE: Low point, 2,280 feet; high point, 3,150 feet

DIFFICULTY: Moderate

TRAILHEADS: Jennings Creek Trail (start) and Round Knob Picnic Area (end)

TRAIL CONNECTIONS: Little Jennings Creek Trail

USE: Hiking, equestrian, mountain bike

TOPOGRAPHIC MAP: USGS Greystone, TN-NC

COMMENTS: The Cowbell Hollow Trail climbs out of the Jennings Creek watershed to reach Round Knob with trail connections to Davis Creek and the Round Knob Connector Road. The trail begins in a rich cove forest and climbs through an interesting open oak and pine forest, then enters a more mature closed oak forest near Round Knob. Reliable water sources can only be found at the beginning and end of the trail.

DETAILS: The trail begins at about 1.2 miles along the Jennings Creek Trail. The Jennings Creek Trail curves right to cross a dry, rocky gully and then becomes the Cowbell Hollow Trail. There is no trail sign, but the trail is quite evident as it climbs up and away from Jennings Creek. Look for the familiar yellow blazes.

The trail follows a small side creek a short distance into Cowbell Hollow along a steep grade through a forest of cove hardwoods (yellow buckeye, yellow poplar, eastern hemlock, sugar maple, flowering dogwood). At 0.1 mile a sign for Round Knob points straight uphill, but the trail passes the sign to reach a switchback at a double blaze. The trail negotiates several switchbacks while climbing an unnamed ridge. Here the forest is composed of red maple, oak, pine, rhododendron, and mountain laurel, with an understory of wintergreen, galax, and trailing arbutus. The trail reaches a gap at 1.2 miles and then descends gently. At 1.4 miles on the right, the terminus of the Little Jennings Creek Trail is marked by a trail sign. Straight ahead is the Round Knob Picnic Area. The trail is badly littered along the last 100 yards approaching the terminus at 1.6 miles. At Round Knob there are picnic tables, toilets, and an excellent piped spring to the left of a shelter with a large stone fireplace. To the right, the Davis Creek Trail terminates at the north end of the parking area, having come 2.8 miles from Shelton Mission Road. To the left, the Round Knob Connector Road climbs south 2.0 miles to the AT.

74. LITTLE JENNINGS CREEK TRAIL (ROUND KNOB BRANCH) (FS TRAIL 195, TI TRAIL 18)

LENGTH: 2.0 Miles

ELEVATION CHANGE: Low point, 1,920 feet; high point, 3,100 feet

DIFFICULTY: Moderate

TRAILHEADS: Jennings Creek Trail (start) and Cowbell Hollow Trail (end)

USE: Hiking, equestrian, mountain bike

TOPOGRAPHIC MAP: USGS Greystone, TN-NC

COMMENTS: This trail provides a nice alternate route to Round Knob from Old Forge. It passes through a mature cove forest along the creek, crossing it frequently, with abundant wildflowers in April and May. This is also known as the Round Knob Branch Trail. Water is available for almost the entire length of the trail. The floods in 2001 have damaged some sections of the trail where it crosses the streams.

Between 0.6 mile and 1.4 mile the trail occasionally follows the streambed for a couple hundred feet and can be very rocky.

DETAILS: The trail begins on the Jennings Creek Trail 0.1 mile from Old Forge Campground. The trail follows Little Jennings Creek (Round Knob Branch) off to the right. There is no sign marking the intersection.

After the intersection, the trail passes through a narrow valley of yellow poplar, red maple, sycamore, and rhododendron. Spring wildflowers grow in profusion. Look for wild iris, violets, Solomon's seal, false Solomon's seal, jack-in-the-pulpit, trillium, and wild ginger (little brown jugs). The trail climbs gently, crossing the creek repeatedly. At 1.0 mile the grade steepens as the valley narrows, and the trail enters a grove of young eastern hemlocks, red maple, and ash (look for a patch of showy orchis).

The Little Jennings Creek Trail continues to follow the creek, but about 100 feet above the valley floor. The trail continues to climb and rejoins the creek, which is now quite small. At 1.6 miles the trail enters a ravine in a rhododendron and laurel slick and begins climbing. The creek disappears and the trail enters an open oak forest at 1.9 miles. At 2.0 miles the trail terminates at the Cowbell Hollow Trail, which enters from the left, having climbed 1.4 miles from Jennings Creek. To the right it is 0.1 mile to the Round Knob Picnic Area.

75. DAVIS CREEK TRAIL (FS TRAIL 19, TI TRAIL 9)

LENGTH: 2.8 miles

ELEVATION CHANGE: Low point, 1,850 feet; high point, 3,100 feet

DIFFICULTY: Moderate

TRAILHEADS: Davis Creek (start) and Round Knob Picnic Area (end)

Type: Hiking

TOPOGRAPHIC MAP: USGS Greystone, TN-NC

COMMENTS: The Davis Creek Trail is a wide path that generally follows an old road up Davis Creek to a former homesite, then climbs steeply up to Round Knob Picnic Area on a footpath. The trail crosses Davis Creek many times. The floods in 2001 have damaged the trail, but only at the stream crossings, making them rockier and wider than before. Water is available from 0.8 mile to 2.3 miles.

DETAILS: The trailhead is on Shelton Mission Road, 0.4 mile northeast of Shelton Mission Church and 1.0 mile from the Shelton Mission Road Trailhead. When coming from the north, look for an old stone foundation near several homes on the right, 1.25 miles off Greystone Road. There is a trail sign off the road that says (incorrectly as to mileage) "Artie Hollow 1.9, Round Knob 2.9." There is room for maybe one car at the trailhead, so it might be better to drive the extra mile to the Shelton Mission Road Trailhead and walk back along the road.

Past the trail sign, the trail ascends along a wide road through a hardwood and pine forest. At 0.1 mile the trail turns right, off the wider road, at a double blaze. The trail then climbs over several low rocky ridges, through a young, second-growth forest. At 0.8 mile a wide trail enters from the right, leading to some private homes. The Davis Creek Trail heads left, joining Davis Creek. The trail then makes many stream crossings. The walking here is very pleasant, along an old road with a gentle grade. The trail passes through a mature, second-growth cove hardwood forest, crossing Davis Creek several more times. At 1.7 miles the rather faint Artie Hollow Trail begins on the right (look for a double blaze on a tree). The Davis Creek Trail continues ahead, crossing Davis Creek a final time. A rather conspicuous road enters from the left at 1.8 miles, heading uphill beside a branch. The Davis Creek Trail continues to the right, crossing the branch and following Davis Creek. Little evidence remains of the wildfires that decimated the area to the left during the drought of the late 1980s. The trail passes a series of sandstone bluffs at 1.9 miles and crosses another branch. The trail then turns left (east) and follows the branch, past an old homesite and through a wonderful grove of large trees. Here the trail begins its ascent of Round Knob. At 2.3 miles the trail splits. The old trail continues straight on the right side of the branch, and the new trail crosses the branch a final time and climbs the opposite bank. The two trails come together again at 2.4 miles and cross a dry branch. At 2.5 miles, the trail enters a young pine forest that is taking over a burned-over area. The Davis Creek Trail continues climbing the ridge on a steep grade before entering a narrow valley. At 2.7 miles the trail splits, with a faint trail following the valley floor and Davis Creek Trail bearing left to climb up and cross a knoll. The trail ends at 2.8 miles at the north end of the picnic area. There is no sign marking the trail. Across the road is the trailhead for the Cowbell Hollow Trail, which leads to Jennings Creek.

76. ARTIE HOLLOW TRAIL (FS TRAIL 18, TI TRAIL 3)

LENGTH: 1.9 miles

ELEVATION CHANGE: Low point, 2,280 feet; high point, 3,400 feet

DIFFICULTY: Difficult

TRAILHEADS: Davis Creek Trail (start) and Phillips Hollow Trail (end)

USE: Hiking

TOPOGRAPHIC MAP: USGS Greystone, TN-NC

COMMENTS: This trail follows an old logging railroad grade up secluded Artie Hollow, past a nice waterfall, and through a fairly mature forest of cove hardwoods. The trail crosses the stream repeatedly, so expect to get your feet wet. This is a very overgrown and little-used trail, which in some sections can be much like off-trail hiking. The floods of 2001 did a lot of damage, especially in the first 0.5 mile, in some areas wiping out whole sections of trail. Some areas require scrambling over large rock dams that were formed in the flood, and downed trees are frequent. This is probably the most difficult trail in the Bald Mountain Ridge Scenic Area.

DETAILS: The trail begins at about 1.7 miles on the Davis Creek Trail or about 1.1 miles from Round Knob. There is no trail sign, so look carefully to the right of the trail just before the last crossing of Davis Creek. There are blue double-blazes just before the intersection. If you are descending from Round Knob, this would be your first major stream crossing.

The trail passes beside Davis Creek briefly, then crosses the branch that leads up Artie Hollow. The trail ascends gently through an open forest of poplar and hemlock to the left of the branch for about 0.2 mile, then begins crossing the stream regularly. The first two crossings have very steep, eroded, and crumbling banks, which can make crossing difficult. At 0.5 mile the trail climbs left slightly away from the branch and passes pretty Mary's Falls, which drops some 30 feet off a sandstone bluff. The trail follows an old logging road, where evidence of rotted ties, spikes, and rails can be seen. The trail now crosses, and sometimes runs through, the branch. The trail is quite overgrown in some places but generally follows the stream. Watch for the blue blazes that are spaced fairly regularly. At 1.2 miles the trail reaches the confluence of two branches in a small opening caused by several blowdowns. The Artie Hollow Trail follows the right fork, ascending to the right of the creek along a ravine. The trail begins ascending away from the stream at 1.3 miles and climbs through a couple of switchbacks, tunneling through dense rhododendron. At 1.4 miles the trail reaches a dry gap on an unnamed ridge. The forest here changes abruptly to pine, laurel, and galax in an old burned-over area. The trail then descends very steeply through rhododendron and young hardwoods and reaches a small branch at 1.6 miles and then turns west, following to the right of the branch and becoming narrow and poorly graded (look for blazes). The trail then crosses the branch and leaves it, skirting the side of a ridge. At 1.9 miles the Artie Hollow Trail terminates at an intersection with the Phillips Hollow Trail. There is no sign marking the intersection. To the left, it is a rough 1.0 mile to the AT. To the right it is about 1.5 miles to the Bullen Hollow Trail.

77. PHILLIPS HOLLOW TRAIL (FS TRAIL 17, TI TRAIL 27)

LENGTH: 2.7 miles

ELEVATION CHANGE: Low point, 1,960 feet; high point, 4,240 feet

DIFFICULTY: Difficult

TRAILHEADS: Shelton Mission Road (start) and AT (end)

TRAIL CONNECTIONS: Artie Hollow Trail

USE: Hiking

TOPOGRAPHIC MAP: USGS Greystone, TN-NC

COMMENTS: The Phillips Hollow Trail provides a pleasant walk, followed by a steep, arduous ascent to the AT along Dry Creek and its tributaries. The upper portion of the trail is very steep and overgrown but is quite scenic, featuring some fine trees, impressive bluffs, and boulder fields. Route-finding ability is necessary, especially in summer, so be sure to carry a map and compass. Water is plentiful for the first 2.2 miles, but camping space is quite limited due to the steepness of the terrain. There is parking for several cars at the Shelton Mission Road Trailhead. Flood damage from the 2001 floods has made creek crossings from 0.4 to 1.6 miles more difficult.

DETAILS: The trail begins at the end of FS 5099 in the middle of extensive flood damage in an open, forested area. The Bullen Hollow Trail also begins from the same parking area, leaving to the right.

The Phillips Hollow Trail goes left, crossing Dry Creek at the stone steps. The trail is marked by old yellow blazes and newer blue blazes as it passes along the valley cut through Cambrian sandstone, which is visible on both sides of the valley. Notice how much more mature the forest is along the creek valley (cove) as compared to several yards up the rugged, boulder-strewn slopes. The trail soon becomes much rougher and reaches the stream confluence of Dry Creek, which goes right, and the east fork, which the trail follows. The USGS topographical map shows the trailhead of a Spruce Thicket Trail at this point, generally following Dry Creek to the vicinity of the Blackstack Cliffs.

No trail is evident here, so follow the blue blazes that mark the Phillips Hollow Trail. At about 0.4 mile the trail crosses and recrosses the creek and then becomes rougher. Look for cross-bedding in the sandstone outcrop on the left.

The trail crosses the East Fork at 0.6 mile, where it enters a flood-damaged section of stream as it ascends through a slightly younger forest. The trail then negotiates another stream crossing and passes through extensive flood damage before passing a series of cascades at 1.1 miles. The trail crosses the creek to the right before passing at 1.3 miles the remains of an old chimney and a young, open forest on the right, which appears to be an old homesite or logging camp. The trail ascends steadily through rhododendron and tall second-growth timber, crossing the creek to the left and reaching the terminus of the Artie Hollow Trail about 250 feet farther at 1.6 miles, which enters at a sharp angle on the left.

The trail continues ahead along a more narrow footpath into a more mature forest and crosses the creek again at a tree with blazes on both sides. The trail leaves the branch and ascends the right side of the valley, skirting a talus slope. The trail here is well constructed into the large rocks, but watch for stinging nettles in the summer. At 2.0 miles the trail rejoins the stream, which now is quite small, and begins ascending steeply, generally following the creek bed. Here the trail is virtually nonexistent in places and is overgrown by rhododendron, making walking difficult. The blazes are less frequent and fainter, but there are occasional flags of surveyor's tape marking the trail. The trail continues to climb steeply through rhododendron along a ravine until 2.2 miles, where it begins to climb the side of the mountain. It reaches the top of the shoulder at 2.5 miles, where the trail turns to the right and becomes gradual and more evident. A faint trail goes left along the shoulder, leading to a rock outcrop, but the views are limited. If you follow this path, be careful of the fragile lichens and mosses covering the rocks. It can take years to repair the damage left by one boot.

Continue ascending gradually along the shoulder, reaching the AT at 2.7 miles. The trail is rather faint in the last 0.1 mile, so look for the faded blue blazes. The old Fox Cabin site is near the end of the trail and is now marked only by a dense briar patch. There is no sign marking the intersection, and this can be a difficult trail to find from the AT, especially in the summer. To the left (east) on the AT it is 1.7 miles to Jerry's Cabin Shelter. To the right (west) it is 1.8 miles to Blackstack Cliffs, offering outstanding views of the TN Valley, and approximately 2.8 miles to the Jones Meadow Trailhead.

78. MARGUERITE FALLS TRAIL (FS TRAIL 189, TI TRAIL 20)

LENGTH: 0.7 mile

ELEVATION CHANGE: Low point, 2,000 feet; high point, 2,600 feet

DIFFICULTY: Moderate (flood damage has created hazardous crossings)

TRAILHEAD: Bullen Hollow Trail (start and dead-end)

USE: Hiking

TOPOGRAPHIC MAP: USGS Greystone, TN-NC

COMMENTS: The Marguerite Falls Trail provides an excellent side trip off the Bullen Hollow and Phillips Hollow trails for a short day hike. The trail follows West Fork through an impressive gorge cut through tilted beds of Cambrian-period sandstone and among large cove hardwoods. The floods of 2001 have damaged several sections of this trail. Many of the crossings are very rocky and slippery. Note that the TI map is seriously wrong on the location of the falls and the length of the trail; it is much shorter than they show.

DETAILS: The trail begins about 250 feet up the Bullen Hollow Trail, just after it begins to climb the base of Reynolds Ridge. The Bullen Hollow Trail leaves to the right, while Marguerite Falls Trail drops slightly downhill to the left. At 0.1 mile the trail splits but comes back together in another 200 feet. The trail crosses West Fork at 0.3 mile, first following the right bank through a flood-damaged section and then passing through the middle of the stream on an island of rocks before crossing to the left. By now the trail has entered into the gorge; notice the vertical sandstone cliffs on the southeast side of the creek. The trail then climbs by large hardwoods to the right of the creek and follows the base of the cliffs along a small talus slope. The trail then rejoins the creek, passing several small waterfalls among sandstone boulders. At 0.5 mile there are good views of Cathedral Rock, an impressive promontory that juts out of the bluffs. Cross the creek to the right and climb a steep slippery slope before reaching Marguerite Falls at 0.7 mile. Marguerite Falls is a very pretty cascade fanning out over thin layers of bedrock. A nice campsite is reached by climbing through the talus to the right of the falls and up the small cliff to the top of the falls. Another small waterfall, Glen Falls, named by Sierra Club hikers, is reached by scrambling up the creek about 0.1 mile farther. Glen Falls, about eight feet high, enters from a branch (Bullen Branch) on the right and drops into a small, secluded, rock-walled glen. If the water is low enough, walk into the glen to its end, where you can see Glen Falls close-up. If the water is too high, you can scramble up the hillside to the right for a view of the falls.

79. BULLEN HOLLOW TRAIL (FS TRAIL 2, TI TRAIL 5)

LENGTH: 4.1 miles

ELEVATION CHANGE: Low point, 1,860 feet; high point, 4,080 feet

DIFFICULTY: Difficult

TRAILHEADS: Phillips Hollow Trail (start) and Low Gap (end)

TRAIL CONNECTIONS: Marguerite Falls

USE: Hiking, equestrian, mountain bike, motorcycle, ATV, 4 WD

TOPOGRAPHIC MAP: USGS Greystone, TN-NC

COMMENTS: This wide, graded trail passes through a diverse assemblage of forest types, from a superb example of closed oak forest to a mature cove hardwood forest in lovely Bullen Hollow. The trail serves as the access to the Marguerite Falls Trail, a fascinating walk through a rugged, steep valley. This trail is unique among the trails in the Bald Mountain Ridge Scenic Area, for it climbs along the ridgetop instead of up the stream valley. Water is available at several locations, and potential campsites are located near the trailhead and in Bullen Hollow. The Bullen Hollow Trail is presently designated by the USFS as an ORV trail. There have been efforts to reclassify it as a hiking trail by the Sierra Club and other conservation groups. Until and if it is reclassified, you may encounter ORVs on this trail.

DETAILS: The trail begins to the right of the Phillips Hollow Trail at the end of FS 5099, in the middle of an extremely flood-damaged area. The Bullen Hollow Trail crosses a rocky gully before beginning to climb the base of Reynolds Ridge. About 250 feet from the trailhead Marguerite Falls Trail begins on the left, following the creek. The trail ascends steadily and is wide and rutted. At 0.3 mile the trail forks twice on a very steep grade, but the various side trails all rejoin as the trail levels, upon climbing out of the steep-sided valley carved by West Fork. The trail enters a dry, open forest of pine, several different oaks, laurel, sourwood, sassafras, and huckleberry. The trail climbs moderately around the south side of Reynolds Ridge, passing good views to the left of Cathedral Rocks on neighboring Rocky Ridge.

The oaks and pine give way to hemlock, maple, and poplar as the trail enters Bullen Hollow, reaching Bullen Branch at 1.3 miles. The trail then climbs out of the hollow and at 1.8 miles turns right to begin climbing more steeply up Henry Ridge through a forest of mature oaks and maple. At 2.6 miles the trail descends gently to a gap with a small bog and reaches a very wide jeep road. From here, follow the road to the right, skirting the top of Henry Ridge, passing fine views of Blackstack Cliffs to the southeast and the TN Valley to the north. The trail rejoins Reynolds Ridge at 3.5 miles at the junction with FS 358 in a wooded gap and a sign for Camp Creek Trail. Look closely for the Bullen Hollow Trail, which leaves the gap to the left, climbing steeply uphill. FS 358 descends from the gap about 150 feet to the junction with FS 358A, which leads to the Kennedy Cabin Trailhead about 0.7 mile away. The Viking Mountain Road is straight ahead, 0.8 mile on FS 358.

From the wooded gap, the trail climbs steeply over a knob, then descends, reaching Low Gap at 4.1 miles at a sign for "Camp Creek Trail, The Oaks Camp." The unofficial Camp Creek Trail, which is maintained by a private camp, continues steeply uphill on the other side of the gap, leading about 0.8 mile to Jones Meadow Trailhead and a connector trail for the AT. There is parking on the side of the road for a few cars. The gated FS 358 is 0.5 mile down Viking Mountain Road.

80. APPALACHIAN TRAIL (JONES MEADOW TO BIG BUTT SECTION) (FS TRAIL 1, TI TRAIL 1)

LENGTH: 6.1 miles

ELEVATION CHANGE: Low point, 4,100 feet; high point, 4,838 feet

DIFFICULTY: Moderate

TRAILHEADS: Jones Meadow (start) and Coldspring Mountain Parking Area (end)

TRAIL CONNECTIONS: Phillips Hollow, Sarvis Cove, and Middle Spring Ridge Trails; Round Knob Connector and Horse Creek Roads

USE: Hiking

TOPOGRAPHIC MAP: USGS Greystone, TN-NC

COMMENTS: The AT skirts the TN-NC state line, which forms the southeastern boundary of the area. This section is quite scenic at either end. The Blackstack Cliffs at the southwestern end offer an outstanding view of the entire area and the TN Valley. The balds on Coldspring Mountain at the northeastern end are an excellent example of southeastern grassy balds and have views of the Appalachians to the southwest. The AT generally follows the ridgecrest of the Bald Mountains, making for very gentle grades. Camping is available at Chestnutlog Gap (Jerry's Cabin), where there is a fine spring; on the balds on Coldspring Mountain; and at a campsite approximately 0.7 mile north from the Jones Meadow access trail (a small spring is located to the right of the trail between the campsite and Whiterock Cliff). Car access is from Jones Meadow; 4 WD vehicles can also access the trail on Horse Creek Road to the Coldspring Mountain Parking Area, although at the time of this writing, the Horse Creek Road was closed to motor vehicles due to flood damage. Horse Creek Road can also be walked (see description above). Vehicles are not allowed on the AT or within an adjacent corridor.

DETAILS: The trail passes below the developed land that formerly belonged to the Viking Mountain Resort, passing numerous springs. This failed development was closed in 1985 after years of financial difficulties. The CNF acquired most of the land and buildings in 1989. The buildings have now been largely dismantled, including a stone lodge and several houses built below the cliffs. At approximately 0.7 mile, there is a campsite on the right side of the trail. About 100 yards past the campsite, an unnamed trail goes right down the hill for about 50 yards, onto an overgrown promontory, while the AT switches back to the left. At 0.8 mile a trail to the right leads about 15 yards to Whiterock Cliff, with fine views to the southeast of the Black Mountains in NC. At 1.0 mile the trail to the left leads 75 yards to the top of Blackstack Cliffs and excellent views. The Blackstack Cliffs, incidentally, are actually composed of gleaming white quartzite that only appear black when viewed from a distance. This white quartzite forms the impressive cliffs that rim the rugged face of the Bald Mountains. The trail continues through dense rhododendron to Bearwallow Gap at 1.2 miles, where the trail bears left and skirts the rocky summit of Big Firescald Knob. The trail follows the level ridgecrest and passes the terminus of the Phillips Hollow Trail at 2.8 miles. This junction may be difficult to find, since there is no sign and the trail is faint, especially in summer. The trail descends gently, passing the terminus of the Round Knob Connector at 3.4 miles near the summit of Bald Mountain (4,360 feet). The trail sign here states that it is 2.0 miles to Round Knob. The Round Knob Connector is mainly an ORV road; through the AT Corridor it is an unmaintained trail that follows an old, overgrown roadbed down to an open ORV road that descends to the Round Knob Picnic Area and Round Knob Road (FS 88).

The trail continues through an open forest, passing the Fork Ridge Trail on the right at 4.2 miles. This trail has climbed 2.0 miles from

Big Creek Road in NC. The AT descends to Chestnutlog Gap (4,150 feet) at 4.5 miles, which is the site of Jerry's Cabin, an AT shelter that sleeps six on wooden bunks. To the left, follow blue blazes to an excellent piped spring at the headwaters of Jennings Creek. Chestnutlog Gap is relatively flat and has a pleasant forest of hemlock and white pine, making it an excellent spot to camp. The trail then leaves the gap along a rerouted section that climbs moderately via switchbacks to reach a grassy bald on Coldspring Mountain at 5.0 miles. The AT is marked by blazed wooden posts and runs through the middle of the bald. At the northern end the trail splits, with the old AT going left and the rerouted AT going right. The Sarvis Cove Trail terminates at 5.3 miles as a small footpath that goes left and crosses the old AT 75 feet away at a "Hiker Trail" sign and blue blazes before continuing down to the Poplar Cove Trail 2.6 miles away. At this point the old AT is marked by green blazes and leads 0.2 mile farther to the terminus of the Horse Creek Road.

From the Sarvis Cove Trail junction the AT continues along the ridgecrest on a rocky trail, crossing a dirt road and entering a small clearing with limited views. At the far left edge of the clearing is a stone memorial to a through-hiker. The AT crosses the dirt road again at 5.7 miles before descending into a rocky ravine. A faint blue-blazed trail goes left, skirting the top of Big Butt and rejoining the AT just after the side trail for Big Butt. The AT climbs up large rocks to a side trail at 6.0 miles that leads off to the left, to the top of Big Butt and 360-degree views. From the junction with the side trail the AT descends 100 feet to the junction with the blue-blazed trail that skirted the summit, from the left. The AT turns right and continues another 250 feet to a dirt road. Straight across the road, the Middle Spring Ridge Trail goes across a bald along the ridgecrest before descending 4.5 miles along Middle Spring Ridge to the Squibb Creek Trail and the Horse Creek Campground. The AT turns right to follow the dirt road, eventually reaching a trailhead at Devil Fork Gap and NC 212 after another 6.7 miles.

81. GREENE MOUNTAIN TRAIL (FS TRAIL 13, TI TRAIL 12)

LENGTH: 3.6 miles

ELEVATION CHANGE: Low point, 2,480 feet; high point, 3,930 feet

TRAILHEADS: FS 98 (start) and Kennedy Cabin (end)

USE: Hiking, equestrian, mountain bike

TOPOGRAPHIC MAPS: USGS Greystone, TN-NC; Davy Crockett Lake, TN-NC

COMMENTS: The trail climbs, then follows, the rocky crest of Greene Mountain. The trail is rather steep for the first mile and is relatively flat thereafter as it travels along the ridgetop. The Greene Mountain Trail is just outside the boundaries of the area but is quite scenic, has outstanding blackberries in season, and often contains evidence of black bear. The Sierra Club has supported adding Greene Mountain to the scenic area. Greene Mountain forms a prominent front to the higher range behind it, the Bald Mountains. Although mostly forested, the trail does afford some fine wintertime views. Since it is largely a ridgetop trail, there are no sources of water. The trail is easy to follow for the most part and is marked with diamond-shaped, yellow metal tags.

DETAILS: The trail begins as a wide, graded path climbing somewhat steeply away from the road. The trail continues climbing steeply through several switchbacks in a second-growth forest, then through a young pine forest that is taking over a burned-over clear-cut. This clearing affords some views to the south and east. Climb through very young pines and sassafras, reentering the woods at 0.7 mile. The trail continues climbing up a side ridge of Greene Mountain, passing through several small saddles. Look for pink ladies' slippers on the dry, rocky stretches during late spring, as well as trailing arbutus, galax, and Indian pipe. The trail reaches the crest of Greene Mountain at 1.6 miles in second-growth of oak and hickory. Giant Solomon's seal, false Solomon's seal, turk's cap lilies, and touch-me-not (jewelweed) grow in profusion, often obscuring the trail. The trail then follows the ridgecrest and descends into an unnamed gap at 2.1 miles. Climbing out of the gap, pass several very large rhododendron and mature hardwoods. The top of Greene Mountain is a rather flat, wide ridge; hereafter, the walking is level and pleasant. Descend gently, passing some views to the southeast of Camp Creek Bald and Jones Meadow and entering into a gap at 3.0 miles, where a grassy woods road enters from the right. The Greene Mountain Trail continues straight ahead (look for metal markers) as an old road. Follow the road along a gentle grade, reaching another intersection at 3.2 miles, and bear left on a larger road. These roads are gated, so they receive very little use. Follow the road for about 0.1 mile, then turn left and cross an earthen barrier, while the main road continues straight ahead. Follow this narrower road past numerous blackberry and blueberry bushes, crossing another road at a large clearing at 3.5 miles. Pass through wooden pylons to reach the end of the trail at 3.6 miles. The trail enters the parking area at the Kennedy Cabin Trailhead on FS 358A to the left of a large metal sign for Kennedy Cabin and a smaller wooden sign that says "Camp Creek Trail, The Oaks Camp." The Camp Creek Trail is maintained by the Oaks Camp, a private camp down at the bottom of the trail in the valley, and leaves the parking area to the right of the signs. The end of FS 358A leads uphill, opposite the signs, a short distance to a grassy bald with views to the north and east. The Kennedy Cabin site is a short distance down the Camp Creek Trail, on a side trail that leads to the right off of the first switchback. There is a spring and some stone remnants. From the parking area it is 0.7 mile along the road to access the Bullen Hollow Trail and FS 358 and another 0.5 mile on the Bullen Hollow Trail to its starting point at Low Gap. The gate for FS 358 is 0.8 mile beyond the junction with FS 358A and FS 358.

82. ROUND KNOB CONNECTOR ROAD (FS 88; NO TI ROAD NUMBER)

LENGTH: 2.0 miles

ELEVATION CHANGE: Low point, 3,100 feet; high point, 4,290 feet

DIFFICULTY: Moderate

TRAILHEADS: Round Knob Picnic Area (start) and AT (end)

USE: Hiking, equestrian, mountain bike, motorcycle, ATV, and 4 WD, except for the last 0.2 mile of the trail up to the AT, which is closed to all use except hiking

TOPOGRAPHIC MAP: USGS Greystone, TN-NC

COMMENTS: The Round Knob Connector is mainly an ORV road (FS 88) that climbs a broad ridge to the base of Bald Mountain and the AT Corridor. Vehicles are thereafter prohibited; a badly rutted trail leads up to the AT. The jeep road receives regular use in the summer months, so use care if you travel this section on foot. There is a campsite at the end of the jeep road.

DETAILS: The road begins at the end of the parking lot for the Round Knob Picnic Area. The Cowbell Hollow Trail ends on the left. The Round Knob Connector follows the jeep road through the gate.

The road ascends on a rutted, wide trail through a second-growth forest of oak, sugar maple, and rhododendron. The road climbs through two switchbacks as it ascends a side ridge, reaching the ridgetop at 0.9 mile. The forest is mostly pine and oak with an understory of mountain laurel, greenbriar, galax, and wintergreen. The road follows the ridgecrest, then descends. Note the angular pieces of white quartzite in the road. At 1.4 miles the road forks in a gap; the right fork leads about 200 yards to a small stream. The Round Knob Connector continues on the left fork and resumes climbing. At 1.8 miles the road ends at a grassy turnaround after cresting a small knob. On the opposite side of the turnaround a "Foot Travel Only" sign marks the wide trail. There is ample camping and/or parking space here. From this point the trail is not maintained but is kept open by frequent use. The trail climbs fairly steeply out of the gap. There is evidence of ORV use all the way to the AT. The trail bears right near the ridgecrest of the Bald Mountains, ending at a wooden sign on the AT that says "Round Knob 2." Bald Mountain is now wooded; however, grassy balds can be found on Coldspring Mountain, past Jerry's Cabin, about 1.8 miles east. To the right (west) it is 0.6 mile along the AT to the Phillips Hollow Trail.

15 Paint Creek

The Paint Creek area does not have any special protected area designations, other than the AT Corridor, and is simply a region within the Nolichucky/Unaka Ranger District. There are 1,749 acres included in the AT Corridor. The area covered generally lies between US 25 and the NC border to the south, and TN 107 to the north and west, with TN 70 and the NC border to the east. The region is popular among locals for hunting, fishing, camping, hiking, canoeing, and swimming.

The flora and fauna are typical of southern Appalachian forests, with pine, oak, hemlock, and hardwood forests. Rhododendron and mountain laurel are common, as well as a wide variety of wildflowers that bloom from spring to late fall. A portion of the region is inside a black bear sanctuary, and a keen eye can find signs of bear, deer, bobcat, fox, opossum, and raccoon. The pileated woodpecker's distinct call and loud drumming is heard frequently. Rattlesnakes are occasionally spotted sunning themselves on the many rock outcroppings. Paint Creek is stocked regularly with rainbow trout and is also home to water snakes and a variety of frogs and salamanders.

HISTORY

The 107-foot Paint Rock, at the end of Paint Creek near the French Broad River, was originally named by explorers in the 1790s who saw images of people and animals in the rock. These may have been pictographs made by Native Americans, but they could also have

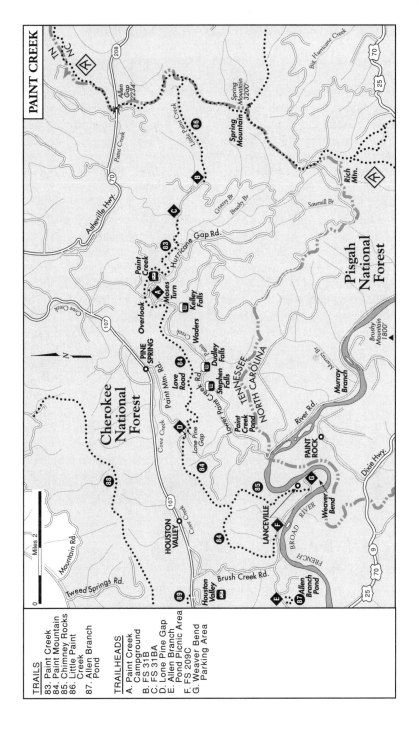

PAINT CREEK

TRAILS
83. Paint Creek
84. Paint Mountain
85. Chimney Rocks
86. Little Paint
    Creek
87. Allen Branch
    Pond

TRAILHEADS
A. Paint Creek
   Campground
B. FS 31B
C. FS 31BA
D. Lone Pine Gap
E. Allen Branch
   Pond Picnic Area
F. FS 209C
G. Weaver Bend
   Parking Area

Cherokee National Forest

Pisgah National Forest

TENNESSEE
NORTH CAROLINA

Miles 2

N

been caused by iron oxide forming shapes that could be recognized as animals.

In 1906, the Patterson Lumber Company began logging 6,500 acres of the Paint Creek area. A steam-powered band saw was set up near Paint Creek, about 4.0 miles away from the French Broad River. Railroads and tramways were used to carry logs from the surrounding mountains down to the mill, where they were cut into lumber. From there, a flume carried the logs alongside Paint Creek and over the French Broad River to the Southern Railroad Line, where they were loaded onto trains and taken to market. A lumber camp near the sawmill provided housing for families and single men as well as a commissary.

A flood in 1914 destroyed the flume bridge over the French Broad River, as well as buildings along the river. The bridge and buildings were never rebuilt, and in 1915 Patterson Lumber Company stopped logging and filed for bankruptcy, probably for reasons other than the flood. The U.S. government bought the original 6,500 acres from Patterson Lumber Company in 1921 for $4.50 per acre. Several other purchases in the surrounding area have added to the overall size of the Paint Creek area.

In July and August of 2001, two powerful storms flooded Greene County, including Paint Creek, Little Paint Creek, and some of the surrounding streams. Since Paint Creek begins in the Bald Mountain Scenic Area, flooding in the Paint Creek area was especially intense, wiping out footbridges, trails, and roads. The USFS and local hiking clubs have repaired many of the damaged sections of trails, but the roads and bridges are unlikely to be repaired unless federal funding is provided. Evidence of the power of fast moving water can be found all along Paint Creek, reminding us to keep an eye on the weather, choose our campsites wisely, and never cross a swollen stream.

TRAILHEADS AND MAPS

To reach the Paint Creek area from Greeneville, go south on TN 70 about 11 miles from US 11E and turn right onto TN 107. The area can also be reached from I-40 near Newport by taking Exit 432 for US 25. Go through Newport, and about 20 miles from I-40 turn left onto TN 107.

Paint Creek Campground, FS 31B, and FS 31BA Trailheads

From the junction of TN 70 and TN 107, go 4.4 miles on TN 107 and turn left onto Rollins Chapel Road. A brown metal USFS sign marks the intersection. If you are driving from Newport, Rollins Chapel

Road is 10.6 miles from the junction of US 25 and TN 107. On Rollins Chapel Road, go 0.5 mile and turn right onto Lower Paint Creek Road. The Lower Paint Creek Road (FS 41) starts as a paved road but turns to gravel before reaching a gap and descending to reach Paint Creek at 1.7 miles. The Paint Mountain Trail crosses the road about 0.4 mile before the road crosses Paint Creek, but there are no parking spaces. The Paint Creek Trail starts on the left just before the bridge over Paint Creek and there is ample parking available in a parking area on the right, just after the bridge. The Paint Creek Campground is on the left. At the time of this writing, the Paint Creek Campground and the Paint Creek Road just after the parking area are closed due to damage from the floods in 2001. It is unlikely that either of these will be opened unless federal funding is found. The closed section of road runs from Paint Creek Campground to the French Broad River.

To reach FS 31B, follow Hurricane Gap Road (FS 31), which starts just past the entrance to Paint Creek Campground and climbs uphill, beginning as a rough, but passable, gravel road. At 4.2 miles past Paint Creek Campground, turn left onto an unmarked FS 31B, just after crossing a small creek. Follow FS 31B for 3.7 miles to reach the Little Paint Creek Trail, just before the road crosses Little Paint Creek, which starts on the right. At the time of this writing, the road ends here. The floods of 2001 washed out the road just before the parking area on the left for Little Paint Creek Trail, so parking is very limited. An interpretive sign still stands at the parking area and gives a good overview of the history of the area.

FS 31BA begins at the parking area for Little Paint Creek and continues another 0.8 mile, following Little Paint Creek all the way to Paint Creek and the Paint Creek Trailhead. At this time FS 31BA is passable only by foot or mountain bike due to the flood damage and will probably remain that way unless funding is found to repair it. Note that Paint Creek Trail is for hiking only.

An alternate route to reach FS 31B and Paint Creek Campground, if coming from NC, is to follow US 25/TN 70 east out of Hot Springs, NC, and turn left about 3.0 miles out of Hot Springs (0.7 mile after passing the AT) onto an unmarked, paved road. This road goes about 100 feet to a T intersection. Turn right at the intersection and go 0.5 mile, turning left onto the gravel Lookout Mountain Road, just before the dead-end. Lookout Mountain Road winds its way around for 4.2 miles before reaching Hurricane Gap. At the sharp curve at the gap, go straight instead of around the left curve to get on Hurricane Gap Road (FS 31) and descend the other side of the gap. Follow Hurricane Gap Road another 1.1 miles to reach the intersection with FS 31B.

Lone Pine Gap Trailhead

From the junction of TN 70 and TN 107, go 5.9 miles on TN 107 and turn left at a small church and a brown metal USFS sign onto Paint Mountain Road. If you are driving from Newport, Paint Mountain Road is 9.1 miles from the junction of US 25 and TN 107 or 3.1 miles past the Cocke County/Greene County line. Paint Mountain Road begins climbing immediately, passing "Road Closed Ahead" signs and soon turns to a rough, but passable, gravel road. It passes a USFS sign and then reaches Lone Pine Gap 2.0 miles from TN 107. There is parking on either side of the gap for several cars and an information sign on the left. Paint Mountain Trail goes toward Paint Creek Campground on a grassy, gated road on the left, and toward Weaver Bend Parking Area on a gated, rocky road that climbs to the right of the road. Paint Mountain Road continues downhill straight ahead but is closed at the bottom of the mountain where it reaches Paint Creek. It will probably not be reopened unless federal funding is found.

Allen Branch Pond Picnic Area, FS 209C, and Weaver Bend Parking Area Trailheads

From the junction of TN 70 (not US 70) and TN 107, go 10.1 miles on TN 107, or 1.0 mile past the Cocke County/Greene County line, and turn left on the unmarked paved Brush Creek Road (FS 209), which, at first, appears to be the driveway to a cabin. If you are driving from Newport, FS 209 is 4.9 miles from the junction of US 25 and TN 107, or 0.3 mile past Houston Valley Recreation Area. The road curves left at the cabin and goes through a USFS gate, winding for 1.8 miles before reaching the junction with FS 209C (the pavement ends near here). Stay straight on FS 209 for another 0.7 mile to go to the Allen Branch Pond Picnic Area, where the trailhead for the Allen Branch Trail is located. From the junction of FS 209 and FS 209C, turn left onto FS 209C and immediately cross Brush Creek to reach the FS 209C Trailhead for the Paint Mountain Trail on the left after 0.8 mile. There is a large, brown metal sign for "Paint Mountain Trail" with an arrow to the left and an information sign. The parking area is large enough for several cars. FS 209C continues another 0.7 mile to reach the very large Weaver Bend Parking Area. You can park here or continue another 0.2 mile, where there is very limited parking at the Chimney Rocks Trail on the left, just before the railroad tracks. You can also access this trailhead from US 70/25. Follow US 70/25 1.2 mile past its junction with TN 107 and turn left on a dirt road (FS

209) just before crossing the French Broad River. Follow FS 209 for 4.2 miles, past the Allen Branch Pond Picnic Area on the right, to the junction with FS 209C described above. Turn right on FS 209C to reach the FS 209C and Weaver Bend Parking Area Trailheads.

TOPOGRAPHIC MAPS: USGS Hot Springs, NC; Paint Rock, TN. TI Map 782, French Broad and Nolichucky Rivers, CNF.

TRAIL DESCRIPTIONS

83. PAINT CREEK TRAIL (FS TRAIL 10, TI TRAIL 23)

LENGTH: 2.9 miles

ELEVATION CHANGE: Low point, 1,750 feet; high point, 2,000 feet

DIFFICULTY: Moderate

TRAILHEADS: Paint Creek Campground (start) and FS 31BA (end)

TRAIL CONNECTIONS: Paint Mountain Trail

USE: Hiking

TOPOGRAPHIC MAP: USGS Hot Springs, NC

COMMENTS: Because of its close proximity to Paint Creek, the Paint Creek Trail was the most heavily damaged of all the trails in the Paint Creek area during the floods of 2001. Some sections were completely washed away, and others have been buried under large piles of dead trees. While the trail is now passable, there are several places where the trail may be difficult to follow. Watch for the blue blazes and watch out for undercut banks and unexpected changes in the character of the trail. While the Paint Creek Trail does not follow the original path of the flume that carried lumber from the sawmill down to the French Broad River, the flume was believed to be located in this area. Water is available along almost the entire length of the trail, and camping is possible between 2.1 and 2.3 miles. A few sandy and rocky flats have also been formed by the flood in the first 1.0 mile, but given the evidence of the power of a thunderstorm, a check on the weather would be wise before camping here.

DETAILS: To reach the trailhead from the parking area across from Paint Creek Campground, cross the bridge over Paint Creek. The trail starts on the right at a USFS trail marker 50 feet away from the bridge, immediately climbing through pines and mountain laurel. At 0.2 mile the trailhead for Paint Mountain Trail is on the left at a wooden sign. The mileages listed in this book differ from the mileages listed on the sign, but, of course, this book is correct. Paint Creek Trail goes to the right at this intersection and levels off, following a contour across a dry, south-facing slope. At 0.5 mile the trail forks, the right fork leading down toward the creek and the left fork going up. Paint Creek Trail follows the left fork up and then descends back down to Paint Creek. At 0.6 mile the trail enters an extremely flood-damaged area. Watch for blue blazes and signs of trail maintenance and stay mostly to the left. After about 200 feet, the trail climbs out of the gully and returns to the original trail, just above the left bank.

At 1.1 miles the trail enters another flood-damaged area. The trail stays on the left side of Paint Creek and descends to within inches of the water for less than 0.1 mile. In high water, this section of trail may be submerged. After a short ascent, the trail forks at 1.3 miles. The left fork is the old and damaged trail and the right fork is the new trail. Follow the right fork and climb steeply, passing through two switchbacks before the trail joins an old railroad grade. The Paint Creek Trail follows the railroad grade to the right for 0.2 mile and then leaves the grade by turning left and climbing steeply uphill.

At 2.1 miles, the trail returns to Paint Creek and parallels it through a dark hemlock forest before crossing the creek. The Paint Creek Trail appears to dead-end at a large debris pile at 2.5 miles, but a small footpath goes down the bank to the left. Cross Paint Creek on a large, fallen hemlock and then follow the bank to the right around the bend in the creek. About 250 feet after the hemlock, the Paint Creek Trail is visible on the other side of the creek. Cross Paint Creek to rejoin the original trail.

At 2.7 miles the Paint Creek Trail crosses Paint Creek to the left. Watch for the cement bridge footings to the right of the path at 2.9 miles. A fairly clear but unofficial trail continues straight ahead, following Paint Creek and eventually climbing to private property near Mundy Gap. Paint Creek Trail crosses Paint Creek at the footings. Take a moment to contemplate just how much water must have been flowing down Paint Creek for it to reach high enough to completely wipe out the bridge as you make the shallow wade that is necessary at this point to get to the trailhead, about 100 feet away. A short washed-out footbridge marks the end of the trail at a gravel parking area at the end of FS 31BA. FS 31BA is closed to motor vehicles due to flood damage, so from here it is another 0.8 mile to reach the nearest parking at FS 31B and the Little Paint Creek Trailhead.

84. PAINT MOUNTAIN TRAIL (FS TRAIL 7, TI TRAIL 24)

LENGTH: 9.6 miles

ELEVATION CHANGE: Low point, 1,250 feet; high point, 2,630 feet

DIFFICULTY: Moderate

TRAILHEADS: Paint Creek Trail (start), Lone Pine Gap (middle), FS 209C (end)

TRAIL CONNECTIONS: Chimney Rocks Trail

USE: Hiking, equestrian, and mountain bike

TOPOGRAPHIC MAPS: USGS Hot Springs, NC; Paint Rock, TN

COMMENTS: The TI map shows Paint Mountain Trail as a hiking trail for most of its length, but the trail has recently been designated as a horse trail for its entire length by the USFS. The trail alternates between foot trail and old roadbed as it climbs the south side of Paint Mountain to Lone Pine Gap. It then follows the ridgeline of Paint Mountain, with several good views, until it descends to the French Broad River. Pine, oak, and rhododendron dominate the forests of this dry mountainside. A young forest of pine is slowly reclaiming Lone Pine Gap, which was burned in 1994 in a forest fire.

Camping is possible at 2.5 miles near a small gap. The nearest water in this area is on private property, so you will need to backtrack about 0.1 to 0.3 mile or more to get water, depending on the dryness of the season. There are fields at 4.0 miles and 5.9 miles, which could be good campsites, but the first field does not have water nearby. The second field is about 0.2 mile from a small pond. Reliable water can be found at 3.1 miles, 6.1 miles, and 9.4 miles.

DETAILS: The Paint Mountain Trail begins at 0.2 mile on the Paint Creek Trail at a wooden sign. The Paint Mountain Trail goes to the left, following a contour away from Paint Creek until it descends to cross FS 41 at 0.2 mile. The trail follows high above Paint Creek, which can be heard but not seen. At this point the trail is a clear but sometimes rocky footpath as it passes rock outcroppings and creek drainages. At 1.9 miles the trail crosses a faint railroad grade before climbing steeply and going through two switchbacks. The trail becomes very rocky and overgrown with mountain laurel. It soon levels off and begins to clear before the trail drops down an eight-foot cliff and resumes its original course.

Two more drainages are crossed before a steep series of four switchbacks leads to a small flat gap at 2.5 miles. The trail can be faint as it goes straight into the gap, so watch for the blue blazes. At 2.7 miles the trail takes a left just before the USFS boundary, which is marked with large, square blue blazes. A white laminated no trespassing sign marks the beginning of private property just before a small pond. After turning left, the trail curves slightly to return to the south side of the ridge.

The trail skirts the edge of the USFS boundary through a section of fallen pines that were the victims of the pine bark beetle. A fresh private road cut is visible to the right. At 3.0 miles a small rock outcrop makes a great spot to stop for lunch or to just enjoy the views to the southwest of TN and NC. From here the trail descends to cross two side creeks through thick rhododendrons before crossing a faint roadbed at 3.5 miles. The trail climbs again and crosses another creek drainage before reaching a grassy roadbed at 4.0 miles. The Paint Mountain Trail turns left to follow the roadbed for about 300 feet and then turns right to leave the roadbed. Look carefully for a faint bluish-white blaze about 15 feet from the road on the right. About 200 feet farther, the trail crosses a small clearing, staying along the right edge.

After crossing the ridge and a switchback, the trail intersects another grassy roadbed at 4.5 miles. A small wooden sign that has been chewed on by a bear marks the intersection and possibly the bear's territory. The Paint Mountain Trail turns left to follow the roadbed along the ridge to a fork in the road at 4.7 miles. In the summer, this area may be overgrown with briars, but a well-timed hike will be rewarded with blackberries and raspberries. Follow the left and lower fork down to the gate and trailhead at Lone Pine Gap and FS 54 at 5.0 miles. USFS trail markers show where the trail enters and leaves the gap. The young forest at the gap allows for great views to the south and west.

From Lone Pine Gap until the junction with Chimney Rocks Trail, the trail is marked with yellow metal diamonds or yellow blazes. The trail crosses the road and climbs a gated, rocky roadbed about 200 feet. A wooden sign marks the intersection where the hiker trail splits off to the left as the horse trail continues ahead along the roadbed. The hiker trail climbs through thick vegetation to a small gap where it rejoins the horse trail and roadbed at 5.2 miles. The Paint Mountain Trail again turns left to follow the roadbed.

From here the trail follows the ridgeline, with several small ups and downs and many slightly obscured views in the winter. At 5.9 miles the trail crosses a small clearing, staying to the right. A small pond is on the left at 6.1 miles, shortly before a fork in the roadbed.

The right fork is overgrown, so the trail takes the left fork to a small gap at 6.3 miles. The horse trail continues straight ahead, climbing steeply out of the gap, while the hiker trail leaves the gap to the right, following a contour. The hiker trail is marked by an obscure small metal sign, nailed to a tree. The two trails rejoin at another small gap at 6.6 miles. Five trails come together in the gap. To the left and going uphill is the horse trail. To the left and going downhill is the gated FS 54B, which leads about 1.3 miles to FS 54. To the right and going up is a very steep trail that follows the ridge. Across the gap is the Paint Mountain Trail, which follows a contour to the southwest to the junction with the Chimney Rocks Trail (FS Trail 154, TI Trail 7) at 6.8 miles. A wooden sign marks the beginning of the Chimney Rocks Trail straight ahead. It is 2.4 miles along the Chimney Rocks Trail to reach FS 209C near the Weaver Bend Parking Area. The Paint Mountain Trail makes a hard right across the ridge to continue following the contour to the west. It passes a small wooden sign marking the Paint Mountain Trail, which is marked by blue blazes for the remainder of the trail.

The Paint Mountain Trail stays on or near the ridgeline until 8.0 miles, where it begins descending a series of switchbacks along a shoulder of Paint Mountain. The switchbacks continue until 9.1 miles where the trail turns left to parallel the now visible FS 209C. At 9.2 miles a side trail leads over to the road. The trail crosses a small creek at 9.4 miles and follows an old roadbed for about 200 feet. The overgrown roadbed continues straight toward FS 209C, while the Paint Mountain Trail curves left to parallel the road until 9.6 miles, where it reaches the trailhead on FS 209C. It enters the parking area from behind the information sign.

85. CHIMNEY ROCKS TRAIL (FS TRAIL 154, TI TRAIL 7)

LENGTH: 2.4 miles

ELEVATION CHANGE: Low point, 1,250 feet; high point, 2,500 feet

DIFFICULTY: Difficult

TRAILHEADS: Weaver Bend Parking Area (start) and Paint Mountain Trail (end)

USE: Hiking, equestrian, and mountain bike

TOPOGRAPHIC MAP: USGS Paint Rock, TN

COMMENTS: This is a very steep, wide, and dry trail that climbs through mostly pine and oak to the junction with the Paint Mountain

Trail. Since it ascends a shoulder on the south side of Paint Mountain, it is also a very hot trail in the summer. The climb is rewarded, though, with views of the French Broad River from high above and the mountains to the southeast. Anyone who is nostalgic for the railroad days will enjoy sitting under the pines on a high rocky outcrop watching the trains work their way along the river far below. Water is not available along the trail, and there are no established campsites. The trail has blueberries and raspberries in season.

DETAILS: The Chimney Rocks Trail begins about 0.2 mile past the Weaver Bend Parking Area on FS 209C, just before the railroad tracks. The trail starts up a gated 4 WD road, at a FS trail marker. It begins climbing immediately, following yellow blazes, and curving to the left through a large field with lots of kudzu before entering the forest at 0.1 mile. A second long field is bypassed by staying to the right along the roadbed. At 0.5 mile, the roadbed curves to the left, while the Chimney Rocks Trail passes a small wooden sign with a yellow blaze on it, straight ahead. The forest becomes noticeably drier, with pine trees becoming more dominant. Many pine trees have fallen or been cut as the result of southern pine beetle damage. The trail climbs back and forth along the ridge, reaching good views of the mountains and the river below between 1.4 miles and 1.6 miles. At 2.0 miles the trail

View of French Broad River from Chimney Rocks Trail. Photograph by Will Skelton.

begins to level off in a forest of mostly oaks, before reaching the junc-tion with Paint Mountain Trail at 2.4 miles. The best views of the French Broad River are near the junction: a huge bend in the river with the historic twin railroad bridges.

A nice loop can be made by turning left and following the Paint Mountain Trail 2.8 miles to the trailhead on FS 209C, and another 0.7 mile to the left along the road, back to the Weaver Bend Parking Area. Going straight from the junction of the Chimney Rocks Trail and the Paint Mountain Trail, it is 1.8 miles to Lone Pine Gap and FS 54, and 6.8 miles to the junction with the Paint Creek Trail.

86. LITTLE PAINT CREEK TRAIL (FS TRAIL 11, TI TRAIL 19)

LENGTH: 2.4 miles

ELEVATION CHANGE: Low point, 2,150 feet; high point, 2,900 feet

DIFFICULTY: Moderate

TRAILHEADS: FS 31B (start) and AT (end)

USE: Hiking

TOPOGRAPHIC MAP: USGS Hot Springs, NC

COMMENTS: The trail follows a former logging railroad bed for most of its length, climbing through lush forests of hemlock and rhodo-dendron before turning to climb to Deep Gap and the AT. The trail crosses Little Paint Creek many times. While most of the crossings can be negotiated without wet feet, the early crossings may require a shal-low wade, especially in wetter months. There are established campsites at the beginning and end of the trail, and water is never very far away. The campsites at the beginning of the trail appear heavily used and could be greatly helped if everyone carried out a little more than they carried in.

DETAILS: The Little Paint Creek Trail starts on the right side of the road, just before the parking area, which is no longer reachable by car. The floods of 2001 washed out the road just below the trailhead. A small wooden sign marks the beginning of the trail. The trail imme-diately crosses the creek and follows a jeep trail for about 100 feet. A USFS trail marker on the right marks where the Little Paint Creek Trail turns off to the right while the jeep trail continues straight ahead. The blue-blazed Little Paint Creek Trail goes toward Little Paint Creek, passing several campsites on the right before the second creek crossing at 0.1 mile.

The trail crosses the creek ten more times before turning right and away from the creek at 2.2 miles. The trail follows a dry gully about 100 yards before entering a series of switchbacks, turning to the left first. The trail can be very faint at this point, so watch carefully for the blue blazes. At 2.3 miles, the Little Paint Creek Trail reaches the top of the climb and runs level, straight for Deep Gap. The trail reaches the gap at 2.4 miles at the junction with the AT. A USFS trail marker and a wooden sign mark the intersection. Straight across the trail is a campsite large enough for a few tents. Water can be found by back-tracking down Little Paint Creek Trail, or by going down the other side of the gap. The second option is not as far, but it is more difficult.

The TI map shows the Deep Gap Hollow Trail leaving down the opposite side of the gap from Little Paint Creek Trail, but there is no evidence of a trail here. To the left, it is 2.0 miles along the AT to reach Allen Gap and TN 70. To the right, it is 3.4 miles along the AT to reach Hurricane Gap and FS 31.

87. ALLEN BRANCH POND TRAIL (FS TRAIL 209, TI TRAIL 2)

LENGTH: 0.4 mile

ELEVATION CHANGE: Low point, 1,500 feet; high point, 1,520 feet

DIFFICULTY: Easy

TRAILHEADS: Allen Branch Pond Picnic Area (loop trail)

USE: Hiking

TOPOGRAPHIC MAP: USGS Paint Rock, TN

DETAILS: The Allen Branch Pond Trail is a very short, flat, gravel nature trail that circles a man-made pond and crosses an earthen dam. Interpretive signs are located along the trail describing the pond's natural history. There are a few benches along the loop, and picnic tables are located at the beginning of the loop. There is a $2 fee for parking at the pond.

16 Meadow Creek Mountain

Meadow Creek Mountain is located just north of TN 107 and Paint Mountain and is divided by the Greene County/Cocke County line; it is in the Nolichucky/Unaka Ranger District. This long, narrow, isolated ridge overlooks the Paint Creek area to the south and east, and

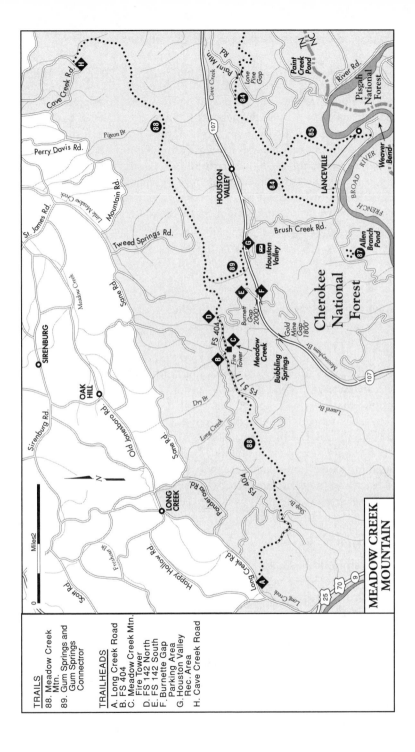

TRAILS
88. Meadow Creek Mtn.
89. Gum Springs and Gum Springs Connector

TRAILHEADS
A. Long Creek Road
B. FS 404
C. Meadow Creek Mtn. Fire Tower
D. FS 142 North
E. FS 142 South
F. Burnette Gap Parking Area
G. Houston Valley Rec. Area
H. Cave Creek Road

MEADOW CREEK MOUNTAIN

the Nolichucky River Valley to the north. The mountains suddenly become foothills on the north side of Meadow Creek Mountain, allowing distant views to the north, especially in the winter. Most of Meadow Creek Mountain is covered by oak forests with patches of pine-oak forests scattered over the mountain. Rhododendron, mountain laurel, blueberry, and huckleberry are common along the ridge, while hemlock and tulip tree are found at its base. Deer, wild turkey, and ruffed grouse are the most commonly seen of the typical southern Appalachian wildlife. While it is popular among hikers and horseback riders, the most popular attraction of Meadow Creek Mountain is its fire tower. There are no protected areas along Meadow Creek Mountain.

HISTORY

Meadow Creek Mountain's most significant history is its use as a site for a fire tower. The current tower is the fifth to stand on the site and may seem sparse by today's standards, with only a small electric stove and fridge, but it is luxurious compared to the original tower. In 1926 the tower was nothing more than a platform between three chestnut trees with a small tent. This tent "office" housed a hand crank telephone that was used to send news of fires that had been spotted. Anyone working in the tower had to live a Spartan lifestyle, since it was a two-mile hike to the tower and water had to be carried up from a spring on the side of the mountain. Starting in the 1980s, airplanes were used for spotting fires, and since then, fire towers are no longer needed. The catwalk that surrounds the tower is open to the public, providing panoramic views, but graffiti and vandalism have taken their toll.

TRAILHEADS AND MAPS

To reach Meadow Creek Mountain from I-40 take Exit 432 for US 25 to Newport. Go through Newport and follow US 25 to cross over the French Broad River on a steel truss bridge. The area can also be reached from Greeneville by going south on TN 70 about 11 miles from US 11E and turning right onto TN 107.

Long Creek Road Trailhead

On US 25 South, go 4.1 miles past the truss bridge over the French Broad River and turn left onto TN 340. (If you are coming from Greeneville on TN 107, this is a right turn 6.1 miles after turning right onto US 25.) Pass Old Long Creek Road on the right after 0.5 mile. After another 0.5 mile, turn right onto Long Creek Road. After 0.4 mile, Long Creek Road crosses a small concrete bridge. The Long Creek Road Trailhead is on the right approximately 50 feet past the bridge. There is enough parking for four or five cars in a pull-off just before an unmarked, gated, USFS road. The Meadow Creek Mountain Trail starts to the left of the gate. There are car campsites on the other side of the bridge and a short distance up the USFS road.

FS 404 Trailhead

From the Long Creek Road Trailhead, continue on Long Creek Road 0.5 mile to the unmarked, gated, gravel FS 404. FS 404 is on the right in a left-hand curve, just after crossing Yellow Spring Branch. Follow FS 404 7.6 miles to a gated road on the right. (From the junction of FS 404 and FS 142 the trailhead is 0.4 mile on the left.) Meadow Creek Mountain Trail goes toward Long Creek Road from behind the gate and toward the fire tower approximately 50 feet past the gate on FS 404. Wooden signs mark the trail in both directions. Parking is available for two to three cars.

Meadow Creek Mountain Fire Tower Trailhead

From the FS 404 Trailhead, continue 0.4 mile to the junction with FS 142. Turn right and go through a gate. The fire tower parking lot is 0.2 mile past the gate. From TN 107, turn right onto FS 142 at the Meadow Creek Fire Tower sign, 1.0 mile past Houston Valley Recreation Area. Continue on FS 142 for 2.8 miles to the junction of FS 142 and FS 404. Stay to the left to reach the fire tower parking lot 0.2 mile ahead. The Meadow Creek Mountain Trail goes toward Long Creek Road from the western end of the lot and follows the gravel FS 142 in the opposite direction. There is ample parking.

FS 142 North Trailhead

From the junction of FS 404 and FS 142, go 0.4 mile east along the ridge. A wooden sign marks the continuation of the Meadow Creek Mountain Trail on the left side of the road just as the road begins to descend off the ridge. From TN 107 turn right onto FS 142 1.0 mile past Houston Valley Recreation Area. The trailhead is 2.4 miles up FS 142, on the right.

FS 142 South Trailhead

From the FS 142 North Trailhead, continue downhill 2.1 miles. The FS 142 South Trailhead is on the left as the road rounds a shoulder to the right. The Gum Springs Connector Trail starts at four upright log posts that block vehicle access to the wide trail. From TN 107 turn right onto FS 142 1.0 mile past Houston Valley Recreation Area. The trailhead is 0.3 mile up FS 142 on the right. There is parking for two to three cars. Larger groups or overflow should use the Burnette Gap Parking Area.

Burnette Gap Parking Area

From the truss bridge on US 25 south, go 10.3 miles and turn left onto TN 107. Follow TN 107 3.6 miles. Turn right onto FS 5110 at Burnette Gap, just past the Meadow Creek Fire Tower Road (FS 142). The parking area is 100 yards up FS 5110. The nearest maintained trails are the Gum Springs Connector Trail, 0.3 mile up FS 142 and Gum Springs Trail, 1.0 mile north on TN 107. The gravel parking area is built for trucks and horse trailers but also provides ample parking for large hiking groups. From Greeneville on TN 107, the parking area is on the left 1.0 mile past the Houston Valley Recreation Area.

View of mountains from Meadow Creek Mountain fire tower. Photograph by Will Skelton.

Houston Valley Recreation Area Trailhead

From the truss bridge on US 25 south, go 10.3 miles and turn left onto TN 107. Follow TN 107 past the Meadow Creek Fire Tower Road (FS 142) to Houston Valley Recreation Area on the right after 4.6 miles. If you are coming from Greeneville on TN 107, the trailhead is 10.4 miles from the junction of TN 70 and TN 107, on the left. There is a $2 day-use fee for parking at the recreation area. Ample parking is available, but, if the gates are closed, there is plenty of parking at the Burnette Gap Parking Area, 1.0 mile south on TN 107. Gum Springs Trail is across the road from the recreation area.

Cave Creek Road Trailhead

From TN 107 north, turn left onto Garret Hill Road 9.3 miles past Houston Valley Recreation Area (on TN 107 south, this is a right turn 1.1 miles from the junction of TN 70 and TN 107). After 1.6 miles, turn left onto the gravel Cave Creek Road. The Cave Creek Road Trailhead is 1.4 miles on the left, just across from a small, yellow USFS boundary sign. The trailhead and trail are unmarked. There is parking for a few cars in a small pull-off on the left, just before the dirt road that Meadow Creek Mountain Trail follows.

TOPOGRAPHIC MAPS: USGS Neddy Mountain, TN; Paint Rock, TN; Cedar Creek, TN. TI Map 782, French Broad and Nolichucky Rivers, CNF.

TRAIL DESCRIPTIONS

88. MEADOW CREEK MOUNTAIN TRAIL (FS TRAIL 6, TI TRAIL 21)

LENGTH: 13.8 miles

ELEVATION CHANGE: Low point, 1,250 feet; high point, 3,050 feet

DIFFICULTY: Moderate

TRAILHEADS: Long Creek Road (start), FS 404, Meadow Creek Mountain Fire Tower, FS 142 North, and Cave Creek Road (end)

TRAIL CONNECTIONS: Gum Springs Trail

USE: Hiking, equestrian, mountain bike

TOPOGRAPHIC MAPS: Neddy Mountain, TN; Paint Rock, TN; Cedar Creek, TN

COMMENTS: Meadow Creek Mountain Trail covers almost the entire length of the ridge, varying from narrow, overgrown paths to gravel roads. Portions of the trail are wide, gradual and easy to follow, while other sections are so overgrown that the trail is nearly imperceptible. Most of the trail is no longer blazed and some intersections are unmarked, so a good map and compass are a necessity.

Reliable water can be found at the Long Creek Road Trailhead and Cave Creek Road trailhead. Once on the trail, water is available at 7.3 miles by going 0.4 mile down Gum Springs Trail and after 12.5 miles (1.3 miles from Cave Creek Road). There are no established campsites along the trail, but campsites can be found at the Long Creek Road Trailhead and Cave Creek Road Trailhead.

DETAILS: The Meadow Creek Mountain Trail begins by climbing along a wide path just to the left of the gate. At 0.3 mile the trail narrows and begins to climb steeply, ascending through a series of short switchbacks. Soon the first views can be seen before reaching the top of a low ridge at 0.6 mile. The trail follows the ridge over a small knob before coming to the end of a dirt road in a small gap. It continues along the road, ascending moderately to another small gap at 1.3 miles. An old overgrown road goes off to the right, while the trail follows the dirt road to the left, staying just off the ridgeline.

At 1.6 miles another dirt road enters from the right. The trail leaves the road at this point and climbs steeply uphill northeast along the shoulder between the two roads. This intersection is unmarked, but the trail is fairly clear. Note that the TI map incorrectly shows the trail leaving the road at its intersection with FS 404.

The Meadow Creek Mountain Trail climbs through a switchback and onto a low ridge, following the ridgeline before climbing steeply to a small gap at 2.7 miles. The trail becomes faint in the gap but turns left to climb along the ridge to the northeast to reach the top of the ridge at 3.0 miles. This section of trail onwards to the grassy road at 4.6 miles is overgrown in sections, although mostly by blueberries, which makes it worth it in the summer. From here the trail becomes much more level with some minor ups and downs and a couple of short switchbacks. It follows the ridgeline to a small knob, where it descends steeply to a small gap and a grassy road at 4.6 miles. There is a wooden sign just before and facing the road that says "Meadow Creek Mountain Trail." Looking back up the hill, you will see one of the few metal yellow diamond blazes found on the trail. The grassy road leads to the left and far right. The Meadow Creek Mountain Trail follows the road to the left, ascending only slightly, to reach another gap at 4.8 miles. A side road goes straight ahead, but the

Meadow Creek Mountain Trail follows the grassy road as it turns left and follows the contour of the mountain to a gate and a junction with FS 404. A wooden "Meadow Creek Mountain Trail" sign stands beside the gate. The trail turns right on FS 404 for approximately 50 feet and then turns steeply uphill past another wooden "Meadow Creek Mountain Trail" sign on a wide path. The Meadow Creek Mountain Fire Tower Trailhead is reached at 5.7 miles in the northwest corner of the parking lot. A wooden sign says "Meadow Creek Mountain Trail, Long Creek Road 5.7 miles."

From the same corner of the lot, another trail leads in a wide spiral a short distance up to the fire tower. There are unobstructed views in all directions from the catwalk that surrounds the top floor of the tower. To continue along the Meadow Creek Mountain Trail, walk across the parking lot and follow FS 142 along the ridge. At 6.3 miles (0.6 mile from the fire tower), another wooden "Meadow Creek Mountain" sign marks the continuation of the trail, just as the road begins to descend off of the ridge. The trail follows the ridgeline down moderately on a wide path, crossing a small meadow at 7.0 miles before reaching a gap and the junction with Gum Springs Trail at 7.3 miles.

At the gap, an unmarked grassy road leaves to the left, while Gum Springs Trail leaves to the right. Wooden signs mark the intersection from three directions. Meadow Creek Mountain Trail continues straight across the gap, skirting to the left of the ridge and following the contour around a knob. The trail narrows and becomes more overgrown. After regaining the ridge, the trail descends briefly to reach a small gap at 7.8 miles. From here the trail climbs gradually over a knob before a steep descent to a gap at 8.7 miles. A grassy road leaves to the left toward Tweed Springs Road. The Meadow Creek Mountain Trail joins the road in the opposite direction, crossing the gap and following the ridge. After a short, steep ascent the trail runs fairly level until it leaves the ridge to the left at 9.5 miles, still following the grassy road as it descends gradually. At 9.6 miles a side trail follows an old road uphill to the right to a small, overgrown clearing. Another 100 feet farther, the grassy road turns hard left as the Meadow Creek Mountain Trail continues straight ahead on an overgrown roadbed.

From this point on the trail receives much less use and less maintenance. Watch carefully for changes in the trail. The trail passes through rhododendron before reaching a narrow gap at 9.8 miles. The roadbed continues downhill to the left of the ridge, but the Meadow Creek Mountain Trail turns right to go straight down the south side of the ridge following a small gully into a pine forest. After a short descent, the trail turns left to follow the contour to a gap at 10.0 miles. The Meadow Creek Mountain Trail turns right to follow the ridge, while a faint trail turns hard right and descends.

The trail leaves the ridge to the left, shortly after leaving the gap, and follows the contour in and out of small stream valleys. The trail continues level to enter a gap from the left at 10.7 miles. The trail becomes faint as it crosses the gap and climbs steeply through an overgrown pine forest. It passes through a switchback before reaching a narrow, rocky ridge at 10.8 miles. Watch for blueberries in the summer as the faint and sometimes completely overgrown trail follows the ridge, climbing gradually.

The trail crosses over the top of a knob at 11.3 miles, descends, and then skirts the next knob to the left as the trail becomes clearer. Another knob is skirted when the trail goes to the right of the ridge before reaching a gap with a large depression on the left side at 12.0 miles. Just beyond the gap, the trail curves left and begins to descend moderately off the ridge to a shoulder.

The trail follows the shoulder down to a switchback at 12.2 miles. Watch carefully for this turn, as a faint trail continues straight ahead and another faint trail dead-ends to the left. Meadow Creek Mountain Trail descends steeply to the right off the shoulder. Four more switchbacks lead to a steep valley at 12.5 miles, where the trail suddenly becomes well maintained. At 12.6 miles, notice the hard work that was done to preserve the trail as it crosses another steep valley that was damaged by a slide. From here the trail descends gradually on a wide trail, passing through two more switchbacks at 12.9 miles. At 13.0 miles an overgrown roadbed goes left, while Meadow Creek Mountain Trail turns right to follow a slightly rutted roadbed around a small shoulder and meets a gravel USFS road at 13.1 miles.

The Meadow Creek Mountain Trail turns hard left onto the USFS Road to follow it down along the ridge. Note that the TI map incorrectly shows the trail as crossing the road repeatedly. The trail follows the road for the rest of its length. Private roads enter from the right at 13.4 miles and 13.7 miles. A road on the left at 13.7 miles, just before the second private road, dead-ends at a campsite. The trail ends at 13.8 miles at Cave Creek Road after crossing a small creek.

89. GUM SPRINGS TRAIL (FS TRAIL 5, TI TRAIL 13)

LENGTH: 1.3 miles

ELEVATION CHANGE: Low point, 1,800 feet; high point, 2,450 feet

DIFFICULTY: Moderate

TRAILHEADS: Houston Valley Recreation Area (start); Meadow Creek Mountain Trail (end)

TRAIL CONNECTIONS: Gum Springs Connector Trail

USE: Hiking (from Houston Valley Recreation Area to junction with Gum Springs Connector Trail); hiking, equestrian, mountain bike (from junction with Gum Springs Connector Trail to Meadow Creek Mountain Trail)

TOPOGRAPHIC MAPS: Paint Rock, TN

COMMENTS: While the Gum Springs Trail provides a somewhat gradual access to the Meadow Creek Mountain Trail, it is also a beautiful, short hike. The clear, wide path climbs past hemlocks, tulip trees, and through rhododendron thickets to reach its namesake. The trail continues past a small flat filled with large ferns to reach the ridgeline of Meadow Creek Mountain at a low gap. There are no campsites along the trail, but water is accessible from 0.6 to 0.9 mile. Parking at the Houston Valley Recreation Area requires a $2 day-use fee. The trail is well marked with blue blazes. Note that the TI map incorrectly shows the entire length of this trail as a mountain bike trail.

DETAILS: Gum Springs Trail begins next to the sign for the Houston Valley Recreation Area. A wooden sign, "Gum Springs Trail, Meadow Creek Mountain Trail 1.3 miles," marks the start of the trail. It begins with a short ascent before it follows the contour of the mountain to the left, following an old roadbed and paralleling TN 107 from a distance. At 0.5 mile the trail turns right just before Gum Springs Branch and the junction with Gum Springs Connector Trail and begins climbing moderately as it parallels the stream through thick rhododendrons. The trail crosses the creek four times before reaching Gum Springs at 0.9 mile. A switchback on the right takes the trail above the roadbed, where it parallels the valley and roadbed as it continues to climb. A wide, flat area is reached at 1.1 mile, where the trail turns left to rejoin the roadbed. The Gum Springs Trail follows the left side of the valley gradually upward until it reaches a gap and the junction with Meadow Creek Mountain Trail at 1.3 miles.

GUM SPRINGS CONNECTOR TRAIL (NO FS OR TI NUMBERS)

LENGTH: 0.3 mile

ELEVATION CHANGE: Low point, 1,950 feet; high point, 2,150 feet

DIFFICULTY: Moderate

TRAILHEADS: FS 142 Trailhead (south) (start) and Gum Springs Trail (end)

USE: Hiking, equestrian, and mountain bike

TOPOGRAPHIC MAPS: Paint Rock, TN

COMMENTS: This trail is an alternate trailhead access to the Gum Springs Trail from the Burnette Gap Parking Area. This trail and its trailhead were constructed to help alleviate safety problems with large trucks and horse trailers parking on the roadsides. The very wide and easy-to-follow Gum Springs Connector Trail did not have any trailhead signs or blazes when hiked in 2003, but it is marked by red flagging tape. There are no established campsites along the trail. Water is available at 0.27 mile.

DETAILS: The Gum Springs Connector Trail leaves FS 142 heading west along a level and wide roadbed through a pine-oak forest. It follows the top of a shoulder to a small grassy area at 0.1 mile with a view looking up at Meadow Creek Mountain and an obscured view over Houston Valley. The trail turns left to descend slightly on a grassy road for 100 feet to a junction. Straight ahead, the roadbed continues for approximately 0.2 mile before it dead-ends. The Gum Springs Connector Trail leaves the junction to the right, descending steeply along the side of the shoulder as it passes through a young hardwood forest. At 0.27 mile the trail nears the bottom of the valley and turns right into a dark forest of hemlock and rhododendron. The trail tunnels through the rhododendron another 175 feet to cross Gum Springs Branch. It reaches Gum Springs Trail 75 feet farther at 0.3 mile. From here Gum Springs Trail is open only to hiking for 0.5 mile to the right to reach TN 107 and Houston Valley Recreation Area. To the left and uphill, Gum Springs Trail is open to hiking, horseback riding, and mountain biking for 0.8 mile to the junction with Meadow Creek Mountain Trail.

17 Devil's Backbone

(Includes Devil's Backbone Backcountry Area and Devil's Backbone Roadless Area)

The Devil's Backbone ridge and Hall Mountain above it are probably the most viewable and accessible of the CNF's protected areas. When driving I-40 into NC from TN, you by necessity look up at these ridges and mountains as you get close to Hartford, TN. The portion nearest the interstate was identified by the USFS as the 4,283-acre Devil's Backbone Roadless Area in the Southern Appalachian Assessment. An area slightly larger than the roadless area is to be protected in the CNF's 2004 plan revision as the 4,341-acre Devil's Backbone Backcountry Area. The area is readily accessible from the trailhead on FS 110 just off I-40 as the Stone Mountain Trail winds its way to the top of the mountain, with outstanding views of the Pigeon River below.

HISTORY

Typical of the southern Appalachian Mountains, this area is in a mostly hardwood forest at relatively low elevation. The Pigeon River

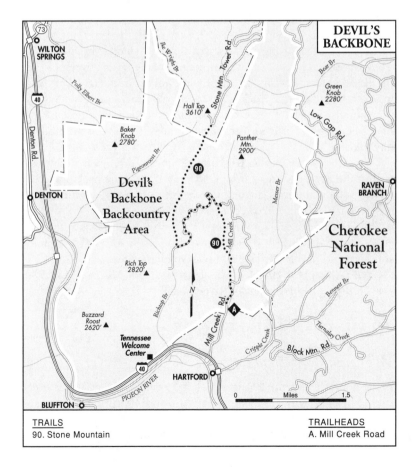

TRAILS	TRAILHEADS
90. Stone Mountain	A. Mill Creek Road

flows at its base along I-40. The high point of this trail is named Hall Top, and the Hall Cemetery is located here just below the actual highest point, on the south side. Several years ago this cemetery was badly overgrown, then it was cleared and a very nice marble marker was placed here, and now it is badly overgrown again. The marker states that the cemetery was established in 1833, and there are several markers for individual graves. Remnants of a former house site can also be found on the ridgetop about a quarter mile north of the high point, but information on it is not available. The high point is now the location of a TN state-owned fire tower and antennas for television and other electronic transmissions.

Like much of the southern Appalachian Mountains, this general area has been logged since early settlers moved into the area until late in the twentieth century. It is recovering and will continue to improve if the USFS will stop cutting the low-quality timber that is common throughout this area. In describing the Stone Mountain Trail, reference will be made to logging grades. These are routes that were once used to remove timber from the area prior to and since it became a NF. They were used by one or more of the following means to remove the timber: skidders, tractors, trucks, mules, horses, and oxen. They vary in width from that of a truck to a very narrow track used by the working animals. Some are quite obvious, but others are very obscure and may be unnoticeable as former logging grades to many of the modern-day hikers.

The 6,660-acre Devil's Backbone Primitive Area was designated within the roadless area in the CNF's 1988 management plan. The CNF's 2004 plan revision continues the protection for a portion of the old primitive area as a backcountry area. However, illegal ORV access continues to be a problem, mainly because the CNF has refused to effectively close FS 110, which allows easy access for ORV's from the southern end of the Devil's Backbone Roadless Area.

TOPOGRAPHIC MAPS: USGS Hartford, TN-NC. TI Map 782, French Broad and Nolichucky Rivers, CNF.

TRAILHEAD AND MAPS

Mill Creek Road Trailhead

Exit I-40 at the Hartford Exit, which is Exit 447, and go to the north side of this highway. If you are going east on I-40, turn left at the end of the exit ramp and go under I-40. Almost immediately turn left (generally west) onto Mill Creek Road, which is mostly unpaved and narrow. Houses are plentiful along this road, so driving it is not a problem. Follow this road 1.0 mile from I-40 and bear left for 0.1 mile to a small parking area. FS 110 and FS Trail 9 are straight ahead. This road, which is also the trail at this point, is gated a few feet from the parking area by the USFS. ORV use is illegal; however, this prohibition is often ignored by some local residents and other users.

TRAIL DESCRIPTION

90. STONE MOUNTAIN TRAIL (FORMERLY DEVIL'S BACKBONE) (FS TRAIL 9, TI TRAIL 34)

LENGTH: 4.8 miles

ELEVATION CHANGE: Low point, 1,480 feet; high point, 3,610 feet

DIFFICULTY: Moderate

TRAILHEAD: Mill Creek Road

USE: Hiking

TOPOGRAPHIC MAP: Hartford, TN-NC

COMMENTS: This trail is described from its lower end at the Mill Creek Road Trailhead to the end of the road on Hall Top that provides access to the Hall Cemetery, and to the fire tower and the antennas on Hall Top's highest point. The trail reaches this road a few hundred feet from the Hall Cemetery, and a short walk of a few hundred feet uphill on the graveled road brings the hiker to the fire tower and antennas. Although the trail is accessible from the fire tower road after several miles of driving on unpaved FS 207 from TN 73, the FS road is best suited to a high clearance vehicle and is not regarded as a trailhead for the purpose of this book. There are no trail markers at the fire tower road.

DETAILS: Follow FS 110 and FS Trail 9 (they are together at this point) as they leave the trailhead and ascend up the gentle sloping road past the USFS gate. A small branch just above the gate may be overflowing the trail in wet weather, but normally it is dry. At 0.3 mile a small branch flows through a culvert under the road and the trail turns left, *off the road,* at this point. Illegal two-wheeled ORVs (motorcycles) also turn left here. Perhaps that is what keeps the trail open, since the USFS does no maintenance on this trail. You can also continue to follow the road for an easier hike and avoid numerous blowdowns; the road traverses around the side of the mountain and rejoins the trail higher up.

The trail follows an old logging grade to mile 0.5, where it crosses Mill Creek. Wading is usually required here, but it is a short, shallow crossing. To follow the trail, continue following the old logging grade to mile 0.9, where the logging grade divides. Bear left. Two small tributaries of Mill Creek are crossed, and at 1.3 miles the trail leaves the creek to ascend a steep slope. An old logging grade bears left up the creek. Keep right and ascend 0.2 mile up this slope (old logging grade

Lower portion of the Devil's Backbone above Pigeon River. Photograph by Will Skelton.

and ORV track) and watch for a vague trail bearing left around the mountain. Follow it a few hundred feet to some major blowdowns. Finding the trail through this tangle is very difficult even for the experienced off-trail hiker. The trail crosses a watercourse, which will be dry most of the time, continuing around the mountain while slowly gaining elevation. In a few hundred feet you emerge in a relatively open woods, but the trail is very obscure. Persevere and at 1.8 miles, after a short, steep climb, you reach FS 110, the road you started on from the trailhead. Turn left uphill on the road, which is a part of the trail, and continue to the top of the ridge at 2.4 miles. If you want to avoid dealing with blowdowns, continue up the steep slope on the ORV track without turning left around the mountain and you will soon reach FS 110. Turn left on the road as noted above and follow it to the top of the ridge.

At the top of the ridge FS 110 continues straight ahead across the ridge, but the trail makes a "U" turn to the right to follow the ridgetop. The ORVs take a shortcut from FS 110 to get to the ridgetop without following it all of the way, as the trail does. The trail is obscure here, but it soon becomes quite obvious when you reach the place where the ORVs come up from FS 110. Such use is illegal, as noted earlier, but is allowed to continue.

The trail is easily followed from here to Hall Top, and there are good distant views when the leaves are down. At mile 4.5 you reach an unofficial dirt road that leads to the Hall Cemetery, which is about 100 feet to the left. Continue straight ahead on this road for a couple hundred feet and you reach a graveled road, FS 207, that provides access to the high point of Hall Mountain, named Hall Top. If you follow this road uphill to the high point where the fire tower and antennas are located, it's at mile 4.8.

18 Miscellaneous Trails

(TI Map 783, South Holston and Watauga Lakes, and TI Map 782, French Broad and Nolichucky Rivers)

91. OLD HOMESTEAD TRAIL (FS TRAIL 603, TI TRAIL 29)

LENGTH: 2.65 miles

ELEVATION CHANGE: Low point, 2,000 feet; high point, 2,550 feet

DIFFICULTY: Moderate

TRAILHEAD: Sink Mountain Boat Ramp

USE: Hiking

TOPOGRAPHIC MAPS: USGS Elk Mills, TN-NC; TI Map 783

TRAILHEAD (SINK MOUNTAIN BOAT RAMP): To access the trail-head, drive TN 67 between Hampton and Mountain City and turn east on TN 167. At 1.9 miles from this junction, turn right on a gravel road (FS 298). At the end of this road at 2.2 miles is the Sink Mountain Boat Ramp and the trailhead.

COMMENTS: The trail is a loop of 2.4 miles with a connection of 0.15 miles to the trailhead, for a total distance of 2.7 miles. The trail

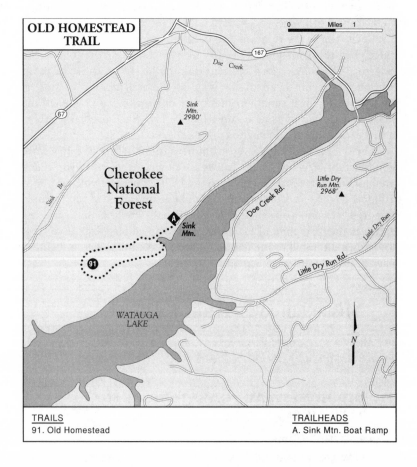

is well marked with blue blazes, but a few sections are steep and some are rocky. There are views of Watauga Lake to the east, especially in winter. Off-trail exploration could continue from the trail.

DETAILS: The trail begins on an old road with the usual dirt berm to impede vehicles. At about 0.1 mile there is a good campsite beside the lake, and the trail narrows. About 200 feet beyond the campsite the trail splits to form a 2.5-mile loop. The right fork is easily followed due to the distinct trail and blue blazes. The left fork can only be followed by observing the blue blazes carefully. The left fork goes a few feet down to a creek and then up the creek about a hundred feet before crossing. After crossing the creek the trail goes straight up the hill a few feet before contouring around the mountain above the lake.

This description will assume a counterclockwise direction around the loop.

Following the right fork, the trail ascends gently beside a usually dry creek bed known as Dry Branch. At 0.4 and 0.6 mile are remains of old homesteads with some interesting ruins. At the second homestead the trail passes through an old open area. Continue straight ahead here and the trail will be picked up at the far side of the homestead.

At 1.2 miles the trail leads to a gap and makes a sharp left turn up the hill. A well-defined trail continues straight through the gap, and care must be exercised to locate the blue blazes leading to the left. At about 1.5 miles the trail reaches the ridgetop, with views of the lake to the east. The trail that continues straight ahead ends in a short distance, but could be used for off-trail hiking down to the lake. At 1.8 miles begin a steep downhill descent following the ridgetop, which is very rocky in spots. At 2.1 miles is a four-pronged hemlock in the middle of the ridge. About 100 yards past this hemlock the ridgetop levels out and the trail angles off the ridge to the right. The trail is not well defined here, so the blue blazes must be followed. The loop is completed at 2.5 miles.

92. WALNUT MOUNTAIN TRAIL (FS TRAIL 135, TI TRAIL 37)

LENGTH: 2.1 miles

ELEVATION CHANGE: Low point, 3,072 feet; high point, 4,250 feet

DIFFICULTY: Moderate

TRAILHEADS: Round Mountain Campground (start); Walnut Mountain AT Shelter (end)

USE: Hiking

TOPOGRAPHIC MAPS: USGS Lemon Gap, NC; TI Map 782

COMMENTS: The Walnut Mountain Trail is a pleasant day hike for campers at the Round Mountain Campground. It can also be combined with sections of the AT to make a longer hike using a car shuttle. A 5.2-mile loop is possible from the campground combining this trail, 1.3 miles of the AT to Lemon Gap, and 1.8 road miles back from Lemon Gap. While the trail is short, the upper portion is steep, so it provides a good workout. Route finding at the upper end is difficult in places where the trail is obscured. A map and compass are a good idea

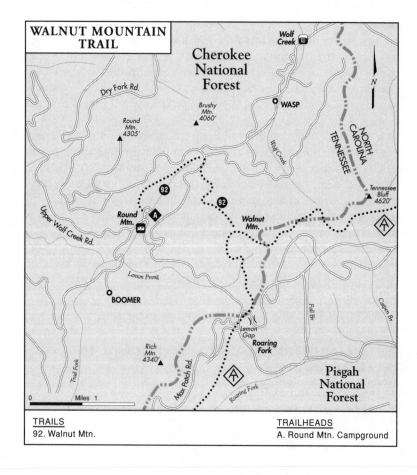

WALNUT MOUNTAIN TRAIL

Cherokee National Forest

Pisgah National Forest

TRAILS	TRAILHEADS
92. Walnut Mtn.	A. Round Mtn. Campground

on a first trip. A sign at the Round Mountain Trailhead (UTM 17S 323463E/3967797N) says 1.1 miles to Rattlesnake Gap and 2.0 miles to the AT; however, our measured mileages are 1.0 and 2.1, respectively. Parking space is available near the entrance to and inside of the campground.

TRAILHEAD (ROUND MOUNTAIN CAMPGROUND): There are two exits from I-40 that may be used to reach this trailhead, TN Exit 435 near Newport and NC Exit 7 at Harmon Den. If you are coming from Knoxville the Exit 435 approach is 11.5 miles shorter and has 7.5 fewer miles of unpaved road. From Ashville, the Harmon Den Exit approach is 34.5 miles shorter.

Coming from the West (Knoxville): Exit I-40 at the second Newport exit, TN Exit 435, and reset your trip odometer to zero. Go left (east) on US 321. At 1.5 miles, turn right on US 25S and 70E at a traffic signal in Newport. Continue east on 70E, passing the Cocke County Courthouse at 2.0 miles. At 13.0 miles from the interstate, turn right on TN 107 at a sign to Del Rio. There is also a sign here pointing right to Lemon Gap. At 19.0 miles, reach the end of TN 107 and turn left on graveled Round Mountain Road. A sign at this intersection points left to Lemon Gap. (The TI map refers to Round Mountain Road as Upper Wolfe Creek Road.) At 24.9 miles go left at a fork. At 25.1 miles from the interstate reach Walnut Mountain Trailhead on the left, just 20 yards before the entrance to Round Mountain Campground.

Coming from the East (Ashville): Exit I-40 at Harmon Den, NC, Exit 7, and reset your trip odometer to zero. Go right (east) on Harmon Den Road (FS 148). At 3.7 miles, bear left at a split. A picnic ground is visible a short distance on the side road. At 6.3 miles reach an intersection with Max Patch Road and Fines Creek Road at Robert Gap. Take a sharp left on Max Patch Road. At 6.6 miles Little Creek Road comes up from the right. Continue straight ahead. At 7.9 miles the AT crosses the road near Max Patch. There is limited parking here for AT hikers. At 8.0 miles pass the Max Patch Trailhead and a larger parking area. At 11.8 miles go through Lemon Gap. The AT is roughly parallel here, just 20 yards to the right. At 13.0 miles continue straight at an intersection where FS 96 branches off to the right. At 13.6 miles from the interstate reach Round Mountain Campground entrance. The trailhead is 20 yards beyond, on the right.

DETAILS: The trail starts on an old road and is fairly wide. The first 0.2 mile parallel the edge of the campground. After 1.0 mile through second-growth forest, reach graveled FS 96. Rattlesnake Gap is visible to the left. Turn left and proceed about 30 yards to the gap.

At Rattlesnake Gap (UTM 17S 324441E/3968791N) turn right on an old road that heads up the ridgecrest. A USFS trail sign here points the way up the Walnut Mountain Trail. This part of the trail is on a previously graveled USFS road and it is well graded. There are views to the northwest of Round Mountain, and to its left (due west) can be seen the gap where the road comes up from Del Rio. Marrow Gap is visible to the right of Round Mountain.

At 1.5 miles (UTM 17S 324614E/3968210N) the trail suddenly turns right off the graded road. This turn comes a few yards after passing a large log that was cut to clear a path through it. There is a trail sign on the right, but it can be obscured by vegetation. While this turn is easy to miss, the trail soon rejoins the roadbed, so the consequences of missing the turn are minor. Evidence of frequent usage indicates most hikers stay on the roadbed. If you see the turn, take it and enjoy the short walk along a stream.

At 1.7 miles (UTM 17S 0324835E/3968110N) the trail rejoins the old roadbed. Turn right, and in about 20 yards come to a split. Take the right fork but immediately ascend a short flight of steps on the left near another Walnut Mountain Trail sign. The trail now ascends the crest of a ridge, at times steeply. At 2.0 miles (UTM 17S 324952E/ 3967787N), at a point where the climb becomes less steep and about 20 or 30 yards before a large rhododendron (the first rhododendron seen on this ridgecrest), the trail bears right between two oak trees and angles up the slope on a heading of about 175 degrees (almost due south). On the right a drainage heads back down to the north, and the trail gradually approaches the center of that drainage. In another 125 yards, reach the center of the drainage near some old apple trees. On the right is a high ridge and, continuing straight ahead, a graded trail now becomes visible heading up the side of that ridge to the southeast. Avoid another old graded trail that turns back and climbs the same ridge heading northwest. At 2.1 miles reach the AT at Walnut Mountain Shelter. To the right (west) it is 1.3 AT miles to the road at Lemon Gap. To the left (east) it is 12.5 AT miles to Hot Springs, NC.

19 Appalachian National Scenic Trail

93. APPALACHIAN TRAIL (FS TRAIL 1, TI TRAIL 1)

The premier trail in the northern CNF has to be the AT. Of the over 2,100 miles covered by the AT, 214.8 miles are found in the CNF between the VA state line and the GSMNP. The northern reaches of this section are located wholly within the CNF. However, after climbing the Highlands of Roan, the trail straddles the boundary between the CNF in TN and the Pisgah NF in NC. The CNF, as of the early 2000s, reports 45,146 acres protected in the AT Corridor.

The CNF portions of the AT contain highly varied and rewarding walking throughout the entire length. The trail follows long wooded ridges, such as on Iron Mountain and the Bald Mountains, passing through northern evergreen forests, high grassy balds, and rhododendron gardens in the Highlands of Roan, or through deep gorges at Laurel Fork and the Nolichucky River. However, some of the most pleasant walking occurs among the numerous old fields, pastures, and small communities of upper East TN.

This part of the AT is maintained by two hiking clubs that are members of the Appalachian Trail Conference: the TN Eastman Hiking and Canoeing Club (http://www.tehcc.org) maintains 122.7 miles from the VA state line to Spivey Gap (as well as the 3.5 miles from the state line north to Damascus, VA). The Carolina Mountain Club (http://www.carolinamtnclub.com) maintains 92.1 miles from Spivey Gap to Davenport Gap. Southwest of Davenport Gap the AT enters Great Smoky Mountains National Park where it is maintained by the Smoky Mountains Hiking Club (http://www.esper.com/smhc). The AT was built and is maintained to established standards; its route is marked with the characteristic white blazes. The overall route is fairly stable, although small relocations to improve it are continually being made.

There are 24 shelters and 33 campsites on this length of the AT. The shelters are three-sided structures sleeping six to eight people and usually spaced five to ten miles apart. Water is available from springs near the shelters and campsites and at other places along the AT. There are 33 road access points, with the distance between them ranging from 1.3 to 13.4 miles. These access points, plus a few side trails, allow hikes of any length to be selected.

Although several especially scenic portions of the AT in the CNF are described in detail in this book, limits of space and the length of this trail allow only a brief summary of the entire AT route through the CNF. For simplicity, the CNF section of the trail has been divided into 16 sections as specified by the Appalachian Trail Conference. For each section, the route is briefly described, giving the amount of climbing, the number of shelters, and a few outstanding features. Each section has road access at each end, and some have intermediate road crossings, as noted.

These 16 sections, routes, and mileage correspond to the sections, routes, and mileage in the *Appalachian Trail Guide to TN-North Carolina;*

the current edition is the eleventh, published in 2001 by the Appalachian Trail Conference (http://www.appalachiantrail.org; see bibliography). The book gives detailed trail descriptions in both directions, plus general historic and descriptive material, with excellent maps. Use of this book is highly recommended for planning hikes on the AT. Note that the Appalachian Trail Conference guidebook mileage may vary slightly from the measured mileage for this book because of trail changes between measurements. The AT within the northern CNF is also shown on TI Maps 782 and 783.

1. *Damascus, VA, to US 421 (Low Gap, TN), 14.8 miles.* Beginning at Damascus Town Hall, the AT ascends 1,400 feet southwest in 3.5 miles to the TN state line at the crest of Holston Mountain. The remaining 11.3 miles of this section are on the crest of Holston Mountain, with no major changes in elevation. The section has one shelter and one intermediate road crossing.

2. *US 421 (Low Gap) to TN 91, 7.0 miles.* From Low Gap, the AT follows the crest of Holston Mountain southwestward for 3.4 miles. It then follows Cross Mountain southeastward for the remaining 3.5 miles. The climb is about 1,800 feet in either direction. This section has one shelter. The Flint Mill section of this book contains a detailed description of this portion of the AT.

3. *TN 91 to Watauga Dam Road, 16.0 miles.* From TN 91 the first mile of the AT goes to the southeast on Cross Mountain. It then turns southwest and follows the crest of Iron Mountain. The trail gains 700 feet in elevation in the first 5.6 miles, has only minor elevation changes in the next 7.0 miles, and descends 1,300 feet in the last 3.0 miles. Much of the route passes through the Big Laurel Branch Wilderness, which is described in detail in the Big Laurel Branch section of this book. The section has two shelters.

4. *Watauga Dam Road to Dennis Cove Road, 12.8 miles.* The AT crosses the top of Watauga Dam, skirts Watauga Lake for 2.3 miles, and then crosses US 321. It next ascends 1,700 feet to the crest of Pond Mountain and drops steeply into Laurel Fork Gorge, up which it then proceeds 2.8 miles, passing Laurel Falls. The section has about 2,900 feet of climb going south to north and 3,200 feet of climb hiking south. Much of this portion of the AT is in the Pond Mountain Wilderness, and that portion is described in detail in the Pond Mountain section of this book. The section has two shelters and two intermediate road approaches.

5. *Dennis Cove to US 19E, 19.4 miles.* The AT climbs 1,000 feet to the crest of White Rocks Mountain, follows its crest for about 4.0

miles, and then passes over numerous small side ridges for 5.9 miles to Walnut Mountain Road. It drops into Sugar Hollow, then ascends into woods and old farms, finally descending through Bishop Hollow and above Bear Branch. The section has much climbing, about 6,500 feet in either direction. The section has one shelter and two intermediate road crossings.

6. *US 19E to Carvers Gap, 13.4 miles.* The AT first climbs 1,900 feet in 2.6 miles to Doll Flats on the TN-NC line, and then another 1,000 feet in 2.4 miles to the summit of Hump Mountain. For the remaining 7.9 miles it continues along the state line on beautifully spacious grassy summits, including Yellow Mountain and Grassy Ridge. Total climbing is 5,700 feet southward and 2,400 feet northward. The Highlands of Roan section of this book describes this portion of the AT in detail. The section has three shelters.

7. *Carvers Gap to Hughes Gap, 4.6 miles.* The first 1.8 miles of the AT are on an old road in dense evergreen woods to Roan High Knob (6,267 feet); the famous rhododendron gardens are found nearby. The remainder, also in woods, descends steeply to Hughes Gap. Total climbing is 820 feet southward and 2,380 feet northward. The Highlands of Roan section of this book describes this portion of the AT in detail. The section has one shelter and one road access near midpoint.

8. *Hughes Gap to Iron Mountain Gap, 8.1 miles.* This section is entirely in woods on the crest of Iron Mountain. The climb is about 2,200 feet southward and 2,600 feet northward. The section has one shelter.

9. *Iron Mountain Gap to Nolichucky River, 19.7 miles.* For the first 7.4 miles, the AT follows the wooded crest of Iron Mountain and Unaka Mountain to Deep Gap (also called Beauty Spot Gap). For the next 4.0 miles to Indian Grave Gap, the trail passes through woods and balds, including Beauty Spot. From there it continues along the ridge and then descends to the Nolichucky River near Erwin, TN. This section has 6,300 feet of climbing going northward and 4,300 feet southward. There are two shelters and one intermediate road crossing, and additional access is available from FS 230, which parallels the trail for part of this section. A detailed description of the AT from Iron Mountain Gap to Indian Grave Gap is included in Unaka Mountain of this book.

10. *Nolichucky River to Spivey Gap, 10.4 miles.* The AT first climbs 1,500 feet up Cliff Ridge in 1.9 miles. Beyond, it follows Temple Ridge and skirts No Business Knob with little change in elevation.

Traveling southward there are 3,300 feet of climbing and 1,500 feet traveling northward. The section has one shelter.

11. *Spivey Gap to Sams Gap, 13.6 miles.* The AT first climbs 1,100 feet near High Rocks in 1.6 miles. It then descends to Whistling Gap and ascends Little Bald in the next 2.7 miles. It continues for 2.5 miles on the crest of the Bald Mountains to Big Bald. Beyond, it descends to Street Gap and the remainder of the section, through hardwoods and old fields. The section has one shelter.

12. *Sams Gap to Devil Fork Gap, 8.2 miles.* The AT first follows the crest of the Bald Mountains through forests and fields for 3.3 miles westward to Rice Gap. Beyond, it goes northward over Frozen Knob, Big Flat, and Sugarloaf Knob to the end of the section. There is one intermediate road crossing and one shelter on this section.

13. *Devil Fork Gap to Allen Gap, 20.2 miles.* The AT first follows the crest of the Bald Mountains northwestward for 5.5 miles to Big Butt. It then heads southwestward on the ridgeline through forest and open areas, passing over Coldspring Mountain, Big Firescald Knob, the rocky face of Blackstack Cliffs, and Camp Creek Bald. Much of the AT in this section is described in detail in the Bald Mountain Ridge section of this book. The section has three shelters and one road crossing.

14. *Allen Gap to Hot Springs, 14.7 miles.* The AT first ascends the Bald Mountain Range ridgeline, climbing 1,400 feet in 6.2 miles to a point near the summit of Rich Mountain. It then descends 1,400 feet in 2.6 miles to Tanyard Gap. Beyond, it passes through woods and open areas to Pump Gap and then Lovers Leap Ridge, descending to the end of the section at Hot Springs, NC. From north to south there are 2,600 feet of climbing, with 3,500 feet from south to north. The section has one shelter and two intermediate road crossings.

15. *Hot Springs to Max Patch Road, 20.0 miles.* In the first 10.1 miles, the AT ascends 3,400 feet to the top of Bluff Mountain. In another 3.7 miles it reaches Lemon Gap. For the next 5.4 miles it generally ascends across side ridges to reach the open summit of Max Patch, a beautiful bald with panoramic views of the adjacent CNF and Pisgah NFs and south to the GSMNP. From north to south, the section has 5,800 feet of climbing, with 1,800 feet from south to north. There are two shelters and two intermediate road crossings in this section.

16. *Max Patch Road to Davenport Gap, 15.3 miles.* The first 10.1 miles of this section of the AT generally follow the crest of Snowbird Mountain along the state line. The trail passes Brown Gap, Groundhog Creek Gap, and Wildcat Top before reaching the western

summit of Snowbird Mountain. This bald contains an FAA structure and provides great views in all directions. Thereafter the trail descends along Painter Branch, reaching I-40 at the Pigeon River in another 3.3 miles. In another 1.9 miles it reaches Davenport Gap. From north to south, there is a net descent of 2,300 feet. This section has one shelter and three intermediate road crossings.

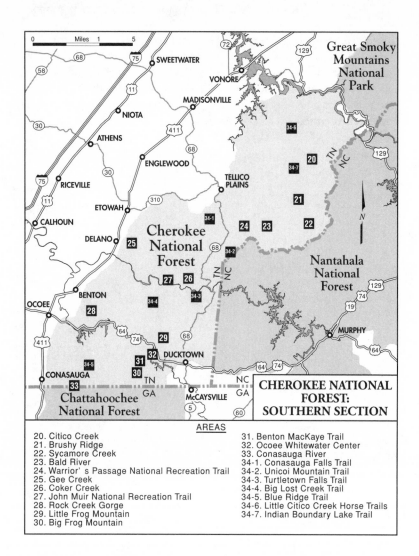

CHEROKEE NATIONAL FOREST: SOUTHERN SECTION

AREAS

20. Citico Creek
21. Brushy Ridge
22. Sycamore Creek
23. Bald River
24. Warrior's Passage National Recreation Trail
25. Gee Creek
26. Coker Creek
27. John Muir National Recreation Trail
28. Rock Creek Gorge
29. Little Frog Mountain
30. Big Frog Mountain
31. Benton MacKaye Trail
32. Ocoee Whitewater Center
33. Conasauga River
34-1. Conasauga Falls Trail
34-2. Unicoi Mountain Trail
34-3. Turtletown Falls Trail
34-4. Big Lost Creek Trail
34-5. Blue Ridge Trail
34-6. Little Citico Creek Horse Trails
34-7. Indian Boundary Lake Trail

Southern Cherokee National Forest

Tellico and Ocoee Rivers
(TI Map 781)

20 Citico Creek

(Includes Citico Creek Wilderness, TN Portion of Joyce Kilmer–Slickrock Wilderness, Joyce Kilmer–Slickrock Wilderness Study Area, and Citico Creek/Joyce Kilmer–Slickrock Roadless Area)

The Citico Creek Wilderness at 16,226 acres is the largest wilderness in the CNF. Its 16 trails, covering more than 57 miles, provide immense opportunities for exploration of the area. The wilderness is dominated by the long, high ridge of the Unicoi Mountains on the east, with three steeply sloped ridges leading west from the main ridge. These ridges, Brush Mountain, Pine Ridge, and Sassafras Ridge, are cut by swift-flowing stream valleys, which drain to the west. The terrain is very rugged, with 90 percent of the slope area exceeding 30 degrees. Elevation ranges from a low of 1,400 feet to a high of 4,600 feet. The area is in Monroe County and the Tellico Ranger District.

Citico Creek Wilderness, along with the contiguous 17,394-acre Joyce Kilmer–Slickrock Wilderness (13,562 acres in NC and 3,832 in TN), constitutes a unique treasure of the Wilderness Preservation System, with many outstanding features, scenic areas, and points of interest. There are numerous ecological, geographic, and trail connections between the two wilderness areas. While this book focuses on the Citico Creek Wilderness, trails in both areas can be linked for extended backcountry trips.

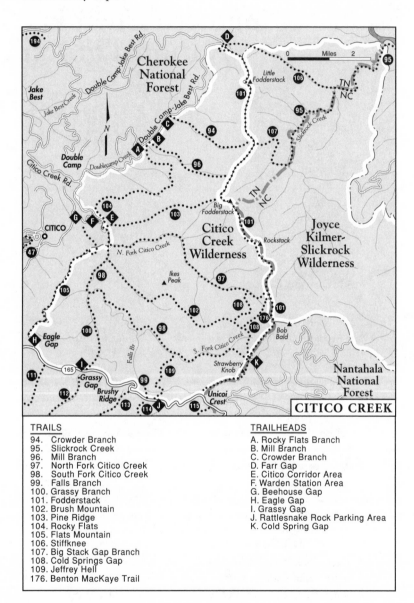

TRAILS
94. Crowder Branch
95. Slickrock Creek
96. Mill Branch
97. North Fork Citico Creek
98. South Fork Citico Creek
99. Falls Branch
100. Grassy Branch
101. Fodderstack
102. Brush Mountain
103. Pine Ridge
104. Rocky Flats
105. Flats Mountain
106. Stiffknee
107. Big Stack Gap Branch
108. Cold Springs Gap
109. Jeffrey Hell
176. Benton MacKaye Trail

TRAILHEADS
A. Rocky Flats Branch
B. Mill Branch
C. Crowder Branch
D. Farr Gap
E. Citico Corridor Area
F. Warden Station Area
G. Beehouse Gap
H. Eagle Gap
I. Grassy Gap
J. Rattlesnake Rock Parking Area
K. Cold Spring Gap

The Citico Creek Wilderness contains the entire upper drainage of Citico Creek, which consists of two major tributaries, the North Fork and South Fork of Citico Creek. In addition, there are at least eight tributary streams in the area. They are characterized by unusually large channels, resulting from the narrow, steep-walled valleys, the steep gradients of the valleys (averaging 13 percent), and the high amount of precipitation (averaging about 70 inches per year). All of these factors contribute to swift, clear-flowing streams, even though they were heavily damaged by logging abuses of the early twentieth century. Eagle and Grassy Branch and some of the upper reaches of streams along the Tellico-Robbinsville Road (now called the Cherohala Skyway) were impacted by the exposure of iron pyrite rock formations and subsequent acid runoff in the construction of the road in the late 1970s.

The Southern Appalachian Assessment by the USFS identified, in addition to the wildernesses, a 1,425-acre Citico Creek/Joyce Kilmer–Slickrock Roadless Area. An area greater than the roadless area is protected in the CNF's 2004 plan revision, including the 1,964-acre Joyce Kilmer–Slickrock Wilderness Study Area.

HISTORY

The area has regained its wilderness character despite a long history of human use. The first humans to use the area were the American Indians. It is not known when this use first began, but there were extensive Cherokee Indian settlements near Citico Creek along the Little Tennessee River during precolonial times. The Indians used the primeval forest and rugged terrain of the Citico Creek area for hunting and other purposes. The name Citico derives from the Cherokee word *sitiku*, meaning place of clean fishing waters. It may still be possible to see artifacts and remnants of campsites left by these early people.

English army lieutenant Henry Timberlake explored nearby in the 1750s. The Cherokee Nation, under much coercion, ceded the area, along with all their holdings east of the Mississippi River, to the United States in 1835 in the Treaty of New Echota. There may have been scattered pioneer families that settled the Citico Creek area in the mid-1800s. The area was owned by wealthy plantation families as a mineral investment and was frequently hunted during this period. Following the Civil War, the land went to northern investors. The Citico Creek area was owned during the late nineteenth century by George Peabody Wetmore, a wealthy US senator from Rhode Island.

The Citico Creek area was acquired by Smoky Mountain Timber and Improvement Company in the early 1900s. The land was surveyed and a railroad line was constructed from the junction of the North and South Forks of Citico Creek to Maryville, TN, where it connected with the Little River Railroad, which came out of the GSMNP. This railroad line was completed about 1910. Logs were removed on smaller tramways built up the stream valleys and on the mountain slopes. Remnants of these tramways and other relics of logging can still be seen in the areas. Names and ownership of the land had changed by the 1920s. Babcock Land and Timber Company and Tellico River Lumber Company continued the timber operations in the early 1920s. In 1925 a disastrous wildfire, fueled by logging slash and debris and exacerbated by very dry weather, burned about half of the Citico Creek Wilderness, especially in the lower elevations. Two people were killed, and many of the structures necessary for timber harvesting were destroyed. The cost of replacement was prohibitive; the timber companies were forced to abandon operations in the higher elevations. Logging continued only along Doublecamp Creek until 1929. This halt to the logging resulted in stands of old-growth forest being left in the inaccessible places that had not yet been cut. In the higher elevations large trees and relatively untouched stands of the primeval forest can still be found. Probably the largest of these are a 187-acre cove hardwood forest near Falls Branch Falls and a 200-acre hemlock-hardwood stand between Glen Gap and the headwaters of Indian Valley Branch.

After the logging period, a number of families settled along the creeks. They farmed some of the areas left cleared by the logging operations and used the balds for summer pasture. The USFS bought the Citico Creek area in 1935 from Babcock and Tellico River Lumber Companies. Only 11 percent of the Citico Creek Wilderness has been harvested since 1935.

Since the 1920s, natural processes have healed much of the damage caused by logging abuses and fire. The remnants of the old-growth forest have been surrounded by second-growth forest. Wildlife has rebounded, and the area is once again renowned for bear, turkey, deer, and other animal life. The much-abused streams once again flow clear and pure, and trout and other water inhabitants abound. The headwaters of Citico Creek are an important habitat for brook trout, since its numerous waterfalls provide barriers to exclude the introduced rainbow trout, with which the brook trout has a hard time coexisting. Several rare animals occur in the area, including the star-nosed mole, woodland jumping mouse, masked shrew, and northern water shrew. Two rare salamanders, the seepage salamander, and *Desmognathus* sp.

are found in the area. The black bear and eastern brook trout found here are considered sensitive species by the USFS. Rare plants found in this location include lesser prickly sedge, Fraser's sedge, a huckleberry known as *Gaylussacia ursina*, Blue Ridge St. John's Wort, Coville's Rush, ginseng, and hedge nettle. As the decades and centuries pass, it is hoped that the wilderness areas, in their protected status, will again approach their primeval condition.

In the 1930s, what is now the Citico Creek Wilderness was considered for wilderness designation by the USFS in a broader proposal for a Citico-Cheoah Primitive Area. This never came to pass, but, as it recovered, the Citico Creek area became known for its natural character. In the 1970s support grew for designating the Citico Creek area as wilderness. The Eastern Wilderness Act, enacted on January 3, 1975, created the Citico Creek Wilderness Study Area and the Joyce Kilmer–Slickrock Wilderness. Subsequently, the Citico Creek Wilderness was designated by Congress in 1984. A 1,060-acre Haw Knob Primitive Area was established in 1988 in the CNF management plan; the primitive area and additional acreage are designated as a wilderness study area in the CNF's 2004 CNF plan revision.

TRAILHEADS AND MAPS

There are two primary approaches to the Citico Creek Wilderness and adjacent areas. A third route uses sections of the other two routes. All routes are accessed from US 411.

One primary route to the area turns off US 411 onto TN 68 in Madisonville, TN. Take TN 68 to the outskirts of Tellico Plains (approximately 14 miles). When TN 68 intersects TN 165, take a left on TN 165. From there, it is a little over a mile to where TN 165 makes a junction with TN 360. Bear right at the junction to stay on TN 165. The following mileages are given for this route measured from this point. TN 165 continues past a group of stores and cabins and passes a CNF sign. The road runs along the south bank and then the north bank of Tellico River. Shortly after passing the Ooesterneck Creek parking area at 4.2 miles, the road forks. The right fork continues along the river past the Tellico Ranger Station and to Bald River Falls. Take the left fork and continue on TN 165 over rolling hills. At 13.7 miles TN 165 intersects with FS 345 on the left. This road leads to Indian Boundary Lake and Recreation Area and, by way of the Citico Creek Road, to the Warden Station Area and the Doublecamp Road area. To reach trailheads along the Tellico-Robbinsville Road (Cherohala Skyway), continue along TN 165.

The other main route is by the Citico Creek Road, which turns off US 411 onto TN 360 at Vonore, TN. After 7.4 miles from Vonore, TN 360 turns right across a bridge. Do not turn right across the bridge, but continue straight on the Citico Creek Road. The pavement ends 16.6 miles from Vonore. At this point do not turn left across Citico Creek on the concrete bridge, but continue on the right side of Citico Creek on the gravel road. Continue on Citico Creek Road (FS 35-1) as it goes deeper into the CNF. Pass through Jake Best Campground at 24.2 miles from Vonore. Doublecamp Road (FS 59) turns left off Citico Creek Road (28.0 miles) at Doublecamp Campground. Citico Creek Road continues up Citico Creek and makes a hairpin turn away from the creek at 29.5 miles. The road (FS 29) that continues straight ahead and crosses the creek goes to the Citico Corridor Area. Continuing on the Citico Creek Road for about 0.1 mile takes you past the turnoff to the Warden Station Area on the left. At 31.9 miles from Vonore, FS 35-1 intersects FS 345 at the entrance to Indian Boundary Recreation Area. Bear left on FS 345 to reach the Tellico-Robbinsville Road (Chero-hala Skyway) (TN 165) after 1.3 miles (33.2 miles from Vonore).

The third route avoids stretches of gravel along the Citico Creek Road and makes use of parts of both of the previous routes. As in the second route, take TN 360 south off US 411 in Vonore. After 7.4 miles stay on TN 360 by turning right across the bridge (this is where you would go straight to go along the Citico Creek Road). At 12.1 miles from Vonore, TN 360 turns left at a stop sign shortly after passing a small sawmill. Continue on TN 360 until it intersects TN 165 (at 22.8 miles from Vonore) shortly after crossing the Tellico River on the outskirts of Tellico Plains. Take a sharp left onto TN 165. Directions and mileages from the first route can be followed from this point.

The best route to take to Citico Wilderness depends on your point of origin, what trailhead you plan to use, and personal preferences. Some factors should be considered. The gravel section of the Citico Creek Road is narrow in places; it is crowded during some weekends of the year; and, depending on the season and the weather, it can be very dusty or rutted. The third route mentioned above, following TN 360, stays entirely in the country and is very scenic. But you may need to keep up with mileages carefully and watch for turnoffs to stay on this route.

Doublecamp Road (FS 59) Trailheads: Rocky Flats Branch, Mill Branch, Crowder Branch, and Farr Gap Trailheads

Four trailheads lie along Doublecamp Road (FS 59), which turns off the Citico Creek Road at Doublecamp Campground. Mileages are given from this turnoff. Trailheads are located on the right (southeast) side of this 6.7 mile road, which ends at Farr Gap, as follows: Rocky Flats Branch Trail (FS Trail 100) at 2.5 miles, Mill Branch Trail (FS Trail 96) at 2.7 miles, Crowder Branch Trail (FS Trail 84) at 3.5 miles, and Fodderstack Trail (FS Trail 95) in Farr Gap at 6.7 miles. The road is gravel but is usually in good condition. Most of the trailheads have limited and informal parking areas, but there are wide places in the road nearby. Farr Gap, which is one trailhead for Fodderstack Trail and is a key access to lower Slickrock Creek in the Joyce Kilmer/ Slickrock Wilderness, has several designated parking places. Note that at Farr Gap, the road turns almost due west, going about 2.0 plus miles before turning generally toward the southwest, leading to a reconnection with Citico Creek Road, for a total distance of approximately 10–12 miles.

Citico Corridor Area Trailhead

There are a number of trailheads in this area and the nearby Warden Station Area. The Citico Corridor Road (FS 29) turns off the Citico Creek Road 2.4 miles northeast from the entrance to the Indian Boundary Recreation Area and 1.6 miles southeast from Doublecamp Road. At the hairpin curve, leave Citico Creek Road and cross the low-water bridge to the corridor. There are a number of forest clearings that are extensively used for car and truck camping. Parking can be found along the Corridor Road. Trailheads for Pine Ridge Trail (FS Trail 99) and Rocky Flats Trail (FS Trail 100) are nearby, although Rocky Flats Trail will be described from the trailhead along Doublecamp Road. The South Fork Trail can also be accessed by following the corridor road for 0.25 mile until it dead-ends into Citico Creek. A rather difficult ford of the creek leads to the old road on the other side that soon becomes the South Fork Trail. However, this trail will be described from the nearby Warden Station Area, which does not require the creek ford.

Warden Station Area Trailhead

To reach the Warden Station Area take the Citico Creek Road toward Indian Boundary for 0.1 mile past the Citico Corridor Area. A turnoff to the left is marked by a trail sign for FS Trail 105. Parking is very limited. There is space for one or two cars to park where the South Fork Trail turns off the road. More parking can be found in the Citico Corridor Area nearby. Ruins of the Warden Station can be found along the early sections of the trail. The trail stays high on the western side of Citico Creek and crosses two small streams. After about 0.5 mile the trail opens up into a large parklike game clearing with some large fruit trees. At the other side of the clearing is an old road that runs along Citico Creek. The South Fork Trail leads off to the right; to the left a short distance the old road crosses Citico Creek to the corridor area. Trailhead connections to the North Fork Citico Creek Trail (FS Trail 98), Ike Camp Branch Trail (FS Trail 97—also known as Brush Mountain Trail), Grassy Branch Trail (FS Trail 91), and Jeffrey Hell Trail (FS Trail 196) lie along the South Fork Citico Creek Trail. The South Fork and North Fork trails will be described from their trailheads in the Warden Station Area. Grassy Branch and Jeffrey Hell trails will be described from their trailheads along the Tellico-Robbinsville Road (Cherohala Skyway).

Beehouse Gap Trailhead

This low gap at 2,580 feet is on the Citico Creek Road 0.9 mile southwest from the Citico Corridor Area and 1.5 miles northeast from the entrance to the Indian Boundary Recreation Area. A trailhead for the Flats Mountain Trail, with space for three or four cars, is in the gap. This trail will be described from its trailhead along the Tellico-Robbinsville Road, ending at Beehouse Gap.

Tellico-Robbinsville Road/Cherohala Skyway (TN 165) Trailheads: Eagle Gap, Grassy Gap, and Rattlesnake Rock Parking Area Trailheads

Access to several trailheads lies along the Skyway (TN 165). This road, which originally would have passed through the present Joyce Kilmer–Slickrock Wilderness, was rerouted to its present path in order to spare that wilderness. Construction of the road disturbed pyrite mineral deposits, which caused acid pollution in some nearby streams. The impact was heavy upon several streams on the other side of the road from Citico Creek Wilderness. Grassy Branch and Eagle Branch on the Citico side of the road sustained damage from this pollution, but both now appear to be fairly undisturbed.

From the intersection of TN 165 and FS 345, take TN 165 as it skirts the southern edge of the Citico Wilderness. Numerous turnoffs along the road give spectacular views of the Citico watershed and of other parts of the Tellico Ranger District. Mileages to trailheads are given from the junction of TN 165 and FS 345. The Flats Mountain Trail (FS Trail 102) Trailhead is at 4.8 miles in Eagle Gap. The Grassy

Branch Trail (FS Trail 91) Trailhead is at 6.2 miles and a large parking area in Grassy Gap. The trailhead for both Falls Branch Trail (FS Trail 87) and Jeffrey Hell Trail (FS Trail 196) is at 8.4 miles near an area known as Rattlesnake Rock Parking Area (note this trailhead is before the Rattlesnake Rock Scenic Overlook).

Cold Spring Gap Trailhead

At the TN-NC state line near Beech Gap (9.85 miles beyond the Indian Boundary turnoff from Tellico-Robbinsville Road), FS 217H turns off to the left. This dirt road travels 1.9 miles through thick forest to a trailhead complex and a former parking area for several cars at Cold Spring Gap near Strawberry Knob. The road is barely passable by even 4 WD vehicles and *is usually closed to motorized vehicles*. Portions of the road have deep ruts, large rocks, and large mud holes. So even if you find it open, save your vehicle and enjoy the easy walk. You will probably make better time. The South Fork Citico (FS Trail 105), Cold Spring Gap (FS Trail 149), Fodderstack (FS Trail 95), Brush Mountain (FS Trail 97), and North Fork Citico (FS Trail 98) trails all have trailheads that can be accessed from Cold Spring Gap (the latter two via Cold Spring Gap Trail). Most of these trails will be described from the other ends of the trails. Only the Brush Mountain and Cold Spring Gap Trails, the latter formerly a section of FS 217H, will be described from Cold Spring Gap. Given the condition of FS 217H and the fact that it is usually closed, you are strongly encouraged to treat the 1.9 miles of FS 217H as a trail and park in the parking area at its junction with the Skyway (TN 165).

TOPOGRAPHIC MAPS: USGS Whiteoak Flats, TN-NC; Big Junction, TN-NC; Tapoco, TN-NC; Santeetlah Creek, NC (the first two maps cover all of the Citico Creek Wilderness); TI Map 781, Tellico and Ocoee Rivers, CNF.

TRAIL DESCRIPTIONS

GENERAL COMMENTS: Most of the trails are on old tramways or roads in the lower elevations and tend to be fairly easy to follow and have reasonable inclines. In the higher elevations the trails are much fainter and are sometimes very steep. Expect to get wet if you are hiking the lower portions of either North Fork Citico Creek or South Fork Citico Creek. Consider carrying a pair of sandals to protect your feet during fords. Some of the upper portions of the trails tend to follow streambeds. Not only can these trails be a muddy mess, but the erosion also adversely impacts the water quality downstream. The upper portions of many of the trails have developed as "paths of least resistance" and are in great need of rerouting.

All of the trails have been blazed at one time or another, traditionally with white paint. On some of the trails these blazes are quite noticeable and easy to follow. On other trails the painted blazes are old and faded, and many of the blazed trees have died and fallen over. The USFS has cleared and reblazed some of the trails since they were hiked for this book, which should make them easier to follow. The new blazes are rectangles cut out of the bark of the trees. As the cuts heal, scar tissue will form that presumably can be followed. So look for these new blazes, as well as the old painted blazes. However, do not depend on their presence for navigation.

The TI Tellico and Ocoee Rivers map provides an excellent overview for hike planning in this area. However, it is only barely adequate for hiking, as the level of detail is not sufficient for route finding and many of the trails are not always obvious. The USFS publishes an excellent topographical map entitled "Joyce Kilmer–Slickrock Wilderness and Citico Creek Wilderness," and copies may be obtained from the CNF (see appendix 2). Alternatively, you can use the USGS quads, but be aware that not all the trails may be marked on these maps.

94. CROWDER BRANCH TRAIL (FS TRAIL 84, TI TRAIL 31)

LENGTH: 2.6 miles

ELEVATION CHANGE: Low point, 1,920 feet; high point, 3,360 feet

DIFFICULTY: Moderate

TRAILHEADS: Doublecamp Road (Crowder Branch) (start) and Fodderstack Trail (end)

USE: Hiking

TOPOGRAPHIC MAP: USGS Whiteoak Flats, TN

COMMENTS: The Crowder Branch Trail follows Crowder Branch from Doublecamp Road to Crowder Place, an old homesite, and on to the Fodderstack Trail. There is a large open area at Crowder Place, as well as an excellent spring, an old orchard, and impressive displays of pink lady's slippers and crested dwarf iris. The trail itself is short but relatively strenuous. It is steep in places and stays in the stream for long stretches, especially near the end. Pay attention in the upper stretch (below Crowder Place) to avoid losing the trail. Nevertheless, the trail is well worth the effort it takes to travel it. The stream is beautiful, the valley contains good examples of cove hardwood forest, and Crowder Place is one of the best campsites in the Citico Wilderness. A very scenic and enjoyable day hike can be negotiated using Crowder Branch Trail, Mill Branch Trail, and the section of the Fodderstack Trail between these two trails.

The trail starts at 3.5 miles on the Doublecamp Road just past a large meadow known as Crowder Field, to the right of the road. There is a parking area/campsite across the road from the trail sign with "No. 84" on it. There is additional parking for one or two cars immediately across a small bridge over Crowder Branch. Additional parking can be found back at the meadow.

DETAILS: The trail crosses Crowder Branch at 0.1 mile and parallels the stream. At 0.2 mile the trail recrosses the branch and follows an old wet roadbed. The trail crosses the branch again and then joins an old roadbed (at 0.4 mile) that follows the branch closely through cove hardwood forest. The trail crosses the branch several times until the trail ascends steeply to the slope above the branch at 0.8 mile. There are more excellent views of the branch as the trail moves up the slope above it. At 1.2 miles the trail descends to a flat area near the creek that could serve as a small campsite.

The trail ascends steeply out of the flat area, crosses a side stream, and rejoins the old roadbed. Below is a towering cove hardwood forest with large, exceptionally straight trees. The trail continues along the left (north) side of Crowder Branch. At 1.7 miles, cross a small side stream and then ascend the slope steeply. At 1.8 miles reach a crossing of Crowder Branch. To follow the established trail, cross here and ascend steeply along its right (south) side. It is possible to continue along the north side on an old roadbed a few yards above the branch. This route is heavily overgrown with rhododendron and is essentially cross-country in many places. However, it avoids some of the sloshing through the streambed that the established trail requires. This alternate route rejoins the main trail near Crowder Place.

The trail is in and out of the stream for much of the remaining distance to Crowder Place. At 2.3 miles, exit the stream to the left and follow it as it enters a clearing at 2.4 miles. Ruins of an old building are to the right. The branch (now a trickle) comes from the covered spring to the left. The spring is very dependable, and there are campsites nearby (UTM 16S 770763E/3924738N). Many more additional sites are available as the trail bears right around the ruins and enters an old meadow, known as Crowder Field. Remnants of three decrepit apple trees still stand in the meadow. The Crowder Branch Trail intersects with the Fodderstack Trail at 2.6 miles. There are also potential camp-sites at this intersection. This junction is 3.04 miles from the Farr Gap Trailhead on the Fodderstack Trail.

95. SLICKROCK CREEK TRAIL (NANTAHALA NF TRAIL 42; NO TI NUMBER)

LENGTH: 13.3 miles (only first 7.4 miles covered)

ELEVATION CHANGE: Low point, 1,150 feet; high point, 1,900 feet for this section; NC terminus is 4,847 feet

DIFFICULTY: Moderate (for the section covered in this book)

TRAILHEADS: US-129 (start) and Stack Gap Branch Trail (end for this section); Naked Ground is NC terminus

TRAIL CONNECTIONS: Stiffknee Trail, Crowder Branch Trail, Big Stack Gap Branch Trail, Mill Branch Trail, Yellowhammer Gap Trail, Nichols Cove

USE: Hiking

Several backpackers negotiate one of many stream fords in the lower reaches of Slickrock Creek in the Joyce Kilmer–Slickrock Wilderness. Photograph by Roger Jenkins.

TOPOGRAPHIC MAPS: USGS Tapoco, NC-TN; Whiteoak Flats, TN

COMMENTS: The lower 8.0 miles of this trail wind along the state line and frequently skirt the extreme eastern edge of that small portion of the Joyce Kilmer–Slickrock Wilderness located in the CNF. It is a great hike, but it can be challenging at times of high water, as there are numerous major fords in the lower section. Bring stream crossing sandals or shoes. Lower Slickrock Creek is noted for its outstanding wildflower displays in springtime. There are numerous campsites along the lower trail, and fishing, we are told, can be wonderful. We have only included the lower end of the trail that is in the CNF. The upper 5.0 miles of the trail involve a lot of challenging climbing (in many places, it will seem more like a rugged off-trail experience) and lie outside the Cherokee.

The trailhead for the Slickrock Creek trail begins about 500 feet down a dirt road that parallels the southern bank of the Little Tennessee River. The road can be reached by taking a turn to the west immediately south of the south end of the US 129 bridge crossing over the Little Tennessee River immediately downstream of Cheoah Dam (UTM 17S 233003E/3926632N). There is parking for a few cars at the trailhead. Do not expect to be alone on the first few miles of your journey—this is a popular place. The trailhead is not described anywhere else in this book. However, it is likely that most readers will access Lower Slickrock Creek trail from one of its many trail connections, either from the TN or NC wilderness areas.

DETAILS: The trail begins near a display board and immediately begins to gain elevation through mixed, low-elevation hardwoods. There are some glimpses of the upper end of Calderwood Lake. At 0.55 miles, the trail arrives at its first junction with the Ike Camp Branch trail, coming in from the left. (It follows Ike Branch through a lovely forest, dotted with hemlocks, and descends from Yellowhammer Gap to rejoin the Slickrock Creek trail. Ike Camp Branch can be used as an alternate approach to lower Slickrock Creek.) At this point, the Slickrock Creek trail, side-hilling around the northeastern face of a 2,200 foot knob, is high (300 feet) above the high-water mark of the lake. The trail continues on and makes a nearly 180-degree bend around a knob, dropping into the valley of Slickrock Creek. It nears the water level of the creek at 1.7 miles. The trail begins a moderate ascent above the creek, traveling at times on an old railroad grade. At 2.8 miles, it is time to get your feet wet, as the old railroad bridge that once spanned the creek is no more. This is the first of many fords of Slickrock creek. On a bright summer day, the pools and cascades are an invitation to play and relax. When the water is high, and it is spitting snow, consider turning around and living to hike another day.

Less than a third of a mile past the first ford, the trail arrives at Lower Falls (UTM 17S 230271E/3927290N). Cascades and plunge pools beckon the warm weather hiker. There are several spots to camp nearby. At 3.6 miles, the trail, again on the old railroad grade, reaches it second official ford. Be aware of the impact of flooding. In the course of updating this book, we noted several places along creeks where banks have washed out to the point where we were forced to ford where 12 years previously there had been plenty of walking room. At 3.8 miles, the trail arrives at its second intersection with the Ike Branch Trail. There is a sign and a large open area for camping. Several artifacts from logging days are present. Just upstream from the intersection is the next ford. This is one of those places where an HBG backpack's plans were altered. A major storm had just moved through, the water was way up, it was lightly snowing, and while the larger members of our party might have held their footing, the current was simply too strong for 100-pound hikers with 25-pound backpacks to keep theirs. As indicated, there is a lot of camping in the area.

At 4.3 miles, on the TN side of the creek, the Stiffknee Trail comes in from the right. There is lovely camping in this area. Prepare to ford the creek for the fourth time. The trail arrives at a junction with the Nichols Cove Trail on the NC side at 4.5 miles. Here you can see the power of flooding. The last 50 meters of Nichols Cove Branch has been washed down to bedrock and is very challenging to negotiate if you are hiking up that trail. The trail moves along near the creek, and at 4.9 miles it is time to ford to the west side again. Next, there is a breather from fords for the next 1.4 miles, but then it is time to take the plunge again.

Wildcat Branch comes in at 5.5 miles, presumably giving its name to the falls you will encounter a mile and a half upstream. The trail winds along the creek, taking the path of least resistance. At 6.7 miles, the trail fords to the west side of the creek, and there is good camping just upstream. As the trail leaves the streambed and starts to climb, you can hear the roar of Wildcat Falls (UTM 17S 227730E/3924580N), which is really spectacular in high-water times. Unfortunately, if you are camped along the creek at such times, the ford immediately above the falls is way too dangerous to attempt, as a slip, which could amount to a nice swim in low water, may carry you over the falls in a strong current. (On one hike for this trail description, very heavy rains during the night forced us to abandon the trail just downstream of this ford and climb 100 feet or more above the streambed, moving cross-country. It took us nearly an hour to make the half mile or so to the Big Stack Gap Branch Trail junction, but it beat swimming over Wildcat Falls.) In low-water times, go ahead and ford—carefully—and prepare for another ford (number nine if you are counting) at 7.4 miles.

Here, in an open area, is a potential campsite and the junction with the Big Stack Gap Branch Trail. For the purposes of this book, this is the end of the trail. However, this could be the start of lots of adventure. You can access the high country by doing the big climb to Naked Ground (terminus of the Slickrock Creek Trail), head to Big Fat Gap along the Big Fat Trail, loop back to lower Slickrock Creek on the Nichols Cove Trail, or ascend to the Fodderstack Trail at the eastern edge of the Citico Creek Wilderness via the Big Stack Gap Branch Trail.

96. MILL BRANCH TRAIL (FS TRAIL 96, TI TRAIL 57)

LENGTH: 2.5 miles

ELEVATION CHANGE: Low point, 1,860 feet; high point, 3,380 feet

DIFFICULTY: Easy

TRAILHEADS: Doublecamp Road (Mill Branch) (start) and Fodderstack Trail (end)

USE: Hiking

TOPOGRAPHIC MAP: USGS Whiteoak Flats, TN

COMMENTS: This trail parallels Mill Branch up the northwest flank of Pine Ridge. However, for most of its length the stream is out of sight and the main stream is crossed only once, although some small side branches are also crossed. The trail is in good condition for most of its length except for some areas near Big Stack Gap. Stretches of the trail are quite steep. An excellent day hike can be put together using Mill Branch Trail, Crowder Branch Trail, and the portion of the Fodderstack Trail between them. Note that there is no marker for Mill Branch Trail on Fodderstack Trail, and a blowdown of large oak branches obscures Mill Branch Trail here. However, Big Stack Gap is easily recognized as the deepest gap on this stretch of the Fodderstack Trail. A beautiful campsite in a grove of large trees dominated by a huge red oak is 0.1 mile down the trail from Big Stack Gap.

The trail begins at 2.7 miles on the Doublecamp Road immediately after crossing Mill Branch on the road. The trail is on the right (east) side of the road and is designated by a trail sign with FS Trail 96. There is limited space for parking at the trailhead. Note that the trail is not marked adequately on the USGS 7.5-minute topographical map.

DETAILS: The trail starts out on an old rail bed through tall hemlock and pines along Mill Branch. There is a clearing on the left that has been used for camping. For the first 0.5 mile the trail is wide, relatively flat, and lined with ferns. The evergreens gradually give way to deciduous trees. The trail runs close to Mill Branch until at 0.5 mile it climbs the slope and leaves the stream far below to the right. A couple of small side streams are crossed at 0.7 and 0.8 mile, and then a pine forest is entered as the trail continues to traverse the slope. At 1.0 mile the trail passes through rhododendron to reach the only major stream crossing (UTM 16S 768195E/3923913N). This is one of the two major forks of Mill Branch. Cross the first fork and ascend very steeply the slope of the ridge. The second fork of Mill Branch flows in the valley below to the right.

The trail continues to ascend along the slope of the ridge from 1.05 miles to 1.75 miles, heading southeast and then east. The trail is steep and without switchbacks but is in good condition. There is evidence that the trail is on the bed of an old narrow-gauge rail spur like those that went up many of the valleys to carry out timber early in the 1900s. At 1.6 miles look for railroad ties exposed in the trail. These particular ties are made of chestnut and are very resistant to decay. At 1.75 miles the trail crosses the brow of the ridge and levels off, remaining relatively level as it passes through the "hanging valley" of this fork of Mill Branch.

At 2.4 miles a grove of large trees lies to the right of the trail. The grove, which contains a large buckeye and several maples and tulip trees, is dominated by a huge northern red oak. There is space for one or more tents in the area surrounded by these trees; water can be obtained in the stream nearby. The trail ascends rather steeply past the grove and enters Big Stack Gap at 2.5 miles. There is room to camp in the gap. The Crowder Branch Trail is 1.2 miles to the left (northeast) along Fodderstack Trail.

97. NORTH FORK CITICO CREEK TRAIL (FS TRAIL 98, TI TRAIL 58)

LENGTH: 5.45 miles

ELEVATION CHANGE: Low point, 1,800 feet; high point, 4,400 feet

DIFFICULTY: Difficult

TRAILHEADS: South Fork Citico Creek Trail (start) and Fodderstack Trail (end)

TRAIL CONNECTIONS: Cold Spring Gap Trail

USE: Hiking

TOPOGRAPHIC MAP: USGS Whiteoak Flats, TN

COMMENTS: Wild and rugged, the North Fork Trail follows the North Fork of Citico Creek from its confluence with the South Fork Citico Creek to near its source below Cherry Log Gap. There are several beautiful waterfalls along the upper portion of the creek. Make no mistake: sometimes the "trail" has more of a feeling of a wilderness route than that of a maintained trail. The adventurous hiker will be rewarded with solitude and some of the wildest and most scenic portions of the Citico Creek Wilderness. Note that the trail crosses Citico Creek many times. Seven of these crossings are in the lower portion of the creek and will likely require a wet ford in all but the very lowest water times. There are several good camping spots in the lower 3.0 miles of the trail. In the last 2.45 miles, camping is limited to small single-tent sites that have appeal only when a bivouac is called for. The trail begins at 0.8 mile on the South Fork Trail at a hiker's sign, just past the ruins of an old concrete building (UTM 16S 765619E/ 3920918N). The trail leaves the South Fork Trail to the left, crossing the South Fork Citico Creek on a wooden bridge.

DETAILS: From the footbridge, the South Fork Citico Creek can be seen flowing into the North Fork Creek to the left. The trail, climbing at a very gentle pace, fords the creek to the left side at 0.5 mile and then back to the right side after about 0.1 mile. The trail, remaining fairly level, continues along the right bank of the creek. A pair of crossings occurs at 1.4 miles and again 0.1 mile later, bringing the trail back to the right side of the creek. At 1.6 miles the trail crosses a tributary stream flowing into the North Fork Creek from the right. A fifth and sixth ford illustrate the power of a southern Appalachian stream when it is flooding. In 1990, when the trail was scouted for the first edition of this book, it was possible to avoid these fords by simply walking along the right stream bank. By 2001, the creek had scoured away the right bank all the way to a cliff. It is possible to avoid some of these fords by doing some serious climbing and bushwhacking. It may be faster to go ahead and just ford the creek.

The trail continues to parallel the creek closely, crossing and recrossing the creek every couple of hundred meters. Some of the fords, when at normal water levels, can be crossed by rock-hopping. The creek is crossed to the left side at 3.2 miles and enters a flat area suitable for camping (UTM 16S 769025E/3919796N). The trail turns sharply left and climbs a very steep slope, after which it intersects an old rail bed and turns right.

After crossing another tributary, the trail continues through a relatively flat area before beginning to climb rather steeply beside the creek. At 3.95 miles the trail passes between two enormous boulders (UTM 16S 769842E/3919353N). As the trail climbs steeply, there is a view of a beautiful waterfall (30 to 40 feet high) and cascade to the right. The trail goes up and over a gigantic moss-covered boulder beside the creek and crosses it to the right side at 4.1 miles. Just shy of 4.7 miles, look for a view of a waterfall ahead through the vegetation. The trail crosses the creek on the lip of this waterfall and reaches another waterfall at 4.8 miles. There is space for a single tent near the base of this waterfall. The trail climbs a steep slope and switchback beside the fall. At 4.84 miles the Cold Spring Gap Trail comes in from the right to join the North Fork Trail (UTM 16S 770870E/3919269N). It is easy to walk past this junction if you do not look back over your right shoulder.

The North Fork Trail continues east-southeast on the right of the creek but soon crosses to the left. At 5.0 miles the trail bears to the left; an old route can be seen bearing to the right back toward the stream. The trail follows an old rail bed, which will have water flowing over it in wet weather. At 5.2 miles the trail is dry and the forest opens up as rhododendron disappears from the understory. The trail climbs steeply between two ridges. Beech, cherry, silverbell, and sugar maple trees are passed as the trail climbs up the hollow and comes out at Cherry Log Gap to intersect the Fodderstack Trail at 5.45 miles. The Fodderstack Trail leads south out of the gap toward Bob Bald and north out of the gap toward Chestnut Knob and Glen Gap.

98. SOUTH FORK CITICO CREEK TRAIL (FS TRAIL 105, TI TRAIL 70)

LENGTH: 8.5 miles

ELEVATION CHANGE: Low point, 1,720 feet; high point, 4,400 feet

DIFFICULTY: Difficult

TRAILHEADS: Warden Station Area (start) and Cold Spring Gap (end)

TRAIL CONNECTIONS: North Fork Citico Creek Trail, Brush Mountain Trail, Grassy Branch Trail, and Jeffrey Hell Trail

USE: Hiking

TOPOGRAPHIC MAPS: Whiteoak Flats, TN; Big Junction, TN

COMMENTS: The South Fork Citico Creek Trail follows the South Fork of Citico Creek from the Warden Station Area to its headwaters below Cold Spring Gap. There is at least one ford in the lower section of the trail that will require care, especially if the creek is high. Sections of the trail may be overgrown with blackberries and grapevines, and portions of the trail may be a challenge to follow unless the trail has received recent maintenance. There are spectacular views of the Citico Creek Gorge in the middle section and a spacious meadow near its end that will accommodate several tents. Spring wildflowers abound along this trail. The trail provides access and connections to several other trails and is a key trail for exploring the Citico Wilderness, as well as being a very scenic and enjoyable hike.

The trailhead for the South Fork Citico Creek Trail begins at the turnoff to the Warden Station Area from the Citico Creek Road 2.3 miles from the Indian Boundary Recreation Area entrance and 1.7 miles from Doublecamp (see the trailhead access for the Warden Station Area, above). Note that this trailhead is not across the low-water bridge at the Citico Corridor Area. It is 0.1 mile up the ridge along the Citico Creek Road toward Indian Boundary past the turnoff to the Corridor Area (UTM 16S 765199E/3921688N). A USFS trail sign with "FS Trail 105" designates the beginning of the trail. There is parking for only two or three cars at the trailhead. It is much better to park across the low-water bridge at the corridor area and walk the 0.1 mile up Citico Creek Road to the trailhead.

DETAILS: Follow the old road until it ends at a dirt barrier. Continue past the barrier as the trail narrows and passes ruins of the Warden Station and a small stream at 0.16 mile. The trail then traverses the steep slope above Citico Creek through rhododendron. Another small stream is crossed at 0.4 mile before reaching a clearing and the remnants of an old orchard at 0.5 mile. Continue through the clearing to reach an old roadbed at 0.6 mile and a wooden trail register. The South Fork Citico Creek Trail turns right along the roadbed. (Back to the left the roadbed crosses Citico Creek and reaches the Citico Corridor area; the concrete low-water bridge at the turnoff from the Citico Creek Road is 0.32 mile away but requires a rather difficult crossing of Citico Creek.)

The trail follows the roadbed along Citico Creek and passes a concrete blockhouse at 0.9 mile. The North Fork Citico Creek Trail turns left across a footbridge at 0.97 mile. The South Fork Citico Creek Trail continues along the right side of the creek. At 1.2 miles a stream enters the creek on the opposite bank; this is Ike Camp Branch. The

Brush Mountain Trail begins at an unmarked creek crossing 250 feet farther upstream (UTM 16S 765475E/3920465N). At 2.13 miles, as you approach an obvious stream crossing, the trail leaves the old roadbed and angles back to the right, up and across the slope to avoid two stream crossings. (If desired, the roadbed can be followed across the two crossings.) The old roadbed is rejoined at 2.39 miles. A small

Backpackers keep a positive attitude during one of several fords along the South Fork of Citico Creek. Photograph by Roger Jenkins.

area with a fire ring and room for a tent is passed at 2.54 miles. (In years past, it was possible to find the Grassy Branch trailhead on this [the right] side of the South Fork. Sometimes you will find the beginning of the trail to be heavily overgrown, and practical access requires that you ford the South Fork [ahead] and then recross it to begin hiking up the Grassy Branch Trail. However, in 2002, the path was completely cleared to a width of three feet, and hikers headed for the Grassy Branch trail who want to avoid fording the South Fork should consider this shortcut, although a less difficult ford of Eagle Branch is required.) The South Fork Trail fords the creek at this point to the left (north) side. At 2.7 miles a stream (Eagle Branch) flows into South Fork Citico Creek on the opposite bank. A short distance later, a side trail to the right leads to a cable strung across the creek; this is the effective trailhead for Grassy Branch Trail. Better footing in the creek may be gained by going about 100 feet downstream of the cable.

At 3.1 miles is a small campsite. The trail leaves the roadbed at 3.5 miles and angles steeply up the slope to the left. At 3.6 miles the trail ascends to the left of a small stream ravine for 0.1 mile. The trail then crosses the stream and proceeds up it. About 50 feet beyond the crossing, despite the presence of a path up the creek bed, do not continue up the streambed. Instead, cut sharply back to the right, go up the slope very steeply, and traverse the ridge steeply until it rejoins the roadbed (or rail bed) at 3.9 miles. At 4.0 miles the trail comes to a fork of the rail beds. The South Fork Trail takes the left fork (note the blazes) and angles upslope of the other roadbed, which appears to go back down to the creek; do not go downward at this point. At 4.2 miles coal can be seen in the trail. At 4.7 miles the slope to the north of the trail is a blackberry slick, presumably due to fires that swept through the area after logging. The trail itself is heavily overgrown with blackberry briars, grape vines, and greenbrier and may be difficult to negotiate unless it has had recent maintenance. This section of the trail affords spectacular views of the South Fork Citico Creek Gorge below. The view is more noticeable when hiking the trail in the opposite direction, so be sure to look back to the west if hiking up the trail. A stream crosses the trail at 5.3 miles. Shortly past the stream turn back for another view over the creek gorge.

The trail rejoins the South Fork Citico Creek, and there is a series of falls and cascades at 5.5 miles. At 5.8 miles is an opening to the left (north) of the trail that has a fire ring and scraps of old iron; space for a tent can be found. Small creeks cross the trail at 5.9 and 6.2 miles. There is a small campsite 100 feet up the second stream. At 6.25 miles the Jeffrey Hell Trail comes in from the right at an unsigned trail junction (UTM 16S 768015E/3917040N), having come from the Tellico-Robbinsville Road. The South Fork Citico Creek Trail continues straight ahead, remaining on the north side of the creek. Cross Citico Creek (wading may be required) to the right (south) side at 7.0 miles. A large grassy meadow beside the trail at 7.4 miles makes a lovely campsite for several tents. Spring beauties abound here in April.

The trail continues through a forest of young, straight tulip trees and through several small streams. The trail continues to cross and be in small streams as it passes through rhododendrons along the old rail bed. Around 8.0 miles, leave the rail bed, ascending moderately. The trail follows the streambed for a short distance and then steeply climbs the adjacent slope. Spring wildflowers, including trout lily and spring beauty, abound in this area in April. The trail continues uphill to the east through rich forest, crosses the stream, and continues steeply through open woods. After a final stream crossing, the trail again ascends steeply up to Cold Spring Gap at 8.6 miles. Congratulations. You made it.

---

99. FALLS BRANCH TRAIL (FS TRAIL 87, TI TRAIL 33)

LENGTH: 1.3 miles

ELEVATION CHANGE: Low point, 3,960 feet; high point, 3,960 feet

DIFFICULTY: Moderate

TRAILHEAD: Rattlesnake Rock Parking Area (start and dead-end)

USE: Hiking

TOPOGRAPHIC MAP: USGS Big Junction, TN

COMMENTS: The Falls Branch Trail is a short but very beautiful trail to the 80 foot Falls Branch Waterfall. The Falls Branch Area was a scenic area before the Citico Creek Wilderness was designated. During this period the trail left directly from the old Sassafras Ridge Road and traveled a fraction of a mile to the falls. After the Tellico-Robbinsville Road was constructed, the trail was rerouted along part of the old Sassafras Ridge Road and the trailhead was placed at the Rattlesnake Parking Area. Be careful along the last section of the trail near the falls as the rocks will be wet, moss-covered, and very slippery.

The trail begins at a parking area on the left of the Tellico-Robbinsville Road near Rattlesnake Rock, 8.4 miles east of the TN 165 and FS 345 junction. USFS hiker's signs with "No. 87" and "No.

196" can be seen leading from the western end of the overlook parking lot. Alternatively, for a shorter hike, park at the scenic overlook at 7.15 miles past the turnoff to Indian Boundary Recreation Area. This scenic overlook is immediately before the "million dollar bridge" (so named because it is rumored to have cost in excess of that amount) that spans a cove on the side of the mountain. A section of the old Sassafras Ridge Road can be found to the west of the bridge. This road joins the other trail to the falls. The old road is heavily overgrown; the other route is recommended for beauty and a more aesthetic approach. Note that this should be considered a one-way hike. Other than the junction at the start, there are no other trails that connect to this one.

DETAILS: Follow the trail that leaves the western side of the parking lot. It is marked with hiker signs for Trail Nos. 196 and 87. The trail goes downhill for 250 feet, at which point the trail divides. Jeffrey Hell Trail (FS Trail 196) turns sharply to the right; Falls Branch Trail (FS Trail 87) bears left. Falls Branch Trail goes through rich northern hardwood forest over the broad, flat, old Sassafras Ridge roadbed. At 0.3 mile there is a switchback. At 0.5 mile, an old roadbed enters from the left. At 0.8 mile is a switchback. At 0.9 mile, look for the trail to turn off to the right at a curve in the roadbed. Watch for blazes. An arrow painted on a large hemlock points toward the falls. The trail passes through rhododendron and then descends along a stream through a cove hardwood forest of large trees. This is part of one of the larger areas of old-growth forest that was never logged. In the spring many wildflowers grow in this area. At 1.1 miles the trail crosses a streambed that may be dry; continue to follow the blazes through a switchback at 1.2 miles.

As the trail levels off there is a view of the falls ahead; the sound of the falls should be loud by this point. Cross a small stream and then go down a steep, slippery slope. The view of the falls continues to get better at points along this approach. Another small stream is crossed, and then the main stream is reached at 1.25 miles. The view of the falls is excellent from this vantage point, but if you want to get closer, cross the stream and pass through a cleft in a large boulder. Follow the trail up the left side of the stream. At 1.3 miles the foot of the falls is reached. Nearby is a birch tree with large arched roots with space to crawl under. Someone has fashioned a rock seat here. There is an excellent view from the rocks below the falls. Do not attempt to climb on the falls, as they are very slick and dangerous.

100. GRASSY BRANCH TRAIL (FS TRAIL 91, TI TRAIL 40)

LENGTH: 2.3 miles

ELEVATION CHANGE: Low point, 3,400 feet; high point, 3,400 feet

DIFFICULTY: Moderate

TRAILHEADS: Grassy Gap (start) and South Fork Citico Creek Trail (end)

USE: Hiking

TOPOGRAPHIC MAPS: USGS Big Junction, TN; Whiteoak Flats, TN

COMMENTS: The Grassy Branch Trail follows Grassy Branch and then Eagle Branch as they descend to South Fork Citico Creek. The trail follows Grassy Branch as it passes through a lovely hanging valley and then flows dramatically out of the valley in a series of falls and cascades to join Eagle Branch. There are a number of inviting pools along Eagle Branch. Two alternate tracks near the end of the trail give a choice of routes for reaching the South Fork Citico Creek Trail.

Construction of the Tellico-Robbinsville Road (Cherohala Skyway) exposed iron pyrites that resulted in acid contamination in the upper portion of Grassy Branch in the 1970s. Mitigation measures were undertaken with some success. Additionally, the small amount of water originating in the polluted area is vastly diluted by the time Grassy Branch reaches Eagle Branch and South Fork Citico Creek. Still, one should not rely on Grassy Branch proper for drinking water (there are old signs along the branch, which have mostly fallen over, warning that the water is contaminated).

The trail begins at a parking area to the left and below the Tellico-Robbinsville Road (Cherohala Skyway) at Grassy Gap, 6.3 miles past the TN 165 and FS 345 junction. There is a parking area to the left just before the Grassy Gap sign.

DETAILS: In a few hundred feet from its start, the trail enters a boggy area. At 0.1 mile the trail passes through dense rhododendron and hemlock. The trail crosses the stream again and is in and out of the water for the next 0.2 mile. At one point the branch runs briefly underground. At 0.3 mile the trail is on the slope above the left side of the stream. During the next mile, the trail and branch gradually enter a hanging valley that has an open understory with herbaceous cover and wildflowers abounding. Two small side streams come in from the left at 0.6 mile and 0.8 mile. Shortly past the second stream, two large hemlocks beside the trail probably predate the logging in the area. The trail crosses and is in Grassy Branch several times during the next 0.5 mile. At 1.1 miles, while the trail is to the right of Grassy Branch, a side stream enters from the east. Since this stream does not have its source near the Tellico-Robbinsville Road, it should be uncontaminated by acid runoff.

At 1.3 miles the branch begins its descent out of the hanging valley as a series of cascades and falls. The trail descends rather steeply along the slope to the right of the branch. As the trail moves away from the branch, look back up the valley for spectacular views of the water falling and cascading out of the hanging valley. At 1.5 miles the trail crosses over the nose of a spur ridge coming down from the right and descends into a small stream channel. As the trail resumes its descent along the slope of the main ridge, Grassy Branch can be seen joining Eagle Branch in the valley below. The trail reaches Eagle Branch at 1.6 miles and crosses it to the left side; it crosses to the right side at 1.7 miles. Pay attention in this area. It is easy to lose the route while focusing on stream crossings. At 1.8 miles is a nice pool in the stream below a small waterfall just after the branch is crossed back to the left side. At 1.9 miles a small stream comes in from the left. Cross Eagle Branch to the right at 2.0 miles.

Continue along the right side of Eagle Branch until it reaches South Fork Citico Creek at 2.3 miles. There is a cable stretched across the creek that can be used with caution to cross. However, you might find easier crossing about 100 feet downstream of the cable. The South Fork Citico Creek Trail is on the other side of the creek at 2.4 miles. The trail junction is at 2.6 miles on the South Fork Citico Creek Trail from the Warden Station Area Trailhead.

If you arrive at the South Fork and decide that the water is too high to safely ford, go back up the trail 0.1 mile and look hard for a crossing of Eagle Branch to the left side. The Eagle Branch crossing is marked by a readily visible rectangular white blaze on a tree on the far side of the creek. After wading, pull yourself up a short steep embankment on the far side. From here an unofficial trail provides an easy bypass of two crossings of Citico Creek. Try to find and follow that trail through rhododendron. Cross Clemmer Cove Branch at 2.3 miles and intersect the South Fork Citico Creek Trail at 2.4 miles before it crosses the creek. Note that this will only avoid a ford of the South Fork if you are heading downstream. Upstream hikers will have to ford immediately.

101. FODDERSTACK TRAIL (FS TRAIL 95, TI TRAIL 36) (INCLUDES STRATTON BALD SPUR TRAIL, NANTAHALA NF TRAIL 54)

LENGTH (FS TRAIL 95): 10.6 miles

ELEVATION CHANGE (FS TRAIL 95): Low point, 2,800 feet; high point, 5,160 feet

DIFFICULTY: Moderate

TRAILHEADS: Farr Gap (start) and Cold Spring Gap (end)

TRAIL CONNECTIONS: Crowder Branch Trail, Big Stack Gap Branch Trail, Mill Branch Trail, Pine Ridge Trail, North Fork Citico Creek Trail, South Fork of Citico Creek Trail, Cold Spring Gap Trail, and Stratton Bald Trail

USE: Equestrian and hiking

TOPOGRAPHIC MAPS: USGS Big Junction, TN; Whiteoak Flats, TN

COMMENTS: This trail runs along the Unicoi Mountain Range dividing Citico Wilderness and Joyce Kilmer–Slickrock Wilderness. It passes near the crests of Little Fodderstack, Big Fodderstack, and

Looking toward Bob's Bald and the eastern boundary of the Citico Wilderness from Hangover Mountain. Photograph by Roger Jenkins.

Rockstack. Bob's Bald, which is a short distance along Stratton Bald Trail in NC's Nantahala NF, offers excellent campsites and spring water. It is one of the finest grassy balds in the southern CNF and offers excellent views. Flame azaleas and phlox bloom profusely in the early summer.

The Fodderstack Trail provides access to several trails in the Citico Wilderness, as well as the Joyce Kilmer–Slickrock Wilderness, and provides the potential for utilizing these for a multiple-day backpack trip. Several small campsites can be found along the trail, and larger sites can be found short distances down the Crowder Branch, Mill Branch, and Stratton Bald trails. Water is usually not found on the trail, but springs are found at Crowder Place and Bob Stratton Bald. In addition, water can be found down the creek drainages off the ridgecrest.

The trail begins at Farr Gap, 6.7 miles along the Doublecamp Road. While it is possible to hike Fodderstack Trail from its southern terminus at the Cold Spring Gap area, that "trailhead" is only accessible by a 1.9-mile walk on the pretty much abandoned roadbed of FS 217H, starting near Beech Gap. The Doublecamp Road is graveled and in fair condition. A parking area near the Fodderstack Trailhead has space for several cars.

DETAILS: The Fodderstack Trail begins at the high point of Farr Gap a short distance up the Doublecamp Road from the parking area. From the gap you can look into the Joyce Kilmer–Slickrock Wilderness. A short distance after the Fodderstack Trail turns right off the road, the Stiffknee Trail (FS Trail 106) turns left (southeast) and descends into the Slickrock Creek watershed. The Fodderstack Trail leads straight ahead through a mixed forest of oak, hickory, tulip trees, sourwood, pine, and maple. The trail gains a ridge after 0.4 mile and turns east along it. The trail remains on the ridge as it turns southeast and goes through forest alternating with old clearings grown up in white pine and blackberries. Good views are possible from some of these clearings, especially in winter.

After 1.0 mile the trail turns south and ascends rather steeply to skirt Little Fodderstack to the west of its summit after 1.5 miles. Look for chestnut sprouts. At 1.7 miles the trail turns sharply from southwest to southeast. An old overgrown trail continues west along the ridge at the switchback. As the main trail continues around Little Fodderstack, a faint trail can be seen to the left following the ridgeline for 0.25 mile to the summit of Little Fodderstack. The main trail ascends to a sister knob of Little Fodderstack at 2.1 miles. From the knob, look back for good views of Little Fodderstack. As one continues beyond the knob along the ridgeline, it may be possible to see

Hangover, a prominent rock outcrop in the Joyce Kilmer–Slickrock Wilderness, to the southeast. The trail reaches a gap at 2.5 miles, with a possible campsite to the left of the trail. A side trail splits off from the main trail at 2.6 miles and goes to the top of a partially cleared knob to the right. The trail reaches the top of another knob at 2.9 miles before descending rather steeply to the gap above Crowder Place at 3.04 miles. The Crowder Branch Trail leaves the gap to the right and passes through Crowder Place, which has numerous campsites and a dependable spring 0.2 mile down the trail from the gap. The trail climbs out of the gap and at 3.2 miles reaches a trail junction with open space that could accommodate several tents. The Big Stack Gap Branch Trail turns left and descends 1.8 miles into Joyce Kilmer–Slickrock Wilderness.

The Fodderstack Trail continues to climb gently past the Big Stack Gap Branch Trail junction along the ridgecrest until it tops out at about 3.7 miles. The trail then steeply descends to Big Stack Gap at 4.2 miles. Mill Branch Trail descends to the right (west) out of the gap. Several very large oaks are in the gap. A large branch of one of these oaks has fallen and has partially obscured the unsigned beginning of Mill Branch Trail.

The trail climbs out of the gap and up the northwest slopes of Big Fodderstack Mountain. At 4.7 miles the trail makes a sharp turn to the left; at this point a trail appears to continue straight ahead, but this "trail" soon disappears. The main trail makes a sharp right within a few yards. The trail heads south but gradually bears to the southwest as it continues to climb around Big Fodderstack. The trail reaches a rocky clearing on the point of a spur ridge at 5.0 miles. The terminus of the Pine Ridge Trail, traversing down the south side of the ridge to the southwest, is reached.

Fodderstack Trail makes a sharp turn to the southeast at the intersection with Pine Ridge Trail and continues up the ridgeline for a short distance before turning east and skirting below the summit of Big Fodderstack. A short bushwhack will take you to the summit (4,200 feet) for good views to the east of the Slickrock Creek Valley. The trail turns back to the southeast and descends along a ridge coming down from Big Fodderstack. Nearby, the TN-NC border leads up from the Slickrock Valley and now shares the ridgeline with the trail. The trail reaches Harrison Gap at 6.19 miles. The gap is long and shallow, with numerous large oaks. The trail steeply ascends out of the gap at 6.6 miles, heading south, and then turns east along a ridgeline where there is evidence of a recent burn. At about 7.0 miles, the trail levels out as it skirts the west side of Rockstack before descending into Glen Gap at

7.3 miles. There is space for one or two tents, and water can be found down the stream drainages on each side of the gap.

The trail climbs out of Glen Gap and ascends along the ridgeline. The trail runs near the state line for the next 2.0 miles. The trail reaches Chestnut Knob at 8.1 miles. Descend gradually through a hemlock grove to Cherry Log Gap at 8.3 miles. Several large, straight black cherry trees are in the gap. This is the terminus for the North Fork of Citico Creek.

The Fodderstack Trail climbs out of Cherry Log Gap moving south along the ridgeline. At 8.6 miles the trail reaches a clearing with large trees that could accommodate two or three tents (UTM 16S 771749E/ 3918965N). If your destination is Bob's Bald, Naked Ground, or Hangover, bear left and ascend the Fodderstack Trail. If your destination is Cold Spring Gap, or Beech Gap on the Cherohala Skyway, bear right, heading slightly downhill, on the newly reconstructed Benton MacKaye Trail. This trail traverses through woods for 1.25 miles to the Cold Spring Gap Trail. There are at least two good water sources and a small campsite along the trail. As the Fodderstack Trail ascends, there are switchbacks at 9.0 miles, 9.1 miles, and 9.3 miles before the trail intersects the Stratton Bald Trail at 9.4 miles. Bob Stratton Bald is in the Nantahala NF at 0.4 mile along the Stratton Bald Trail (FS Trail 54), which turns left (east) at the intersection.

The Stratton Bald Trail, a hiking trail, and the Bob Stratton Bald to which it leads are in NC but make a good side-hike or camping area. The bald is often referred to as "Bob's Bald," and maps label it as both "Bob Bald" and "Stratton Bald." The correct name is probably "Bob Stratton Bald," since it was named after Robert B. Stratton, a mountain man who lived nearby in the late 1800s. He reportedly bought 100 acres of Swan Meadows for $9.40 in 1872. The portion of the original bald that remains clear is 5,280 feet high and provides one of the best views in the entire area. The GSMNP is in the distance to the north with the Slickrock Creek valley below. The USFS clears the bald periodically, so there are numerous grassy campsites with reliable water on the southeast edge of the grassy area, about 100–200 feet back in the trees.

The Fodderstack Trail turns right (southwest) from the Stratton Bald Trail junction and passes through blackberries and rhododendron as it descends down the backbone of the ridge. A short section that followed an eroded gully at 9.7 miles was replaced and revegetated in 1990; avoid the replaced section. There are a number of large, gnarled trees on this section of the trail; a particularly large tree is reached at about 9.8 miles. The forest opens up considerably before descending steeply at 10.1 miles. The trail continues to descend steeply along the ridge for 0.5 mile to end at Cold Spring Gap at 10.6 miles.

102. BRUSH MOUNTAIN TRAIL (FS TRAIL 97, TI TRAIL 16)

LENGTH: 4.4 miles

ELEVATION CHANGE: Low point, 1,980 feet; high point, 4,400 feet

DIFFICULTY: Difficult

TRAILHEADS: Cold Spring Gap (start), South Fork Citico Creek Trail (end)

USE: Hiking

TOPOGRAPHIC MAPS: USGS Whiteoak Flats, TN; Big Junction, TN

COMMENTS: This trail has outstanding scenery and conveys a sense of wild remoteness and isolation. There are signs of logging and a small-gauge railroad along Ike Camp Branch, and the presence of an old, four-cylinder engine block suggests the earlier existence of a road. In the middle and upper portions of the trail there are signs of bear and boar among some beautiful forest stands and isolated large trees. However, this trail receives relatively low usage and there is little evidence of trail maintenance. Numerous brush thickets and fallen trees present a challenge in off-trail scrambling and wilderness route finding. While not recommended for novice hikers, experienced off-trail hikers equipped with USGS quadrangle maps and a compass (and preferably a GPS) can follow the path and will love the challenge. The trail is shown as a dashed line on the USGS quadrangle maps, and, while the line is imprecise, it does show the general route. The trail is marked with occasional blazes, some of which are white paint, some orange, and some are very old blazes made with an ax or a knife.

The lower trailhead is reached by hiking 1.1 miles up South Fork Citico Trail (Trail 105) from its trailhead on the Citico Creek Road just west of the turnoff to the Citico corridor area. The upper trailhead is reached by hiking north from the Beech Gap Trailhead 1.8 miles on the Fodderstack Trail (FS Trail 95) to Cold Spring Gap and then another 1.5 miles north on the Cold Spring Gap Trail (FS Trail 149). An appealing Brush Mountain day hike (for experienced route finders) is to leave a car at the lower end and start hiking at Beech Gap. In this manner the difficulties of rugged terrain, route finding, and added length at start and finish are not compounded by the need to climb some 2,500 feet. The following details are based on the top-to-bottom plan. We have done the trail both ways, and each direction has its own challenges.

DETAILS: Starting at Beech Gap, hike northeast on the Fodderstack Trail (FS Trail 95) that, at this point, is an old jeep road. In 1.8 fairly level miles, come to Cold Spring Gap, where three trails meet. A sharp left would take you down the South Fork Citico Trail (FS Trail 105) and a half right turn uphill is the continuation of FS Trail 95. Instead, take a half left and continue on the old jeep road that, at this point, becomes the Cold Spring Gap Trail (FS Trail 149). After 1.5 fairly level miles on this trail (3.3 miles from Beech Gap) FS Trail 149 turns to the right through a saddle and heads east. Here (UTM 16S 770208E/3918257N) the Brush Mountain Trail (FS Trail 97) starts on the left, heading west-northwest along the left side of a knob. (Note: The USGS map, Big Junction, TN, shows both a trail and an old road intersecting FS Trail 97 in this area. The westernmost route, a purple dashed line, is the actual route now followed by the Cold Spring Gap Trail. The short sections of trail indicated by dotted black lines in this area have been abandoned.) The remaining mileages in this description of FS Trail 97 start at this point.

A blackberry bush patch may obscure the start of the trail. Walk around the side of the patch to begin hiking the trail. In just 0.3 mile, after passing that first knob, descending a ridgecrest, and passing to the right of another knob, the trail circles around the ridge to the left. Be alert here (UTM 16S 769711E/3918304N) so as to not head off down the ridge to the northwest. The hiking direction here is changing from due west to southwest and the trail soon becomes parallel to the nearby ridgecrest that runs in the same general line. At 0.6 mile the trail turns sharply left and climbs steeply about 50 vertical feet to the ridgecrest. Continue southwest along the crest. At 0.8 mile, the trail appears to go straight ahead along a ridgeline. Watch for a white double change of direction blaze. Turn sharply right (16S 769181E/3917925N) and drop off the crest about 40 vertical feet, then bear left at another double blaze, now headed west at a constant elevation of about 4,100 feet for approximately two hundred yards, then bearing to the northwest and descending. At 1.0 mile, come into a saddle (UTM 16S 768917E/3918012N) and exit to the north, passing to the right of a low knob. (Note: The USGS map contours do not indicate a saddle at this point.) At 1.1 miles the trail joins an old roadbed and becomes easier to follow.

At 1.2 miles another old roadbed comes down from the left rear. If you were hiking in the opposite direction at this point, you would take the left fork. At 1.3 miles, the trail curls around to the left through a saddle overgrown with rhododendron. This saddle, at 3,860 feet, is clearly shown on the USGS map. Just on the other side of the rhododendron, the trail turns sharply right, leaving the old roadbed, and climbs steeply. There is a large orange blaze on a tree at this turn. At 1.4 miles reach the crest of a peak that is southwest of peak 4,013. At 1.5 miles reach the crest of peak 4,013 (USGS map shows a height of 4,013 feet.) At this crest (UTM 16S 768435E/3918486N) turn right and descend to the north, soon bearing left to head northwest. Ike's Peak is directly ahead to the northwest and the trailheads in the general direction of that peak for the next 0.7 mile. At 1.9 miles reach a stream in the middle of a rhododendron thicket. This stream is one of two branches that join to form Ike Camp Branch lower down the mountain. FS Trail 97 descends the other one, farther northwest, so continue northwest, climbing steeply away from the branch. At 2.2 miles arrive in a saddle just southeast of Ike's Peak. Here (UTM 16S 767791E/3919229N) the trail turns to the left and descends along the branch. From here to the end (UTM 16S 767270E/3918917N), locating the route is simply a matter of finding the path of least resistance on either side of, or in, the stream. Sometimes an old road grade shows where the trail probably was at one time, but travel is slow through rocky streambed stretches.

At 2.8 miles the other branch joins from the left (UTM 16S 767149E/3918862N), and the stream turns from southwest to northwest. (If hiking uphill, be sure to take the left fork.) Soon after that confluence, the trail follows an old road grade on the north bank and gradually diverges to about 50 or 60 yards from the stream. At 3.3 miles the trail crosses to the south side of Ike Camp Branch. It again follows an old roadbed and continues to do so almost to the end, although at 3.9 miles it crosses to the north side and soon back again to the south side.

At 4.4 miles reach the end of FS Trail 97 on South Fork Citico Creek. Look for the easiest place to cross. In low-water periods one can rock-hop, but for much of the year this will be a wet crossing. Use a stick for support and proceed carefully!

The actual junction with FS Trail 105 is on the far (west) side of the South Fork (UTM 16S 765476E/3920475N) at a point 0.1 mile upstream from the mouth of Ike Camp Branch. From there it is 1.1 miles to the FS Trail 105 trailhead and another 0.2 mile to the Citico Creek Road. On the way, FS Trail 105 passes a junction with the North Fork Citico Trail (FS Trail 98) at 0.4 mile from Ike Camp Branch and it passes another split, at 0.7 mile, where FS Trail 105 branches left to stay on the west side of the creek until the trailhead.

103. PINE RIDGE TRAIL (FS TRAIL 99; NO TI NUMBER)

LENGTH: 3.55 miles

ELEVATION CHANGE: Low point, 1,720 feet; high point, 4,000 feet

DIFFICULTY: Moderate

TRAILHEADS: Warden Station Area (start) and Fodderstack Trail (end)

USE: Equestrian and hiking

TOPOGRAPHIC MAP: USGS Whiteoak Flats, TN

COMMENTS: The Pine Ridge Trail follows Pine Ridge to its junction with the Fodderstack Trail near the top of Big Fodderstack Mountain. It offers a great way to reach the middle of the Fodderstack trail and to make interesting loop hikes. For most of its length the trail follows the southern flank of Pine Ridge just below its backbone as it climbs steadily to the east-northeast. The middle portion of the trail goes through a series of small coves along the ridge side, alternating with the exposed south slope. There are some excellent views of the North Fork drainage along this trail. Iris and phlox bloom on the lower portion of the trail in the spring, and flame azaleas can be seen in late June on the middle portion of the trail. The trail is relatively dry, although a small stream is crossed on the lower portion, and a spring occurs in the last mile. Do not expect to camp along the trail. There are only very occasional flat areas.

The trail starts in the Citico Corridor Area about 0.1 mile up the dirt road from the concrete low-water bridge. Look for a horse-trail sign on the left. A hiker's trail sign is a few feet past the first sign. The two trails that turn off to the left join after a few feet.

DETAILS: The trail will appear to fork after a very short distance. Take the right fork; the left fork dead-ends. At 0.1 mile the trail comes to an overlook over Citico Creek. At 0.2 mile the trail crosses a beautiful small stream and then begins to climb up the slope and away from Citico Creek. At 0.4 mile the trail enters a small cove. At 0.5 mile the trail turns sharply north. Huckleberries are along the trail here. The trail turns sharply to the east again at 0.56 mile as it goes through a mixed pine and hardwood forest. At 1.8 miles there is a potential campsite downslope to the right; there are signs this site has been used as a hunter's camp in the past. But do not count on any water nearby.

The trail crosses a dry drainage at 2.31 miles; there are several large trees in this area. At 2.6 miles the trail slants across the steep side of the ridge with rock outcrops above the trail and then goes around a ridge point where there is a potential campsite on the point of the ridge to the right. At 2.7 miles there are views through the trees of the North Fork of Citico drainage. A spring emerges below the trail at 2.8 miles, but it could be seasonally dependent. At 3.3 miles the trail angles north; there is a view of Big Fodderstack Mountain to the east through the pines. The trail passes through a section overgrown with mountain laurel and has great views before intersecting with the Fodderstack Trail at 3.55 miles. From here the Fodderstack Trail goes northeast toward Crowder Place and southeast toward Glen Gap.

104. ROCKY FLATS TRAIL (ROCKY FLATS BRANCH) (FS TRAIL 100, TI TRAIL 65)

LENGTH: 4.5 miles

ELEVATION CHANGE: Low point, 1,880 feet; high point, 2,960 feet

DIFFICULTY: Moderate

TRAILHEADS: Doublecamp Road (Rocky Flats Branch) (start) and Citico Creek Corridor (end)

USE: Hiking

TOPOGRAPHIC MAP: USGS Whiteoak Flats, TN

COMMENTS: You will need some skill in route following to hike this trail, but you will be rewarded with solitude, interesting terrain, and impressive ruins of an old homestead. It is well worth the effort if you enjoy the challenge. The trail is probably somewhat easier to follow starting from Doublecamp Road rather than in the opposite direction. The trail intersects the road at mile 2.5, before the road crosses Mill Branch. The trail starts on the right (southeast) side of the road at a sign for FS Trail 100. There is parking for two or three cars on the opposite side of the road. This is also known as Rocky Flats Trail. Note that this trail is not marked on some USGS 7.5-minute topographical maps.

DETAILS: The trail climbs uphill heading southeast; no blazes are visible. After turning east briefly, the route continues southeast through second-growth mixed hardwoods and pine. After 0.5 mile the trail turns south along an old roadbed. At 0.7 mile the trail is almost blocked by young trees; bear to the right through the trees and then downhill toward the south. At 0.9 mile the trail leaves the roadbed and heads southwest to the right of a small stream. Look for sporadic blazes.

The trail passes several rock structures in ruins and through the remains of an old house. An almost intact chimney is to the right of the trail; ruins of another chimney are to the left of the trail. The trail enters the stream at 1.1 miles, heading downstream. Go through the stream for about 60 feet and look for a white blaze and an old roadbed on the left side of the stream. Follow the road. A huge old chestnut log lies across the trail at 1.2 miles. It has footholds cut in its side to climb over. Follow blazes to the south and then to the southeast. Go through a patch of ferns and start up a broad valley. Turn sharply right just past the ferns at 1.3 miles (there is no blaze, but the turn is 150 feet past the last blaze).

The trail proceeds steeply upslope. Look for a blaze about 200 feet upslope; turn sharply right (northwest) just past the blaze. The trail follows the contour of the slope and passes over a ridge at 1.4 miles. It then descends into and crosses a dry drainage with hemlocks and poplars towering above. The trail is now heading northwest. At 1.6 miles pass through a dense stand of young pine and hemlock. The trail heads downhill into another dry drainage and turns right (southwest) along the slope of the opposite side of the drainage; watch for blazes. Go over a small ridge at 1.7 miles and head southwest and then south. The trail encounters and parallels a small stream for a short distance before entering the stream at 1.9 miles. It emerges about 30 feet downstream on the opposite bank.

Backpacker inspects a stone chimney at a former homesite on the Rocky Flats trail in Citico Creek Wilderness. Photograph by Roger Jenkins.

Head uphill through rhododendron. At 1.95 miles cross a small drainage and head sharply uphill (southwest). The trail tops out on a ridge and takes a sharp left to the south back along the slope of the ridge. Notice white quartz boulders at 2.1 miles. Continue around the contour of Pine Ridge, heading generally west, topping spur ridges and descending into dry drainage channels. Look closely for the sporadic blazes.

At 2.9 miles the trail descends into a valley with a small stream after making two switchbacks. Cross the stream and turn right (west). Follow the stream as it bears to the southwest. The trail crosses the stream three more times and at 3.4 miles goes down the middle of the stream for about 40 feet and emerges on the left of the stream. Cross the stream two more times. As the trail tops the ridge at 3.55 miles, turn sharply left to the northeast and climb the rocks along the ridgecrest. You will need to look closely for this turnoff, as the trail appears to continue straight along the ridge. If you continue straight along the ridge on the alternate trail, there is a view of Citico Creek to the left. The alternate trail then continues around the ridge and reaches Citico Creek after 0.2 mile. If you cross Citico Creek on the alternate trail, you will reach the Citico Road approximately halfway between Doublecamp and the Citico Corridor area. This is where the designated trail formerly ended.

Continuing along the designated trail, climb steeply over rocks on the ridgecrest to the northeast. Spectacular views of Citico Creek are below to the right. The trail runs along the dry south slope above Citico Creek. At 3.8 miles the trail flattens out and runs through open hardwoods. At 4.3 miles the trail again comes out on the dry south slope above Citico Creek. At 4.4 miles the trail crosses a small stream and descends along the stream through rhododendron. At 4.5 miles the trail comes out in a meadow in the Citico Corridor area. A trail sign by a large forked tulip tree indicates FS Trail 100.

105. FLATS MOUNTAIN TRAIL (FS TRAIL 102, TI TRAIL 35)

LENGTH: 6.1 miles

ELEVATION CHANGE: Low point, 1,960 feet; high point, 3,860 feet

DIFFICULTY: Moderate

TRAILHEADS: Eagle Gap (start); Beehouse Gap (end)

USE: Hiking

TOPOGRAPHIC MAPS: USGS Whiteoak Flats, TN; Big Junction, TN

COMMENTS: The Flats Mountain Trail follows the ridge of Flats Mountain from its high point near Eagle Gap down along the edge of the Citico Creek Wilderness to Beehouse Gap outside the wilderness. There are wonderful views of Indian Boundary Lake and much of the Tellico Ranger District, as well as views into the Citico Creek Wilderness, especially when leaves are off the trees.

When hiked from Eagle Gap to Beehouse Gap, as described, the trail is practically all downhill and particularly enjoyable, with many outstanding vistas. Hawks can often be sighted in the higher elevations. Wildflowers of many kinds may also be found in the spring and summer. Water is generally not available on the Flats Mountain Trail, and few campsites are available, so this trail is better suited for a day hike than for backpacking. By doing a bit of road walking, the trail can be connected to others in the Citico Creek watershed for a nice backpacking trip. If a backpack trip is undertaken, water may be found in a spring at 1.3 miles or off trail on the lower portion of the trail.

The trail begins at Eagle Gap on the Tellico-Robbinsville Road (Cherohala Skyway), 4.7 miles east of TN 165 and FS 345 junction (Indian Boundary turnoff). A paved road at the gap (UTM 16S 0762869E/3917053N) leads up the ridge to a large, gravel parking area that cannot be seen from the highway.

DETAILS: Follow the jeep road uphill from the parking area. After a locked gate at 0.1 mile, the trail continues up the ridgecrest on the road until at 0.6 mile it reaches a second open field. These two fields are wildlife management clearings. In 2001, the first field was allowed to become overgrown while the second was mowed and experimentally planted in chufa, a legume. Chufa grows a nut, or kernel, on the root, similar to the peanut plant. It makes excellent food for wild turkeys, which easily can scratch up the roots. However, since it is not native to the area, the turkeys must learn to recognize it from the plant foliage. The USFS plans to observe and, if necessary, will disk harrow the field to bring some of the roots to the surface. The hope is that the turkeys will learn to get the food while the wild hogs do not. If the experiment succeeds, the USFS will plant chufa in the other field here and in other areas.

At the end of the second field the road ends and the trail enters the woods at a registration box. This is the highest point reached on the trail. Just 0.3 mile beyond that box (1.0 mile from the trailhead) a side trail to the left leads down to rock outcroppings from which there are tremendous views to the northwest of Indian Boundary Lake, Tellico Lake, and, in the distance, the TN Valley. There will be a number of other views of this panorama as the trail winds down the mountain, but the view from these rocks is by far the best.

Continuing northeast along the main trail, two sharp switchbacks occur at 1.1 miles, and the trail traverses across the mountain to the east. At 1.3 miles there is another switchback to the left and the trail now traverses back across to the northwest. There is a spring here that has a good flow in slightly dry seasons, but a prolonged dry spell may require descending the streambed some distance to find water. Another switchback to the left (southwest) occurs at 1.7 miles. There will be several more of these switchbacks in the next mile. In each case, after turning sharply left and dropping off the ridgecrest the trail then turns back to the right to gradually regain the crest at a lower elevation. Watch for those left turns carefully, as some of them still show signs of the old trail that continued steeply, straight down the ridgecrest.

At 2.0 miles the trail passes through a stand of table mountain pine where an opening in the trees provides a view of the Citico Creek watershed to the east. Another opening on the right at 2.5 miles provides a good view of the Unicoi Mountains. The trail goes through a gap at 3.2 miles and then tops out on a knob covered with table mountain pine at 3.4 miles.

The trail now makes a steep, straight descent. Big Fodderstack can be seen straight ahead. Soon there is a good view to the right of the Citico area and the last views to the west of Indian Boundary Lake. At 3.9 miles the trail turns sharply back to the right and descends off the ridge. The sounds of Citico Creek can be heard below. At 4.2 miles the trail turns back toward the northeast. At 5.3 miles it passes a blowdown area with good views to the north. The trail continues northwest through mixed pine and hardwoods until, at 6.1 miles, it emerges at Beehouse Gap (UTM 16S 0764420E/3921888N). A USFS sign gives the elevation at Beehouse Gap as 2,580 feet, but this should be 1,960 feet.

106. STIFFKNEE TRAIL (FS TRAIL 106, TI TRAIL 74) (INCLUDES SLICKROCK CREEK TRAIL, NANTAHALA NF TRAIL 42)

LENGTH: 3.4 miles

DIFFICULTY: Moderate

ELEVATION CHANGE: Low point, 1,400 feet; high point, 2,840 feet

TRAILHEAD: Farr Gap (start) and Slickrock Creek Trail (end)

USE: Hiking

TOPOGRAPHIC MAPS: USGS Tapoco, TN-NC; Whiteoak Flats, TN

COMMENTS: Stiffknee Trail is one of three trails connecting the trail systems of the contiguous Citico Creek Wilderness and Joyce Kilmer–Slickrock Wilderness (the others are Big Stack Gap Branch and Stratton Bald; see Fodderstack Trail for details on these). It is also the only trail in the Haw Knob Primitive Area and only slightly touches the primitive area.

DETAILS: The trail starts on the east side of the Farr Gap parking area and is marked. It is outside the wilderness boundary for 0.8 mile as it traverses down the side of a ridge, in and out of small coves. The trail is poorly graded, so watch your footing. At 0.8 mile it reaches Stiffknee Gap just below Stiffknee Top. At this point it is skirting the edge of the primitive area to the northeast. The trail then enters the Joyce Kilmer–Slickrock Wilderness and descends into the headwaters of Little Slickrock Creek. After reaching the creek, the trail follows it for slightly over 2.0 miles to Slickrock Creek. The trail is initially a rocky footpath beside the creek, but after 2.4 miles the trail appears to follow an old railroad bed. The creek is crossed five times.

As the trail arrives at Slickrock Creek, it intersects the Slickrock Creek Trail (Nantahala NF Trail 42). You can use this to go both up and downstream. It is the longest (13.3 miles) and one of the most beautiful of the Joyce Kilmer–Slickrock Wilderness trails as it winds its way along Slickrock Creek from Lake Cheoah to the high mountains above the valley. The elevation gain along the way is substantial— 3,700 feet; however, most of this gain is in the last 5.0 miles. On its final assault on Naked Ground (its terminus), it becomes quite rugged and demanding to hike, especially with a full backpack. This trail is entirely in the Nantahala NF. To the left (downstream) the trail leads to Lower Falls at about 1.2 miles from the junction of Stiffknee and Slickrock trails. Continue on downstream to Calderwood Lake, then to the east along the lake. The trailhead at US 129 is reached at 4.3 miles. To the right (upstream) from the Stiffknee-Slickrock trails junction, you will pass the spectacular Wildcat Falls in about 2.7 miles. About another half mile upstream on the right (west) is the Big Stack Gap Branch Trail, which leads up to the Fodderstack Trail and the Citico Creek Wilderness. Shortly thereafter the climbing will begin, and at 13.3 miles the trail reaches Naked Ground and the Haoe Lead Trail (FS Trail 53). To the right (west) 0.6 mile on the Haoe Lead Trail you will reach the Stratton Bald Trail (FS Trail 54). Another 1.3 miles on the Stratton Bald Trail will lead you across the scenic Bob Stratton Bald to the Fodderstack Trail and the Citico Creek Wilderness.

---

107. BIG STACK GAP BRANCH TRAIL (FS TRAIL 139, TI TRAIL 13) (INCLUDES STRATTON BALD SPUR TRAIL, NANTAHALA NF TRAIL 54)

LENGTH: 1.8 miles

ELEVATION CHANGE (FS TRAIL 95): Low point, 1,900 feet; high point, 3,406 feet

DIFFICULTY: Moderate

TRAILHEADS: Fodderstack Trail (start) and Slickrock Creek Trail (end)

TRAIL CONNECTIONS: Fodderstack Trail and Slickrock Creek Trail

USE: Equestrian and hiking

TOPOGRAPHIC MAP: USGS Whiteoak Flats, TN

COMMENTS: The Big Stack Gap Trail is one of the primary connectors between the Citico Creek Wilderness and the Joyce Kilmer Slickrock Wilderness. There is no water along the trail's higher elevation stretch, but as it descends toward Slickrock Creek, you may be able to find some flowing in the coves. Note that this trail may not appear on some USGS 7.5-minute topographical maps.

DETAILS: The Big Stack Gap Branch Trail is a hiking trail that provides access to Slickrock Creek and the Joyce Kilmer–Slickrock Wilderness trail system. It is blazed with bear-preserve signs and initially follows a ridge down into Slickrock Valley. At 0.6 mile it drops off the ridge to the south and descends across a series of coves to Big Stack Gap Branch. Before this drop, there are some nice views of the Slickrock Creek valley when the leaves are off the trees. The trail then follows an old logging skid road along the branch to its end at 1.8 miles at Slickrock Creek. The Slickrock Creek Trail (FS Trail 42) goes left (north) 2.7 miles downstream to the Stiffknee Trail (FS Trail 106; see description below), which turns left and leads back up out of the valley to Farr Gap. FS Trail 42 continues along Slickrock Creek for 1.8 miles to Lake Cheoah and on to a trailhead at US 129. The Slickrock Creek Trail goes right (south) up Slickrock Creek to its headwaters and up a steep climb to Naked Ground and a junction with the Stratton Bald Trail (FS Trail 54), a distance of approximately 6.0 miles.

108. COLD SPRING GAP TRAIL (FS TRAIL 149, TI TRAIL 27)

LENGTH: 3.2 miles

ELEVATION CHANGE: Low point, 3,840 feet; high point, 4,400 feet

DIFFICULTY: Easy

TRAILHEADS: Cold Spring Gap (start) and North Fork Citico Creek Trail (end)

TRAIL CONNECTIONS: Brush Mountain Trail

USE: Equestrian (one-way), hiking

TOPOGRAPHIC MAPS: USGS Big Junction, TN; Whiteoak Flats, TN

COMMENTS: The Cold Spring Gap Trail follows the roadbed of the former road (FS 217H) that now ends at Cold Spring Gap. The trail follows the contours of Brush Mountain and connects the Fodderstack Trail, the South Fork Citico Creek Trail, and the North Fork Citico Creek Trail; the Brush Mountain Trail intersects the Cold Spring Gap Trail about halfway between the other trails. The trail is broad and in excellent condition. It makes a good connector for long hikes in the area. There are usually numerous signs of bear along this trail, indicating that they, too, use the trail as a connector.

The Cold Spring Gap Trailhead is at Cold Spring Gap, which is 1.9 miles from Beech Gap, at the turnaround to FS 217H past Strawberry Knob. This road at present is barely passable to cars and even 4 WD vehicles, with sections having deep ruts, large exposed rocks, and large mud holes. On those rare occasions where you might find the old road open, you still may not want to risk getting your vehicle stuck. Leave it parked near Beech Gap and hike the road. The trail begins at vehicle barriers on the north side of the gap, opposite from where the road enters. The Fodderstack Trail enters the gap from the northeast; the South Fork Citico Creek Trail enters the gap from the northwest. Two other old roadbeds also enter the gap from the southwest and the southeast.

DETAILS: Follow the trail over the mounds of dirt that act as vehicle barriers. The flat, wide, gravel trail passes through mixed hardwoods and hemlock forest. At 0.75 mile one of the sources of the South Fork Citico Creek flows under the trail. The trail climbs after crossing the creek but soon levels off again. At 1.3 miles (UTM 16S 770416E/3918125N) there is a large clearing growing up in blackberries. In the summer of 2004, there was a huge blowdown in this clearing.

To the right, there is a newly reconstructed segment of the Benton MacKaye Trail. It follows the approximate route of the long-abandoned upper Brush Mountain Trail that connects with the Fodderstack Trail after 1.25 miles. To stay on the Cold Spring Gap Trail, bear left, work your way through the brush, and regain the old road bed. At 1.4 miles note a large hemlock growing to the left of the trail. (Note that at about this point, UTM 16S 770427E/3918109N, it appears that, judging from the flagging with plastic tape, someone is trying to relocate the trail off the old roadbed to cross the base of a long hairpin turn in the trail. This "shortcut" ends near UTM 16S 770404E/3918215N. However, we recommend that you stay on the roadbed. It is smoother going, and you will be less likely to miss the head of the Brush Mountain Trail.) At 1.5 miles reach another clearing growing up in blackberries; the Brush Mountain Trail enters this clearing from the left (16S 770210E/3918254N). Follow the Cold Spring Gap trail as it continues to curve around the mountain. (When we were mapping this trail with GPS tracking, we noted that in many places along the trail the map showed the trail being located slightly to the west or east of where it actually was. This is a good example of why you cannot take maps for granted).

At 1.7 miles an old roadbed comes in from the left to join the trail at a clearing. At 1.9 miles is a very large birch tree where a small stream crosses the trail. Shortly after the tree is another clearing. Through thick blackberries on the right of the trail is a roadbed that joins the abandoned connector trail that leads up the mountain to Fodderstack Trail. Another clearing occurs at 2.4 miles, and shortly afterward one of the headwater streams for the North Fork Citico Creek crosses under the trail. The trail goes through a grove of very large hemlocks at 2.6 miles. At 2.98 miles there is a small clearing with a fire ring. At 3.0 miles the trail narrows, passes over dirt vehicle barriers, and descends steeply to reach one of the main branches of the North Fork Citico Creek at 3.2 miles. The North Fork Citico Creek Trail has come up the stream from the left and proceeds upward to the right. This junction is at 4.84 miles on the North Fork Citico Creek Trail from the South Fork Citico Creek Trail Trailhead. Cherry Log Gap and the Fodderstack Trail are 0.6 mile to the right along the North Fork Citico Creek Trail.

109. JEFFREY HELL TRAIL (FS TRAIL 196, TI TRAIL 48)

LENGTH: 2.2 miles

ELEVATION CHANGE: Low point, 3,320 feet; high point, 3,960 feet

DIFFICULTY: Moderate

TRAILHEADS: Rattlesnake Rock Parking Area (start) and South Fork Citico Creek Trail (end)

USE: Hiking

TOPOGRAPHIC MAP: USGS Big Junction, TN

COMMENTS: The Jeffrey Hell Trail follows an old roadbed as it gradually descends through Jeffrey Hell toward the South Fork Citico Creek. Jeffrey Hell gets its name because of the dense growth of rhododendron and mountain laurel that makes off-trail hiking difficult. There is also the legend that a man named Jeffrey went looking for his hunting dogs in the area. Before he left, he made the statement, "I'll find them if I have to go to hell to get them." He was never seen again. The first part of the trail descends very gradually and is fairly easy hiking. However, the last 0.5 mile of the trail leaves the roadbed and heads very steeply downhill to intersect the South Fork Citico Creek Trail. There are few places to camp along the Jeffrey Hell Trail, but it is a good route to obtain access to the middle portion of the South Fork Citico Creek Trail quickly or when the lower portion of that trail is inaccessible because the creek is high.

The trail begins at a parking area on the left of the Cherohala Skyway (formerly the Tellico-Robbinsville Road) near Rattlesnake Rock, 8.4 miles east of the TN 165 and FS 345 junction. USFS hiker's signs with "No. 87" and "No. 196" can be seen at a trail leading from the west side of the overlook parking lot. There is abundant parking at the overlook.

DETAILS: The two trails head downhill together for a very short distance until they intersect an old roadbed. The Falls Branch Trail turns left. The Jeffrey Hell Trail turns sharply right and descends gradually along the roadbed past some rather large buckeye and silverbell trees. A stream passes under the trail at 0.5 mile through a culvert left from the old road. There is a rock wall bordering the trail across the stream. The stream, Falls Branch, flows down the small valley to Falls Branch Falls, which is accessed from the Falls Branch Trail. The Jeffrey Hell Trail continues around the contours of the mountain, heading in a generally northerly direction.

A grove of large hemlocks is passed to the left of the trail at 1.2 miles. An old road or trail can be seen to the left at 1.5 miles. A small clearing is reached at 1.7 miles. The old roadbed turns left to the southwest; the trail bears right, leaves the roadbed, and heads very steeply downhill to the northeast. As the trail descends the slope, turn east at a double-blazed tree. An old oil drum can be seen beside the trail. A small stream is reached at 1.8 miles. The trail is in and out of the water for the next 0.4 mile as the trail continues to descend the slope more gradually. Logging cables and cinders from the old tramway that came up the South Fork Citico Creek during logging days can be seen in this stretch of trail. An eroded streambed that contains considerable amounts of cinders is reached right before South Fork Citico Creek is crossed. The South Fork Citico Creek Trail is reached at 2.2 miles after the creek is crossed, a point 6.25 miles up the South Fork Citico Creek Trail from the Warden Station Area Trailhead.

21 Brushy Ridge

(Includes Brushy Ridge Roadless Area and Brushy Ridge Backcountry Area)

The 7,389-acre Brushy Ridge Roadless Area is overshadowed by the wilderness neighbors that it generally lies between, the Citico Creek Wilderness to the north and the Bald River Gorge Wilderness to the south. However, it contains some outstanding scenery and hiking in its own right. The roadless area was identified in the USFS's Southern Appalachian Assessment. Portions of that roadless area are protected in the CNF's 2004 plan revision as the 6,075-acre Brushy Ridge Backcountry Area. The area is bordered on the north by Sassafras Ridge and the Cherohala Skyway (also known as the Tellico-Robbinsville Road, especially when it was being constructed; in TN it is TN 165 and in NC it is NC 143). On the south, it is bordered by North River and the North River Road (FS 217). Between the Cherohala Skyway and North River Road is a beautiful area of forest, streams, and ridges. Six trails begin along the North River Road and ascend along stream valleys through the area to the Cherohala Skyway along Sassafras Ridge. These stream valleys are separated by ridges that intersect Sassafras Ridge at right angles. With vehicle shuttles, numerous hikes are possible from the Cherohala Skyway to the North River Road. The area is in Monroe County, TN, and the Tellico Ranger District.

The area is just south of the Cherohala Skyway and the Citico Creek Wilderness and shares many of the same plants and animals. Cove hardwood forest spreads up the stream valleys; oak complexes

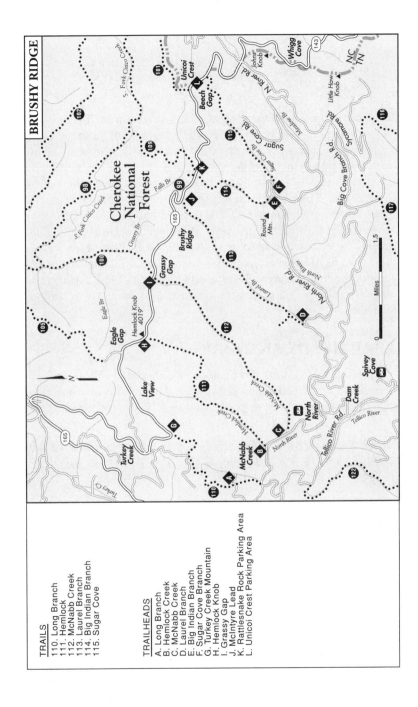

BRUSHY RIDGE

TRAILS

110. Long Branch
111. Hemlock
112: McNabb Creek
113: Laurel Branch
114: Big Indian Branch
115: Sugar Cove

TRAILHEADS

A. Long Branch
B. Hemlock Creek
C. McNabb Creek
D. Laurel Branch
E. Big Indian Branch
F. Sugar Cove Branch
G. Turkey Creek Mountain
H. Hemlock Knob
I. Grassy Gap
J. McIntyre Lead
K. Rattlesnake Rock Parking Area
L. Unicoi Crest Parking Area

dominate the slopes; pines are mixed with oaks on the ridges; and pines rule the dry south slopes.

HISTORY

Most of the area is covered in second-growth forest, having been logged extensively in the early twentieth century. Old narrow-gauge tramways from this period were used to harvest the timber. The rail beds from these tramways form the trails along the streams in the lower elevations of Brushy Ridge today. Construction on the Tellico-Robbinsville Road along the higher elevations of the area during the 1970s exposed iron pyrites that drained into Hemlock Creek and McNabb Creek, resulting in severe water-quality degradation in these streams. Neutralization structures have been built at the headwaters of these streams to help correct the problem. The CNF designated 4,220 acres of the roadless area as a primitive area in its 1988 management plan. A total of 6,075 acres is protected as a backcountry area in the CNF's 2004 plan revision.

TRAILHEADS AND MAPS

It is possible to access all of the trails in the area from either the North River Road or the Cherohala Skyway. For detailed alternate directions to the Cherohala Skyway, see the Citico Creek Wilderness section above.

North River Road Trailheads: Long Branch, Hemlock Creek, McNabb Creek, Laurel Branch, Big Indian Branch, and Sugar Cove Branch Trailheads

Turn off US 411 onto TN 68 in Madisonville, TN. Take TN 68 to Tellico Plains (approximately 14.0 miles). When TN 68 intersects TN 165 in the middle of Tellico Plains, take a left (east) on TN 165. This road, the Cherohala Skyway, continues past a group of stores and cabins and passes a CNF sign. The road runs along the south bank and then the north bank of the Tellico River. Shortly after passing the Ooesterneck Creek Parking Area at 5.4 miles, turn right onto the paved Tellico River Road (FS 210). Continue along the Tellico River Road past the Tellico Ranger Station and past Bald River Falls on the right. At 10.1 miles from TN 165, turn left off the Tellico River Road onto the North River Road (FS 217) just before a bridge. Long Branch Trailhead is 0.6 mile on the North River Road. Hemlock Creek Trailhead is 1.3 miles on the North River Road; McNabb Creek Trailhead is 1.7 miles on the North River Road; Laurel Branch Trailhead is 4.9

miles on the North River Road; Big Indian Branch Trailhead is 7.7 miles on the North River Road; and Sugar Cove Branch Trailhead is 8.0 miles on the North River Road. FS 217 can also be reached from the east by turning right (north) off the Tellico River Road onto FS 217 or by turning right off of TN 165 at Stratton Gap and then turning left to go under the bridge. Sugar Cove Trail is 4.7 miles from Stratton Gap on the North River Road.

Cherohala Skyway Trailheads: Turkey Creek Mountain, Hemlock Knob, Grassy Gap, McIntyre Lead, Rattlesnake Rock Parking Area, and Unicoi Crest Parking Area Trailheads

To access the trailheads along the Cherohala Skyway, stay on TN 165 when the Tellico River Road turns right just after the Ooesterneck Creek Parking Area and continue on TN 165 over rolling hills. At 15.0 miles TN 165 intersects with FS 345. This road leads to Indian Boundary Recreation Area. To reach trailheads along the Cherohala Skyway, continue along TN 165. From the intersection of TN 165E and FS 345, continue on TN 165E as it skirts the southern edge of the Citico Creek Wilderness. Numerous turnoffs along the road give spectacular views of the Citico watershed and of the Tellico Ranger District of the CNF. At 16.8 miles the Turkey Creek Overlook is on the right. The Turkey Creek Mountain Trailhead for the Long Branch Trail is 1.3 miles past the Turkey Creek Overlook on TN 165; the Hemlock Knob Trailhead is 2.4 miles from the Turkey Creek Overlook on TN 165; Grassy Gap and the McNabb Creek Trail are 4.6 miles from the Turkey Creek Overlook on TN 165; McIntyre Lead and the Laurel Branch Trail are 6.0 miles from the Turkey Creek Overlook on TN 165; Rattlesnake Rock Parking Area and the Big Indian Branch Trail are 6.7 miles from the Turkey Creek Overlook on TN 165; and the Unicoi Crest Parking Area and Sugar Cove Trail are 8.5 miles from the Turkey Creek Overlook on TN 165.

TOPOGRAPHIC MAPS: USGS Big Junction, TN-NC; Bald River Falls, TN-NC. TI Map 781, Tellico and Ocoee Rivers, CNF.

TRAIL DESCRIPTIONS

110. LONG BRANCH TRAIL (FS TRAIL 103, TI TRAIL 54)

LENGTH: 2.6 miles

ELEVATION CHANGE: Low point, 1,750 feet; high point, 2,900 feet

DIFFICULTY: Moderate

TRAILHEADS: Long Branch (start) and Turkey Creek Mountain (end)

USE: Hiking

TOPOGRAPHIC MAPS: USGS Big Junction, TN-NC; Bald River Falls, TN-NC

COMMENTS: Despite the name, the trail leaves Long Branch almost immediately, paralleling the creek from almost 0.25 mile away. This trail is easy to follow as it passes first through hemlock and rhododendron and then mostly through pine forests after it leaves the creek. The scars of forest fires are visible at 0.8 mile and 1.8 miles. After the first 0.1 mile, there is no water source on the trail.

DESCRIPTION: The Long Branch trail begins on the west side of Long Branch, heading north. After 100 feet, the trail turns west away from Long Branch and follows a small creek. After crossing the creek, the trail goes up a switchback at 0.3 mile. At 0.5 mile, it crosses directly over an old FS road. The trail climbs moderately up, curving in and out of small valleys. At 1.3 miles, the trail joins an old railroad grade and turns right for 80 feet. Then the trail turns left and goes uphill, leaving the railroad grade as it goes downhill and off to the right. At 1.8 miles there are good views to the south in an area of fire-scarred trees. The trail forks 100 feet after these views. The left fork goes uphill 200 feet to FS 2051A. The Long Branch Trail follows the right fork downhill for a short distance, then climbs to the east. At 2.3 miles, the trail turns north and parallels the ridge on the east side. The Turkey Creek Mountain Trailhead on Cherohala Skyway is reached at 2.6 miles at a large grassy area with ample parking.

III. HEMLOCK TRAIL (HEMLOCK CREEK TRAIL) (FS TRAIL 101, TI TRAIL 43)

LENGTH: 3.35 miles

ELEVATION CHANGE: Low point, 1,760 feet; high point, 3,800 feet

DIFFICULTY: Moderate

TRAILHEADS: Hemlock Creek (start) and Hemlock Knob (end)

USE: Hiking

TOPOGRAPHIC MAPS: USGS Big Junction, TN-NC; Bald River Falls, TN-NC

COMMENTS: This is a beautiful, gradual trail in its lower sections as it follows Hemlock Creek. The trail at this point follows an old roadbed or narrow-gauge rail bed. The trail crosses the creek a number of times before it veers away from the stream at about the halfway point. The last half of the trail is very steep, occasionally rocky, and largely unmaintained. There is no water on the last 1.25 miles of the trail. This is also known as Hemlock Creek Trail.

DETAILS: The trail begins on the north side of the road at a small parking area and a sign for FS Trail 101. Follow the nearly level trail as it passes through second-growth forest. At 0.35 mile, rock-hop across Hemlock Creek. Continue along the trail, making several easy crossings of Hemlock Creek and small side branches. At 0.74 the trail has been damaged by flood. It goes through a rocky, overgrown section on the left bank for 50 feet before rejoining the railroad grade. This is repeated at 0.84 mile at another flood-damaged section. There is a large flat area suitable for camping nearby. The trail continues along the creek, crossing several times as it begins a gentle ascent.

At 1.7 miles the old rail bed fades into a well-marked trail. At 1.8 miles, with the creek to the left, the trail angles sharply to the right. It ascends moderately up a ravine but quickly becomes much steeper. This section is quite strenuous and the trail is obscure. Stick to the ravine and look for white blazes on trees. At 2.0 miles the trail climbs up the side and crosses the top of a 10 foot waterfall. Continue following the drainage up to a spring at 2.1 miles.

The trail reaches a small saddle at 2.2 miles. Continue a more moderate ascent along a spur, coming to several small saddles. The trail along this section is better marked but begins to become overgrown. The trail stays on the ridge until it ends its ascent at 3.26 miles. The trail traverses left and leads through a tangle of thorns to Hemlock Knob and the Cherohala Skyway at 3.35 miles. The trail is marked by a sign for FS Trail 101. Parking is available along the shoulder of the road.

112. MCNABB CREEK TRAIL (FS TRAIL 92, TI TRAIL 56)

LENGTH: 3.7 miles

ELEVATION CHANGE: Low point, 1,800 feet; high point, 3,400 feet

DIFFICULTY: Moderate

TRAILHEADS: McNabb Creek (start) and Grassy Gap (end)

USE: Hiking

TOPOGRAPHIC MAPS: USGS Big Junction, TN-NC; Bald River Falls, TN-NC

COMMENTS: McNabb Creek Trail is a scenic trail that follows McNabb Creek for most of its distance. There are many creek crossings. The trail ascends gently for the first two-thirds of its length; it then becomes moderately steep for the last third. There is minor flood damage on the trail at 1.7 miles and 2.3 miles. The upper reaches of McNabb Creek, while appearing to be clear, are contaminated by acid drainage from iron pyrite exposed by the construction of the Tellico-Robbinsville Road.

DETAILS: The trail begins on the north side of the North River Road just past the McNabb Creek Group Camp. Follow the dirt road that turns off the road to the left, just before the bridge. The trail starts at the end of the turnaround loop and is marked by a sign for FS Trail 92. Follow the gently ascending trail as it follows an old railroad grade through second-growth forest of rhododendron and conifers. Frequent crossings of McNabb Creek, a beautiful mountain stream, require rock-hopping or shallow wading. Although water along these lower stretches may be drinkable, hikers should note the comments above on acid drainage.

At 0.03 mile there is a small campsite on the left. At 0.64 mile is a level campsite to the left of the trail next to the creek; there is another campsite at 1.88 miles, below the trail near the creek. At 2.4 miles the trail becomes rocky and overgrown. The trail becomes steep and the railroad grade ends. The trail turns right to join another railroad grade at 2.5 miles and then ascends more gradually. The McNabb Creek Valley becomes much narrower; this section is easy hiking.

At 2.9 miles the trail turns left to leave the railroad grade, ascends 20 feet, and then turns right to join another railroad grade. The trail is now passing through a mixed forest of hardwoods, conifers, and rhododendrons as it crosses the creek two more times. At 3.24 miles, after crossing a small branch, the trail begins a steep ascent. A rusted metal sign that says "Danger Contaminated Water Do Not Use" is encountered, after which you come to a small dam across McNabb Creek, which is much smaller at this point.

After crossing to the left side of the creek, at 3.4 miles cross back to the right, avoiding the faint trail that follows the creek. The rerouted trail follows a series of switchbacks up the right side of the creek before paralleling it from well above. The trail climbs gradually, eventually traversing the hillside on the east side of the creek, paralleling the highway for a short distance through open forest. At 3.6 miles the trail reaches a railroad grade and turns left. After 30 feet it turns to the right to leave the railroad grade and ascend the hillside. After 100 feet it switches back to the left and emerges on the Cherohala Skyway at 3.7 miles next to a sign for FS Trail 92, 10 feet behind the guardrail. There is a small area on the road shoulder for parking. About 150 yards west of the trailhead is a sign: "Grassy Gap— Elevation 3,400 feet." Grassy Gap provides beautiful views to the

Small cascade in the upper reaches of the McNabb Creek Trail in the Brushy Ridge Area. Photograph by Roger Jenkins.

south. A road at the gap heads down the north side of the ridge to a large parking area with a trailhead for the Grassy Branch Trail into Citico Creek Wilderness.

113. LAUREL BRANCH TRAIL (FS TRAIL 93, TI TRAIL 51)

LENGTH: 3.0 miles

ELEVATION CHANGE: Low point, 2,000 feet; high point, 3,800 feet

DIFFICULTY: Moderate

TRAILHEADS: Laurel Branch (start) and McIntyre Lead (end)

USE: Hiking

TOPOGRAPHIC MAP: USGS Big Junction, TN-NC

COMMENTS: Laurel Branch Trail is pleasant for the first two-thirds of its length and involves several stream crossings. The trail becomes fairly steep during the last third of its length. Good displays of spring wildflowers can be found.

DETAILS: The trail begins on the north side of the road at a bridge over Laurel Branch, where there is a sign designating FS Trail 93. Follow the trail, which follows an old rail bed, through second-growth forest consisting mostly of rhododendron and pine. After 50 yards, a small trail on the left leads to a campsite. At 0.1 mile, enter a small clearing. A side trail goes off to the left for 0.25 mile to a gate on North River Road, about 150 yards southwest of the trailhead. Laurel Branch Trail turns to the right and crosses the clearing. There are small wooden footbridges over Laurel Branch at 0.2 mile and 0.7 mile. The trail crosses the creek several times in the first 2.6 miles. These crossings are usually easily negotiated over rocks. At 1.4 miles, there is a storage tank and pipeline on the right. The trail leaves the old rail bed at 1.6 miles. The rail bed turns to the left and uphill, while Laurel Branch Trail veers to the right. The trail becomes less distinct in places but is clearly marked.

The trail crosses the branch several more times. At 2.5 miles the grade becomes considerably steeper. In the spring, this is a good section to see Dutchman's breeches, trillium, and wild geraniums.

The trail becomes more obscure at 2.6 miles; look carefully for trail blazes. The trail becomes steeper and is not graded or maintained, and during wet weather it would be difficult to negotiate. At 2.7 miles the trail goes through a series of switchbacks before crossing the spring where Laurel Branch begins. When leaves are off the trees during the winter, a good view down the valley can be glimpsed at 2.9 miles. The long, grassy trailhead parking area is reached at 3.0 miles on McIntyre Lead on the south side of Cherohala Skyway. A USFS sign designates FS Trail 93.

114. BIG INDIAN BRANCH TRAIL (FS TRAIL 94, TI TRAIL 11)

LENGTH: 1.7 miles

ELEVATION CHANGE: Low point, 2,600 feet; high point, 3,950 feet

DIFFICULTY: Moderate

TRAILHEADS: Big Indian Branch (start), Rattlesnake Rock Parking Area (end)

USE: Hiking

TOPOGRAPHIC MAP: USGS Big Junction, TN-NC

COMMENTS: This short climb makes up for its lack of distance with its diversity, splitting its length between mountainside, shoulder line, and stream, and passing through pine and hardwood forests. A small campsite is found just 250 feet from the beginning. Water is available for the first mile of the trail and also at 1.5 miles, from a small creek that may be unreliable during dry periods.

DETAILS: The trail begins on the north side of the road, just below Indian Branch, with a USFS sign designating FS Trail 94. It crosses over the earthen berm and follows the creek, crossing it several times in the first mile. At 1.0 mile, the trail turns left to leave Indian Branch and climbs up toward the shoulder. At 1.2 miles, the trail goes through switchbacks just before reaching the shoulder at a small gap. A faint trail leads off to the left (southwest). The Big Indian Branch Trail turns right to follow the top of the shoulder. At 1.3 miles, the trail leaves the top of the shoulder, curving to the right while continuing to climb. At 1.6 miles the trail goes through more switchbacks before reaching the end of the trail at 1.7 miles on the south side of the Cherohala Skyway. A USFS sign behind the guardrail designates FS Trail 94.

115. SUGAR COVE TRAIL (SUGAR COVE BRANCH TRAIL) (FS TRAIL 89, TI TRAIL 75)

LENGTH: 2.2 miles

ELEVATION CHANGE: Low point, 2,800 feet; high point, 4,450 feet

DIFFICULTY: Difficult

TRAILHEADS: Sugar Cove Branch (start), Unicoi Crest Parking Area (end)

USE: Hiking

TOPOGRAPHIC MAP: USGS Big Junction, TN-NC

COMMENTS: The first mile of Sugar Cove Branch Trail climbs moderately, but the last mile becomes very steep. Much of the trail passes through lush cove hardwood forest, paralleling the stream. This offers a cool respite from the heat of summer but may also be very overgrown. It is well marked in the overgrown areas and easy to follow. Water is available for all but the last 0.5 mile. There are no established campsites.

DESCRIPTION: Begin at the small pull-off 0.1 mile southwest of the bridge over Sugar Cove Branch. The trail starts on the south side of the road at a wooden sign for "Sugar Cove Trail No. 89." It begins by climbing east toward Sugar Cove Branch and then paralleling the stream from high above. The trail passes two cascades before crossing the creek at 0.5 mile.

The trail continues to follow Sugar Cove Branch until it turns left at 1.1 miles and climbs steeply to an old railroad grade. It then follows the railroad grade to the right until 1.4 miles, where it turns left again and leaves the railroad grade. While this area may be overgrown enough to obscure the trail in the summer, the trail is well marked. The trail continues to head east-northeast, paralleling the stream.

At 1.7 miles the trail turns right slightly to gain a small shoulder and then climbs very steeply straight up the shoulder to the end of the trail at 2.2 miles. The trail ends at the Unicoi Crest Parking Area on the Cherohala Skyway, just below the guardrail across the road from the north end of the parking area. It is marked with a USFS sign for FS Trail 89 and a wooden sign that says "Sugar Cove."

22 Sycamore Creek

(Includes Sycamore Creek Roadless Area and Sycamore Creek Backcountry Area)

The Sycamore Creek area is similar to the Brushy Ridge area in its proximity to other better-known protected areas and its location just south of the Cherohala Skyway. Much of the area is contained in a 6,994-acre roadless area identified by the USFS in its Southern Appalachian Assessment. Most of the roadless area is protected as a 6,284-acre backcountry area in the CNF's 2004 plan revision. The area is located in Monroe County, TN, and the Tellico Ranger District, in the uppermost reaches of the Tellico River, generally east of Tellico Plains. It is bounded on the east by the TN-NC state line and lies between FS 2417 and FS 61B to the north and Tellico River Road (FS 210) to the south. The steep mountain slopes are covered with typical southern Appalachian hardwoods, pine, rhododendron, dog hobble, mountain laurel, and a wide variety of other flora. The fall colors are gorgeous, and the area supports a wide variety of wildlife typical of the southern mountains of Appalachia, including the larger species such as black bear, deer, wild hogs, and possibly turkey. Hunting is a favorite activity in the area.

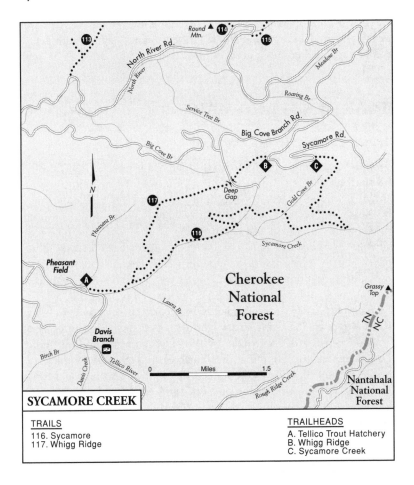

SYCAMORE CREEK

TRAILS
116. Sycamore
117. Whigg Ridge

TRAILHEADS
A. Tellico Trout Hatchery
B. Whigg Ridge
C. Sycamore Creek

There are two maintained trails in the area. Off-trail access is also available from the southeast from a dirt road along Rough Ridge Branch, starting from the end of the Tellico River Road, with a topographical map being essential. The Davis Creek, Big Oak Cove, and Stateline USFS campgrounds are near the area.

HISTORY

Like much of the Tellico River basin, the area was heavily logged in the early part of the twentieth century. However, it has recovered quite well from abusive logging practices of that time and provides a unique recreational opportunity without roads or trails. Nearby and just to the east of the area in NC's Nantahala NF is the Snowbird Creek Backcountry Area with over 30 miles of trails; that area can be reached by off-trail hiking. The 2,970-acre Rough Ridge Primitive Area was designated in the CNF's 1988 management plan. A significantly larger 6,284-acre backcountry area is protected in the CNF's 2004 plan revision.

TRAILHEADS AND MAPS

Tellico Trout Hatchery Trailhead

From I-75 turn onto TN 68 to go through Madisonville, TN. Take TN 68 to Tellico Plains (approximately 14.0 miles from Madisonville). When TN 68 intersects TN 165 in the middle of Tellico Plains, take a left (east) on TN 165. This road, the Cherohala Skyway, continues past a group of stores and cabins and passes a CNF sign. The road runs along the south bank and then the north bank of the Tellico River. Shortly after passing the Ooesterneck Creek Parking Area at 5.4 miles, turn right onto the paved Tellico River Road (FS 210). Continue on this road past the Tellico Ranger Station and past Bald River Falls on the right. At 10.1 miles from TN 165, pass the junction with North River Road (FS 217), staying straight to go over the bridge and stay on Tellico River Road. The road passes several campsites and the Tellico Lodge area before arriving at the Tellico Trout Hatchery on the left (a bridge crosses the river to the hatchery) and the Pheasant Field Picnic Area just beyond the bridge on both the left and right at 5.2 miles from the junction with North River Road. There is a large parking area for the picnic area on the left.

Sycamore Road Trailheads: Whigg Ridge and Sycamore Creek Trailheads

At the time of this writing, Sycamore Road (FS 61B) and Big Cove Branch Road (FS 61) were not accessible due to road construction on FS 61. FS 61 begins on the North River Road at 1.0 mile southwest of the junction of North River Road and Cherohala Skyway (also known as Tellico-Robbinsville Road). There are detailed instructions to this junction in the Brushy Ridge section above. From the junction of FS 61 and North River Road, FS 61 goes southwest for approximately 1.5 miles where the road splits. Big Cove Branch Road leads off to the right and Sycamore Road leads left. It is approximately 0.75 mile to the Whigg Ridge Trailhead and another 0.5 mile to the Sycamore Creek Trailhead.

TOPOGRAPHIC MAPS: USGS Big Junction, TN-NC. TI Map 781, Tellico and Ocoee Rivers, CNF.

TRAIL DESCRIPTIONS

116. SYCAMORE TRAIL (FS TRAIL 163, TI TRAIL 76)

LENGTH: 5.75 miles

ELEVATION CHANGE: Low point, 2,100 feet; high point, 4,250 feet

DIFFICULTY: Moderate

TRAILHEADS: Tellico Trout Hatchery (start) and Sycamore Creek (end)

USE: Hiking

TOPOGRAPHIC MAP: USGS Big Junction, TN-NC

COMMENTS: This is a very pleasant climb that winds moderately up through hardwood and hemlock forests, following an old railroad bed (and later a logging road) most of its distance. The trail is easy to follow, but is only intermittently marked with white blazes. There are two campsites along the trail. The first campsite is at 1.0 mile, which is large enough for about three tents, and the second is at 4.2 miles and is large enough for several tents lined up along the old roadbed. Reliable water sources are accessible regularly for the first mile and again at 4.2 miles. Less reliable water sources can be found at 2.75 miles, 3.25 miles, and possibly 5.5 miles.

DETAILS: The Sycamore Trail begins as a gravel road on the far side of the bridge to the Tellico Trout Hatchery. A USFS trailhead marker and a gate show the beginning of the trail as it follows the Tellico River a short distance upstream before slightly turning to follow Sycamore Creek. A cabin is located on the other side of the creek, near the mouth. The gravel road quickly reaches a junction with several jeep trails and ends near a small dam at 0.1 mile; the foot trail only begins at this point. The trail passes through/over several rock/earth berm ORV barriers during the first mile. Whigg Ridge Trail begins on the left at 0.4 mile at a USFS trailhead marker. Sycamore Trail continues climbing gradually, paralleling Sycamore Creek through rhododendrons and hardwoods, passing a campsite at 1.0 mile.

At 1.9 miles, the trail and the roadbed it is following switchback to the left, about 100 yards past an old iron rail with the stamp "Roane Steel 1880" and just after crossing a small side creek. Be careful to turn left here, as a small but clear trail continues alongside Sycamore Creek straight ahead; it will probably be blocked by a few branches people have placed on the ground. The roadbed splits at 2.25 miles but comes together again a short distance later before a sharp switchback to the right; an old road continues straight ahead. As you make the turn to the right, look for three blazes carved on a tree. The middle one has the numbers "165" and "U" shaped arrows. At 3.0 miles the roadbed splits again. This time the right fork goes downhill steeply to the southeast, while the Sycamore Trail follows the left fork uphill. The trail reaches a small gap at 3.5 miles, where the roadbed forks again. The Sycamore Trail follows the left fork and follows the contour for a while before beginning to climb again.

At 4.2 miles the roadbed forks at a switchback. The Sycamore Trail follows the left fork around the switchback, while the right fork leads straight approximately 0.1 mile to a campsite alongside Sycamore Creek. That campsite is a wonderful place, with level sites located on the old roadbed overlooking Sycamore Creek and the junction of a couple of streams that cascade into a pool just above the camp. Note an old foot bridge (two logs and a cable) just below the pool; available maps provide no clue as to the destination of the now grown-over trail on the other side of the bridge. The Sycamore Trail continues to climb moderately to 4.75 miles, where it rounds the end of a shoulder and then climbs the last mile to the trailhead on the gravel Sycamore Road (FS 61B) at 5.75 miles. It reaches the trailhead on a grassy roadbed that climbs up from below the trailhead to a junction with a jeep trail that enters from the east. From the trailhead, Sycamore Road goes uphill (dead-end) to the northwest and downhill (toward FS 61) to the southwest. There is enough parking for about four cars. The Whigg Ridge trailhead is 0.5 mile downhill on Sycamore Road.

117. WHIGG RIDGE TRAIL (FS TRAIL 86, TI TRAIL 84)

LENGTH: 3.0 miles

ELEVATION CHANGE: Low point, 2,200 feet; high point, 4,050 feet

DIFFICULTY: Difficult

TRAILHEADS: Sycamore Trail (start) and Whigg Ridge (end)

USE: Hiking

TOPOGRAPHIC MAP: USGS Big Junction, TN-NC

COMMENTS: The Whigg Ridge Trail climbs steeply first through rhododendron and hardwoods before passing through a pine forest that has been heavily damaged by the pine bark beetle. Downed trees are common in this area and may require detours or scrambling. The pines give way to hardwoods and hemlocks as the trail gets closer to the rocky ridgeline. This is a fairly obvious trail for most of its length and is well marked with white blazes. There are no reliable water sources along the trail and no established campsites.

DETAILS: Whigg Ridge Trail begins at 0.4 mile up the Sycamore Trail at a USFS trail marker. It begins by climbing steeply a short distance and then curving to the right to climb moderately along the mountainside before entering a small valley. At the top of the valley, the trail turns sharply to the right and then again to the left to leave the valley at 0.3 mile and climb more steeply along the shoulder. For several hundred yards the blowdowns are rather severe and make for

View from Whigg Meadow at the upper end of the Sycamore Creek drainage after an early snow. Photograph by Betty Petty.

difficult walking in 2003. The blowdowns resulted from southern pine beetle infestation. At 1.2 miles the trail turns slightly left to begin climbing along the side of the mountain until it reaches a small gap at 1.6 miles. From the gap the Whigg Ridge Trail turns right to follow the ridge for the remainder of the trail. At 2.2 miles it crosses over the gated section of Big Cove Branch Road at Deep Gap and begins to climb very steeply up a series of short switchbacks. At 2.8 miles the Whigg Ridge Trail levels before reaching the end of the trail at Sycamore Road at 3.0 miles. The parking area is 300 feet to the right with plenty of parking.

OFF-TRAIL HIKING OPPORTUNITIES

To gain off-trail access into the area from the south, continue up the Tellico River road about 3.0 miles from the Tellico Trout Hatchery Trailhead and bridge to near the TN-NC state line and the USFS Stateline Campground, where there is adequate parking. The Tellico River Road is on the north side of the river at this point. The dirt log-

Day hiker enjoys the views from Whigg Meadow, at the upper end of the Sycamore Creek drainage. Photograph by Roger Jenkins.

ging road (FS 210G) up Rough Ridge Creek, which is closed to public vehicles, goes northeast from the Tellico River Road, starting just west of Rough Ridge Branch, and provides access to the area from the southeast. There are no maintained trails in this area.

23 Bald River

(Includes Bald River Gorge Wilderness, Upper Bald River Wilderness Study Area, Bald River Gorge Backcountry Area, and Bald River Roadless Area)

The Bald River watershed is one of the true gems of the CNF, with almost an entire watershed above the scenic Bald River Falls protected in various types of land management categories. The 3,721-acre Bald River Gorge Wilderness is the most accessible portion of the area, but there is much more. The USFS in its Southern Appalachian Assessment identified a total of 9,112 acres in the Bald River Roadless Area. The CNF's 2004 plan revision provides for the protection of a 1,735-acre Bald River Gorge Backcountry Area and a 9,112-acre Upper Bald River Wilderness Study Area. These areas together mean that this huge Bald River watershed is essentially protected from logging and additional road building, except for 175 privately owned acres near Sandy Gap. This watershed is in the upper region of the Tellico River basin, generally east of Tellico Plains in Monroe County, TN, and in the Tellico Ranger District. The wilderness is the steep-sided gorge north of FS 126, extending north to, but not including, a few acres around Bald River Falls at FS 210. The wilderness study area includes the watershed basin south of FS 126.

The large size and outstanding beauty of the area make the watershed a significant recreation, wildlife, and scientific resource. Little Bald, Beaverdam Bald, Sled Runner Gap, Rocky Top, Round Top, Hazelnut Knob, and Sandy Gap are landmarks located on the TN-NC state line ridge, which forms the southern boundary. Waucheesi Bald, which dominates the high ridgeline to the southwest, is accessible by car from Basin Gap. Sandy Gap is accessible by car from TN 68 at the Hiwassee River using USFS roads in the Shuler Creek watershed.

Bald River, originating on the north side of Little Bald at the southeast corner of the area, is relatively small but is clean, cold, fast-moving, and very attractive. Several tributaries such as Henderson Branch, Brookshire Creek, Kirkland Creek, Waucheesi Creek, and Big Cove Branch contribute their share of clean, cold water. Cascades are

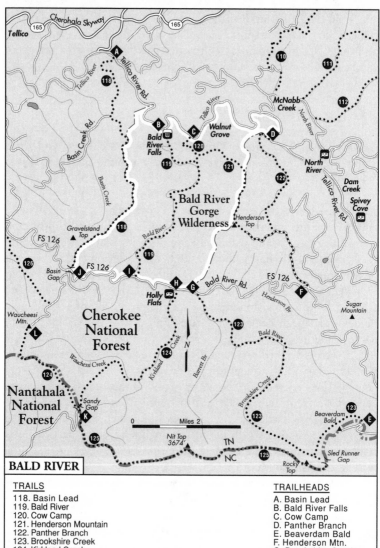

BALD RIVER

TRAILS
118. Basin Lead
119. Bald River
120. Cow Camp
121. Henderson Mountain
122. Panther Branch
123. Brookshire Creek
124. Kirkland Creek
125. State Line

TRAILHEADS
A. Basin Lead
B. Bald River Falls
C. Cow Camp
D. Panther Branch
E. Beaverdam Bald
F. Henderson Mtn.
G. Brookshire Creek
H. Kirkland Creek
I. Cantrell Parking Area
J. Basin Gap
K. Sandy Gap
L. Waucheesi Mtn.

numerous, contributing significantly to the beauty of the area. Trout thrive here, as do trout fishermen who prefer a challenge in a wilderness setting. During late fall and early winter, hunting is a major activity in the area.

The mountain slopes are covered with typical southern Appalachian hardwoods, pine, rhododendron, dog hobble, mountain laurel, and a wide variety of other flora. Wildflowers are plentiful and the fall colors are gorgeous. The area supports a wide variety of wildlife typically found in the southern Appalachians, including large species such as black bear, deer, wild hogs, and turkey.

Bald River Falls, at the north end of Bald River (just outside of the wilderness), where it flows under the Tellico River Road, is one of the most impressive waterfalls in TN. The Bald River Trailhead is here, and this trail is the most heavily used in the area. FS 126, a gravel road passable by cars, traverses the area from Green Cove Gap on the east to Basin Gap on the west. Holly Flats Campground is on this road, which provides good access to the Upper Bald River Area where the Brookshire Creek Trail and the Kirkland Creek Trail are located. Located to the northeast of Henderson Top (Henderson Mountain) there is a small watershed with a very good trail, Panther Branch.

Fisherman risks slippery footing at the base of Bald River Falls. Photograph by E. Kenneth McDonald.

Note that TI Trail 42, Gravelstand Top, located just west of the Basin Lead Trail and outside of the Bald River Gorge Wilderness, is incorrectly shown on the TI map as a hiking trail. It is an official motorized trail for all-terrain vehicles.

HISTORY

Much of this area was logged during the early part of the twentieth century, utilizing a railroad extending up the Tellico River. The major timber company was Babcock Lumber Company, owned by two brothers from Pittsburgh, PA. Starting at the railhead of the Tellico railroad in 1905, they pushed their logging railway up the gorge of the Tellico River to Bald River. The railroad into the Bald River watershed left the main track on the Tellico River a short distance below Bald River Falls, gaining elevation to get above the falls and the cliff on the west side of the falls. They constructed a trestle across the river well above the falls and continued construction upstream to the headwaters of Bald River and several of its tributaries. The trail that now follows the river and the two major trails in the area use much of this old logging grade. When the timber in the Bald River watershed was cut, the railroad was continued up the Tellico to North River and so on until virtually all the drainage basin of the Tellico River was cut.

Beaverdam Bald above the Bald River watershed. Photograph by Will Skelton.

Farming in this remote area was impractical even for the hardy mountaineers that inhabited this region of TN and NC in bygone days. There is no obvious evidence of farming in the gorge area along the Bald River Trail, but the lay of the land along FS 126 and in the small valleys south of this road is such that it could have supported subsistence mountain farms, as did most of the Appalachian Mountains. There is evidence today that such a farm did exist in the headwaters of Brookshire Creek near Beaverdam Bald, and two other remote cabin sites are found on Brookshire Creek. An area-wide archaeological survey would probably disclose further evidence of other mountain farms, logging camps, and possibly sites used by the Cherokee Indians. One Cherokee cemetery is reported to be located on Indian Ridge, which is between Kirkland and Brookshire Creeks.

With the depletion of timber resources and the withdrawal of logging railroads, the area recovered its wilderness character. Some timber harvesting has occurred since the 1960s: several clear-cuts south of Henderson Top and a clear-cut in the head of Bald River. Efforts to protect the entire watershed under the provisions of the Wilderness Act of 1964 began in the early 1970s but were unsuccessful. After a lengthy struggle by conservationists, the 3,721-acre Bald River Gorge Wilderness was added to the wilderness system in 1984 and 10,460 acres were designated as primitive areas in the CNF's 1988 management plan

View of the Upper Bald River watershed after a rain. Photograph by Roger Jenkins.

(although portions allowed limited timber harvesting). The CNF's 2004 plan revision provides for the protection of most of the prior primitive areas, but as a wilderness study area and a backcountry area.

The area is popular for hunting, fishing, camping, hiking, horseback riding, and pleasure driving on FS 126. The trails in the area utilize many of the old logging grades, except for the Cow Camp and Henderson Mountain trails. NC's Nantahala NF Trail 82 borders the roadless area on the state line ridge from Sled Runner Gap to Sandy Gap and makes loop trips possible. This trail, although virtually unmaintained by the USFS, is easy to follow by experienced hikers from Sled Runner Gap, just south of Beaverdam Bald, to Sandy Gap. The trail is generally described in the descriptions of the Brookshire Creek and Kirkland Creek trails.

TRAILHEADS AND MAPS

The trails are described from their low-elevation ends, the most practical starting point. Most of the trailheads are located on the paved Tellico River Road (FS 210) and the unpaved FS 126, the east end of which connects to FS 210. This junction is about 19.0 miles upstream on the Tellico River Road from the west side of Tellico Plains at the intersection of TN 68 and TN 165. Driving directions for these trailheads start at this intersection. The Beaverdam Bald Trailhead, which provides access to the south end of the Brookshire Creek Trail and east end of the State Line Trail (FS Trail 82), a Nantahala NF Trail, is described from the intersection of FS 24 with FS 210 near the Big Oak Grove Campground on the Tellico River. The trailhead for the west end of the State Line Trail and the south end of the Kirkland Creek Trail at Sandy Gap is described from the intersection of the Shuler Creek Road with TN 68 where TN 68 crosses the Hiwassee River.

Tellico River Road (FS 210) Trailheads

From the intersection of TN 165 and TN 68 on the west side of Tellico Plains, TN, follow TN 165 up the Tellico River to a junction at mile 5.2. This is the intersection of TN 165 and FS 210, the Tellico River Road. The following trailheads are along FS 210.

BASIN LEAD TRAILHEAD

Keep right up the Tellico River on FS 210, 4.4 miles to Turkey Creek where there is a small parking area. Turkey Creek flows under a small bridge at this location. About 200 feet downstream below this confluence the piers of a former footbridge can be found, and you may still see remnants of the former bridge on the riverbank across the river. The north end of the Basin Lead Trail is directly across the river at the piers.

The bridge was washed out in the early 1990s, and according to the District Ranger the CNF does not intend to replace it. Replacing the bridge is expensive, but the CNF could relocate the lower (north) end of the Basin Lead Trail by moving the trailhead upstream about 0.9 mile, where FS 210 crosses the Tellico River. At this point they could construct a short length of trail going uphill and northwest to connect to the current Basin Lead Trail. This relocated section would be much less than 0.9 mile in length, since the lower end of the trail at the river goes uphill to the southeast. There is ample parking for this relocated trailhead.

A loop trip can be made using this trail and the Bald River Trail that is 1.9 miles farther up the river, at Bald River Falls. The parking area for the south end of both of these trails is on FS 126 and is also 1.9 miles apart. For a loop trip, start at the lower end of the Basin Lead Trail (Tellico River end) and go up the Basin Lead Trail to Basin Gap, at FS 126. Travel east on FS 126 to the Bald River Trail. Follow this trail to Bald River Falls, at FS 210, the Tellico River Road. A car shuttle between the two trailheads on FS 210 is desirable.

BALD RIVER FALLS TRAILHEAD

From the Basin Lead Trailhead described above, continue up the Tellico River 1.9 miles to a small parking area on the east side (upriver) of Bald River Falls. You cannot miss the falls. A large sign marks the location of parking for the Bald River Falls Picnic Area. Trail marker 88 marks the north end of the Bald River Trail (FS Trail 88). Primitive toilet facilities are available here. In late spring, summer, and early fall, it may be difficult to find a parking space. Roadside parking, where the shoulder permits, is usually acceptable. The trailhead is 11.4 miles from the west side of Tellico Plains. The south end of the trail is on FS 126 just east of where the Bald River flows under this road. The trailhead for this end is on the west side of the bridge and is called the Cantrell Parking Area Trailhead.

COW CAMP TRAILHEAD

Continue on FS 210 about 1.0 mile upstream from the Bald River Falls Trailhead to a bridge and cross the bridge to the east (upstream) end to park. This trailhead is 12.4 miles from the intersection of TN 68 and TN 165 on the west side of Tellico Plains. Park on the shoulder between the pavement and the river. There is parking space for about four cars here but no facilities. A smaller parking area is on the shoulder about 100 feet downstream of the bridge. The north end of the trail is behind the guardrail at the west (downstream) end of the bridge. A small trail marker identifies this as FS Trail 173, and a small wooden stairway behind the guardrail helps you over a steep embankment onto the trail proper. This trailhead also serves as the trailhead for the Henderson Mountain Trail. The north end of the Henderson Mountain Trail is at an unmarked junction, with the Cow Camp Trail on the ridgecrest about 0.6 mile from the Tellico River Road.

PANTHER BRANCH TRAILHEAD

The Panther Branch Trailhead provides access to FS Trail 162 from the Tellico River Road 15.8 miles from the junction of TN 68 and TN 165 on the west side of Tellico Plains. There is plenty of parking space, and a footbridge provides an easy crossing of the Tellico River. This trail, the Henderson Mountain Trail, and the Cow Camp Trail make a good loop, but a car shuttle is advised, since there are 3.4 miles of road between the two trailheads on the river. If you are hiking the loop, start at the Cow Camp Trailhead, go up the Cow Camp Trail to the junction with the Henderson Mountain Trail, follow the Henderson Mountain Trail to the south end of the Panther Branch Trail, then go down the Panther Branch Trail to the trailhead on the Tellico River. The junction of the Henderson Mountain Trail with the south end of the Panther Branch Trail is on a logging road, FS 40832, a part of which is also a part of the Henderson Mountain Trail.

BEAVERDAM BALD TRAILHEAD

Beaverdam Bald is reached by FS 24, a rough, unpaved road, from FS 210, the Tellico River Road. This end of FS 24 is about 22.2 miles from the intersection of TN 68 and TN 165 on the west side of Tellico Plains and a high clearance vehicle is needed. This road leaves FS 210 near the Big Oak Cove Campground, proceeds generally south to the TN-NC state line, then generally west along the state line, past Little Bald and Grassy Gap to Beaverdam Bald. The distance from the Tellico River is unknown, and a USFS map may be necessary to follow this road. On the east side of Beaverdam Bald the road forks, with the left fork going to the top of Beaverdam Bald at elevation 4,259 feet, where there is a wildlife management clearing. Take the right fork, which ends shortly at another wildlife management clearing. Park here at the edge of the clearing. The trail sign marking the south end of the Brookshire Creek Trail is directly ahead, across the saddle at about 3,960 feet elevation. This saddle is a good campsite for backpackers making a loop from the Bald River using the Brookshire Creek Trail, the State Line Trail, and the Kirkland Creek Trail.

This trailhead provides access to the State Line Trail, FS Trail 82, at Sled Runner Gap. To reach the State Line Trail follow the Brookshire Creek Trail around Beaverdam Bald about 0.4 mile, where this trail makes a sharp right turn. Just before this turn a path to the left goes about 0.1 mile, generally southeast to Sled Runner Gap. Here an old ORV trail enters from the east and continues north to Beaverdam Bald. An unmarked trail goes generally south and swings to the west. This is the State Line Trail, FS Trail 82, which leads to Sandy Gap at the south end of the Kirkland Creek Trail.

Upper Bald River Road (FS 126) Trailheads

Follow TN 165 from the intersection of TN 68 and TN 165 on the west side of Tellico Plains, 5.2 miles to the junction of this highway and FS 210, the Tellico River road. Turn on FS 210 and follow it another 13.8 miles to FS 126 and turn right on this road. This is 19.0 miles from Tellico Plains. The Holly Flats Campground is located on FS 126 about 5.4 miles from FS 210, between Kirkland Creek and the Cantrell Parking Area Trailheads. It is a good place to stay overnight and day hike the Bald River, Brookshire Creek, and Kirkland Creek Trails. There is a fee charged for camping in the campground. The following trailheads are on FS 126.

HENDERSON MOUNTAIN TRAILHEAD

Follow FS 126 to the top of the ridge, 2.1 miles from FS 210. This is the Henderson Mountain Trailhead. Gated logging roads are on both sides of FS 126. On the right (north) is FS 40832, which is also a part of the Henderson Mountain Trail, (FS Trail 107). There is plenty of parking space.

BROOKSHIRE CREEK TRAILHEAD

Follow FS 126 to the top of the ridge at 2.1 miles from FS 210 and continue straight ahead 3.0 miles to a clearing where the Brookshire Creek Trail is on the left (south) side of the road at the confluence of Henderson Branch and Bald River. This is 24.1 miles from the intersection of TN 68 and TN 165 on the west side of Tellico Plains. A trail marker identifies this trail as FS Trail 180. Primitive camping is permitted here and there is considerable evidence of such camping; there are no facilities. For a backpacking loop trip, use this trail, the State Line Trail (Nantahala NF Trail FS 82), and the Kirkland Creek Trail

(FS Trail 85). The Kirkland Creek Trailhead on FS 126 is only 0.4 mile downstream from the Brookshire Creek Trailhead on FS 126.

KIRKLAND CREEK TRAILHEAD

Follow FS 126 to the top of the ridge at 2.1 miles from FS 210 and continue straight ahead 3.4 miles to a small parking area on the left (south) side of the road near the confluence of Kirkland Creek and Bald River. A trail marker identifies this trail as FS Trail 85. If you are making the loop trip mentioned above, you will arrive at FS 126 here and walk upstream on the road 0.4 mile to the starting point.

CANTRELL PARKING AREA TRAILHEAD

Follow FS 126 to the top of the ridge at 2.1 miles from FS 210 and continue straight ahead 4.3 miles to a parking area on the right (north) side of the road immediately after crossing Bald River on a small bridge. The south end of the Bald River Trail is back upstream of the bridge about 100 feet (6.4 miles from FS 210), where a trail marker identifies this trail as FS Trail 88. A sign also says that the trail is maintained by a Boy Scout troop from Chattanooga.

BASIN GAP TRAILHEAD

Follow FS 126 to the top of the ridge at 2.1 miles from FS 210 and continue straight ahead 4.3 miles to a parking area on the right (north) side of the road immediately after crossing Bald River on a small bridge. This is the Cantrell Parking Area Trailhead. The Holly Flats Campground was passed at 5.9 miles from FS 210. Continue on FS 126 uphill 1.9 miles to the top of the ridge at Basin Gap. On the right (north side) is the south end of the Basin Lead Trail, FS Trail 161, which at this point is an old logging grade. Parking space is adequate. On the left (south side) are two USFS roads that have a common junction with FS 126. The westernmost, and most used of these, is FS 126C, which is the access road to Waucheesi Mountain and the Warrior Passage Trail's southern end.

WAUCHEESI MOUNTAIN ROAD TRAILHEAD

From the Basin Gap Trailhead described above, drive up FS 126C. The road is sometimes gated but is generally open. It is suitable for 2 WD vehicles if you drive with care. At 0.8 miles the Warrior's Passage Trail descends steeply to the right; there are a couple of signs indicating the trail. At 1.3 miles on the right are several communications towers. The summit is reached at 1.6 miles. A large grassy area has been cleared on the summit, and there is another communications tower and a small cinderblock building on the north side of the summit.

SANDY GAP TRAILHEAD (ACCESS FROM TN 68)

Sandy Gap is the trailhead for two trails, the south end of the Kirkland Creek Trail and the west end of the Nantahala NF Trail 82. The access road to Sandy Gap turns off of TN 68 at an unmarked junction at the north end of the Hiwassee River bridge, 1.5 miles north of the Farner, TN post office, and 1.1 miles southeast of the Womble Branch Trailhead for the John Muir Trail. This junction is in TN (mile 0.0) and is also Monroe County Road 37, and FS 311. The road proceeds up the Hiwassee River, which is somewhat difficult to see when leaves are present, and at mile 2.0 a sign announces that you are leaving the CNF. This is very close to the state line. At the unmarked state line this road becomes NC state road 1322 (SR 1322) and at mile 2.3 it bears away from the river, turning up Shuler Creek. You are in NC at this point, and the road to Sandy Gap remains in NC to its end at Sandy Gap on the state line.

At mile 3.8 the road splits and to the right is a small bridge. A sign at the split refers to the Appalachian Baptist Church, but no church is in sight. About 150 feet straight ahead (the left branch of this junction) a sign marks Shuler Creek Road and SR 1322. Follow Shuler Creek Road. A gate identifying the entrance to Circle Valley Ranch is on the right side of the road at mile 5.5. At mile 7.1 the Joe Brown Highway, SR 1326, comes in from the left, continues ahead about 300 feet with Shuler Creek Road and turns right. This is the end of Shuler Creek Road. A sign indicates that Burrell Mountain Road, SR 1325, continues straight ahead. Take this road, continuing upstream. A road to the left at mile 9.4 is FS 62. Continue on Burrell Mountain Road to a junction at mile 9.6, where it bears right across a bridge. To the left is Evans Road, SR 1327, and a No Outlet sign. Take Evans Road. At mile 10.0 is a sign saying that you are entering the Nantahala NF, and at mile 10.4 the road divides. Evans Road, SR 1327, is to the left and Quinn Road, SR 1328, is to the right. Continue on Evans Road. About 100 feet ahead a small sign identifies Evans Road as FS 50. Continue to Sandy Gap at mile 13.8.

As you drive into the gap the State Line Trail, Nantahala NF Trail 82, is to the right (generally southeast), and at this point it is an ORV trail unidentified by either a road or a trail number. Straight ahead (generally east) is the long abandoned Kirkland Creek Trail descending steeply down the side of the ridge. To the left (generally northwest) on a relatively level old logging grade, is the Kirkland Creek Trail (FS Trail 85), where there is a trail marker. Going uphill northwest is another long abandoned trail and logging grade that leads to Waucheesi Mountain.

TOPOGRAPHIC MAPS: USGS Bald River Falls, TN-NC; Unaka, TN-NC. TI Map 781, Tellico and Ocoee Rivers, CNF.

TRAIL DESCRIPTIONS

118. BASIN LEAD TRAIL (BASIN GAP TRAIL) (FS TRAIL 161, TI TRAIL 4)

LENGTH: 6.1 miles

ELEVATION CHANGE: Low point, 1,300 feet; high point, 2,940 feet

DIFFICULTY: Difficult

TRAILHEADS: Basin Lead (start); Basin Gap (end)

USE: Hiking

TOPOGRAPHIC MAP: USGS Bald River Falls, TN-NC

COMMENTS: Many of the trails in the CNF are either poorly maintained or not maintained at all. The Basin Lead Trail is in the latter category. In fact it does not appear to have been maintained since it was officially designated as a CNF trail. Aged blazes (paint or ax) occasionally exist, with long stretches in between, where the obscure trail is little more than a wildlife track or on an old logging grade with unmarked junctions. It is a trail for the experienced off-trail hiker who does not object to going through, over, under, and around blowdowns or to searching for obscure and sometimes non-existent trails. Aged ax-cuts or badly peeled paint blazes on dead trees, and the saw-cut ends of blowdowns that appear to be decades old, are clues to the trail's location. It is suggested that the hiker travel with a companion who has the right attitude about off-trail hiking. Start early and plan to finish late. Carry a 1:24,000 scale topographical map with contour intervals no greater than 40 feet (other maps are inadequate). If you have a GPS unit, use it to at least know where you are if you lose the trail. Have fun.

A loop can be made using this trail, FS 126 going between the Basin Gap Trailhead and the south end of the Bald River Trail, the Bald River Trail to FS 210 (Tellico River Road) and, FS 210 from Bald River Falls downstream to the starting point.

DETAILS: Your first obstacle is to wade the Tellico River, which can be dangerous during high water levels. Wade it close to its confluence with Turkey Creek and follow the river bank downstream to the broken bridge piers or the end of the former bridge remnants if they are still there (mile 0.0). A pair of sandals or wading shoes are advised for making this crossing. Search for the end of the trail on the bank at the former bridge piers and begin traversing around the mountain going upstream while gaining elevation. Several switchbacks are made as the trail gains elevation, and at mile 1.9 a ridgecrest is reached where there is little or no slope for a short distance. In many places the trail is very obscure and difficult to find even when there are no leaves on the trees and the low-growing plants have succumbed to cold weather. Occasional blazes, as described above, are found. Blowdowns are plentiful. About 200 feet farther an old firebreak is reached that follows the ridgetop. Another 600 feet brings you to the point where the firebreak leaves the ridgetop (goes downhill to the west) and there is no evidence of a trail in the dead and living brush and blackberry vines.

Stay with the ridgetop until the grade steepens at mile 2.1 and look for obscure signs of the trail going straight uphill. At the time this trail was last measured there was a very old, badly peeled white blaze on a small dead pine. It may have fallen by the time you read this. Continue uphill about 100 feet and again look for the very obscure trail, bearing left (east) around the ridge and gaining elevation. You are now going around a small knob. At mile 2.3 you may see there is an old blaze on a pine on the side of the ridge. If the leaves have fallen, you can see the Tellico River by looking back. You reach a small gap at mile 2.6. About 300 feet ahead from the small gap is an old logging road that leads to a higher point on the ridge at mile 3.1. Follow this old road.

After going down an easy grade to a small gap at mile 3.2 another old logging road joins this trail and is on the right (west) side. Go left around the knob. At mile 3.9 is a small gap where the larger, more recently constructed logging road bears right (generally west) around the ridge on a relatively level grade. A much older and smaller logging grade with some obstructions also bears right around the ridge but gains elevation to go around a knob; follow this one. At mile 4.2 on this logging grade, the grade and the trail disappears. Continue ahead on the right (west) side of a rock outcrop and look for a very obscure trail going around the knob, bearing generally southeast, and descending to a gap. Descend to the gap and continue down on the east side of the gap to an old logging grade. This is mile 4.3. If you have made it this far, the remainder of the trip is easy. Continue on this logging grade to mile 6.1, Basin Gap.

119. BALD RIVER TRAIL (FS TRAIL 88, TI TRAIL 3)

LENGTH: 4.8 miles

ELEVATION CHANGE: Low point, 1,380 feet; high point, 1,860 feet

DIFFICULTY: Easy

TRAILHEADS: Bald River Falls (start); Cantrell Parking Area (end)

TRAIL CONNECTIONS: Cow Camp Trail

USE: Hiking

TOPOGRAPHIC MAP: USGS Bald River Falls, TN-NC

COMMENTS: If you are hiking only the Bald River Trail, it is suggested that you start at the Bald River Falls Trailhead. The lower end of it can be used in combination with the Cow Camp Trail for a short loop or the Basin Lead Trail and FS 126 for a much longer loop.

The trail passes through a largely deciduous forest with some white pine and hemlock mixed in. Rhododendron, mountain laurel, and dog hobble, along with conifers, provide an adequate amount of green color in winter. The trail utilizes an old logging grade in some locations, but other parts of it are a narrow tread. The logging railroad that went up this river switched back and forth across the waterway to avoid large cuts for the roadbed in very steep riverbanks. To avoid trail bridges, which are subject to being washed out and are costly to maintain, the trail stays on the east bank and uses the former logging grade when it is on the east side of the river. The rhododendron encroaches on the trail in some locations but is not a serious problem. Wildflowers and fall colors adorn the landscape in season.

Easy access to the river is provided for those who trout fish. The river is small but relatively clean since there is only one small campground and an unpaved road, FS 126, upstream. It tumbles over numerous cascades and rock ledges on its way to the Tellico River. Several small sites suitable for backpacking campsites exist along the river. This trail receives heavy use except in late fall, winter, and early spring.

To make a loop hike using the Basin Lead Trail, start on the Basin Lead Trail (see the description of that trail). A short loop hike can be make starting on this trail (Bald River Trail) at Bald River Falls, going up it 1.4 miles to an unmarked trail junction with the Cow Camp Trail. Turn north here and follow the Cow Camp Trail 0.25 mile up to the crest of the ridge where there is an unmarked junction with the north end of the Henderson Mountain Trail (FS Trail 107). It is then downhill to the Tellico River Road and 0.9 mile downriver on the road to the Bald River Falls Trailhead. See the description of the Cow Camp Trail.

DETAILS: Starting at the trailhead (mile 0.0), take the obvious and heavily used trail up the ridge, past a Bald River Wilderness sign, to a small "beachlike" picnic area above the falls. This is, however, a dangerous area, and you should not enter the water. There are a couple of unauthorized "memorials" to people on the beach area, with plastic flowers and plaques. The old logging railroad, which extended up Bald River, crossed the river near this point above the falls; the railroad continued down the south side of the Tellico River and you can still see the cuts for the railroad. After a short distance it descends down near the river, and the Tellico River Road currently follows much of the railroad route. Continue upriver on the old logging grade; in late March and early April there is abundant purple wake-robin trillium along this part of the trail. At mile 0.5 the trail will turn left and switchback up a steep hillside. Do not follow an obvious trail that goes straight ahead as it leads to a dead-end. Instead, follow the narrow trail up to a rock outcrop on the nose of a ridge at 0.6 mile. The river makes a U-bend around the base of the rocks, cascading over several rock ledges. An unmaintained manway leads out onto the rocks, where there is a good view of a large cascade a short distance upstream. The trail goes a few feet steeply up the nose of the ridge then turns upstream and descends to the large double waterfall at mile 0.7. The upper falls drops about 20 feet to a pool, then a larger falls of about 30 feet drops to another larger pool. With the exception of Bald River Falls, this waterfall and a series of cascades near the end of the trail are the most outstanding waterfalls/cascades easily visible from the trail.

At 1.4 miles there is an unmarked trail junction where the Cow Camp Trail joins the Bald River Trail. If making the short loop mentioned above, the obscure Cow Camp trail goes uphill in a normally dry watercourse. After about 200 feet the Cow Camp Trail turns left out of the watercourse onto a steep hillside and continues through mountain laurel, pine, and small hardwoods to the ridgecrest. At 0.24 mile from Bald River on the Cow Camp Trail, near a large oak about three feet in diameter, there is an obscure, unmarked junction with the Henderson Mountain Trail (FS Trail 107). Turn northwest on the Cow Camp Trail to return to the Tellico River Road.

From the junction with the Cow Camp Trail, the Bald River Trail descends to the old logging grade; just after reaching the river look to the right for an excellent campsite located on the old railroad bed, overlooking several cascades. Most of the larger and more noisy cascades and waterfalls are located downstream of the Cow Camp Trail junction; the river becomes quieter and calmer as you continue, with several notable exceptions. The trail continues upstream, reaching the small Pawpaw Cove Creek at 1.8 miles. At 2.3 miles, and for a few hundred feet beyond, there are old stumps and downed trees cut by beavers. In the spring of 2003 there were also fresh cuts that had been made in this area. A cast steel brake shoe, an artifact from the days of railroad logging in this watershed, may be seen at mile 3.0. When the leaves are down, Big Cove Branch can be seen entering Bald River at mile 4.2, on the west side of the river.

Along the way several small branches cross the trail, but all are easily crossed. The trail crosses the end of a low ridge at mile 4.5 and descends back to the river. Bald River is a very attractive stream anywhere, but here there is an exceptionally attractive scene of a large cascade, pool, and large rocks in the river and on the banks. This is the second of the most outstanding waterfalls/cascades above Bald River Falls that are easily visible from the trail. A protruding rock ledge allows you to, carefully, walk out for a wonderful view of the cascades upstream.

Just after a Bald River Wilderness sign, the end of the trail is reached at mile 4.8 on FS 126, the road that traverses the Bald River watershed. The river is on the south side of the road at this point, but just a very short distance to the west it flows under the road on its way to Bald River Falls. The Cantrell Parking Area is on the west side of the river, where there is adequate parking.

120. COW CAMP TRAIL (FS TRAIL 173, TI TRAIL 30)

LENGTH: 0.8 mile

ELEVATION CHANGE: Low point, 1,500 feet; high point, 1,940 feet

DIFFICULTY: Easy

TRAILHEADS: Cow Camp Trail (start); Bald River Trail (end)

TRAIL CONNECTIONS: Bald River Trail, Henderson Mountain Trail

USE: Hiking

TOPOGRAPHIC MAP: USGS Bald River Falls, TN-NC

COMMENTS: This is a short trail crossing low on the north end of the ridge that defines the east side of the Bald River watershed. It ends at an unmarked trail junction on the Bald River Trail (FS Trail 88). The trail passes through a mixed pine and hardwood forest with some rhododendron and mountain laurel. One small watercourse is crossed shortly after leaving the road at the Cow Camp Trailhead. This trail provides access to the Henderson Mountain Trail's northern end on the ridgetop at 0.6 from the Cow Camp Trailhead. This junction is unmarked, but there is a large oak tree about three feet in diameter at the junction. The Henderson Mountain Trail goes up the ridge and the Cow Camp Trail continues across the ridge, descending to the Bald River in about 0.25 mile. This trail provides a short loop trip by using it and the lower 1.4 miles (north end) of the Bald River Trail. Doing this loop from either of the two trailheads makes a good loop, but some hikers may have a problem finding the junction of the two trails on the Bald River Trail if they start the loop by going up the Bald River at the falls.

DETAILS: After parking at the upstream end of the bridge, across the Tellico River from where the trail starts up the mountain, walk back across the bridge, step over the guardrail onto the wooden stairway (six or seven steps), and you are on the trail. The trail follows an easy grade southwest along a small stream course, which may be dry in summer, for about 0.25 mile. It then switches back to the left, going around a small ridge and gaining elevation until it reaches the ridgecrest at 0.6 mile, with an elevation gain of about 440 feet. Here is the junction with the Henderson Mountain Trail mentioned above and described below. The Cow Camp Trail continues across the ridge, descending to the Bald River Trail at another unmarked junction about 0.8 mile from the starting point. To make the loop mentioned above, go down the Bald River Trail about 1.4 miles to the Tellico River Road and then 0.9 mile up the road to the starting point.

121. HENDERSON MOUNTAIN TRAIL (FS TRAIL 107, TI TRAIL 45)

LENGTH: 5.8 miles (includes the lower 0.6 mile of Cow Camp Trail)

ELEVATION CHANGE: Low point, 1,940 feet (this low point is on the ridge at a junction with the Cow Camp Trail; the elevation change from FS 210 to this junction is 440 feet); high point, 2,580 feet

DIFFICULTY: Moderate

TRAILHEADS: Cow Camp Trail (start); Henderson Mountain (end)

TRAIL CONNECTIONS: Cow Camp Trail (start); Panther Branch Trail (end)

USE: Hiking

TOPOGRAPHIC MAP: USGS Bald River Falls, TN-NC

COMMENTS: This trail is best hiked from the Cow Camp Trailhead on the Tellico River Road. This requires hiking the first 0.6 mile of the Cow Camp Trail to get to the north end of the Henderson Mountain Trail, where it joins the Cow Camp Trail. See the Cow Camp Trail description to get to this point. The location of the trail (Cow Camp Trail) from the road to this junction is obvious. From this junction (north end of Henderson Mountain Trail) the Henderson Mountain Trail follows an unnamed ridge, generally east, to Cow Camp Lead, from which this unnamed ridge extends. It then follows Cow Camp Lead and Maple Camp Lead to the Henderson Mountain Trailhead, at the junction of roads FS 40832 and FS 126. FS 40832 is on Maple Camp Lead, and the last 2.5 miles of the Henderson Mountain Trail are on this logging road.

Along Cow Camp Lead and Maple Camp Lead, from the junction with the Cow Camp Trail to FS 408832, the trail is often obscure. It is an opening with no tread construction and has seen little or no maintenance since it was originally established. It is marked with aged blazes and occasional evidence of someone having cut some blowdowns or underbrush many years ago. It makes virtually no compromise in its grade as it follows the ridgecrest, and there are no campsites or water along the trail. The trail is forested with hardwoods and some pine. On a clear day, when the leaves are down, there are some good views of the distant mountains. Wild turkey have been seen along this trail.

DETAILS: As noted above, follow Cow Camp Trail to the northern end of Henderson Mountain Trail. It is on the ridgecrest where there is a large oak tree about three feet in diameter with an arrow carved on it. Turn east, following the trail along the ridgecrest and over low knobs. The trail then descends to the left through an area of blowdowns and begins to contour around to the right (south) to arrive at a saddle on the ridgecrest. It continues uphill, bears right at an indistinct turn to reach a shoulder on the ridge, then bears back to the left. Here it continues up a steep grade following the ridge, eases again, and soon reaches the top of an unnamed knob at 0.8 mile. The trail descends to a shallow gap at 1.0 mile and continues on with alternately steep and easy grades to 1.6 miles, where it reaches Cow Camp Lead. Here there will be very good views of the mountains to the east, north, and west when the leaves are down. Henderson Top is visible straight ahead at about 0.75 mile.

Turning south on Cow Camp Lead, it is easy going to 2.2 miles, where there is a steep grade ascending Henderson Top. Continue up the steep grade to 2.3 miles, where the trail veers left and continues around Henderson Top to begin a descent at 2.4 miles. Descend generally along the ridgecrest to the southeast. There are no blazes here, and the trail is obscure. In fact, most of this trail, from Cow Camp

Trail to FS 40832, is obscure, particularly when the leaves are on the trees. A logging road south of the trail (downhill on the right) soon appears, and at 2.7 miles you exit the woods onto FS 40832, where there is a trail marker for FS 107, facing south. FS 40832 is a graveled logging road that goes generally southeast to FS 126, and FS Trail 107 is on this road from here to FS 126.

At 3.3 miles the south end of the Panther Branch Trail (FS Trail 162) joins the Henderson Mountain Trail on FS 40832 at a small clearing on the east side of the road (trail). There is a trail marker here near the road for FS Trail 162 and another about 100 feet down the clearing at the edge of the woods, on the east side of the clearing. Continuing ahead on FS 40832 (FS Trail 107) to mile 5.8, the south end of FS 107 is reached at the road (Henderson Mountain Trailhead), FS 126. The actual hiking distance is 6.4 miles from Tellico River Road, which includes the first 0.6 mile of Cow Camp Trail.

122. PANTHER BRANCH TRAIL (FS TRAIL 162, TI TRAIL 61)

LENGTH: 2.5 miles

ELEVATION CHANGE: Low point, 1,700 feet; high point, 2,640 feet

DIFFICULTY: Easy

TRAILHEADS: Panther Branch (start); Henderson Mountain (end)

TRAIL CONNECTIONS: Henderson Mountain Trail

USE: Hiking

TOPOGRAPHIC MAP: USGS Bald River Falls, TN-NC

COMMENTS: It is suggested that this trail be hiked from the Panther Branch Trailhead on the Tellico River to the Henderson Mountain Trail on FS 40832. Return back down the Panther Branch Trail or down the Henderson Mountain Trail and Cow Camp Trail, or continue on FS 40832, which is also a part of the Henderson Mountain Trail, generally south to the Henderson Mountain Trailhead on FS 126. The latter two choices would require a car shuttle or some very long road walking to get back to the Panther Branch Trailhead.

After crossing the Tellico River on a footbridge the trail passes through a hardwood forest with rhododendron and some pine, following Panther Branch upstream. While there seems to be little or no maintenance by the USFS, the trail is used enough to keep it open and easy to follow. In 2001, blowdowns were not a problem. The rhododendron encroaches on the trail in some locations but is not bothersome. The Panther Branch watershed is very attractive and fall colors will enhance the beauty of it. It would be an enjoyable winter trip.

DETAILS: Cross the footbridge at the Panther Branch Trailhead. The trail is obvious as it bears to the right to follow Panther Branch upstream. At times the trail is an old logging grade, which is quite common in the heavily logged Appalachian Mountains. This watershed has recovered very well and there is no evidence of any recent logging. Some creek crossings are required, but they are not difficult, except after substantial rains. Some wading may be required depending on the amount of rainfall.

The last 0.4 mile before reaching the opening at the south end of the trail is quite steep. This opening is along side FS 40832, which at this point is also the Henderson Mountain Trail and is relatively level. The Panther Branch Trail joins this trail here. Backpackers could use this opening as a campsite, since there is a spring just a few yards downhill in the rhododendron. At the trail junction the hiker could turn right (generally south) on the Henderson Mountain Trail and follow it and the Cow Camp Trail back to the Tellico River or turn left and follow the Henderson Mountain Trail on FS 40832 to FS 126.

123. BROOKSHIRE CREEK TRAIL (FS TRAIL 180, TI TRAIL 15)

LENGTH: 6.2 miles

ELEVATION CHANGE: Low point, 1,950 feet; high point, 3,950 feet

DIFFICULTY: Moderate

TRAILHEADS: Brookshire Creek (start); Beaverdam Bald (end)

USE: Hiking, equestrian

TOPOGRAPHIC MAPS: USGS Bald River Falls, TN-NC; Unaka, NC-TN

COMMENTS: This provides a very scenic route to the Beaverdam Bald and Sled Runner Gap area on the TN-NC state line. A trip to this area and back from the Brookshire Creek Trailhead at the confluence of Bald River and Henderson Branch on FS 126 can be made easily in one day. A good backpack loop is provided by this trail, FS Trail 82, and the Kirkland Creek Trail (FS Trail 85). FS Trail 82 is a Nantahala NF trail that generally follows the state line from Sled Runner Gap west to Sandy Gap at the head of Kirkland Creek, where it connects to the south end of the Kirkland Creek Trail.

CNF trails are often poorly maintained or unmaintained, so be prepared to make your way through, over, and around blowdowns on the trail. There are several stream crossings, at least one of which requires wading. The trail uses old logging grades for most of its length, passing through a hardwood forest with some pine and a generous amount of rhododendron. Wildflowers are plentiful in the spring and the fall colors are beautiful. Fly fishermen may find the Bald River part of this trail route interesting, and hunting is permitted in the area. During hunting season, hunters and hunting dogs may be encountered on the trail.

DETAILS: Starting at FS 126 you must immediately cross Henderson Branch, then continue up Bald River (on river right) generally going southeast on an old logging grade. A dry crossing of Henderson Branch can be made most of the time. The trail is close to Bald River and is easy hiking. A variety of deciduous trees and undergrowth with some pine line the trail. At 1.1 miles the trail crosses Bald River and wading is required. Continue upstream (on river left) to 2.3 miles, where there is a beautiful cascade. At 2.4 miles there is a small waterfall about 15 feet high.

About 20 yards beyond this the old Bald River logging grade crosses Brookshire Creek, which comes in from the west, at some very attractive cascades on Brookshire Creek. Just before reaching this crossing the Brookshire Creek Trail turns northwest (right) up a steep embankment, staying on the west side of Brookshire Creek, where the former logging grade is not present. The former logging grade continues up Bald River for some distance, but just above the confluence of Bald River and Brookshire Creek there is a switchback to get the logging grade into the Brookshire Creek drainage. At 2.7 miles the trail returns to the logging grade on Brookshire Creek. At 2.9 miles the trail crosses the creek and continues a short distance up a steep grade, but at no time is the trail difficult.

An old cabin site is found on the east side of the trail at 4.1 miles, and at 4.7 miles more attractive cascades are found. In spring, wildflowers are everywhere, and since the trail is always in a hardwood forest, fall colors are beautiful. Another old cabin site can be found at 5.0 miles, and at 5.7 miles there are some rock walls and evidence of yet another former cabin site and mountain farm.

A few yards beyond this point the trail makes a sharp switchback to the east. Very close to this point an old manway continues on a heading of approximately 120 degrees to Sled Runner Gap, about 0.1 mile away. Here and old ORV trail enters from the east and continues north to Beaverdam Bald. An unmarked trail goes generally south and swings to the west. This is the State Line Trail (FS Trail 82), mentioned earlier, which is under the jurisdiction of the Nantahala NF. A suggestion for backpacking this loop: start on the Brookshire Creek Trail. Contrary to some maps, including the TI map, the official Brookshire Creek Trail does not go to Sled Runner Gap.

At the switchback mentioned above, the trail continues to the edge of a wildlife management clearing at mile 6.2, where there is a trail marker. When this trail was measured in late 2001, the marker erroneously referred to FS Trail 180. It should have referred to FS Trail 80. This is the Beaverdam Bald Trailhead for the Brookshire Creek Trail. Do not drive across the clearing to get to this point. There is no parking area here. Instead, park on FS 24 where it enters the clearing on the east side. It is just a few hundred feet to the trail marker. At mile 6.5, in the clearing, there is a saddle that makes a good campsite for those who want to backpack the loop mentioned at the beginning of this trail description. This saddle is a short distance west-northwest of the 4,259-foot Beaverdam Bald.

FS 24 enters the wildlife management clearing from the northeast, providing access from the Tellico River near the Big Oak Cove Campground. See the description above of the route to the Beaverdam Bald Trailhead. Water can be found below FS 24 about 500 feet east of the edge of the clearing where FS 24 enters it. Continuing a little farther east along FS 24 a junction in the road is reached where you can turn back west and continue up to the top of Beaverdam Bald. There is another wildlife management clearing here.

A suggestion for backpacking the Brookshire Creek–Kirkland Creek Loop: start on the Brookshire Creek Trail, camp at the wildlife management clearing mentioned above, go back to Sled Runner Gap, follow the State Line Trail west to Sandy Gap, then take the Kirkland Creek Trail down to the Bald River and FS 126. A short walk on FS 126 will bring you back to the Brookshire Creek Trailhead. The current Kirkland Creek Trail goes northwest from Sandy Gap on an old logging grade, not downhill to the northeast, as shown on some maps still in use. There is no water on the State Line Trail or at Sandy Gap.

124. KIRKLAND CREEK TRAIL (FS TRAIL 85, TI TRAIL 50)

LENGTH: 4.6 miles

ELEVATION CHANGE: Low point, 1,880 feet; high point, 2,580 feet

DIFFICULTY: Moderate

TRAILHEADS: Kirkland Creek, Sandy Gap

USE: Hiking

TOPOGRAPHIC MAP: USGS Bald River Falls, TN-NC

COMMENTS: This trail provides a very scenic and easy route to Sandy Gap on the TN-NC state line, although several shallow creek crossings (about 10) must be waded during most of the year. A trip to Sandy Gap and back from the Kirkland Creek Trailhead at the confluence of Bald River on FS 126 can be made easily in one day. A good backpack loop is provided by this trail, FS 82, and the Brookshire Creek Trail. To hike this loop trip, start on the Brookshire Creek Trail. See the comments concerning trail conditions to be expected on the Kirkland Creek Trail under the Brookshire Creek Trail description above. Nantahala NF Trail 82 is also included in this book.

Take a pair of wading shoes and wear them continuously when hiking the Kirkland Creek and Waucheesi Creek sections of this trail. If you are starting at the Kirkland Creek Trailhead, wear your wading shoes or take off your boots, since you must wade Bald River about 50 feet from the trailhead, just upstream of the Kirkland Creek and Bald River confluence.

The trail uses old logging grades for most of its length, passing through a hardwood forest with some pine and a plenty of rhododendron, which does not seriously obstruct the trail. Wildflowers are plentiful in the spring and the fall colors are beautiful. There is only one relatively short section where the trail is not on an old logging grade. Fly fishermen should find the Kirkland Creek part of this route interesting. Hunting is permitted in the area, so hunters and hunting dogs may be encountered along the trail during the hunting season.

Those who are familiar with the USFS roads in the Tellico District will know shorter routes to the Sandy Gap and Kirkland Creek Trailheads described in this trail guide. Others may want to get a FS compartment map and do some exploration of the state, county, and USFS system roads that will save some driving distance.

The TI map shows the Kirkland Creek Trail continuing from Sandy Gap along the ridgeline northwest to Sixmile Gap, then up to Waucheesi Mountain. This is an error; as of 2004, there is no official trail between Sandy Gap and Waucheesi Mountain. However, the planned route of the Benton MacKaye Trail (see that trail description) will, when constructed, follow the ridgeline from Sixmile Gap to Sandy Gap, then the State Line Trail on to Beaverdam Bald. Although not an official trail, the route between Sandy Gap and Waucheesi

Mountain is passable and is described under the State Line Trail below, since it is a logical part of that trail.

DETAILS: After crossing Bald River, about 50 feet from the trailhead, the trail follows old logging grades most of the way to Sandy Gap and only leaves these logging grades on Waucheesi Creek to climb a short distance to a ridgetop where other old logging grades take you to Sandy Gap. Look carefully shortly after leaving Bald River and you will see some evidence of an effort made many years ago, prior to the first edition of this guide book, to improve the trout habitat on the first 0.5 mile or so of Kirkland Creek.

It is quite level along this part of the stream and could have once supported subsistence farming. No cabin sites are obvious from the trail, but a little exploring in some of the wide, flat areas may reveal evidence of past habitation. Supposedly, an Indian burial site exists on a ridge at the head of this stream. If so, this little valley may have been inhabited or used to some extent by Indians prior to the coming of early settlers. The real Warrior Passage Trail would have followed the ridge where FS Trail 82 is now located and would be above the burial site if it actually exists.

There are some good backpack camping sites along Kirkland Creek, and a suitable site can be found near where you leave Waucheesi Creek to get to the ridgetop, where old logging grades will lead you to Sandy Gap. Water is never a problem until you leave Waucheesi Creek. Wildflowers are plentiful in the spring, and in the fall this hardwood forest will show a typical display of very colorful Appalachian foliage.

At 1.7 miles the trail veers from south to southwest, indicating that you are nearing the Waucheesi Creek part of the watershed. After a couple of creek crossings and at mile 2.1 you wade Waucheesi Creek. The confluence of Kirkland Creek and Waucheesi Creek is out of sight to the east, through the rhododendron shortly before making this creek crossing. Old topographical maps show the trail continuing up Kirkland Creek, as does the TI map, and the logging grade this trail followed can be found if you wish to search for it. You are now traveling west up Waucheesi Creek. The grade will steepen a little before reaching a creek crossing at mile 2.7, where there are some large slippery rocks and a cascade visible upstream. The valley is very narrow in this area. At mile 2.8 the valley widens into a large relatively flat area, and the creek may be overflowing its right bank into the trail.

Continue to mile 2.9, where the trail turns south away from the stream and soon reaches the base of the ridge at mile 3.0. The trail is obscure, typical of CNF trails, so look carefully for blazes. If you have been wearing wading shoes and carrying hiking boots, this is the place to change them. The trail goes steeply up the side of the ridge through an open wooded area, reaching the top at mile 3.1. Here you will find another old logging grade going westward along the ridge. The logging grade on the creek was the original logging access to this area. The one on the ridge was constructed much later. Except in wet weather, there is no water between the Waucheesi Creek and Sandy Gap. The trail continues on the old logging grades as it makes its way along the ridge or around the mountain, swinging to the south with mostly easy grades up and down. A saddle on the ridgecrest is reached at mile 3.4, and the trail continues across the saddle on a wider logging grade. Other logging grades leave this saddle, so follow the more obvious one across the saddle. Very old painted blazes can sometimes be found, but you must look carefully. Sandy Gap is reached at mile 4.6, where there is a trail marker for FS Trail 85. This is the Sandy Gap Trailhead, which can be reached from TN 68 on the Hiwassee River and also at the end of FS 50. If you are familiar with the backroads, it can also be reached by way of Joe Brown Highway, a USFS road from TN 68 that is much closer to Tellico Plains than the Hiwassee River.

The old Kirkland Creek Trail ends here and can be found dropping steeply downhill on the TN side of the gap. If you decide to take a shortcut on this old trail to the official Kirkland Creek Trail at the confluence of Kirkland Creek and Waucheesi Creek be prepared to bushwhack through extensive rhododendron, briars, other assorted undergrowth, and soggy bottomland.

The Nantahala NF Trail 82 follows the state line ridge from Sandy Gap to Sled Runner Gap near the Brookshire Creek Trail and can be used to make the backpacking loop mentioned above and in the Brookshire Creek Trail description. There is no trail marker for this trail, but it goes uphill to the southeast on a very rough old logging grade that is now being used by ORVs. It is also the access to an inholding of about 175 acres, one corner of which is at Sandy Gap.

During wet weather, water can be found about 0.4 mile before reaching Sandy Gap on the Kirkland Creek Trail, and backpacking tents can be set on the logging grade before reaching the gap if you wish to spend the night here. See the comments section above for the extension of the Kirkland Creek Trail beyond Sandy Gap to Waucheesi Mountain that is shown on the TI map.

125A. STATE LINE TRAIL (NANTAHALA NF TRAIL 82) (SANDY GAP TO SLED RUNNER GAP SECTION)

LENGTH: 6.7 miles

ELEVATION CHANGE: Low point, 2,580 feet; high point, 4,000 feet

DIFFICULTY: Moderate

TRAILHEADS: Sandy Gap and Brookshire Creek Trail

USE: Hiking

TOPOGRAPHIC MAPS: USGS Bald River Falls, TN-NC, Unaka, TN-NC

COMMENTS: This is a Nantahala NF trail that essentially runs along the TN-NC state line between Sandy Gap and Sled Runner Gap, near the southern end of the Brookshire Creek Trail. It is not marked at either of these locations. Occasionally an old "NC Wildlife Game Lands" sign will be seen. Like many CNF trails in the area, it sees no maintenance. When the leaves are down, great views of mountains in all directions can be seen and in the fall the hardwood forest colors will be unsurpassed. An unofficial route going generally northwest about 0.1 mile from Sled Runner Gap connects to the Brookshire Creek Trail. See the section on that trail to find the connection. Do not rely on the TI map for this connection. Although it is not a CNF trail, it is included in this trail guide because it provides a link for an excellent backpack loop using the Brookshire Creek Trail and the Kirkland Creek Trail. It is suggested that those making this backpack trip start with the Brookshire Creek Trail, since camping at the south end of this trail near Beaverdam Bald is much better. There is no water source on FS 82, and there may or may not be water at about 0.4 mile northeast of Sandy Gap on the Kirkland Creek Trail. Also, there is a 1,280 feet loss of elevation going toward Sandy Gap. See the Kirkland Creek Trail section on creek crossings if you are planning this trip.

The following details of this trail are given from Sandy Gap to Sled Runner Gap because the Sandy Gap Trailhead is accessible by ordinary automobile and those making a day trip on this trail would start here.

DETAILS: At Sandy Gap start hiking up the ORV track, formerly a logging grade, to the southeast out of Sandy Gap. This old road is also an access to a piece of private property near the gap. At 0.2 mile the road splits, keep right up the ridge, where good views will be seen on clear days, vegetation permitting. At 0.4 mile there is another fork that bears left. The trail continues up the steep ridge as it climbs over the knoll to descend into Hipps Gap. The trail climbs steeply out of this gap but soon levels off and turns northeast. When a split in the trail is reached, bear right (the two routes unite at 1.4 miles). The trail soon leaves the ridge on the right side, swinging around the side of the mountain and reaching another ridge just above Moss Gap at 1.9 miles. Here the trail makes an abrupt turn to the left up the side of the ridge, away form Moss Gap, bearing north-northeast. Evidence of ORV use is found here, apparently coming up from Moss Gap. The trail soon levels, swings east, and reaches Hazelnut Knob at 2.5 miles. On the way to Hazelnut Knob watch for a stone with "1812/1816" carved on it.

Note: When hiking from Sled Runner Gap to Sandy Gap (opposite from how the trail is described here), it is very important to pay close attention to the trail from the east side of Hazelnut Knob to the right, west of Moss Gap. On the east side of Hazelnut Knob a very obvious and illegal ORV trail comes uphill from the south. Do not descend there. Instead, continue straight ahead on a less obvious trail that immediately begins to ascend Hazelnut Knob. After crossing Hazelnut Knob, the trail makes an obscure V turn (not a U turn) to the right (north). As of 2004, there was a large oak tree with two large grapevines where the turn is made. The trail continues to be obscure for a short way after the turn but then becomes more obvious. At the V turn, a more obvious route continues down into Moss Gap. In Moss Gap an unofficial trail continues up the ridge on the other side of the gap, *while another unofficial trail* descends from the gap to the left.

Continue on the ridgecrest to a split in the ORV tracks to begin a by-pass around the high point of Nit Top. There are several intersecting and paralleling ORV tracks, but continue generally eastward to by-pass the crest of Nit Top. Round Top is ahead at 4.1 miles, where the trail bears northeast. ORV tracks are obvious here going south and southeast downhill. Do not follow them. An unnamed peak with an elevation of 3,698 feet is a short distance northeast of Round Top. The trail continues along the ridgetop, generally in an easterly direction, gaining some elevation to reach the high point of Rocky Top (about 4,000 feet elevation) at mile 6.4. This is the highest point between Sandy Gap and Sled Runner Gap. Brookshire Creek may be heard in the ravine to the left. The trail descends on an easy slope, curving to the north, and arrives in Sled Runner Gap at 6.7 miles, the official end of the trail.

The trail formerly continued on past the gap and up the steep ridge to Beaverdam Bald, where there is a wildlife management clearing that connected the trail to FS 24. Due to ORVs coming up to Sled Runner

Gap from the NC side and going up to Beaverdam Bald, and FS 24, the USFS cut numerous trees across the trail, making it difficult to hike. The trail has now grown up in young trees and blackberry vines, so the ORVs no longer take this route. However, by turning to the left, northwest, in Sled Runner Gap a route can be found that connects to the Brookshire Creek Trail in about 0.1 mile. This route was apparently created by motorcyclists, and they may still be using them. Once on the Brookshire Creek Trail, turn right and follow the trail up toward a wildlife management clearing and the south end of the Brookshire Creek Trail; FS 24 can be easily reached from there. See the Brookshire Creek Trail for more information on this option, particularly if you are backpacking.

125B. STATE LINE TRAIL (WAUCHEESI MOUNTAIN TO SANDY GAP SECTION)

LENGTH: 2.3 miles

ELEVATION CHANGE: Low point, 2,580 feet; high point, 3,692 feet

DIFFICULTY: Moderate

TRAILHEADS: Sandy Gap and Waucheesi Mountain

USE: Hiking

TOPOGRAPHIC MAPS: USGS Bald River Falls, TN-NC

COMMENTS: The TI map shows the Kirkland Creek Trail continuing from Sandy Gap along the ridgeline northwest to Sixmile Gap and then up to Waucheesi Mountain. This is an error, and there is no official trail between Sandy Gap and Waucheesi Mountain. However, the State Line Trail logically continues from Sandy Gap to Waucheesi Mountain, and much of that route will be followed by the Benton MacKaye Trail. FS 126C, the access road up to the Waucheesi Mountain Trailhead, is steep and little used. It would make a perfect mountain bike ride and is not bad for hiking. There are wonderful views to the west as you climb the ridge toward the summit. The road surface is mainly packed dirt with a little gravel, and there is a steep drop to the right for much of the way. The lookout tower on topographic maps is long gone from the summit, and the only structure is a communications tower and a small cinderblock building. A couple of acres are clear and grassy and the views are spectacular. Except when looking out toward the Tennessee Valley, where there are some houses, the view is of nothing but mountains, particularly the Upper Bald River Basin and the

Citico Creek Wilderness in the far distance. You are almost certain to see soaring birds from the summit. Just down the road a short ways, a wild turkey was observed gliding from the ridge several miles down into the valley. Even more impressive, in April of 2003 a bald eagle was observed gliding along the ridge just above the summit.

The trail is best hiked from Waucheesi Mountain to Sandy Gap because it is a gradual descent most of the way. A shuttle car at Sandy Gap is impractical because of the shuttle distance, which necessitates doubling back to Waucheesi Mountain or doing a loop hike on several Upper Bald River Trails. The shorter loop would be to follow the State Line to Sandy Gap and descend to a shuttle car on FS 126, the Bald River Road, using the Kirkland Creek Trail. A larger, and probably backpacking, loop would be to follow the entire State Line Trail to Beaverdam Bald and then descend to FS 126 on the Brookshire Creek Trail. The best time for hiking the entire State Line Trail is probably when the leaves are off the trees, since the views are pretty much constant at that time. However, because of the sparse vegetation on many of the ridges, there are also views in the summer. After reaching Sixmile Gap, the trail is periodically marked with blazes cut by chainsaws to mark an illegal ORV route. The trail is completely dry to Sandy Gap so you should carry water.

DETAILS: The trail begins at the southern side of the grassy area on the summit of Waucheesi Mountain. Although somewhat grown over, there is an obvious trail that descends steeply down the ridge toward Sixmile Gap. At this point you are looking directly down to Sixmile Gap and the peak on the other side. The trail goes first through a pile of trees, which resulted from the clearing of the bald, and some small new growth. You will shortly see a "closed to vehicles" sign; ORV use of the trail has been a persistent problem.

Sixmile Gap is reached at 0.3 mile (UTM 16S 0752811E/3906441N). This is the junction with the proposed Benton MacKaye Trail that goes left and right at this point. ORV users have cleared a path in both directions, and as of 2003 the Benton MacKaye Trail is flagged with blue ribbons, with construction to follow. A short 0.3-mile walk to the right will lead to the north end of a ridge that the Benton MacKaye trail will follow to the south.

Continue on the State Line Trail to the left from Sixmile Gap. The trail traverses out the side of a ridge that makes a giant "U" from Sixmile Gap. Look to your left as you leave the gap and you will see the ridgetop you are headed toward. There are obvious signs of an old foot trail along the route, but, as of 2003, there are also "improvements" by ORV users. The trail follows the ridgetop as it winds a circuitous route down to Sandy Gap.

At 0.83 mile, just before ascending up to the knoll opposite Waucheesi Mountain, the Benton MacKaye Trail, when constructed, will leave the ridgetop and traverse down to the left. This route will provide a more gradual descent to a gap at 1.2 mile. However, as of 2003 that route is only flagged, so continue on the ORV route to the top of the knoll at 0.9 mile. The ridgetop is a nice place for a rest, and you are at this point directly opposite Sixmile Gap. There are wilderness-type views in every direction, and Waucheesi Mountain is very visible on the northwest skyline; indeed, if you park there, you can probably see your car.

A series of knolls and gaps follow as the ridgeline gradually drops down toward Sandy Gap. The ridgeline is the TN-NC state line, and you will periodically see "North Carolina Game Lands" signs. At 1.3 miles the ORV route goes left while the trail goes straight up the ridge, although the two routes shortly converge. Again, at 1.5 miles the ORV route goes straight up the ridge, while the trail diverges to the left around the side of the ridge. The two routes converge again at 1.6 miles in a shallow gap. At this point, the foot trail goes through the gap and down the other side (if you came down the ORV route, take a right at this point). The ORV route continues along the ridgetop above the foot trail. Until the foot trail is upgraded to the Benton MacKaye, you will encounter blowdowns. However, especially if you are coming up from Sandy Gap, the foot trail is the better choice because, although the ORV route is shorter, it is very steep.

At 1.95 miles the foot trail rejoins the ORV route at the base of a knoll (turn right on a level ridgetop). After 100 feet, the trail begins dropping toward Sandy Gap and signs of an old road become obvious. Earthen barriers, used to stop vehicular traffic, begin to appear. At 2.13 miles an abandoned road turns back to the left, just after the trail descends another steep knoll. At 2.25 miles the road makes a deep cut into the side of the ridge. After a final ORV barrier Sandy Gap is reached at 2.3 miles (UTM 16S 0754461E/ 3904773N). A USFS "Closed to Vehicles" sign is posted at the trailhead. The Kirkland Creek Trail cuts sharply back to the left and below the State Line Trail, while the State Line Trail continues up the ORV road on the other side of the gap.

24 Warrior's Passage National Recreation Trail

The Warrior's Passage Trail is one of two national recreation trails on the CNF; the other is the John Muir Trail in the Ocoee/Hiwassee Ranger District (there is also the Overmountain Victory National Historic Trail in the Nolichucky/Unaka Ranger District). The CNF's 2004 plan revision does not appear to provide a protected corridor for the Warrior's Passage Trail. The trail is located in the Tellico Ranger District in Monroe County, TN.

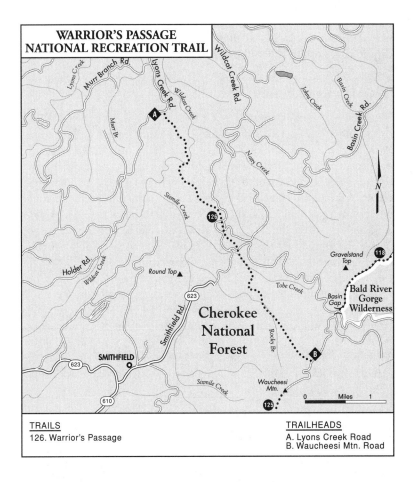

WARRIOR'S PASSAGE NATIONAL RECREATION TRAIL

Cherokee National Forest

TRAILS
126. Warrior's Passage

TRAILHEADS
A. Lyons Creek Road
B. Waucheesi Mtn. Road

HISTORY

The original Warrior's Passage Trail served Cherokee Indians traveling between villages, British soldiers who built Fort Loudon, and South Carolina traders eager to reach the Overhill towns. Some adventurers, interested in the gold once found in nearby Coker Creek, used the trail to cross the southern Appalachian Mountains. Like the Tellico River area, the area through which the trail passes was logged in the nineteenth century as well as in the twentieth century, but the trail is attractive for most of its distance. Under the 1988 CNF management plan, the trail was protected by a 200-foot-wide corridor. Local Boy Scouts maintained the trail for some time. However, in spite of its national designation, this trail has more recently not been well maintained. When measured in the early 2000s the original route was not passable in some places and alternative routes are being used, although the alternate routes are in the vicinity of the original routes.

TRAILHEADS AND MAPS

This trail is described from its lower end on FS 76, Lyons Creek Road, to its higher end on FS 126C, Waucheesi Mountain Road. There is no good parking area at either end of these locations. One car can be parked at either end without impeding the traffic of these narrow unpaved roads, but it would be preferable to park some distance from either of these trail ends. At the lower end (northwest), there is a somewhat wider place on FS 76 about 0.3 mile before reaching the obscure trail marker where the trail leaves this road. At the upper end, the top of Waucheesi Mountain is an excellent place to park and provides excellent high-elevation views on a clear day. It is 0.8 mile from the upper end of the trail on FS 126C to the top of the mountain.

The CNF includes as part of the trail the 2.9 miles along FS 76 from TN 165 to the Lyons Creek Road Trailhead on FS 76, giving it a length of 8.1 miles. The hiker would normally drive this road section, leaving the trail's distance that would normally be hiked at 5.2 miles. The CNF also shows the length at 10.0 miles, but this is either inaccurate or the lack of maintenance makes the location of the additional mileage unclear.

Lyons Creek Road Trailhead

Starting at the intersection of TN 68 and TN 165 on the west side of Tellico Plains, follow TN 165 to County Road 671 at mile 2.3. County Road 671 is Lyons Creek Road and also FS 76. Turn right on

FS 76 and drive 2.9 miles to an obscure USFS trail marker on the left (east) side of the road. Park about 200 feet up the road from this sign or about 0.3 mile back downhill below this marker. The Boy Scout signpost that once marked the trail here is gone.

Waucheesi Mountain Road Trailhead

Follow the directions, using FS 126, to the Basin Gap Trailhead at Basin Gap in the Bald River section above. Turn uphill (south) onto FS 126C and follow it 0.9 mile to the Waucheesi Mountain Road Trailhead, the southeastern end to the Warrior's Passage Trail. One car can park here, very close to the shoulder of the road, without impeding traffic. You may continue another 0.8 mile to the top of Waucheesi Mountain, where there is plenty of parking space and excellent views on a clear day. Note that FS 126C may be gated in the winter.

TOPOGRAPHIC MAPS: USGS Bald River Falls, TN-NC. TI Map 781, Tellico and Ocoee Rivers, CNF.

TRAIL DESCRIPTION

126. WARRIOR'S PASSAGE NATIONAL RECREATION TRAIL (FS TRAIL 164, TI TRAIL 82)

LENGTH: 5.2 miles

ELEVATION CHANGE: Low point, 1,380 feet; high point, 3,200 feet

DIFFICULTY: Moderate

TRAILHEADS: Lyons Creek Road (start); Waucheesi Mountain Road (end)

USE: Hiking

TOPOGRAPHIC MAP: USGS Bald River Falls, TN-NC

COMMENTS: This trail is described from the lower end (Lyons Creek Road Trailhead) to the upper end on the road from Basin Gap to Waucheesi Mountain (FS 126C), the Waucheesi Mountain Road Trailhead. This trail is marked with aged blazes and are sometimes difficult to find. They may be ax or paint blazes. When this trail was measured, there was some evidence of blowdowns having been cut. Road crossings require close attention. The trail uses many old logging grades, some very old and others of more recent vintage. Very close attention is required to make all of the necessary turns. The CNF lists the trail as being 10.0 miles long, and the TI map shows it as 8.1 miles, but we could not find more than the 5.2-mile portion described below. Although a National Recreation Trail, it is not well maintained, as with many other CNF trails. As indicated above, both the USFS (but not the TI map) include 2.9 miles of a USFS road, FS 76, as part of the trail; we do not describe that portion. The USFS (but not the TI map) also includes a short 0.8 mile section of FS 126C to the top of Waucheesi Mountain, and we likewise do not describe that portion in detail.

If you are hiking from the Lyons Creek Road Trailhead to the Waucheesi Mountain Road Trailhead, as is recommended, the southeastern (higher) end of the trail is on FS 126C, the road to Waucheesi Mountain. It is suggested that you continue on to the top of Waucheesi Mountain using FS 126C, where on a clear day the views will be outstanding. Fall colors will add to the beauty along the trail and especially to the views from Waucheesi Mountain.

DETAILS: The trail leaves FS 76 on the east side and goes downhill on an old logging grade. In just a few hundred feet the logging grade splits. Keep right. Continuing downhill the trail leaves the logging grade at about 0.3 mile to follow a small watercourse that may be dry most of the time. Look for a painted blaze on a pine tree in the brush and blowdowns in the creek bed. The trail crosses the streambed

Hiker at upper trailhead sign for the Warrior's Passage Trail. Photograph by Will Skelton.

after a few hundred feet and begins to ascend the right bank of the watercourse. Look for blazes. The trail crosses a small ridge, descends into another watercourse, and then bears left down this watercourse. In a few hundred feet the trail leaves this watercourse on the right side and continues around the side of the mountain. At 0.6 mile the trail reaches the nose of a small ridge and turns right, uphill on an easy slope, but stays to the left of the ridgecrest. Blazes may be found. An old logging grade is reached at the top of a ridge where the trail turns left down the crest of the ridge. After a few hundred feet the trail leaves this ridge on the right side and descends to Wildcat Creek at 0.9 mile. It is not as complicated as it appears, but due to the lack of maintenance and aging of the blazes, careful observation is necessary.

Make a U-turn and continue downstream on Wildcat Branch to a crossing at a pool at 1.0 mile. This is a very attractive place, the best on the trail. The trail continues directly across the pool, which can be easily crossed up- or downstream. Cross the stream and return to the trail to ascend steeply up the hillside from the pool to an old logging grade on the ridge. Continue uphill to a split in the logging grade and bear right off the ridge. The trail descends on the logging grade to a small stream and continues up this stream to mile 1.5, where the logging grade makes a U-turn to the right, leaving the stream. Do not follow the logging grade at this point but continue up the watercourse to a wide place where the watercourse divides. Follow the right branch (upstream), generally south. After going a short way up the watercourse, the trail bears right and steeply up the hillside to reach the ridgecrest at mile 1.7.

The trail soon comes within 100 feet of a road on the east side of the trail, FS 384. An older logging grade parallels FS 384. Stay on the trail west of the road, losing sight of it for a short distance but soon arriving at the older logging grade. Cross the grade and bear left, generally following FS 384. At 2.3 miles the trail crosses FS 384, ascends to a ridgecrest, then descends back to FS 384 and crosses it again. After this crossing, the trail descends to a gently sloping valley. It continues up the valley, where it crosses a small stream and then continues on an old logging grade that soon leaves the streambed on the right. At mile 3.0, the trail turns sharply left uphill, leaving the logging grade, and reaches the ridgecrest in a few hundred feet. The trail goes up the ridge, which steepens quickly and after some switchbacks reaches another logging grade. Here it continues left around the hillside on this logging grade, which is relatively level. At mile 3.6 the trail bears right up toward the ridgecrest, leaving the logging grade and continuing to Mule Pen Gap at mile 3.7.

A large burned area was in evidence here in the early 2000s and there is a logging road junction here. To the left is an older gated logging road. There was also a trail marker post here at the time the trail was measured. The trail follows the newer logging road generally south (on the right side of the ridge) through the burned area to mile 3.9, then it bears steeply to the left, uphill off of the logging road to the ridgecrest. After a steep climb for a short distance the trail levels and a small saddle on the ridge is reached where another old logging grade is found. Following this grade a few yards, the trail then makes an abrupt turn uphill to the left. Look carefully. The brush in the old logging grade is more prevalent beyond this point.

The trail climbs steeply up the ridge from the abrupt turn on an obscure route with switchbacks for a short distance, passing through an old burn and fallen pines. The slope eases for a very short distance then steepens again to ascend without switchbacks to mile 4.7. While ascending from the last logging grade watch carefully for old blazes and sawed stumps and stubs from long past trail maintenance.

Here the trail bears left around the mountain on an easy grade and an obvious trail to reach a flat area. It then turns uphill on a steep ridge with a series of long switchbacks. The trail may be obvious, but, again, watch for blazes and evidence of past maintenance. You reach FS 126C at mile 5.2, the Waucheesi Mountain Road Trailhead. For really great views on a clear day, continue another 0.8 mile to the top of Waucheesi Mountain.

25 Gee Creek

(Includes Gee Creek Wilderness)

Gee Creek, a rugged, hanging valley cut out of the extreme western "Chilhowee" face of the southern Appalachians, was the first officially designated wilderness completely in the CNF, receiving that status in 1975. The creek's watershed is easily visible from US 411 just north of the Hiwassee River Bridge. What you see is a V-shaped cut in the steep, otherwise continuous face of Starr and Chestnut Mountains. The creek and its major tributary, Poplar Springs Branch, begin as northeast-to-southwest streams, parallel to and behind Starr Mountain. Only in the last 0.5 mile of Gee Creek does the watershed abruptly turn some 60 degrees to cut east-west through the ridge face. Were it not for Gee Creek, Chestnut Mountain would simply be the end of Starr Mountain and deserve no separate name. Although the wilderness is located at the southern end of Starr Mountain, the entire

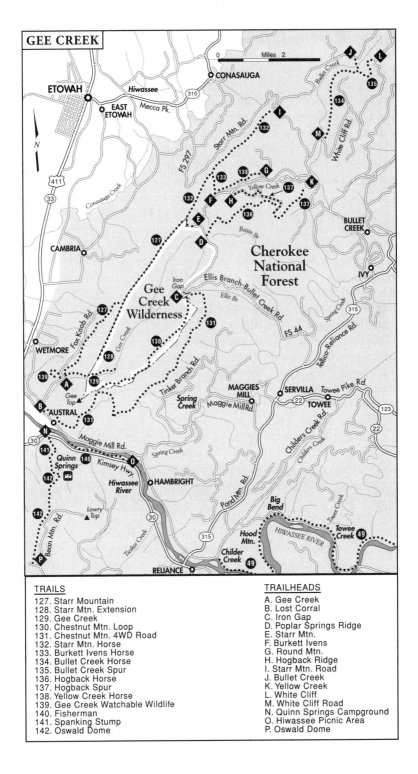

GEE CREEK

Miles 2

ETOWAH
Hiwassee
EAST ETOWAH
Mecca Pk.
CONASAUGA

Hiwassee
Starr Mtn. Rd.
FS 297
Conasauga Creek

Cherokee National Forest

Gee Creek Wilderness

Iron Gap
Ellis Branch-Bullet Creek Rd.
Ellis Br
FS 44

Basin Br.
Yellow Creek

Bullet Creek
White Cliff Rd.

BULLET CREEK
IVY
Spring Creek
315

WETMORE
Fox Knob Rd.
Gee Creek
Gee Top
AUSTRAL
Tinker Branch Rd.
Spring Creek
MAGGIES MILL
Maggie Mill Rd.
Childers Creek Rd.
SERVILLA
Towee Pike Rd.
TOWEE
22
123
22
Childers Creek

Quinn Springs
Maggie Mill Rd.
Kimsey Hwy
Spring Creek
HAMBRIGHT
Hiwassee River
Lowry Top
Pond Mtn. Rd.
Big Bend
Towee Creek
Towee Creek
49

Bean Mtn. Rd.
Tucker Creek
30
315
Hood Mtn.
Childer Creek
HIWASSEE RIVER
RELIANCE
49

TRAILS
127. Starr Mountain
128. Starr Mtn. Extension
129. Gee Creek
130. Chestnut Mtn. Loop
131. Chestnut Mtn. 4WD Road
132. Starr Mtn. Horse
133. Burkett Ivens Horse
134. Bullet Creek Horse
135. Bullet Creek Spur
136. Hogback Horse
137. Hogback Spur
138. Yellow Creek Horse
139. Gee Creek Watchable Wildlife
140. Fisherman
141. Spanking Stump
142. Oswald Dome

TRAILHEADS
A. Gee Creek
B. Lost Corral
C. Iron Gap
D. Poplar Springs Ridge
E. Starr Mtn.
F. Burkett Ivens
G. Round Mtn.
H. Hogback Ridge
I. Starr Mtn. Road
J. Bullet Creek
K. Yellow Creek
L. White Cliff
M. White Cliff Road
N. Quinn Springs Campground
O. Hiwassee Picnic Area
P. Oswald Dome

mountain is covered here because of numerous nearby trails outside the wilderness.

The small 2,493-acre wilderness includes virtually the entire watershed of Gee Creek. Its three trails represent three entirely different experiences. Because of its easy accessibility to major highways, the Gee Creek Trail itself is the nearest thing to instant exposure to wilderness a hiker will find in the CNF. From an elevation of 2,100 feet at the headwaters of Gee Creek and Poplar Springs Branch, the system loses 1,100 feet of elevation within the wilderness, down to 1,000 feet elevation at the Gee Creek Trailhead. Most of this elevation drop is fairly evenly distributed over 4.0 to 5.0 miles of watershed, but the last 350 feet is suddenly, lavishly lost in the final 0.5 mile, creating many waterfalls, some 20 to 25 feet high, along the Gee Creek Trail. Hemlock, tulip trees, and rhododendron fill the lowest elevations of the gorge, while the higher elevations are dominated by Virginia pine, white oak, and red oak, with some hickory. The highest point is the 2,560-foot crest of Chestnut Mountain.

The Gee Creek area also contains a cave, some impressive bluffs, and is near the Hiwassee River. From the Gee Creek Campground it is possible, for those with the proper equipment and experience, to go whitewater canoeing, caving, rock climbing, and hiking all in one weekend. Note that, because of the wilderness's small size, overnight camping is not allowed.

The flat top of Starr Mountain continues on another six miles northeast of the wilderness boundary, with additional hiking opportunities on several well-maintained horse trails. The eastern slope of Starr Mountain is the watershed of Yellow and Bullet Creeks. Bullet Creek leaves the steep slopes of Starr Mountain toward the east as Bullet Creek Falls. South of Starr Mountain and immediately south of the Hiwassee River is Bean Mountain. Starr Mountain and Bean Mountain would be the same mountain if the Hiwassee River had not split them apart by a gorge that makes for a very scenic view from Highway 411. The very top of Bean Mountain is known as Oswald Dome. This is the location of the radio antennas seen across the Hiwassee River when traveling south of Highway 411.

HISTORY

The oldest signs of man in the area are the remains of a concrete flume and rock crusher on the lowest section of Gee Creek, vestiges of an iron-mining venture during the years 1825–60. The mine was operated by TN Copper Company, whose employees sought a certain type of iron ore used as an additive in copper smelting. They lived in the nearby, now deserted, community of Austral. There are also said to be scattered mining holes still visible. The USFS says the entire drainage was logged as recently as 45 years ago, but some large trees, mostly hemlock, were left in the gorge. Starr Mountain, the first buffer to the prevailing westerly winds over the TN Valley, was the scene of many forest fires in the 1920s. In the early 1970s (prewilderness) three wildlife-management clearings were made on Chestnut Mountain, but they have blended into the forest and are not noticeable from the trail.

Starr Mountain, which forms the western boundary of the wilderness designation, is named for Caleb Starr, a young Pennsylvanian Quaker who moved into the area from NC after the Revolutionary War. Caleb and his descendants were historical figures in TN and, subsequently, Oklahoma. Caleb married Nancy Harlan, granddaughter of Nancy Ward, known as the "Wild Rose of the Cherokees." He owned Starr Mountain and amassed a fortune in land, livestock, and slaves. The area was then under Cherokee jurisdiction, but Caleb's son, James Starr, persuaded President Jackson to sign a treaty that gave 640 acres to white settlers. The following unrest culminated in the Trail of Tears. Since the Starrs were part Indian, the entire family, including Caleb and Nancy, moved to Oklahoma. James was later murdered for his role in selling out the Cherokees. Tom Starr, Caleb's son, and Sam Starr, Caleb's grandson, became notorious outlaws in the Southwest; Tom started killing at age 19 to avenge the death of his father, and Sam rode with the well-known Younger gang. Another relative, Henry Starr, was also an infamous southwestern outlaw, as was Sam's wife, Belle Starr. There was a large three-story hotel, known as the White Springs Hotel, located on the north end of Starr Mountain in the late 1800s.

Oswald dome is named for Dr. Flex Oswald, who came to Polk County around 1880 from Belgium and had a cabin on the north side of Bean Mountain. Dr. Oswald wrote several books but was spoken of with suspicion by the local people, as he seemed to keep to himself and seldom mixed with the local people.

The Gee Creek Wilderness was designated in 1975 as part of the Eastern Wilderness Areas Act. Written testimony supporting the wilderness was submitted to the US Congress by HBG of the Sierra Club members Jim Anker, Ray Payne, and Will Skelton; Will's submission included photographs from an HBG outing in the area. In the CNF's 1988 management plan, an additional 1,400 acres to the southeast of the wilderness were protected as a primitive area; unfortunately, such protection is not continued in the CNF's 2004 plan revision.

In addition to the USFS, another source of information for hiking in this area is the TN State Park Ranger's office building at the Gee

Creek Campground and Picnic Area (just before the turnoff to Lost Corral Trailhead, described below).

TRAILHEADS AND MAPS

Gee Creek Trailhead

Turn east off US 411 on Gee Creek Road exactly 5.0 miles south of the old Etowah train depot and 1.3 miles north of the Hiwassee River bridge. On the opposite side of US 411 are County 163 to Calhoun and the Delano Branch of the Benton Banking Company. After immediately crossing some railroad tracks the road turns right. The road follows along the left side of the railroad tracks through a small community and then turns away from the tracks to the left (1.4 miles from US 411). Follow the road until the pavement runs out at 1.9 miles. Continue on the dirt road until you come to the trailhead (2.2 miles from US 411). There is a bulletin board with a map of the area and a small parking lot. To the left, you will find the trailhead for Starr Mountain Trail only about 30 yards up the road on the right-hand side (you may even be able to see the first of the white trail blazes from the parking area). To the right is the Gee Creek Trailhead.

Lost Corral Trailhead

Turn east off US 411 on Spring Creek Road at the Gee Creek Campground sign 0.4 mile north of the Hiwassee River. Follow the paved road across Gee Creek, and pass the state ranger's office on the left at 0.8 mile. At 0.1 mile past the ranger's office turn left on a dirt road, cross railroad tracks, and immediately take the right fork. Just beyond the railroad tracks is a large dirt parking area. On the left back corner of the parking area is the access to Gee Cave. (Do not enter the cave without using the proper equipment and checking in with the USFS in advance.) On the right back corner of the lot is a gate that is the trailhead for the Chestnut Mountain 4 WD road (FS 2004). The trailhead for the Chestnut Mountain Loop Trail (FS Trail 104) is 1.8 miles up the 4 WD road.

Ellis Branch–Bullet Creek Road (FS 44) Trailheads: Iron Gap, Poplar Springs Ridge, and Starr Mountain Trailheads

Beginning at the TN 315 bridge at Reliance, travel north 5.1 miles to a junction with gravel FS Road 44 on the left at Servilla Baptist Church. This is known as the Ellis Branch–Bullet Creek Road. It is a rough 4.3 miles to Iron Gap, a trailhead for the Chestnut Mountain Loop Trail (FS Trail 104) and the Chestnut Mountain 4 WD road (FS 2004). There is a bulletin board at the beginning of the trail about 75 feet from the road. At 6.1 miles on the right is the Poplar Springs Ridge Trailhead at gated FS 1106. This is the southern terminus of the Hogback Horse Trail. At 6.2 miles on FS 44 is the Starr Mountain Trailhead on the left at a sharp right turn of the road; this is the trailhead for the Starr Mountain Horse Trail (FS Trail 120). A trailhead for the Starr Mountain Foot Trail (FS Trail 190) is 0.4 mile up the Starr Mountain Horse Trail. Additional trailheads farther north on FS 44 are described below.

Ellis Branch–Bullet Creek Road (FS 44) Trailheads: Yellow Creek, Round Mountain, Hogback Ridge, Burkett Ivens, Starr Mountain, and Poplar Springs Ridge Trailheads

This section describes how to reach the trailheads on FS 44 from the north and Tellico Plains. As described above, FS 44 makes a big loop up to Starr Mountain and back down again; this description is of the northern approach to the loop. To reach these trailheads from Reliance and the south, see the description for the Iron Gap, Poplar Springs Ridge, and Starr Mountain Trailheads above. Travel south on TN 315 from TN 68 at Tellico Plains toward Reliance 10.9 miles to a junction with Monroe County 653 (this is a paved road also known as FS 44 and Ellis Branch–Bullet Creek Road and is shown as FS 44 on the TI map). Turn west off TN 315 onto County 653/FS 44. There is a USFS sign here pointing west to parking and horse trails. After 0.8 mile reach an intersection and continue west (straight-ahead) on TN 653/FS 44. At 1.7 miles from TN 315 pass an intersection with TN 652. Continue straight ahead another 0.1 mile to a point where the paved road turns left. Here, continue straight ahead on a dirt road that is the continuation of FS 44.

At 3.1 miles from TN 315 reach the Yellow Creek Trailhead, which is the eastern trailhead for Hogback Spur Horse Trail (FS Trail 126A) on the left. There is no gate or trail sign here, but there is a sign indicating the road is closed to vehicular traffic. At 0.1 mile beyond the trailhead there is a gated USFS road on the left and in another 0.1 mile an intersection with FS 220 on the right. At 4.1 miles, on the right, reach the Round Mountain Trailhead that is the eastern trailhead for the Yellow Creek Horse Trail (FS Trail 123); there is a gated road (FS 11215) and a trail sign identifying the trail and its mileage. At 5.1 miles from TN 315, reach the Hogback Ridge Trailhead. This is the western trailhead, on the left, for the Hogback Spur Horse Trail

(FS Trail 126A). There is no sign, but there is a gate at the start of a graveled road. Just 0.1 mile farther on, at 5.2 miles, is the Burkett Ivens Trailhead for the Burkett Ivens Horse Trail (FS Trail 122) on the right. A trail sign gives the name and mileage of the trail. This is also the western trailhead for the Yellow Creek Horse Trail (FS Trail 123).

The trailheads described above on FS 44 from the south can be reached by continuing on FS 44. At 6.2 miles from TN 315, reach a hairpin turn and Starr Mountain Trailhead; this is the southern trailhead for the Starr Mountain Horse Trail (FS Trail 120; also described above). Again, there is no sign, but there is a closed gate at the entrance to a gravel road. At 6.6 miles reach the Poplar Springs Ridge Trailhead that is the southern trailhead for the Hogback Horse Trail (FS 126). There is no trail sign at this gated road, but there is a sign identifying the road as FS 1106. All of these trailheads have some parking space, either at the trailhead or within several hundred yards on FS 44.

Bullet Creek, Starr Mountain Road, White Cliff, and White Cliff Road Trailheads

From TN 68 at Tellico Plains take TN 315 and begin measuring mileage. At the junction with TN 310 go straight ahead on TN 310 and continue measuring mileage. At 6.2 miles turn left on gravel FS 297 (Starr Mountain Road) and reset mileage to 0. For the north trailhead of FS Trail 121 continue on FS 297 to the junction of FS 220 at 2.5 miles. Continue on FS 297 for 1.7 miles from the junction of FS 297 and FS 220 to the Bullet Creek Trailhead for the Bullet Creek Horse Trail (FS Trail 121) on the left (UTM 16S 0734443E/3912014N). There is a large parking area just beyond the trailhead. By continuing on FS 297 past the Bullet Creek Trailhead, you can reach the ending, or north, trailhead for FS Trail 120, called here the Starr Mountain Road Trailhead. This trailhead is on FS 297 at 3.9 miles past its junction with FS 220 described above. The horse trail is on the left where the road makes a sharp right turn just short of the fire tower on top of Starr Mountain. As of the early 2000s, FS 297, known as Starr Mountain Road, is not passable down the west side of Starr Mountain. It is understood there are plans to improve this road in the future.

For FS Trail 121A and the south trailhead of FS Trail 121, turn left off of FS 297 onto FS 220. At 0.5 mile from the junction the White Cliff Trailhead for the Bullet Creek Spur Trail (121A) is on the right, but there is no good parking (UTM 16S 731719E/3911448N). For the FS Trail 121 south trailhead, continue on FS 220 to where it crosses

Bullet Creek on a concrete bridge. The White Cliff Road Trailhead is just before the bridge on the right. There is parking on the opposite side of the road from the trailhead. The TI map published in 2001 is incorrect as to the location of this trailhead.

Quinn Springs Campground and Oswald Dome Trailheads

The lower, or beginning, trailhead for the Oswald Dome Trail is at Quinn Springs Campground 1.6 miles east of US 411 on TN 30. There is ample parking just to the left of the area entrance. The Fisherman Trail also starts near Quinn Springs Campground; the trailhead is at the back right corner of a parking lot located just across US 411 from the campground entrance. For the upper, or ending, trailhead for the Oswald Dome Trail, follow Oswald Dome Road (FS 77) north from the Chilhowee Mountain Campground to its junction with FS 77C. Turn left at this junction, and the Oswald Dome Trailhead (UTM 16S0722335E/ 3896932N) is on the right just a few hundred feet before reaching the radio antennas. There is plenty of parking beside the road.

Hiwassee Picnic Area Trailhead

The eastern end of the Fisherman Trail is accessed from the Hiwassee River Picnic Area on TN 30, 3.2 miles from US 411. The trailhead is actually 0.1 mile west of the picnic area on the shoulder of US 411. The picnic area is a fee parking area, although there is also room for a couple of cars at a pull-off 175 feet west of the trailhead. The trail can also be accessed near its middle at the Taylors Island Picnic area on the riverside of TN 30 at 2.3 miles from 411.

TOPOGRAPHIC MAPS: USGS Oswald Dome, TN; Etowah, TN; Mecca, TN. TI Map 781, Tellico and Ocoee Rivers, CNF.

TRAIL DESCRIPTIONS

127. STARR MOUNTAIN TRAIL (FS TRAIL 190, TI TRAIL 72)

128. STARR MOUNTAIN EXTENSION (SPUR) TRAIL (FS TRAIL 190A, TI TRAIL 72A)

LENGTH: 4.9 miles (FS Trail 190)

ELEVATION CHANGE: (FS Trail 190) Low point, 950 feet; high point, 2,270 feet

DIFFICULTY: Moderate

TRAILHEADS: Gee Creek (start) and Starr Mountain (end)

TYPE: Hiking

TOPOGRAPHIC MAPS: USGS Oswald Dome, TN; Etowah, TN

COMMENTS: The Starr Mountain Trail was constructed in the mid-1980s by linking together a series of preexisting jeep tracks and trails at various levels of the mountain. It is not the trail shown on the 1967 vintage Etowah topographical map. The lowest section of the trail goes through an area of utter devastation caused by clear-cutting, fire, and pine beetle damage. As the trail climbs Starr Mountain the clear-cut area is left behind for a fine mixed hardwood forest. There are many good views of the Tennessee Valley in winter and a few in the summer. There are a few sections on the mountainside where the trail crosses old rockslides, making footing difficult; however, in all but a very few steep sections the trail is graded, well marked, and well maintained. In the summer there is virtually no water on Starr Mountain, and there is a good deal of poison ivy.

DETAILS: From the trailhead just above and to the left of the parking area, climb the short switchback, following the first of the "dotted i" white blazes. After about 100 yards, the trail turns right along a logging road. At 0.2 mile the trail leaves the logging road with a sharp left turn up a bank. Use care here not to keep following the old road. The trail has been rerouted at this point to go around a clear-cut made in 1991. The area has also been burned and heavily attacked by pine beetles, making for a very unappealing landscape.

At about 0.9 mile the pine beetle damage is left behind and a mixed hardwood forest is entered. At 1.2 miles is an area overgrown with vines and briers, but in 2003 they were well cut back from the trail. There are good views here, with the Huber Chemical plant in the foreground. Through this overgrown area the trail makes one short but steep switchback to the right. It will immediately put you on another old track headed left.

The trail is now headed in a northeasterly direction along the slope of Starr Mountain, gently gaining altitude. At 1.4 miles a knoll on the side of the mountain is crossed and the forest becomes quite beautiful. At 1.6 miles there is an old blowdown area, again covered with vines, giving good views of the Tennessee Valley in clear weather. At slightly over 2.0 miles, the Starr Mountain ridgecrest, ruggedly fitted with house-sized boulders, comes into view through the trees on the right. At 2.7 miles the trail begins a series of switchbacks as the ridgecrest is approached. This is the only steep section of any length on the Starr

Mountain Trail. At almost due north the town of Etowah can be seen through the trees. At 2.8 miles, the trail tops out on the ridgecrest of Starr Mountain, at 2,300 feet elevation, and turns left (north). From here on, the trail simply follows the nearly level ridgecrest to the northeast.

At the point the trail reaches the ridgecrest, you can turn right (south) and hike along the mountain crest for about 1.8 miles, gently downhill, to the point of Starr Mountain; however, the views are disappointing. This short dead-end trail is the Starr Mountain Extension (Trail No. 190A).

Within a few hundred yards after reaching the crest and turning left, the Starr Mountain Trail passes what may be the highest point of the ridge at 2,380 feet, just to the left of the trail. There are many areas along this ridgetop section where good views may be had in winter by walking a few steps to the west. The trail passes a property corner marker—a USGS benchmark beside a steel post and rock painted bright red—at 3.25 miles and 2,330 feet elevation. At roughly 3.6 miles the trail enters a beautiful, heavily shaded section of ridgecrest with many large rocks, offering panoramic views of the countryside.

At 4.7 miles the mountain becomes a true knife-edge ridge, and the trail, entering a pretty grove of pines, slopes down to the right of the ridgecrest. At this point, you should begin watching the trail blazes carefully. Within a few yards the trail will suddenly cut up the ridge to the left, through some knee-high rocks, to follow the ridgecrest once again. There is a blazed pine tree on the left at the point of the turn, but it is easy to miss. Follow what looks like the main track straight ahead into a maze of blowdowns and frustration. At 4.9 miles the trail ends at the Starr Mountain Horse Trail. It is 0.4 mile to the right on the horse trail to the Starr Mountain Trailhead on FS 44. It is then 2.2 miles to the right on FS 44 to the Iron Gap Trailhead.

129. GEE CREEK TRAIL (FS TRAIL 191, TI TRAIL 38)

LENGTH: 1.9 Miles

ELEVATION CHANGE: Low point, 920; high point, 1,400 feet

TRAILHEAD: Gee Creek (start and dead-end)

TYPE: Hiking

DIFFICULTY: Moderate

TOPOGRAPHIC MAPS: USGS Oswald Dome, TN; Etowah, TN

COMMENTS: The Gee Creek Trailhead is at the same location as the Starr Mountain Trailhead, 2.2 miles from TN 411. This is a dead-end trail that follows Gee Creek closely for 1.9 miles. The first 0.8 mile is easy walking on a very open trail, ending at a very enchanted section of Gee Creek Gorge. There is a whole series of beautiful back-to-back waterfalls framed by hemlocks in a very steep sided gorge. The last 1.1 miles is more difficult, being a narrow but easily followed trail on the sides of the gorge, and crossing the creek eight times. This section of the trail should not be attempted in periods of high water. Off-trail hikers can continue on to FS 44.

DETAILS: From the parking lot at the bulletin board, take the wide trail to the right, which is an old road. At 0.5 mile the trail leaves the old road to the right and crosses to the right side of Gee Creek on a wooden footbridge. At 0.6 mile ruins of the old Tennessee Copper Company are seen on the right. A few hundred feet beyond these ruins is a covered concrete flume through which the entire creek flows. Just above the flume is the series of beautiful waterfalls. Children must be closely controlled here, as the steep side of the gorge above the waterfalls makes for a dangerous situation.

At 0.8 mile, the trail crosses the creek for the first time between two 20–25 foot waterfalls. Although the trail crosses back in a few hundred feet, do not attempt to avoid these two crossings by bushwhacking across the face of the gorge. The gorge contains hard rock

A double-cascade waterfall on the Gee Creek Trail. Photograph by Will Skelton.

formations covered by a thin layer of vegetation, which will slide off easily, making for a bad fall. Do not continue the hike if the water at the first ford is too high for a safe crossing.

The trail continues up the steep side of the gorge, and although the trail is not blazed it is very easy to follow. At approximately 0.9 mile is what would be a very nice campsite; however, camping is not allowed in the Gee Creek Wilderness. Just above this area, on the opposite side of Gee Creek, but in plain view of the trail, is a very unusual side-stream waterfall that slants on a 45-degree angle from the upper left to lower right down a perfectly cut channel in the rock.

The fifth creek crossing is very easy and the trail levels out somewhat. There are large hemlocks in the bottom of the gorge here and the last three creek crossings are also easy. The trail ends on the right side of the creek after the eighth crossing, just upstream from a short boggy area. There is a large flat area here and very faint signs of an old trail continuing up the creek. However, the official trail ends here, and only individuals with off-trail hiking experience should continue on up the valley, where FS 44 is located.

130. CHESTNUT MOUNTAIN LOOP TRAIL (FS TRAIL 104, TI TRAIL 20)

LENGTH: 3.8 miles (FS Trail 104 only)

ELEVATION CHANGE: Low point, 1,520 feet; high point, 2,560 feet

DIFFICULTY: Moderate

TRAILHEADS: Chestnut Mountain 4 WD road (start); Iron Gap (end)

TYPE: Hiking, equestrian

TOPOGRAPHIC MAPS: USGS Oswald Dome, TN; Etowah, TN; Mecca, TN

COMMENTS: The trail officially begins 1.8 miles up FS 2004; however, because most hikers will hike to this trail on FS 2004, the route is described from the beginning of the 4 WD road at the Lost Corral Trailhead. The 4 WD road is very rough and is absolutely not suitable for ordinary automobiles. All the elevation gain is in the first 3.0 miles; the stretch on top of Chestnut Mountain is mostly level or a gentle downhill slope. Beyond the point where the trail leaves the 4 WD road there is a real sense of solitude all the way to Iron Gap. The trail is well defined and easy to follow. The name of the trail would cause a hiker to expect a loop, and indeed the TI map shows a loop along the crest of Chestnut Mountain. However, there is no signed or visible loop on the ground as of 2003. Note that there is also a Chestnut Mountain Loop Trail in the Ocoee Whitewater Center section and a Chestnut Mountain Trail in the Big Frog Mountain Wilderness.

DETAILS: Begin at the gatepost at the back right corner of the Lost Corral parking lot. Follow the jeep trail to the right (FS 2004), ignoring a path to the left. Near the beginning, and in the winter, the Hiwassee River can be observed on the right. At 0.8 mile, after some rather steep sections, the 4 WD road enters the watershed of Coffee Creek, which drains from the gap between Gee Knob and Chestnut Mountain. The trail comes within sight of Coffee Creek at 1.0 mile.

At 1.8 miles and at 1,520 feet elevation the trailhead for the Chestnut Mountain Loop Trail is on the left (UTM 16S 0724911E/3902239N). It is marked with the standard FS fiberglass stake with the number 104. There are also three wooden posts here to block vehicles from the trail. The trail is an old road all the way to Iron Gap and is marked with the "dotted i" blaze. The gap between Gee Knob and Chestnut Mountain is reached at 2.1 miles. This is the boundary of the Gee Creek Wilderness Area, so there is a sign and an old registration box here. The trail makes a sharp right here and is well marked with another fiberglass stake. The trail immediately becomes rockier, wilder, and steeper as it begins the climb up Chestnut Mountain. At 2.3 miles—in winter—good views of the entire Gee Creek Gorge are visible. Later the views include the Hiwassee River and the Tennessee Valley south of the nose of Starr Mountain. The views last all the way to the top of Chestnut Mountain. At 2.8 miles the trail begins some fairly steep switchbacks that will abruptly end at the top of the mountain.

The highest elevation, the top of Chestnut Mountain, is reached at 3.3 miles. From this point, it will take less than half the time to get to Iron Gap that it took to reach the top of the mountain; it is all downhill, or level, and gently graded. At 3.7 miles the old trail crosses the first of two springs spaced only a few dozen yards apart. However, they do not run in dry seasons. From here the trail is a relatively uneventful, but very pleasant, walk down the top of Chestnut Mountain, gradually easing off to the left (west) of the crest.

At 5.1 miles the trail begins a sharper descent. A sizable stream crosses the trail at 5.4 miles. Just beyond the stream the trail is strewn with several table-sized boulders that look oddly out of place. From here the trail begins a short, much steeper descent to Iron Gap. Just before the gap is an FS sign-in box, a row of posts to prevent vehicle entrance, and a short section of road that serves as a parking area. The gap and FS 44 are reached at 5.6 miles. The elevation here is about 1,900 feet. To the left on FS 44 it is 2.6 miles to the Starr Mountain Trailhead. To the right is the end of the 4 WD road (FS 2004) from which the Chestnut Mountain Loop Trail began. This makes a good return route of 7.6 miles back to the Lost Corral Parking Area. However, the 4 WD road is not in the Gee Creek Wilderness Area so the forest is not nearly as pristine.

131. CHESTNUT MOUNTAIN 4 WD ROAD (FS 2004, TI TRAIL 22)

LENGTH: 7.6 miles

ELEVATION CHANGE: Low point, 750 feet; high point, 2,000 feet

DIFFICULTY: Moderate

TRAILHEADS: Lost Corral (start); Iron Gap (end)

TOPOGRAPHIC MAPS: USGS Oswald Dome, TN; Etowah, TN; Mecca, TN

COMMENTS: This is a well-used 4 WD road that ends at the same location that the Chestnut Mountain Loop Trail begins, therefore providing an ideal round-trip hike of 9.6 miles, beginning at Iron Gap. The trail is poorly marked with the "dotted i," but because of the heavy 4 WD traffic there is no trouble following it. Part of the 4 WD road is also described under the Chestnut Mountain Loop Trail above. Note that there is also a Chestnut Mountain Trail in the Big Frog Mountain section (FS Trail 63; TI Trail 21).

DETAILS: The trail begins at the Lost Corral Trailhead. It is easily noticed beside a large bulletin board. The trail is rocky and steep for about the first 2.5 miles. The trail is then reasonably level and a pleasant walk. At 0.85 mile there are the remnants of an old trail leading off to the left at a right angle. At 1.8 miles is a junction with the Chestnut Mountain Loop Trail (FS Trail 104) on the left. This junction is well marked (UTM 16S 0724911E/3902239N). At 2.0 miles there is a white metal cross nailed to a tree on the right side of the trail with the inscription "James Newman 1967–Sept. 7, 2001." At 5.1 miles there is a viewpoint with an excellent view to the east. At 7.6 miles the trail ends at Iron Gap.

132. STARR MOUNTAIN HORSE TRAIL (FS TRAIL 120, TI TRAIL 73)

LENGTH: 3.5 miles

ELEVATION CHANGE: Insignificant

DIFFICULTY: Easy

TRAILHEADS: Starr Mountain (start); Starr Mountain Road (end)

USE: Hiking, mountain bike, equestrian

TOPOGRAPHIC MAP: USGS Mecca, TN

COMMENTS: This trail is a well-maintained USFS road behind locked gates and is a very pleasant hiking trail even though it is open to horses. It follows the top of Starr Mountain and is almost level its entire length. There are views to the west in winter.

DETAILS: The trail begins at a locked gate on the west side of FS 44, where it makes a sharp hairpin turn. There is plenty of parking room in front of the gate. The trail goes gently uphill for 0.4 mile to the junction with the Starr Mountain Trail (FS Trail 190). At 0.65 mile there is an overlook on the west side of the trail with a well-worn trail going straight down the slope of Starr Mountain. At 1.5 miles on the right is a junction with the Burkett Ivens House Trail (FS Trail 122). At 0.37 mile from the end of the trail at the Starr Mountain Road there is a locked gate.

133. BURKETT IVENS HORSE TRAIL (FS TRAIL 122, TI TRAIL 18)

LENGTH: 0.6 mile

ELEVATION CHANGE: Low point, 1,750 feet; high point, 2,100 feet

DIFFICULTY: Easy

TRAILHEADS: Burkett Ivens (start); Starr Mountain Horse Trail (end)

USE: Hiking, equestrian, mountain bike

TOPOGRAPHIC MAP: USGS Mecca, TN

COMMENTS: The trail is well defined and easily followed, although it is now seldom used. It has a moderate grade for its entire length and is blazed with the common "dotted i."

DETAILS: There is a small cleared area at the trailhead on the downhill side of FS 44 to park several cars; however, the slope is slippery in wet weather. The trail begins on a recent logging road and immediately crosses Yellow Creek. At 640 feet from the road the trail makes a sharp left off the logging road (UTM 16S 0729358E/ 3908678N). Care must be used to find this turn-off, as it is not marked. The balance of the trail is very easy to follow as it leads up to the Starr Mountain Horse Trail.

134. BULLET CREEK HORSE TRAIL (FS TRAIL 121, TI TRAIL 17)

135. BULLET CREEK SPUR TRAIL (FS TRAIL 121A, TI TRAIL 17A)

LENGTH: Bullet Creek Horse Trail, 2.7 miles; Bullet Creek Spur Trail, 0.7 mile

ELEVATION CHANGE: Bullet Creek Horse Trail, low point, 1,700 feet, high point, 1,820 feet; Bullet Creek Spur Trail, low point, 1,700 feet, high point, 1,910 feet

DIFFICULTY: Easy

TRAILHEADS: Bullet Creek Horse Trail: White Cliffs Road (start) and Starr Mountain Road (end); Bullet Creek Spur Trail: White Cliff (start) and Bullet Creek Horse Trail (end)

USE: Hiking, equestrian, mountain bike

TOPOGRAPHIC MAP: USGS Mecca, TN

COMMENTS: Even though this is a horse trail, it is a very pleasant and well-maintained trail for hiking. It generally follows the eastern side of Bullet Creek, finally crossing to the western side just before the northern end. The trail could be muddy in wet weather.

DETAILS: The Bullet Creek Horse Trail begins as an old logging road just to the east of the concrete bridge where FS 220 crosses Bullet Creek. The logging road is shown on the TI map, but the trail is shown almost 2.0 miles to the northeast of its proper location. The logging road soon ends, but the trail continues in the bottomland of the creek. The junction with Bullet Creek Spur is 0.5 mile from the northern end of the trail (UTM 16S 734443E/3912014N). This junction is well marked. The spur does not stay in the creek bottom but goes generally uphill to FS 220. FS Trail 121 continues to its termination at the Starr Mountain Road (FS 297).

136. HOGBACK HORSE TRAIL (FS TRAIL 126, TI TRAIL 46)

LENGTH: 2.5 miles

ELEVATION CHANGE: Low point, 1,900 feet; high point, 2,130 feet

DIFFICULTY: Easy

TRAILHEADS: Poplar Springs Ridge (start); Hogback Spur Horse Trail (end)

USE: Equestrian, hiking, mountain bike

TOPOGRAPHIC MAP: USGS Mecca, TN

COMMENTS: The Hogback Horse Trail descends northward from FS 44 along the crest of Hogback Ridge to an intersection with Hogback Spur Horse Trail (FS Trail 126A). Most of the trail is on graveled FS 1106 that is gated to prevent vehicular traffic. The trail is easy to follow, and, when leaves are down, there are pleasant views of Pine and Brown Mountains to the east and of Starr Mountain to the west. Note: The TI map incorrectly shows the Hogback Spur Trail (Trail 126A) ending at an old USFS road near the northern end of FS Trail 126. Actually, Trail 126A continues on that old USFS road west to a trailhead at FS 44.

DETAILS: Starting at the southern end, the trail gradually descends along the ridgecrest. It passes several clearings, including one with a small pond, the only water to be found on the trail. At 2.1 miles the gravel road ends and the trail continues straight ahead into the woods. It then follows an older roadbed, but at 2.2 miles it turns sharply off that old roadbed at a horse trail sign with an arrow pointing right. The trail then curves around to the left and again reaches the ridgecrest. In this area there are a few, very old, white blazes. At 2.5 miles reach an intersection with another graveled USFS road. This is the northern end of the Hogback Horse Trail and its junction with Hogback Spur (FS Trail 126A). To the left on the gravel road, which is the Hogback Spur Trail, it is 1.2 miles to the west end of the Hogback Spur Trail at FS 44; to the right it is 1.5 miles to the east end of the Hogback Spur Trail, also on FS 44.

137. HOGBACK SPUR TRAIL (FS TRAIL 126A, TI TRAIL 46A)

LENGTH: 2.6 miles

ELEVATION CHANGE: Low point, 1,550 feet; high point, 1,900 feet

DIFFICULTY: Easy

TRAILHEADS: Hogback Ridge (start); Yellow Creek (end)

USE: Equestrian, hiking, mountain bike

TOPOGRAPHIC MAP: USGS Mecca, TN

COMMENTS: Hogback Spur provides access to the northern end of the Hogback Horse Trail. There are more parking spaces available at the western end of the spur, which is the start of the description below. The trail has a gentle grade for its entire route, and toward the eastern end there are some nice views down into the valley below. Note: The TI map incorrectly shows this trail ending at an old USFS road near the northern end of FS Trail 126. Actually, Trail 126A continues on that old USFS road west to a trailhead at FS 44.

DETAILS: Starting at the western end of Hogback Spur, proceed on a gradually ascending graveled road. At 1.1 miles reach the intersection with Hogback Horse Trail (FS Trail 126) on the right, which climbs the ridgecrest to the south for 2.5 miles to its southern end at FS 44. There are signs here indicating the mileages in three directions. The actual distance from here to the eastern end of Hogback Spur is 1.5 miles and to the southern end of Hogback Horse Trail is 2.5 miles. One of the signs identifies Hogback Horse Trail as FS Trail 106 and the eastern end of Hogback Spur as FS Trail 1123.

Continuing east on the old road and the Hogback Spur Trail, at 1.4 miles (0.3 mile past that intersection) the graveled USFS road ends and the trail now follows an older roadbed. At 2.0 miles there is a large Yucca plant, indicating the possible existence of an earlier homesite. In this area one can see down into the broad valley to the east, where there are several homes and farms. At 2.2 miles there is a survey marker indicating the boundary between the CNF on the east and a private inholding to the west. At 2.5 miles reach an open wildlife field. In middle of the field the trail intersects an old road and turns left on that road. It is the road used by the USFS to access the wildlife field. At 2.6 miles reach the end of Hogback Spur at its eastern trailhead on FS 44.

138. YELLOW CREEK HORSE TRAIL (FS TRAIL 123, TI TRAIL 86)

LENGTH: 1.2 miles

ELEVATION CHANGE: Insignificant

DIFFICULTY: Easy

TRAILHEADS: Round Mountain (start); Burkett Ivens (finish)

USE: Hiking, mountain bike, equestrian

TOPOGRAPHIC MAP: USGS Mecca, TN

COMMENTS: The trail starts and ends on FS 44 and parallels the road for its entire length. The trail is in a very poor state of maintenance, so it is difficult to follow, and in general there are much better trails for hiking in the area.

DETAILS: The trail begins at a locked gate on FS 11215 where it joins FS 44 (UTM 16S 0730910E/390886N). At 730 feet on FS 11215 the trail makes a sharp left off the road. The trail is then marked with the common "dotted i" blazes, but the blazes are very old and difficult to see as of this date. The trail ends at the same trailhead as the Burkett Ivens Horse Trail, but the trail would be extremely difficult to find beginning at this end. To find it look for blazes on the right immediately after crossing the creek.

139. GEE CREEK WATCHABLE WILDLIFE TRAIL (FS TRAIL 151, TI TRAIL 39)

LENGTH: 0.7 mile

ELEVATION CHANGE: Insignificant (50 feet)

DIFFICULTY: Easy

TRAILHEAD: Gee Creek

USE: Hiking

TOPOGRAPHIC MAP: USGS Oswald Dome, TN

COMMENTS: This is a loop trail constructed in 1994 by Etowah city school children for the purpose of observing wildlife. The trail does traverse varied types of vegetation from open areas to dense woods. There are several bird boxes along the way, but in the year 2001 the trail was in poor condition.

DETAILS: The trail begins on the west side of the Gee Creek Road 500 feet from the end of the road at the Gee Creek Trailhead. The beginning of the trail is well marked with a large bulletin board. A single trail begins at the bulletin board, but in a few hundred feet it splits to make a loop.

140. FISHERMAN TRAIL (FS TRAIL 167, TI TRAIL 34)

LENGTH: 1.4 miles

ELEVATION CHANGE: Insignificant

DIFFICULTY: Easy

TRAILHEAD: Quinn Springs Campground (start); Hiwassee Picnic Area (end)

USE: Hiking

TOPOGRAPHIC MAP: USGS Oswald Dome, TN

COMMENTS: This is a well-blazed (with the "dotted i") and maintained trail along the shore of the Hiwassee River. Some sections are much used by fishermen and are clear, but other sections, especially where the trail passes under power lines, may be somewhat grown over by brush and briers.

DETAILS: The trail begins at a parking area across TN 30 from the USFS Quinn Springs Campground. The trail then follows close along the shore of the river for its entire length, crossing small streams on wooden bridges and, in two locations, crossing over piles of driftwood deposited during periods of unusually high water. At 0.7 mile the trail passes only a few feet from the back of Taylors Island Picnic Parking Area, and a large gravel parking lot for the picnic area gives convenient access to the middle section of the trail. At about 1.3 miles the trail is forced close to TN 30 by a shallow channel of the river, requiring the trail to end on the shoulder of the highway 0.1 mile before the Hiwassee Picnic Area.

141. SPANKING STUMP TRAIL (FS TRAIL 169, TI TRAIL 71)

LENGTH: 0.27 mile

ELEVATION CHANGE: Insignificant

DIFFICULTY: Easy

TRAILHEAD: Quinn Springs Campground (start and end)

USE: Hiking

TOPOGRAPHIC MAP: USGS Oswald Dome, TN

COMMENTS: This is a short forest walk with sign posts pointing out interesting aspects of the forest. This trail is especially inviting during the fall color season.

DETAILS: The trailhead is to the right of the parking area as one enters the Quinn Springs area from TN 30. It is located just across the loop road from the restroom building. A few feet from the beginning the trail splits and makes a loop.

142. OSWALD DOME TRAIL (FS TRAIL 80, TI TRAIL 60)

LENGTH: 4.0 miles

ELEVATION CHANGE: 2,250 feet

DIFFICULTY: Moderate

TRAILHEADS: Quinn Springs Campground (start); Oswald Dome (end)

USE: Hiking

TOPOGRAPHIC MAPS: USGS Oswald Dome, TN; Etowah, TN; Mecca, TN

COMMENTS: This is a very well-maintained and well-graded trail from Quinn Springs camping area on the Reliance Road to the top of Oswald Dome on Bean Mountain. Oswald Dome is the top of the spectacular mountain straight ahead as one approaches the Hiwassee River on Highway 411 from the north. The trail ends at the radio antennas that can be seen from the highway. In winter there are good views to the west and north, but they are obscured by vegetation in summer. The 2001 edition of the TI map is incorrect where it shows the trail intersecting and following FS 1004 for a few tenths of a mile. The trail does not come within sight of a road until its end at the top of Oswald Dome.

DETAILS: The trail begins at Quinn Springs Campground on TN 30. When turning off TN 30 the parking area for the trail is just to the left. The trailhead is on the south side of the parking area. The first 2.7 miles of the trail is a steady uphill grade to the almost flat top of the mountain. Then the trail levels out to a very moderate grade. The trail is generally through mixed deciduous forest with some stands of Virginia pine that have been heavily attacked by pine beetles. The trail ends at the Oswald Dome Road a few hundred yards from the radio antennas on the summit. There are no views from the summit.

26 Coker Creek

(Includes Coker Creek Scenic Area)

Coker Creek is a small, 443-acre scenic area in Polk County, TN, and the Ocoee/Hiwassee Ranger District near the Hiwassee River. It protects an especially scenic portion of Coker Creek before it flows into the Hiwassee River. The most outstanding sight in the scenic area is Coker Creek Falls, a series of ledge falls, up to 40 feet high, that rival any other falls in the CNF. The falls are located in a narrow, densely forested gorge, with evergreens along Coker Creek and deciduous trees on the slopes. The scenic area itself is a small part of a large valley through which Coker Creek flows to the Hiwassee River. The larger, and unprotected, valley is bounded on the west by Duckett Ridge Road (FS 22), on the east by TN 68 and Unicoi Mountain, and on the south by the Hiwassee River. The Unicoi Mountain Trail (FS 83) runs along Unicoi Mountain, providing outstanding views of the gorge and the Hiwassee River Valley. The scenic area is designated in the CNF's 2004 plan revision.

The forest is second growth, and hardwood species typical of the southern Appalachians dominate the area along with some large old-growth hemlock and white pine. Vegetation also includes sassafras, ginseng, flame azalea, mountain mint, mountain laurel, rhododendron, the uncommon Carolina hemlock, Fraser's sedge, and Allegheny cliff fern. Many wildflowers bloom from early spring through fall. Sandberry,

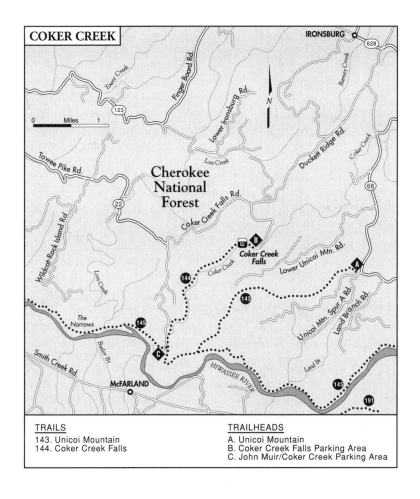

TRAILS
143. Unicoi Mountain
144. Coker Creek Falls

TRAILHEADS
A. Unicoi Mountain
B. Coker Creek Falls Parking Area
C. John Muir/Coker Creek Parking Area

blackberry, and blueberry can also be found. Most wildlife species of the southern Appalachians are present, including a large number of wild turkeys.

HISTORY

Just north of the scenic area, near Ironsburg and beside Coker Creek, a few foundation stones remain from the Tellico (formerly Carroll) Ironworks. Carroll Ironworks purchased the ironworks from the Cherokee Indians, who originally built "the works" prior to the War of 1812. During the winter of 1863, General Sherman's army destroyed the ironworks. Panning for gold occurred in the Coker Creek area before the 1847 California Gold Rush, with Coker Creek being one of the few TN gold-producing areas. An operation partially owned by T. F. Peck proved quite profitable. Just before 1900, a railroad was built in the area and was a major factor in attracting large timber operations during the first quarter of the twentieth century. W. C. Heyser, then C. A. Scott, and finally Babcock Logging Company cut over much of the area during that period. In 1933, 85,000 or more acres were sold to the USFS by the timber companies, forming the core of the current Tellico Wildlife Management Area. The Coker Creek Community commemorates that past and sponsors an annual Autumn Gold Festival featuring gold panning and other festival-type activities.

A 375-acre scenic area was originally designated in the CNF's 1988 management plan and such designation is continued for a slightly larger area in the 2004 plan revision. The Unicoi Mountain Trail is not within a protected area under the current plan. Conservationists have long requested the CNF to protect more of the wonderful natural area bounded by the Hiwassee River, Coker Creek, and TN 68, but such requests have consistently been denied.

TRAILHEADS AND MAPS

Unicoi Mountain Trailhead

Follow TN 68 south from Tellico Plains, TN, through the Coker Creek Community. South of the community, about 12.5 miles from Tellico Plains, note the Ironsburg Methodist Church on the right. Start keeping mileage there. At 0.1 mile farther, note on the left the Calvary Baptist Church. At 3.5 miles from the Ironsburg Methodist Church, the highway takes a sharp left turn downhill. At the turn, on the right, is a small parking area with a gated logging road going downhill. On the uphill side of the logging road is a series of dirt mounds (barriers to ORVs). A trail is visible in the center of the mounds heading up the ridge; this is the Unicoi Mountain Trail (FS 83).

Note that another 0.3 mile down TN 68 brings you to the Unicoi Mountain motorcycle trail on the left side of the road, heading up the mountain to Buck Bald. Although a motorcycle trail, it is not used very much by ORVs and is a scenic hike. Another 2.2 miles on TN 68 brings you to the John Muir Trail (FS Trail 152). Womble Branch runs into the Hiwassee River near this point; the trailhead is on the right where TN 68 first comes down to the Hiwassee River.

Duckett Ridge Road Trailheads: Coker Creek Falls Parking Area and John Muir/Coker Creek Parking Area

Follow TN 68 south from Tellico Plains, TN, for about 12.5 miles through the Coker Creek Community. South of the community, note the Ironsburg Methodist Church on the right. Start measuring mileage here. Just beyond this church, opposite the Calvary Baptist Church, turn right onto County 628. At 0.9 mile take a left turn onto County 626. This is also FS 22, known as the Duckett Ridge Road, but the only sign at the intersection is the County 626 sign. On the left at the intersection is the Ironsburg Cemetery. Continue to the right at 1.4 miles, where County 625 turns to the left. The pavement ends at 1.6 miles; at 3.8 miles turn left on FS 2138. As of the early 2000s there was no sign at this intersection except for the number 2138. FS 2138 descends steeply one mile to a parking area beside Coker Creek (UTM 16S 0739643E/3897589N). Use care in descending this road in wet weather, as it may be difficult to drive back out. The trail (FS Trail 183) proceeds downstream from the parking area. There is space for a few tents near the creek.

If you continue on Duckett Ridge Road, past the FS 2128 intersection for 1.6 miles, you will reach an intersection with FS 22 making a sharp right turn. Take the left road, which is FS 22B. It goes downhill another 1.6 miles to a parking area above the creek (UTM 16S 0737578E/3855780N). This is the John Muir/Coker Creek Parking Area. The John Muir Trail (FS Trail 152) goes west, toward the Hiwassee River, from the right side (west) of this parking area. A bad road continues a short distance down to the creek, where there is an area used for ORV camping. At the end of the road, about 0.2 mile from the parking area above the creek, are two trailheads. Coker Creek Trail (FS Trail 183) proceeds straight ahead up the left side of Coker Creek. The eastern portion of the John Muir Trail crosses

Coker Creek on a wooden bridge built during the summer of 1990. It proceeds up Coker Creek a very short distance on an old logging road, then turns back to the south and up to a gap. At about 0.45 mile from the bridge there is a trail up the ridge to the left; this is the Unicoi Mountain Trail (FS Trail 83). A sign marks the trailhead as "Unicoi Mountain Trail No. 83, State Highway 68 4." The John Muir Trail continues to the right through the gap.

TOPOGRAPHIC MAPS: USGS McFarland, TN; Farner, TN. TI Map 781, Tellico and Ocoee Rivers, CNF.

TRAIL DESCRIPTIONS

143. UNICOI MOUNTAIN TRAIL (FS TRAIL 83, TI TRAIL 80)

LENGTH: 4.25 miles

ELEVATION CHANGE: Low point, 1,240 feet; high point, 2,080 feet

DIFFICULTY: Moderate

TRAILHEADS: John Muir/Coker Creek Parking Area(start) and Unicoi Mountain (end)

TRAIL CONNECTIONS: John Muir Trail

USE: Hiking

TOPOGRAPHIC MAPS: USGS McFarland, TN; Farner, TN-NC

COMMENTS: This is an easy, well-defined trail marked with the common white square over a white rectangle. The trail is described from the John Muir/Coker Creek Parking Area, off the Duckett Ridge Road, to TN 68 but can easily be hiked in either direction; if you arrange a shuttle, you will not have to backtrack. Trail mileage is given from the parking area, not the junction with the John Muir Trail Trailhead, where the official trail begins. There are good views in winter.

DETAILS: The trail (initially on the John Muir Trail) begins at the upper end of the creekside camping area at a trail sign marked with a hiker logo and the number "152." The trail immediately crosses Coker Creek on a very well-built wooden bridge. Immediately on the other side of Coker Creek, the trail proceeds left up the ridge on an old logging road. Note that the old road comes in from the right after having crossed the creek; this road formerly provided ORV access to this side of Coker Creek. At 0.06 mile there is another hiker logo and John

Muir Trail sign, together with another sign for Trail 152. Just beyond those signs, the trail swings sharply around to the right and heads gradually upward across a series of ridges. Where the trail turns sharply right, there are signs of an old road proceeding up Coker Creek, to the left. To the right the trail gradually leaves the Coker Creek gorge bottom and its hemlock forest and climbs into a mixed deciduous forest.

At 0.45 mile there is a junction where the Unicoi Mountain Trail officially begins. The John Muir Trail, FS Trail 152, makes a right turn here and is well marked. The Unicoi Mountain Trail makes a sharp left turn at a huge beech tree and heads up the ridge. It is also marked with a hiker logo and number "83." In addition, there is a mileage sign pointing out the two trails: "Unicoi Mountain Trail No. 83, State Highway 68 4; John Muir Trail No. 152, State Highway 68 5." An old road proceeds straight across the gap behind the mileage sign. Use care not to follow it. At 0.6 mile the top of the ridge is reached, and the trail simply crosses and traverses around to the right of a knoll toward a gap. At 0.7 mile the trail passes above and to the left of the gap previously mentioned and continues to traverse along the side of the ridge. Above the gap is a profusion of small white pines that are particularly scenic on winter hikes when hardwood leaves are gone. The abundant white pines continue and get larger under a canopy of large deciduous trees. Toward the TN 68 end of the trail there will also be a profusion of small white pines. Wildflowers are plentiful on this trail in the spring and include wild iris, several varieties of trillium, lady's slippers, and maidenhair ferns. Poison ivy is also present, especially at the TN 68 end of the trail.

At 1.0 mile the trail reaches the top of the ridge and crosses a gap, proceeding now to the left side of the ridge and a knoll on the ridge. After going around the knoll, the trail reaches a beautiful gap between two knolls on the ridge, flat and wide, at 1.15 miles. This is an especially nice place with the sound of the Hiwassee River wafting up from below and a portion of the river visible on the right side of the trail. Straight ahead is another knoll with large white rock outcrops visible in the winter. It would be a great campsite if water were carried from below. This is the closest the trail comes to the Hiwassee River. The trail proceeds past the gap around the left side of the knoll, from which a view is available in winter. The hardwood forest here is especially impressive, with very little undergrowth.

At 1.35 miles the trail returns to the ridgetop, which is fairly level at this point. The Hiwassee River is still off to the right. The trail soon leaves the ridgetop and traverses along the left side of the ridge, looking steeply down into the Coker Creek gorge. The trail proceeds slightly downward to another gap at 1.6 miles. At this point the valley on the right is narrow, with the opposite ridge quite close. The trail then heads up the ridge on the other side of the gap, traversing to the left. After going around a small knoll, the trail ascends very gradually, and in almost a straight line, toward a side ridge running down into the Coker Creek gorge.

At 2.0 miles the ridgetop is reached. Here the handsome forest ends and a 20-odd-year-old clear-cut begins. This is a textbook illustration of the difference in a mature forest and an old clear-cut, with small trees very close together. There is a dim trail leading out the ridge to the left, where there are great views looking west, with Chestnut Mountain and Oswald Dome Mountain looming prominent on the horizon. At 2.2 miles, the clear-cut ends and the woods resume.

At 2.6 miles you will reach the top of the ridge at a point between the two highest knolls on the ridge, one to the left at 2,160 feet, and the other to the right at 2,120 feet. At this point, the trail simply crosses over the ridge and traverses down on the other side below the knoll to the left. In the winter the views are outstanding from this point looking south over the Hiwassee River gorge to the mountains on the horizon. At 2.9 miles, you will reach a gap and will see an old logging road coming up from the right. The trail proceeds down the

One of a series of cascades that make up Coker Creek Falls. Photograph by Will Skelton.

old logging road straight ahead, to the left side of the ridge. The trail follows this old road all the way to TN 68.

At 3.0 miles, the trail reaches the top of the ridge and proceeds along it. The trail at this point is wide and almost level, making for very easy walking. The trail gradually follows the ridge, traversing around knolls and leading slightly upward. At 3.35 miles, the trail begins descending, continuing along the ridgetop. White oaks blanket the right side of the trail at this point. The trail is consistently almost on top of the ridge, with great wintertime views both to the left and right. At 3.67 miles, the trail leaves the ridgetop and heads down the right side of the ridge. After a short distance the trail begins to descend more steeply, down toward TN 68. Near the end of the trail is a series of earthen bumps designed to keep out ORVs. Just beyond the third of these bumps is the trailhead sign "Unicoi Mountain Trail No. 83; Coker Creek 5." Finally, at 4.25 miles, you will reach the last of the earthen mounds, and you will see TN 68 directly ahead with a gravel logging road proceeding down to the right.

144. COKER CREEK FALLS TRAIL (FS TRAIL 183, TI TRAIL 26)

LENGTH: 2.7 miles

ELEVATION CHANGE: Low point, 940 feet; high point, 1,360 feet

DIFFICULTY: Moderate

TRAILHEADS: Coker Creek Falls Parking Area (start) and John Muir/Coker Creek Parking Area (end)

TYPE: Hiking

TOPOGRAPHIC MAPS: USGS McFarland, TN; Farner, TN-NC

COMMENTS: The distinguishing feature of this trail is Coker Creek Falls, which is located just downstream from the parking area. The trail is well marked with two white blazes, a square blaze above a rectangular blaze. It is also fairly open, and is very easy to hike. The roaring of Coker Creek is almost always present. It can be hiked easily in either direction but is described from the Coker Creek Falls Parking Area to the John Muir/Coker Creek Parking Area.

DETAILS: The trail proceeds down Coker Creek from the parking lot. There is no sign at the beginning of the trail. Due to vandalism the USFS has found it necessary to place their signs down the trail just out of sight of the parking areas. A sign 125 feet from the parking area indicates "Coker Creek Falls Trail No. 183, John Muir Trail No. 152 3."

Coker Creek Falls is located just downstream at 0.1 mile from the parking area and the initial trail sign. You will hear their roar before you reach them and will be impressed by the series of spectacular waterfalls as you walk down the trail. The falls are formed by rock ledges that extend completely across the creek, 75 feet or so. There are four major ledge falls that vary in height from 5 to 40 feet, with shoals between the falls. Dense evergreen trees cover both banks and accentuate the white water and roaring noise. A short side trail, with log handrails, goes down to the lower, and largest, fall.

Below the falls at 0.2 mile the trail heads up to the top of a ridge and away from the creek. You will see occasional views of additional, smaller falls and will constantly hear the roar of the creek as you proceed along this trail. The trail then dips down to the creek and back up on the side of the gorge, then back down and back up again. Thereafter, a series of steep switchbacks lead down toward the creek. At 1.1 miles there is a good campsite beside a small tributary stream coming in from the right. On the other side of the small stream is one long switchback up the hill to the side of the gorge. The trail at this point follows the steep gorge side, in some cases looking almost directly down at Coker Creek below.

The trail then descends to another small tributary creek coming in from the right at 1.7 miles and continues just above Coker Creek. It thereafter descends even lower down toward Coker Creek, where the creek has somewhat flattened. The trail at this point (1.8 miles) runs level and straight along an old logging road. However, at 2.2 miles the trail leaves the old road, which is washed out in a bend of Coker Creek ahead, and goes up the side of the ridge to the right. It then descends again down to the old road and more level walking. However, the old road and trail almost immediately angle up the hill to the right and then turn sharply to the right. About 50 feet beyond the sharp turn to the right, the trail leaves the old road with a sharp turn to the left. Be careful and do not continue up the old road. After what is essentially a Z-series of turns, you should be following the white blazes down Coker Creek. The trail then goes down into and around the creek ravine, then down the Coker Creek gorge above Coker Creek.

After a short distance the trail returns again down to the creek and ends at 2.7 miles at a junction with the John Muir Trail. This junction is at a large flat area 200 yards from the John Muir/Coker Creek Parking Area and is described in the "Trailheads and Maps" section. A sign here reads "Coker Creek Falls Trail No 183, Coker Creek Falls 3; John Muir Trail No 152, State Highway 68 6." However, as this sign is just out of view from the trail junction, one

Hiker admires huge beech tree in Coker Creek area. Photograph by Will Skelton.

must walk a few feet up a steep hill on the blazed Coker Creek Falls trail to view the sign.

Although the Coker Creek Trail officially ends at the junction with the John Muir Trail, the Hiwassee River can be reached by following the John Muir Trail a short distance west of the parking area, where an unmaintained trail branches to the left and continues a short distance to the river. The trip is rewarding, especially in winter, but the main flow of the river at this point is routed underground in a tunnel between Apalachia Dam and Apalachia Power House. Use care on this unmaintained trail, as it can be dangerous.

27 John Muir National Recreation Trail

The John Muir National Recreation Trail was built in 1972 through the efforts of the Youth Conservation Corps and the Senior Community Service Employment Program. The trail follows the scenic Hiwassee River, named after the Cherokee Indian word *ayuwasi* (meadow). The first 3.0-mile section is designed for senior citizens and is quite easy to walk. This section of the river is known for trout fishing and canoeing. As many as 50,000 whitewater rafters use the river every year, and it is one of the nation's outstanding scenic streams. The trail is in the Ocoee/Hiwassee Ranger District in Polk County, TN. The CNF's 2004 plan revision provides for a protected corridor for the trail. The CNF lists the trail as being 17.0 miles long, whereas our measurements show 19.0 miles.

HISTORY

The trail was named for Sierra Club founder John Muir; he traveled this section of the Hiwassee River during a walk from Kentucky to Florida and documented the walk in his book *A Thousand Mile Walk to the Gulf*. On September 19, 1867, after crossing from TN to Murphy, NC, John Muir wrote the following:

> My path all today led me along the leafy banks of the Hiwassee, a most impressive mountain river. Its channel is very rough, as it crosses the edges of upturned rock strata, some of them standing at right angles, or glancing off obliquely to right and left. Thus a multitude of short, resounding cataracts are produced, and the river is restrained from the headlong speed due to its volume and the inclination of its bed.

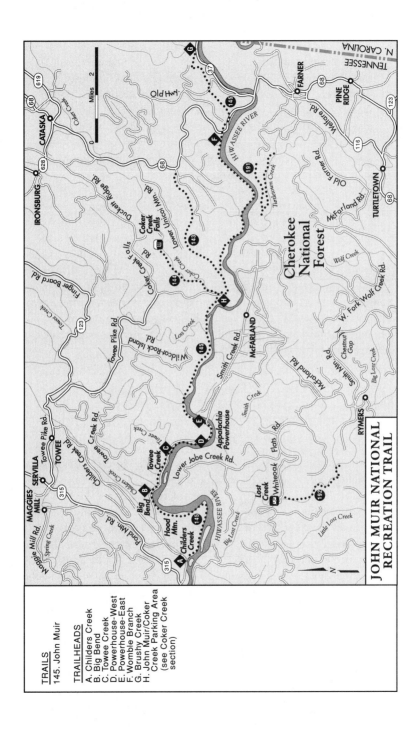

TRAILS
145. John Muir

TRAILHEADS
A. Childers Creek
B. Big Bend
C. Towee Creek
D. Powerhouse-West
E. Powerhouse-East
F. Womble Branch
G. Brushy Creek
H. John Muir/Coker
   Creek Parking Area
   (see Coker Creek
   section)

JOHN MUIR NATIONAL
RECREATION TRAIL

All the larger streams of uncultivated countries are mysteriously charming and beautiful, whether flowing in mountains or through swamps and plains. Their channels are interestingly sculptured, far more so than the grandest architectural works of man. The finest of forests are usually found along their banks, and in multitude of falls and rapids the wilderness finds a voice. Such a river is the Hiwassee, with its surface broken to a thousand sparkling gems, and its forest walls vine-draped and flowery as Eden. And how fine the songs it sings!

There is a great variety of wildlife present along the trail, including songbirds, as well as grouse and wild turkey. The larger animals are beaver, raccoon, fox, deer, and wild boar. Water-related wildlife is especially prevalent along this trail. A wide variety of wildflowers may be found, including squaw root, bloodroot, toothwort, fire pink, columbine, stargrass, trillium, white and yellow trout lilies, rattlesnake plantain, wild sorrel, dog hobble, bishop's cap, fairy wand, little brown jug, yuccas, and wild ginger. The trail is protected by a minimum 200-foot corridor pursuant to the 1988 CNF management plan. Protection is continued in the CNF 2004 plan revision.

TRAILHEADS AND MAPS

West Section Trailheads: Childers Creek, Big Bend, Towee Creek, Powerhouse-West and Powerhouse-East Trailheads

From the north, take US 411S through Etowah, TN, cross the Hiwassee River, go 0.5 mile, and turn left on TN 30. From the south follow US 411N and turn right on TN 30 just before crossing the Hiwassee River. Go 5.7 miles on TN 30 and turn left onto TN 315 at the bridge that crosses the river (Reliance Bridge). At the end of the bridge, take the first road to the right (FS 105). The mileage to the trailheads will be measured from this point. The Childers Creek Trailhead is on the right at 0.5 mile. Turn right onto FS 108 at 1.2 miles (the sign on the building is Reliance Visitors Center and the sign on the road is Childers Creek Road). Take the right fork at 1.5 miles. The Big Bend Trailhead is at 2.5 miles. The Towee Creek Trailhead is at 2.5 miles. The Powerhouse-West Trailhead is at 4.6 miles. The Powerhouse-East Trailhead is at 4.8 miles. The footbridge across the river to the Apalachia Power House is a short distance on a gravel road from the Powerhouse-East parking area.

East Section Trailheads: Womble Branch and Brushy Creek Trailheads

TN 68 runs south from Coker Creek, TN, to Ducktown, TN, crossing the Hiwassee River just below Apalachia Lake. From Coker Creek proceed south on TN 68 into Polk County. After mile marker 3, where the road comes down to Hiwassee River and takes a distinct bend to the southeast along the river, the Womble Branch Trailhead is an unmarked pull-off on the left at 3.7 miles. Womble Branch runs into the Hiwassee River at this point. To hike west, walk across TN 68 and proceed downstream on the trail along the Hiwassee River. The trail mileage to Childers Creek Trailhead is 15.8 miles from this point. To hike east, climb the steep bank on stairs from the trailhead. From Ducktown, drive north on TN 68, pass the Farner Post Office, cross the Hiwassee River, and at 2.6 miles from the post office the Womble Branch Trailhead will be on the right just as the road turns north away from the river.

The Brushy Creek Trailhead is the eastern end of the trail and is located on County 37 (Schuler Creek Road), which joins TN 68 on the north side of the bridge across the Hiwassee River. Following County 37 from TN 68, the junction with FS 311 is at 0.3 mile, the Brushy Creek Trailhead is at 1.7 miles, and the NC state line is at 2.1 miles. The trailhead is unmarked and has a large kudzu patch on the left. There is just enough room to pull a car off the road at the concrete bridge that crosses Brushy Creek at the end of the kudzu. The trailhead can be found on the left about 100 yards down the jeep road that cuts through the kudzu. The road is extremely muddy in wet weather. The trail climbs over the ridge and goes downstream to Womble Branch Trailhead (3.2 miles) and Childers Creek Trailhead (19.0 miles).

OTHER TRAILHEADS: See Coker Creek section for trailheads in that area.

TOPOGRAPHIC MAPS: USGS McFarland, TN; Farner, TN-NC. TI Map 781, Tellico and Ocoee Rivers, CNF.

TRAIL DESCRIPTION

145. JOHN MUIR NATIONAL RECREATION TRAIL (FS TRAIL 152, TI TRAIL 49)

LENGTH: 19.0 miles

ELEVATION CHANGE: Low point, 600 feet; high point, 1,200 feet

TRAILHEADS: Childers Creek (start) and Brushy Creek (end)

TRAIL CONNECTIONS: Coker Creek Trail, Unicoi Mountain Trail

TYPE: Hiking

TOPOGRAPHIC MAPS: USGS McFarland, TN; Farner, TN-NC

COMMENTS: The trail is identified with either the number "152" (although some USFS maps show it as FS Trail 108) or "JM" for John Muir. The entire trail essentially follows the north bank of the Hiwassee River. The CNF lists the trail mileage as 17.0 miles and the TI map shows 20.7, but we measured the identifiable portion of the trail as 19.0 miles.

DETAILS: The trail begins at Childers Creek Trailhead. There is a footbridge across Childers Creek, and the trail starts off in a southeasterly direction through a meadow, with the river in the distance. After a short way, it passes the first of many towering bluffs on the left, with the Hiwassee River directly on the right. The rock formations consist of micaceous quartzite, quartz schist, mica slate, and mica schist. When the water level is low enough, the rock formations create exciting but only moderately difficult rapids for canoeists and rafters.

At 1.5 miles the trail begins to head north and moves away from the river through large stands of hemlocks, with rhododendrons covering the bluffs. Before long it leaves the river completely and passes through a marshy area. The trail eventually widens as it goes along an old logging trail. At 3.0 miles, it reaches the Big Bend Trailhead. There are roadside facilities available.

The trail proceeds along the road to mile 3.3 and then climbs the bluff next to the road. In 2001, the trail was frequently blocked by fallen trees and needed maintenance. At mile 3.9, the trail reaches a nice rockhouse and shortly after reaches an overlook with a good view of the river and countryside. The trail reaches the Towee Creek Trailhead at mile 4.2. The trail follows the road to mile 4.7. In this section, fishermen have created a network of trails and the main trail is not well marked. The Powerhouse-West Trailhead is at mile 5.3 and the trail is on the road to the Powerhouse-East Trailhead at mile 5.6. The trail follows the gravel road with the sign "Employees only. No parking beyond this point."

At mile 5.7, there is a suspension footbridge that goes over the Hiwassee River to the Apalachia Power House. Do not cross the bridge; instead, the trail continues down under the bridge along the north side of the river (the side opposite the power plant). At mile 5.8, there is a sign: "John Muir Trail. 152. Coker Creek 4. State Highway

68 10." At mile 6.6, the trail goes on the north side of Big Rock Island and has high rocks on both sides of a narrow canyon. There are signs of beaver in this area. At mile 6.8, the trail begins a series of nine switchbacks to the left, then to the right. The trail returns to the river for a brief stretch at mile 7.1, then heads back into the forest of hemlocks, popular, redbuds, dogwoods, yellow buckeyes, ash, ironwoods, sycamores, and cucumber magnolias.

At 7.3 miles, the main trail has a switchback to the left at a "No. 152" trail marker (UTM 16S 0734822E/3896755N). A well-used side trail continues straight ahead that goes down to the river. There are some very interesting rock formations caused by water erosion; these are definitely worth exploring. This section of the river is called the Narrows. Once the trail begins the series of switchbacks at the FS Trail 152 sign, it climbs up the side of the mountain and follows the contour of the bluffs. The trail occasionally provides a glimpse of the river several hundred feet below. The trail reaches the end of the Narrows and descends back down to the river level at mile 8.1. The trail crosses Loss Creek at mile 8.5.

At mile 9.3, the trail reaches an overlook with a magnificent view of the river. It begins heading back down the bluffs with another series

Footbridge across Hiwassee River near Apalachia Power Plant. The John Muir Trail goes underneath the far end of the bridge. Photograph by Roger Jenkins.

of switchbacks for another 0.3 mile. Near the bottom (at mile 9.6), the John Muir Trail merges with a trail from the right that goes down along Coker Creek to its junction with the Hiwassee River. This short but difficult side trail provides a scenic close-up view of the river, bluffs, and Coker Creek. The John Muir Trail quickly reaches the Duckett Ridge Road (FS 22B) at mile 9.7. The trail follows the road down to Coker Creek and to the left up Coker Creek past some primitive vehicle campsites. At the end of the camping area (mile 9.8) the Coker Creek Trail goes straight ahead, while the John Muir Trail forks off to the right across Coker Creek (UTM 16S 0737603E/3896054N). A bridge constructed in 1989 allows a dry crossing.

Once again the trail heads into the forest. In late spring, a wide profusion of mountain laurel, flame azalea, and rhododendrons will be in bud, and the rhododendrons will be in full bloom in early summer. About 0.45 mile from Coker Creek (mile 10.3) there is a trail junction (UTM 16S 0737410E/3895701N). The Unicoi Mountain Trail (FS Trail 83) begins here and proceeds left up the ridge. An old road continues across the gap behind the mileage sign that reads "Unicoi Mtn Trail No. 83, State 68 4; John Muir Trail No. 152, State 68 5." At the junction, continue following the John Muir Trail marker back around to the right, down a long-forgotten roadbed. Cross the small streambed and begin going up the side of the mountain, following its contours.

At 11.5 miles, the trail begins a series of switchbacks down the mountainside. At mile 13, after you have descended to the Hiwassee River, a good lunch spot can often be found on the dry, exposed rock in the middle of the river. The river at this point is mainly diverted, hence the dry rocks; it flows in a huge pipe downstream to the Apalachia Power House to make electricity. The final leg of the trail goes through the forest and along an old roadbed. At times the ferns and poison ivy almost cover the trail. It can be very soggy and sometimes downright muddy after abundant rainfall. At mile 15.8, the trail reaches the Womble Branch Trailhead.

The trail enters Miller Cove at mile 16.2 and has a well-marked crossing of FS 311 at mile 16.9 (UTM 16S 0744448E/3896541N). In the early 2000s, the trail could not be followed through forest that had recently burned. The trail was lost near mile 18.5 (UTM 16S 0745625E/3897229N). The trail descends using switchbacks to an unnamed road and follows it 100 yards to the Brushy Creek Trailhead (UTM 16S 0745872E/3897049N). The total length of the trail is 19.0 miles.

28 Rock Creek Gorge

(Includes Rock Creek Gorge Scenic Area)

This 244-acre Rock Creek Gorge Scenic Area is one of the CNF's oldest scenic areas. Rock Creek, a clear mountain stream with 11 waterfalls along its rugged gorge path, is the focal point of this area. One of

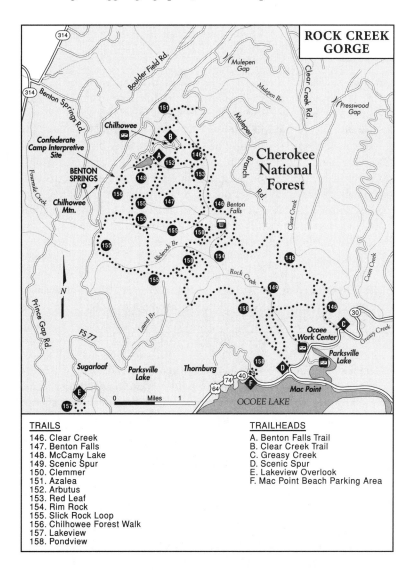

ROCK CREEK GORGE

Cherokee National Forest

TRAILS	TRAILHEADS
146. Clear Creek	A. Benton Falls Trail
147. Benton Falls	B. Clear Creek Trail
148. McCamy Lake	C. Greasy Creek
149. Scenic Spur	D. Scenic Spur
150. Clemmer	E. Lakeview Overlook
151. Azalea	F. Mac Point Beach Parking Area
152. Arbutus	
153. Red Leaf	
154. Rim Rock	
155. Slick Rock Loop	
156. Chilhowee Forest Walk	
157. Lakeview	
158. Pondview	

the falls drops 60 feet over a sheer rock bluff while another cascades 180 feet. The area is close to the picnicking, swimming, camping, and hiking opportunities and developments on Chilhowee Mountain and is within hiking distance of Lake Ocoee developments. The area is also very popular for mountain biking. Adjacent to the scenic area is the 5.2-mile Clear Creek Trail and the 1.6-mile Benton Falls Trail. The scenic area is designated in the CNF's 2004 plan revision and is located in the Ocoee/Hiwassee Ranger District in Polk County, TN, near Lake Ocoee.

HISTORY

Once many of the Cherokee Indians were driven out of this area in 1838, settlers moved in to develop the area for pasture land and agriculture. The two best-known settlers, McCamy and Cronin, built Benton Springs Road up Chilhowee Mountain. During the Civil War there was a Confederate camp nearby, and the area had its share of Civil War homicides. In early 1865, it is reported that Civil War troops were ambushed on Benton Springs Road. One of these legendary soldiers managed to crawl down the mountain to the Greasy Creek community to get help. Years later, a resort area was developed on Chilhowee Mountain and tourists came from surrounding states to enjoy the cooler summer temperatures and the fresh spring water provided by Benton Springs.

The scenic area was first designated for protection in 1965 because of its popularity with local tourists for recreation. This designation was continued in the CNF's 1988 management plan for a 220-acre area. The CNF's 2004 plan revision continues that designation for a slightly larger area. Conservationists have long requested the CNF to protect more of the huge complex of trails located on Chilhowee Mountain, but such requests have consistently been denied. The Clear Creek Trail and Benton Falls Trail are not within the protected scenic area, but, under the CNF management plan, a forest corridor should be maintained along each trail (some past clear-cuts remain evident on the Clear Creek Trail).

TRAILHEADS AND MAPS

Chilhowee Recreation Area Trailheads: Benton Falls Trailhead and Clear Creek Trailhead

The usual approach to Chilhowee Recreation Area is from the west. Starting from the intersection of US 411 and US 64, drive east on US

64. Look for FS 77 on the left at the Ocoee District Ranger Station that is 2.7 miles past the sign marking the entrance to the CNF. If approaching from the east, drive west on US 64 and look for FS 77 on the right after driving some distance along Ocoee Lake. Turn onto paved FS 77, which is signed by number and is also known as Oswald Road (although the name is not signed). Benton Falls Trailhead and Clear Creek Trailhead are located off FS 77.

Benton Falls Trailhead: Drive 7.1 miles on FS 77 past several over-looks and past the historical marker indicating the old Confederate Camp. Turn right into the Chilhowee Recreation Area that is clearly indicated by a large sign. Go 0.5 mile to a parking lot for Lake McCamy. There is a large wooden map that shows the location of the lake, campgrounds, and trails. There is a user fee for this area, but it is best to park at the lake. The lake is popular for swimming in the hot summer months, so you may have to park away from the area. The trailhead is immediately to the left of the dam and swimming area. Two signs clearly indicate the beginning of the trail.

Clear Creek Trailhead: Continue by taking a left turn through a gate at the Lake McCamy parking lot described above and proceed down the hill, past all the camping loops, to the dump station at a dead-end circle. The Clear Creek Trailhead (UTM 16S 718373E/ 3892280N) is off to the left of the dump station. As there is no park-ing area at this trailhead (and the gate may be closed in winter), you will likely need to park in the Lake McCamy parking lot described above and walk 0.5 mile down the road past the camping loops to the trailhead.

Greasy Creek Trailhead

When approaching the area from the west, start at the intersection of US 411 and US 64 and drive east on US 64. Pass the entrance to the CNF and continue 2.7 miles to the Ocoee Ranger Station on the left. Continue another 2.1 miles to TN 30. Turn left. Approaching from the east, drive west on US 64; look for TN 30 shortly after crossing a bay of Ocoee Lake; turn right. Go 1.0 mile on paved TN 30 to the trailhead on the left. Landmarks for the trailhead include a parking area on the right just before the trailhead and a bridge that crosses Clear Creek just before it flows into Greasy Creek immediately beyond the trailhead.

Scenic Spur Trailhead

Follow US 64 going east past the Ocoee Dam. The Ocoee Ranger Station is on your left a couple of miles past the dam. From the ranger station, follow US 64 2.3 miles. Turn left on TN 30 that is plainly marked by highway signs. Take the first gravel road to your left. This is only a short distance from US 64. Follow the gravel road for 0.1 mile to a parking lot. Signs at the lot indicate the Scenic Spur Trail. This is also the trailhead for the Clemmer Trail.

Lakeview Overlook

Lakeview Overlook is located on FS 77 described above. From US 64 immediately east of the entrance to the Ocoee/Hiwassee Ranger District Office, turn left on paved FS 77. Drive 2.3 miles on FS 77 and park at the Lakeview Overlook, which is the first overlook on the left.

Mac Point Beach Parking Area

The Mac Point Beach Parking Area is on Lake Ocoee. From the intersection of US 64 and FS 77 immediately east of the Ocoee/Hiwassee Ranger District Office, drive east on US 64 for 1.8 miles to Mac Point Beach and park in the beach parking lot. The Pondview Trail begins to the north of the parking area at a locked gate across gravel FS 33102.

   TOPOGRAPHIC MAPS: USGS Oswald Dome, TN; Caney Creek, TN; Parksville, TN. TI Map 781, Tellico and Ocoee Rivers, CNF.

TRAIL DESCRIPTIONS

146. CLEAR CREEK TRAIL (FS TRAIL 79, TI TRAIL 24)

   LENGTH: 5.2 miles

   ELEVATION CHANGE: Low point, 880 feet; high point, 2,000 feet

   DIFFICULTY: Moderate

   TRAILHEADS: Chilhowee Recreation Area (start) and Greasy Creek at TN 30 (end)

   USE: Hiking, mountain bike

   TOPOGRAPHIC MAP: USGS Oswald Dome, TN; Caney Creek, TN

   COMMENTS: The Clear Creek Trail provides a moderately difficult hike from the Chilhowee Recreational Area to TN 30. For a moderately more demanding hike, consider beginning near Greasy Creek at TN 30 and walking the opposite direction to the recreation area. That trailhead is also signed. The trail largely follows old roadbeds through a second-growth forest of deciduous and evergreen trees, skirting the north side of the Rock Creek Gorge on Chilhowee Mountain. The trail is marked with red "dotted i" blazes and is easy to follow. Wildflowers in the spring and wild berries in the summer are abundant along the old roadbeds. In winter and early spring, when leaves are off the trees, this trail offers scenic views of the Hooper Mountain Range, Lake Ocoee, Sugarloaf Mountain, and the Big Frog Mountain Wilderness to the south. Stay alert and listen and watch for bikers who also use this trail. The width of the trail ranges between two and six feet, and its surface is often smooth natural sand, although there are some rough areas with many exposed tree roots and sharp rocks. The first section of the trail from Chilhowee Recreation Area is marred by an area near the trail that was clear-cut a number of years ago. The pine beetle infestation of recent years has killed many pine trees throughout this area, forcing the CNF to cut down trees for the safety of those using the trails. The result of the tree cutting is distracting even though some views have been enhanced. Wooden bridges are provided for several creek crossings, but at other times wading or crossing on rocks is necessary. Beware of extremely slippery rocks. An initial elevation gain of 190 feet is misleading because there is an overall loss of 820 feet from the trailhead to the end. Plant life on the trail varies significantly because of the change in elevation. The trail ends at Greasy Creek on TN 30 where a bridge and a picnic/parking area on the far side of the road make good landmarks if hikers choose to use a car shuttle.

DETAILS: The Clear Creek Trail passes through mixed evergreen and deciduous second-growth forest. Both the short Chilhowee Recreation Area Azalea Trail and the Arbutus Trail join the Clear Creek Trail briefly during the first 0.3 mile. Watch the trail signs and at 0.3 mile take the left fork. Cross a creek on a small wooden bridge at 0.4 mile. Just past the bridge, to the left of the trail, several acres were completely cleared and plowed under in 1990 in order to create a seed orchard. The orchard is managed by the USFS for research and propagation of native plant seeds. Franklin Spring Branch, a tributary of Rock Creek, parallels the trail in this area. When it cannot be seen, the creek can be heard as it tumbles down its rocky course.

At 0.7 mile cross a second small wooden bridge and continue to follow the well-marked trail. At 1.1 miles you may be able to hear the sound of Rock Creek as it pours over Benton Falls off to the right on the opposite side of Rock Creek Gorge. At 2.1 miles Clear Creek Trail comes to a T intersection and continues onto an old roadbed to the left. To the right is Rim Rock Trail, which intersects at 1.0 mile with the popular Clemmer mountain biking trail. Step across a small creek at 2.3 miles and follow the trail as it snakes uphill to the 2.7 miles mark, which is the highest point of the trail (elevation 2,000 feet). Spectacular panoramic views are possible from this section.

The trail begins a descent at 2.9 miles and then becomes steeper, rockier, and more narrow at 3.1 miles. As the steep descent begins, enjoy a view of the Hooper Mountain Range on the left. At this point you may hear Clear Creek down in the gorge. The trail again winds uphill from 3.7 miles to 3.8 miles, descends with a switchback at 3.9 miles, intersects with Clemmer Trail at 4.3 miles and then levels out for a while beginning at 4.4 miles as it follows an old road cut into a hillside. Another descent leads to the trail's lowest elevation (880 feet) at 4.8 miles where you step across a narrow creek. Cross 15-foot-wide Clear Creek at 5.0 miles and then again at 5.1 miles. Wading is recommended because the rocks are slippery. Finally, the trail joins an old road and follows Clear Creek to end at Greasy Creek on TN 30.

147. BENTON FALLS TRAIL (FS TRAIL 131, TI TRAIL 8)

LENGTH: 1.6 miles

ELEVATION CHANGE: Low point, 1,600 feet; high point, 1,880 feet

DIFFICULTY: Easy

TRAILHEAD: Chilhowee Recreation Area (start and dead-end)

USE: Hiking

TOPOGRAPHIC MAP: USGS Oswald Dome, TN

COMMENTS: The Benton Falls Trail is an easy trail, sometimes level and sometimes downhill, which proceeds 1.6 miles through a mixed deciduous forest. The trail dead-ends at Benton Falls, a 65-foot waterfall, which makes the walk well worthwhile. This well-worn trail varies from four to six feet wide. The only difficulties are presented by areas where the trail is rocky and by the somewhat steep descent on rock stairs at the end of the trail to the falls. The trail is marked with blue blazes.

DETAILS: The trail begins at the Lake McCamy Dam with a sharp right turn and a short descent below the dam. It then levels off to continue along the forest floor beside a small creek that flows out of the swimming lake. Turn left at the visitor registration stand and continue on level trail through mostly deciduous forest of secondary growth. At 0.2 mile cross through a power-line right-of-way with high wires overhead. Undergrowth on the forest floor is relatively sparse on the first

Benton Falls. Photograph by Will Skelton.

part of the trail, but medium and large gray boulders litter the area, on trail and off trail. A thick carpet of ferns can be found to the left of the trail at 0.4 mile. Natural sand is found in some locations along the trail.

At 1.0 mile, the trail begins a gradual descent, and at 1.1 miles the Red Leaf Trail (FS Trail 144) dead-ends at Benton Falls Trail from the left. Within sight on the left is a large blackberry bush; look for ripe berries in June and July. The trail curves to the right and becomes quite wide. At 1.35 miles large rhododendron bushes are located to the left below you. Soon afterward a sign warns of slippery footing around the falls and points out that three people have been hospitalized as a result of falling while climbing the rocks at the falls.

A sharp left turn begins the sudden and final descent to the bottom of the falls on a trail now much narrower and rockier. Just after a switchback at 1.45 miles, a side trail to the left leads to the top of the falls. Thereafter, a log fence railing prevents hikers from stepping off the left edge of the trail. Rocks taken from the immediate area have been embedded to serve as steps. At 1.55 miles, the trail levels out; look up to enjoy beautiful Benton Falls. The falls drops from a high rock ledge down a rock face onto another rock ledge and then into a small pool littered with medium and large gray boulders.

148. MCCAMY LAKE TRAIL (FS TRAIL 72, TI TRAIL 55)

LENGTH: 0.3 mile

ELEVATION CHANGE: Negligible

DIFFICULTY: Easy

TRAILHEAD: Chilhowee Recreation Area

USE: Hiking, mountain bike

TOPOGRAPHIC MAP: USGS Oswald Dome, TN

DETAILS: From the parking area at Chilhowee Campground, head toward the beach area. Go left toward the dam. Stone steps lead up to the dam and to the McCamy Lake Trail. Cross the dam initially. At the junction go right following the trail marker. This trail follows the shoreline of the lake. At 0.3 mile, you will come to a junction. If you continue straight, you will arrive at Loop A of the campground. Here you may elect to cross the bridge to your right to continue the loop around the lake, bearing right after you cross the bridge. This short path will lead you back to the beach area.

149. SCENIC SPUR TRAIL (FS TRAIL 78, TI TRAIL 67)

LENGTH: 1.7 miles

ELEVATION CHANGE: Low point, 880 feet; high point, 1,080 feet

DIFFICULTY: Easy

TRAILHEAD: Scenic Spur

USE: Hiking

TOPOGRAPHIC MAPS: Oswald Dome, TN; Caney Creek, TN

COMMENTS: The Scenic Spur Trail is a good but narrow dirt trail through heavy forest. It dead-ends at an interesting little waterfall and cascade. Hiking the trail requires hopping the rocks across the stream leading from this waterfall in two places.

DETAILS: At the parking lot, a sign indicates "Scenic Spur 1.7 mi." From the parking lot, take the trail uphill for 0.15 miles following both white and green blazes. At the intersection where the Clemmer Trail leads to the left, go straight ahead on the Scenic Spur Trail as indicated by the sign. From this point, the Scenic Spur Trail has only white blazes. The trail continues through heavy forest for a short downhill stretch and parallels a dry creek bed. Then, it begins an easy, but steady uphill grade. At 0.6 mile, cross an old road. At 0.9 mile, begin hiking alongside the stream. At 1.1 miles, cross the stream on large rocks. Leave the stream and continue. From here to the waterfall, the uphill grade is somewhat steeper than before. At 1.5 miles, cross the stream once more on rocks to the left bank. The trail from here to the end is rather rocky. At 1.6 miles, look to the right to a series of cascades. The trail crests on a rock ledge next to an approximately 20-foot-high waterfall with numerous cascades downstream. You can go down to the stream. Be careful on the rocks; where they are wet they are quite slippery.

150. CLEMMER TRAIL (FS TRAIL 302, TI TRAIL 25)

LENGTH: 4.4 miles

ELEVATION CHANGE: Low point, 880 feet; high point, 1,680 feet

DIFFICULTY: Moderate

TRAILHEADS: Benton Falls Trail and Scenic Spur

USE: Hiking, mountain bike

TOPOGRAPHIC MAPS: USGS Oswald Dome, TN; Caney Creek, TN

COMMENTS: The Clemmer Trail (referred to as "Clemmer Bike Trail" on most of the signs) is a moderate trail, mostly downhill, that proceeds 4.4 miles through a mixed deciduous forest. The trail ends at a parking lot off TN 30 a few yards from US 64 as it passes along Ocoee Lake. This well-worn trail is almost never less than six feet wide and for part of its length is an old, once graveled, road. In a few places it is slightly rocky. Although parts of the trail are marked with green blazes, the markings are not consistent. From its beginning at the Benton Falls Trail, the Clemmer Trail is mostly, but not always, either level or downhill.

DETAILS: The trail begins at a sign 1.45 miles along the Benton Falls Trail. There is a sign reading "Clemmer Bike Trail" at the point where the Clemmer Trail splits from the Benton Falls Trail. At 0.1 mile, cross a small stream and gain a bit of altitude for the next few hundred yards. At 0.3 mile a sign points to the right to a side trail that leads to the Slick Rock Trail (the sign reads "SL ROCK"). At this junction, continue straight ahead and cross another creek. At 0.8 mile, Rim Rock Trail comes in from the left. Continue straight ahead on Clemmer Trail. At this point, the trail becomes marked with green blazes. The forest above the trail becomes more open, and the trail skirts a steep slope and returns to more dense forest. At 1.1 miles, cross a babbling brook. At 1.3 miles, an unmarked trail goes off to the left. This is a stretch of side trail that will return to the main trail in another 0.3 mile. For this 0.3-mile stretch, the green blazes disappear.

The side trail just mentioned is a dirt trail that goes through the forest and passes through some mountain laurel and rhododendron. There are no views down into the gorge to be had from this trail, but both the trail and the vegetation have a different character from the main Clemmer Trail. This side trail is 0.6 mile long from its beginning to its return to the Clemmer Trail, compared to a distance of 0.3 mile if one stays on the Clemmer Trail. This side trail is marked with brown blazes that seem to have been painted over older green blazes.

At 1.6 miles, the side trail comes back in from the left. At 1.7 miles, cross a wooden bridge. A trail comes in from the right at the far side of this bridge. The sign for this trail indicates that it goes to Slick Rock ("SL ROCK"). Angle to the left following the Clemmer Trail. At 2.2 miles, cross a stream. At about 2.4 miles, begin to pass mountain laurel. From approximately 2.8–3.0 miles, the trail skirts along a slope with views down into the gorge. There is a nice view of the gorge and mountains to the east at 3.1 miles. At 3.3 miles, the trail widens significantly. From here to most of the way to the other end, the trail follows an old road. The downhill grade steepens and becomes rather steady. The road was once graveled along much of the remaining distance.

At 4.3 miles, reach a sign pointing to the left that reads "Clemmer Trail 302." The road continues straight ahead and, no doubt, leads to a trailhead for mountain bikers. Take the left turn indicated by the sign and enter the forest. After a few feet, a trail leads to the left to Scenic Spur. Bear right and follow the dirt trail through heavy forest. The trail has both green and white blazes. The Clemmer trail ends at the Scenic Spur parking lot at 4.4 miles. This can be used as an alternate trailhead if one wishes to follow the Clemmer Trail from the bottom to the top in the reverse direction from that indicated in this section.

151. AZALEA TRAIL (FS TRAIL 140, TI TRAIL 2)

LENGTH: 2.0 miles

ELEVATION CHANGE: Negligible

TRAILHEAD: Chilhowee Recreation Area

DIFFICULTY: Easy

USE: Hiking, mountain bike

TOPOGRAPHIC MAP: USGS Oswald Dome, TN

DETAILS: This easily traversed trail begins just left of the gate to Loops C, D, E, and F of the Chilhowee Campground and travels through a deciduous forest. The trail initially parallels the campground road situated to the right. In July an abundant crop of blueberries is available during the first part of this trail. At 0.9 mile you will come to an intersection with an unmarked trail on the left. A trail sign indicates that the Azalea Trail continues to the right. At 1.2 miles and for several yards you will pass through an area of dense rhododendron. At the intersection at 1.7 miles, a right turn will take you back to the campground. A left turn at this junction will take you to the Arbutus and Clear Creek trails.

152. ARBUTUS TRAIL (FS TRAIL 141, TI TRAIL 1)

LENGTH: 0.7 mile

ELEVATION CHANGE: Negligible

DIFFICULTY: Easy

TRAILHEAD: Chilhowee Recreation Area

USE: Hiking, mountain bike

TOPOGRAPHIC MAP: USGS Oswald Dome, TN

DETAILS: This short, easy trail begins at the dump station at the end of the road leading to loops D, E, and F in the Chilhowee Campground and ends at the intersection of Clear Creek Trail. The trail passes openings in the forest that were created to enhance wildlife habitat. Damage as a result of the pine bark beetle is evident on this trail, and the USFS has cut numerous trees.

153. RED LEAF TRAIL (FS TRAIL 144, TI TRAIL 62)

LENGTH: 0.3 mile

ELEVATION CHANGE: Negligible

DIFFICULTY: Easy

TRAILHEAD: Arbutus Trail or Benton Falls Trail

USE: Hiking, mountain bike

TOPOGRAPHIC MAP: USGS Oswald Dome, TN

COMMENTS: This 0.3-mile trail serves as a connector between the Arbutus Trail and the Benton Falls Trail and is simply a short walk through a second-growth forest.

154. RIM ROCK TRAIL (FS TRAIL 77, TI TRAIL 63)

LENGTH: 1.0 mile

ELEVATION CHANGE: Low point, 1,750 feet; high point, 1,800 feet

DIFFICULTY: Moderate

TRAILHEADS: Clemmer Trail (start) and Clear Creek Trail (end)

USE: Hiking, mountain bike

TOPOGRAPHIC MAP: USGS Oswald Dome

COMMENTS: The Rim Rock Trail connects the Clemmer and Clear Creek Trails. The trail drops to the bottom of Rock Creek Gorge to cross the creek, so be prepared for some rock-hopping.

DETAILS: At 0.8 mile along the Clemmer Trail, turn left to begin the Rim Rock Trail, which is marked with white blazes. After a short passage though rhododendron thickets, the trail bears farther to the left to descend beside rock outcroppings into the Rock Creek Gorge. The trail reaches Rock Creek at 0.5 mile, 1,400 feet elevation. After an easy rock-hop across the creek, the trail immediately turns to the right to climb out of the gorge. At 0.9 mile the trail reaches the rim. Turning leftward, the Rimrock Trail levels out as it passes through a wooded area to meet the Clear Creek Trail at 1.0 mile. A turn to the left leads 1.7 miles to the head of the Clear Creek Trail.

155. SLICK ROCK LOOP TRAIL (NO FS NUMBER, TI TRAIL 68)

LENGTH: 7.7 miles

ELEVATION CHANGE: Low point, 1,860 feet; high point, 2,150 feet

DIFFICULTY: Moderate

TRAILHEADS: Benton Falls Trail (start of upper Slick Rock Trail); Clemmer Trail (lower Slick Rock Trail)

USE: Hiking, mountain bike

TOPOGRAPHIC MAP: USGS Oswald Dome, TN

COMMENTS: The Slick Rock Loop Trail consists of several pathways linked together by a couple of old USFS roads The hike described below follows a long loop, 7.1 miles long, formed by the upper, lower, and middle Slick Rock Loop Trail in combination with a portion of the Clemmer Trail. The round-trip distance from the Benton Falls Trailhead at Lake McCamy is 7.7 miles.

DETAILS: Follow the Benton Falls Trail 0.3 mile from Lake McCamy. Turn right at the sign for the upper Slick Rock Trail, which is an old USFS road, FS 4032, to begin the loop. Yellow blazes mark this portion of the trail. It follows an old roadbed that winds gently upward through pine woodlands. The upper Slick Rock Trail enters a wildlife field at 0.8 mile. Turn right and cross along the top of the wildlife field to reenter the woods. Light green blazes now mark the trail as it turns left near a metal post labeled "Slick Rock" to follow another old USFS road (FR 0902) graced with mountain laurel. At 1.4 miles, the trail takes an abrupt turn leftward off the old road. The USFS road (FR 0902) continues on a short distance to meet the paved road leading to the Chilhowee Campground.

The Slick Rock Trail, now a footpath, heads in a southerly direction, offering glimpses of Matlock Valley and Sand Mountain beyond. As the trail bears eastward, it eases downhill. At 2.2 miles, the trail crosses the first of two wooden footbridges over Slickrock Branch. It is not clear why the trail is named Slick Rock when the creek it is named after is one word. The pathway moves up and away from the stream to end at FR 5050 at 3.0 miles. A metal post labeled "Slick Rock" denotes the intersection. Sporadic light blue blazes mark the gravel road. Note: A left turn onto FR 5050 will lead to the middle section of the Slick Rock Trail, 0.4 mile away. Turn right onto the road to complete the long loop hike. Walk a short distance along the roadbed. At 3.2 miles, take a sharp left turn off the road onto another footpath.

The lower Slick Rock Trail, marked with light green blazes, continues through the woods to end at 3.4 miles at the Clemmer Trail. A wooden sign on the Clemmer Trail points out directions to the campground and the Slick Rock Trail. Turn left on the Clemmer Trail, marked with dark green blazes. Continue on the Clemmer Trail past the trailheads for the Rim Extension Trail at 3.7 and 4.0 miles and for the Rimrock Trail at 4.2 miles. Signs at 5.2 miles indicate the directions to Benton Falls, the campground, and the middle Slick Rock Trail. Turn left onto the middle Slick Rock Trail that is marked with light blue blazes.

The middle Slick Rock Trail travels westward and leaves the woods to enter a wildlife field at 5.8 miles. Turn left a short distance beyond onto a gravel road (FR 5050) marked with light blue blazes. Metal posts labeled "Slick Rock" indicate these turns. At 5.9 miles, turn right onto the pathway marked by a small rock cairn and remnants of a wooden sign labeled "S. Rock." The middle Slick Rock Trail climbs uphill along a rocky path marked with yellow blazes. The trail arrives at the bottom of the first wildlife field seen on this hike. Stay to the right of the field and continue to its top to close the loop at 6.3 miles. Retrace the path of the upper Slick Rock Trail to the Benton Falls Trail at 7.1 miles and turn left to return to Lake McCamy at 7.7 miles.

156. CHILHOWEE FOREST WALK TRAIL (FS TRAIL 130, TI TRAIL 23)

LENGTH: 0.4 mile loop

ELEVATION CHANGE: Low point, 1,900 feet; high point, 1,960 feet

DIFFICULTY: Easy

TRAILHEADS: Chilhowee Recreation Area

USE: Hiking

TOPOGRAPHIC MAP: USGS Oswald Dome, TN

COMMENTS: The Chilhowee Forest Walk is one of the few trails in the Chilhowee Recreation Area that is closed to mountain bikes. Because of this closure it is much less used than other Chilhowee trails. To reach the trail from the Benton Falls Trailhead, follow the blue-blazed bike trail for 0.1 mile past the beach access for McCamy Lake to the far end of McCamy Dam at a well-signed trail junction.

DETAILS: At the junction at the far end of the McCamy Lake Dam there are trails leading left, right, and straight ahead. The Lake Trail leads right to encircle McCamy Lake, while the Benton Falls Trail leads left to the main Chilhowee trail network. The Forest Walk is the less used trail heading straight. In 30 feet the trail forks. Go left and follow the better defined trail. The trail is marked with white "i" blazes. It traverses the slope of a small ridge within sight of a power line and crosses a small wood bridge at 0.25 mile. The return path remains above the lake. The loop closes at 0.4 mile. You can retrace your route to the parking area or explore another of the myriad trails nearby.

157. LAKEVIEW TRAIL (FS TRAIL 300; NO TI NUMBER)

LENGTH: 0.3 mile loop

ELEVATION CHANGE: Low point, 1,720 feet; high point, 1,720 feet

DIFFICULTY: Easy

TRAILHEADS: Lakeview Overlook

USE: Hiking

TOPOGRAPHIC MAPS: USGS Caney Creek, TN; Parksville, TN

COMMENTS: The Lakeview Trail is one of the two Ocoee/Hiwassee Ranger District Ocoee Scenic Byway Trails. These short loops are well disguised. No blazes or signs mark the trails. In fact, there is nothing by way of signage to indicate these are maintained or system trails. However, the trail is obvious on the ground and is a trail worth visiting, if only to give you a good excuse for stopping at the spectacular Lakeview Overlook. FS 77 climbs steeply from Ocoee Lake so the overlook looms high above the water. The marina is directly below, and straight ahead is Ocoee Dam No. 1, just to the right of the conical peak of Sugarloaf.

DETAILS: The trail offers no views beyond those available at the overlook. To start the hike look for a signboard 100 feet to the left of the overlook and follow a path into the forest beyond it. In 100 feet the loop splits. Take the right fork to follow the loop counterclockwise. The trail will loop around a low ridge through a young forest with views of FS 77 before closing at 0.3 mile. Go right to return to the parking area.

158. PONDVIEW TRAIL (FS TRAIL 301; NO TI NUMBER)

LENGTH: 0.6 mile loop

ELEVATION CHANGE: Low point, 870 feet; high point, 880 feet

DIFFICULTY: Easy

TRAILHEADS: Mac Point Beach Parking Area

USE: Hiking

TOPOGRAPHIC MAP: USGS Caney Creek

COMMENTS: Like the Lakeview Trail, the Pondview Trail is an Ocoee Scenic Byway Trail. Also like the Lakeview Trail, Pondview is somewhat of a mystery. No blazes mark the trail, and no signs point out its start or intersection. When walked in 2002, parts of the trail were heavily overgrown and covered with fallen trees. The trail could be handy for someone wanting to fish the pond, but without any clue that it exists, few feet will walk it. Road noise from US 64 and constant gunfire from the Thornburg Shooting Range will encourage most hikers to find a quieter trail.

DETAILS: From US 64 walk north on gravel FS 33102 for 300 feet. Turn right off the road onto an older, heavily overgrown road. At 0.1 mile the loop splits where a foot trail enters on the right. Follow the old road to the left around the pond to 0.2 mile where a lone post marks a turn down to the shoreline. Rejoin the old road (which now has the remnant of an asphalt coating) in a short distance, then drop off again to descend some wooden stairs at 0.3 mile. Here a sign identifies Mac Point Pond by a turnout alongside US 64. Walk along the mowed area between US 64 and the pond. At 0.4 mile turn away from the pond and follow a path to close the loop at 0.5 mile. Turn left to return to the parking area.

29 Little Frog Mountain

(Includes Little Frog Mountain Wilderness, Little Frog Mountain Wilderness Study Area, and Little Frog Mountain Roadless Area)

The Little Frog Mountain Wilderness is immediately adjacent to the busy Ocoee River Corridor and provides a respite from the crowds and vehicles in the corridor. The wilderness contains 4,666 acres and the CNF's 2004 plan revision designates an additional 977-acre wilderness study area. Those 977 acres were also identified by the

USFS as the Little Frog Roadless Area in its Southern Appalachian Assessment. From its highest point at Sassafras Knob, at 3,322 feet, to approximately 1,200 feet at the Ocoee River near Powerhouse No. 3, the area is one of beauty and variety. It offers a taste of wilderness to the novice or the experienced backpacker. The trails will lead you along ridges, through gaps, across streams, and down into a beautiful valley while traveling through a second-growth forest. Dry Pond Lead and Little Frog Mountain form a horseshoe-shaped valley that isolates Pressley Cove, giving it a wild character. Many species of flowering plants, trees, and shrubs are present, including the flame azalea, mountain laurel, rhododendron, trailing arbutus, trout lily, crested dwarf

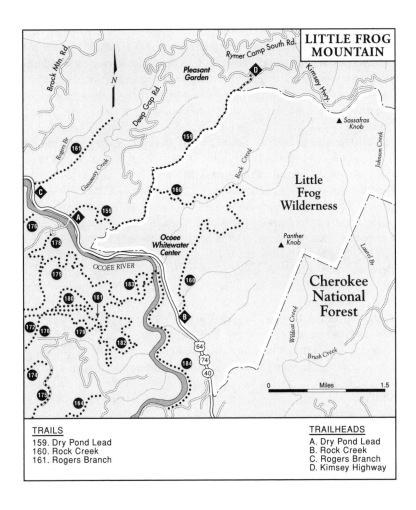

TRAILS
159. Dry Pond Lead
160. Rock Creek
161. Rogers Branch

TRAILHEADS
A. Dry Pond Lead
B. Rock Creek
C. Rogers Branch
D. Kimsey Highway

iris, mayapple, bloodroot, toothwort, magnolia, dogwood, and red-
bud. A panoramic view of this area could formerly be seen from the
Sassafras Knob fire tower, which was dismantled in 1989. The solitude
and splendor of the area is in sharp contrast with the devastation in
the Copperhill/Ducktown area just to the east and the heavily used
Ocoee River boating areas. The area is located east of Cleveland, TN,
in Polk County and the Ocoee/Hiwassee Ranger District.

HISTORY

Much of the area has been cut in the past, but only a few obvious
signs remain, and even those are now rapidly disappearing. The word
ocoee is a Cherokee Indian term meaning "apricot vine place" (trans-
lation: maypop or passion flower plant). The passion flower plant produces a pulpy seed capsule that was eaten by the Indians. It was the
place-name of a Cherokee settlement on the Ocoee River west of Little
Frog and Chilhowee mountains. Cherokee settlements at Ducktown
and Turtletown were immediately east of Little Frog Mountain. The
steep walls of the Ocoee gorge made both settlement and foot travel
there impossible for the Cherokees, so a network of trails connected
the settlements across the mountain passes of Little Frog. During the
1938 removal, some Cherokees hid on Little Frog Mountain and managed to escape removal. Most eventually moved onto Qualla Boundary,
but one family, the Catts, continued to live in the Cold Spring Gap
area of Little Frog Mountain, where their descendants remain today.

Jenkins Grave Gap is named for Thomas Jenkins, a settler from
Cherokee County, NC, who lived his adult life on the waters of Brush
Creek. After his wife died and his daughter married, he became despon-
dent and eventually became one of Polk County's first paupers. He
lived at the poorhouse in Benton but would frequently return to Brush
Creek, where his wife was buried. It was on one of these trips that he
froze to death in 1854. His grave is about 100 yards off FS 68 between
Sassafras Knob and Dry Pond Lead Trailhead. The grave of Viola
Morgan is also there; her tombstone reads "Nov. 17, 1897." She was
a young girl of sixteen out gathering chestnuts in November with rel-
atives. The party set fire to the grass to uncover the chestnuts and
Viola caught her dress on fire and burned to death near the spot where
she is buried.

Perhaps the most interesting historical aspect of the Little Frog
Wilderness is its location northwest of the infamous Ducktown/
Copperhill copper-processing plants. Sulfuric acid emissions from
those industries reduced the landscape for several miles around to a

desertlike appearance. The damage to the wilderness was slight because of the protection afforded by the ridge of Little Frog Mountain and the prevailing northwest winds. Pine reforestation efforts in the barren areas have been recently successful; only a core area around the smelting plants remains barren. However, these same trees are now threatened by the current raging infestation of pine beetles in the region.

The Kimsey Highway (FS 68), located to the north of the area and basically following the old Indian path, was started in 1914, but the contractor soon went bankrupt. Dr. Lucius Kimsey of Ducktown pushed for finishing the road until Polk County completed the construction in 1920. For some time the Kimsey Road was the only road between the Copper Basin and the TN Valley. A road built along the Ocoee River to haul copper was abandoned sometime after a railroad was constructed in 1890, leaving only the Kimsey Road. The road along the Ocoee River was reconstructed in the late 1920s or early 1930s, and the Kimsey Road fell into disuse. There are some current efforts to relocate US 64 away from the Ocoee River because of congestion during rafting season and the winding nature of the road.

Little Frog Mountain Wilderness was designated by Congress in 1984 after having been a wilderness study area for two years. As noted

Rhododendrons alongside a small cascade in the Little Frog Wilderness. Photograph by Roger Jenkins.

above, the CNF has recommended that the wilderness be expanded to include the Little Frog Wilderness Study Area.

TRAILHEADS AND MAPS

Dry Pond Lead Trailhead

This trailhead, on US 64, is approximately 18.6 miles east of the US 64/US 411 and east of Cleveland, TN. Drive up the Ocoee River on US 64 to Powerhouse No. 3, which is about 0.5 mile above Ocoee Dam No. 2 and a launch. The trailhead marker, "Dry Pond Lead, No. 76," is on the north side of US 64 directly across from Powerhouse No. 3 and Thunder Rock Campground. Parking for the trail is a small parking area across the bridge from US 64 beside Powerhouse No. 3 or, if full, the parking area at Thunder Rock Campground. Walk back across the bridge and US 64 to the trailhead. The trailhead can also be approached from Ducktown, TN, by following US 64 westward to Powerhouse No. 3 for 7.6 miles from the TN 68/US 64 junction.

Rock Creek Trailhead

This trailhead, on US 64, is approximately 21.3 miles east of the US 64/US 411 intersection. It is also 2.7 miles east from Powerhouse No. 3 and Thunder Rock Campground. Parking for the trail is at the trailhead on an old paved road to the left of US 64. The trailhead is approximately 20 yards beyond and to the right of a mound of dirt placed across the old road. The trail descends sharply to the left of the "Rock Creek No. 125" trail sign. If you approach from the east, the trailhead is on the right side of US 64 at 4.9 miles west of the US 64/TN 68 junction in Ducktown, TN.

Rogers Branch Trailhead

This trailhead is about 0.5 mile west (downstream) on US 64 from the Dry Pond Lead Trailhead (see above). The Ocoee Dam No. 2, a boat launch ramp, and a parking area are on the south side of US 64; the trailhead, unmarked, is on the north side and difficult to see.

Kimsey Highway Trailhead

The Kimsey Highway, a 15-mile-long gravel USFS road, stretches from the west in the vicinity of Greasy Creek eastward across the CNF, north of the area, to TN 68 and provides access to the Dry Pond Lead Trail and the old Sassafras Lookout Tower site. Drive north about 4.4 miles on TN 68 from the intersection of US 64 with TN 68 at Ducktown, TN. When a railroad track crosses TN 68, begin looking on the left (west) for the Kimsey Highway (initially County 68 and subsequently FS 68). County 68 will turn left on the opposite side of the road at Vic's Auto Parts. There is also a small green sign for Kimsey Highway. If you approach from the north on TN 68, drive 8.9 miles south from the Hiwassee River Bridge; County 68 will turn right at Vic's Auto Parts store. The Kimsey Highway is paved at first and then becomes gravel. Turn left at two road intersections near the top of the mountain. About 5.5 miles from TN 68, the gated FS 68A veers sharply to the left and provides a 0.75 mile walk up to the former Sassafras Knob Lookout Tower site and the wilderness boundary. Continue west on the Kimsey Highway to 7.4 miles, where the Dry Pond Lead Trailhead is on the left. The trail is initially a gated road and is marked with a sign and bulletin board. Parking space is available for about four cars.

From the west, travel US 64 east into the Ocoee Gorge. Turn left on TN 30, toward Greasy Creek. Follow TN 30 for 4.3 miles and turn right on Greasy Creek Road. Follow Greasy Creek Road for 0.7 mile to a right turn onto Kimsey Mountain Highway. After 1.8 miles the road forks and Kimsey Mountain Highway goes to the left. The pavement ends in another one-half mile. The Dry Pond Lead Trailhead is on the right 6.2 miles from the fork in the road. On the way you will pass another USFS road on the left going to Lost Creek, and at 4.9 miles you will cross under a TVA power line. Note: Information about current conditions may be obtained at the Ocoee District Ranger Station. The ranger station is 2.9 miles inside the CNF boundary heading east on US 64 from Cleveland.

TOPOGRAPHIC MAPS: USGS Ducktown, TN. TI Map 781, Tellico and Ocoee Rivers, CNF.

TRAIL DESCRIPTIONS

159. DRY POND LEAD TRAIL (FS TRAIL 76, TI TRAIL 32)

LENGTH: 4.5 miles
ELEVATION CHANGE: Low point, 1,150 feet; high point, 2,840 feet

DIFFICULTY: Moderate

TRAILHEADS: Dry Pond Lead (start) and Kimsey Highway (end)

TRAIL CONNECTIONS: Rock Creek Trail

USE: Hiking

TOPOGRAPHIC MAP: USGS Ducktown, TN

COMMENTS: The Dry Pond Lead Trail forms the northwestern boundary of the Little Frog Mountain Wilderness. The trail ascends through a second-growth forest with a variety of flowering plants, trees, and shrubs. This trail and the Rock Creek Trail provide the shortest access to Pressley Cove and Rock Creek, an area of peaceful beauty with its emerald green moss-covered logs, swift-flowing streams, and small sparkling waterfalls. One trip into Pressley Cove will heighten the appreciation of hiking in a wilderness area. The Benton-MacKaye Trail exits the Big Frog area into Thunder Rock Campground, crosses the bridge over the Ocoee, and follows Dry Pond Lead for most of its length, 4.0 miles. The Rock Creek Trail intersects the Dry Pond Lead Trail at 1.9 miles. From this intersection, Pressley Cove and Rock Creek are 0.8 mile east. The Dry Pond Lead Trail is quite dry, as the only water sources are down in the valleys off the trail, with some difficulty of access. At 3.1 miles to the left is a depression, usually dry, that provides the name of both the ridge and the trail.

DETAILS: The Dry Pond Lead Trail starts directly across from the Ocoee No. 3 Powerhouse and Thunder Rock Campground. The trail immediately starts uphill on a very steep but short climb out of the Ocoee gorge, with a small creek on the right. Shortly there is a visitor's trail registry on the left. The trail ascends with switchbacks 0.3 mile to a TVA transmission line right-of-way connecting Ocoee Powerhouse No. 3 with the Apalachia Power House to the northwest. From here there is a good view down the right-of-way of Powerhouse No. 3 and the large, light-green steel surge tank. The trail reaches the rim of the Ocoee Gorge at 0.5 mile. From here the trail continues fairly level, gently ascending, while crossing small ridges and through gaps. At 0.6 mile it turns to the right and passes through a pine forest with ferns literally covering the ground, a bit of enchanted forest. At 1.9 miles a large wooden post marks the intersection with the Rock Creek Trail, which drops down to the right. The sign may be attached to the post or may be lying on the ground, depending on the mood of the resident bear in the area.

The Dry Pond Lead Trail continues straight northward, begins to ascend, and traverses left, following the western side of the ridge. At 2.3 miles there is a different valley to the left with a view of Brock Mountain across the way. At 2.35 miles, an old road cut crosses the trail. This old road will be intertwined with the trail for the next 1.5 miles. Follow the Benton-MacKaye diamond white trail blazes painted on the trees. Toothwort blooms along this stretch of the trail in the spring. At 2.6 miles the trail levels out and passes a scattered outcropping of white quartz. This is an attractive stone with a rating of 7 on a hardness scale (with 10 being the hardest). Quartz is harder than some knife blades. At 3.6 miles the trail ascends through a scattered pine thicket, then tops out at 3.7 miles and becomes level as it veers east of the ridgetop.

The trail passes a boundary sign at 4.0 miles and enters an abandoned wildlife opening that is now filled with locust trees and briers. The crest of Dry Pond Lead has turned eastward at this point and will rapidly gain elevation as it continues toward Sassafras Knob. The Lost Creek section of the Benton-MacKaye Trail branches to the northwest, descending toward Pleasant Garden and Deep Gap. The trail crosses the opening diagonally (northeasterly) and exits from the crest at 4.1 miles. It then descends on an old roadbed and reaches the Kimsey Highway Trailhead at 4.5 miles. The last half mile or so of the trail has been relocated twice, more recently in 1987.

160. ROCK CREEK TRAIL (FS TRAIL 125, TI TRAIL 64)

LENGTH: 5.5 miles

ELEVATION CHANGE: Low point, 1,450 feet; high point, 2,320 feet

DIFFICULTY: Moderate

TRAILHEADS: Rock Creek (start) and Dry Pond Lead Trail (end)

USE: Hiking

TOPOGRAPHIC MAP: USGS Ducktown, TN

COMMENTS: The Rock Creek Trail winds through the center of the wilderness, bordered on the east by Little Frog Mountain and on the west by Dry Pond Lead. This trail offers the variety one would expect while hiking in the TN foothills of the southern Appalachians. The trail winds through a second-growth forest with flowering trees, plants, and shrubs along the way, leading across creeks, over ridges, and through gaps. The trail leads into a beautiful valley called Pressley Cove. While descending into the valley, the trail passes rhododendrons, holly, and hemlock, with the swift-flowing Rock Creek undulating through its center.

DETAILS: The trail descends to the left of the Rock Creek Trail sign and crosses a small branch at 0.7 mile. Just past the branch there is a trail registry on the side of the trail. A short distance down the trail at 0.1 mile is a leaning beech tree growing to the left. It is a handsome tree with smooth gray bark and sawtooth leaves. The beech also produces small edible nuts in the fall. The trail descends and passes a rhododendron thicket on the left, next to a small stream, at 0.3 mile. In late spring the rhododendron, particularly those along the stream banks, put on a spectacular display of large blossoms. Along this section of the trail the beautiful crested dwarf iris also grows. The trail crosses two more splendid creeks a few yards apart at 0.4 mile, the latter being Laurel Creek, which is the largest. The stream may be between five to eight feet wide, depending on the time of the year. Try to keep your feet dry, as there is a lot of trail ahead. From here the trail ascends gradually to a gap at 2.7 miles before descending into Pressley Cove. Along the way at 0.4 mile there is a switchback to the left, and the light-green steel surge tank at Ocoee Powerhouse No. 3 is visible west of the trail. This section also has beautiful winter views of Big Frog Mountain.

The trail continues ascending, and at 1.9 miles the trail becomes rocky. At 2.1 miles it follows the side of a ridge with a deep valley to the left of the trail. Listen for the sounds of the pileated woodpecker, the largest of the North American woodpeckers, echoing through the valley or along its ridges. Also inhabiting the area are deer, black bear, wild hog, turkey, and various types of small game.

The trail crosses to the east side of the ridge for the final time, and at 2.7 miles it turns west through a gap and follows an old logging road for about 150 yards down a hollow. The trail then makes a 135-degree turn to the left and exits the roadbed (the road continues in an arc to the left up a knob, where it disappears; a couple of dim blazes might lead you incorrectly up the knob). Just after you leave the road there is a small spring off the trail to the left; it may be hard to find. The trail continues down and bears slightly to the right beneath the knob as it enters the upper elevations of picturesque Pressley Cove with Rock Creek flowing through its center. The trail then makes a gradual descent into Pressley Cove.

As you descend into the valley, the cool air will rise to greet you. The trail crosses a feeder stream and then arrives at a beautiful mountain creek, Rock Creek, at 4.0 miles. This is an excellent place to have lunch. The area is an open wooded cove with a scattering of older second-growth trees and thickets of rhododendron overhanging the swift-flowing Rock Creek. Lean back and enjoy the beauty of Pressley Cove. Crossing Rock Creek will usually require wading; it is about 10 feet wide where the trail crosses and 6 to 12 inches deep, depending on the amount of rainfall. The trail follows Rock Creek for a short distance. At 4.3 miles there is a perfect open vista of a picturesque 5-foot waterfall to the left of the trail. The trail crosses a feeder stream at 4.5 miles, and at 4.7 miles the trail ascends to leave Rock Creek. It continues to ascend until it terminates at 5.5 miles into the Dry Pond Lead Trail. To the left the Dry Pond Lead Trail continues 1.9 miles to US 64 across from the Ocoee Powerhouse No. 3.

161. ROGERS BRANCH TRAIL (FS TRAIL 138; NO TI NUMBER)

LENGTH: 2.3 miles

ELEVATION CHANGE: Low point, 1,140 feet; high point, 1,640 feet

DIFFICULTY: Moderate

TRAILHEAD: Rogers Branch (start and dead-end)

USE: Hiking

TOPOGRAPHIC MAP: USGS Ducktown, TN

COMMENTS: Although this trail is not in the Little Frog Mountain Wilderness, it is nearby and includes a beautiful creek section similar in appearance to some in the Citico Wilderness. As of the early 2000s, the trail has not been maintained in many years and is in very rough condition. However, it is scheduled for rehabilitation and may be in better shape by the time this book is published. While this trail is rated as moderate because of its short length, it does have a challenging area when the ground is composed of very unstable shale. The trail begins on the north side of US 64 across from the Ocoee Recreation Area/ Rogers Branch Put-In. The trailhead is unmarked and difficult to see. On the south side of US 64 is the boat put-in and, to the east, upriver, a parking area. Do not park on US 64 or in the put-in area to the west. Your car may be ticketed or towed. The parking area to the east is a fee area and belongs to the TN State Park System. USFS parking permits are not valid there. This area is extremely congested during water releases on the Ocoee, but it is empty the rest of the time.

DETAILS: The trail initially proceeds up a gently sloped hollow with steep sides along Rogers Branch. Trees and large rhododendron bushes shade the trail. After about 200 yards, the main trail begins a climb to the left and a side trail continues straight to a vantage point between two successive small waterfalls. The trail crosses the creek three times on slippery rocks. Two small switchbacks at about 0.5 mile lead up out of the hollow onto a knobby ridgetop where the forest alternates between pine and hardwood. Galax, trailing arbutus, and partridge berry may be seen on the ground. To the northwest, two old clear-cuts appear as a uniform stand of pine on the side of Brock

Mountain. The trail continues on the ridge, swings east, and does a switchback (currently obscured by a large blown-down tree) in order to pass to the left (west) of a knoll at approximately 1.0 mile. Thereafter, the trail follows the ridgecrest for a way, eventually crosses to the right of the ridgetop, side-hilling around an area of loose shale, and descending into the Gassaway Creek valley, but it does not reach the creek. Instead, it follows the west side of Gassaway Creek for a short distance and ends at 2.3 miles. The trail ends rather abruptly in a grove of hemlock trees near the head of Gassaway Creek. Brock Mountain is to the left (northwest), and Dry Pond Lead is to the right (southeast).

OFF-TRAIL HIKING OPPORTUNITIES

A trail known as the Little Frog Mountain Trail once existed along the crest of Little Frog Mountain. It started west of a small ridge itself to the west of the point where Brush Creek crosses under US 64 at a shooting range. It ran westward up a lead to the Little Frog Mountain crest, just bypassing Boyd Gap, and then proceeded northward along the ridge to Sassafras Lookout Tower. An old road out of Jenkins Grave Gap can access it from the top more easily than the route from Sassafras Knob. The trail was around eight miles long but is now densely overgrown in the middle mainly with green briar, partially as the result of intense fires that swept up the west side of the ridge at Boyd Gap in 1978 and 1983. While both ends of the trail are open, any attempt to follow it should be considered off-trail hiking. The fire tower has been removed. Winter views from the ridgetop of Little Frog Mountain are good but obscured the rest of the year. The top of Panther Knob has a spectacular wintertime panoramic view of the Ducktown/Copperhill area to the east, Ocoee No. 3 dam to the south, the US 64 bridge over Brush Creek to the near south, and the upper Whitewater course on the Ocoee to the southwest, contrasting with the wilderness to the west.

30 Big Frog Mountain

(Includes Big Frog Wilderness, TN portion of Cohutta Wilderness, Big Frog Wilderness Study Area, and Big Frog Roadless Area)

The Big Frog Wilderness and the adjacent Cohutta Wilderness (principally in GA) together form a 45,059-acre wilderness tract. This is the

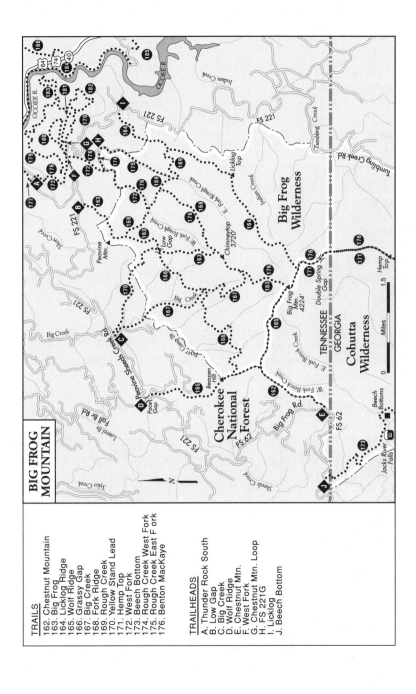

BIG FROG MOUNTAIN

TRAILS

162. Chestnut Mountain
163. Big Frog
164. Licklog Ridge
165. Wolf Ridge
166. Grassy Gap
167. Big Creek
168. Fork Ridge
169. Rough Creek
170. Yellow Stand Lead
171. Hemp Top
172. West Fork
173. Beech Bottom
174. Rough Creek West Fork
175. Rough Creek East Fork
176. Benton MacKaye

TRAILHEADS

A. Thunder Rock South
B. Low Gap
C. Big Creek
D. Wolf Ridge
E. Chestnut Mtn.
F. West Fork
G. Chestnut Mtn. Loop
H. FS 221G
I. Licklog
J. Beech Bottom

largest designated wilderness tract on USFS lands in the eastern United States and is an incredible resource for the hiker. Big Frog Wilderness, the southernmost wilderness in the CNF, is an 8,082-acre area encompassing the slopes of Big Frog Mountain, at 4,224 feet the highest point in Polk County, TN. The mountain dominates the view to the southeast from Parksville Lake (Ocoee Lake). A few acres (89) of the Big Frog Wilderness are located in GA's Chattahoochee NF and 7,993 acres are in the CNF. The USFS's Southern Appalachian Assessment identified an additional 365 acres as the Big Frog Roadless Area, and the CNF's 2004 plan revision recommends those acres as a wilderness study area. Also in the CNF are 709 acres of GA's 35,268-acre Cohutta Wilderness, contiguous to the Big Frog Wilderness. The TN areas are located in the Ocoee/Hiwassee Ranger District.

For hikers, the area has perhaps the greatest variety of trail types of any of the CNF wilderness areas, including a 5.0-mile stretch of perfect contour trail along a 50-degree slope (Grassy Gap), something very rare in the East. The Big Frog, Wolf Ridge, and Licklog Ridge trails all rank among the finest in the CNF.

Several loop hikes are possible. One of the most popular overnight hikes combines the Big Frog and Benton MacKaye Trails. Shorter loops for day hikes include Big Creek–Grassy Gap–Yellow Stand Lead and the East and West forks of Rough Creek from FS 221G. The hiker should be aware, however, that Big Frog is considerably drier than most other wilderness areas of the CNF. Bring plenty of water in the summer and expect hot temperatures even at the higher altitudes. You may want to hike the trails in the spring or fall for more availability of water and cooler temperatures. For experienced hikers the area is excellent for winter hiking.

All of the TN area is within the 52,825-acre TWRA designated Ocoee Bear Reserve. The old black-on-orange WMA signs may be seen from several of the trails. Bears were restocked in the 1970s from the GSMNP. Their sign is fairly common today in the wilderness. The USFS restocked ten deer in the Ocoee area in 1937; these expanded to a substantial population by 1952 when TWRA began to allow hunting. The herd is now considerably smaller, and only an occasional deer may be seen in the wilderness and on other USFS lands in Polk County.

Feral hogs, or domestic hogs gone wild, used to populate the Ocoee area. Woodrow Beckler, who is probably the last person who remembers living at the Dutch Settlement on the northwest of the wilderness, said that everyone let their pigs run loose. When the sow had a litter, the piglets were marked so that they could be identified and released to forage in the mountains. They would stay away for periods of two or three months, and if there was a good supply of acorns the sow would return alone. Beckler said that several times local hunters killed wild hogs that bore his mark. In the 1960s European wild hogs, or Russian boar, were trapped from the GSMNP and released in Ocoee/Hiwassee Ranger District and other areas south of the park. Today the hogs largely have the Russian characteristics, with protruding tusks and dark coloration, although occasionally one has a white strip down his side reflecting domestic interbreeding.

Wild turkeys in the area make their presence most evident in the late winter when there is mast in the higher elevations. Pothole scratches in the leaves are the result of turkeys searching for acorns. Some unusually large bobcats have also been seen in the area. Although the area borders the state of GA, it is still well outside the range of lower-altitude venomous snakes, like the cottonmouth or pygmy rattlesnake. Timber rattlesnakes, however, are fairly common, as are copperheads. The area around the Big Creek camping area, at the border of the wilderness, is home to some unusually large (40-plus inches) copperheads.

Lower elevations are forested heavily with Virginia pine. Upland hardwoods include white oak, red oak, and hickory. A tree species not regularly encountered by hikers in more northern areas of the CNF is the white pine, with its extra-long, blue-green needles. There are also beech, basswood, birch, red maple, black gum, and silverbell. Some large black cherry trees can be seen from the Big Frog and Wolf Ridge trails. Some tulip (what many call poplar) and oak in the coves along the slopes of Big Frog have already reached impressive size.

Dr. Gene Wofford of the University of Tennessee Botany Department surveyed the Big Frog Mountain area in 1981. He found four rare species of plants: catchfly, purple hyssop, cow parsnip, and rattlesnake root. Paul Somers of the TN Heritage Program also hiked the area in 1982 and observed the rare bushpea and bush honeysuckle. Zack E. Murrell completed a two-year study of plants on Big Frog Mountain under the direction of Dr. Wofford in 1987. Of the 479 species identified, only 22 were nonnative or introduced, reflecting little disturbance by human activity. Three species were found to be at the southernmost point of their range. The rugged topography and high rainfall at Big Frog maintain a more typically northern flora. The observant hiker will notice color variations in many flower species that differ from those seen in the GSMNP and the northern CNF. Trillium, iris, and azalea all display surprisingly different color variations.

Hikers will still find Big Frog trails often wild and woolly. Trails signs are frequently missing, footways can be indistinct, trail junctions can be obscure, and none of the trails have been blazed in modern times.

HISTORY

J. Felton Stanley, retired from the USFS, and the late Ed Manges, fisheries biologist for TWRA, were among our sources of information on the early history of Big Frog. Magnus was with the USFS and TVA during the Great Depression years. Stanley worked for both the USFS and the CCC. In 1990, Felton Stanley was 80 years of age and had an exceedingly sharp memory, down to individual personalities of many of the CCC men and specific hikes they took in the old days.

At the turn of the century, Big Frog Mountain and the surrounding areas were virtually trackless. An old wagon road from GA reached as far as Sylco Creek watershed, to the west of Big Frog Mountain. From that road an even smaller road led up to the Dutch Settlement, a community of German- and French-speaking settlers located near Pace Gap. The community was established in the 1840s, apparently to raise grapes and make wine. The settlement was sometimes called "Vineland," but the wine was not a commercial success. According to Roy Lilland, Polk County historian, *dutch* was a corruption of the German *deutch*. Rosine Parmentier and her sister and brother-in-law were the investors behind the settlement. She lived in New York City but visited the area in 1852 and kept an extensive journal of the trip. The Beckler family was the last to leave the Dutch Settlement, doing so in 1927. Their cabin was torn down in 1940.

Pace Gap was named for the Pace family, who lived near the current Big Creek Trailhead. In the small triangle formed by Pace Branch, Big Creek, and FS 221 is the foundation of the old Pace cabin, which was occupied until sometime around World War I, and stood in ruin until well into the 1920s.

The trails of Big Frog are essentially the fruits of labor of many young men in the CCC camps of the 1930s. Three trails, however, preceded the CCC: they were the Big Frog (or Peavine), Licklog Ridge, and Wolf Ridge trails. Wolf Ridge Trail is probably the oldest, dating back to 1914–15. Big Frog and Licklog Ridge were both built during the late 1910s and 1920s. For pre-CCC creations, these trails are excellent, properly graded and switchbacked, having none of the painfully steep, "straight from here to up yonder" stretches so typical of old-timer trails in Tellico and other areas of the CNF.

The CCC entered the picture in the 1930s, improving Big Frog, Licklog Ridge, and Wolf Ridge trails and adding most other trails presently in the system. Some were works of art: the Grassy Gap Trail is a perfect contour trail, laid out by surveyor's compass and string along a 50- to 60-degree slope and kept to within 200 feet of elevation all the way around the base of Big Frog. Rarely has any government agency had the manpower and time to lay out such a trail. The result was a trail system rivaled only at Citico Creek Wilderness in the CNF.

The young men of the CCC were supposed to be 17 to 21 years of age, but "some of them fibbed on their ages," Stanley says, because money was so scarce. The government provided each CCC man with work clothes and paid all of his doctor and dentist bills. A regular worker was paid $30 per month, while an assistant leader got $36 and a leader $45.

The men were stationed at two CCC camps of 210 men apiece, one at Sylco to the west and the other at Tumbling Creek to the east, toward Copperhill. Each is now the site of a USFS campground. The CCC built what are now FS 221 and the Sheeds Creek Road and improved the old preexisting road in Sylco Valley. The Big Creek Road, which follows Big Creek itself from the Big Creek Campground down to the Ocoee River, was built by the Conasauga River Lumber Company and the USFS around 1947–48. Most of the other roads between Big Frog Wilderness and the Ocoee River are recent, built in the big timber-cutting period since the 1970s. The TN Power Company built Ocoee Powerhouse No. 1 in 1912, creating Parksville (Ocoee) Lake. The famous flume line from the lake to Powerhouse No. 2 was completed in 1913 and was completely rebuilt in the early 1980s.

Until 1936 the CNF extended far into GA, including much of what is now Chattahoochee NF. In 1936 the GA portion of the CNF was realigned along state lines and became the Chattahoochee NF. Before the realignment, Felton Stanley and others of the Cherokee branch of the USFS ranged well into GA. Stanley was part of the team that walked from Sylco Camp up Wolf Ridge and down what is now Hemp Top Trail to determine where to put the Hemp Top fire tower, which for half a century provided incredible views down into the Cohutta Mountain area. Stanley made the final decision. By then it was getting dark, and they had no provisions for the night; "so we just turned around and hiked back up Big Frog, down Wolf Ridge through the old Dutch Settlement clear back to Sylco Creek Camp that night," Stanley says. They made a round-trip in a single day of nearly 30 miles, much of it on a rough manway trail and all of it in the old-style leather walking boots. And they had no flashlights.

The west peak of Big Frog Mountain, the highest point of the area, once had a fire tower built of heavy timbers reaching treetop level. The tower was built by Frank Payne, whose grandson, Bud Payne, was the sheriff of Polk County from 1982 to 1990. The tower was in bad repair by the 1950s and was designated to be torn down, but the USFS never got around to it. Several campers from the YMCA's Camp Ocoee climbed the tower and did the job for them: the tower collapsed. It caused only moderate injuries to the campers, but considerable embarrassment to all concerned; the part of the tower still standing was then hastily torn down. Frank Payne was an early USFS warden who lived near Tumbling Creek in the valley to the east side of Big Frog. He had a camp at a dry pond on Peavine Ridge south of the present day FS 221.

The USFS maintains the Big Frog Mountain trail system in a "primitive condition." However, it is only in recent years that the trails have been significantly maintained at all. Old-time hikers of the 1950s and 1960s remember trailheads and junctions with no signs whatsoever. The upper stretches of Big Creek Trail, for example, were virtually impossible to identify. The Grassy Gap Trail was only the faintest of paths, used a few times each year by the most experienced hikers.

Jacks River Falls in the extreme northern Cohutta Wilderness. Photograph by Betty Petty.

Today there are some user-friendly trail signs, wilderness signs, and information "booths" at most trailheads, though these features have limited life spans. The USFS refurbished most of the trails in 1978 and others in the early 1990s.

For many years the trails of the area were "maintained" solely by the use of hikers from YMCA Camp Ocoee, Boy Scout Camp Cherokee, and locals from Polk County who hiked up the mountain each year for the "Ramp Tramp." For most of the twentieth century, Big Frog Mountain has been a part of the fabric of experience at Camp Ocoee. The camp, on the shores of Parksville Lake, was founded in 1923 by Glen "Chick" Ellis, who died at the age of 99 in 1992. Generations of campers and counselors, mostly from the Chattanooga and Cleveland area, walked the Big Frog trails during the low-maintenance years of the 1940s, 1950s, and 1960s.

Big Frog Mountain was for many years the goal of the annual Polk County "Ramp Tramp." From 1958 until the mid-1980s people would hike to the top of the mountain in April, when wild mountain onions, known as ramps, could be harvested. At the top of the mountain a meal of cornbread, meat, fried potatoes, ramps, and eggs was prepared, using a jeep road to bring up supplies. The Ramp Tramp was started when James Passmore, Bud Payne (then Polk County sheriff), John DeWeese, and Jimmie Passmore took Fred Colby, a state 4-H Club leader from Knoxville, to the top of Big Frog Mountain to look for ramps. The idea was originally conceived by Mrs. Dennis Blevins, former Polk County home economics agent. When the area was designated as a wilderness, several methods were used to get the supplies to the mountaintop, including a helicopter. However, because of a heart-attack fatality on the hike in 1978, the difficulty of moving supplies to the mountaintop, and frequent rains on the mountain, the Ramp Tramp was converted to a festival and held at a campground. It is now held on the last Saturday in April at Camp McCroy (a former CCC camp site) on TN 30.

The Cohutta Wilderness was designated by the US Congress in 1974 and, in the same bill, 4,626 acres in the CNF were designated as a wilderness study area. The higher elevations of the Big Frog Wilderness (5,055 acres) were designated as wilderness in 1984. The acreage was expanded in 1986 to the current 8,082-acre wilderness. A total of 365 acres outside the wilderness is recommended as a wilderness study area by the CNF's 2004 plan revision. A 1,460-acre primitive area was designated on the western slopes of the wilderness in 1988 in the CNF management plan; such protection is deleted from the CNF's 2004 plan revision. Big Frog Mountain rated a "21" during the USFS's wilderness inventory in the late 1970s, the highest of the CNF's inventoried roadless areas. The USFS said it rated highest on "natural integrity, apparent naturalness, and opportunity for solitude." The area provides about as remote a wilderness experience as a hiker can have in the southeast. Only the GSMNP and a few areas in Pisgah and Nantahala forests in NC can offer as much solitude.

In 1996, the USFS published the map "Cohutta and Big Frog Wilderness, Georgia-Tennessee," which showed the trail network and surrounding roads on a topographic map. The map corrected the CNF's renaming of the Grassy Gap Trail, eliminating much confusion. In the 1990s the Benton MacKaye Trail was also extended south of the Rough Creek Trail by using part of the formerly unofficial West Fork Rough Creek Trail (now called the West Fork Trail) to reach FS 221. The Benton MacKaye was then routed down the former bed of FS 45 to intersect FS 45 at the south end of the Thunder Rock Trail.

TRAILHEADS AND MAPS

The Big Frog Wilderness is circled on the west, north, and east by USFS roads 62 and 221. Under most conditions these dirt roads are easily driven in passenger cars. However, in winter snow or inclement weather, these roads should be avoided. The most convenient access to most of the Big Frog trailheads is from the north from US 64 along the Ocoee River via FS 45. FS 45 starts near the Ocoee Power Plant Number 3 at a sign for the Thunder Rock Campground. This turn is 18.5 miles east of the junction of US 64 and US 411, and it is 8.1 miles west of the junction of US 64 and TN 68. To reach FS 221 drive 3.0 miles north on FS 45 to a T-junction, passing the Thunder Rock South Trailhead at 1.2 miles, The FS 45 and FS 221 junction is well signed. To the left, the West Fork Trailhead is 0.4 mile, the Chestnut Mountain Loop Trailhead is 0.6 mile, FS 221G is 1.6 miles, and the Licklog Trailhead is 3.4 miles. To the right, the Low Gap Trailhead is 0.5 mile, the Big Creek Trailhead is 5.4 miles, the Wolf Ridge Trailhead is 7.4 miles, and FS 62 is 10.0 miles.

FS 221 can also be reached from the east via TN 68, 2.1 miles south of the intersection of TN 69 and US 64 at the Ocoee Basin Federal Credit Union. Turn west off TN 68 onto the paved Grassy Creek Road. Follow the paved road for 5.7 miles until it crosses a bridge and reaches a signed intersection with gravel FS 65 leading south and gravel FS 221 leading east. Turn right on FS 221 to reach the CNF Tumbling Creek Campground in 2.0 miles. The Licklog Ridge Trailhead is another 3.6 miles beyond the campground.

From the west, FS 221 can be reached via FS 55 from US 64 at Cherokee Corner. Turn south on the Cookson Creek Road at a convenience store 2.5 miles east of the overpass on US 64 above US 411. The road turns to dirt at 4.2 miles, after passing the King Slough Boat Ramp and the YMCA Camp and entering the CNF. After 0.6 mile of gravel road, bear right at an intersection with FS 302, then stay left at an unmarked junction that follows immediately. Keep to the main road past numerous unmarked intersections to reach the CNF Sylco Campground in another 6.7 miles. The junction with FS 221 is 0.4 mile past the campground and is a total of 11.9 miles from US 64. A right turn at this junction will lead to the trailheads for the Conasauga River Corridor and Jacks River Trail. Keep left and drive 1.8 miles to reach the junction with FS 62, which leads to the Chestnut Mountain Trailhead. Another 2.6 miles ahead on FS 221 is the Wolf Ridge Trailhead.

FS 221 and 62 can also be reached more directly from the west via US 411, as described in the trailhead directions for the Beach Bottom Trail and Conasauga River Corridor.

Thunder Rock South Trailhead

The Thunder Rock South Trailhead is located 1.2 miles south of US 64 on FS 45. The Thunder Rock Trail begins by a sign on the west bank of the road. This trail is part of the Benton MacKaye Trail. The West Fork and Benton MacKaye Trails leave the opposite side of the road at the unmarked intersection with the old abandoned bed of FS 45. There is room for several cars to pull out at the trailhead.

Low Gap, Big Creek, and Wolf Ridge Trailheads

From the junction of FS 221 and 45 turn right and drive west for 0.5 mile to the Low Gap Trailhead, which is the starting point for the Big Frog Trail. The parking area is on the south side of FS 221 and has room for several vehicles. The Big Creek Trailhead is located 4.9 miles west of the Low Gap Trailhead (5.4 miles from the junction of FS 221 and 45), just across the bridge over Big Creek and past the gated entry to the Yellow Stand Lead Trail. There is a large parking area. The large expanse of flat areas and easy access to water make this trailhead a popular informal camping area on weekends.

The Wolf Ridge Trailhead is located 2.0 miles beyond Big Creek (7.4 miles west of the junction of FS 221 and 45), just west of Pace Gap. A small parking area and information sign are located on the south side of FS 221.

Chestnut Mountain Trailhead

The Chestnut Mountain Trailhead is located on FS 62, 4.1 miles south of the intersection of FS 62 and 221 (14.1 miles west of the junction of FS 221 and 45). This trailhead is also 1.7 miles east of the Beach Bottoms Trailhead. There is a small parking area with an informational sign and room for overflow parking along FS 62. The Chestnut Mountain Trail begins on the left of the trailhead at a gate.

West Fork, Chestnut Mountain Loop, FS 221G, and Licklog Trailheads

At the junction of FS 221 and 45 turn left and drive east on FS 221 for 0.4 mile to the West Fork Trailhead. Park north of the road beside a gate across the route of old FS 45, which is both the West Fork and Benton MacKaye trails, though neither is marked in this direction. The West Fork Trail and Benton MacKaye trails continue north of the road beside a large sign. The new Quartz Loop Trail begins at the northeast corner of this intersection.

The Chestnut Mountain Loop Trailhead is 0.2 mile east of the West Fork Trailhead and 0.6 mile from the intersection of FS 45 and 211. The Chestnut Mountain Loop Trail begins on the south side of the road at a sign for the trail and for the Ocoee Whitewater Center by following old FS 1330.

FS 221G begins on FS 221 1.2 miles past the West Fork Trailhead (1.6 miles east of the FS 221 and 45 junction). The junction and road are unsigned. FS 221G is a rough dirt road passable by skilled drivers with good insurance. The road ends in 0.6 mile, where it is washed out at an old bridge across Rough Creek. The Rough Creek East Fork route begins to the left across the creek, and the Rough Creek West Fork route begins to the right across the creek. There is a good campsite to the right along the west fork.

The Licklog Ridge Trailhead is 1.8 miles past the start of FS 221G (3.4 miles east of the junction of FS 221 and 45). The trailhead is marked by a carsonite post and small signboard. Parking is available on the north side of the road at the entrance to bermed and unsigned FS 1330B.

Beech Bottom Trailhead

Turn east off of US 411 onto Ladd Springs Road, which is also TN 313, about 6.5 miles south of the US 411/US 64 intersection. The junction is easily missed. There is a gas station on the west side and signs for Ladd Springs Road and TN 313, which goes northwest to Cleveland. It is also possible to approach this intersection by taking the US 64 bypass in Cleveland to TN 78 south. Turn left onto Ladd Springs Road (TN 313) and follow it straight across US 411.

Drive east on Ladd Springs Road and through an intersection at Ball Play Road. At 3.9 miles the pavement ends and the road becomes FS 221. Follow FS 221 across Iron Mountain to the Jacks River Bridge and Trailhead at 9.1 miles, where new modern camping facilities are being developed by the USFS. Continue down the very lovely Alacusy Valley to the intersection with Big Frog Road (FR 62) at 10.2 miles. FR 62 may be gated in bad weather. Make a sharp right turn up the mountain to reach the large parking area for the Beech Bottom Trail at 14.5 miles. This trailhead is in the CNF and is a fee area.

To reach the trailhead from the south (or if you miss the Ladd Springs turnoff from the north and cross the state line) on US 411, turn right onto Old GA 2 (FS 16), just before the beautiful old stone Cisco Baptist Church. Continue on FS 16 past the end of the pavement, bear right at a fork, and pass the Hopewell Church. Cross the Conasauga River, continuing straight ahead 8.7 miles to the Jacks River Bridge. Continue up the Alaculsy Valley on FS 221, following the directions from the north.

TOPOGRAPHIC MAPS: USGS Caney Creek, TN; Ducktown, TN; Epworth, TN-GA; Hemp Top, TN-GA. TI Map 781, Tellico and Ocoee Rivers, CNF. A USFS map of the area entitled "Cohutta and Big Frog Wilderness," May 1996, Recreation Guide R8-RG-203, is available from the Cherokee and Chattahoochee NFs.

TRAIL DESCRIPTIONS

162. CHESTNUT MOUNTAIN TRAIL (FS TRAIL 63, TI TRAIL 21)

LENGTH: 1.9 miles

ELEVATION CHANGE: Low point, 2,160 feet; high point, 3,040 feet

DIFFICULTY: Easy

TRAILHEADS: Chestnut Mountain (start) and Wolf Ridge Trail (end)

USE: Hiking, equestrian

TOPOGRAPHIC MAPS: USGS Hemp Top, GA-TN; Caney Creek, TN

COMMENTS: The Chestnut Mountain Trail is one of the shortest and most popular routes to the summit of Big Frog Mountain. Combined with the Wolf Ridge Trail, hikers can make a 7.4-mile round-trip summit hike. The trail begins on an old road and follows the border of the Cohutta Wilderness for its entire length. Though open to horses, there is no evidence of their use on the trail.

The trailhead is at the old Van Arthur place, acquired by the USFS in 1946, and is a short distance from the TN-GA line. An old road continues straight from the parking area. The Chestnut Mountain Trail leaves left at a metal gate. There is a similarly named Chestnut Mountain Loop Trail that is part of the trail system at the Ocoee Whitewater Center and also a Chestnut Mountain Loop Trail and Chestnut Mountain 4 WD road in the Gee Creek area.

DETAILS: Within 100 yards the trail passes a register box for the wilderness. The unmarked trail climbs gently along the old road through a pine-oak forest that offers winter views to the right of Big Frog Mountain. At 1.2 miles the trail appears to fork. The left branch is a steep and strenuous "shortcut," while the main route bears right and follows the road around a switchback to the left. The shortcut rejoins the main trail on the ridgecrest at 1.7 miles. Reach a signed junction with the Wolf Ridge Trail at 1.9 miles at a dry ridgetop campsite.

163. BIG FROG TRAIL (BENTON MACKAYE TRAIL) (FS TRAIL 64, TI TRAIL 10)

LENGTH: 5.6 miles

ELEVATION CHANGE: Low point, 2,120 feet; high point, 4,224 feet

DIFFICULTY: Moderate

TRAILHEADS: Low Gap (start) and Wolf Ridge and Licklog Ridge Trails (end)

USE: Hiking

TOPOGRAPHIC MAP: USGS Caney Creek, TN

COMMENTS: Big Frog Trail is the premier footpath of the Big Frog Wilderness. The character of the trail changes many times as it passes from the drier pine woods near the trailhead at FS 221 through shaded switchbacks leading to the scrub oak forests at Chimneytop and finally to Big Frog itself. You may see signs of bobcat, bear, coyote, or deer along the route. As with most of the trails in the area, this one is best hiked in the spring or fall; water can be hard to find in dry summers. The trail is marked with a few ancient white, red, or ax blazes. The trail is also known as the Peavine Ridge Trail after the ridge it follows. From the top of Big Frog Mountain to the junction with the Fork Ridge Trail it is also part of the Benton MacKaye Trail. Big Frog is the most popular trail in the wilderness: it was the only trail in TN to receive even a "moderate" use rating on the 1996 wilderness map. Most hikers use it for a round-trip day hike or overnight hike to the summit. However, Big Frog intersects seven other wilderness trails, providing many loop opportunities. One appealing 12.0 mile overnight trip is to climb on the Big Frog Trail to an overnight site near the mountaintop and return to FS 221 via the Benton MacKaye Trail. This route requires only a one-mile vehicle shuttle or road walk.

Low Gap Trailhead is located 0.5 mile west on FS 221 from the FS 45 and 221 junction. Unfortunately, there are two Low Gaps along the route; the trailhead and the Low Gap at the junction with the Yellow Stand Lead and Grassy Gap trails. To minimize confusion, this description will use "lower" Low Gap Trailhead for the trailhead and "upper" Low Gap Junction for the trail junction. "Upper" Low Gap is called Hall Camp Gap on some older maps. Beyond the trailhead on FS 221 there are excellent views north, including all of Little Frog Mountain and Chilhowee Mountain as the result of clear-cutting in the late 1970s.

DETAILS: The trail begins to the right of the parking area at a signboard and trail register. The ridge on the skyline to the left is Licklog Ridge. Begin by following old FS 5065, which is blocked by berms. At 0.2 mile, go right and up where a split leads to an old wildlife opening. At 0.6 mile the old road ends in a stand of Virginia pines. Keep right and continue uphill. Enter the wilderness at 0.7 mile where the trail begins to level off.

At 1.5 miles another road splits off to the left. Just beyond is the signed junction with the Rough Creek Trail, which enters from the left. There is a small campsite here with water available from a pond 0.1 mile down the Rough Creek Trail. Continue right on a remarkably level section of trail to reach a signed four-way junction with the Grassy Gap and Yellow Stand Lead trails at "upper" Low Gap Junction at 2.4 miles. Yellow Stand Lead Trail on the right descends 2.3 miles to the Big Creek Trailhead. The middle trail is Grassy Gap, which follows along contour 1.7 miles to a junction with the Big Creek Trail. There is water in a small hemlock-filled draw about 150 yards to the left and a small campsite just beyond the junction. Some of the shrubby plants on the east side of the gap are buffalo nuts, which have poisonous green-cased nuts in the late summer; they are about two inches long with five little protrusions in a circular pattern around the bottom end of the nut.

Follow the left trail, which is the only one to climb from the gap. In its first 2.4 miles, Big Frog Trail has climbed only 350 feet. But this is about to change because the Fork Ridge Trail intersection 1.3 miles

Backpacker lumbers up the Big Frog Trail in early springtime. Photograph by Suzanne McDonald.

ahead is about 900 feet higher. At 3.2 miles watch for a sharp right turn on the ridgecrest. Then the trail arcs to the left, passing through a dark area carpeted with May apples and, if they're blooming, some of the most deeply colored purple trillium you will see. Reach the signed intersection with the Fork Ridge and Benton MacKaye trails that enters to the left at 3.7 miles. Fork Ridge leads 1.8 miles to a junction with the Rough Creek Trail. From this point to the summit, the Big Frog Trail is part of the Benton MacKaye Trail. Straight ahead is the very steep Rough Creek (East Fork) watershed and, in the distance, Licklog Ridge. Both of these features will be on your left for most of the remainder of the trail. Big Frog Trail turns sharply to the right (it has to) and begins a dramatically different segment as it ascends and begins following the narrow crest of Chimneytop Ridge.

The Big Frog Trail follows a knife-edge crest beginning at 3.9 miles, where the ridgetop is only a few feet wide. The escarpment drops several hundred feet on each side. Trees are stunted and the canopy is thin. Grasses and herbaceous material cover the ground, but there are also saw briars, blackberry vines, and hawthorn bushes to impede your travel. Some of the 10-foot-high shrubs are Carolina buckthorn, which are sometimes covered with bright red berries for a short while in the late summer before they darken. The easternmost peak of Big Frog is visible to the south. A few yards down the trail an excellent view to the left (southeast) opens up, and on a good day you can see over the crest of Licklog Ridge far into the distance to Brasstown Bald, the highest point in GA. Up over the ridgecrest, to the north, is Chilhowee Mountain. The trail climbs to the very crest of the knife-edge ridge.

At 4.0 miles, the trail turns to the right off the east side of the crest to pass 75 yards below and to the right of the peak of Chimneytop. There are many trillium and sweet white violets here. After going to the west side of the ridge, you come out on a second knife edge at 4.3 miles in the "saddle" between Chimneytop and the north peak of Big Frog Mountain, which is straight ahead. In this saddle is the unsigned junction with the top of the Big Creek Trail. This faint path is marked only by two small rock cairns.

Reach another narrow crest at 4.4 miles that has good views off either side. The finest views from Big Frog Trail are seen from this point, a good spot for lunch. The towns of Copperhill, TN, and McCaysville, GA, are to the east. Over the top of Licklog Ridge, to the southeast, is Brasstown Bald. Pass through a short tunnel of rhododendron before reaching a spartan campsite on the north peak of Big Frog at 4.9 miles, where the grade finally begins to ease. The next 0.5

mile or so is incredibly level, following the shelf between the "tent poles" of Big Frog, which from the distant west (the Ocoee Lake and Cleveland area) looks exactly like a giant pup tent, with the "entrance flap" (Chimneytop) facing north. Some also feel it looks more like a huge frog. There is a spacious campsite on the west side of the crest. A very large black cherry tree is some 30 yards down off the ridge to the right at 5.5 miles.

At 5.6 miles the Big Frog Trail ends at the rarely signed junction with the Licklog Ridge and Wolf Ridge trails at a well-used campsite. Note that this junction is just below the crest and can easily become overgrown and is thereby not obvious. Wolf Ridge Trail heads south and then turns west, but its start is offset about 10 feet west of the end of the Big Frog Trail on the opposite side of the campsite. Licklog Ridge Trail follows the main path east.

Ninety degrees to the right from the end of the Big Frog Trail is a side trail leading about 60 yards to the highest point of Big Frog Mountain at 4,224 feet. There was once an old fire tower on the peak. Look to the west; contemplate that the next mountain anywhere near the size of the Big Frog/Cohutta system—in the entire US from this

Backpacker reviews his maps in camp at the very summit of Big Frog Mountain. Photograph by Suzanne McDonald.

point west—is somewhere in the Black Hills of South Dakota or the mountains of Big Bend in Texas. Big Frog Mountain and its GA sisters, Cowpen, Bald, and Grassy Mountains, are the westernmost 4,000-foot peaks of the Appalachians. An outstanding campsite and spring are located just 0.2 mile to the left down the Licklog Ridge Trail. The spring is unreliable in dry weather.

164. LICKLOG RIDGE TRAIL (FS TRAIL 65, TI TRAIL 52)

LENGTH: 5.9 miles

ELEVATION CHANGE: Low point, 1,760 feet; high point, 4,224 feet

DIFFICULTY: Moderate

TRAILHEADS: Licklog Ridge (start) and Big Frog and Wolf Ridge Trails (end)

USE: Hiking

TOPOGRAPHIC MAPS: USGS Hemp Top, GA-TN; Caney Creek, TN; Ducktown, TN

COMMENTS: This trail follows the crest of Licklog Ridge from FS 221 to the top of Big Frog Mountain. It traverses a forest dominated by pine and oak. There are some good views east to Ocoee No. 3 Lake and west across the East Fork of Rough Creek. The trail, which is little used and partly overgrown and brushy, is also known as the Licklog Trail. The top 0.6 mile on Big Frog Mountain is part of the Benton MacKaye Trail. The trailhead is 3.3 miles west of the junction of FS 45 and 221 on FS 221. There is parking for several cars at a turnout at the start of unmarked FS 1330B at an old clear-cut. The trail begins opposite the parking area.

DETAILS: The most difficult part of this trail is navigating through an old clear-cut at the start of the trail. From FS 221, walk 50 yards to a signboard and register box. In 0.1 mile, reach an intersection where three old logging roads split off. Follow the left-most road uphill for 40 yards, then turn right off the road onto a foot trail. If all goes well, you will cross under a TVA power line at 0.2 mile. Beyond the power line the trail is marked by a few ancient white or red paint blazes and some ax blazes of similar vintage. You will also see some old signs marking the edge of a wildlife management area.

At 1.0 mile, pass a sign indicating that you are now in the Big Frog Wilderness. Gain the ridgecrest and enjoy a view of Ocoee Lake No. 3 before reaching a signed junction with the Rough Creek Trail at 1.5 miles. Rough Creek leads right 1.4 miles to the Fork Ridge Trail. The

5.9
-1.5
4.4

Licklog Ridge Trail rounds a small knoll and follows the ridgecrest with more views of Ocoee Lake.

At 2.2 miles, move right off the crest and enjoy views of Peavine Ridge. After another stretch directly on the crest move to the left side at 3.5 miles. Cross the head of a small dry stream before returning to the crest, at a series of fine overlooks of Chimneytop at 4.2 miles. From one opening the TN Valley and Walden Ridge are visible over the shoulder of Peavine Ridge.

Reach the crest of Groundhog Ridge at 4.8 miles. A faint manway leading down the ridge is blocked by a low wall of rocks. Regain the crest of Licklog Ridge just before reaching the signed junction with the Hemp Top and Benton MacKaye trails at 5.3 miles. There is a small campsite here with room for three or four tents. The Benton MacKaye Trail leads south here to follow the Hemp Top Trail for 0.8 mile to Double Springs Gap at the GA-TN line. To the north, the Benton MacKaye Trail will follow the Licklog Ridge Trail to the summit of Big Frog Mountain.

From this junction the trail turns northwest toward Big Frog Mountain. At 5.5 miles there is a large, but sloping, campsite in a small saddle. At 5.7 miles there is a small spring on the left side of the trail in a rock area. This spring is usually flowing year round and makes the summit of Big Frog an enticing camping area. Small campsites are also located downhill from the spring. The trail ends at 5.9 miles at the junction with the Wolf Ridge and Big Frog Trails at another well used campsite. In 2002, the junction was marked only by a post. The Big Frog and Benton MacKaye Trail is the well-marked trail leading right. A faint trail heading straight goes 60 yards to the site of an old lookout tower on the true summit. The Wolf Ridge Trail is the faint path leading downhill to the left from the far side of the campsite.

165. WOLF RIDGE TRAIL (FS TRAIL 66, TI TRAIL 85)

LENGTH: 4.5 miles

ELEVATION CHANGE: Low point, 1,660 feet; high point, 4,224 feet

DIFFICULTY: Moderate

TRAILHEADS: Wolf Ridge (start) and Big Frog and Licklog Ridge Trails junction (end)

USE: Hiking, equestrian (from Chestnut Mountain Trail to Big Frog Mountain)

TOPOGRAPHIC MAP: USGS Caney Creek, TN

COMMENTS: The Wolf Ridge Trail offers the second shortest route to the top of Big Frog Mountain. However, most use of the trail is by hikers using the Chestnut Mountain route to the summit. Wolf Ridge is a moderate 9.0-mile round-trip to the summit. It can also be combined with the Grassy Gap and Big Frog Trails for a 12.9-mile loop that visits the summit, too. The Wolf Ridge Trail begins on gated FS 221E, which turns off FS 221 0.3 mile south of the junction with FS 374 at Pace Gap. The trailhead is 7.4 miles west of the junction of FS 221 and FS 45. It is marked by a large brown sign reading "Wolf Ridge Trail No. 66." There is a USFS bulletin board, trail register, and parking.

A small stone monument commemorating John Curbow was formerly located on the Wolf Ridge Trail on a level spot about 1.0 mile above the Chestnut Mountain Trail intersection. Curbow was an organizer of the annual Ramp Tramp, a walk to the top of Big Frog Mountain. He died in a farming accident after returning home from the Ramp Tramp in 1968. The monument was installed in the mid-1970s but disappeared in 1980.

DETAILS: The Wolf Ridge Trail begins at a gate across FS 221E. It follows the road past a register box to a right turn at 0.3 mile that is marked only by a low sign. The trail from this point to the junction with Chestnut Mountain is marked by old red or white paint blazes. At 0.5 mile, switchback to the left at an unexpected turn. Reach the crest of Wolf Ridge at 0.9 mile. Like many of the ridgetops in the wilderness area, this dry crest supports a forest of pines and oak. At 1.4 miles begin to skirt the edge of an old clear-cut that is now choked by an impenetrable thicket of small pines. Just past the clear-cut stands a three-foot-wide oak.

At 2.0 miles a sign indicates that the Grassy Gap Trail leaves the ridge to the left to reach the Big Creek Trail in 3.3 miles. The Wolf Ridge Trail continues straight but is unmarked from this point on. Leave the ridgecrest to the right just before reaching the signed junction at 2.7 miles with the Chestnut Mountain Trail, which leads to FS 62 in 1.9 miles.

The Chestnut Mountain junction is in a small level saddle that could make a dry emergency campsite. Turn left at this junction to follow the Wolf Ridge Trail. Climb steadily on the crest to a small knoll at 3.2 miles. Beyond the knoll is a broad level area in an open hardwood forest where dry camping is possible. The knoll is the former site of the John Curbow Monument, but all that now remains are a few pieces of concrete block.

The climbing resumes at 3.5 miles. As the trail nears the top of the mountain, it again becomes steep, rocky, and somewhat overgrown. At

4.5 miles reach the junction with the ends of the Big Frog and Licklog Ridge trails at a campsite near the summit of Big Frog Mountain. The main trail to the right is the Licklog Ridge Trail that passes a spring in 0.1 mile. The main trail to the left is the Big Frog Trail leading 5.6 miles to "lower" Low Gap Trailhead. A faint trail turning sharper left from the barren signpost at the junction leads 60 yards to the site of the former Big Frog summit lookout tower.

166. GRASSY GAP TRAIL (FS TRAIL 67, TI TRAIL 41)

LENGTH: 5.0 miles

ELEVATION CHANGE: Low point, 2,400 feet; high point, 2,440 feet

DIFFICULTY: Moderate

TRAILHEADS: Wolf Ridge Trail (start) and Big Frog Trail (end)

USE: Hiking

TOPOGRAPHIC MAP: USGS Caney Creek, TN

COMMENTS: The Grassy Gap Trail was formerly known as the Barkleggin Trail. This trail has been radically reconfigured since the first edition of this guide. The trail as now described is a five-mile contour route from Grassy Gap on Wolf Ridge to "upper" Low Gap Junction on the Big Frog Trail. The trail section from the crossing of Big Creek up Bark Legging Lead to the Big Frog Trail at Chimneytop is now considered part of the Big Creek Trail.

Grassy Gap provides a rare opportunity for hikers to travel five miles along contour with practically no elevation gain. But do not be deceived into thinking the trail is easy. This is one of the least used trails in the wilderness. The trail has received little maintenance in recent years, and much of the footway is very narrow and sloping. The trail is often obscured by blowdowns, though the CNF does periodically clear downed trees. Heavy underbrush might completely hide the trail in summer. There are few blazes to mark the way, but the trail remains at nearly a constant elevation for its entire length.

DETAILS: The trail begins 2.0 miles down the Wolf Ridge Trail where a new sign marks a left turn onto the Grassy Gap Trail. It is marked by old and rare white paint blazes. Grassy Gap stays on the 2,400-foot contour through an open hardwood forest that offers sporadic views of Wolf Ridge. At 0.3 mile cross the first streambed. Some very large tulip poplar and oak—up to four feet in diameter—adorn this little watershed. In 75 to 100 years hikers will truly appreciate the creation of Big Frog Wilderness when they view Joyce Kilmer

Memorial–size trees here. Weave in and out of three more narrow stream valleys and dry ridges before reaching a rock-hop over Penitentiary Branch at 1.5 miles. The valley of Penitentiary Branch is the broadest along the trail, but even here the landscape is too steep and lumpy for camping.

Watch for the change from oak to pine forest as you round the nose of the ridges. Cross one small valley and reach a rock retaining wall built into a remarkably steep slope at 2.6 miles. The effort required of the CCC crews to dig five miles of this trail into these steep slopes was amazing. Unfortunately, it would take nearly the same effort to repair much of this worn footway. At 3.1 miles cross a side branch of Big Creek. The trail beyond this crossing is faint and obscured by blowdowns but is marked by a pair of broad, ancient ax blazes. The trail remains well disguised until it descends to a signed junction with the Big Creek Trail at 3.3 miles.

At this junction, the well-defined Big Creek Trail leads 2.3 miles down the creek to the Big Creek Trailhead. The well-defined trail climbing to the right above, and almost parallel to the Grassy Gap Trail, is the Big Creek Trail leading 1.8 miles to the Big Frog Trail near Chimneytop. The Grassy Gap Trail is an obscure path continuing straight ahead across the creek.

From the Big Creek junction, the Grassy Gap Trail continues at the same elevation. It crosses three small creeks and offers some leafy views of ridges to the west. At 5.0 miles it reaches a four-way intersection with the Yellow Stand Lead and Big Frog trails at "upper" Low Gap Junction. The signed Yellow Stand Lead Trail turns left to descend 2.3 miles to the Big Creek Trailhead. The well-defined Big Frog Trail continues straight down 2.4 miles to lower Low Gap Trailhead and turns right to climb to the top of Big Frog Mountain in 3.2 miles.

167. BIG CREEK TRAIL (FS TRAIL 68, TI TRAIL 9)

LENGTH: 4.1 miles

ELEVATION CHANGE: Low point, 1,400 feet; high point, 3,600 feet

DIFFICULTY: Moderate

TRAILHEADS: Big Creek (start) and Big Frog Trail (end)

USE: Hiking

TOPOGRAPHIC MAP: USGS Caney Creek, TN

COMMENTS: The Big Creek Trail climbs from FS 221 to the Big Frog Trail near Chimneytop. It has been rearranged since the first edition of this book by swapping segments with the Grassy Gap Trail. The second segment of Big Creek now climbs up Bark Legging Lead to the Big Frog Trail from the junction with Grassy Gap. This is still the most diverse trail in the wilderness. The lower section is a gentle streamside walk with plenty of potential campsites, while the upper trail climbs steadily up the steep slopes below Chimney Top. The Big Creek Trailhead is on FS 221, 5.4 miles from the junction with FS 45. The trailhead has ample parking and is a popular car camping area. The lower part of the Big Creek Trail can be combined with Yellow Stand Lead and north part of the Grassy Gap Trail for a pretty 6.3-mile day hike.

DETAILS: The trail begins as a wide old roadway. At 0.1 mile there is a trail register. The trail turns right off the road at 0.2 mile to follow a route above the creek on the steep hillside. At 0.8 mile return to an old road at stream level next to a spacious campsite. The trail crosses Peter Camp Branch at 0.9 mile and enters the wilderness.

After crossing the creek, keep following the trace of an old road that is sporadically marked with faint white paint blazes. Turn right off the road onto a narrow footpath at 1.3 miles. The trail crosses an upper branch of Big Creek at 2.2 miles, then makes a switchback to the left. At 2.3, miles reach a poorly marked four-way junction next to a side branch of Big Creek.

Though only one route is immediately obvious here, two trails actually cross at this point. The only sign here lies on the ground and indicates that Peavine Road (FS 221) is 2.25 miles and Low Gap is 2.0 miles. To the left the northeast section of the faint Grassy Gap Trail crosses the side branch along contour and leads 1.7 miles northeast to the Yellow Stand Lead and Big Frog trails at upper Low Gap Junction. This section was once considered part of the Big Creek Trail. Follow the Grassy Gap Trail left if you are trying to follow the 6.3-mile loop back to the Big Creek Trailhead. Another faint footpath turns sharp right in the elbow of the Big Creek Trail. This is the southwest section the Grassy Gap Trail that leads southwest for 3.3 miles to an intersection with the Wolf Ridge Trail at Grassy Gap.

The Big Creek Trail turns gently right and climbs the most obvious trail for 1.8 miles to join the Big Frog Trail near Chimneytop. The trail continues to be marked by rare white blazes as it ascends more steeply toward Big Frog Mountain. The first of a pair of switchbacks is partially obscured by blowdowns. At 2.6 miles is an open area with views. Recross the main stream of Big Creek and gain Bark Legging Lead, which is covered with pine and galax and offers welcome views of the surrounding ridges. At 3.8 miles, cross the now dry head of Big

Creek and enter an open and sunny grove of sugar maples that promises to be a wonderland during the spring wildflower bloom. The final climb to the crest of Chimneytop is on a very obscure trail. From the final crossing of Big Creek the trail angles left up the slope. No blazes mark this route. Reach the junction with the Big Frog Trail at 4.1 miles. The junction is marked only by two small rock cairns. From this point it is 1.3 miles right to the summit of Big Frog Mountain and 4.3 miles left to lower Low Gap Trailhead.

168. FORK RIDGE TRAIL (BENTON MACKAYE TRAIL) (FS TRAIL 69, TI TRAIL 37)

LENGTH: 1.8 miles

ELEVATION CHANGE: Low point, 2,280 feet; high point, 3,360 feet

DIFFICULTY: Moderate

TRAILHEADS: Rough Creek Trail (start) and Big Frog Trail (end)

USE: Hiking

TOPOGRAPHIC MAP: USGS Caney Creek, TN

COMMENTS: The Fork Ridge Trail begins at the Rough Creek Trail 0.6 mile from either the east or west forks of Rough Creek. This dry trail follows the crest of Fork Ridge through a pine-oak forest. For the entire length it is part of the Benton MacKaye Trail and can be used as part of a loop hike between the Big Frog and Benton MacKaye trails.

DETAILS: The Fork Ridge Trail begins at a junction with the Rough Creek Trail on the crest of Fork Ridge. In 2002 the junction was marked by a post but only fragments of a sign. The trail leads directly up the crest of Fork Ridge for the first 0.1 mile before branching left to climb up the east slope. Parts of the lower trail are narrow and sloping and can make for difficult walking. At 0.9 mile, cross the crest to the west side. In spring, violets, pussy toes, and trailing arbutus bloom here. At 1.8 miles, reach a signed junction with the Big Frog Trail. The summit of Big Frog is 1.9 miles to the left, and the lower Low Gap Trailhead is 3.7 miles to the right.

169. ROUGH CREEK TRAIL (BENTON MACKAYE TRAIL) (FS TRAIL 70, TI TRAIL 66)

LENGTH: 2.9 miles

ELEVATION CHANGE: Low point, 1,840 feet; high point, 2,480 feet.

DIFFICULTY: Moderate

TRAILHEADS: Licklog Ridge Trail (start) and Big Frog (end)

USE: Hiking

TOPOGRAPHIC MAP: USGS Caney Creek, TN

COMMENTS: Rough Creek Trail is a useful, but little used, connector between Licklog, Fork, and Peavine ridges and between the east and west forks of Rough Creek. The vegetation is varied, with oak and pine growing on the drier ridgetops and hemlock, rhododendron, and other moist-area species in the creek drainages. Either direction the trail is hiked involves descending a high ridge, crossing a stream, ascending and descending another ridge, crossing a second stream, and climbing a ridge to the trail's end. Hiked on its own, the trail is more diverse than other trails in the wilderness, which are either confined solely to ridgetops or stream bottoms. Only widely scattered and faint white paint blazes mark the trail.

The trail begins 1.5 miles up the Licklog Ridge Trail from FS 221 at a signed junction. Between the Fork Ridge and West Fork Trails, Rough Creek Trail is part of the Benton MacKaye Trail.

DETAILS: From the signed junction on Licklog Ridge, the Rough Creek Trail descends steadily down the east slope of the ridge. At 0.2 mile a faint overgrown road enters from the right. The trail descends to cross two branches of the east fork, which are easy rock-hops under most conditions. Beyond the crossings, the trail climbs the bank to reach the bed of the Rough Creek East Fork Trail and a small cairn at 0.8 mile.

The Rough Creek East Fork Trail is a well-defined roadbed that can be followed at least two miles upstream. Rough Creek Trail turns right on the roadway and follows it downstream for a short distance to 0.9 mile. Here another small cairn marks the point where the trail climbs the steep bank and begins the climb of Fork Ridge. After a moderate climb through a forest dominated by pine and oak, reach the unsigned junction with the Fork Ridge and Benton MacKaye trails at 1.5 miles. The Fork Ridge and Benton MacKaye trails lead left 1.8 miles to the Big Frog Trail.

The Benton MacKaye Trail now follows the Rough Creek Trail off the ridge down toward the West Fork. The trails ford the West Fork of Rough Creek in a dense grove of rhododendron and hemlock where a small side stream joins the West Fork. Bear left at the crossing and reach the old roadbed of the West Fork Trail at a cairn at 2.0 miles.

Just upstream from the cairn, the roadway is washed out at the site of a culvert bridge over the west fork. The roadway continues upstream

0.5 mile on a route that was considered part of the Rough Creek West Fork manway in the first edition of this book. Though several blow-downs and a vigorous growth of young hemlock sometimes block the way, the walk offers continuous views of the creek.

To continue on the Rough Creek Trail, turn right at the cairn and walk 100 feet north of the junction with the West Fork Trail to a cairn that marks where the Rough Creek Trail leaves the West Fork and Benton MacKaye trails. Turn left here and begin a moderate climb through a pine forest. You can tell that the upper slopes of the ridge have been clear-cut by the dense packing of the small stubby regrowth, and by the absence of any large trees. At 2.6 miles, climb up a bank onto an old logging road. At 2.8 miles pass a small pond on the left that was built in the 1970s as a helicopter water-loading source for firefighting. Where the old road then splits, the trail follows the left fork to the signed intersection with the Big Frog Trail at 2.9 miles. From this point it is 1.5 miles right to lower Low Gap Trailhead and 4.1 miles left to the top of Big Frog Mountain. Just below the intersection is a small campsite that could be used in conjunction with the small fire pond.

170. YELLOW STAND LEAD TRAIL (FS TRAIL 73, TI TRAIL 87)

LENGTH: 2.3 miles

ELEVATION CHANGE: Low point, 1,400 feet; high point, 2,430 feet

DIFFICULTY: Moderate

TRAILHEADS: Big Creek (start) and Big Frog Trail (end)

USE: Hiking

TOPOGRAPHIC MAP: USGS Caney Creek, TN

COMMENTS: The Yellow Stand Lead Trail begins just across the concrete bridge over Big Creek from the Big Creek Trailhead, where a metal gate blocks former FS 3367-01. Much of trail lies outside the wilderness, and the lower reaches follow an old logging road. This little-used trail is best hiked as part of a 6.3-mile loop hike with the Big Creek Trail.

DETAILS: Begin by hiking past the metal gate on the old logging road. At 0.2 mile an overgrown route branches to the left up a side draw. Continue following the main road until you reach the end of the road and a former trailhead parking area at 0.9 mile. At this point, a sharp left turn leads to a wildlife opening, while the main road bears right. The Yellow Stand Lead Trail turns more gently left here on a side road to reach the old sign board and register box.

Just beyond the old trailhead, the trail makes a left turn off the side road and travels up the crest of Yellow Stand Lead. At 1.1 miles another faint side trail leaves to the left in a stand of small pines and sugar maples. Reach a violently destroyed wilderness boundary sign at 1.4 miles. The trail continues up the ridge past two leafy overlooks to reach a signed four-way junction with the Big Frog and Gassy Gap trails at 2.3 miles at upper Low Gap Junction. To complete the 6.3-mile loop with the Big Creek Trail, turn sharp right on the signed Grassy Gap Trail, which leads 1.7 miles to the Big Creek Trail. The two most obvious trail branches here are parts of the Big Frog Trail, which lead right 3.2 miles up to the summit of Big Frog Mountain, and left 2.4 miles down to the lower Low Gap Trailhead.

171. HEMP TOP TRAIL (FS TRAIL 145, TI TRAIL 44)

LENGTH: 0.8 mile

ELEVATION CHANGE: Low point, 3,200 feet; high point, 4,100 feet

DIFFICULTY: Moderate

TRAILHEADS: Licklog Ridge Trail (start) and Double Spring Gap (end)

USE: Hiking, equestrian

TOPOGRAPHIC MAP: USGS Hemp Top, GA-TN

COMMENTS: Hemp Top is the only trail that connects the trail systems in the Big Frog and Cohutta Wilderness areas. Here we describe the trail only to the state line at Double Springs Gap. Most hikers use this trail to access the springs and campsite at Double Springs Gap. In Georgia, Hemp Top becomes Chattahoochee NF Trail 62 and continues past the former fire tower site to a trailhead at Dally Gap. The entire route of the Hemp Top is part of the Benton MacKaye Trail, which continues south through the Chattahoochee NF for 80 miles to Springer Mountain, also the southern terminus of the AT.

DETAILS: The Hemp Top Trail begins at a signed junction with the Licklog Ridge Trail, 0.6 mile east of the top of Big Frog Mountain. The junction is located by a small dry campsite. Signs indicate that the Licklog Ridge Trail heads north and that the combined Licklog Ridge and Benton MacKaye trails lead west. Hemp Top is the unmarked trail leading south; it is hard to believe such a trail is the major connector to Cohutta. If you are hiking south from Big Frog Mountain, the Hemp Top Trail turns off to the right.

Hemp Top Trail begins to descend the ridge almost immediately after it leaves Licklog Ridge Trail. The trail drops and drops with little relief, losing 500 to 600 feet of elevation about as fast as if you had bushwhacked down the mountain. The trail is marked only by a few ancient wildlife management area signs that have been partly swallowed by their host trees. At 0.8 mile reach Double Springs Gap, where a wooden sign facing GA welcomes hikers to TN and the CNF. Springs on either side of the gap can be reached within 200 feet down well-trod trails. From this point it is about 1.2 miles on the Benton MacKaye Trail to an old fire tower site, 3.0 miles to the Penitentiary Branch Trail, 4.5 miles to a split with the Benton MacKaye Trail, and 5.5 miles to Dally Gap.

172. WEST FORK TRAIL (BENTON MACKAYE TRAIL, FS TRAIL 303, TI TRAIL 83)

LENGTH: 3.8 miles

ELEVATION CHANGE: Low point, 1,440 feet; high point, 1,880 feet

DIFFICULTY: Moderate

TRAILHEADS: Thunder Rock South (start) and Rough Creek Trail (end); the trail also crosses FS 221 at the West Fork Trailhead

USE: Hiking; mountain bikes are allowed north of FS 221

TOPOGRAPHIC MAPS: USGS Caney Creek; TN; Ducktown, TN

COMMENTS: The new West Fork Trail provides a connection for the Benton MacKaye Trail between the Rough Creek Trail and the south end of the Thunder Rock Trail at FS 45. Part of the trail south of FS 221 follows old West Fork logging road, and another part is a foot trail that was built in the mid-1990s. Two old culverts on the roadway south of FS 221 are washed out, and the stream must be rock-hopped at these points. North of FS 221 the trail follows the route of old FS 45, which is still a well-conditioned roadway and is open to mountain bikes. The half mile of trail immediately north of FS 221 is part of the Ocoee Whitewater Center trails.

There is a new trailhead on FS 221 located 0.4 mile east of the junction of FS 221 and 45 that also serves the Chestnut Mountain Loop and Quartz Loop trails that are part of the Ocoee Whitewater Center trail system. The first 1.2 miles of this trail can be combined with the Thunder Rock and Thunder Rock Express trails to form a 5.0-mile loop from the Thunder Rock Campground on trails partly shared with mountain bikes.

The West Fork Trail partially replaces the old Rough Creek West Fork manway as described in the first edition of this book. From FS 45 to the West Fork of Rough Creek it is marked with new white diamond paint blazes.

DETAILS: The West Fork Trail begins at the Thunder Rock South Trailhead on FS 45, 1.2 miles south of US 64. Between FS 45 and FS 221 it follows the bed of former FS 45 on a gentle ascent. At the start, the trail follows the open roadbed through an area that is very shrubby in summer. At 0.2 mile is a grave site on the right of the trail that is marked by bricks and concrete block. Make a hairpin turn to the left at 0.5 mile and resume a gentle climb. At 0.8 mile an older, rougher road enters downhill from the right. The forest here is more mature than is typical of the area north of FS 221. The dense canopy and open forest make for pleasant walking even in summer.

Just beyond a grove of hemlocks at 1.2 miles, reach a signed intersection with FS 33641, which is also signed as the C loop of the Ocoee Whitewater trails. The tan-blazed Chestnut Mountain Loop Trail shares this route north to FS 221. At 1.6 miles reach the West Fork Trailhead at FS 221. To the right on FS 221 it is 0.4 mile to the junction of FS 221 and 45. The Chestnut Mountain Loop Trail turn left onto FS 221 for 0.2 mile to the Chestnut Mountain Loop Trailhead, while the Quartz Loop Trail begins left along the ridgecrest.

The West Fork Trail continues across FS 221, where it is marked with white "i" and diamond blazes. The first half mile follows an old logging road along the crest of a small ridge. At 2.1 miles, turn right off the road to follow the east side of a small stream. Keep the stream on your right as the trail winds gently downhill. At 2.6 miles, reach the old West Fork logging road at a junction marked by a small cairn. There are no more blazes past this junction. To the left the road leads downstream 0.5 mile to FS 221G and is called the Rough Creek West Fork Trail. The West Fork and Benton MacKaye trails turn right here and follow the wide, open road.

Cross two small side streams and stay right where a side road branches left at 2.7 miles. The trail along the creek is beautiful walking, with views of the creek interspersed with clusters of rhododendron and hemlock. The trail crosses the West Fork at 3.2 and 3.3 miles. Culverts protecting the road have now been washed away, and the creek must be rock-hopped. At 3.8 miles, reach an unmarked junction with the Rough Creek Trail that leads right 0.9 mile to the Big Frog Trail on Peavine Ridge. In another 100 feet the West Fork Trail ends where the Rough Creek Trail turns left off the roadway to ford the West Fork. The roadway extends another 50 feet to a third washed-out culvert, where there is a small campsite.

Though the West Fork Trail ends at this point, it is possible to cross the stream at the third culvert and continue to follow the roadway along the West Fork. Though some sections are heavily overgrown with young hemlocks and many blowdowns block the way, the route is still easy to follow. At 0.3 mile past the third culvert there is a fourth culvert that is still intact. The road appears to end in 0.5 mile at a turnaround.

173. BEECH BOTTOM TRAIL (FS TRAIL 304, TI TRAIL 6)

LENGTH: 4.0 miles

ELEVATION CHANGE: Low point, 1,380 feet; high point, 1,640 feet

DIFFICULTY: Moderate

TRAILHEAD: Beech Bottom Trailhead

USE: Hiking

TOPOGRAPHIC MAP: USGS Hemp Top, GA-TN

COMMENTS: The Beech Bottom Trail begins in the CNF in TN but very quickly passes into the Chattahoochee NF and the Cohutta Wilderness in Georgia. It provides the easiest access to the spectacular Jacks River Falls because it is primarily an old roadbed and does not have a major river crossing. All other trails into this area cross the Jacks River at least once, and the Jacks River Trail to which this trail connects crosses the river 44 times! This trail is beautiful and easily hiked at all seasons of the year, and that leads to its only major drawback. It is the most heavily used trail in the region and is usually crowded both with campers and hikers. While this trail is only four miles long, it is 4.6 miles to Jacks River Falls.

DETAILS: The trail begins across FS 62 from the trailhead parking lot. There is a fee box and an information kiosk at the trailhead. At 0.3 mile is a Cohutta Wilderness sign, which is also the GA-TN state line. The walking is gently downhill and easy on an old roadbed. The first small stream is crossed at one mile. The trail climbs gently to a crest at 1.5 miles, then it rolls gently along the ridgetop and around several switchbacks. The first sound of the falls is at 2.4 miles. At 3.0 miles you are directly above the falls and can hear them distinctly. Because this is such a high-use area, there are many short-cut trails around the switchbacks. One shortcut straight down to the falls begins here. Do not take these shortcuts because they contribute to erosion problems and can be dangerous.

At 3.3 miles arrive at Beech Bottom. The trail turns sharply to the right to cross Beech Creek. Beech Bottom was the site of a hunting lodge, and before that it was a logging camp. It is much used as a primitive campsite today. After crossing Beech Creek, the trail seems to split into several branches through a rocky flat area. All these little trails shortly come together and continue through Beech Bottom. At 3.5 miles there is a sign on the right that says "Foot Travel Only" and another short cut, made semiofficial by the sign, heads off down Beech Creek to the falls.

Beech Bottom Trail continues straight ahead, climbing slightly and skirting the ridge on the side of the bottoms until it ends at the intersection with the Jacks River Trail at 4.0 miles. Turn right on the Jacks River Trail and continue 0.6 mile to the Jacks River Falls. Along the way you will pass the intersection (if you can find it on the other side of the Jacks River) with the Hickory Ridge Trail and a primitive campsite where Beech Creek flows into the Jacks River. Remember that the Cohutta Wilderness is a bear haven, and you will need to practice leave-no-trace camping to prevent any incidents with bears.

174. ROUGH CREEK WEST FORK TRAIL (NO FS OR TI NUMBERS)

LENGTH: 0.5 mile

ELEVATION CHANGE: Low point, 1,560 feet; high point, 1,680 feet

DIFFICULTY: Easy

TRAILHEADS: FS 221G (start) and West Fork/Benton MacKaye Trail (end)

USE: Hiking

TOPOGRAPHIC MAP: USGS Ducktown, TN

COMMENTS: This route is the remains of a prewilderness-era logging road along the West Fork of Rough Creek. As described in the first edition of this guide, Rough Creek West Fork Trail extended south from the end of FS 221G for 2.6 miles to the road's end at a small turnaround. The middle section of the trail is now part of the new West Fork Trail, which is also the route of the Benton MacKaye Trail north out of the wilderness to FS 221. The south end of the old route is now described with the West Fork Trail, so only the north end between FS 221 and the West Fork Trail is described here. Rough Creek West Fork Trail can be combined with Rough Creek East Fork Trail and the West Fork and Rough Creek trails for a scenic 4.8-mile loop hike.

DETAILS: From the end of FS 221G, cross Rough Creek at the site of a washed-out culvert. On the far side of the creek, follow an unsigned old roadway to the right. In 300 feet pass a trail register, where there is a view down to campsites along the creek. The route continues on the wide, level roadway, reaching a concrete bridge and the Big Frog Wilderness Boundary at 0.2 mile. The route ends at 0.5 mile, where the West Fork and Benton MacKaye trails join the roadway from the right. The roadway continues ahead for 1.3 miles as the West Fork Trail and then for another 0.5 mile as an unsigned route. Possibilities exist on up the West Fork for off-trail hiking (see below).

175. ROUGH CREEK EAST FORK TRAIL (NO FS OR TI NUMBERS)

LENGTH: 4.0 miles

ELEVATION CHANGE: Low point, 1,560; high point, 2,600 feet

DIFFICULTY: Easy

TRAILHEADS: FS 221G (start) and Rough Creek Trail (end)

USE: Hiking

TOPOGRAPHIC MAP: USGS Ducktown, TN

COMMENTS: Like the Rough Creek West Fork Trail, this route is the remains of a prewilderness-era logging road along the East Fork. Still in remarkably good condition, the old roadbed remains one the area's most heavily used footpaths. The East Fork is the start of a scenic 4.8-mile loop from the FS 221G trailhead. The loop, which connects the Rough Creek Trail with the Rough Creek East and West Fork trails is one of the few short and easy day hikes possible in the Big Frog Wilderness.

DETAILS: From the end of FS 221G, cross Rough Creek at the site of a washed-out culvert. On the far side of the creek, follow an unsigned old roadway straight ahead, up and over a few berms across the start of the road. At 0.1 mile are the remains of a sign for a trail register. At 0.2 mile there is a small waterfall on the East Fork. For most of the way the old roadbed is wide and clear, though hemlock and rhododendron may crowd the trail. Though there are some fallen trees across the trail, most are easily passed. The footing remains remarkably clear. Pass a pleasant campsite below the trail at 0.4 mile.

At 1.7 miles, reach an obscure intersection with the Rough Creek Trail, which enters from the right down a steep bank. The Rough Creek Trail leaves the roadway to the left at 1.8 miles, where it is marked by a small cairn. The old roadway continues for another 2.2 miles along the East Fork, where it ends at an old clearing and provides opportunities for off-trail hiking (see below).

OFF-TRAIL HIKING OPPORTUNITIES

The East Fork and West Fork of Rough Creek provide good valleys to hike up, often on old logging roads that remain clear and usable. From the Rough Creek Trail's junction with either the East or West Fork, simply turn upstream and follow the old logging roads up the creek; a portion of these routes are described above under the Rough Creek East Fork and Rough Creek West Fork Trails. After some distance the old roadbeds will end and you will have to travel cross-country. However, the terrain is often so open and rocky that it is relatively easy for an experienced off-trail hiker to find a route toward Big Frog Mountain. Probably the best of the off-trail hikes (best as an overnight backpack) is all the way up the East Fork to the summit of Big Frog Mountain, with a return on the Big Frog Trail. There are rumored to be some small stands of virgin timber that the loggers missed near the summit of Big Frog Mountain.

31 Benton MacKaye Trail

176. BENTON MACKAYE TRAIL (FS TRAIL 2, TI TRAIL 7)

The northern CNF has the AT as its premier long-distance trail. Although the southern CNF has some fine trails, it has lacked a truly long-distance hiking trail. This shortcoming may be remedied over the next decade as the Benton MacKaye Trail marches up from GA into the heart of the southern CNF and on to the GSMNP. The FS Trail number will be, appropriately, 2, while the TI Trail number will be 7. By way of background, the Benton MacKaye is already a well-known hiking trail in GA. Its origins date all the way back to the origins of the AT. Benton MacKaye, who is credited with originating the idea of a foot trail from GA to Maine, originally proposed that the AT route would have a southern terminus at Mount Mitchell in NC. In the intermediate planning stages, the route was changed to the western crest of the Appalachians through Monroe and Polk counties in the CNF. However, when the AT was built in the 1930s, it was more convenient to follow a more eastern route through NC.

However, in 1979 the organizers of the Benton MacKaye Trail Association (http://www.bmta.org) revived the idea of a footpath along the western ridges of the Blue Ridge Mountains. Their idea was a trail looping south from the AT in the GSMNP, through the CNF into GA, and reconnecting with the AT at Springer Mountain. The route of the southern loop would therefore roughly parallel the AT, with the AT on the east and the Benton MacKaye Trail on the west. Substantial additional long-distance hiking opportunities would be provided, thus easing pressure on the AT. Long-distance hiking access would be afforded to some scenic locations in the CNF and the Nanatahala and Chattahoochee NFs. The organizers formed an association and began clearing the trail in 1980.

The GA portion of the trail is complete, from Springer Mountain to the TN-GA state line, as is the TN portion through the Big Frog Wilderness to the Ocoee River and US 64, for a distance of 92.8 miles. In TN the trail has, to date, primarily followed existing trails in the Big Frog Mountain and Ocoee Whitewater Center areas; see those sections for more detailed descriptions of the trail. Generally, from the TN-GA state line at Double Springs Gap, the trail follows the Hemp Top Trail for 0.8 mile to Licklog Ridge Trail. It then follows Licklog Ridge Trail for 0.6 mile to the top of Big Frog Mountain. The trail descends Big Frog via the Big Frog (1.9 miles) and Fork Ridge (1.8 miles) trails. It then turns west and follows the Rough Creek Trail for 0.6 mile to the new West Fork Trail, which takes it for 2.3 miles to FS 221. North of FS 221 the Benton MacKaye Trail follows part of the new West Fork Trail for 1.6 miles to FS 45. From FS 45 it follows the Thunder Rock Trail for 1.2 miles to the Thunder Rock Campground and then follows FS 45 to the current northern end at US 64. The CNF expects the Benton MacKaye Trail to follow the route of the Dry Pond Lead Trail north of US 64. Maps of both the GA and completed TN portions of the trail are available from the Benton MacKaye Trail Association.

However, although much has been done, especially in GA, the trail remains very much a trail in progress. It is ultimately envisioned to extend for 280 miles. Although the association plans to continue to follow existing trails where possible, substantial additional trail construction will be required. The projected route will continue through many of the areas in this book, generally along the TN-NC state line, to a crossing of Cheoah Dam near Deals Gap and into the GSMNP. In the GSMNP the trail will cross the AT, then continue as a lower elevation trail alternative to the AT, using existing trails, to rejoin the AT at Davenport Gap on the northern end of the GSMNP. The result will be a huge figure eight formed by both the AT and the Benton MacKaye Trail.

The approved route north of the Ocoee River is generally as follows: From the Ocoee River the trail will pass through the Little Frog Wilderness and then to the western end of the Hiwassee River for a crossing at Reliance (TN 315), then on the John Muir Trail up the Hiwassee River. The trail will then head over toward the state line at Unicoi Gap and generally follow the state line and the Unicoi Mountains northward. The route will traverse the State Line Trail in the Bald River area, leaving the state line on the Brookshire Creek Trail to the Bald River, ascending over the Sugar Mountain Lead, and descending to the Tellico River. The Sycamore Trail will be used to ascend again to a route, generally on the Fodderstack Trail, between the Citico Creek Wilderness and the Joyce Kilmer–Slickrock Wilderness. A descent into Slickrock Creek will follow, then over to the Cheoah Dam crossing of the Little Tennessee River and up to Deals Gap. Into the GSMNP, the trail will join the Lakeshore Trail and continue north on other trails to Davenport Gap. All but 10 miles will be on public lands, and the new trail construction is limited as the result of using existing trails. There is one shelter on private land located in GA, but, unlike the AT, no other shelters are planned to preserve the primitive nature of the trail.

After some initial reluctance about the trail in the CNF, the USFS has now agreed to cooperate with the extension of the trail through the southern CNF. By a public notice dated February 14, 2003, the USFS commenced its formal planning process. On December 17, 2003, the CNF and Nantahala National Forest supervisors approved the extension of the Benton MacKaye Trail through both forests. The first construction work trip was held on December 23, 2003. The approved route utilizes 63 miles of existing trails and requires 22 miles of new construction. Over half of the new construction was completed in mid-2004, and the entire trail is expected to be completed in 2005. Accordingly, by the time a third edition of this book is published, there will most likely be a much more detailed section on the Benton MacKaye Trail.

32 Ocoee Whitewater Center

The Tanasi Trail system around the Ocoee Whitewater Center is a recent addition to the CNF trail network. Built after the 1996 Summer Olympic Games, the trails represent a welcome effort to expand the recreational opportunities available in the Ocoee region and to provide a year-round use for the CNF's beautiful new visitors center on the upper Ocoee. The Whitewater Center trails are multiple use and are therefore open to horses and mountain bikes as well as hikers. These are some of the first trails the USFS has built especially for mountain

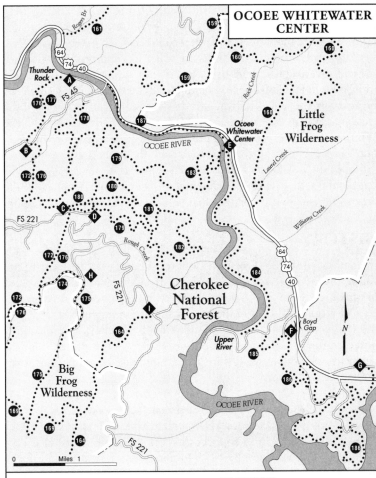

OCOEE WHITEWATER CENTER

Thunder Rock

Ocoee Whitewater Center

Little Frog Wilderness

OCOEE RIVER

Cherokee National Forest

Big Frog Wilderness

Boyd Gap

Upper River

OCOEE RIVER

Rogen Br
Rock Creek
Laurel Creek
Williams Creek
Rough Creek

FS 45
FS 221

0   Miles   1

TRAILS
177. Thunder Rock
178. Thunder Rock Express
179. Chestnut
180. Quartz Loop
181. 1330 Bypass
182. River View Loop
183. Bear Paw Loop
184. Old Copper Road
185. Boyd Gap
186. Brush Creek
187. Thunder Rock-Whitewater Center Connector

TRAILHEADS
A. Thunder Rock
B. Thunder Rock South
C. West Fork
D. Chestnut Mtn. Loop
E. Ocoee Whitewater Center
F. Boyd Gap
G. Brush Creek Shooting Range Rd.
H. FS 221G (see Big Frog section)
I. Licklog (see Big Frog section)

biking, which is the main activity here. Of the trails built by early 2002 only the Old Copper Road, Thunder Rock, and perhaps Quartz Loop trails are more likely to appeal to hikers than bikers.

The Whitewater Center trails are still a work in process. Many of the trails were constructed over the fall and winter of 2001–2. Some trails built in late 2002 have, as of mid-2003, yet to be assigned names or numbers by the CNF. Trail names, signs, and even locations of the existing trails may change, so visitors should be sure to stop by the Whitewater Center to get the latest trail information before heading out. The CNF plans to continue to expand the trail system. A rehabilitation of the Boyd Gap Trail is expected, and other new trails may be built in the area. The CNF's 2004 plan revision designates much of the area as a scenic byway corridor that will allow some timber harvesting.

HISTORY

In contrast to the Big Frog and Cohutta Wilderness Areas just to the south, the Ocoee River Basin has been strongly impacted by the hand of man over the last 150 years. From the mining of copper to the logging of virgin forests, and the harnessing of the mighty Ocoee River, the basin has been stripped of many of its natural features. Now, however, the Ocoee is beginning to recover from the effects of industrialization, and a move toward recreational use of the basin is leading the way.

European settlers first discovered copper ore in 1847 near the modern town of Ducktown. The ore at the surface was remarkably rich, and the mining district quickly boomed. The miners built the Old Copper Road in 1953 to connect the mines to the railroad in Cleveland, TN, 33 miles away. By 1855 14 mines were operating and smelting of ore had begun at the site. The forests around the mines were cut to provide timbers for the mines and fuel for the smelters.

Once the rich, near-surface ores were exhausted, the mines lay idle until new technology allowed extraction of the lower grade, deeper, and sulfide-bearing ores. By the late 1890s the miners were able to treat the sulfide ores, though zinc, found in nearly the same concentration as copper, and the small amounts of silver and gold in the ore were still not recovered. To keep the workings from flooding, 500,000 gallons of water was pumped from the mines every day. By the mid-1870s all the timber in the basin was gone, and later a 50-square-mile area was completely stripped of vegetation.

Later innovations allowed the miners to capture and sell some of the sulfuric acid that was produced as a byproduct of the copper smelting. However, the smelters still vented an acidic gas that killed nearly all the vegetation within Copper Basin. The combination of acid smelter discharge and the logging of the forests combined to reduce much of the basin to a nearly lifeless moonscape by the 1920s, when runoff from the barren land also became a problem. At this point, over ten million tons of ore had been mined. Enough material was being removed daily to fill a container 30 feet on a side. The miners would eventually dig down over 2,000 feet below the earth's surface in their quest for precious ore. In the 1930s US Highway 64 was built over much of the route of Old Copper Road. An expansion of the highway in 1957 left only three miles of the old route intact.

Ducktown grew to become the most important metal mining district in the southeastern United States. The Burra Mine alone produced over 15 million tons of copper ore by the time it closed in 1959 after nearly 60 years of operation. The last mines in the district were closed in 1987, though the chemical plants continued to produce sulfur dioxide until 2000.

Reclamation of this environmental calamity still continues. Once known as a barren area so devastated that it could be recognized from outer space, much of the district has at least been partly revegetated. A small area around the Burra Open Pit has not been reclaimed, in order to preserve an example of the devastation that once claimed the entire district.

Along with its rich timber and mineral resources, the Ocoee Basin has been harnessed for hydroelectric power. In 1912, Ocoee Dam No. 1 was built creating the huge Ocoee No. 1, or Parksville Lake, at the west end of the river gorge. Two other pairs of dams and powerhouses have been constructed upstream along the river. The famous flume that diverts water to powerhouse 2 and sits high above the river on the south bank is easily seen from many spots on US 64. It was built in 1913 and rebuilt in the 1980s. The TN Valley Authority bought dams 1 and 2 in 1939, and built the third dam and powerhouse in 1941.

All three dams work in a similar manner. Water is captured upstream at a dam and diverted from the river by a system of flumes and tunnels. Once at the powerhouse, the water is dropped down through turbines to generate power and then released briefly for the short trip to the next dam. Together the three dams on the Ocoee can produce 67,000 kilowatts of electricity, enough to power over 13,000 homes.

When the city of Atlanta was awarded the 1996 Olympic Summer Games, one of the challenges facing the organizing committee was to find a world-class course worthy of the kayak and canoe slalom events. The stretch of the Ocoee River below Powerhouse No. 2 was a popular whitewater run, but organizers soon focused on the potential of an unused section of the river below Ocoee Dam No. 3. Because most river water was diverted from the channel directly to Power Station No. 3, this section was not an established run but could be modified to suit the needs of the competition.

Using the natural characteristics of the river as much as possible, the CNF, TN Valley Authority, and the Olympic Committee were able to construct a scenic and challenging course fit for Olympians. In fact, the course was so well received that TVA diverts water from Powerhouse No. 3 to the river strictly for whitewater enthusiasts on 20 weekend days a year.

The 1996 Summer Olympic Games had a huge long-term impact on the Ocoee area. The already popular river gained a new notoriety from hosting such a prestigious event. Planners saw a means of revitalizing a languid local economy with a healthy dose of recreation dollars. At the height of the period of optimism following the games a 150,000-acre National Recreation Area was proposed around the river that would include the Big Frog, Little Frog, and Gee Creek Wilderness areas. However, this proposal died due to lack of support from local governments and opposition from timber interests.

In 2001 over 200,000 people floated the middle section of the Ocoee on commercial trips. The upper river is also run by private boaters and 22 commercial outfitters who pay a premium to TVA to help offset the cost of lost power production on the few days when water is released each summer.

Facilities from the games are now used by the CNF's Ocoee Whitewater Center. The CNF expanded the recreation options around the river by beginning the construction of a new Tanasi trail system. In 1998 the Old Copper Road Trail and Bear Paw Trails were opened. These trails were built for multiple uses, including mountain biking and horse riding, as well as hiking. Next to be built was the Chestnut Loop, which gave the area enough trails to start attracting mountain bike racers.

In 2001 the CNF expanded the Tanasi system by adding four new trails. Expansion continues with the planned rehabilitation of the trail at Boyd Gap and plans to link the system to a proposed greenway in Ducktown, TN.

TRAILHEADS AND MAPS

Thunder Rock Trailhead

The Thunder Rock Trailhead is between campsites T23 and T24 in the Thunder Rock Campground. The campground is 1.8 miles west of the

Whitewater Center, on the south side of the Ocoee River, just south of Ocoee Power Station No. 3. Hikers should park in the free designated area at the campground entrance, near the registration area. Just beyond the campground turnoff on FS 45 is the north end of the Thunder Rock Express Trail where a TVA access road ends at a gate. There is no parking at this point. The 1.5 miles paved Thunder Rock–Whitewater Center Connector Trail starts near the campground (at the highway side of the Ocoee River Bridge at Ocoee No. 8 Powerhouse) and leads to the Ocoee Whitewater Center.

Thunder Rock South, West Fork, and Chestnut Mountain Loop Trailheads

These three trailheads are not maintained by the CNF. FS 45 begins at US 64 by the Ocoee Power Station No. 3 at a sign for the Thunder Rock Campground. The Thunder Rock South Trailhead is located 1.2 miles south of US 64 on FS 45. Here is the south end of the Thunder Rock Trail and the north end of the West Fork Trail. Both trails are part of the Benton MacKaye Trail.

The West Fork and Chestnut Mountain Loop trailheads can be reached by driving 3.0 miles south on FS 45 from US 64. Turn left at the junction of FS 45 with FS 221 and drive east on FS 221 for 0.4 mile to the West Fork Trailhead. Park north of the road beside a gate across the route of old FS 45, which is now the West Fork, Chestnut Mountain Loop, and Benton MacKaye Trails, though none is marked in this direction. The West Fork Trail and Benton MacKaye trails continue south of the road beside a large sign. The new Quartz Loop Trail begins at the northeast corner of this intersection.

The Chestnut Mountain Loop Trailhead is 0.2 mile west of the West Fork Trailhead on FS 221 and 0.6 mile from the intersection of FS 45 and 221. The trail begins on the south side of the road at a sign for the trail and for the Ocoee Whitewater Center. The trail begins by following old FS 1330, which is blocked by a gate.

Ocoee Whitewater Center

The Ocoee Whitewater Center is located on US 64 6.3 miles west of the junction of US 64 and TN 68 and 20.9 miles east of the overpass on US 64 above US 411. The center is a fee area. In 2002 the fee was $3 per day. There is short-term metered parking in front of the center, and day-use parking farther downstream. A system of concrete walkways on both sides of the river leads from the parking area to the center. There is a large pedestrian bridge over the Ocoee on the east side of the center. Old Copper Road Trail begins on the north side of the bridge and the Bear Paw Loop begins on the south side of the bridge. The 1.5-mile paved Thunder Rock–Whitewater Center Connector Trail starts at the Whitewater Center and leads to the Thunder Rock Campground.

Boyd Gap Trailhead

The paved Boyd Gap Vista Road is located 1.8 miles east of the Whitewater Center on the south side of US 64. The road leads 0.2 mile to a turnaround where public access ends. The views from the trailhead across the Ocoee to Licklog Ridge and Tumbling Creek are some of the finest in the region. Trailheads for the Brush Creek Gap Trail, constructed in 2002, and the Boyd Gap Trail are located here.

Brush Creek Shooting Range Road Trailheads

Continue on US 64 from the turn off to Boyd Gap Vista Road described above for 0.8 mile east to an old paved road on the left with a sign reading "Brush Creek Shooting Range." The ending trailhead for the Brush Creek Trail is 0.4 mile down this road just before a bridge crossing Brush Creek. There is also an additional trailhead for the Brush Creek Trail accessing a 0.1 mile spur off the main trail. The trailhead is 0.1 mile down an FS road (FS 332102) that turns south from US 64 just opposite the Brush Creek Shooting Range Road. The trailhead is on the left just as FS 332102 forks. This spur joins the main trail 0.5 mile from its end at the Shooting Range Road.

TOPOGRAPHIC MAPS: USGS Caney Creek, TN; Ducktown, TN. Note that since these trails are new, they will not yet appear on USGS maps. TI Map 781, Tellico and Ocoee Rivers, CNF, shows only the Chestnut Mountain Loop, Bear Paw, and Thunder Rock Trails. You can pick up a specific area trail map at the Whitewater Center or from http://www.chattbike.com.

TRAIL DESCRIPTIONS

177. THUNDER ROCK TRAIL (FS TRAIL 305, TI TRAIL 77

LENGTH: 1.2 miles

ELEVATION CHANGE: Low point, 1,160 feet; high point, 1,440 feet

DIFFICULTY: Easy

TRAILHEADS: Thunder Rock Campground (start); Thunder Rock South (end)

USE: Hiking

TOPOGRAPHIC MAPS: USGS Ducktown, TN; Caney Creek, TN

COMMENTS: Though not officially part of the Ocoee Whitewater Center trail system, this hiking-only trail provides a useful connection from the river at Thunder Rock Campground to the Whitewater Center trails. The Thunder Rock Trail was built in the 1990s to connect the north end of the Benton MacKaye Trail, and the Big Frog Wilderness, to the CNF campground at Thunder Rock, and to the Ocoee River. The trail is an excellent addition to the CNF trail system and provides year-round access to the trails above the Ocoee. The trail is well marked with white diamond paint blazes.

Hikers who are not staying in the campground should park at the free hiker parking area located across from the registration station at the campground entrance. Parking here will add about one-quarter mile each way to your hike. Hikers can make a 5.0-mile loop around the West Fork, Chestnut Mountain Loop, and Thunder Rock trails, if they do not mind sharing part of the route with mountain bikes. The entire trail is part of the Benton MacKaye Trail. BMT hikers can follow the white blazes south along FS 45 over the Ocoee River to the north end of the trail at US 64.

DETAILS: The Thunder Rock Trail begins at the far end of the campground loop between sites T23 and T24. From the campground the trail heads downstream along the floodplain of the Ocoee River. At 0.2 mile use a wooden bridge to pass over an overflow channel. Beyond the bridge the trail begins a steady climb up the bank meandering around seven switchbacks. At 0.8 mile reach a marked T-junction with an old logging road and turn left. At 0.9 mile, keep left at a split in the road.

The trail skirts the edge of a larger old logging road at 1.0 mile. Be sure to keep left at this signed junction. At 1.1 miles a sign directs you off the road and onto level trail that reaches FS 45 and the Thunder Rock South Trailhead at 1.2 miles. The Benton MacKaye and West Fork Trails continue across the road, reaching FS 221 in 1.6 miles. On FS 45 it is 1.2 miles left down to the Thunder Rock Campground and 1.8 miles right up to the junction of FS 45 and 221.

178. THUNDER ROCK EXPRESS TRAIL (NO FS OR TI NUMBERS)

LENGTH: 1.5 miles

ELEVATION CHANGE: Low point, 1,200 feet; high point, 1,560 feet

DIFFICULTY: Moderate for hiking; moderate-difficult for mountain bikers

TRAILHEADS: Chestnut Mountain Loop Trail (start); Thunder Rock (end)

USE: Hiking, mountain bike

TOPOGRAPHIC MAPS: USGS Ducktown, TN; Caney Creek, TN

COMMENTS: The Thunder Rock Express Trail is destined to become a favorite of both hikers and mountain bikers. Hikers based at Thunder Rock Campground will cherish the chance to make a 5.0-mile loop combining the Express with the Thunder Rock, West Fork/Benton MacKaye, and Chestnut Mountain Loop trails.

Among mountain bikers the trail's curvaceous descent has already made it a favorite. The tight turns and never too steep grades make for an exhilarating drop from the Chestnut Mountain Loop Trail down to FS 45. This is as close to technical single track as the usually contour hugging Whitewater Center trail system gets. In fact, riders descending the trail should keep in mind the possibility that other riders, or hikers, may be climbing the trail. It appears most riders descend the express, ride up FS 45, then return to the Chestnut Mountain Loop Trail via the north end of the West Fork/Benton MacKaye Trail. This side trip adds 2.8 miles, and a considerable elevation change, to the Chestnut Mountain Loop. Note that an identically named Chestnut Mountain Loop Trail is located in the Gee Creek section (FS Trail 104; TI Trail 20).

DETAILS: The green-blazed Thunder Rock Express Trail begins on the north lobe of the Chestnut Mountain Loop Trail at a signed junction 2.7 miles west of the junction with the connector trail with the Bear Paw Loop, and 0.8 mile east of the point where the West Fork/Benton MacKaye Trail splits from Chestnut Mountain. The trail starts as a wide single track that follows a pine-covered ridgecrest north. But the trail soon drops to the west side of the ridge and begins an adrenaline-inducing plunge toward the Ocoee River. The tight turns, consistent drop, and narrow trail keep this endorphin-fest going long enough to make even die-hard hikers want to trade in their boots for two wheels.

At 1.0 mile is a wooden bridge over a small creek in a grove of hemlock trees. Just beyond the bridge, those who have thrown caution to the wind will pay the price where the trail makes a sharp right turn around a rocky ridge. In 2002 the turn was protected with safety netting, but it would be better to use your brakes here than to find out if the netting really works. At 1.4 miles is a second wooden bridge. Just 100 feet beyond the bridge the trail turns left onto a gravel TVA road. The trail ends at 1.5 miles at a gate and a junction with FS 45. Turn right on FS 45 to reach Thunder Rock Campground in 0.3 mile. To the left it is 0.9 mile uphill to the FS 45 Trailhead and another 1.2 miles (still uphill) on the West Fork/Benton MacKaye Trail to rejoin the Chestnut Mountain Loop Trail.

179. CHESTNUT MOUNTAIN LOOP TRAIL (NO FS NUMBER, TI TRAIL 19)

LENGTH: 6.0 miles

ELEVATION CHANGE: Low point, 1,480 feet; high point, 1,880 feet

DIFFICULTY: Moderate

TRAILHEADS: West Fork Trailhead (start) and Chestnut Mountain Loop (end). The trail is most often accessed from the Whitewater Center via the Bear Paw trail.

USE: Hiking, mountain bike

TOPOGRAPHIC MAPS: USGS Ducktown, TN; Caney Creek, TN

COMMENTS: The Chestnut Mountain Loop Trail is the backbone of the Ocoee Whitewater Trail system. All the mountain biking trails intersect this loop, and nearly every ride in the area will use some part of this trail. The loop is a mix of wide single track and old two-track logging roads suitable for beginning riders with plenty of stamina, but exciting enough to hold the attention of jaded veterans. The narrow single track on the north side of the loop is the favorite ride of many local bikers. The trail makes a wide loop around Chestnut Mountain, holding to contour as best it can. The main 6.0-mile loop is rarely done alone. Most often it is accessed via the Bear Paw Loop, which adds 2.1 miles. The River View Loop adds 3.1 miles, while the Quart Loop adds 2.2 miles and the Thunder Rock Express-FS 221-West Fork trails loop adds 2.8 miles and a serious climb.

Do not confuse the Ocoee Whitewater Center's Chestnut Mountain Loop Trail with the similarly named Chestnut Mountain Trail in the Big Frog Wilderness or with the Chestnut Mountain Loop and Chestnut Mountain 4 WD road near the Gee Creek Wilderness.

DETAILS: From the west end of the spur that connects the Chestnut Mountain Loop to the Bear Paw Trail take the left fork to follow the trail clockwise. Here the loop trail follows FS 1330, a wide two-track road marked by tan paint blazes. Climb steadily to reach a signed east junction with the blue-blazed River View Loop Trail at 0.5 mile. Keep right on FS 1330 to reach the signed junction with the orange-blazed 1330 Bypass at 0.7 mile. If single track is your thing, turn right on the bypass and save yourself 0.3 mile. Those who stay on FS 1330 will reach the signed west junction with the River View Loop Trail at 0.9 mile.

At 1.9 miles the 1330 Bypass joins the main trail within sight of both a gate across FS 1330 and the Chestnut Mountain Loop Trailhead on FS 221. Turn right up FS 221 to reach the West Fork Trailhead at 2.1 miles. Here the signed West Fork/Benton MacKaye Trail south into the Big Frog Wilderness is foot travel only. The Quartz Loop Trail leaves from the northeast corner of the trailhead. The Chestnut Mountain Trail leaves the trailhead to the north on an old road that was formerly part of FS 45. Until this road forks at 2.5 miles the Chestnut Mountain Loop, West Fork, and Benton MacKaye trails all share this old roadway.

At the split, the West Fork and Benton MacKaye trails go left toward FS 45, while Chestnut Mountain turns right onto old FS 33641, which also may be signed Loop C. Enjoy a fast, easy descent to a four-way junction at 3.3 miles. Here the green-blazed Thunder Rock Express Trail leaves left, an abandoned logging road goes straight, and Chestnut Mountain Loop bears right. The trail narrows to a single track while traversing steep slopes in a pretty forest of mostly second-growth hardwoods. At 5.0 miles an old spur road joins from the right. Another spur joins from the left at a sharp turn at 5.2 miles. At 6.0 miles close the loop at the intersection with the connecting trail between Chestnut Mountain Loop and Bear Paw trails.

180. QUARTZ LOOP TRAIL (NO FS OR TI NUMBERS)

LENGTH: 1.9 miles

ELEVATION CHANGE: Low point, 1,880 feet; high point, 2,040 feet

DIFFICULTY: Easy

TRAILHEADS: The trail is a semiloop, which starts and ends at the West Fork Trailhead.

USE: Hiking, mountain bike

TOPOGRAPHIC MAPS: USGS Ducktown, TN; Caney Creek, TN

COMMENTS: The Quartz Loop Trail was constructed in the fall of 2001 by the CNF as an addition to the Whitewater Center Trail system. The trail has a semiloop (or Lasso) shape, with a short feeder segment leading to the main loop, which circles the highest knob in the area between FS 221 and the Ocoee River. The entire circuit covers 2.2 miles. It offers better summer vistas than other Whitewater Center trails and is less used by mountain bikers, making it an attractive option for those seeking a short loop hike in the area.

DETAILS: The start of the gray-blazed Quartz Loop Trail is by a carsonite post on the northeast side of the West Fork Trailhead. The trail begins as a wide single track leading east along the ridgecrest. At 0.1 mile it turns left onto gated TVA Road 5157. Follow this dirt two-track road up and over a small knoll where milky white quartz veins outcrop to give the loop its name. At 0.2 mile cross a power line cut where a maintenance road leads right. Just beyond is a signed junction where the yellow-blazed Quartz Loop Spur Trail goes right 0.1 mile down to the 1330 Bypass. At 0.3 mile the loop begins at a signed four-way junction where an abandoned two-track road is the middle fork.

To follow the Quartz Loop counterclockwise, take the right fork, which is a wide single track. At 0.4 mile an overgrown roadway joins on the left. When this trail was ridden in late spring 2002 the treadway had recently been dug and made for rather rough riding. No doubt with use it will become better packed and smoother. At 0.7 mile is a power line cut with views south toward Rough Creek and down to the 1330 Bypass. Cross an overgrown road on the crest of the ridge and swing around to the north slopes of the knob. Here in the cooler shaded forest you will pass two lush fern gardens and more hemlock trees than on the sunnier south slopes.

At 1.2 miles the loop recrosses the power-line cut with views northwest toward the Ocoee River. Cross the overgrown ridgecrest road once more before closing the loop at 1.9 miles. To return to the trailhead, turn right and retrace your route for another 0.3 mile.

181. 1330 BYPASS TRAIL (NO FS OR TI NUMBERS)

LENGTH: 1.0 mile

ELEVATION CHANGE: Low point, 1,800 feet; high point, 1,840 feet

DIFFICULTY: Easy

TRAILHEADS: Chestnut Mountain Loop Trail near the Chestnut Mountain Trailhead on FS 221 (start), Chestnut Mountain Loop Trail (end)

USE: Hiking, mountain bike

TOPOGRAPHIC MAPS: USGS Ducktown, TN; Caney Creek, TN

COMMENTS: The orange-blazed 1330 Bypass Trail is one of the new additions to the Whitewater Center Trail system that was constructed in the fall of 2001. The trail provides a single track alternative to the south lobe of the Chestnut Mountain Loop Trail where that trail follows old FS 1330, which is a two-track dirt road. Combined with the Chestnut Mountain Trail, it provides an opportunity for a short 2.0-mile loop from FS 221.

DETAILS: The 1330 Bypass begins on the south lobe of the Chestnut Mountain Loop Trail at a signed junction just 150 feet from FS 221. The trail is a wide, well-constructed single track. At 0.1 mile it intersects the yellow-blazed Quartz Loop Spur, which leads left 0.1 mile left to the Quartz Loop Trail. At 0.5 mile reach a power-line cut where riders on the Quartz Loop may be seen on the hillside above. Just beyond the cut is an even better overlook, with views extending south to Big Frog Mountain and Peavine Ridge. At 1.0 mile the trail ends at an intersection with the Chestnut Mountain Loop Trail, at a point midway in between the two Chestnut Mountain/River View junctions.

182. RIVER VIEW LOOP TRAIL (NO FS OR TI NUMBERS)

LENGTH: 3.5 miles

ELEVATION CHANGE: Low point, 1,520 feet; high point, 1,800 feet

DIFFICULTY: Moderate

TRAILHEADS: Chestnut Mountain Loop Trail (start); Chestnut Mountain Loop Trail (end)

USE: Hiking, mountain bike

TOPOGRAPHIC MAPS: USGS Ducktown, TN; Caney Creek, TN

COMMENTS: The River View Loop Trail is the fourth of the new trails constructed in the fall and winter of 2001. River View is an interior trail, adding 3.1 miles onto the Chestnut Mountain Loop for those who choose to explore it. The loop is hillier than other Whitewater Center trails, so riders should factor in both extra effort and extra distance. The origin of the trail name is somewhat of a mystery. In summer, at least, there are no obvious river views.

DETAILS: To ride the loop clockwise, begin at the signed east intersection with the Chestnut Mountain Loop Trail at a point 0.5 mile from the Chestnut Mountain/Bear Paw junction. Turn left onto the blue-blazed trail, which is a wide single track for the entire distance. The trail begins with a fast descent along a ridge but soon swings off the crest to follow the twists and turns of the steep slopes above Rough Creek. At 0.9 mile the trail forks. Both forks will lead to the same spot; the light-blue blazed trail leading left just takes an extra 0.1 mile to get there. At 1.1 mile is the far end of the light-blue trail.

Continue on the curvy single track to the first of two quick crossings of a power-line cut at 2.5 miles. Cross a grass-covered former logging road at 3.0 miles. The trail ends at 3.5 miles at a signed intersection with the Chestnut Mountain Loop Trail at a point 0.4 mile west of the starting point and 1.0 mile east of the Chestnut Mountain Loop/FS 221 intersection.

183. BEAR PAW LOOP TRAIL (NO FS TRAIL NUMBER, TI TRAIL 5)

LENGTH: 1.5 miles

ELEVATION CHANGE: Low point, 1,300 feet; high point, 1,560 feet

DIFFICULTY: Easy to moderate

TRAILHEADS: Ocoee Whitewater Center (start and end)

USE: Hiking, mountain bike

TOPOGRAPHIC MAPS: USGS Ducktown, TN; Caney Creek, TN

COMMENTS: The Bear Paw Loop Trail is the major connecting route from the Ocoee Whitewater Center to the trail system above on Chestnut Ridge. Because of the heavy use of the Whitewater Center, and the popularity of the trail system among mountain bikers, Bear Paw is a heavily used trail. Since the trail is a semiloop (a short feeder trail leads to the loop), a round-trip hike on the trail covers 1.9 miles. The Bear Paw Trail is marked by green painted dotted "i" blazes.

DETAILS: The trail begins on the south side of the Ocoee River, across the foot bridge, which is located in back of the Whitewater Center. On the far side of the bridge turn left onto the wide trail bed. The trail heads upstream along the river for 0.2 mile before turning right and climbing alongside a narrow side stream. At 0.4 mile the trail forks at the start of the loop.

Go left at the fork and immediately cross a wooden bridge. After some moderate climbing, reach another signed trail intersection at the far end of the loop at 0.8 mile. To the left is a 0.2 mile connector to the Chestnut Mountain Loop Trail. The connector trail is marked with tan paint "i" blazes. The Bear Paw Trail follows the green blazes to the right. The trail follows the ridgecrest with views through the trees of the Little Frog Wilderness across the Ocoee River. At 1.2 miles a false trail branches left to a cliff top. Just beyond is a rest bench with a commanding view of the Whitewater Center and Ocoee River. Descend gradually to reach the start of the loop at 1.5 miles. To return to the Whitewater Center, turn left and walk 0.4 mile to the bridge over the Ocoee River.

184. OLD COPPER ROAD TRAIL (FS TRAIL 306, TI TRAIL 59)

LENGTH: 2.4 miles

ELEVATION CHANGE: Low point, 1,300 feet; high point, 1,340 feet

DIFFICULTY: Easy

TRAILHEADS: Ocoee Whitewater Center (start); FS 334 (end)

Whitewater rushes over one of the many famed rapids along the Old Copper Road that parallels the Ocoee River. Photograph by Roger Jenkins.

USE: Hiking, mountain bike

TOPOGRAPHIC MAPS: Ducktown, TN; Caney Creek, TN

COMMENTS: The Old Copper Road Trail is one of the few trails in the Ocoee Whitewater system that will appeal more to hikers than mountain bikers. The flat riverside route is steeped in history. The road, built from 1851 to 1853 using mostly Cherokee labor, gave miners in Ducktown an access road for shipping their copper ore to the nearest railroad, which was then in Cleveland, TN. Most of the route was obliterated by the construction of US 64 in the 1930s. In 1957 the highway was improved, leaving only the three-mile section upstream from the Whitewater Center intact. After the 1996 Olympic Games the CNF began the process of restoring the old roadbed to resemble its original condition. The current route ranges from a wide trail to lightly graveled road.

Because there is normally no public access to FS 334, most hikers will need to retrace their route from the road back to the Whitewater Center for a 4.8-mile round-trip hike. The generally flat terrain along the trail is suitable for novice mountain bikers; however, some sections are rocky and rooted enough to challenge beginners.

DETAILS: The Old Copper Road Trail begins at the southeast corner of the parking area in front of the Ocoee Whitewater Center by a large sign. The trail begins with a crossing of a small stream that is lined with large, flat stones. The first mile is blessed with a number of fine river views, should you be lucky enough to walk the trail during a rare release of water. Be aware that because of these releases water levels in the river can rise suddenly with no warning. At 0.9 mile the trail uses a wooden bridge to cross a small stream near a cascade.

At 1.3 miles the trail crosses a service road. At 2.0 miles a short boardwalk leads out to a wetland where an interpretive sign discusses the role of beaver in the river ecosystem. Just beyond is another wooden bridge, which marks the start of a short but steep hill. After crossing two more bridges reach the end of the trail at 2.4 miles at a gravel path and restroom along FS 334, which is the access road for the upper Ocoee River run. To the left it is 0.6 mile uphill to the lower end of the Boyd Gap Trail.

185. BOYD GAP TRAIL (NO FS OR TI NUMBERS)

LENGTH: 0.7 mile

ELEVATION CHANGE: Low point, 1,440 feet; high point, 1,680 feet

DIFFICULTY: Moderate

TRAILHEADS: Boyd Gap (start); FS 334 (end)

USE: Hiking, mountain bike

TOPOGRAPHIC MAPS: Ducktown, TN; Caney Creek, TN

COMMENTS: Boyd Gap is currently the least used of the trails around the Ocoee Whitewater Center. However, the CNF plans to rehabilitate the trail for mountain biking in the near future. If the CNF is able to connect the Ocoee trails to a proposed greenway system to the east in Ducktown, Boyd Gap will then become a useful connector between the two systems. When hiked in the early 2000s the trail was not blazed and there was little to distinguish it from other abandoned dirt roads in the forest. The lower end is signed.

DETAILS: From the parking area at the Boyd Gap Overlook, walk south across the mowed area to the start of an old dirt road that begins at the edge of the trees. This point may be marked by a sign or a post. The slopes just below the overlook were clear-cut, and the forest remains a chaos of second growth. At 0.2 mile a power line and rugged service road are visible to the right of the trail. At 0.4 mile turn left onto this old road and follow it for 250 feet before turning right onto another rutted old road. Descend gradually on a trail that could become very shrubby in summer, to reach a T-junction with FS 334 at 0.8 mile. To the right the road leads back up to US 64. To the left it is 0.6 mile downhill to the east end of Old Copper Road Trail.

186. BRUSH CREEK TRAIL (NO FS OR TI NUMBERS)

LENGTH: 6.7 miles

ELEVATION CHANGE: Low point, 1,460 feet; high point, 1,760 feet

DIFFICULTY: Easy

TRAILHEADS: Boyd Gap (start); Brush Creek Shooting Range Road (end)

USE: Hiking, mountain bike

TOPOGRAPHIC MAP: USGS Ducktown, TN

COMMENTS: This is a very level and easy-to-walk bicycle trail meandering around and following the contours on a small peninsula between US 64 and Ocoee No. 3 Lake. The trail is generally in hardwood forest, but there are extensive areas of pines that have been attacked by pine beetles. There are several good views of Ocoee No. 3 Lake with Big Frog Mountain in the distance.

DETAILS: We describe this trail beginning at the Boyd Gap Trailhead. Take the trail to the left at the turnaround located at Boyd Gap. The trail begins through a cut in the ridge, evidently for an old road. At 0.4 mile come to a fork in the trail; take the left fork here. At 1.1 miles, cross a creek on a wide wooden bridge just below the highway. The trail then turns to the right and follows this attractive creek downstream. At about 1.3 miles observe the first of a long string of wildlife management clearings across the creek. These clearings are followed up a small tributary stream until it is crossed at 1.7 miles on another wide bridge. Immediately after, a primitive FS road is crossed that is used to access the wildlife management clearings.

The trail then goes back downstream until the creek flows into Ocoee No. 3 Lake at 2.4 miles. The lakeshore is then generally followed with excursions inland to follow the contours of the shoreline. At 3.0 miles is an especially appealing scene as the trail crosses a low ridge with a good view of the lake. At 3.9 miles is the first of several views of the lake with Big Frog Mountain in the background. At 5.1 miles FS 332102 is crossed as the trail veers away from the lake.

At 6.1 miles the trail forks with the left fork going uphill 0.1 mile for an intersection with FS 332102 at 0.1 mile from US 64 (see Brush Creek Shooting Range Road Trailhead description). The right fork of the trail crosses US 64 by going under the high bridge across Brush Creek. The trail ends 0.5 mile from the intersection at the paved, but little used, Brush Creek Shooting Range Road.

187. THUNDER ROCK–WHITEWATER CENTER CONNECTOR TRAIL (NO FS OR TI NUMBERS)

LENGTH: 1.5 miles

ELEVATION CHANGE: Insignificant

DIFFICULTY: Easy

TRAILHEADS: Thunder Rock Campground (start); Ocoee Whitewater Center (end)

USE: Hiking, mountain bike

TOPOGRAPHIC MAP: USGS Ducktown, TN

COMMENTS: This is not a wilderness trail but a convenient paved route for hikers or bikers to travel between the Thunder Rock Campground and the Ocoee Whitewater Center.

DETAILS: The trail begins at the highway side of the Ocoee River Bridge at Ocoee No. 3 Powerhouse. The first 0.7 mile of the trail is an extension of the shoulder pavement of US 64; however, it is separated from the road by a metal guardrail. Another metal guardrail is on the riverside of the trail. At 0.7 mile the trail continues alongside the Whitewater Center parking lot. Here the trail is separated from traffic by only a white line on the pavement.

At 1.1 miles the trail moves off the parking lot to a paved sidewalk closer to the river and through the rocky riverbed. There is a picturesque bridge here that crosses the river and provides an alternate but slightly longer route to the Whitewater Center. This bridge leads to a trail on the far side of the river that returns via a similar bridge upstream from the Whitewater Center. There are picnic tables on the far side of the river near the bridge. The trail on the near side of the river continues through the riverbed, close to the river, for another 0.4 mile to the Whitewater Center.

33 Conasauga River

(Includes Conasauga River Scenic Corridor)

The Conasauga and Jacks rivers originate in the mountains of northern GA; they join together just after flowing into TN at the northern end of the Alaculsy Valley. The river continues westward as the Conasauga River through the CNF; after leaving the CNF, it curves to the south, under US 411, and back into GA. Because of its relatively unpolluted mountain source, the Conasauga is a clear, clean river as it flows through TN. The portion in TN east of US 411 is a part of TN's Scenic River System. A portion within the CNF (1,110 acres) is designated as an Eligible Wild River in the CNF's 2004 plan revision. That designation will protect the river corridor for consideration for inclusion in the National Wild and Scenic Rivers System. The TN portion is in the Ocoee/Hiwassee Ranger District in Polk County.

The Conasauga is noted for numerous darters and chubs, and 22 species of fish not found elsewhere in TN have been recorded. The TN portion of the river is generally an easy trip for canoeists when the water is high enough and provides a scenic trip. The Conasauga River Trail follows the river for 2.6 miles.

HISTORY

The Conasauga River was involved in the earliest explorations of North America; it is likely that Hernando de Soto and his expedition camped near the Cherokee village of Conasauga on June 1, 1540. To get to the town, de Soto probably crossed the Conasauga River. The watersheds of the Conasauga and Jacks rivers were the site of intensive logging of virgin timber during the 1920s and 1930s; logging was then dependent on railroads for transportation. The railroad came to the town of Conasauga on US 411, where the sawmill was located just after the turn of the century. A trunk line was extended east along the Conasauga River into the mountains and to the Alaculsy site at the Jacks River and Conasauga River junction. The 1920s were spent logging the upper Conasauga from a camp known as Bray Fields; the Jacks River timber was cut in the 1930s from another camp at Beech Bottoms (in the Cohutta Wilderness). The loggers then turned to the north slopes of Big Frog Mountain, with trucks being used to haul timber to Alaculsy for loading on railroad cars. The rails along the

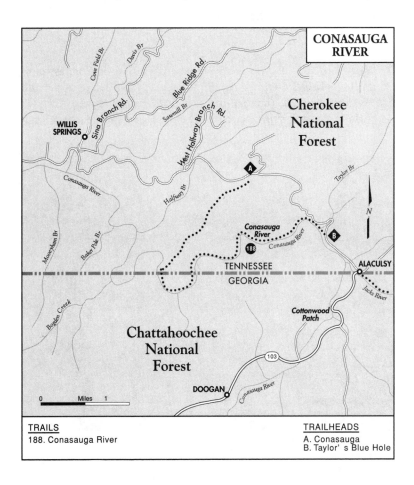

TRAILS
188. Conasauga River

TRAILHEADS
A. Conasauga
B. Taylor' s Blue Hole

Conasauga River were removed in 1942, leaving a rail bed that the Conasauga River Trail now follows along the river.

A scenic corridor along the Conasauga River was designated in the 1988 CNF management plan, and such designation is continued in the CNF's 2004 plan revision. This category protects areas with high visual sensitivity and a high degree of public interest and generally prohibits timber harvesting. The USFS has established several designated campsites along the north shore of the Conasauga, between the bridge at Alaculsy and the trailhead at Taylor's Blue Hole. There are picnic tables, tent pads, parking spaces, and privies. These camps, along with the Cottonwood Patch Campground across the river in Georgia, make this a nice, remote car-camping location.

TRAILHEADS AND MAPS

Conasauga Trailhead

Turn east off US 411 onto Ladd Springs Road about 6.5 miles south of the US 411/US 64 intersection at Ocoee, TN. There is a Ladd Springs Road sign at the turn-off, and TN 313 heads west from US 411 where Ladd Springs Road heads east. Drive southeast on Ladd

Rapids along the Conasauga River. Photograph by Will Skelton.

Springs Road 3.9 miles where the pavement ends and FS 221 continues as a gravel road. Proceed on FS 221 about 6.8 miles from US 411 to the Conasauga Trailhead on the right (UTM 16S 0713991E/3875675N). There is a turn-off at this trailhead where an old road heads south up the hill. White blazes show where the trail heads to the southwest along the ridge.

Taylor's Blue Hole Trailhead

Continue past the Conasauga Trailhead for 1.7 miles (a total of 8.5 miles from US 411) to the Taylor's Blue Hole Trailhead, which is marked by a metal sign for FS Trail 61 (UTM 16S 0715379E/3874741N). This will be the first time FS 221 reaches the river. This trailhead is also 0.6 mile from the bridge across the Jacks River; GA County 16 is on the other side of the bridge, while FS 221 is on the north side. A parking area, picnic tables, and information board are located about 50 yards off FS 221 at the trailhead.

TOPOGRAPHIC MAPS: Parksville, TN; Tennga, TN-GA. TI Map 781, Tellico and Ocoee Rivers, CNF.

TRAIL DESCRIPTION

188. CONASAUGA RIVER TRAIL (FS TRAIL 61, TI TRAIL 29)

LENGTH: 4.6 miles

ELEVATION CHANGE: Low point, 880 feet; high point, 1,480 feet

DIFFICULTY: Easy

TRAILHEADS: Taylor's Blue Hole (start); and Conasauga (end)

USE: Equestrian, mountain bike, hiking

TOPOGRAPHIC MAPS: USGS Parksville, TN; Tennga, TN-GA

COMMENTS: The trail follows the abandoned railroad bed along the river for 2.6 miles, where it turns to the northeast and follows a ridge to the Conasauga Trailhead. A 6.3-mile loop can be completed without a car shuttle if you walk back on FS 221 to the Taylor's Blue Hole Trailhead. The road has occasional traffic.

DETAILS: The railroad bed is gently sloped and easy walking. The adjacent Conasauga River is 50 to 125 feet wide at normal flow and has some whitewater rapids. The escarpment is steep on both sides of the river at first with one hillside of large white pines on the south side.

A few large hemlocks are located along the trail adjacent to the large pools and rapids, but most of the trees are small hardwoods and pines. An improvised swimming hole is located at 0.5 mile. At 2.6 miles (UTM 16S 0712474E/3873943N), the trail turns sharply to the right and away from the railroad bed. There are signs here indicating a right turn for the Conasauga River Trail and pointing straight ahead for the Iron Mountain Trail. (You can proceed straight ahead on the old roadbed for 0.2 mile to the former location of a railroad bridge. The Iron Mountain Trail fords the river at this point; see below.) The Conasauga River Trail, after turning right, goes up a ridgecrest with shallow soils; the oaks and Virginia pines are often somewhat stunted. There are at least half a dozen patches of small ground pine (also called club moss) near the trail on the ridge. The trail leaves the protected corridor as it follows the ridge. The Conasauga Trailhead is reached at 4.6 miles.

If the river level is normal or lower, you can ford it and hike another 2.6 miles downstream along the old roadbed parallel to the river. This section of the roadbed is not a maintained trail, but it is well used and is a pleasant walk. The ford is about 100 feet wide and about 32 inches deep in the middle (at normal flow). Do not attempt to make this ford when the water level is high or if you are not comfortable with fording streams. Just 0.1 mile across the river, the Iron Mountain Trail turns left and heads southeast and the roadbed continues west, downstream for 2.6 miles, where it ends at a vehicle exclusion barrier (UTM 16S 0710979E/3875493N). The Iron Mountain Trail is in Georgia's Chattahoochee NF and is beyond the scope of this book. Its main trailhead is at the Cottonwood Patch Campground and information on it is available from the Cohutta Ranger District of the Chattahoochee NF (706/695-6736).

34 Miscellaneous Trails (Southern CNF)

(TI Map 781, Tellico and Ocoee Rivers)

189. CONASAUGA FALLS TRAIL (FS TRAIL 170, TI TRAIL 28)

LENGTH: 1.2 miles

ELEVATION CHANGE: Low point, 1,040 feet; high point, 1,880 feet

DIFFICULTY: Moderate

TRAILHEAD: Conasauga Falls

USE: Hiking

TOPOGRAPHIC MAPS: USGS Tellico Plains, TN; TI Map 781

TRAILHEAD: To reach the Conasauga Falls Trail, go south from Tellico Plains on Route TN 68. Measure the mileage from the intersection of Route 68 and TN 165 at Tellico Plains. At 2.3 miles turn right on an asphalt road. There is a USFS sign at the intersection pointing right to Conasauga Falls. The first mile of the asphalt road has some severely broken pavement areas. It then becomes a dirt road with some very bad ruts and rocks. A 4 WD drive, high road-clearance vehicle would be desirable. At 2.3 miles from TN 68 come to the trailhead

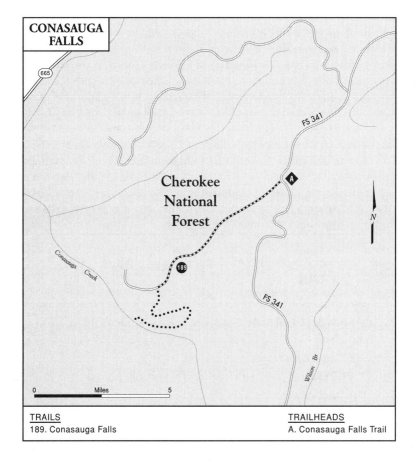

CONASAUGA
FALLS

665

FS 341

Cherokee
National
Forest

A

N

Conasauga Creek

189

FS 341

Wilson Br

0   Miles   5

TRAILS
189. Conasauga Falls

TRAILHEADS
A. Conasauga Falls Trail

for the Conasauga Falls Trail. There is a trail sign on the right where the trail starts on an old road.

COMMENTS: Conasauga Falls is near the headwaters of the Conasauga Creek, a different stream from the Conasauga River. The creek rises near Tellico Plains and eventually empties into the Hiwassee River about 5.0 miles upstream from the mouth of the Ocoee River. The Conasauga River rises in the Cohutta Wilderness of north Georgia, flows north into TN, then west and back south into GA. It eventually empties into the Oostanaula River near Calhoun, GA. This trail would be rated easy were it not for the steep descent and return climb, and the very steep scramble at the bottom.

DETAILS: The first half mile of the trail follows the old road at a fairly constant elevation. The road is not gated and, as of July 2001, is open to vehicular traffic even though the sign indicates it is for hiking. It has several serious mud holes, and unless you have a high road-clearance and/or 4 WD vehicle, it is best to walk the road. (The USFS has future plans to close it to vehicular traffic.) At the road's end, the trail becomes a manway descending into the woods to the left. The falls can be heard as you enter the woods. The trail descends the steep hillside through two switchbacks. Toward the lower end of the trail, Conasauga Creek can be seen below, with its long series of small falls and cascades. At 1.1 miles from the trailhead and some 800 feet below the old road, the manway ends. Here, a 20-foot scramble down a steep bank brings one to the stream below the main falls. From this vantage point the falls are beautiful. Like the Coker Creek Falls, they are a series of falls and cascades made as the creek flows down over a series of rock formations between two steep hillsides. The largest falls are about 20 feet high and about 30 feet wide.

190. UNICOI MOUNTAIN TRAIL (FS TRAIL 117, TI TRAIL 81)

LENGTH: 7.1 miles

ELEVATION CHANGE: Low point, 1,600 feet; high point, 3,200 feet

DIFFICULTY: Difficult

TRAILHEAD: Joe Brown Highway (North and South)

USE: Equestrian, mountain bike, hiking

TOPOGRAPHIC MAPS: USGS Tellico Plains, TN; USGS Farner, TN; TI Map 781

TRAILHEADS: FS Trail 117 is one of two Unicoi Mountain Trails. It is 3.2 miles northwest (on TN 68) of the other one, FS Trail 83. To reach FS Trail 117, travel south on Route TN 68 from Tellico Plains. Start measuring mileage in Tellico Plains at the intersection of TN 68 and TN 165 (Cherohala Skyway). After 9.3 miles turn left on the Joe Brown Highway. There is no sign for this highway, but it is a paved road that intersects 68 where County Road 617 enters from the right. Go 0.3 mile into Joe Brown Highway and come to a dirt road entering from the left. This is the first (north) trailhead for FS Trail No 117 (UTM 16S 0746393E/3904346N). To reach the south trailhead, continue south on Joe Brown Highway another 1.9 miles to a hairpin turn where FS Trail 117 enters from the left (south trailhead; UTM 16S

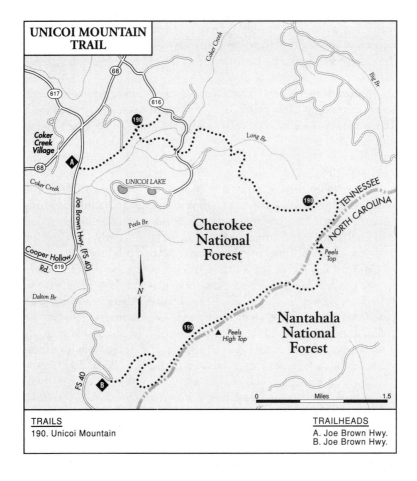

TRAILS	TRAILHEADS
190. Unicoi Mountain	A. Joe Brown Hwy.
	B. Joe Brown Hwy.

0746888E/3901791N). The last mile or so is a dirt road, but it can be traveled by passenger cars. A third trailhead exists to the east on CO 616, but there is no parking space there.

COMMENTS: This trail provides good views on both sides of Unicoi Mountain, well worth the sometimes steep ascent. Care must be taken to avoid wrong turns on intersecting trails.

DETAILS: Starting a hike at the north trailhead, proceed east on the dirt road about a hundred yards to a left curve where the trail continues straight into the woods and past some cleared areas. The double white blazes (white square over a white rectangle) start to appear here. At 0.6 mile from Joe Brown Highway the trail enters another cleared area and immediately turns right. This turn (UTM 16S 0747129E/ 3904777N) is easy to miss. The old road continues straight ahead a quarter mile to the third trailhead on county road 616, but the main trail turns south here, crosses the field and enters the woods. There are two small trail signs in the open field, but they are difficult to see from the old road. A tree on the north side of the old road bears the double blaze on both sides.

Just inside the woods the trail fords Coker Creek and Long Branch and heads east up a low ridge. At 0.7 mile the trail crosses a paved road. The white blazes continue at regular intervals. At 2.0 miles begin a steep ascent. A half mile later the trail crests a ridge, descends, and comes to a trail junction. An unmarked but well-established trail turns off to the right, while FS Trail 117 ascends to the left, at times very steeply.

At 3.3 miles there is another trail junction. This turn (UTM 16S 0749796E/3904139N) is also easy to miss. FS Trail 117 doubles sharply back to the right, heading southwest up the ridge, while an unnamed but well-established trail continues straight ahead to the northeast. There are no white blazes on either of the two trails beyond this junction.

At 3.9 miles the wide trail ends and is replaced by a narrow manway that continues through an overgrown gap and then down a ridge. At 4.5 miles come in to Peels Gap. At 4.9 miles there is another trail junction. Here, continue along the ridge to the southwest, avoiding the trail that heads down off the ridge on the right. Just after this split, the double white blazes again begin to appear. The trail continues southwest, descending gradually on the southeast side of Peels High Top.

At 6.0 miles, enter a cleared, grassy area and turn sharply right onto a wide, well-graded, and grassy jeep road. Avoid the other road on the far right. Descend the jeep road for one-half mile and find the spot on the left where FS Trail 117 drops off the road into the woods. There are no signs at this turn, and the narrow opening into the woods is barely visible. Beyond the turn-off, the jeep road continues to descend along Dalton Branch ravine, then bends left, crossing the branch over a high culvert, and ascending gradually on the other side. If you find yourself ascending, you have missed the turn. Go back and look for the opening. After turning off the jeep road, the trail descends steeply to Dalton Branch and follows it downstream. At 7.1 miles reach the south trailhead, the end of FS Trail 117.

191. TURTLETOWN FALLS TRAIL (FS TRAIL 185, TI TRAIL 78)

LENGTH: 3.6 miles

ELEVATION CHANGE: Low point, 1,200 feet; high point, 1,640 feet

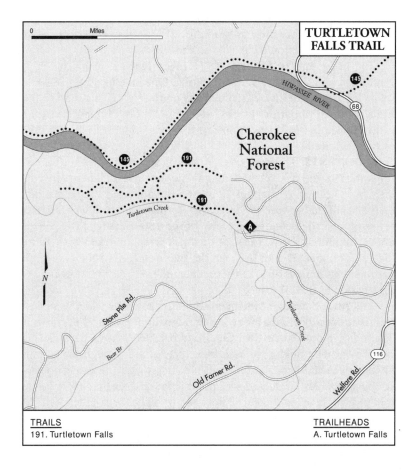

TRAILS
191. Turtletown Falls

TRAILHEADS
A. Turtletown Falls

DIFFICULTY: Easy

TRAILHEADS: Turtletown Creek and FS 1166

USE: Hiking

TOPOGRAPHIC MAPS: USGS Farner, TN; TI Map 781

TRAILHEADS: Proceed south on TN 68 from Tellico Plains 19.5 miles to the Hiwassee River Bridge. Cross the bridge, go another 1.6 miles, and turn right on Underwood Road. Alternatively, go north on TN 68 from the intersection with TN 123 near Turtletown, TN and in 4.0 miles turn left on Underwood Road. The Farner Post Office is at this intersection and there is a sign for the Farner Presbyterian Church. Go west on Underwood Road 0.3 mile and turn left on Duggan Road; go another 0.1 mile and turn left on Old Farner Road (the sign says Farner Road). In another 0.5 mile (0.9 mile from TN 68) a sign points right to Turtletown Creek Scenic Area. Turn right and proceed 1.5 miles on FS 1166, turn left on FS 11651, and reach the trailhead at the road end. Just before the trailhead the road fords a small branch. At the trailhead, Turtletown Creek is on the left.

The other end of FS Trail 185 can be reached using a 4 WD vehicle on which scratches do not matter. One mile into FS 1166 at a sharp left turn, a branch road connects on the right. This road to the right is the continuation of FS 1166, while FS 11651 goes left to the main trailhead. It is 2.0 miles on that brushy section of FS 1166 to the second trailhead.

COMMENTS: This trail offers a very pleasant hike with a beautiful waterfall and a lovely cascade at the lower falls. The main falls include a sheer drop of about 20 feet on the north side and a cascade on the south. In between is a large rock formation. The lower falls is a series of cascades where the creek drops about 20 to 30 feet over about a hundred yards. Most of this trail is well marked with white blazes. A connector trail between the two branches of the main trail permits a 3.8-mile loop hike that renders the second trailhead unnecessary. Details describe the loop.

DETAILS: Starting at the main trailhead, follow a wide, well-used trail that initially climbs along a low ridge. In a few hundred yards it descends again to Turtletown Creek and parallels it downstream. This initial section is obviously used by vehicles, even though there is an intended vehicle barrier at the trailhead. It is a nice hike along a fairly sizable creek. At 0.5 mile, there are some fallen trees that prevent further vehicle travel, and the trail now climbs higher above the creek. At 0.7 mile come to a split where the connector trail goes up to the right. Trail signs indicate that FS Trail 185 goes in all three directions from this junction. Go left here and, at 1.1 miles, reach the start of several switchbacks that take the trail down to the stream below the falls. At the bottom, turn left about 30 yards to the falls.

Leaving the falls, instead of going back up the switchbacks, continue on the trail downstream. At 1.3 miles (0.1 mile from the falls) the trail begins to climb along the stream bank. At 1.5 miles, as you cross a ridge, the sound of the creek is suddenly gone. Enjoy the momentary quiet. At 1.9 miles reach a junction with an old road. To the left it is 0.1 mile to the lower falls. While two vantage points are there, neither one provides an optimum overlook of the cascades. Aggressive viewers and photographers can get a better view by scrambling down the bank below the cascades.

Leaving the lower falls, return 0.1 mile to the junction where the trail came to the old road. Now go straight up the old road instead of returning by the previous trail. At 2.2 miles (0.2 mile from the lower falls) cross a power line, bear right, and continue up the ridgecrest in the woods. This is Shinbone Ridge and a look at the map shows that it is aptly named. The power line is roughly over the Appalachia

Turtletown Falls on its namesake trail, across the Hiwassee River from the John Muir Trail. Photograph by George Ritter.

Tunnel, a huge 8.5-mile-long underground aqueduct that carries water from Apalachia Dam to the Apalachia Powerhouse. After generating power there, the water augments the Hiwassee River flow for the boaters and floaters. At 2.9 miles reach a low saddle where an old road intersects on the right (UTM 16S 0741405E/3894727N). Here a trail sign indicates the hiking symbol in all three directions. Straight ahead it is another 0.6 mile to the second trailhead. However, this is the connector and our loop hike turns right. Follow the connector 0.2 mile to its other end, where a left turn brings you back to the main trailhead in another 0.7 mile.

192. BIG LOST CREEK TRAIL (FS TRAIL 109, TI TRAIL 12)

LENGTH: 1.7 miles

ELEVATION CHANGE: Low point, 950 feet; high point, 1,000 feet

DIFFICULTY: Easy

TRAILHEAD: Lost Creek Campground

USE: Hiking

TOPOGRAPHIC MAPS: USGS McFarland, TN; TI Map 781

TRAILHEAD: Proceed south on TN 30 from the intersection with TN 315 in Reliance, TN 1.7 miles to the intersection with FS 103 (Lost Creek Road). There is a sign at the intersection pointing left to Big Lost Creek Campground. Alternatively, proceed north on TN 30 from US 64 at Lake Ocoee 7.3 miles to the intersection with FS 103 and turn right at the sign. After 4.8 miles on FS 103, cross the bridge over Little Lost Creek. It is then another 2.2 miles (7.0 miles from TN 30) on FS 103 to the trailhead at Lost Creek Campground.

COMMENTS: This short trail is a nice walk for campers at Lost Creek Campground. Fishermen use the lower end and keep it open. The upper end is heavily overgrown. The campground has 15 first-come-first-served sites with parking spaces, tent pads, and tables. Water and privies are available.

DETAILS: A "Trail 109" sign with the hiker symbol marks the trailhead just east of bridge over Big Lost Creek. After fording Mary Branch, the trail starts upstream on an old roadbed along the east side of Big Lost Creek. There are numerous side trails leading to the creek bank. At 0.5 mile there is a detour to the right around a small pond and the trail begins to show fewer signs of use. At 0.7 mile the trail jogs right and angles toward the creek, which it fords. At 1.1 miles from the trailhead, still following the old roadbed, pass a flat area suitable for a backcountry camp. Parts of the trail here on the west side of the creek are overgrown with rhododendron and dog hobble and there are downed trees to scramble through. At 1.3 miles come to a large pool where the creek flow bends from northwest to northeast. Here, climb up a few feet to the right and continue on a higher section of the old roadbed. At 1.7 miles come to a pair of large blowdowns. The trail beyond disappears in heavy growth and this is the place to turn around.

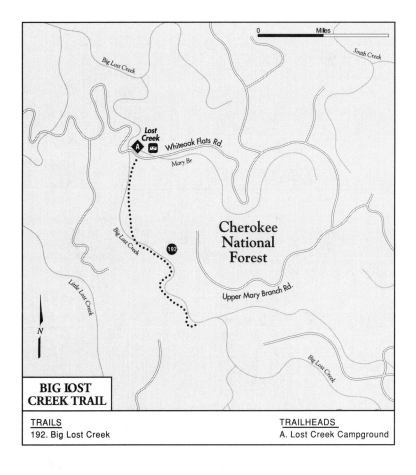

BIG IOST CREEK TRAIL

TRAILS
192. Big Lost Creek

TRAILHEADS
A. Lost Creek Campground

193. BLUE RIDGE TRAIL (FS TRAIL 62, TI TRAIL 14)

LENGTH: 2.9 miles

ELEVATION CHANGE: Low point, 1,150 feet; high point, 1,550 feet

DIFFICULTY: Moderate/easy

TRAILHEADS: FS 99 Blue Ridge; Blue Ridge Gap

USE: Equestrian, mountain bike, hiking

TOPOGRAPHIC MAPS: USGS Caney Creek, TN; USGS Parksville, TN; TI Map 781

TRAILHEADS: *FS 99 Blue Ridge Trailhead:* Coming from Ocoee, proceed west on US 64 from the intersection with US 411. Go 2.4

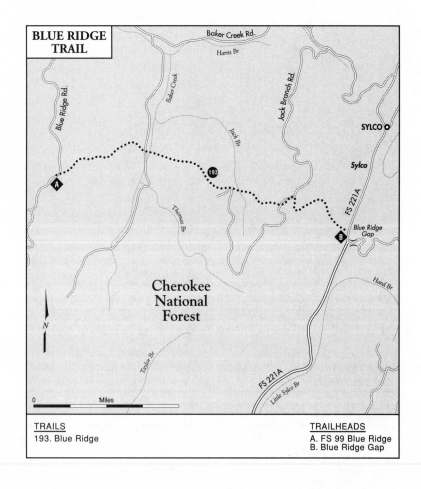

miles to Cherokee Corner and turn right on Cookson Creek Road. The turn is just after an Exxon gas station. At 3.5 miles from US 64 bear right, following the road, which now becomes FS 55. At 4.0 miles the pavement ends. At 4.5 miles turn right on FS 55. At this junction, FS 302 starts, heading east, while FS 55 turns south. Immediately after this right turn take the left fork to stay on FS 55. Proceed another 1.9 miles on FS 55 (6.4 miles from US 64) and turn right on FS 99. In 2.3 miles (8.7 miles from US 64) the road crests a ridge and the trailhead is just beyond on the left. There are no trail signs or blazes, but there is a vehicle barrier at the start of an old road.

Blue Ridge Gap Trailhead: This trailhead for the Blue Ridge Trail can be reached from the Ocoee area to the north or from the Conasauga River Corridor to the south. Coming from Ocoee, proceed initially as in the directions to the FS 99 trailhead. Instead of turning right on FS 99, continue straight ahead on FS 55 another 4.6 miles (11.0 mile from US 64) to the Sylco Creek Campground. Go another 0.2 mile to the trailhead on the right. Here there is a trail sign for FS Trail 62 and a USFS bulletin board. Coming from the Conasauga River Corridor, proceed north on FS 221 and 221A from the Bridge at Alaculsy. In 3.0 miles come to an intersection at the start of FS 55 and proceed straight ahead on FS 55 another 0.1 mile to the trailhead on the left.

COMMENTS: This remote trail offers a pleasant hike through interesting second-growth forest areas. It is relatively short, but climbing the two ridges provides some aerobic exercise. There are a few white blazes, but they appear only occasionally. This is a nice hike for campers staying at the Sylco Creek Campground or at the designated campsites on the Conasauga River.

DETAILS: Heading west to east, the trail first ascends slightly and then descends, at times steeply, to Baker Creek, which is reached in 0.9 mile. Partway down there are some nice views to the east of Sylco Ridge (which the trail later crosses) and of Chimneytop and Big Frog Mountains, farther east in the Big Frog Wilderness. On reaching the Baker Creek area, the trail intersects an old road. Here a sharp turn to the right must be made, heading upstream parallel to the creek. If the turn is missed, an old cabin and another, newer one soon appear. Turn back and find the missed right turn. Baker Creek rises a little over a mile south of here, at Baker Creek Spring. It flows north, eventually emptying into the Baker Creek Inlet of Parksville Lake (Lake Ocoee).

Only 70 yards after that right turn the trail turns left and fords Baker Creek. Avoid the old road that continues upstream on the west side. After fording Baker Creek, the trail turns left again and then bends around to the right, heading up an unnamed stream between two hills. At 1.5 miles an old, USFS road grade can be seen above on the right. At 1.6 miles the trail passes close to that road grade before descending to cross Jack Branch in a pleasant glen of rhododendron at 1.8 miles. At 2.1 miles cross another section of that road grade and soon reach the crest and start descent of Sylco Ridge. At 2.9 miles the trail ends at FS 55 near Blue Ridge Gap.

194. LITTLE CITICO CREEK HORSE TRAILS (FS TRAILS 165-1, 2, 3, 4, TI TRAILS 53-1, 2, 3, 4)

The Little Citico Horse Trails cover an area to the east of Citico Creek and northwest of the Citico Creek Wilderness. Most of these trails fol-

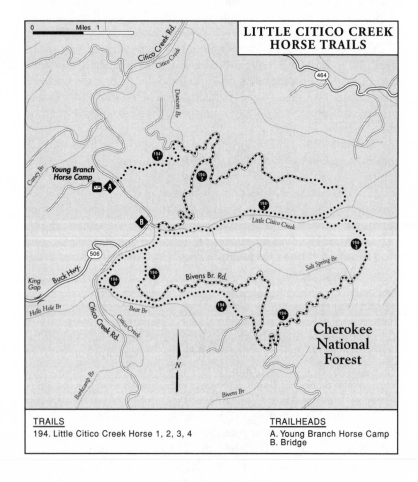

TRAILS
194. Little Citico Creek Horse 1, 2, 3, 4

TRAILHEADS
A. Young Branch Horse Camp
B. Bridge

low old logging or USFS roads, many of which were graveled but are now somewhat overgrown. Because they are wide, well graded, and flat, they are ideal for equestrians and are attractive to mountain bikers. Hikers and backpackers might find them less interesting than, for example, the hiking trails in the Citico Creek Wilderness. These trails are all connected, and a variety of pleasant riding loop trips are possible by combining two or more in one outing. They are all marked with white blazes, but care is needed at several points where a wrong turn is possible. There are many other old roads and trails in the area, and illegal ORV usage has made some of them appear to be maintained trails. This is especially true in the area to the northeast near private land.

TRAILHEADS: There are two main access routes to the Little Citico Horse Trails, both starting from the BP station on US 411 in Vonore, TN. Turn east at that point on Route TN 360. At 7.4 miles from Vonore, TN 360 turns right across a bridge. At this point the first access route continues straight ahead on the Citico Creek Road, county road 455. At 16 miles from Vonore, the hard road ends. At this point do not turn left across the bridge but continue straight ahead on the gravel road, FS 35-1. At 19.5 miles from Vonore reach Young Branch Horse Camp Trailhead. Another 0.7 mile straight ahead is the Bridge Trailhead.

The alternate access route has more turns and may be difficult to follow, but it avoids a badly rutted 3.0 mile section of FS 35-1 north of Young Branch Horse Camp. (The two routes are about the same distance.) The alternate route turns right across the bridge when TN 360 turns right 7.4 miles from Vonore. At 12.1 miles from Vonore, TN 360 turns left at a stop sign. Turn left and continue on TN 360 another 1.1 miles to the point where County Road 504 intersects from the left. Turn left on 504 and go 1.7 miles to a fork where County Road 506 goes left. Take the left fork and proceed 5.1 miles over the Buck Highway to the Citico Creek Road. (A sign at the fork points left to the Buck Highway and says it is 4.0 miles to the Citico, but the measured distance is 5.1.) The last mile of the Buck Highway is a graveled road that is sometimes steep, but there are no significant ruts or potholes. On reaching the Citico Creek Road, go left 0.2 mile to the Bridge Trailhead and another 0.7 mile to the Young Branch Horse Camp Trailhead.

Young Branch Horse Camp Trailhead: The trailhead for 165-1 is just opposite the southern (upstream) entrance to the horse camp. A sign on the gate to the horse camp says "Reservation required" and a phone number is listed: "253-2520." The horse camp is fairly large, with six parking spaces, concrete picnic tables, a horse rack, and a privy. There is very little day parking available at this trailhead. The USFS does not want vehicles parked on the vegetation along the road, and the campsite parking is reserved for campers. Day hikers should look for nearby parking at wide spaces on the gravel or dirt road surface but off the road itself and not blocking a gate. More parking is available 0.7 mile upstream at the Bridge Trailhead. Using Young Branch Horse Trailhead requires a ford of Citico Creek. At times of low water the ford is relatively easy. The water is about 15 inches deep (or less) and the creek is about 25 yards wide. The level can rise quickly, however, and can make a return crossing dangerous. An unseen rain farther up the watershed the night before has been known to increase the level from 15 inches at 10 a.m. to 32 inches at 3:00 p.m. Be prepared to detour 4.3 miles via the bridge trailhead if your return is blocked by rising water. (It is 2.1 miles back up 165-1 to the intersection with 165-2, where a right turn brings you down that trail to the bridge in 1.5 miles. It is another 0.7 mile on the road back to the trailhead at Young Branch Horse Camp.)

Bridge Trailhead: This is the main trailhead for Horse Trails 165-2, 3, and 4, and, because of the ford and the lack of day parking at the Young Branch Horse Camp Trailhead, equestrians use the Bridge Trailhead almost exclusively. A graveled road heads east from the Citico Creek Road at a point 0.7 mile upstream from Young Branch Horse Camp and 0.2 mile down from the Buck Highway intersection. The road immediately crosses Citico Creek on a bridge and there is room on the far side for parking several vehicles and/or trailers.

194-1 LITTLE CITICO HORSE TRAIL (FS TRAIL 165-1, TI TRAIL 53-1)

LENGTH: 2.3 miles

ELEVATION CHANGE: Low point, 900 feet; high point, 1,280 feet

DIFFICULTY: Easy (except during high water)

TRAILHEADS: Young Branch Horse Camp Trailhead (start) and FS Trail 165-2 (end)

USE: Equestrian, mountain bike, hiking

TOPOGRAPHIC MAPS: USGS Whiteoak Flats, TN; TI Map 781

DETAILS: The first 50 yards of the trail leads to Citico Creek, which one must ford to follow this trail (see the warning under the

"Trailheads" section above). Just across the creek the trail turns right off a cleared area and enters the woods. Inside the woods bear left, avoiding an old road heading up to the right. At 0.2 mile, after two switchbacks, the trail joins an old road, which it follows up the side of the ridge, then along the crest and continuing in an easterly direction. At 0.8 mile cross a weedy, open area and avoid a side trail heading up to the right.

At 1.3 miles reach a wide, graveled, USFS road, on which the trail turns right. To the left, the service road descends about a mile to a dead-end. (Note: the TI map lists the mileage for this trail as 1.5, implying that it ends at this road; however, the trail actually continues another 0.8 mile up this road to an intersection with FS Trail 165-2. There are no blazes on the gravel road section of 165-1, but there are signs at both ends bearing the trail number FS Trail 165-1.)

At 1.9 miles another USFS road enters from the left or north (UTM 16S 0762624E/3930992N). Keep to the right at this split, as 165-1 heads due east, then turns south. At 2.3 miles reach the gate at the intersection with 165-2. This is the end of FS Trail 165-1 (UTM 16S 0762600E/3930584N). (Note: The gate is across the end of 165-1, not across 165-2 as shown on the TI map.)

194-2 LITTLE CITICO HORSE TRAIL (FS TRAIL 165-2, TI TRAIL 53-2)

LENGTH: 7.1 miles

ELEVATION CHANGE: Low point, 900 feet; high point, 1,400 feet

DIFFICULTY: Moderate

TRAILHEADS: Bridge Trailhead (start and end)

USE: Equestrian, mountain bike, hiking

TOPOGRAPHIC MAPS: USGS Whiteoak Flats, TN; TI Map 781

DETAILS: Two dirt roads leave the trailhead. Straight ahead is the start of 165-2, and to the right are the start of 165-3 and the end of the loop made by 165-2. The description of 165-2 follows a clockwise direction, starting straight ahead after crossing the bridge. At about 100 yards there is a gate closing the road to vehicles. Most of FS Trail 165-2 is a well-graded, gravel road, with very few weeds. At 1.5 miles FS Trail 165-1 intersects from the left, behind a closed gate (UTM 16S 0762600E/3930584N). 165-2 continues straight ahead. At 2.7 miles reach an open area on the right with the remains of an old sawmill. At

3.3 miles, after passing through areas of an old forest fire (circa 1994–95) reach the remains of a USFS gate and the end of the gravel road. The trail continues straight ahead on a slightly rutted road.

At 3.5 miles the road turns to the right, heading south. Here the TI map shows a spur trail heading north to a connection with TN 467, but the spur trail is nearly impassable. The USFS does no maintenance on it and does not consider it to be an official trail. It is not usable by equestrians or mountain bikers, and only those hikers skilled in route finding should attempt to use it.

At the turn, and 50 yards later, avoid ORV trails entering from the left. At 3.6 miles enter a clearing where the trail bends left, continuing on the old road. At 4.0 miles another ORV trail enters from the left. At 4.4 miles, after descending the ridge, come to the intersection with the eastern end of FS Trail 165-3 (UTM 16S 0764545E/3929720N). FS Trail 165-2 continues straight ahead following downstream along Little Citico Creek but is now a narrow creekside trail instead of a hillside road. At 7.1 miles, after five easy fords of Little Citico, come to the intersection with the western end of 165-3. Turn right and proceed 100 yards to the trailhead, completing the loop.

194-3 LITTLE CITICO HORSE TRAIL (FS TRAIL 165-3, TI TRAIL 53-3)

LENGTH: 7.4 miles

ELEVATION CHANGE: Low point, 900 feet; high point, 1,800 feet

DIFFICULTY: Difficult

TRAILHEADS: Bridge Trailhead (start) and FS Trail 165-2 (end)

USE: Equestrian, mountain bike, hiking

TOPOGRAPHIC MAPS: Whiteoak Flats, TN; TI Map 781

DETAILS: The trail starts by taking the right hand road just across the bridge. In 100 yards come to a split where 165-2 goes left and 165-3 goes to the right. Go right and follow the narrow trail along the hillside above Citico Creek. At 0.6 mile come to the split where FS Trail 165-3 goes left and FS Trail 165-4 goes right (UTM 16S 0761384E/3929102N). Turn left and begin gradual ascent on old road. At 1.1 miles come into a cleared area that is the beginning of a graveled USFS road (Bivens Branch Road). Here the TI map shows a side trail heading southwest to a connection with FS Trail 165-4, but the side trail is nearly impassable. The USFS does no maintenance on it and does not consider it to be an official trail. It is not usable by equestrians or mountain bikers, and only those hikers skilled in route finding should attempt to use it.

The trail now follows Bivens Branch Road. At 3.9 miles the eastern end of FS Trail 165-4 enters from the right, coming down the ridge (UTM 16S 0763418E/3927828N) At 4.3 miles come to a broken gate at an intersection where a road enters from the left. The road to the left, which is gated to prevent vehicular traffic, is the continuation of trail 165-3. Turn left (UTM 16S 0763700E/3927719N). At 6.1 miles, come into a cleared area where FS Trail 165-3 leaves the USFS road. Look for the trail sign where the trail enters the woods at the far left of the clearing. Avoid the old road continuing down to the right.

At 6.5 miles crest a ridge and begin a sometimes steep, winding descent into the Little Citico Creek valley. At 7.3 miles ford the creek and at 7.4 miles reach the junction with FS Trail 165-2 (UTM 16S 0764545E/3929720N). To the left it is 2.7 miles on 165-2 to the trailhead at the bridge, to the right the other side of the FS Trail 165-2 loop brings you to the bridge trailhead in 4.4 miles.

194-4 LITTLE CITICO HORSE TRAIL (FS TRAIL 165-4, TI TRAIL 53-4)

LENGTH: 2.4 miles

ELEVATION CHANGE: Low point, 900 feet; high point, 1,450 feet

DIFFICULTY: Easy

TRAILHEADS: Bridge Trailhead (start) and FS Trail 165-3 (end)

USE: Mountain bike, hiking, equestrian

TOPOGRAPHIC MAPS: Whiteoak Flats, TN; TI Map 781

DETAILS: The first 0.6 mile is traveled on FS Trail 165-3. At 0.6 mile from the bridge come to the split where FS Trail 165-3 goes left and FS Trail 165-4 goes right (UTM 16S 0761384E/3929102N). Go right, cross the small branch, and continue upstream above the east bank of Citico Creek. Mileage for FS Trail 165-4 is now given from this starting point. Note: this initial section of FS Trail 165-4 is not shown on the TI map.

In 0.5 mile the trail leaves the Citico Creek and heads east upstream along Bear Branch. In about 50 yards it crosses the branch. Here the TI map shows a side trail heading northeast to a connection with FS Trail 165-3, but, while the side trail appears open at this junction, it quickly becomes overgrown and nearly impassable. The USFS does no maintenance on it and does not consider it to be an official trail. It is impassable by equestrians or mountain bikers and only those hikers skilled in route finding should attempt to use it. There are trail signs on both sides of the branch crossing that show the correct route for FS Trail 165-4. The trail continues east alongside, and sometimes in, the branch as it gradually ascends the narrow, densely shaded valley.

At 1.3 miles another small branch enters from the right, and the old road grade of FS Trail 165-3 is visible above on the left. FS Trail 165-4 soon leaves the branch and ascends the crest of a ridge through more open woods. At 2.1 miles come to an intersection with another old logging road. Go left, following the white blazes. At 2.4 miles after descending the ridge, come to the intersection with Trail 165-3 (UTM 16S 0763418E/3927828N). To the left it is 3.9 miles on FS Trail 165-3 back to its start. To the right it is 3.5 miles on FS Trail 165-3 around to its intersection with FS Trail 165-2.

195. INDIAN BOUNDARY LAKE TRAIL (FS TRAIL 129, TI TRAIL 47)

LENGTH: 3.5-mile loop

ELEVATION CHANGE: Low point, 1,780 feet; high point, 1,780 feet

DIFFICULTY: Easy

TRAILHEAD: Indian Boundary Campground Swimming Area

USE: Hiking, mountain bike

TOPOGRAPHIC MAPS: USGS Whiteoak Flats, TN; Rafter, TN

TRAILHEAD: To reach the Indian Boundary Campground and its swimming area from the junction of TN 68 and TN 165 in Tellico Plains, turn east onto TN 165, which will become part of the Cherohala Skyway. Drive 14.8 miles east and turn left at a well-marked intersection onto FS 345. In 1.2 miles the road forks, with the left branch leading into the Indian Boundary Area. From this point drive 1.3 miles, generally bearing right at major junctions and following the well-signed route to the Indian Boundary Swimming Area. Park at the large lot. Indian Boundary is a fee area. In 2002 the day-use charge was $2 per vehicle.

COMMENTS: The deservedly popular and highly scenic Indian Boundary Lake Trail is located adjacent to the largest camping area in the southern part of the CNF. The trail draws campers and day trippers who have come to the area to picnic, boat, fish, and swim in this small, lovely body of water. For its entire length the trail hugs the lakeshore, seldom rising or falling more than a few feet in elevation.

The trail is also one of the best maintained in the Cherokee. It is wide, well-cleared, and covered with a layer of fine gravel. Though most visitors walk around the lake, the easy grades and smooth surface make Indian Boundary a perfect trail for those seeking some easy mountain biking.

DETAILS: From the parking area for the swimming area look for a gravel path running between the parking area and the beach. To follow the trail clockwise around the lake turn left on the path. Though the trail is not blazed, the fine gravel covering the footway will guide you around the lake. Many short wood bridges span potentially wet drainages.

Work your way through the picnic and campground areas taking care to follow the gravel path, which will never stray too far from the

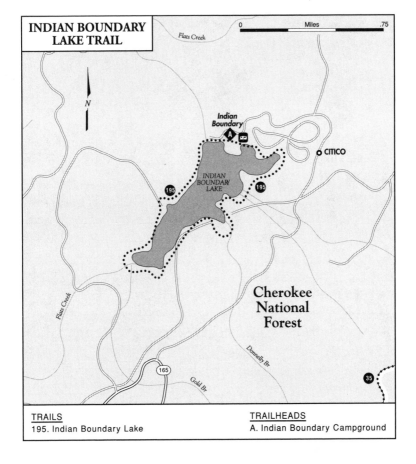

INDIAN BOUNDARY LAKE TRAIL

0   Miles   .75

Flats Creek

N

Indian Boundary

CITICO

INDIAN BOUNDARY LAKE

Cherokee National Forest

Flats Creek

Donnelly Br

Gold Br

TRAILS	TRAILHEADS
195. Indian Boundary Lake	A. Indian Boundary Campground

lakeshore. At 0.8 mile cross the road leading to the boat launch site. You will pass the ends of two other dirt roads before crossing the inlet of the lake on a wooden bridge at 2.4 miles. At 3.3 miles reach the dam across Flats Creek. You cross this narrow barrier between two fences that seem especially designed to comfort those who otherwise might dread the high, exposed crossing. The trail ends back at the swimming beach at 3.5 miles. Though it is not required that you take a swim after your hike, no summer visitor will be able to pass up the opportunity for a refreshing dip after their trip.

Appendix 1

Available Maps
and Sources

There are two principal maps available from the CNF: one of the northern CNF and one of the southern CNF. They are called "Forest Visitor Maps," and each is available for $8 ($16 for both north and south) from the CFAIA, Map Order, PO Box 2010, Cleveland, TN 37320, or contact the CNF through its map Web page, at http://www.southern-region.fs.fed.us/cherokee/maps2003/index. These very general maps show the USFS roads and developed facilities but do not show all of the boundaries of the areas in this book or the details of such areas. The CNF also has a map of the Joyce Kilmer–Slickrock Wilderness, the Cohutta Wilderness, and the trails of Nolichucky, available for $6, $7, and $6, respectively, from the above address.

A book of helpful general maps, particularly for access roads, is the *Tennessee Atlas and Gazetteer*, which includes all of the CNF; it is available at local bookstores or from DeLorme Mapping Company, at 800/561-5105. A similar map book is *Tennessee County Maps*, available at local bookstores or from County Maps, Puetz Place, Lyndon Station, WI 53944.

The CNF works in partnership with the Cradle of Forestry in America Interpretive Association (CFAIA), who provides interpretive literature, maps, and other items for sale at many USNF facilities throughout the South. Sales outlets are located in each CNF office, the Ocoee Whitewater Center, and Coker Creek Village on Highway 68.

Of course, the best maps to use for hiking are the USGS topographical maps. How one obtains and uses these maps now is just another example of how things have changed since the first edition of this book was written. In 1992, the only option for obtaining topographical maps was to purchase them, either in person or by phone or mail, directly from a map dealer. Of course, you can still do that, but there are many other options, most of which offer a huge convenience factor. Depending on personal taste, the recommendation of hikers or mountain bikers who are really serious about their maps is to purchase digital mapping software. There is another section of this book that describes the use of these products in concert with handheld GPS units but, put simply, such software permits you to generate the classic USGS quad, customized for your outing, in minutes on your home computer and color printer. There are several products available. Two of the ones used most widely seem to be TOPO!, available from National Geographic Maps (http://maps.nationalgeographic.com/topo), and Terrain Navigator, available from Map Tech (http://www.maptech.com).

If you are in a hurry, have access to the Internet, and do not own one of these products, there are other ways in which you can obtain "free" maps. For example, some Web sites, such as TopoZone (http://www.topozone.com), enable one to print out a copy of the interactive topo map displayed on their site. The maps are not large, and they do not have coordinate grids printed on them, but they may do in a pinch. Other Web sites actually offer free downloads of scanned 7.5 minute topographical quads. These are called digital raster graphics, or DRGs. Do a search on the Internet for these. One particularly useful site is the Tennessee Spatial Data Server (http://63.148. 169.50/). This site has a wealth of information on it. Just look for the quad you need, download it, and print it out. You should note, however, that the DRGs available for download are so-called collarless DRGs, meaning that they lack the white border with the coordinates and other scale information on the actual map. The Web site is designed for geographic information systems (GIS) users, and each map comes with a "World File," which supplies that information to GIS software package that a typical GIS professional would use. Again, not perfect, but better than nothing. If you can find DRGs that cover the forest that are not collarless, all the better.

Like much in life, you usually get what you pay for. There are a number of sites on the Web that offer downloads of DRGs for a small fee (usually $2–$3 each). One such site is the GIS Data Depot (http:// data.geocomm.com). Another approach is a membership fee site that offers unlimited downloads of user-customized maps. One example is MapCard (http://www.mapcard.com). The above sites also offer aerial photographs of the areas covered by their maps. Keep in mind that by their very nature, maps have a lot of information on them, and so file size can be an issue for individuals with a slow Internet connection.

Of course, you can always go out and purchase the paper USGS topographic maps directly, available from the USFS, local hiking equipment shops, and several other sources, including the following:

The Map Store
2024 Dutch Valley Rd.
Knoxville, TN 37918
865/688-3608

TVA Map Store
101 Haney Building
311 Broad St.
Chattanooga, TN 37402
423/751-6277

Timely Discount Topos
9769 West 119th Dr.
Broomfield, CO 80021
800/821-7609
http://www.usgstopomaps.com

US Geological Survey
Washington, DC 20242
http://topomaps.usgs.gov/ordering_maps.html

Note: These topographic maps often do not show the boundaries of the areas in this book.

Appendix 2

US Forest Service Offices

The following CNF offices are open from 8:00 A.M. to 4:30 P.M., Monday through Friday, excluding holidays.

CNF Forest Supervisor's Office
2800 North Ocoee St.
PO Box 2010
Cleveland, TN 37320
423/476-9700
http://www.southernregion.fs.fed.us/cherokee/

Watauga Ranger District
PO Box 400
Unicoi, TN 37692
423/735-1500

Nolichucky/Unaka Ranger Station
124 Austin St., Ste. 3
Greenville, TN 37745
423/638-4109

Tellico Ranger District
250 Ranger Station Rd.
Tellico Plains, TN 37385
423/253-2520

Ocoee/Hiwassee Ranger District
Route 1, Box 348D
Benton, TN 37307
423/338-5201

The Nantahala and Pisgah NFs in NC are managed from one location in Asheville; their information is National Forests in NC, PO Box 2750, 160A Zillicoa St., Asheville, NC 28802; 828/257-4200; http://www.cs.unca.edu/nfsnc. The Southern Region of the USFS, which includes the CNF, is located in Atlanta: USDA Forest Service, Southern Region, 1720 Peachtree Rd., NW, Atlanta, GA 30309; http://www.southernregion.fs.fed.us. Another agency that is important in connection with the CNF is the TN Wildlife Resources Agency; they are in charge of hunting and fishing in the national forest. Their address is East TN (Region IV), 3030 Wildlife Way, Morristown, TN 37814; 423/587-7037; http://www.state.tn.us/twra.

Outings and Issues Groups

Members of the Harvey Broome Group of the TN Chapter of the Sierra Club hiked the trails and wrote this book. The group has been a longtime advocate of wilderness and preservation of the CNF and also regularly conducts outings in the CNF. The Harvey Broome Group can be reached online at http://tennessee.sierraclub.org/broome/index.htm. Current group officers can be obtained from the national Sierra Club's Web site, at http://www.sierraclub.org, or by writing Sierra Club at National Headquarters, 85 Second St., 2nd Floor, San Francisco, CA 94105. Their phone number is 415/977-5500. The Harvey Broome Group is one of several groups in the TN Chapter of the Sierra Club, including the State of Franklin Group in the upper East TN area (http://tennessee.sierraclub.org/sofg/index.htm).

Other primarily local groups that are involved in CNF issues and/or conduct hiking outings in the CNF are the following:

Appalachian Trail Conference
PO Box 807
Harpers Ferry, WV 25425
http://www.appalachiantrail.org

Carolina Mountain Club
PO Box 68
Asheville, NC 28802
http://www.carolinamtnclub.com

Benton MacKaye Trail
Association
PO Box 53271
Atlanta, GA 30355
http://www.bmta.org

Chattanooga Hiking Club
P.O. Box 1443
Chattanooga, TN 37401
http://www.chattanooga.net/hiking

Cherokee Forest Voices
1101 Antioch Rd.
Johnson City, TN 37604
423/929-8163
Fax 423/232-9485
cfvcatherine@worldnet.att.net

Cherokee Hiking Club
2349 Varnell Rd.
Cleveland TN 37311

Chota Canoe Club
PO Box 8270
University Station
Knoxville, TN 37996
http://www.korrnet.org/chota

Foothills Land Conservancy
614 Sevierville Rd.
Maryville, TN 37804
865/681-8326
http://www.foothillsland.org

Greenville Hiking Club
http://www.greenevillehikers.xtn.
net

Hiwassee Hiking Club
c/o Carlene Hill
410 Lynn Ave.
Athens, TN 37303-3720

Mid-Appalachian Highlands
Club, Inc.
PO Box 702
Elizabethton, TN 37644
http://jat.esmartweb.com/
hikers/mid-app-hiland-club.htm

Southern Appalachian Forest
Coalition
46 Haywood St., Ste. 323
Asheville, NC 28801
828/252-9223
safc@safc.org

Southern Appalachian Highlands
Conservancy
34 Wall St., Ste. 802
Asheville, NC 28801
828/253-0095
www.appalachian.org

Smoky Mountain Hiking Club
PO Box 1454
Knoxville, TN 37901
http://www.esper.com/smhc

Tennessee Citizens for Wilderness
Planning
130 Tabor Rd.
Oak Ridge, TN 37830
http://www.korrnet.org/tcwp

Tennessee Eastman Hiking and
Canoeing Club
Building 310
Eastman Rd.
Kingsport, TN 37662
http://www.tehcc.org

Tennessee Scenic Rivers
Association
PO Box 159041
Nashville, TN 37215
http://www.paddletsra.org/index
2.htm

Tennessee Trails Association
PO Box 41446
Nashville, TN 37204-1446
http://www.tennesseetrails.org
University of Tennessee Canoe
and Hiking Club
http://web.utk.edu/~canoehik

Western North Carolina Alliance
70 Woodfin Place, Ste. 326
Asheville, TN 28801
828/258-8737

Appendix 4

Outdoor Equipment Retail Stores

Be sure to call ahead for current information.

BRISTOL, VA

1021 Commonwealth Ave.
Bristol, VA 24201
540/466-8988
http://www.mountainsportsltd.com

CHATTANOOGA

Rock Creek Outfitters
100 Tremont St.
Chattanooga, TN 37405
423/265-5969
http://www.rockcreek.com

2200 Hamilton Place Blvd.
7-B Hamilton Crossing
Chattanooga TN 37421
423/485-8775

CLEVELAND

Extreme Outdoors
185 Inman St. E
Cleveland, TN 37311
423/728-2709 or 423/728-4810

DAMASCUS, VA

Mt. Rogers Outfitters
110 Laurel Ave.
Damascus, VA 24236
276/475-5416
http://www.mtrogersoutfitters.com

GATLINBURG

Happy Hiker
865/436-6000
905 River Rd., Ste. 5
Gatlinburg, TN 37738
http://www.happyhiker.com

JOHNSON CITY

Mahoney's
830 Sunset Dr.
Johnson City, TN 37604
423/282-5413

The Peerless Center
2513 N. Roan St.
Johnson City, TN 37604
423/282-8889

KNOXVILLE

River Sports Outfitters
2918 Sutherland Ave.
Knoxville, TN 37919
615/523-0066

Blue Ridge Mountain Sports
Village Green Center
11537 Kingston Pike
Knoxville, TN 37922
865/675-3010

Kingston Pike Center
4610 Kingston Pike
Knoxville, TN 37919
865/588-2638
http://www.brmsstore.com

Earth Traverse Outfitters
1815 Sutherland Ave.
Knoxville, TN 37919
865/523-0699

MARYVILLE

Little River Trading Co.
2408 E. Lamar Alexander Pkwy.
Maryville, TN 37804
865/681-4141

Appendix 5

Protected Areas
and Acreages

There are approximately 640,000 total acres in CNF as of January 30, 2004 (340,969 in the northern and 298,998 in the southern CNF). Many of these acres are protected in a variety of land management categories, some more permanent than others. In this book we have highlighted most of the protected areas, especially wilderness, scenic, and backcountry areas. As of 2004, designated wilderness areas constitute 10.37 percent of the total CNF acreage (66,389 acres), while the recommended wilderness study areas and the scenic and backcountry areas constitute 15 percent of the total.

Roadless areas were identified by the USFS prior to the 2004 planning process. Such identification did not protect the areas until President Clinton's Final Rule for Roadless Area Conservation issued on January 12, 2001. However, the Bush administration as of 2004 is attempting to revise such executive order so as to allow timber harvesting in such areas.

Wilderness areas are designated by Congress pursuant to the Wilderness Act of 1964 and provide the best permanent protection for the natural resources of an area from development, road building, and clear-cutting; however, most recreational uses such as hunting (in national forests but not national parks), fishing, horseback riding, hiking, and camping are allowed.

Wilderness recommendations are made by the USFS when management plans are revised. It requires an act of Congress to actually make the designations. However, areas recommended for that designation would be managed very much like wilderness until they are designated by Congress or for the life of the plan.

Scenic areas are protected only by the current CNF management plan and can be changed when the plan is revised; pending any change, however, the management is only slightly less protective than wilderness designation.

Backcountry or primitive areas are likewise protected only by the CNF management plan; they are generally managed without timber harvest or additional road building. However, different subcategories of backcountry designation permit different levels of activity. The least restrictive subcategory allows salvage logging, road reconstruction, temporary road construction, and ORV use on existing ORV trails. The most restrictive subcategory prohibits logging and road construction/reconstruction and ORV use. In the CNF's 1988 management plan these areas were called "Semi-Primitive, Nonmotorized (or Motorized) Recreation Areas" or "Primitive Areas." In the 2004 plan revision they are called "Remote Backcountry Recreation— Nonmotorized (or Few Open Roads) Areas" or "Backcountry Areas."

Rare communities, special or unique area designations, Appalachian Trail Corridor, and *scenic corridors* offer protection of species habitats, scenic values, and backcountry values to different degrees and with different emphasis. They are all valuable designations that last for the life of the management plan.

Relevant dates: August 4, 1988, is the date on which the old CNF management plan was implemented. The revised-draft plan was released on March 21, 2003, and the final plan was released on January 30, 2004. Wilderness bills were signed into law on October 30, 1984 (southern CNF), and October 16, 1986 (northern CNF).

The chart below lists most of the protected areas in the CNF, arranged by the section numbers for each area in this book, and shows the management category, acreage, and county of location for each area. We have also provided in parenthesis the specific prescription numbers (management categories) for each of the areas, as specified in the 2004 management plan.

NORTHERN CNF

1 ROGERS RIDGE (4,753 acres inventoried roadless plus 180 acres on Jefferson NF)

Johnson County

Area	Acres (1988 Plan)	Acres (2004 Plan)
Rogers Ridge Scenic (4F)	3,865	5,530
Rogers Ridge Backcountry (12A)	1,390	2,548

2 IRON MOUNTAIN (3,431 acres inventoried roadless plus 853 acres on Jefferson NF)

Johnson County

Area	Acres (1988 Plan)	Acres (2004 Plan)
London Bridge Backcountry (12B)	2,550	3,416
London Bridge Backcountry (12A)		1,239
Iron Mountain Backcountry (12B)		544
Eligible Recreation River (2B3)		665
Iron Mountain Rare Communities (9F)		1,117

3 BEAVERDAM CREEK (5,130 acres inventoried roadless + 1,133 acres on Jefferson NF)

Johnson and Sullivan Counties

Area	Acres (1988 Plan)	Acres (2004 Plan)
Beaverdam Creek Backcountry (12B)	1,145	2,792
Eligible Recreation River (2B3)		1,113
Appalachian Trail Corridor (4A)		3,194

4 FLINT MILL (9,629 acres inventoried roadless)

Johnson, Sullivan, and Carter Counties

Area	Acres (1988 Plan)	Acres (2004 Plan)
Stoney Creek Scenic Area (4F)	3,920	2,606
Flint Mill Backcountry (12B)	2,620	7,981
Appalachian Trail Corridor (4A)		1,660

HICKORY FLAT BRANCH (included in this book as part of Big Laurel Branch)

Johnson and Carter Counties

Area	Acres (1988 Plan)	Acres (2004 Plan)
Hickory Flat Branch Backcountry (12A)		4,220
Appalachian Trail Corridor (4A)		2,176
Rare Community (9F)		102

5 Big Laurel Branch (5,589 acres inventoried roadless)

Johnson and Carter Counties

Area	Acres (1988 Plan)	Acres (2004 Plan)
Big Laurel Branch Wilderness (1A)	6,332	6,360
Big Laurel Branch Recommended Wilderness Addition (1B)		4,930
Big Laurel Branch Backcountry (12A)		1,297
Appalachian Trail Corridor (4A)		462

6 Pond Mountain

Carter County

Area	Acres (1988 Plan)	Acres (2004 Plan)
Pond Mountain Wilderness (1A)	6,929	6,929

7 White Rocks Mountain

Carter County

Area	Acres (1988 Plan)	Acres (2004 Plan)
Appalachian Trail Corridor (4A)		2,866

8 Doe River Gorge

Carter County

Area	Acres (1988 Plan)	Acres (2004 Plan)
Doe River Gorge Scenic Area (4F)	1,783	2,652

Slide Hollow (4,195 acres inventoried roadless; included in this book as part of White Rocks Mountain)
Carter County

Area	Acres (1988 Plan)	Acres (2004 Plan)
Slide Hollow Backcountry (12A)		2,464
Appalachian Trail Corridor (4A)		1,498
Rare Community (9F)		22
Eligible Recreation River (2B3)		627

9 Highlands of Roan
Carter County

Area	Acres (1988 Plan)	Acres (2004 Plan)
Highlands of Roan Special Management Area (4K)	2,867	4,601
Rare Communities (9F)		397

Stone Mountain (5,373 acres inventoried roadless; included in this book as part of Unaka Mountain)
Carter and Unicoi Counties

Area	Acres (1988 Plan)	Acres (2004 Plan)
Stone Mountain Backcountry (12B)		5,457

10 Unaka Mountain
Unicoi County

Area	Acres (1988 Plan)	Acres (2004 Plan)
Unaka Mountain Wilderness (1A)	4,496	4,496
Unaka Mountain Scenic Area (4F)	910	708
Unaka Mountain Backcountry	1,248	
Appalachian Trail Corridor (4A)		1,912

11 Nolichucky River Corridor North
Unicoi County

Area	Acres (1988 Plan)	Acres (2004 Plan)
Appalachian Trail Corridor (4A)		2,189
Eligible Scenic River (2B2)		363
Nolichucky Backcountry	1,970	
Rare Communities (9F)		197

12 Nolichucky River Corridor South
Unicoi County

Area	Acres (1988 Plan)	Acres (2004 Plan)
Appalachian Trail Corridor (4A)		3,076
Eligible Scenic River (2B2)		394
Rare Communities (9F)		27

13 Sampson Mountain (3,069 acres inventoried roadless)
Unicoi, Greene, and Washington Counties

Area	Acres (1988 Plan)	Acres (2004 Plan)
Sampson Mountain Wilderness (1A)	7,992	7,992
Sampson Mountain Recommended Wilderness Addition (1B)		3,069
Sampson Mountain Backcountry (Motorized)	6,308	
Coldspring Mountain Backcountry	380	
Flint Mountain Backcountry	480	

14 Bald Mountains (11,744 acres inventoried roadless + 10,971 in Pisgah)
Greene County

Area	Acres (1988 Plan)	Acres (2004 Plan)
Bald Mountain Ridge Scenic Area (4F)	8,653	8,696
Bald Mountain Backcountry (12A)		3,833
Appalachian Trail Corridor (4A)		953

15 Paint Creek
Greene County

Area	Acres (1988 Plan)	Acres (2004 Plan)
Appalachian Trail Corridor (4A)		1,749

16 Meadow Creek Mountain (no protected areas)

17 Devil's Backbone (4,283 acres inventoried roadless)
Cocke County

Area	Acres (1988 Plan)	Acres (2004 Plan)
Devil's Backbone Backcountry (12B)	6,660	4,341

18 **Miscellaneous Trails** (see individual trail description)

19 **Appalachian Trail**
Cocke, Greene, Unicoi, Unicoi, Carter, Johnson, and Sullivan Counties

Area	Length (1988 Plan)	Acres (2004 Plan)
Total Appalachian Trail Corridor	Over 150 miles	36,076
Appalachian Trail Corridor not included in above areas		14,341

SOUTHERN CNF

20 **Citico Creek/Joyce Kilmer–Slickrock** (1,425 acres inventoried roadless)
Monroe County

Area	Acres (1988 Plan)	Acres (2004 Plan)
Citico Creek Wilderness (1A)	16,226	16,226
Joyce Kilmer–Slickrock Wilderness (1A) (plus 13,562 in Nantahala NF)	3,832	3,382
Joyce Kilmer–Slickrock Recommended Wilderness Addition (1B)		1,964
Haw Knob Backcountry	1,060	

21 **Brushy Ridge** (7,389 acres inventoried roadless)
Monroe County

Area	Acres (1988 Plan)	Acres (2004 Plan)
Brushy Ridge Backcountry (12B)	4,220	6,075
Rare Communities (9F)		684

22 **Sycamore Creek** (6,994 acres inventoried roadless)
Monroe County

Area	Acres (1988 Plan)	Acres (2004 Plan)
Sycamore Creek Backcountry (12B)	2,970	6,284
Rare Communities (9F)		1,504

23 Bald River (9,112 acres inventoried roadless)
Monroe County

Area	Acres (1988 Plan)	Acres (2004 Plan)
Bald River Gorge Wilderness (1A)	3,721	3,721
Bald River Gorge Backcountry (12B)	10,460	1,735
Upper Bald River Recommended Wilderness (1B)		9,112

24 Warrior's Passage National Recreation Trail
Monroe County

Area	Length (1988 Plan)	Length (2004 Plan)
Warrior's Passage Trail	10 mi.	10 mi.

25 Gee Creek
Polk and McMinn Counties

Area	Acres (1988 Plan)	Acres (2004 Plan)
Gee Creek Wilderness (1A)	2,493	2,493
Gee Creek Backcountry	1,400	

26 Coker Creek
Polk County

Area	Acres (1988 Plan)	Acres (2004 Plan)
Coker Creek Scenic Area (4F)	375	443

27 John Muir National Recreation Trail
Polk County

Area	Acres (1988 Plan)	Acres (2004 Plan)
John Muir National Recreation Trail	17 mi.	17 mi.

28 Rock Creek Gorge
Polk County

Area	Acres (1988 Plan)	Acres (2004 Plan)
Rock Creek Gorge Scenic Area (4F)	220	244
Scenic Byway Corridor (9A)		1,382

29 Little Frog Mountain (977 acres inventoried roadless)
Polk County

Area	Acres (1988 Plan)	Acres (2004 Plan)
Little Frog Mountain Wilderness (1A)	4,666	4,666
Little Frog Mountain Recommended Wilderness Addition (1B)		977

30 Big Frog Mountain (365 acres inventoried roadless)
Polk County

Area	Acres (1988 Plan)	Acres (2004 Plan)
Big Frog Wilderness(1A) (plus 89 acres in Chattahoochee NF)	7,993	7,993
Big Frog Recommended Wilderness Addition (1B)		365
West Big Frog Backcountry	1,460	

31 Benton MacKaye Trail (no separately designated acres)

32 Ocoee Whitewater Center (no wilderness, scenic, or backcountry areas; much of it is designated as a Scenic Byway Corridor, Prescription 7A, which allows some timber harvesting)

33 Conasauga River
Polk County

Area	Acres (1988 Plan)	Acres (2004 Plan)
Conasauga Eligible Wild River (2B1)		1,110
Conasauga Eligible Recreational River (2B3)		121

34 Miscellaneous Trails (see individual trail descriptions)

Miscellaneous Total Acreage Amounts:

Total Northern and Southern CNF Wilderness Acreage	66,389
Total Northern and Southern CNF Scenic, Backcountry (Primitive), and Miscellaneous Protected Area Acreage (1988 plan)	94,284
Total Northern and Southern CNF Protected Areas included in 2004 Plan (Not Including Designated Wilderness)	147,370
Total Northern and Southern CNF Recommended Wilderness Study Area Acreage (2004 Plan)	20,417

Total Northern and Southern CNF Scenic Acreage (2004 Plan)	20,879
Total Northern and Southern CNF Backcountry Acreage (2004 Plan)	54,360
Total Northern and Southern CNF Roan Mountain Acreage (2004 Plan)	4,601
Total Northern and Southern CNF Rare Community Acreage (2004 Plan)	6,591
Total (Northern CNF) Appalachian Trail Corridor (4A)	36,076
Total Northern and Southern CNF Wild, Scenic, and Recreational Rivers (2B)	4,446

Appendix 6

Threatened, Endangered, and Sensitive Species

Federally listed endangered species are recognized by the US Fish and Wildlife Service as being in danger of becoming extinct. Federally listed threatened species are recognized by the US Fish and Wildlife Service as being in danger of becoming endangered. Sensitive species are plant and animal species identified by the regional forester for which global population viability is a concern.

THREATENED AND ENDANGERED SPECIES LIST FOR THE CNF (FEDERAL LISTING)

Taxa Group	Scientific Name	Common Name	Status
Arachnid	*Microhexura montivaga*	Spruce-fir moss spider	E
Bird	*Haliaeetus leucocephalus*	Bald eagle	T
Fish	*Cyprinella caerulea*	Blue shiner	T
Fish	*Etheostoma percnurum*	Duskytail darter	E
Fish	*Noturus baileyi*	Smoky madtom	E
Fish	*Noturus flavipinnis*	Yellowfin madtom	T
Fish	*Percina antesella*	Amber darter	E
Fish	*Percina jenkinsi*	Conasauga logperch	E
Fish	*Percina tanasi*	Snail darter	T
Mammal	*Glaucomys sabrinus coloratus*	Carolina northern flying squirrel	E
Mammal	*Myotis grisescens*	Gray bat	E

Mammal	*Myotis sodalis*	Indiana bat	E
Mollusk	*Alasmidonta raveneliana*	Appalachian elktoe	E
Mollusk	*Epioblasma florentina florentina*	Yellow blossom pearly mussel	E
Mollusk	*Epioblasma florentina walkeri*	Tan riffleshell	E
Mollusk	*Lampsilis altilis*	Fine-rayed pocketbook	T
Mollusk	*Pleurobema georgianum*	Southern pigtoe mussel	E
Mollusk	*Villosa trabalis*	Cumberland bean pearly mussel	E
Nonvascular plant	*Gymnoderma lineare*	Rock gnome lichen	E
Vascular plant	*Geum radiatum*	Spreading avens	E
Vascular plant	*Hedyotis purpurea montana*	Roan Mountain bluet	E
Vascular plant	*Isotria medeoloides*	Small whorled pogonia	T
Vascular plant	*Pityopsis ruthii*	Ruth's golden aster	E
Vascular plant	*Solidago spithamaea*	Blue Ridge goldenrod	T
Vascular plant	*Spiraea virginiana*	Virginia spiraea	T

REGIONAL FORESTER'S SENSITIVE SPECIES LIST FOR THE CNF

Taxa Group	Scientific Name	Common Name
Amphibian	*Desmognathus caroliniensis*	Carolina mountain dusky salamander
Amphibian	*Desmognathus santeetlah*	Santeetlah dusky salamander
Amphibian	*Eurycea junaluska*	Junaluska salamander
Amphibian	*Plethodon aureolus*	Tellico salamander
Amphibian	*Plethodon teyahalee*	Southern Appalachian salamander
Amphibian	*Plethodon welleri*	Weller's salamander
Bird	*Falco peregrinus*	Peregrine falcon
Bird	*Lanius ludovicia migrans*	Migrant loggerhead shrike
Fish	*Etheostoma acuticeps*	Sharphead darter
Fish	*Etheostoma brevirostrum*	Holiday darter
Fish	*Etheostoma vulneratum*	Wounded darter
Fish	*Ichthyomyzon greeleyi*	Mountain brook lamprey
Fish	*Percina burtoni*	Blotchside logperch
Insect	*Cheumatopsyche helma*	Helma's net-spinning caddisfly
Insect	*Gomphus consanguis*	Cherokee clubtail
Insect	*Gomphus viridifrons*	Green-faced clubtail
Insect	*Macromia margarita*	Mountain river cruiser
Insect	*Megaleuctra williamsae*	William's giant stonefly

Insect	*Ophiogomphus alleghaniensis*	Allegheny snaketail
Insect	*Ophiogomphus edmundo*	Edmund's snaketail
Insect	*Ophiogomphus incurvatus*	Appalachian snaketail
Insect	*Speyeria diana*	Diana fritillary
Mammal	*Corynorhinus rafinesquii*	Rafinesque's big-eared bat
Mammal	*Microtus chrotorrhinus carolinensis*	Southern rock vole
Mammal	*Myotis leibii*	Eastern small-footed bat
Mammal	*Sorex palustris puntculatus*	Southern water shrew
Mollusk	*Fusconaia barnesiana*	TN pigtoe
Mollusk	*Lasmigona holstonia*	TN heelsplitter
Mollusk	*Lasmigona subviridis*	Green floater
Mollusk	*Lexingtonia dolabelloides*	Slabside pearlymussel
Mollusk	*Pallifera hemphilli*	Black mantleslug
Mollusk	*Paravitrea placentula*	Glossy supercoil
Mollusk	*Pleurobema hanleyianum*	Georgia pigtoe
Mollusk	*Pleurobema oviforme*	TN clubshell
Mollusk	*Strophitus connasaugaensis*	Alabama creekmussel
Mollusk	*Villosa nebulosa*	Alabama rainbow
Mollusk	*Villosa vanuxemensis umbrans*	Coosa combshell
Reptile	*Clemmys muhlenbergi*	Bog turtle
Nonvascular plant	*Acrobolbus ciliatus*	A liverwort
Nonvascular plant	*Aneura maxima (=A. sharpii)*	A liverwort
Nonvascular plant	*Aspiromitus appalachianus*	A hornwort
Nonvascular plant	*Bartramidula wilsonii*	Dwarf apple moss
Nonvascular plant	*Bazzania nudicaulis*	Bazzania moss
Nonvascular plant	*Brachydontium trichodes*	Peak moss
Nonvascular plant	*Cephalozia macrostachya* spp. *australis*	A liverwort
Nonvascular plant	*Cephaloziella massalongi*	A liverwort
Nonvascular plant	*Cheilolejeunea evansii*	A liverwort
Nonvascular plant	*Chiloscyphus appalachianus*	A liverwort
Nonvascular plant	*Diplophyllum apiculatum* var. *taxifoliodes*	A liverwort
Nonvascular plant	*Diplophyllum obtusatum*	A liverwort
Nonvascular plant	*Ditrichum ambiguum*	A moss
Nonvascular plant	*Drepanolejeunea appalachiana*	A liverwort
Nonvascular plant	*Entodon concinnus*	Lime entodon
Nonvascular plant	*Fissidens appalachiensis*	Appalachian pocket moss
Nonvascular plant	*Frullania appalachiana*	A liverwort
Nonvascular plant	*Frullania oakesiana*	A liverwort
Nonvascular plant	*Homaliadelphus sharpii*	Sharp's homaliadelphus
Nonvascular plant	*Hydrothyria venosa*	An aquatic lichen

Nonvascular plant	*Lejeunea blomquistii*	A liverwort
Nonvascular plant	*Lejeunea dimorphophylla*	A liverwort
Nonvascular plant	*Leptodontium excelsum*	Grandfather Mountain leptodontium
Nonvascular plant	*Leptohymenium sharpie*	Mount Leconte moss
Nonvascular plant	*Lophocolea appalachiana*	A liverwort
Nonvascular plant	*Marsupella emarginata* var. *latiloba*	A liverwort
Nonvascular plant	*Megaceros aenigmaticus*	A hornwort
Nonvascular plant	*Metzgeria fruticulosa (= M. temperata)*	A liverwort
Nonvascular plant	*Metzgeria furcata* var. *setigera*	A liverwort
Nonvascular plant	*Metzgeria uncigera*	A liverwort
Nonvascular plant	*Nardia lescurii*	A liverwort
Nonvascular plant	*Pellia X appalachiana*	A liverwort
Nonvascular plant	*Plagiochila austinii*	A liverwort
Nonvascular plant	*Plagiochila caduciloba*	A liverwort
Nonvascular plant	*Plagiochila echinata*	A liverwort
Nonvascular plant	*Plagiochila sharpii*	Sharp's leafy liverwort
Nonvascular plant	*Plagiochila sullivantii* var. *spinigera*	A liverwort
Nonvascular plant	*Plagiochila sullivantii* var. *sullivantii*	Sullivant's leafy liverwort
Nonvascular plant	*Plagiochila virginica* var. **caroliniana**	A liverwort
Nonvascular plant	*Plagiochila virginica* var. *virginica*	A liverwort
Nonvascular plant	*Plagiomnium carolinianum*	Carolina plagiomnium
Nonvascular plant	*Platyhypnidium pringlei*	A moss
Nonvascular plant	*Polytrichum appalachianum*	Appalachian haircap moss
Nonvascular plant	*Porella wataugensis*	Watauga porella
Nonvascular plant	*Radula sullivantii*	A liverwort
Nonvascular plant	*Radula voluta*	A liverwort
Nonvascular plant	*Riccardia jugata*	A liverwort
Nonvascular plant	*Sphenolobopsis pearsonii*	A liverwort
Nonvascular plant	*Sticta limbata*	A foliose lichen
Nonvascular plant	*Taxiphyllum alternans*	Japanese yew-moss
Nonvascular plant	*Tortula ammonsiana*	Ammons's tortula
Vascular plant	*Aconitum reclinatum*	Trailing white monkshood
Vascular plant	*Aster georgianus*	Georgia aster
Vascular plant	*Berberis canadensis*	American barberry
Vascular plant	*Botrychium jenmanii*	Dixie grapefern
Vascular plant	*Buckleya distichophylla*	Piratebush
Vascular plant	*Calamagrostis cainii*	Cain's reed grass
Vascular plant	*Cardamine clematitis*	Small mountain bittercress
Vascular plant	*Carex misera*	Wretched sedge
Vascular plant	*Carex roanensis*	Roan sedge

Vascular plant	*Cimicifuga rubifolia*	Appalachian bugbane
Vascular plant	*Collinsonia verticillata*	Stoneroot
Vascular plant	*Coreopsis latifolia*	Broadleaf tickseed
Vascular plant	*Danthonia epilis*	Bog oat-grass
Vascular plant	*Delphinium exaltatum*	Tall larkspur
Vascular plant	*Diervilla rivularis*	Riverbank bush-honeysuckle
Vascular plant	*Fothergilla major*	Large witchalder
Vascular plant	*Gentiana austromontana*	Appalachian gentian
Vascular plant	*Geum geniculatum*	Bent avens
Vascular plant	*Glyceria nubigena*	Great Smoky Mountain mannagrass
Vascular plant	*Helianthus glaucophyllus*	Whiteleaf sunflower
Vascular plant	*Heuchera longiflora* var. *aceroides*	Maple-leaf alumroot
Vascular plant	*Hymenophyllum tayloriae*	Taylor's filmy fern
Vascular plant	*Hypericum graveolens*	Mountain St. Johnswort
Vascular plant	*Hypericum mitchellianum*	Blue Ridge St. Johnswort
Vascular plant	*Ilex collina*	Longstalked holly
Vascular plant	*Juglans cinerea*	Butternut
Vascular plant	*Lilium grayi*	Gray's lily
Vascular plant	*Lysimachia fraseri*	Fraser's yellow loosestrife
Vascular plant	*Minuartia godfreyi*	Godfrey's stitchwort
Vascular plant	*Monotropsis odorata*	Sweet pinesap
Vascular plant	*Penstemon smallii*	Small's beardtongue
Vascular plant	*Platanthera integrilabia*	White fringeless orchid
Vascular plant	*Potamogeton tennesseensis*	TN pondweed
Vascular plant	*Prenanthes roanensis*	Roan Mountain rattlesnakeroot
Vascular plant	*Pycnanthemum beadlei*	Beadle's mountain mint
Vascular plant	*Rosa obtusiuscula*	Appalachian Valley rose
Vascular plant	*Rugelia nudicaulis*	Rugel's Indianplantain
Vascular plant	*Saxifraga caroliniana*	Carolina saxifrage
Vascular plant	*Scutellaria arguta*	Hairy skullcap
Vascular plant	*Scutellaria saxatilis*	Rock skullcap
Vascular plant	*Sedum nevii*	Nevius's stonecrop
Vascular plant	*Sida hermaphrodita*	Virginia fanpetals
Vascular plant	*Silene ovata*	Blue Ridge catchfly
Vascular plant	*Stachys clingmanii*	Clingman's hedge-nettle
Vascular plant	*Thaspium pinnatifidum*	Cutleaved meadow parsnip
Vascular plant	*Thermopsis mollis* var. *fraxinifolia*	Ashleaf goldenbanner
Vascular plant	*Trillium rugelii*	Illscented trillium
Vascular plant	*Trillium simile*	Jeweled trillium
Vascular plant	*Tsuga caroliniana*	Carolina hemlock

Appendix 7

Waterfalls

Many spots in the CNF provide stunning views of beautiful waterfalls. This section is a summary of those waterfalls. Most are described elsewhere in the book; refer to the listed trail name/number description or, for those with no trail, the location description. The falls are listed in general geographic order, starting in the north.

Waterfall	Location	Trail Name	Guidebook Trail Number
Northern CNF			
Gentry Creek	Rogers Ridge	Gentry Creek	1
Backbone Falls	Beaverdam Creek	Backbone Rock	4
Blue Hole	Watauga District, CNF	Off Panhandle Road	None
North Fork Stony	Flint Mill	North Fork of Stony Creek	None
Sulpher Spring Branch	Flint Mill	Off Trail	None
Laurel	Pond Mountain	AT	21
Firescald Branch	Pond Mountain	Laurel Fork	29
Dennis Cove	Pond Mountain	Laurel Fork	29
Coon Den	Pond Mountain	Coon Den Falls	134
Red Fork	Unaka Mountain	Red Fork Falls	46
Rock Creek	Unaka Mountain	Rock Creek Falls	41
Dick Creek	Unaka Mountain	Dick Creek	49
Buckeye	Sampson Mountain	Clark Creek	None
Sill Branch	Sampson Mountain	Sill Branch	92
Squib Creek	Sampson Mountain	Squib Creek	57
Pete's Branch	Sampson Mountain	Pete's Branch	69

Mary's (Davis Creek)	Bald Mountains	Artie Hollow	76
Marguerite	Bald Mountains	Marguerite Falls	78
Glen	Bald Mountains	Marguerite Falls	78

Southern CNF

Wildcat	Joyce Kilmer–Slickrock	Slickrock Creek	95
Lower Falls	Joyce Kilmer–Slickrock	Slickrock Creek	95
N. Fork Citico Creek	Citico Creek	North Fork Citico Creek	97
Falls Branch	Citico Creek	Falls Branch	99
Bald River	Bald River	Bald River	119
Upper Bald River	Bald River	Brookshire Creek	123
Brookshire Creek	Bald River	Brookshire Creek	123
Gee Creek	Gee Creek	Gee Creek	129
Conasauga	Ocoee/Hiwassee Ranger District, CNF	Conasauga Falls	189
Coker Creek	Coker Creek	Coker Creek Falls	144
Turtletown	Ocoee/Hiwassee Ranger District, CNF	Turtletown Falls	191
Benton	Rock Creek Gorge	Benton Falls	147

Appendix 8

Grassy Balds

One of the greatest thrills of hiking is to reach the summit of a mountain and view the gorgeous panorama of surrounding mountains and valleys. This appendix is a summary of CNF summits that provide the most spectacular of such views. Most are called "balds" because of their history of having no or few trees, which allows panoramic views. There is much debate about the origins of balds, from ancient fires to clearings made by Indians and early settlers. Whatever their origin, however, they usually reforest without some means of keeping them clear. Accordingly, most of the current balds are managed for openness and mechanically mowed; many other balds have already become forested. You will often see remnants of old balds: grassy areas along the mountaintops and ridges. Most of the grassy balds are described elsewhere in the book; refer to the listed trail name/number description below or, for those with no trail, the location description. The balds are listed in general geographic order, starting in the north.

Bald	Location	Trail Name	Guidebook Trail Number
Northern CNF			
Rogers Ridge	Rogers Ridge	Rogers Ridge Horse Trail	2
Hump Mountain	Highlands of Roan	AT	34
Little Hump Mountain	Highlands of Roan	AT	34
Jane Bald	Highlands of Roan	AT	34
Round Bald	Highlands of Roan	AT	34
Pleasant Garden	Unaka Mountain	AT	40

Beauty Spot	Unaka Mountain	AT	None
Big Bald	Not in this book; AT Spivey Gap, NC, to Sams Gap, TN-NC, section	AT	None
Coldspring Mountain	Bald Mountains	AT	80
Max Patch	Not in this book; AT Hot Springs, NC, to Max Patch Road section	AT	None
Snowbird Mountain	Not in this book; AT Max Patch Road to Davenport Gap section	AT	None
Hall Top	Devil's Backbone	Stone Mountain Trail	90

Southern CNF

Bob Stratton Bald	Joyce Kilmer–Slickrock	Fodderstack	101
Waucheesi Bald	Bald River	Warrior's Passage	126
Beaverdam Bald	Bald River	Brookshire Creek	123

Contributors

Lamar Alexander, US Senator (TN), Washington, DC. He was US Secretary of Education from 1991 to 1994, President of the University of Tennessee from 1988 to 1991, and Governor of Tennessee from 1979 to 1987. He was elected governor after a one-thousand-mile walk across the state. He is from Maryville and has long been a passionate supporter of the GSMNP and the CNF.

Barbara J. Allen, Administrative Assistant, Knoxville, TN (Sampson Mountain). She is a past Chair of the Harvey Broome Group of the Sierra Club. Her activities include backpacking, hiking, canoeing, and bicycling.

Daniel Dunlap, Student, Knoxville, TN (Big Laurel Branch and Pond Mountain). His work was done for BSA rank advancement to Eagle Scout. The members of BSA Troop 155 helped him on his sections. Interests include, backpacking, music, and scouting.

John Dunlap, Biologist, University of Tennessee, Knoxville (Beaverdam Creek, Doe River, Iron Mountain, Nolichucky River North). His interests include backpacking, hiking, photography, bicycling, and travel.

Steve Dyer, Dental Technologist, Knoxville, TN (White Rocks Mountain). He is a past Vice Chair of the Harvey Broome Group of the Sierra Club. His interests include conservation and preservation of public lands, greenway development, hiking, backpacking, and canoeing.

John R. Finger, Emeritus Professor of History at the University of Tennessee, Knoxville (Human History). His interests include hiking and backpacking, other travel, and fishing.

Will Fontanez, Director, Cartographic Services Laboratory, Geography Department, University of Tennessee, Knoxville. He was assisted in preparing the maps for this book by Will Albaugh, Staff Cartographer. Will is a national-level men's gymnastics official and enjoys outdoor activities and woodworking.

Gary Hugh Irwin, Forest Ecologist, Southern Appalachian Forest Coalition, Asheville, NC (Vegetation, portions of Political History and Appendixes). He was Coordinator of Cherokee Forest Voices, a CNF citizen watchdog organization, for eight years and has been a leader in CNF and regional forest management issues as a Sierra Club activist. His interests include photography, nature study, and hiking.

Roger A. Jenkins, Analytical Chemist, Bozeman, MT (many of the photographs, Some Warnings and Advice, Maintaining and Protecting the Trails, Maps and GPS Information, Highlands of Roan, and Citico Creek). He has served as Chairman of the Sierra Club's TN Chapter and Harvey Broome Group and has been a leader on wilderness preservation issues. His activities include hiking, backpacking, photography, and downhill skiing.

Kathleen Kitzmiller, Librarian and Environmental Engineer, Knoxville, TN (Nolichucky River Corridor South and several other trails). Her interests include hiking, backpacking, and reading.

Lance N. McCold, Mechanical Engineer, Oak Ridge National Laboratory, Knoxville, TN (Wildlife). His interests include photography, hiking, and nature study.

Susie McDonald, Web Applications Developer, Science Applications International Corporation, Bozeman, MT (some photographs and cowriter of Roan Mountain and Citico Creek). She has been active in environmental causes in East Tennessee for thirty years, and is a former Chairman of the Harvey Broome Group of the Sierra Club.

Steve McGaffin, Environmental Educator, Knoxville, TN (Bald Mountains, Paint Creek, Meadow Creek Mountain, Brushy Ridge, and Sycamore Creek). His interests include hiking, backpacking, biking, climbing, caving, sailing, natural history, and travel.

Ray Payne, retired Mechanical Engineer, Oak Ridge National Laboratory, Knoxville, TN (Devil's Backbone, Bald River, and Warrior's Passage National Recreation Trail). He has served as Chairman of Great Smokies Wilderness Advocates, President of the Great Smoky Mountain Hiking Club, Chairman of the Sierra Club's Tennessee Chapter, and Chairman of the Sierra Club's Appalachian Region Conservation Committee. He has been a leader on Wilderness preservations issues in the CNF and the GSMNP. His outdoor interests include hiking, backpacking, and canoeing.

Betty J. Petty, Computer Programmer/Analyst, TVA, Chattanooga, TN (Little Frog Mountain and the book's index). She is the Chattanooga Hiking Club newsletter editor, Web master, and representative to the Cumberland Trail Conference Executive Board. Her interests include hiking, backpacking, photography, music, Scottish history, Native American culture/religions, and especially the health and welfare of the CNF.

David Reiser, Senior Research Engineer, Knoxville, TN (John Muir National Recreation Trail). He is the Conservation Chair of the Harvey Broome Group of the Sierra Club and his interests include the Cumberland trail, energy policy, and day hiking

George G. Ritter, Retired President of Performance Development Corporation, Oak Ridge, TN (Unaka Mountain, AT, Conasauga River, Miscellaneous Trails Southern CNF, and the Waterfalls and Grassy Balds Appendixes). He hiked over two hundred miles in the preparation of this book. He is a Director and Treasurer of the Smoky Mountains Hiking Club and is an avid hiker.

Hiram Rogers, Financial Analyst, Knoxville, TN (Big Frog Wilderness, Ocoee Whitewater Center). He is the author of the guidebook *Exploring the Black Hills and Badlands: A Guide for Hikers, Mountain Bikers, and Cross-country Skiers, 50 Hikes in Kentucky,* and *Backroad Bicycling the Blue Ridge and Great Smokies.* His activities include hiking, trail running, and mountain biking.

William H. Skelton, Attorney with Bass Berry and Sims, PLC, Knoxville, TN (Volume Editor, Political History, Rogers Ridge, and other unattributed sections). He served as Coordinator of the CNF Wilderness Coalition during the CNF Wilderness campaigns and has been Chairman of the Sierra Club's Tennessee Chapter and Harvey Broome Group. He was Vice Chairman of Gov. Lamar Alexander's Commission on Tennesseans Outdoors and is currently Chairman of the Knoxville Greenways Commission. His interests include backpacking, running, and travel.

Emery E. Soler, Computer Programmer, Knoxville, TN (Rock Creek Gorge). He has served as Chairman of the Harvey Broome Group of the Sierra Club. His interests include development of greenways, hiking, and bicycling.

Beverly Smith, Demand Analyst, Knoxville, TN (Beaverdam Creek, Doe River, Iron Mountain, Nolichucky River North). She has served as Chair of the Harvey Broome Group of the Sierra Club and as an organizer of the Greater Smoky Mountains Coalition. Her interests include hiking, backpacking, bicycling, and travel.

Trygve J. Tolnas, Retired Electrical Engineer, Maryville, TN (Coker Creek, Gee Creek, Flint Mill and Miscellaneous Trails Northern CNF). His interests include hiking, backpacking, wilderness canoeing, and wilderness preservation.

James E. Wedekind, Geologist, Middleton, WI (Geology). He is a former Knoxvillian and is a contributing author to *Hiking Trails of the Smokies*. His interests include the Sierra Club (John Muir Group), hiking and backpacking, paddling, fishing, skiing, and he still brews an occasional homemade beer.

Other Contributors. Although the above individuals were the principal contributors, others provided help with the book. Several hiked trails and prepared individual trail descriptions, including Susan M. Lackey, retired Banker, Cleveland, TN; Mary Anne Hoskins, University Administrator, University of Tennessee, Knoxville; and John Kirkpatrick, Engineer, Oak Ridge National Laboratory, Oak Ridge, TN. Julie McCoig, Legal Secretary, Dandridge, TN, was invaluable in typing various portions of the manuscripts. Emily Skelton, High School Teacher, Alcoa, TN, updated the wildlife section. Melissa Brenneman, Reference Librarian, Lawson McGhee Library, Knoxville, TN, updated the bibliography. Diane Madison, Knoxville, TN, reviewed a portion of the book.

We also want to recognize the people who made major contributions to the first edition of this book, although they were not involved in this edition: James Blackstock, Dennis R. and Marty L. E. Danilchuk, Daniel P. Dillon, Dana Eglinton, Emily Ellis, Tom Gatti, Russ Griffith, Robert Harvey, Ray Hunt, Martha J. Ketelle, Kirk Johnson, Dan MacDonald, Noel P. McJunkin, David McPeak, Barbara J. Muhlbeier, Darrol Nickels, Arthur S. Smith, Mary A. Vavrik, Kenneth S. and Helen Scott Warren, Janice McMillian, Cata Folks, Jo Wetherall, Margaret Olson, and Jacyne Woodcox. Other contributors to the prior edition included Karen Young, Kirk Johnson, Patricia Horton, Rebecca Dotson, Janice Irwin, Carolyn Hahs, Samantha and Kevin Pack, Jacyne Woodcox, John Denton, Hartwell Herring, Janet Goodwin, Sam Brocato, Reese Scull, Andrew Schiller, and Paul Somers.

Bibliography

Alsop, Fred J., III. *Birds of the Smokies*. Gatlinburg, TN: Great Smoky Mountains Natural History Association, 1991.

Appalachian Trail Guide to Tennessee-North Carolina. 12th ed. Harpers Ferry, WV: Appalachian Trail Conference, 2002.

Brandt, Robert S., and Tennessee Chapter Staff Sierra Club, eds. *Tennessee Hiking Guide*. Rev. ed. Knoxville: Univ. of Tennessee Press, 1988.

Braun, E. Lucy. *Deciduous Forests of Eastern North America*. Philadelphia: Blakiston Co., 1950.

Brewer, Carson. *Just Over the Next Ridge: A Traveler's Guide to Little-Known and Out-of-the-Way Places in Southern Appalachia*. Newly updated and expanded ed. Knoxville: Knoxville News-Sentinel, 1992.

Brown, Fred, Nell Jones, and Thomas Perrie. *The Georgia Conservancy's Guide to the North Georgia Mountains*. 2nd ed. Atlanta: Longstreet Press, 1999.

Bull, John, John F. Farrand Jr., and Lori Hogan. *National Audubon Society Field Guide to North American Birds: Eastern Region*. 2nd rev. ed. New York: Alfred A. Knopf, 1994.

Campbell, Carlos, et al. *Great Smoky Mountains Wildflowers*. 5th ed., rev. and expanded. Northbrook, IL: Windy Pines Publishing, 1995.

Chew, V. Collins. *Underfoot: A Geologic Guide to the Appalachian Trail*. 2nd ed. Harpers Ferry, WV: Appalachian Trail Conference, 1993.

Collins, Henry Hill, Jr. *Harper and Row's Complete Field Guide to North American Wildlife, Eastern Edition*. New York: Harper and Row, 1981.

de Hart, Allen. *North Carolina Hiking Trails*. 3rd ed. Boston: Appalachian Mountain Club Books, 1996.

Fernald, Merritt Lyndon, and Alfred Charles Kinsey. *Edible Wild Plants of Eastern North America*. Rev. by Reed C. Collins. New York: Dover Publications, 1996.

Fletcher, Colin, and Chip Rawlins. *The Complete Walker IV*. New York: Knopf, 2002.

Forgey, William W., MD. *Wilderness Medicine: Beyond First Aid*. 5th ed. Guilford, Conn.: Globe Pequot Press, 1999.

Foster, Stephen, and James A. Duke. *A Field Guide to Medicinal Plants and Herbs of Eastern and Central North America*. 2nd ed. Boston: Houghton Mifflin, 2000.

Gorman, Stephen. *Winter Camping*. Boston: Appalachian Mountain Club Books, 1991.

Gove, Doris. *50 Hikes in the Tennessee Mountains: Hikes and Walks from the Blue Ridge to the Cumberland Plateau*. Woodstock: Backcountry Guides, 2001.

Graydon, Don, and Kurt Hanson, eds. *Mountaineering: The Freedom of the Hills*. 6th ed. Seattle: Mountaineers Books, 1998.

Hart, John. *Walking Softly in the Wilderness*. 3rd ed. San Francisco: Sierra Club Books, 1998.

Homan, Tim. *Hiking Trails of Joyce Kilmer–Slickrock and Citico Creek Wildernesses*. 2nd ed. Atlanta: Peachtree Publishers, 1998.

———. *The Hiking Trails of North Georgia*. 3rd ed. Atlanta, Ga.: Peachtree Publishers, 1997.

———. *Hiking Trails of Cohutta and Big Frog Wildernesses*. Atlanta, Ga.: Peachtree Publishers, 2000.

Kemp, Steve. *Trees and Familiar Shrubs of the Smokies*. Gatlinburg, TN: Great Smoky Mountains Natural History Association, 1993.

Kricher, John C. *A Field Guide to Eastern Forests, North America*. Boston: Houghton Mifflin, 1998.

Malter, Jeffry Lowell. "The Flora of Citico Creek Wilderness Study Area, Cherokee National Forest, Monroe County, Tennessee." Master's thesis, Univ. of Tennessee, Knoxville, 1977.

Manning, Harvey. *Backpacking: One Step at a Time*. 4th ed. New York: Vintage Books, 1986.

Jardine, Ray. *Beyond Backpacking: Ray Jardine's Guide to Lightweight Hiking*. LaPine, OR: AdventureLore Press, 2000.

Means, Evan, and Bob Brown. *Hiking Tennessee Trails*. 5th ed. Old Saybrook, CT: Globe Pequot Press, 1999.

Muir, John. *A Thousand Mile Walk to the Gulf*. Ed. William F. Bade. Boston: Houghton Mifflin, 1917.

Murray, Kenneth. *Highland Trails: A Guide to Scenic Trails: Northeast Tennessee, Western North Carolina, Southwest Virginia*. 3rd ed. Johnson City, TN.: Overmountain Press, 1997.

Murrell, Zack Ernest. "The Vascular Flora of Big Frog Mountain, Polk County, Tennessee." Master's thesis, Univ. of Tennessee, Knoxville, 1985.

Thieret, John W., William H. Niering, and Nancy C. Olmstead. *The Audubon Society Field Guide to North American Wildflowers, Eastern Region*. 2nd ed., rev. New York: Alfred A. Knopf, 2001.

Peterson, Lee. *A Field Guide to Edible Wild Plants of Eastern and Central North America*. Boston: Houghton Mifflin, 1978.

Peterson, Roger Tory, and Virginia Marie Peterson. *A Field Guide to the Birds of Eastern and Central North America.* 5th ed. Boston: Houghton Mifflin, 2002.

Price, Steve. *Wild Places of the South.* Charlotte, N.C.: East Woods Press, 1980.

Roberts, Harry. *Movin' On: Equipment and Techniques for Winter Hikers.* Rev. ed. Boston: Stone Wall Press, 1991.

Ross, Cindy, and Todd Gladfelter. *A Hiker's Companion: 12,000 Miles of Trail-Tested Wisdom.* Seattle: Mountaineers, 1993.

Stupka, Arthur. *Wildflowers in Color.* New York: Harper and Row, 1965.

Sulzer, Elmer G. *Ghost Railroads of Tennessee.* Indianapolis, IN: Vane A. Jones Co., 1975.

Sutton, Ann, and Myron Sutton. *Eastern Forests.* New York: Alfred A. Knopf, 1985.

Whitaker, John O., Jr. *The National Audubon Society Field Guide to North American Mammals.* Rev. ed. New York: Alfred A. Knopf, 1996.

Wilkerson, James A., MD, ed. *Medicine: For Mountaineering and Other Wilderness Activities.* 5th ed. Seattle: Mountaineers Books, 2001.

Wilson, Jennifer Bauer. *Roan Mountain: A Passage of Time.* Winston-Salem, NC: John F. Blair, 1991.

Wofford, Eugene B. *Sensitive Plants of the Cherokee National Forest.* N.p.: US Dept. of Agriculture, Forest Service Southern Region, 1981.

Woods, Frank W., and Royal. E. Shanks. "Natural Replacement of Chestnut by Other Species in the Great Smoky Mountains National Park." *Ecology* 40 (1959): 349–61.

Index to Areas, Trailheads, and Trails

FS Trail = US Forest Service trail number
TI Trail = Trails Illustrated Map trail number

AREAS

TRAILHEADS

TRAILS

Cherokee National Forest Hiking Guide was designed and typeset on a Macintosh computer system using QuarkXPress software. The body text is set in 9.75/12 Sabon. This book was designed and typeset by Ellen Beeler and manufactured by McNaughton Gunn, Inc.